Reader's Digest

GREAT WORLD ATLAS

THE
READER'S DIGEST
ASSOCIATION

Pleasantville, New York

READER'S DIGEST GREAT WORLD ATLAS

FIRST EDITION

PUBLISHED BY
THE READER'S DIGEST ASSOCIATION, INC.
Pleasantville, New York

© 1963 by THE READER'S DIGEST ASSOCIATION, INC.

Reproduction in any manner, in whole or in part, in
English or in other languages, is prohibited. All rights reserved.
Printed in the United States of America

Relief maps on pages 24-29 © Babson Institute
Relief maps on pages 15, 22-23 and 30-41 © Aero Service Corp.
Maps on pages 46-136 and 146-147 © John Bartholomew & Son Ltd.

Library of Congress Catalog Card Number: Map 63-10

ACKNOWLEDGMENTS

Special Consulting Editors

CHARLES B. HITCHCOCK

M.A., D.SC. (Hon.), Director, American Geographical Society, New York, N. Y.

and

FRANK DEBENHAM

O.B.C., M.A., D.SC. (Hon.), Emeritus Professor of Geography, Cambridge University, Cambridge, England

---

The Reader's Digest expresses its gratitude to the following, who have generously contributed to and advised on the preparation of this Atlas:

J. B. Allen, B.SC., PH.D., F.G.S., Overseas Geological Surveys, London

American Geographical Society, New York, N. Y.

Peter Bartholomew, John Bartholomew and Sons, Ltd., Edinburgh

Franklyn M. Branley, ED.D., Associate Astronomer, The American Museum—Hayden Planetarium, New York, N. Y.

William Briesemeister, Senior Cartographer, American Geographical Society, New York, N. Y.

British Broadcasting Corporation, London

Wm. Collins, Sons & Co., Ltd., London

David J. deLaubenfels, PH.D., Associate Professor of Geography, Syracuse University, Syracuse, N. Y.

F. W. Dunning, B.SC., F.G.S., Geological Survey and Museum, London

Rhodes W. Fairbridge, B.SC., D.SC., Professor of Geology, Columbia University, New York, N. Y.

Anthony W. Gatrell, London

George H. Hamlin, Jr., Aero Service Corporation, Philadelphia, Pa.

James G. Hawk, Babson Institute, Babson Park, Mass.

Institut de la Statistique et des Études Économiques, Paris

Preston E. James, PH.D., Professor of Geography, Syracuse University, Syracuse, N. Y.

Robert Jastrow, PH.D., Adjunct Professor of Geology, Columbia University; Director, Institute for Space Studies, National Aeronautics and Space Administration, New York, N. Y.

E. A. Jobbins, B.SC., F.G.S., Geological Survey and Museum, London

H. C. King, M.SC., PH.D., F.R.A.S., F.B.O.A., The London Planetarium, London

H. A. G. Lewis, Directorate of Military Survey, War Office and Air Ministry, London

Library of Congress, Washington, D.C.

Lick Observatory, Mount Hamilton, Calif.

Longmans, Green & Co., Ltd., London

Mississippi Valley Association, St. Louis, Mo.

Mount Wilson Observatory, Mount Wilson, Calif.

John Newbauer, Editor, *Astronautics*, American Rocket Society, Inc., New York, N. Y.

Thomas D. Nicholson, PH.D., Assistant Chairman and Astronomer, The American Museum—Hayden Planetarium, New York, N. Y.

Palomar Observatory, Mount Palomar, Calif.

Nicholas Panagakos, Science Editor, Institute for Space Studies, National Aeronautics and Space Administration, New York, N. Y.

G. Etzel Pearcy, B.E., M.A., PH.D., The Geographer, Department of State, Washington, D. C.

E. Penkala, London

James S. Pickering, Assistant Astronomer, American Museum—Hayden Planetarium, New York, N. Y.

The Polar Institute, London

Erwin Raisz, Cambridge, Mass.

C. S. Roetter, LL.B., London

C. A. Ronan, M.SC., F.R.A.S., Royal Society, London

Scientific Liaison Office, Australia, New Zealand, Canada

E. C. Slipher, D.SC., LL.D., Lowell Observatory, Flagstaff, Ariz.

David Stern, PH.D., Theoretical Division, National Aeronautics and Space Administration, Greenbelt, Md.

United Nations Information Centre, London

United Nations Statistical Office, New York, N. Y.

U.S. Department of Commerce, Bureau of the Census, Washington, D.C.

U.S. Department of Interior, Washington, D.C.

U.S. Naval Photographic Interpretation Center, Washington, D.C.

U.S.S.R. Academy of Science, Moscow

William Warntz, PH.D., Research Associate, American Geographical Society, New York, N. Y.

Bernard Workman, M.A., London

Yerkes Observatory, Williams Bay, Wisconsin

We also wish to thank all the others—geographers, cartographers, designers, editors and technicians—who gave valuable assistance in the preparation of this Atlas.

Illustrations on page 15: Lunar flight—based on a drawing, courtesy of American Rocket Society, Inc., New York, N. Y. Earth-Mars flight—based on a drawing, courtesy of Jet Propulsion Laboratory, California Institute of Technology, Pasadena, Calif. Earth-Venus flight—based on a drawing, courtesy of American Rocket Society and Jet Propulsion Laboratory. Mars—from tricolor separation negatives made July 4, 1954, by the National Geographic Society-Lowell Observatory Expedition to the Lamont-Hussey Observatory, Bloemfontein, South Africa, by E. C. Slipher; color print prepared by the Air Force Aero-nautical Chart and Information Center, St. Louis, Mo. Venus—photo, Mount Wilson and Palomar Observatories. Jupiter—original photograph by E. C. Slipher; color copy by J. B. Edson, Lowell Observatory. Page 17: far side of the Moon—Sovfoto, Moscow.

Aero Service Corporation, Philadelphia, Pa., a division of Litton Industries, produces many three-dimensional relief maps, including those photographed on pages 15, 22-23 and 30-41, as well as special maps for space navigation. It is the largest aerial mapping company in the world.

The three-dimensional relief maps of the North Atlantic and North Pacific Ocean floors, photographed on pages 42-44, were prepared by the United States Naval Photographic Interpretation Center, Washington, D.C.

The Fairbridge Geotectonic World Map, pages 138-139, is reproduced by courtesy of Rhodes W. Fairbridge, with special acknowledgment to Professor H. W. Menard and Professor Bruce C. Heezen. The photograph of the relief model on page 140 is also reproduced by courtesy of Professor Fairbridge.

The maps on pages 146-147 are based on the work of Preston E. James and others.

EDITED BY THE SPECIAL BOOK DIVISION OF READER'S DIGEST

DeWitt Wallace and Lila Acheson Wallace, Founders and Publishers

Alfred S. Dashiell, Editor

Editors: Elliott W. Schryver, Senior Editor
Peter Glemser, London
Letitia B. Kehoe, Charles Spain Verral, Anthony Wethered
Copy Editors: Paul A. Hirschman, Winifred F. Courtney

Art: Kenneth Stuart, Director
Edwin B. Kolsby
Edmund D. Smith, Jr., Murray J. Miller
Photographers: Joseph D. Barnell, William Sonntag

CONTENTS

PART ONE

THE UNIVERSE AND THE EARTH

PART TWO

THE COUNTRIES OF THE WORLD

CONTENTS

CONTENTS

PART THREE

THE WORLD ABOUT US

PART FOUR

INDEXES

From the center of the Earth to the outermost limits of space

Paradise is somewhere in the Far East, Jerusalem is the center of all nations, and the world itself is a flat disk surrounded by vast oceans. So the monks, mapmakers of the Middle Ages, saw the world they lived in.

Today our knowledge of the world has been greatly enriched through scientific discovery, travel and exploration. This Atlas has drawn upon the sum of that knowledge, accumulated through many lifetimes of research.

In *The Universe and the Earth*, Part One of this Atlas, we first view our Earth in space. Incurably inquisitive, man searches continually into every facet of our world and other worlds beyond. He knows that the Sun, around which our planet revolves, is a minor star at the edge of the Milky Way. A galaxy of many millions of stars, the Milky Way is itself only one among a million other galaxies moving in the infinity of space where traditional concepts of distance and time are meaningless.

The universe is a vision that dwarfs the globe on which we live and makes our tiny planet seem insignificant, but here life has been created and has developed. As yet we do not know whether the delicate balance of conditions which has made evolution possible on this planet has ever occurred on any other.

In the opening section of this Atlas, maps made from scientifically designed models show us how our world would appear to an observer hundreds of miles above the surface. Great mountain peaks stand out in sharp contrast to the worn surfaces of older ranges and the plains traversed by mighty rivers. The levels of the ocean floor tell the history of submerged lands and of deeps only recently explored.

Next come *The Countries of the World*. Towns and cities, rivers and railways can all be found easily, for the coloring is subdued and the place names are clear. Together with the relief section, these maps complete a picture of the landscape of our Earth and of the places where we live.

The third Part portrays *The World About Us*. The marvel of its creation cannot be told by any single map or chart. Each feature in this section of the Atlas has been devised to illustrate a most important aspect of the Earth — the evolution of the terrain beneath our feet and man's exploration of it, patterns of climate and vegetation, facts about world population and about the Earth's natural features. Each subject is linked to another, for none of the world's wonders or problems can be seen or understood in isolation.

If this Atlas is new in its manner of presenting geographically the facts about Earth and life and space, it is also new in another way: it provides the background for, and it points the way to, the discoveries and explorations that lie in the future.

The Editors

PART ONE

THE UNIVERSE AND THE EARTH

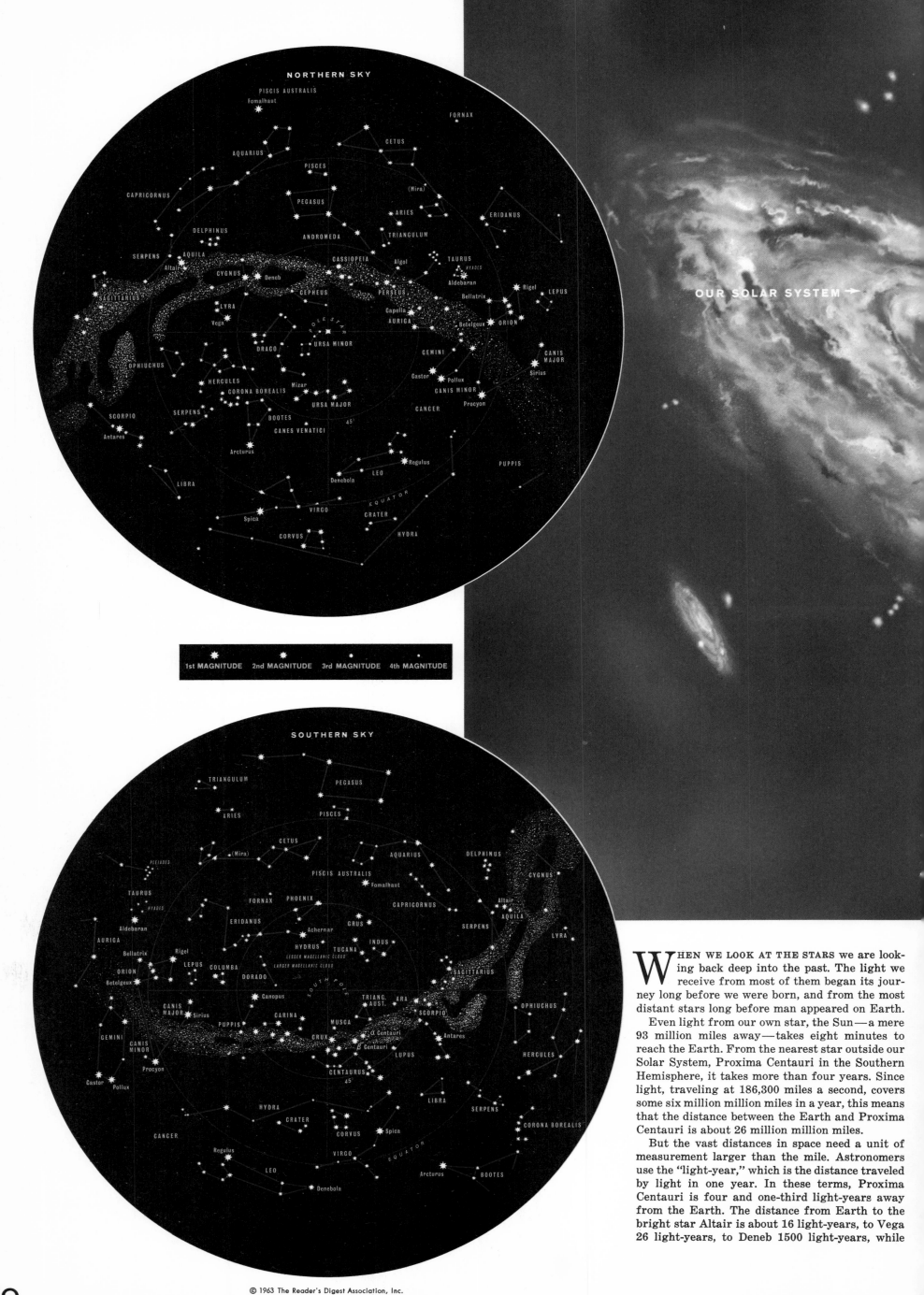

NORTHERN SKY

PISCIS AUSTRALIS
Fomalhaut
FORNAX
CETUS
AQUARIUS
PISCES
CAPRICORNUS
PEGASUS
(Mira)
ARIES
ERIDANUS
DELPHINUS
ANDROMEDA
TRIANGULUM
SERPENS
AQUILA
CASSIOPEIA
Algol
TAURUS
HYADES
Altair
CYGNUS
Deneb
PERSEUS
Aldebaran
SAGITTARIUS
CEPHEUS
Bellatrix
Rigel
LEPUS
LYRA
Capella
ORION
OPHIUCHUS
Vega
POLE STAR
AURIGA
Betelgeux
DRACO
URSA MINOR
GEMINI
CANIS
MAJOR
HERCULES
Mizar
Castor
Pollux
Sirius
CORONA BOREALIS
CANIS MINOR
SCORPIO
SERPENS
URSA MAJOR
CANCER
Procyon
Antares
BOOTES
45°
CANES VENATICI
LIBRA
Arcturus
Regulus
PUPPIS
LEO
Denebola
VIRGO
EQUATOR
CRATER
Spica
HYDRA
CORVUS

1st MAGNITUDE   2nd MAGNITUDE   3rd MAGNITUDE   4th MAGNITUDE

SOUTHERN SKY

TRIANGULUM
PEGASUS
ARIES
PISCES
CETUS
PLEIADES
(Mira)
AQUARIUS
DELPHINUS
TAURUS
PISCIS AUSTRALIS
CYGNUS
HYADES
FORNAX
PHOENIX
Fomalhaut
CAPRICORNUS
Altair
ERIDANUS
GRUS
SERPENS
AQUILA
Aldebaran
Achernar
INDUS
AURIGA
HYDRUS
TUCANA
LYRA
Bellatrix
Rigel
LESSER MAGELLANIC CLOUD
SAGITTARIUS
ORION
LEPUS
COLUMBA
LARGER MAGELLANIC CLOUD
Betelgeux
DORADO
SOUTH POLE
OPHIUCHUS
Canopus
TRIANG.
AUST.
ARA
CANIS
MAJOR
Sirius
CARINA
SCORPIO
GEMINI
PUPPIS
MUSCA
α Centauri
Antares
CANIS
MINOR
CRUX
β Centauri
LUPUS
HERCULES
Procyon
CENTAURUS
Castor
Pollux
45°
LIBRA
HYDRA
SERPENS
CRATER
CANCER
CORVUS
Spica
CORONA BOREALIS
Regulus
VIRGO
EQUATOR
LEO
Arcturus
BOOTES
Denebola

OUR SOLAR SYSTEM →

WHEN WE LOOK AT THE STARS we are looking back deep into the past. The light we
receive from most of them began its journey long before we were born, and from the most
distant stars long before man appeared on Earth.

Even light from our own star, the Sun—a mere
93 million miles away—takes eight minutes to
reach the Earth. From the nearest star outside our
Solar System, Proxima Centauri in the Southern
Hemisphere, it takes more than four years. Since
light, traveling at 186,300 miles a second, covers
some six million million miles in a year, this means
that the distance between the Earth and Proxima
Centauri is about 26 million million miles.

But the vast distances in space need a unit of
measurement larger than the mile. Astronomers
use the "light-year," which is the distance traveled
by light in one year. In these terms, Proxima
Centauri is four and one-third light-years away
from the Earth. The distance from Earth to the
bright star Altair is about 16 light-years, to Vega
26 light-years, to Deneb 1500 light-years, while

© 1963 The Reader's Digest Association, Inc.

OUTER SPACE: THE BOUNDLESS SKY

© 1963 The Reader's Digest Association, Inc.

some stars of the Milky Way are so distant their light takes thousands of years to reach us.

The stars vary greatly in size. Some, called super-giants, make our Sun seem a dwarf. Others are only a few thousandths of the Sun's size.

Stars also vary considerably in brightness, and so are graded into different "magnitudes." A star of the first magnitude is 100 times brighter than a star of the sixth magnitude.

The brighter stars—such as Rigel and Regulus —are not necessarily the nearest to us. Several very faint stars are in fact nearer to Earth than most of the bright ones.

From earliest times, men have grouped the stars under names of animals and legendary heroes. A few of these constellation figures, as they are called, such as Orion and Corona Borealis (the Northern Crown), do look something like the figures they are supposed to represent, though most call for powerful feats of imagination.

Because the Earth rotates on its axis, the stars —like the Sun by day—*appear* to wheel from east to west across the sky. In the Northern Hemisphere, only Polaris seems to stand still because it is almost directly above the North Pole.

With the unaided eye, we can see from 2000 to 2500 stars on a clear night. Binoculars will show thousands more, and a large telescope can reach out to thousands of millions of stars. Most of these lie in the bright girdle of our own galaxy, the Milky Way.

The Milky Way is a vast rotating system of a hundred billion stars. It is just one galaxy among billions of others in the Universe. The galactic structures in the Universe range from single galaxies to mammoth clusters containing as many as 500 galaxies.

Although the cluster of galaxies to which our Milky Way belongs is comparatively small (it has only 19 members), our galaxy itself ranks among the larger of the known stellar systems. The distance across it is 100,000 light-years.

In the illustration we see the Milky Way Galaxy from the viewpoint of an observer out in space. In the foreground near the bottom of the picture are two huge masses of stars and nebulae known as the Magellanic Clouds. Our galaxy lies 156,000 light-years beyond the Large Magellanic Cloud and 163,000 light-years beyond the Small Magellanic Cloud. The Andromeda Galaxy (far left), with a diameter greater than 100,000 light-years, appears small because it is two million light-years beyond the Milky Way.

Clusters of hundreds and thousands of stars move as units around the galaxy. Reddish stars are concentrated toward the center of the formation, blue stars in the outer portions. Dark gases and interstellar dust are grouped so close together here and there that starlight from beyond cannot be seen. Our Solar System—the Sun and nine planets—is just a faint dot in one of the spiral arms of the Milky Way, some 27,000 light-years from the center.

As man probes deeper into a Universe that may be boundless, the number of galaxies seems to grow as vast as the space through which they speed.

THE Sun dominates and dwarfs its solar family of the nine major planets and the several thousand smaller ones called "asteroids." Jupiter, the largest dependent planet of the Sun, is no more than a speck by comparison with it, and Jupiter is roughly 1300 times the size of the Earth. The Sun comprises over 99.87 percent of the entire mass in our Solar System. Yet, despite the comparative smallness of the planets and the enormous distances of empty space that separate them from the Sun and from one another, the Sun keeps them under strict control.

Revolving around it in elliptical orbits, these planets are held in their course by the gravitational attraction of the Sun, and are kept from being drawn into it by the speed with which they move through space. The closer they are to the Sun, the faster they move. Mercury—at an average distance of 36 million miles, the planet nearest the Sun—takes only about 88 days to travel around it, at a speed of 107,280 miles per hour. Mercury always faces the Sun with the same side. Venus, 67 million miles from the Sun, takes 224.7 days to complete its solar orbit at a speed of about 78,000 miles per hour. Evidence recorded by Mariner II spacecraft indicates that Venus, like Mercury, may keep the same face to the Sun. Or it may turn so slowly that its day and night roughly equal its year—the direction of its rotation being opposite to that of the other planets. If this is so, on Venus the Sun rises in the west and sets in the east, and the outer heavens remain fixed.

The Earth, 92,900,000 miles from the Sun, in its yearly orbit travels at a speed of 66,600 miles per hour. Pluto, now thought to be more than twice as large as was once estimated, is the most distant known planet. 3671 million miles from the Sun, Pluto takes just over 248 years at a speed of 10,440 miles per hour to make one journey around it.

Six of the planets have one or more moons revolving about them, with twelve belonging to Jupiter, nine to Saturn, five to Uranus, two each to Neptune and Mars and one to Earth. Two of Jupiter's moons, Callisto and Ganymede, are very large, exceeding even the planet Mercury in size.

Traveling in a great orbital belt between Mars and Jupiter are the uncounted numbers of asteroids. They range in size from a few yards in diameter to several hundreds of miles. The largest on record is Ceres, 480 miles in diameter. Asteroids have no moisture or air, and therefore no life as we know it can exist on them.

It is doubtful, indeed, if such life can exist on any planet except Earth. Mercury is so close to the Sun that the temperature on its sunlit side is estimated to reach 700° F. Venus, although almost twice as far from the Sun as Mercury, is believed to have a surface temperature of 800° F. uniformly distributed by strong winds. This high temperature may be due to the greenhouse effect of Venus' thick cloud covering, which traps the Sun's heat. Jupiter, Saturn, Uranus, Neptune and Pluto are all too cold to sustain life, and their surfaces are enveloped by layers of the poisonous gases methane and ammonia.

There has been much speculation as to whether a form of life exists on Mars. This planet has an atmosphere with water vapor and carbon dioxide present. The white caps at the Martian poles, probably hoarfrost, vanish in the summer and reappear in the winter. There are also seasonal color changes in what appears to be a kind of vegetation. The belief that the hundreds of miles of Martian "canals" were the work of intelligent beings has now been discounted. However, many authorities agree that some primitive life forms may exist on Mars.

A planet that has long aroused great interest is the giant of the Solar System, Jupiter. Spinning on its axis faster than any other planet, Jupiter has the shortest day of all, less than 10 hours in length. This rapid rotation has caused a bulging of its equator and a flattening of the polar regions. Striking in appearance with its great irregular bands of yellow and brown, Jupiter is best known for its mysterious Great Red Spot, which was discovered in 1665 and about which little is known.

Saturn with its vast rings is one of the most interesting and beautiful planets. The rings, 170,000 miles in diameter, are extremely thin—not more than 10 miles thick—and are composed of millions of small particles, all performing as independent satellites as they speed around the mother planet.

WHERE EARTH

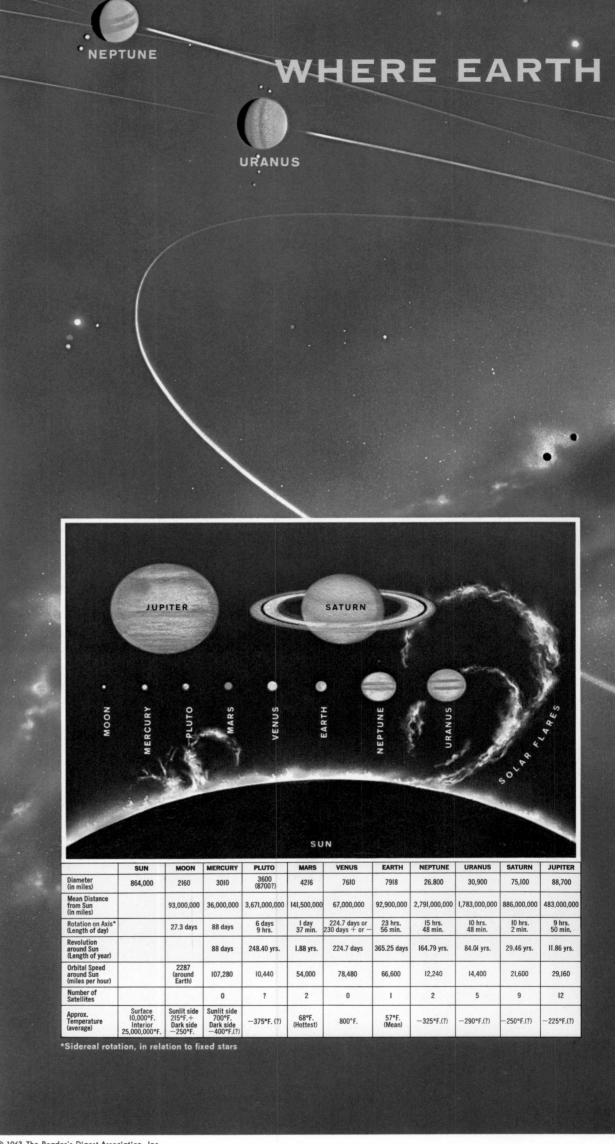

	SUN	MOON	MERCURY	PLUTO	MARS	VENUS	EARTH	NEPTUNE	URANUS	SATURN	JUPITER
Diameter (in miles)	864,000	2160	3010	3600 (8700?)	4216	7610	7918	26,800	30,900	75,100	88,700
Mean Distance from Sun (in miles)		93,000,000	36,000,000	3,671,000,000	141,500,000	67,000,000	92,900,000	2,791,000,000	1,783,000,000	886,000,000	483,000,000
Rotation on Axis* (Length of day)		27.3 days	88 days	6 days 9 hrs.	1 day 37 min.	224.7 days or 230 days + or −	23 hrs. 56 min.	15 hrs. 48 min.	10 hrs. 48 min.	10 hrs. 2 min.	9 hrs. 50 min.
Revolution around Sun (Length of year)			88 days	248.40 yrs.	1.88 yrs.	224.7 days	365.25 days	164.79 yrs.	84.01 yrs.	29.46 yrs.	11.86 yrs.
Orbital Speed around Sun (miles per hour)		2287 (around Earth)	107,280	10,440	54,000	78,480	66,600	12,240	14,400	21,600	29,160
Number of Satellites		0	?	2	0	1	2	5	9	12	
Approx. Temperature (average)	Surface 10,000°F. Interior 25,000,000°F.	Sunlit side 215°F.+ Dark side −250°F.	Sunlit side 700°F. Dark side −400°F.(?)	−375°F. (?)	68°F. (Hottest)	800°F.	57°F. (Mean)	−325°F.(?)	−290°F.(?)	−250°F.(?)	−225°F.(?)

*Sidereal rotation, in relation to fixed stars

© 1963 The Reader's Digest Association, Inc.

Another spectacular part of our Solar System is provided by comets. More than a million comets swing around the Sun in flat elliptical orbits. Some take only a few years to make the trip, but most have periods so lengthy that their return cannot be accurately predicted. The head of a comet, sometimes 50,000 miles wide, is composed mainly of dust and gases. When a comet comes near the Sun on its orbital flight, the gaseous matter in the head streams out to form a great glowing tail sometimes millions of miles long. This tail vanishes when the comet speeds away from the Sun. One of the most famous comets is named after the English astronomer Edmund Halley. He observed it in 1682 and accurately predicted its return every 76 years. Halley's Comet was last seen in 1910 and should be visible again in 1986.

Also racing through interplanetary space in regular orbits are billions upon billions of particles called meteorids. Some scientists believe that these bits of stone or metal, whose average size is no larger than a grain of sand, are fragments left

BELONGS: THE SOLAR SYSTEM

PLUTO

MERCURY

VENUS

SUN

MARS

ASTEROID BELT

MOON

EARTH

JUPITER

SATURN

THE SUN AND ITS PLANETS IN THE WINTER OF THE YEAR 2000

from disintegrated comets. When these particles plunge into the Earth's atmosphere they grow white hot and vaporize, becoming "shooting stars." Once in a while a mass of cosmic matter weighing tons plunges through the atmosphere to bury itself in the surface of the Earth. These large meteorites probably originate in the asteroid belt.

The composition of our Earth and its distance from the Sun seem to have provided exactly the right conditions in which an advanced form of life could develop. The life-giving energy of the

Sun, the source of all the heat and light in our Solar System, is generated by nuclear fusions in the Sun's interior. These raise the temperature deep inside the Sun to perhaps as high as 25,000,-000°F. So tremendous is the radiation rate of the Sun's energy that it loses millions of tons in weight every second. This rate of loss has been going on for five billion years, and the likelihood is that another five billion years will pass before the Sun's fuel is finally consumed and our great mother star winks out forever.

© 1963 The Reader's Digest Association, Inc.

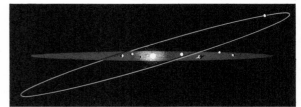

The planets of our Solar System not only travel around the Sun in the same direction, they also all lie in practically the same plane. Pluto is the exception. That faraway planet follows a path that is tilted 17 degrees from "the plane of the ecliptic," which is the name of the plane in which our Earth revolves.

THE REACH INTO SPACE

FOR THOUSANDS OF YEARS man has gazed up at the sky and wondered what lay beyond. Early astronomers studied the pinpoints of light in the heavens and drew star charts. They examined the Moon and the planets, too, as best they could. They learned much, yet the geography of space remained a mystery that would never be really solved until man found a way to travel to the celestial regions and explore and map them himself. But, unlike the birds he observed, man was bound to the ground by a mysterious force he later called "gravity."

When, in 1783, the balloon was invented, it was thought that a means had been found to break free. Within the next century daring "aerostatists" did soar to the upper limits of the breathable atmosphere and scientists succeeded in sending up recording devices to still greater heights. Even so, the balloon proved not to be the answer. The balloon needed the pressure of air to make it rise. It could not function in the vacuum of space.

In 1903 the Wright brothers flew the first engine-driven heavier-than-air machine and another era of sky adventuring began. But the great ocean of space beyond the atmosphere was still unreachable. The airplane, too, was helpless at extreme heights. It could not fly without air flowing across its wings, nor could its internal-combustion engine operate without air.

Finally, after 25 years of experimentation, the modern rocket was developed. Carrying its own oxygen, the rocket needed no air to make its fuel burn. Neither did it need air to buoy it up, or air for its jet stream of exhaust gases to push against. The rocket operated on the principle contained in Sir Isaac Newton's Third Law of Motion: *For every action there is an equal and opposite reaction.* It "kicked" itself forward in the same manner that a gun recoils when it is fired. The rocket functioned even better in the vacuum of space than in the atmosphere of Earth.

It was the rocket, then, that introduced the space age. This amazingly simple device, invented by the Chinese over 700 years before, now stood ready to carry man's recording instruments—and man himself—into the outer deeps of space. On October 4, 1957, such an engine launched an artificial satellite, Sputnik I, into orbit around the Earth—the first man-made object to gain freedom from the remorseless force of gravity.

Since the launching of the first satellite, a great many others have been sent speeding into space. Packed with delicate instruments, these satellites perform a multitude of tasks. They have discovered belts of radiation encircling the Earth, relayed trans-oceanic messages, measured the Earth's shape and located tropical storms long before their existence would otherwise have been suspected.

The first man-carrying satellite was placed in orbital flight around the Earth by the Russians on April 12, 1961. Numerous other manned flights have followed, some orbiting the Earth many times and covering hundreds of thousands of miles.

To launch a rocket, a great amount of thrust is necessary. Thrust is the propelling force produced by the exhaust stream of a rocket motor and is measured in pounds. The thrust force of a rocket must be much greater than the total rocket weight (including fuel and pay load) before the rocket lifts. Early rocket motors developed a mere 100 pounds of thrust. But by the end of World War II, 56,000 pounds were being delivered by the German V-2 rockets, which bombed London. During the early 1960s there were giant rocket engines rated at over a million pounds. Huge "solid-fuel" boosters are supplementing the liquid-fuel types. Nuclear energy, the ultimate power source, is also being harnessed.

We are, in fact, in a new era of manned space voyages—landings on the Moon, visits to our nearest neighbors, Mars and Venus, and even to the satellites of Jupiter. Our most ancient dreams are at the point of realization, and what the future holds for coming generations is barely imaginable.

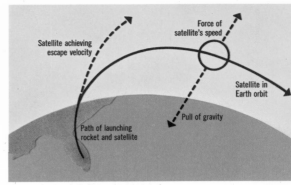

© 1963 The Reader's Digest Association, Inc.

THE LAUNCHING OF A SATELLITE INTO ORBIT

A satellite in orbit maintains a balance between the gravitational attraction of the Earth, which is trying to pull the satellite down from the sky, and its own speed. To be launched into orbit around the Earth, a satellite must be accelerated to 18,000 miles per hour at an altitude of 100 to 200 miles. This speed produces in the satellite the exact amount of centrifugal force necessary to counteract the pull of gravity. When this balance of forces occurs, the satellite is in orbit, whirling around the Earth once every 90 minutes on an elliptical path.

If the satellite were to slow down, the balance of the two forces would be upset, with the gravitational attraction becoming dominant. The satellite would then be drawn toward the Earth.

If the opposite occurred—if the speed of the satellite should increase—its centrifugal force would become the stronger of the two pulls. This would result in the elliptical orbit of the satellite becoming more and more elongated as the satellite moved farther away from the Earth. At the speed of 25,000 miles per hour the satellite would attain "escape velocity" and travel out into space, never to return.

In orbital flight, with his rocket engines shut off, an astronaut experiences a state of "weightlessness." He and his satellite are falling "freely" around the Earth with nothing to resist their plunge. The feeling of weight will return to the astronaut only when some resisting force begins to operate, such as the firing of rockets or the re-entry into the Earth's atmosphere.

© 1963 The Reader's Digest Association, Inc.

FLIGHT PATH OF AN ORBITING SATELLITE

The flight path of a satellite in orbit around the Earth is plotted on a map of the world as a wavy track—not as a straight line. While the satellite is swinging around the Earth at an angle to the Equator, the Earth itself is rotating on its own axis beneath the satellite. Therefore the satellite is never observed continuously along one circumference of the globe, but appears to swing intermittently north and south as it goes.

Each time the satellite completes a circuit (in 90 minutes for a 200-mile-altitude orbit), the Earth will have turned about 25 degrees under it. Thus, on its second trip the satellite will pass, not over its launching site, but over a point about 25 degrees to the west of this site.

Every subsequent orbit will bring about a similar 25-degree shift westward until, after approximately 16 orbits, the satellite (unless redirected) repeats its first orbital path. The track of each orbit will cross the previous track twice.

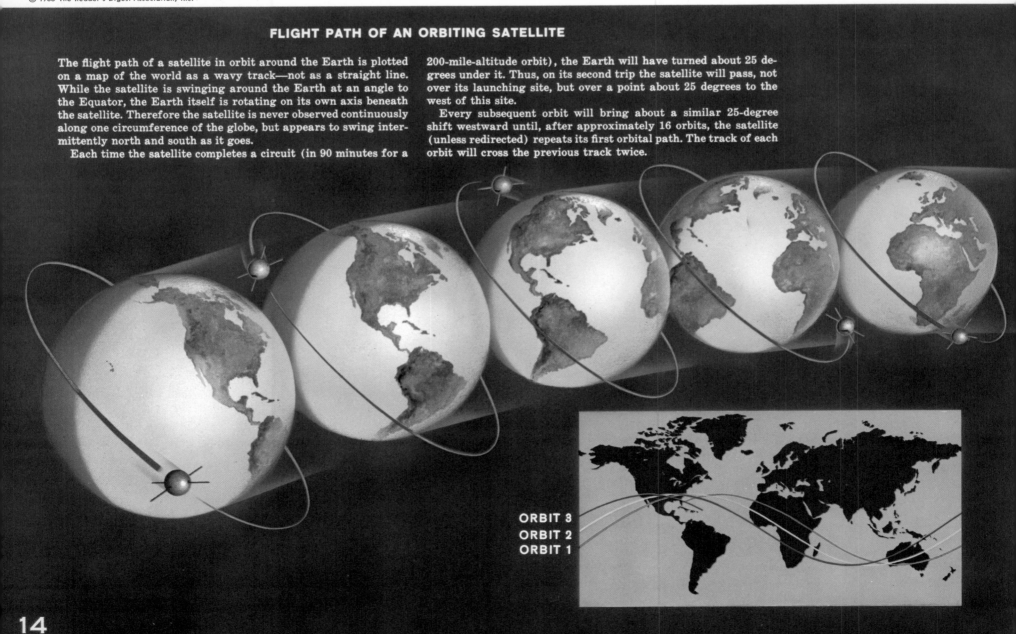

ORBIT 3
ORBIT 2
ORBIT 1

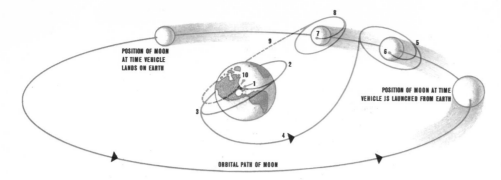

LUNAR FLIGHT

A number of flight patterns for a journey to the Moon have been plotted. The one illustrated here involves the use of a small lunar excursion vehicle, termed a "bug." The parent spacecraft carrying three astronauts and the bug is launched (1) by a three-stage rocket into an orbit (2) around the Earth at an altitude of 100 miles. At the proper moment for a Moon shot the third stage is fired (3) to give the spacecraft escape velocity. The spacecraft is sent on a 70-hour journey (4) to the Moon. Upon arrival in the Moon's vicinity, the craft is maneuvered into a 100-mile-high orbit (5) around the Moon. Two of the crew now enter the bug, de-

tach it from the mother ship and land on the Moon (6). After a period of exploration the lunar astronauts re-enter the bug and take off (7). Because of the low gravitational pull of the Moon (one sixth of Earth's gravity), relatively little thrust is needed. The bug links up with the mother craft (8), the Moon explorers enter the main ship, and the bug is cut loose and abandoned. The astronauts head back for the Earth in the mother craft (9) and a landing is made (10).

Another favored lunar flight plan involves an Earth-orbiting fuel tanker rather than the bug, but the excursion path is the same.

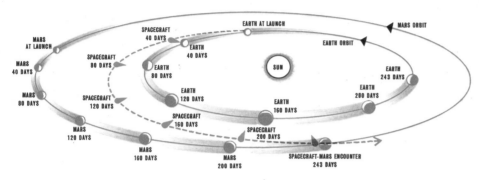

INTERPLANETARY FLIGHT PATHS

When a space vehicle leaves Earth to travel to another planet, it must first attain escape velocity (25,000 miles per hour). The craft then becomes, in effect, an independent satellite of the Sun, traveling in an orbit planned to intersect that of the planet to be visited.

If the objective is Mars or any of the other outer planets, the space vehicle must be launched from Earth in the same direction as the Earth's orbital movement around the Sun (see diagram above). This gives the vehicle an independent velocity greater than that of the Earth (Earth's orbital speed is 66,600 miles per hour). As a result, the spacecraft will travel outward, away from the Sun, with enough speed to counter the gravitational pull of the Sun. The spacecraft's orbit can be timed to intersect the path of an outer planet, such as Mars, at a given point in space. The duration of a flight to Mars would be about 243 days.

If the space vehicle is to rendezvous with an inner planet, such as Venus, the procedure is reversed (see diagram below). To go inward to-

ward the Sun, the vehicle must travel at less than the Earth's orbital speed. It is therefore launched counter to the direction of the Earth's orbital movement. This lowers the craft's speed below that of the Earth, even though the space vehicle will still travel around the Sun in the same direction as the Earth. The spacecraft will now pass inward toward the Sun and can be timed so that it will meet the oncoming Venus in approximately 108 days.

By extremely careful calculations and aiming, such orbits can be designed so that a space vehicle will rendezvous with any one of the planets, using very little more energy than is required to leave the Earth. Such a maneuver is called a "Hohmann transfer" after the engineer who developed the theory in the 1920s. Venus and Mars probes have been undertaken, using this type of orbit strategy, and plans are being made for sending instrument probes to Jupiter. The first manned landing on that planet will be made probably on one of Jupiter's "moons" rather than on Jupiter itself.

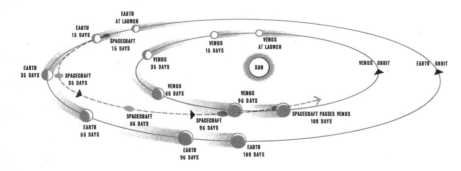

Planet	Minimum Distance from Earth (miles)	Maximum Distance from Earth (miles)	Surface Gravity (compared to 100 Earth pounds)	Escape Velocity (miles per hour)	Approximate Transit Time from Earth
Mercury	49,100,000	136,900,000	38 lbs.	9360	110 days
Venus	25,700,000	160,900,000	88 lbs.	23,040	108 days
Earth			100 lbs.	25,000	
Moon	221,463	252,710	16 lbs.	5400	72 hours
Mars	34,000,000	247,000,000	39 lbs.	14,400	243 days
Jupiter	362,000,000	597,000,000	265 lbs.	133,200	2.7 years
Saturn	773,000,000	1,023,000,000	117 lbs.	79,200	6 years
Uranus	1,594,000,000	1,946,000,000	92 lbs.	46,800	16 years
Neptune	2,654,000,000	2,891,000,000	123 lbs.	50,400	31 years
Pluto	2,605,000,000	4,506,000,000	16 (?)lbs.	5400 (?)	46 years

THE MOON has thousands of craters pitting its surface. Hell Crater, shown here in model form, is small by lunar standards (20 miles in diameter) and has a cluster of mountains at the center of its sunken floor. Such a crater may be chosen as a landing area for the first U.S. manned Moon flight.

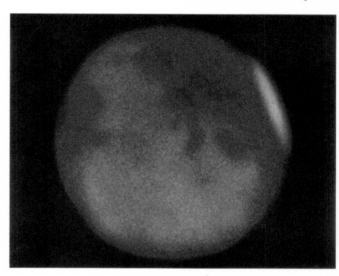

MARS, when studied by telescope, reportedly reveals canal-like lines that do not show up in photographs. The patches of color in this picture are believed to be zones of vegetation. The white area, one of the polar caps, is thought to be covered by a thin coating of ice.

VENUS' surface is an inferno darkened by a curtain of clouds. According to recent radar studies, there are sandy or dusty mountains and plains dotted with molten pools. The brightest of the planets seen from Earth, Venus appears smallest when full and largest when crescent-shaped.

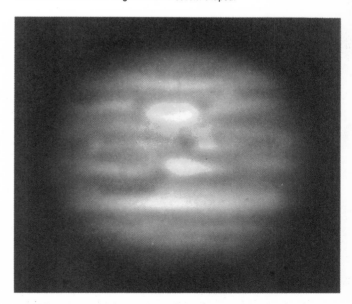

JUPITER is renowned for its Great Red Spot, over 30,000 miles long and 7000 miles wide. The Spot undergoes strange color changes (as in this photograph, where it appears almost white). The dark bands circling Jupiter are believed to be atmospheric, the yellowish areas to be the planet itself.

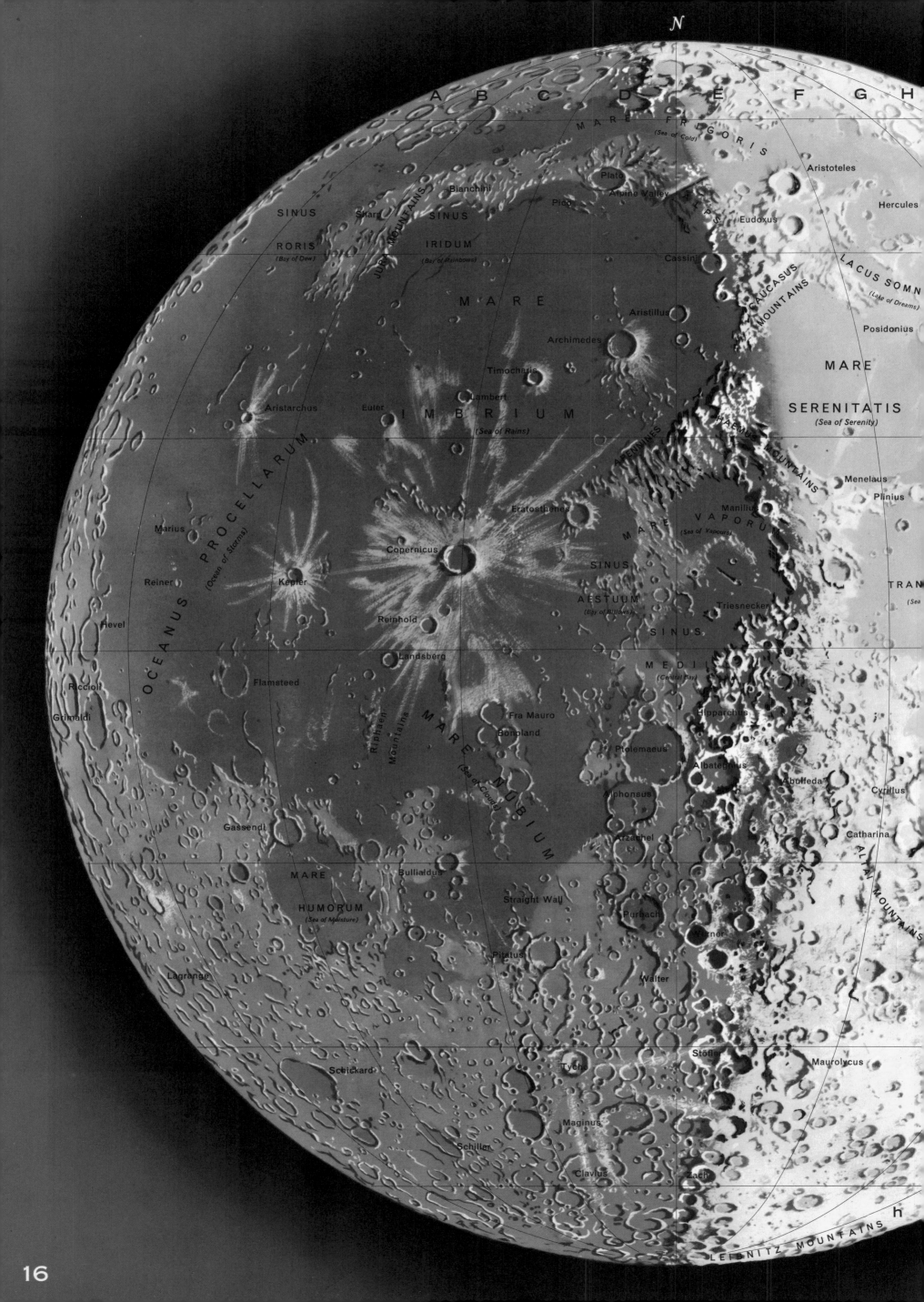

N

A B C D E F G H

MARE FRIGORIS
(Sea of Cold)

Aristoteles

Plato   Hercules
SINUS   Sharp   Bianchini   Alpine Valley
RORIS   SINUS   Pico   Eudoxus
(Bay of Dew)   IRIDUM   Cassini
                             (Bay of Rainbows)   LACUS SOMN
                                                                                                 (Lake of Dreams)
M A R E   Aristillus
                                                                                           Posidonius
                              Archimedes
                      Timocharis   MARE

                           Lambert   SERENITATIS
        Aristarchus   Euler   I M B R I U M   (Sea of Serenity)
                             (Sea of Rains)

                                                                                           Menelaus
    Marius   Manilius
                                      Eratosthenes   (Sea of Vapours)   Plinius
                                                              VAPORUM
            Copernicus   SINUS
    Reiner   Kepler   AESTUUM   TRAN
                                                      (Bay of Billows)   Triesnecker   (Sea
    Hevel   Reinhold
                                                   SINUS
                                          Landsberg
                                                   MEDI
                                          Flamsteed   (Central Bay)
    Riccioli   Hipparchus
                               Riphaen   Fra Mauro
    Grimaldi   Mountains   Bonpland   Albategnius
                                           Ptolemaeus   Abulfeda
                                    MARE NUBIUM   Alphonsus   Cyrillus
                                    (Sea of Clouds)
            Gassendi   Arzachel   Catharina

                                    Bullialdus
        MARE   ALTAI MOUNTAINS
        HUMORUM   Straight Wall
        (Sea of Moisture)   Purbach
                                                   Werner
                        Pitatus
        Lagrange   Walter

                                                                                   Maurolycus
                                          Stöfler
            Schickard
                          Tycho   Zach
                    Maginus
        Schiller
                        Clavius

16

LEIBNITZ MOUNTAINS   h

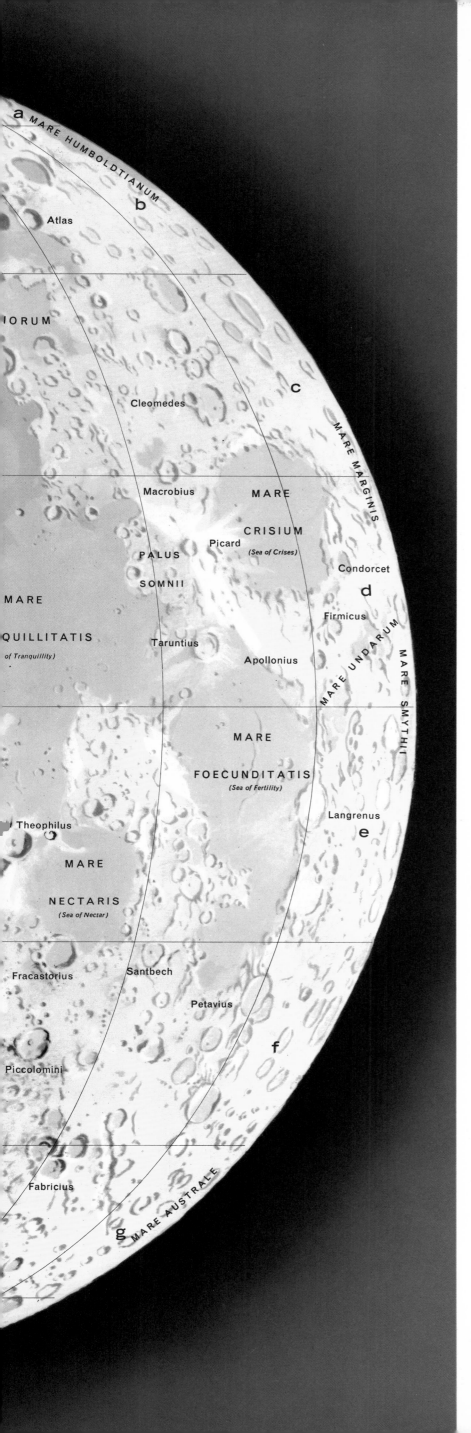

THE MOON

EARTH'S NATURAL SATELLITE

THE MOON IS UNIQUE in our Solar System. Many planets have satellites, but these are small in relation to their mother planets. The Moon is the only satellite of a size comparable to its planet, Earth.

The large map shows the near side of the Moon, which always faces the Earth; the far side is therefore never seen from Earth. As the Moon orbits the Earth, its periods of sunlight (its "day") and darkness (its "night") are each a half-month long.

To the naked eye the Moon seems to be made up of bright and darker patches. The bright parts are mountains and craters which catch the light of the Sun; the large darker areas are the low-lying plains. Once thought to be seas, these plains are still called by such names as Mare Imbrium (Sea of Rains) and Oceanus Procellarum (Ocean of Storms), though in fact the Moon is entirely without water.

High, sharp-peaked mountains, similar to the Apennines, rise to 20,000 feet. The highest are the Leibnitz Mountains, near the Moon's south pole, which reach 35,000 feet, higher than Mount Everest.

The most striking features are the many thousands of craters, named after philosophers and men of science. Possibly caused by the impact of meteorites, they range in size from pits a mile or less across, to magnificent walled plains such as Clavius, which is some 150 miles in diameter. Two of the finest, Copernicus and Tycho, are both over 50 miles across and have walls rising to heights above two miles. From these two craters and some others, bright streaks radiate for thousands of miles across mountains and valleys. Their origin is unknown; they may be some whitish material that welled up through cracks in the Moon's crust, or surface deposits thrown out when the craters were formed.

With a diameter about one quarter of the Earth's, the Moon has a surface area less than half that of the Atlantic Ocean. Its gravitational pull is correspondingly smaller, only about one sixth of the Earth's.

The Moon is without atmosphere, its gravity being too weak to hold down gas in any quantity. There is no erosion due to weather, and the Moon's features have therefore undergone little major change since they were formed. There is no sound, which is a vibration transmitted through air. With no atmosphere to protect it from the Sun by day or to imprison the heat by night, the Moon has great extremes of temperature. At the equator, the daytime temperature at the Moon's surface rises to 215°F., higher than that of boiling water, and at night the temperature sinks to −250°F. Under these conditions no life as we know it can exist.

Average distance from Earth......238,900 miles	Mass in terms of Earth 1:81
Diameter .... 2160 miles (Earth's diameter 7918 miles)	Sidereal Period ....27.3 days (approx.) (time taken to make one complete circuit of Earth)
Density ....3.3 times that of water (Earth's density 5.5 times that of water)	Synodic Period ....29.5 days (approx.) (interval between one new Moon and the next)

THE FAR SIDE OF THE MOON

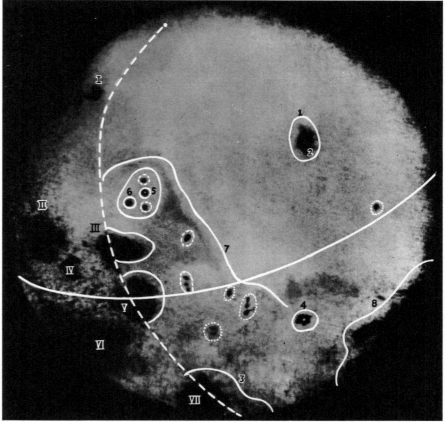

In October 1959 the Russian lunar probe Lunik 3 photographed the far side of the Moon. The above photograph shows the features classified and named by the Soviets: 1 — The Sea of Moscow; 2 — Gulf of the Astronauts; 3 — Continuation of the Southern Sea; 4 — Tsiolkovsky Crater; 5 — Lomonosov Crater; 6 — Joliot-Curie Crater; 7 — Soviet Mountains; 8 — Sea of Dreams.

The solid line indicates the Moon's equator. The broken line divides the hemispheres of the Moon seen and unseen from Earth. Features on the visible side are: I — Sea of Humboldt; II — Sea of Crisis; III — Border Sea; IV — Sea of Waves; V — Sea of Smyth; VI — Sea of Fertility; VII — Southern Sea. Areas circled with a dotted line are still being studied for classification.

© 1963 The Reader's Digest Association, Inc.

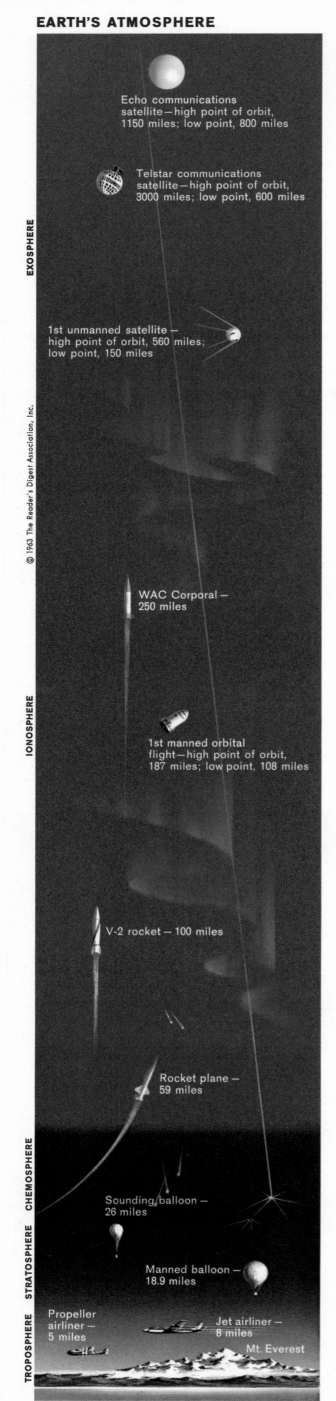

EARTH'S ATMOSPHERE

Echo communications satellite—high point of orbit, 1150 miles; low point, 800 miles

Telstar communications satellite—high point of orbit, 3000 miles; low point, 600 miles

1st unmanned satellite—high point of orbit, 560 miles; low point, 150 miles

WAC Corporal—250 miles

1st manned orbital flight—high point of orbit, 187 miles; low point, 108 miles

V-2 rocket—100 miles

Rocket plane—59 miles

Sounding balloon—26 miles

Manned balloon—18.9 miles

Propeller airliner—5 miles

Jet airliner—8 miles

Mt. Everest

© 1963 The Reader's Digest Association, Inc.

EXOSPHERE

IONOSPHERE

CHEMOSPHERE

STRATOSPHERE

TROPOSPHERE

Earth's atmosphere, the blanket of gases surrounding the planet, is the factor that, more than any other, enables life to exist. Without its protective insulation, temperatures would swing from unbearable cold at night to unbearable heat during the day. No one knows how far above the Earth the atmosphere extends, but it is probably at least 1000 miles. The air is not a uniform mass but can be divided into layers, each with its own characteristics.

The air here is so rarefied that its density is only one million-millionth of that at ground level. Air particles move freely, some escaping into the near-vacuum of outer space.

In the ionosphere the air particles are electrically charged (ionized) by the Sun's ultraviolet radiation, and congregate in four main layers: D, E, F_1 and F_2. It is these layers which reflect radio waves back to the ground.

F_2 Layer (150-250 miles)

The glowing auroras (northern and southern lights) are caused by streams of fast electrons and protons impinging upon the ionosphere. The auroras occur at varying heights between 40 and 600 miles.

F_1 Layer (90-150 miles)

It is mainly in the lower ionosphere that meteors burn up as they meet the increased air resistance. F_2 and F_1 layers reflect short radio waves. E layer reflects long radio waves. Also called the Heaviside layer, it is the lowest stable layer. D layer is unstable and unpredictable.

E Layer (60-90 miles)

Hydroxyl zone, where water vapor is broken up by sunlight into hydrogen atoms and molecules of one hydrogen and one oxygen atom (hydroxyl).

D Layer (45-60 miles)

The chemosphere is defined mainly by an accumulation of ozone gas at a height of 20 to 30 miles. Ozone absorbs some of the Sun's ultraviolet rays and is the Earth's main defense against the Sun's harmful effects. Cosmic particles from space collide with molecules at various heights in Earth's atmosphere.

Throughout the 10-mile-thick layer of stratosphere, the temperature varies little, and is usually about −70° F. At the lower boundary, the tropopause, the direct effects of Earth's weather are not usually felt.

From the ground to the tropopause the temperature drops steadily from about 59° F. at sea level (in temperate zones) to about −70° F. at seven miles (the average height of the troposphere), while the air thins out rapidly with increasing height.

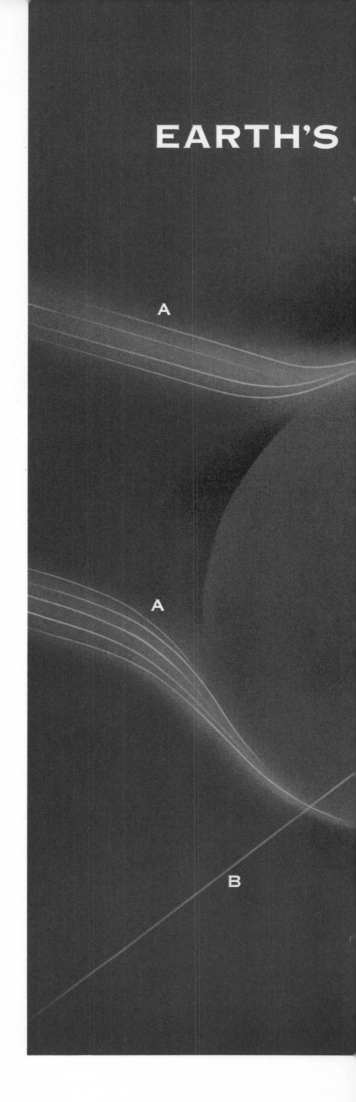

EARTH'S

THE EARTH IS A GREAT MAGNET. The holding force of its magnetic field, arching from pole to pole, entraps a vast belt of radiation about the Earth. This zone is called the Van Allen Belt, named after Dr. James A. Van Allen, whose dramatic discovery came in 1958 when he launched recording instruments aboard the first U.S. Explorer satellites. It was discovered then that high-energy protons and electrons are held within the belt. Such trapped particles may be produced when strong cosmic rays which penetrate the Earth's atmosphere collide with molecules of air.

The Van Allen Belt is broad—its inner limit about 600 miles above the Earth and its outer limits reaching some 35,000 miles into space. Crescent-shaped, its rim dips down toward the North

ENVIRONS

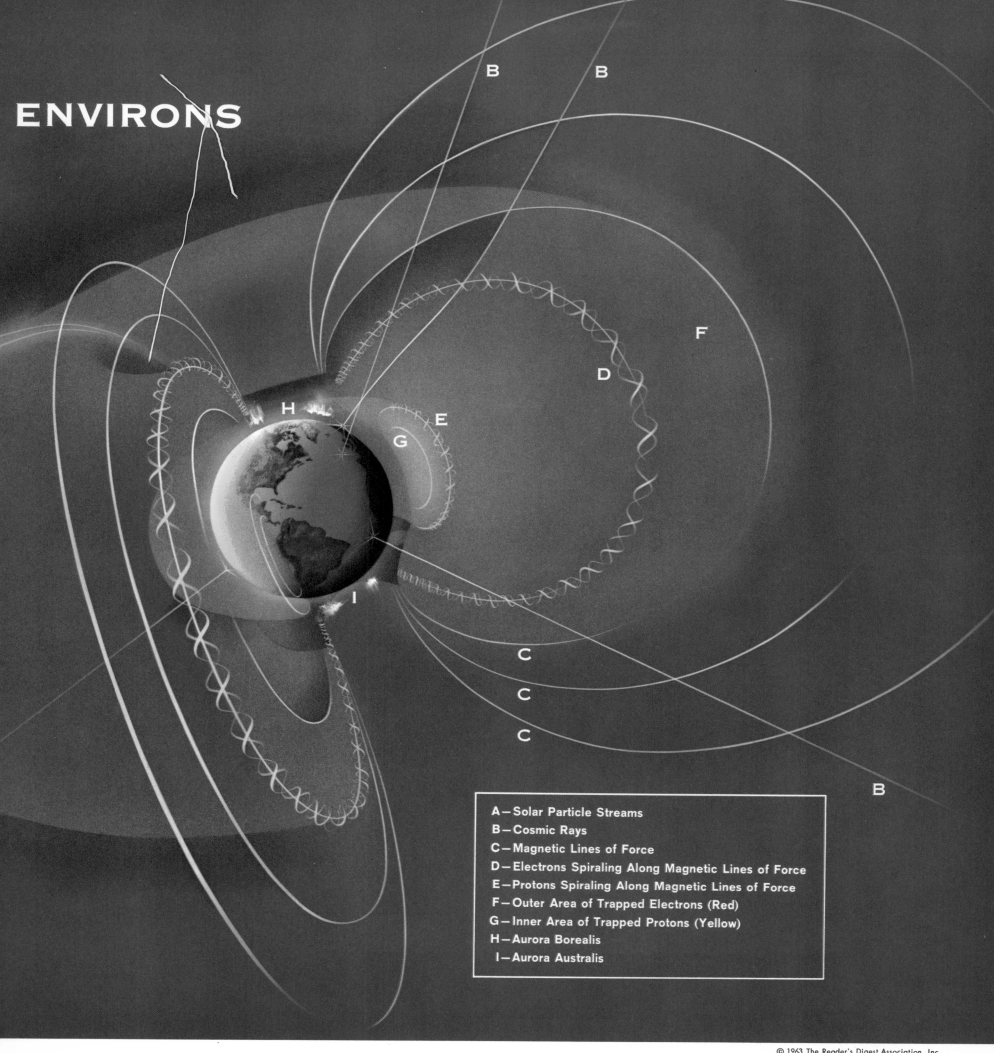

A — Solar Particle Streams
B — Cosmic Rays
C — Magnetic Lines of Force
D — Electrons Spiraling Along Magnetic Lines of Force
E — Protons Spiraling Along Magnetic Lines of Force
F — Outer Area of Trapped Electrons (Red)
G — Inner Area of Trapped Protons (Yellow)
H — Aurora Borealis
I — Aurora Australis

© 1963 The Reader's Digest Association, Inc.

and South Poles, where the Earth's magnetic field is most powerful. The Van Allen Belt poses a serious problem for the space traveler. Manned orbital flights are safe enough at 200 miles or so above the Earth, far under the inner rim of the belt. But when a manned spacecraft sets out for the Moon, Venus or Mars, great care will have to be taken to shield the humans aboard from the lethal effect of radiation until the zone has been passed.

The vast ocean of space that surrounds our Earth is ever active. Through it surge currents and tides of heat, light and many other kinds of radiation. These powerful streams of energy come almost entirely from one source—the Sun.

The Sun is more than a ball of raging hot gases.

It is a tremendous thermonuclear furnace, slowly fusing hydrogen atoms into helium to produce incredible amounts of energy.

The substance of the Sun is never still. Short-lived eruptions, gigantic and dark, are constantly appearing across its face. Every 11 years these sunspots—looking like whirlpools—become especially numerous. Some are so large they could swallow up our Earth a hundred times over.

During the solar eruptions, great flares leap from the vicinity of the sunspots and slash out hundreds of thousands of miles across space. The flares spew out clouds of X rays and high-energy particles in all directions. Shooting toward the Earth, traveling at tremendous speeds, they strike the magnetic field and are deflected to the North

and South Poles. Here, fast electrons and protons, possibly escaping from the Van Allen Belt, interact with the upper atmosphere to produce one of the grand mysteries of the Earth—the aurora borealis and aurora australis, or the northern and southern lights. Unusually brilliant displays of these luminous arcs and draperies are caused when, following a large sunflare and a heavy bombardment of high energy particles, magnetic storms agitate the Earth's magnetic field.

Much information has been gathered about the sunflare particles, gamma rays, X rays and all the others that make up the electro-magnetic spectrum. A great deal more must be learned before man embarks on his first voyage beyond the terrestrial limits of the Earth.

THE MASS OF LAND

In full summer, from a point above central eastern Europe, the whole range of the Earth's surface structure can be seen. To the north a great plain stretches from the North Sea across Europe into Siberia, and finally merges into the close-packed ice floes of the Arctic. To the south an immense desert barrier sweeps from the shores of the Atlantic in a giant scimitar curve across the north of Africa, Arabia, Turkestan and to the Gobi. In Asia the mountains broaden out from the Caucasus to form the great wall of the mighty Himalayas with the Tibetan plateau behind them; and farther south lie the hot and densely populated lands of southern Asia.

In winter a view from the same point would reveal a dramatically unbroken sheet of snow stretching from the northern plain of Poland to the Pacific, demonstrating how the cold intensifies as the land recedes from the maritime western edges and reaches into the heart of the continent.

AROUND

These are views of the world as no man has ever seen it—a world exposed as a blanket of water; as a globe roofed in ice; as illusions of light and shadow. Here the world is seen in perspective,

WHERE MEN LIGHTEN THE DARKNESS

At night, populated areas prick out patterns of light. Centered on London there is a half-world in which live nine tenths of the people on the Earth. At night, lights in western Europe form a bright galaxy, for this region contains 85 towns with populations of 200,000 or over. In the eastern United States glow the lights of 40 such cities.

Because of the tilt of the Earth's axis, London can never be at the center of the Earth's dark hemisphere. The situation shown here represents midnight in London about December 22, when London is nearest to the center of the Earth's own shadow.

Already in China, Japan and Indonesia the homes of many millions of people are in daylight.

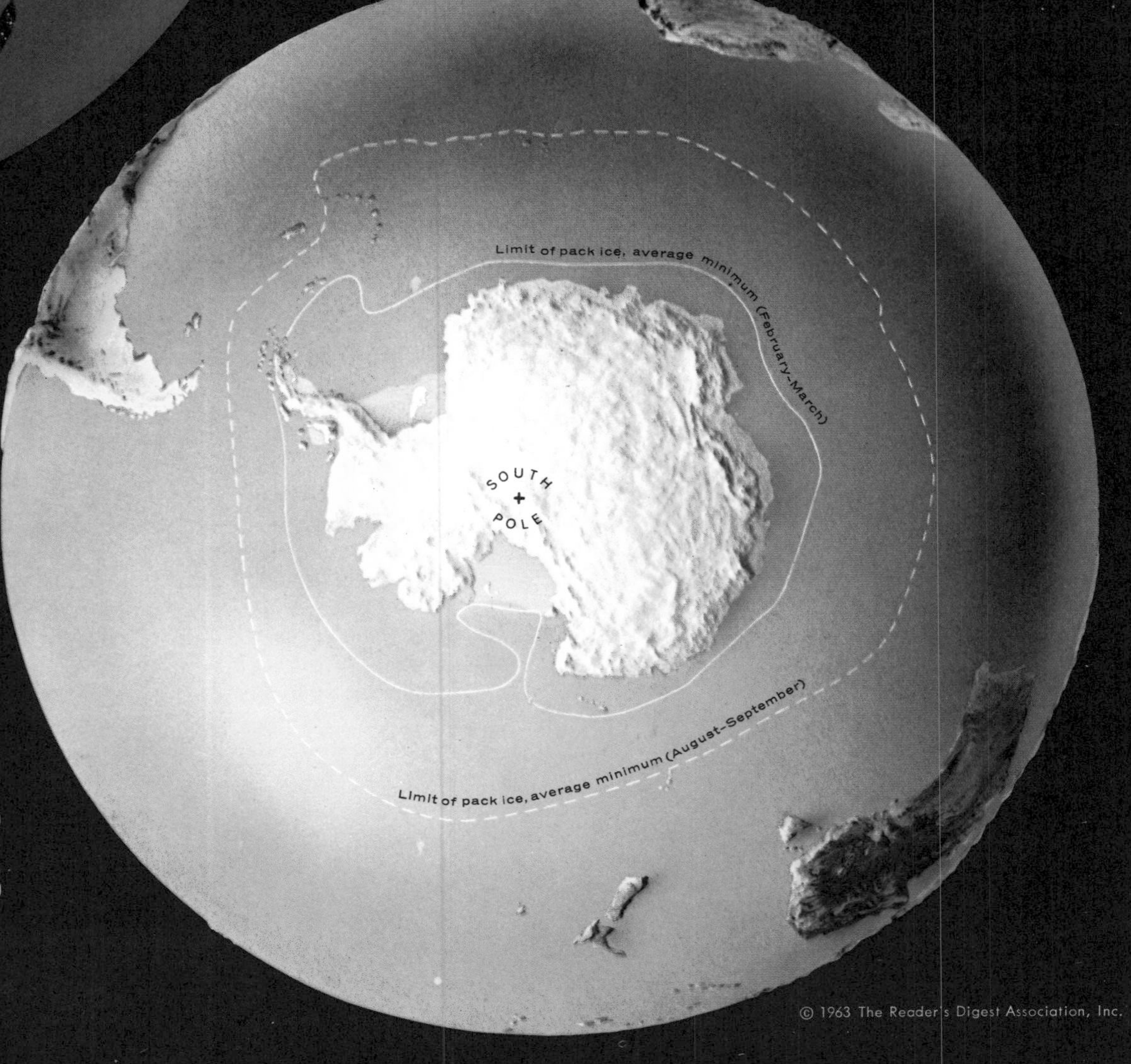

A CONTINENT OF ICE

Seen from a point over the South Pole, the Southern Hemisphere seems to be dominated by the shining ice cap that covers an island larger than Europe. In almost every direction the horizon is sea, although the tips of three continents extend into this half-world. Cape Horn is 2350 miles from the South Pole; Buenos Aires is 3800 miles from it; the Cape of Good Hope lies a similar distance away; Christchurch in New Zealand and Hobart in Tasmania, the largest towns near to the Pole, are 3200 miles away.

The ice continent is itself uninhabited, and the stormy southern seas are deserted except for icebergs broken adrift from the polar ice cap.

SOUTH + POLE

Limit of pack ice, average minimum (February-March)

Limit of pack ice, average minimum (August-September)

© 1963 The Reader's Digest Association, Inc.

THE WATER PLANET

Tahiti is at the center of this half-world that is almost all water. To the east and south of Tahiti are thousands of square miles of the Pacific Ocean without a single island or reef. In the western Pacific, groups of tiny islands gleam white in the sunlight; far to the north lies Hawaii, a solitary stepping-stone on the 6200-mile hop from North America to Asia. Solid land masses are far away. To the southwest is Australia—with Sydney 3801 miles from the island of Tahiti. The vast semicircle of the Americas serrates the opposite skyline; Vancouver is 4888 miles from Tahiti, Panama 5180, Cape Horn 4950, Tokyo 5893.

Compare this hemisphere with the one to its left. There, millions of people live in the heart of Asia. Here, in the water hemisphere, live only a few hundred thousand people, thousands of miles from any sizable land.

THE WORLD

night and day, and from four directions. Hold these pages 18 inches from your eyes. Each of the half-worlds will reveal the Earth the same size you would see it if you were 25,000 miles out in space.

DAWN ADVANCES

Part of the world is in shadow: dawn is just reaching the Americas. The first rays of the rising sun break on the hills of Nova Scotia and Brazil, while the glaciers of Greenland are already in full daylight. It is nine in London and breakfast is over, four in the morning in New York, an hour after midnight in San Francisco and noon in Baghdad.

Only at the equinoxes in March and September does every place in the world have an equal number of hours of darkness and light. In June the tilt of the Earth's axis brings full daylight all round the clock to the North Pole. It is then midsummer in the Northern Hemisphere and midwinter in the Southern.

THE ROOF OF THE WORLD

The North Pole, with its waste of broken ice, is the hub of this view. The floating ice of the North Pole merges into the frozen northlands of Russia and Canada. Below comes the belt of coniferous forest which rings the world from the Atlantic Ocean to the Pacific and, jumping the 50-mile gap between Siberia and North America, sweeps on again from the Pacific Ocean to the Atlantic. Below the forest region, great towns describe another circle round the globe—Leningrad 2070 miles from the North Pole, Glasgow 2360, Quebec 3000 and Edmonton 2520. Along this ring the railways, highways and air routes make a web of communications that continues across the oceans by ship and plane. Far on the horizon lies the belt of desert and mountain between temperate and tropical lands.

ST. OF JUAN DE FUCA
C. Disappointment
Seattle
MT. RAINIER 14,410
COAST RANGES
Columbia R.
CASCADE
Portland
MT. HOOD 11,245
45°
Snake R.
SAWTOOTH MTS.
MT. CLEVELAND 10,124
ROCKY
BITTERROOT RANGE
BLUE MTS.
Salmon R.
SACAJAWEA PK. 10,033
SALMON RIVER MTS.
Boise
Yellowstone
Billings
ABSAROKA RANGE
BANNETT PEAK 13,785
Snake River Plain
BIG HORN MTS.
MOUNTAINS

C. Mendocino
MT. SHASTA 14,162
LASSEN PEAK 10,457
COAST RANGES
SIERRA
Humboldt R.
Pyramid Lake
Great Salt Lake
Salt Lake City
South Pass
WASATCH RANGE
KINGS PEAK 13,498
LARAMIE RANGE
MEDICINE BOW PK. 12,005
Cheyenne
Pt. Arena
Sacramento R.
Donner Pass
Reno
California Trail
SHOSHONE MTS.
NEVADA
ARID ZONE
WHEELER PEAK 13,058
LONGS PEAK 14,255
ROCKY
San Francisco
San Joaquin R.
MT. WHITNEY 14,495
COAST RANGES
MT. ELBERT 14,420
Denver
PIKES PEAK 14,109
Pt. Sur
DIABLO RANGE
Colorado R.
Grand Canyon
Pt. Arguello
Mojave Desert
HUMPHREYS PK. 12,633
Painted Desert
SAN JAN MTS.
MOUNTAINS
Los Angeles
SAN BERNARDINO MT. 11,485
SANTA CATALINA I.
Colorado R.
Salton Sea
Phoenix
Albuquerque
Santa Fe Trail
San Diego
GALIURO MTS.
SACRAMENTO MTS.
Pecos R.
Pta. Banda
GUADALUPE PEAK 8751
Rio Grande
CERRO LA ENCANTADA 10,100
GULF OF CALIFORNIA
Llano Estacado
Edwards Plateau
30°
SIERRA MADRE OCCIDENTAL
SMOKY PEAK 7895
SIERRA MADRE ORIENTAL
BOLSON DE MAPIMI
MEXICO
Rio Grande

Columbia R.
120°
ROCKY MTS.
CANADA
100°
N
Red R.
Missouri R.
Platte R.
North Platte
Republican R.
Arkansas
Oklahoma City

PACIFIC OCEAN

For Alaska see page 30.

160°   155°
KAUAI I.
OAHU I.
Honolulu
MOLOKAI I.
PACIFIC   OCEAN
MAUI
20°   20°
HAWAII
50   0   100 Miles
HAWAII I.
160°   155°

THE COUNTRIES of the world, as they might be seen by an astronaut, appear on the relief maps on this and the following pages. Looking down, we see the snow- and ice-covered regions edging the Arctic Ocean; the Antarctic, bleak and formidable in its cold isolation; the lands becoming warmer as we approach the Equator; the shadowy forms of hills rising above the general level of the Earth; the great mountain ranges in all their ruggedness, forming immense natural barriers as they sweep across the continents regardless of man-imposed boundaries; the low-lying plains, some richly fertile, others wide, arid wastes.

In magnificent relief, we see the coastline, sometimes falling abruptly, sometimes sloping gently,

STATES

L. of the Woods
Fargo
Duluth
ISLE ROYALE
LAKE SUPERIOR
Sault Ste. Marie
MANITOULIN I.
BEAVER I.
LAKE MICHIGAN
LAKE HURON
Minneapolis St. Paul
Milwaukee
Chicago
Detroit
LAKE ERIE
Cleveland
Sioux Falls
Des Moines
maha
Kansas City
St. Louis
L. of the Ozarks
Indianapolis
Cincinnati
Louisville
BOSTON MTS.
OUACHITA MTS.
Little Rock
Memphis
Dallas
Jackson
Birmingham
Atlanta
Houston
New Orleans
ATCHAFALAYA BAY

L. Abitibi
Gouin Reservoir
Lake St. John
Québec
L. Nipissing
Ottawa R.
Montreal
St. Lawrence R.
MT. MANSFIELD
Montpelier
MT. WASHINGTON
Concord
Portland
ADIRONDACK MTS.
MOUNT MARCY
Toronto
L. ONTARIO
CATSKILL MTS.
Hartford
Providence
Boston
Cape Cod
MARTHAS VINEYARD
NANTUCKET
Montauk Pt.
LONG ISLAND
New York
Trenton
Pittsburgh
Philadelphia
Baltimore
Cape May
Washington
Richmond
CHESAPEAKE BAY
Norfolk
C. Charles
Charleston
BLUE RIDGE
Roanoke
Raleigh
C. Hatteras
C. Lookout
APPALACHIAN
CLINGMANS DOME
BLUE RIDGE
MOUNTAINS
Columbia
Cape Fear
Cape Romain
Savannah R.
Altamaha
C. San Blas
Cape Canaveral
Lake Okeechobee
Miami
BAHAMA IS.
FLORIDA KEYS
Cape Sable

GULF OF MEXICO

ATLANTIC OCEAN

Missouri R.
Mississippi R.
Ohio R.
Wabash R.
Tennessee R.
Cumberland R.
Red R.
Pearl R.
Chattahoochee R.

50 25 0   50   100   150   200 Miles

Relief map copyright: Aero Service Corp., Philadelphia 20, Pa., a Division of Litton Industries

down into the sea, which gives a clear pattern of
the shapes of continents in their early evolution.
We become aware of the vastness of the oceans,
the great depths in many of them, and their submerged peaks and mountain ranges.

LAND ELEVATIONS

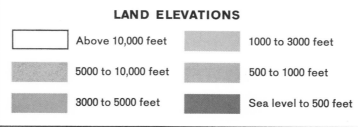

	Above 10,000 feet		1000 to 3000 feet
	5000 to 10,000 feet		500 to 1000 feet
	3000 to 5000 feet		Sea level to 500 feet

This map and the reliefs on pages
30-35 and 42-44 are vertically magni-
fied 20 times. On the maps on pages
24-29 and 36-37 the vertical magnifi-
cation is 30 times; on pages 38-41
it is 25 times.

THE APPALACHIAN RANGE

THE APPALACHIAN RANGE, the oldest chain in the United States, sweeps from Canada 1500 miles southward to central Alabama. It includes the White Mountains of New Hampshire, the Green Mountains of Vermont, the Alleghenies, the Blue Ridge Mountains, the Black Mountains, the Great Smokies and lesser ranges. These form the divide that separates the rivers flowing into the Atlantic Ocean from those entering the Gulf of Mexico.

A number of these rivers have cut deep valleys known as "gaps," among which are the Delaware Water Gap, the Shenandoah Valley and the Cumberland Gap. (There are also wind gaps.) Through the Cumberland Gap, on the borders of Kentucky, Tennessee and Virginia, Daniel Boone blazed one of the principal routes to the west in 1775 — the Wilderness Road.

Other early routes through the mountains were the Forbes Road, between what are now Harrisburg and Pittsburgh, and the National — or Cumberland — Road from Maryland to Illinois, worn by generations of settlers.

The Appalachians have been worn down by the weathering of centuries, and the highest of them — such as Mount Washington in New Hampshire and Mount Mitchell in North Carolina — do not exceed 7000 feet.

An unusual feature of the chain is its longitudinal system of valleys, known as the Great Appalachian Valley, extending north to separate the Appalachians from the Adirondacks and south to divide the Alleghenies from the Blue Ridge.

The Alleghenies have been among the most productive of American mountains, their slopes in the neighborhood of Pittsburgh yielding coal, coke and — once — the iron ore that contributed to the rise of such men as Andrew Carnegie.

Indeed, the Pittsburgh coal seam, discovered by Colonel James Burd in 1759, proved richer in value than any other mineral source ever worked by man. It covers some 5700 square miles in four states. Great labor unions found their origin here among the workers in mining and steel. The first petroleum well was drilled in this region in 1859.

Historically, too, these mountains have been significant. The Appalachians kept the early settlers confined to the Atlantic Coast and delayed the opening of the west. On the other hand, they provided a natural barrier from would-be attackers across the mountains — the Indians and the French — and brought about the denser settlement of the coastal lands.

The combination of protection from enemies and the community spirit fostered among Americans forced to live close together brought the original 13 colonies to a higher degree of development than might otherwise have been the case. The Appalachian barrier therefore played a role in the ultimate success of the American Revolution.

The view to the right shows the upper Appalachians from northern New Hampshire to Pennsylvania. The Great Lakes are seen in the distance. Below, one follows the range from Pennsylvania to Tennessee.

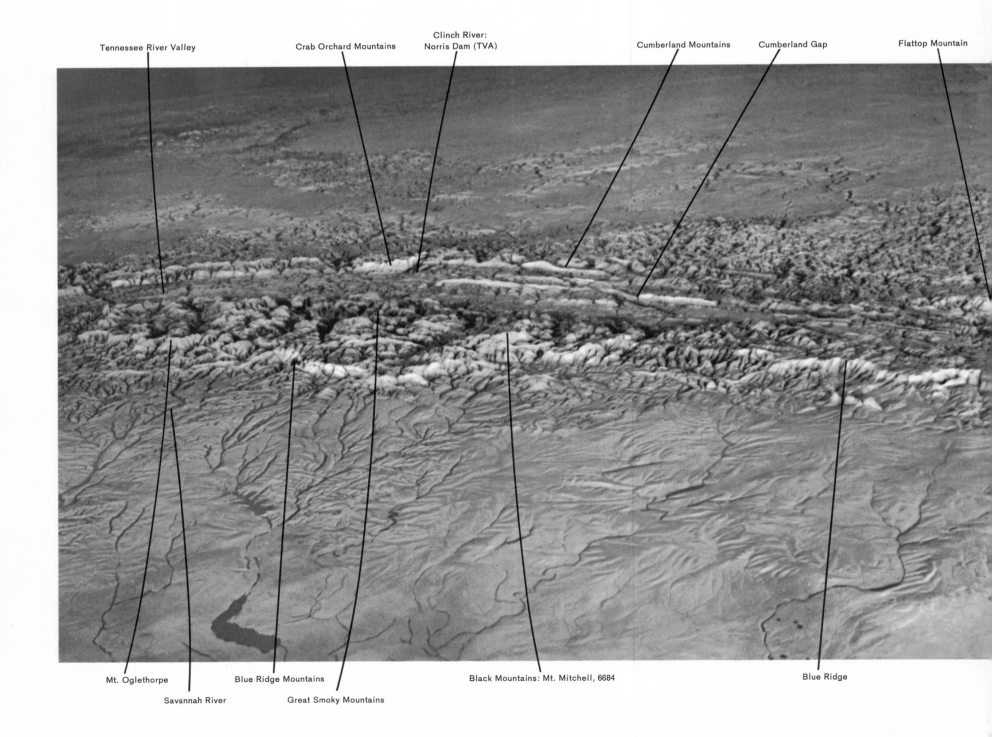

Tennessee River Valley — Crab Orchard Mountains — Clinch River: Norris Dam (TVA) — Cumberland Mountains — Cumberland Gap — Flattop Mountain

Mt. Oglethorpe — Savannah River — Blue Ridge Mountains — Great Smoky Mountains — Black Mountains: Mt. Mitchell, 6684 — Blue Ridge

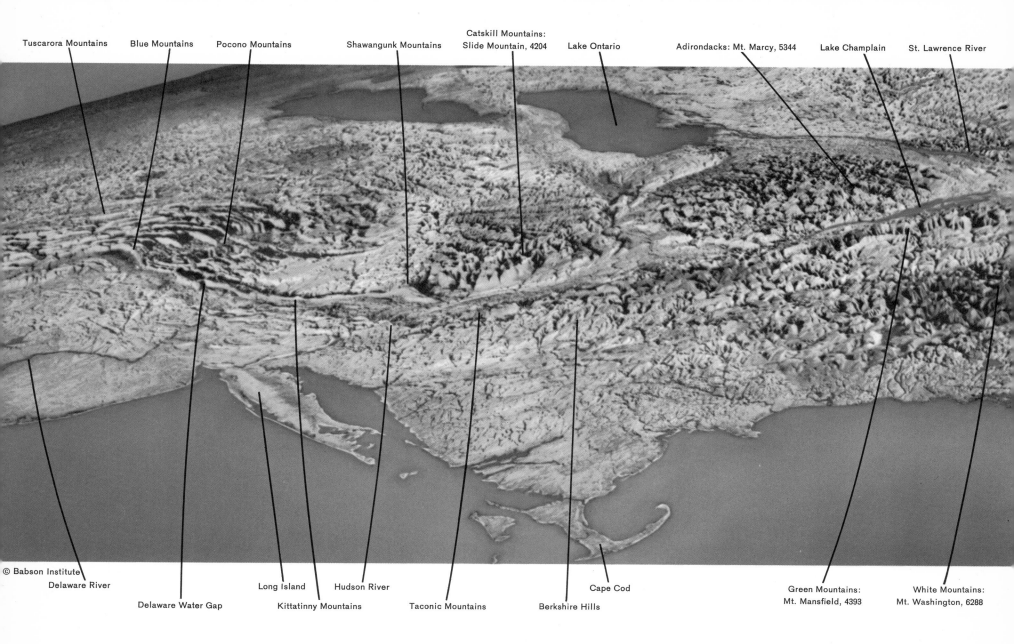

Tuscarora Mountains Blue Mountains Pocono Mountains Shawangunk Mountains Catskill Mountains: Slide Mountain, 4204 Lake Ontario Adirondacks: Mt. Marcy, 5344 Lake Champlain St. Lawrence River

© Babson Institute
Delaware River Delaware Water Gap Long Island Hudson River Kittatinny Mountains Taconic Mountains Berkshire Hills Cape Cod Green Mountains: Mt. Mansfield, 4393 White Mountains: Mt. Washington, 6288

© Babson Institute

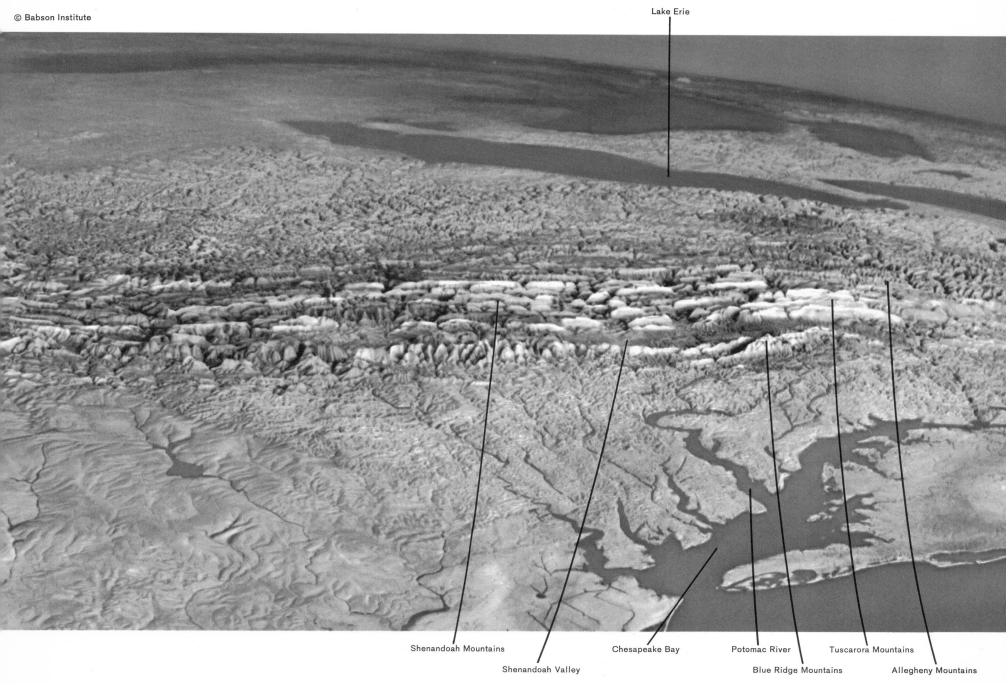

Lake Erie

Shenandoah Mountains Shenandoah Valley Chesapeake Bay Potomac River Blue Ridge Mountains Tuscarora Mountains Allegheny Mountains

THE ROCKY MOUNTAINS

THE ROCKY MOUNTAINS, the newest range in the United States, extend some 2800 miles, of which 1290 are below the Canadian border. The latter mark the Continental Divide, which separates the rivers flowing into the Gulf of Mexico from those emptying into the Pacific Ocean.

The highest peaks below Canada are found in Colorado, which has more than 250 mountains of over 13,000 feet and 55 of over 14,000 feet.

Early American pioneers such as Zebulon Pike and the much-traveled John C. Frémont endured hazardous journeys to cross the mountain barriers. South Pass on the Oregon Trail and Raton Pass on the Santa Fe Trail provided passage through the Rockies for later settlers and adventurers traveling westward.

Great rivers, such as the Yukon, the Mackenzie, the Columbia, the Missouri, the Arkansas, the Colorado and the Rio Grande, rise in this range to water the continent.

The views shown here are taken looking westward from eastern Wyoming (top) and eastern Colorado (bottom).

Mt. Shasta, 14,162 — Snake River Plain — Wind River Range: Gannett Peak, 13,785 — Great Salt Lake — Bridger Basin — South Pass (Oregon Trail) — Wind River — N. Platte River — Absaroka Range

Painted Desert — San Francisco Peaks, 12,794 — Grand Canyon — Gunnison River Valley — Spanish Peaks, 13,623 — Raton Pass (Santa Fe Trail) — Sangre de Cristo Range: Blanca Peak, 14,390 — San Luis Valley — Arkansas River — Pikes Peak, 14,109 — San Juan Mountains: Summit Peak, 13,272

Teton Mountains   Sawtooth Range   Yellowstone National Park   Snowy Range   Mt. Rainier, 14,410   Bitterroot Range

Bighorn River

Yellowstone River

Powder River   Bighorn Range: Cloud Peak, 13,175   Bighorn Basin

© Babson Institute

Great Salt Lake Desert   Wasatch Range

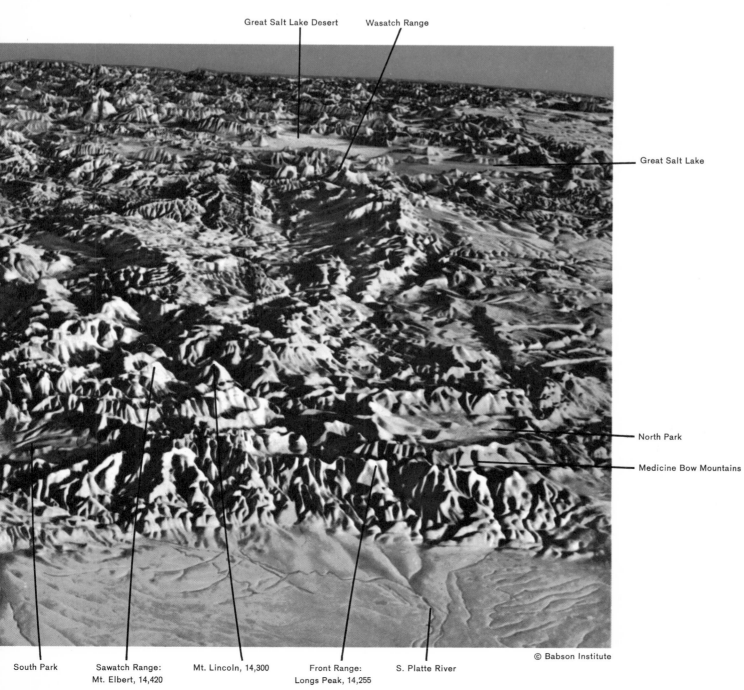

Great Salt Lake

North Park

Medicine Bow Mountains

South Park   Sawatch Range: Mt. Lincoln, 14,300   Front Range: S. Platte River
Mt. Elbert, 14,420   Longs Peak, 14,255

© Babson Institute

THE WESTERN COASTAL RANGES

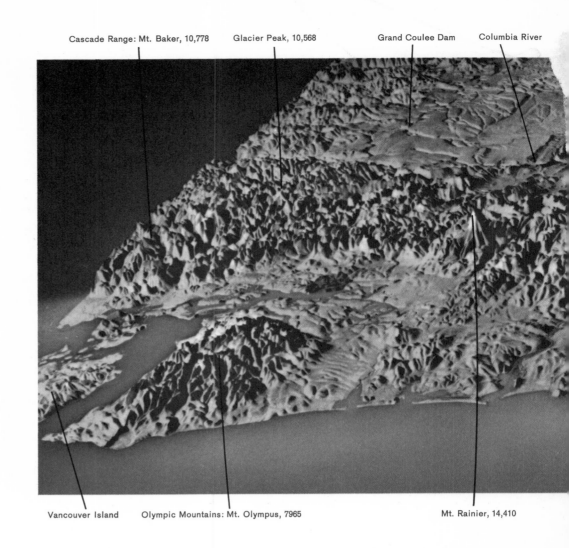

THE WESTERN COASTAL MOUNTAINS of the United States stretch from Oregon through California, descending into Mexico. Bordering the Pacific are the Coast Ranges. In Washington they include the wild fastnesses of the Olympic Mountains. Farther inland are the Cascade Mountains, of which one, Mount Rainier, rises to a snow-clad peak two and a half miles above sea level.

The Cascade Range continues into Oregon. Through the Blue Mountains of this state, along the valley of the Columbia River, wound the Oregon Trail, blazed by early fur traders. One of these was John Jacob Astor, who founded Astoria at the Columbia River's mouth in 1811. Washington and Oregon and the states east of them are shown to the right.

Below are views of California and the states to the east. The Coast Ranges here are the area of earthquakes, of which the most famous was that at San Francisco in 1906. Inland are the majestic Sierra Nevadas. Mount Whitney (14,495 feet), in this range, is the highest peak below Canada.

Cascade Range: Mt. Baker, 10,778   Glacier Peak, 10,568   Grand Coulee Dam   Columbia River

Vancouver Island   Olympic Mountains: Mt. Olympus, 7965   Mt. Rainier, 14,410

Santa Rosa Range   Great Salt Lake   Shoshone Mountains   Pyramid Lake   Donner Pass   Lake Tahoe   Sierra Nevada Range   Yosemite National Park   White Mountains

© Babson Institute

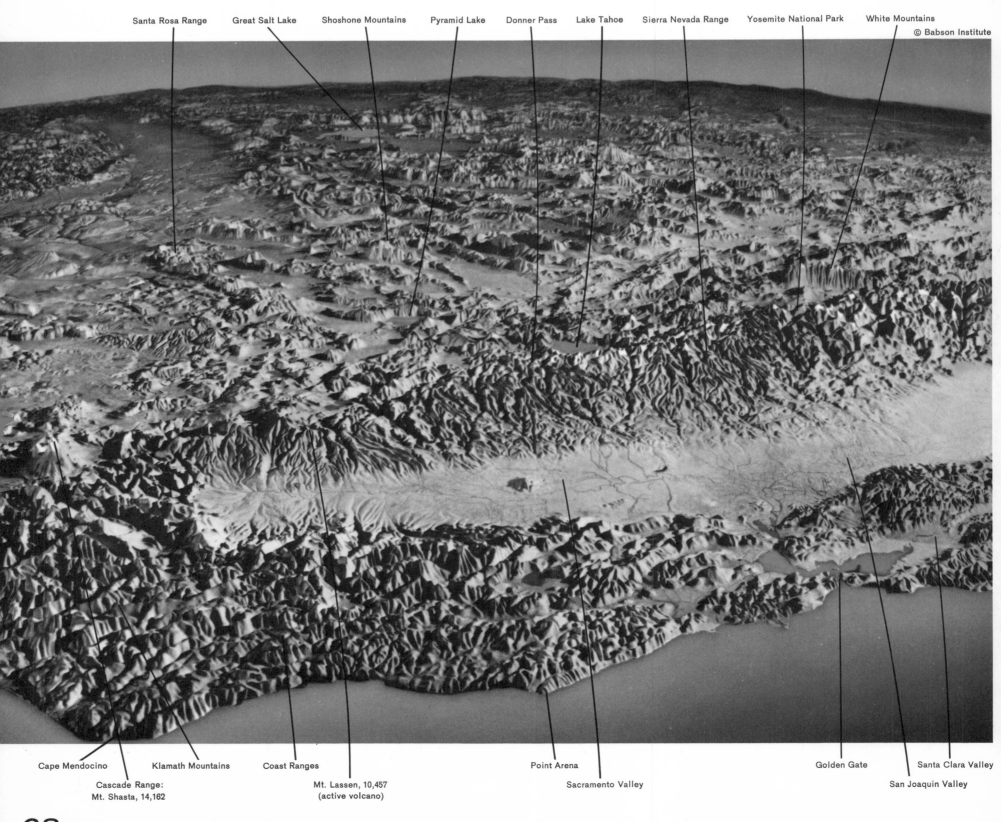

Cape Mendocino   Klamath Mountains   Coast Ranges   Point Arena   Golden Gate   Santa Clara Valley

Cascade Range: Mt. Shasta, 14,162   Mt. Lassen, 10,457 (active volcano)   Sacramento Valley   San Joaquin Valley

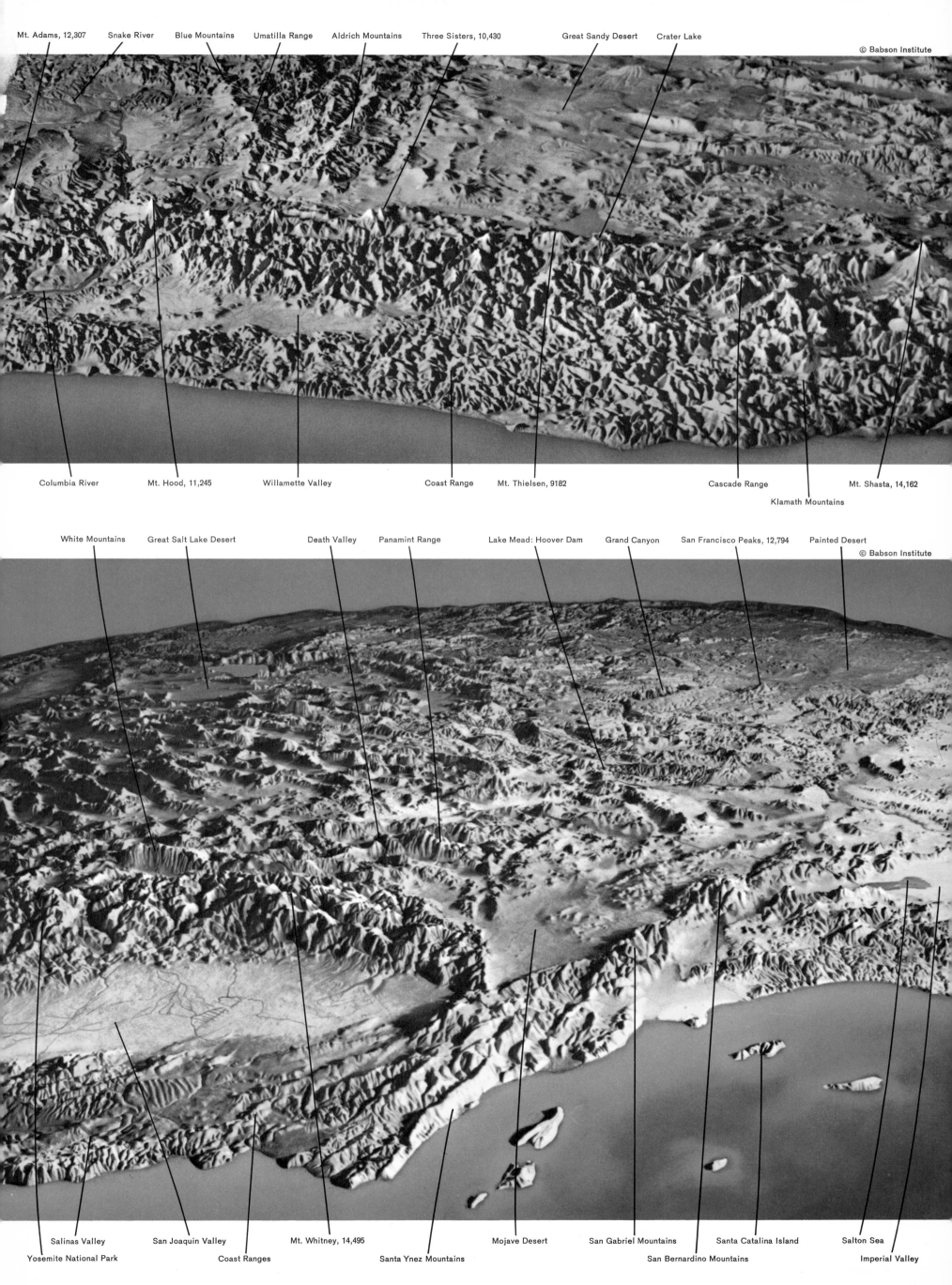

Mt. Adams, 12,307   Snake River   Blue Mountains   Umatilla Range   Aldrich Mountains   Three Sisters, 10,430   Great Sandy Desert   Crater Lake

© Babson Institute

Columbia River   Mt. Hood, 11,245   Willamette Valley   Coast Range   Mt. Thielsen, 9182   Cascade Range   Mt. Shasta, 14,162

Klamath Mountains

White Mountains   Great Salt Lake Desert   Death Valley   Panamint Range   Lake Mead: Hoover Dam   Grand Canyon   San Francisco Peaks, 12,794   Painted Desert

© Babson Institute

Salinas Valley   San Joaquin Valley   Mt. Whitney, 14,495   Mojave Desert   San Gabriel Mountains   Santa Catalina Island   Salton Sea

Yosemite National Park   Coast Ranges   Santa Ynez Mountains   San Bernardino Mountains   Imperial Valley

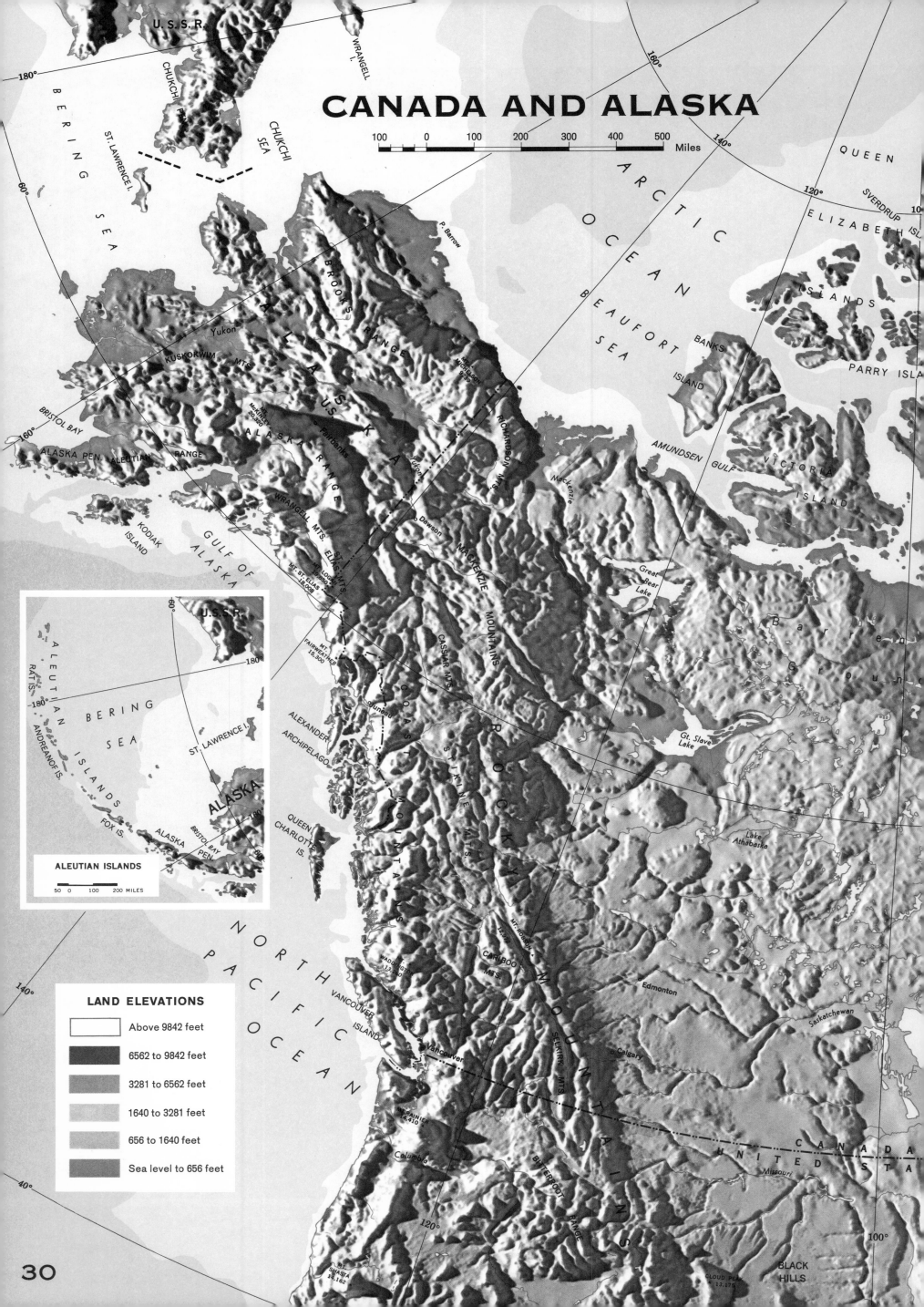

CANADA AND ALASKA

100   0   100   200   300   400   500
Miles

LAND ELEVATIONS

- Above 9842 feet
- 6562 to 9842 feet
- 3281 to 6562 feet
- 1640 to 3281 feet
- 656 to 1640 feet
- Sea level to 656 feet

U.S.S.R.

WRANGELL I.

CHUKCHI PEN.

CHUKCHI SEA

ST. LAWRENCE I.

BERING SEA

BRISTOL BAY

ALASKA PEN.   ALEUTIAN RANGE

KODIAK ISLAND

KUSKOKWIM MTS.

Yukon

ALASKA

ALASKA RANGE

McKINLEY 20,320

Fairbanks

BROOKS RANGE

U.S.A.

MICHELSON 9,239

Dawson

Yukon

MT. LOGAN 19,850

WRANGELL MTS.   ST. ELIAS MTS.

MT. ST. ELIAS 18,008

GULF OF ALASKA

MT. FAIRWEATHER 15,300

Juneau

P. Barrow

ARCTIC   OCEAN

BEAUFORT SEA

BANKS ISLAND

RICHARDSON MTS.

Mackenzie

MACKENZIE MOUNTAINS

CASSIAR MTS.

COAST MOUNTAINS

STIKINE MTS.

ALEXANDER ARCHIPELAGO

QUEEN CHARLOTTE IS.

VANCOUVER ISLAND

Vancouver

NORTH   PACIFIC   OCEAN

Columbia

MT. RAINIER 14,410

MT. SHASTA 14,162

QUEEN

SVERDRUP

ELIZABETH IS.

PARRY ISL.

AMUNDSEN GULF

VICTORIA ISLAND

Great Bear Lake

Barren Ground

Gt. Slave Lake

ROCKY

MOUNTAINS

MT. ROBSON

CARIBOO MTS.

WADDINGTON 13,260

SELKIRK MTS.

Lake Athabaska

Edmonton

Saskatchewan

Calgary

BITTERROOT RANGE

Missouri

CANADA

UNITED STATES

BLACK HILLS

CLOUD PEAK 13,175

60°

160°

180°

140°

120°

100°

40°

ALEUTIAN ISLANDS

50   0   100   200 MILES

U.S.S.R.

ALEUTIAN ISLANDS

RAT IS.

ANDREANOF IS.

FOX IS.

BERING SEA

ST. LAWRENCE I.

ALASKA

BRISTOL BAY PEN.

ALASKA PEN.

60°

180°

30

ICELAND

Reykjavik

20°

DENMARK STRAIT

Relief map copyright: Aero Service Corp., Philadelphia 20, Pa., a Division of Litton Industries

40°

G R E E N L A N D

I C E   C A P

80°

80°

Thule

ELLESMERE ISLAND

DEVON I.

BAFFIN

BAY

60°

DISKO I.

DAVIS

STRAIT

40°

MELVILLE
PEN.

FOXE
BASIN

BAFFIN   ISLAND

N O R T H

KEEWATIN
PEN.

SOUTHAMPTON
I.

HUDSON   STRAIT

UNGAVA
BAY

A T L A N T I C

H U D S O N

UNGAVA
PEN.

L A B R A D O R

O C E A N

B A Y

NEWFOUNDLAND

Gander

James

Bay

Lake
Winnipeg

GULF OF

ST. LAWRENCE

LAURENTIDE   MTS.

St. Lawrence

Winnipeg

Québec

NOVA   SCOTIA

Halifax

80°

Mississippi

Montreal

APPALACHIAN

MOUNTAINS

60°

Ottawa

LAKE   SUPERIOR

LAKE
MICHIGAN

LAKE
HURON

Toronto

L. ONTARIO

31

SOUTH AMERICA

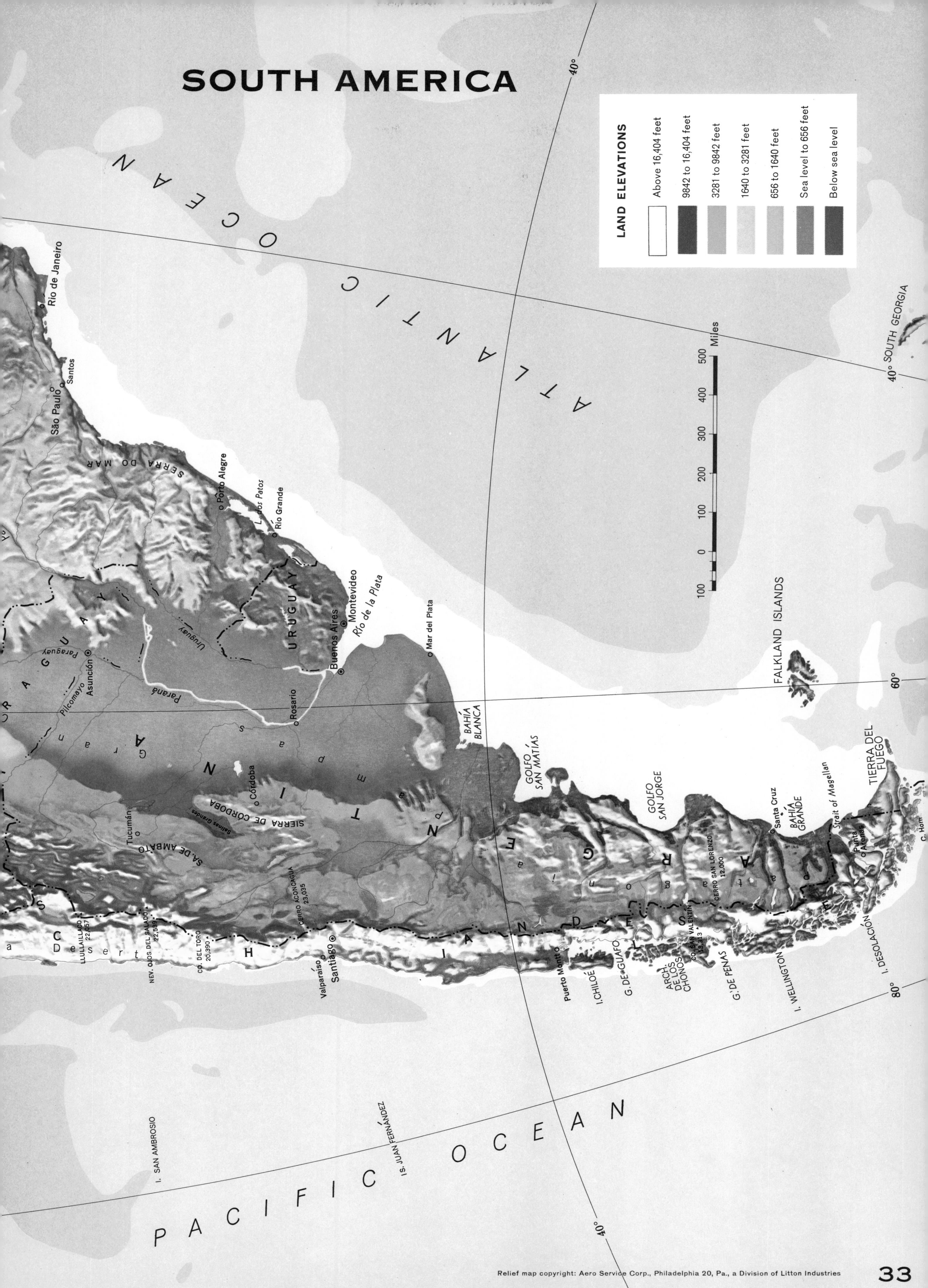

ATLANTIC OCEAN

PACIFIC OCEAN

Relief map copyright: Aero Service Corp., Philadelphia 20, Pa., a Division of Litton Industries

LAND ELEVATIONS

Above 16,404 feet	
9842 to 16,404 feet	
3281 to 9842 feet	
1640 to 3281 feet	
656 to 1640 feet	
Sea level to 656 feet	
Below sea level	

Miles

500
400
300
200
100
0
100

Rio de Janeiro
Santos
São Paulo

SERRA DO MAR
Porto Alegre
L. dos Patos
Rio Grande

URUGUAY
Montevideo
Buenos Aires
Río de la Plata
Mar del Plata

Uruguay

PARAGUAY
Asunción
Pilcomayo
Paraguay
Paraná
Rosario

G r a n   C h a c o

A R G E N T I N A

SIERRA DE CÓRDOBA
Córdoba
Salinas Grandes
Tucumán
S. DE AMBATO
CERRO ACONCAGUA
23,035

P a t a g o n i a

BAHÍA BLANCA

GOLFO SAN MATÍAS

GOLFO SAN JORGE

Santa Cruz
BAHÍA GRANDE

Strait of Magellan

TIERRA DEL FUEGO

Punta Arenas

C. Horn

I. DESOLACIÓN

I. WELLINGTON

G. DE PENAS

ARCH. DE LOS CHONOS

G. DE GUAFO

I. CHILOÉ

Puerto Montt

CERRO SAN LORENZO
12,000

CERRO SAN VALENTÍN
13,313

A N D E S   M T S.

LLULLAILLACO
22,057
D e s e r t
NEV. OJOS DEL SALADO
22,539
CO. DEL TORO
20,390

Valparaíso
Santiago

FALKLAND ISLANDS

SOUTH GEORGIA

40°

40°

40°

60°

80°

I. SAN AMBROSIO

IS. JUAN FERNÁNDEZ

33

EUROPE

75 50 25 0   100   200   300
Miles

Relief map copyright: Aero Service Corp., Philadelphia 20, Pa., a Division of Litton Industries

0°

60°

20°

ICELAND

Reykjavik

NORWEGIAN SEA

20°

ATLANTIC OCEAN

40°

FAERÖE IS.

SHETLAND IS.

ORKNEY IS.

IRELAND

Dublin

Edinburgh

UNITED KINGDOM

London

ENGLISH CHANNEL

NORTH SEA

NORWAY

Bergen

Oslo

L. Vänern

SWEDEN

Stockholm

GULF OF BOTHNIA

FINL

GULF

BALTIC SEA

DENMARK

NETHERLANDS

BELGIUM

Bonn

LUXEMBOURG

Frankfurt

Rhine

Berlin

GERMANY

POLAND

Warsaw

Oder

Prague

CZECHOSLOVAKIA

BAY OF BISCAY

FRANCE

Massif Central

Paris

Bern

SWITZERLAND

MONT BLANC 15,771

Rhône

Danube

AUSTRIA

Vienna

HUNGARY

Budapest

Y U G O S L A V I A

Belgrade

PORTUGAL

SPAIN

Madrid

PYRENEES

Barcelona

Lisbon

40°

BALEARIC ISLANDS

CORSICA

SARDINIA

ITALY

Rome

MT. VESUVIUS 4190

ADRIATIC SEA

Tirana

ALBANIA

0°

TYRRHENIAN SEA

IONIAN SEA

GREECE

20°

M E D I T E R R A N E A N   S E A

Algiers

Tunis

SICILY

MALTA

34

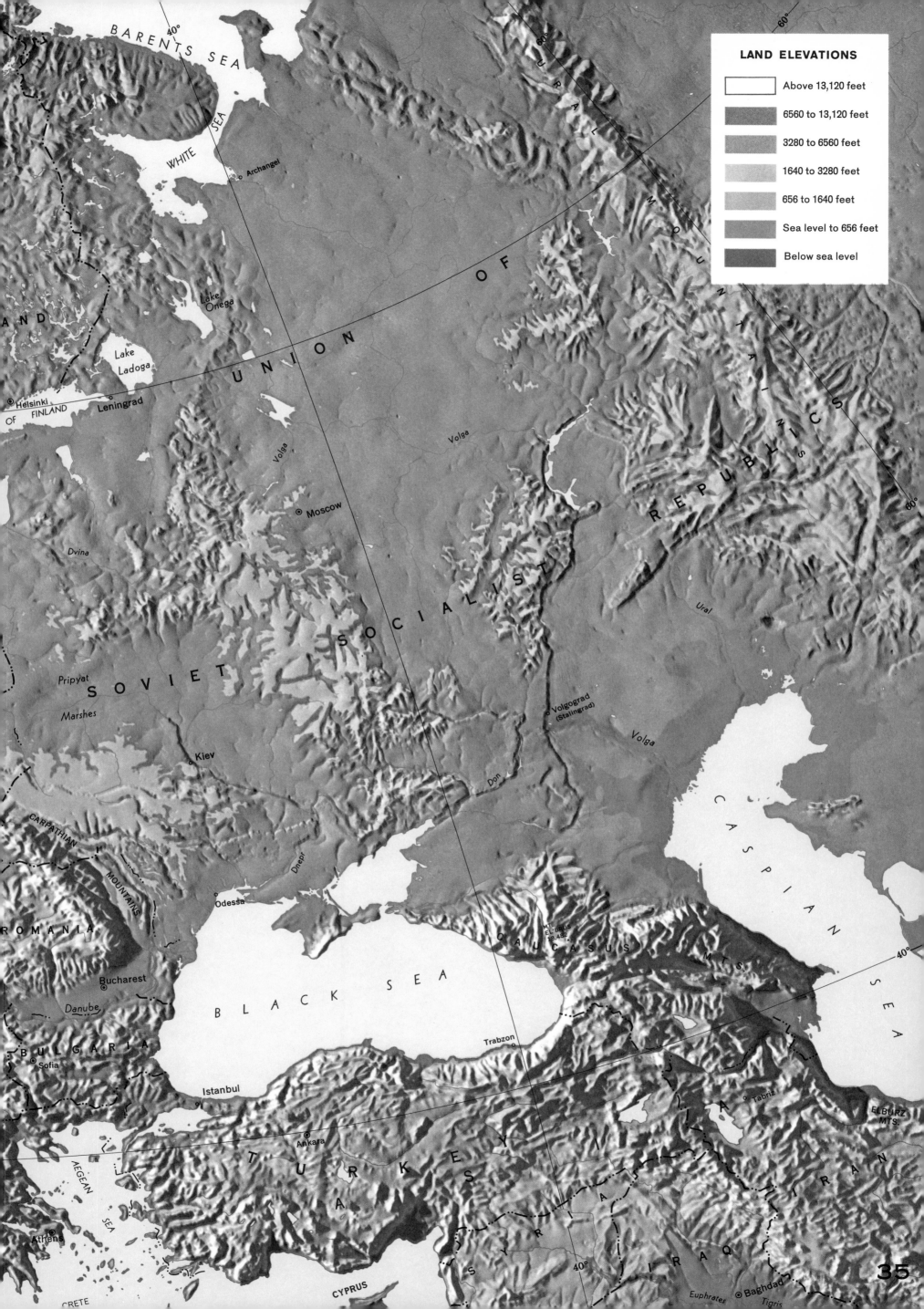

LAND ELEVATIONS

	Above 13,120 feet
	6560 to 13,120 feet
	3280 to 6560 feet
	1640 to 3280 feet
	656 to 1640 feet
	Sea level to 656 feet
	Below sea level

BARENTS SEA

WHITE SEA

Archangel

Lake Onega

Lake Ladoga

Helsinki

FINLAND

Leningrad

UNION OF

U R A L   M O U N T A I N S

Volga

Volga

Moscow

Dvina

Ural

S O V I E T   S O C I A L I S T   R E P U B L I C S

Pripyat

Marshes

Kiev

Volgograd (Stalingrad)

Volga

Don

CARPATHIAN

MOUNTAINS

Dnepr

Odessa

C A S P I A N

ROMANIA

Bucharest

Danube

BULGARIA

Sofia

B L A C K   S E A

CAUCASUS

MT. ELBRUS

El. 18,481

MTS.

S E A

Trabzon

Istanbul

Ankara

T U R K E Y

Tabriz

ELBURZ

MTS.

AEGEAN

SEA

S Y R I A

I R A N

Athens

I R A Q

Euphrates

Baghdad

CRETE

CYPRUS

Tigris

35

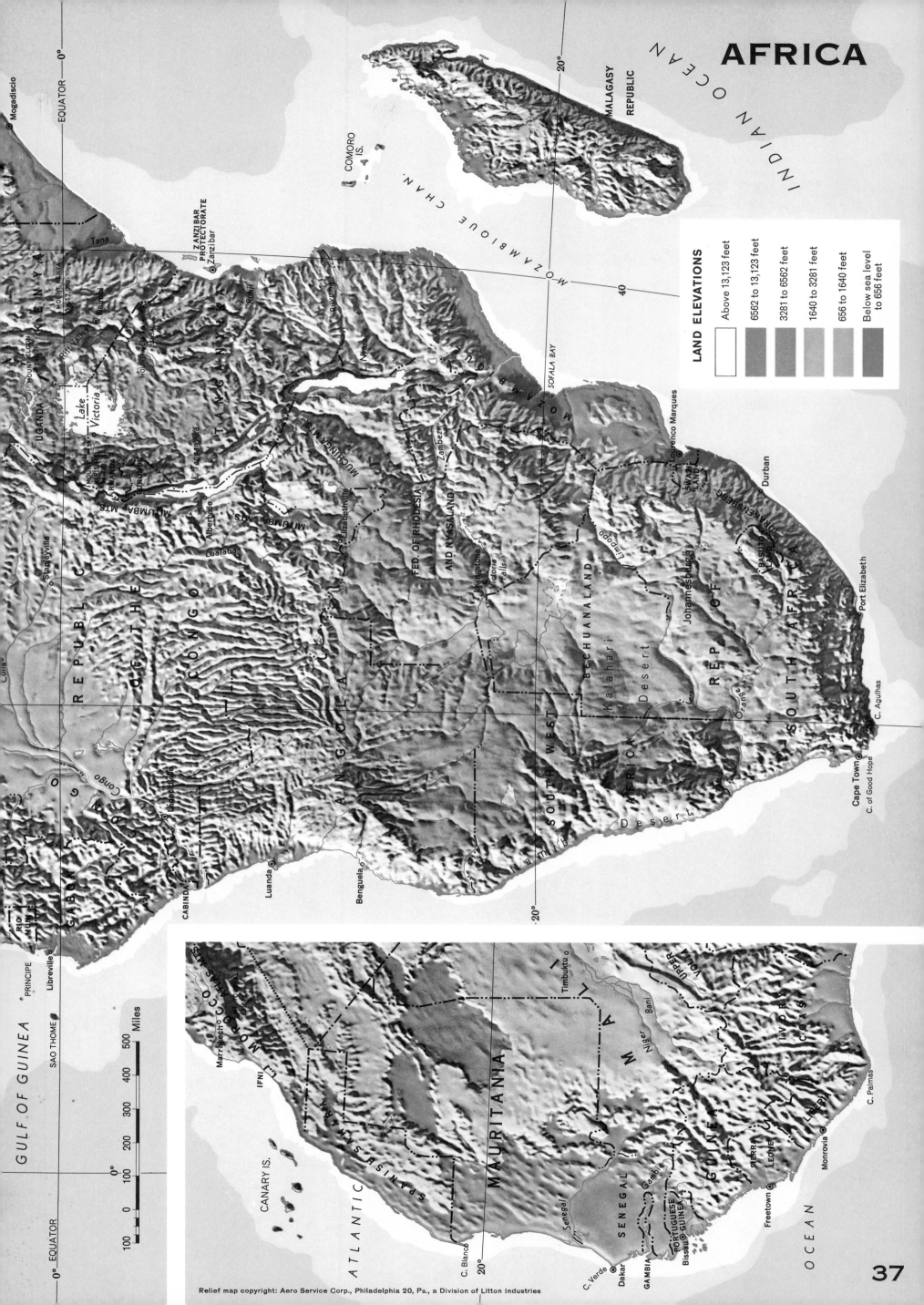

AFRICA

INDIAN OCEAN

MALAGASY REPUBLIC

MOZAMBIQUE CHAN.

COMORO IS.

ZANZIBAR PROTECTORATE
○ Zanzibar

○ Mogadiscio

EQUATOR 0°

K E N Y A

MOUNT KENYA
17,058

Tana

○ Nairobi

Rift Valley

MOUNT ELGON
14,175

UGANDA

Lake Victoria

MOUNT KILIMANJARO
19,565

MT. MERU

RWANDA

BURUNDI

T A N G A N Y I K A

Ruvuma

MUCHINGA MTS

Rukwa

Tanganyika

MITUMBA MTS

MITUMBA MTS

Alberville ○

Lualaba

SOFALA BAY

Lourenço Marques

SWAZI LAND

Durban

DRAKENSBERG

BASUTO LAND

Port Elizabeth

○ Stanleyville

R E P U B L I C   O F   T H E   C O N G O

Léopoldville ○

Congo

GABON

RIO MUNI

CABINDA

Luanda ○

Benguela ○

A N G O L A

Elizabethville ○

FED. OF RHODESIA AND NYASALAND

Zambezi

Livingstone ○
Victoria Falls

Limpopo

Johannesburg ○

BECHUANALAND

Kalahari Desert

S O U T H   W E S T   A F R I C A

Namib Desert

Orange

R E P.   O F   S O U T H   A F R I C A

Cape Town ○
C. of Good Hope

C. Agulhas

LAND ELEVATIONS

☐	Above 13,123 feet
▦	6562 to 13,123 feet
▦	3281 to 6562 feet
▦	1640 to 3281 feet
▦	656 to 1640 feet
▦	Below sea level to 656 feet

GULF OF GUINEA

PRINCIPE

SAO THOME

Libreville ○

0°

EQUATOR 0°

Miles
500
400
300
200
100
0
100

A T L A N T I C   O C E A N

CANARY IS.

Marrakech ○

ANTI-ATLAS MTS

IFNI

GRAND ATLAS MTS
13,661

M O R O C C O

SPANISH SAHARA

C. Blanco

C. Verde ○
Dakar

SENEGAL

Senegal

GAMBIA

Gambia

PORTUGUESE GUINEA
Bissau ○

M A U R I T A N I A

Timbuktu ○

M A L I

Niger

Bani

UPPER VOLTA

Niger

I V O R Y   C O A S T

GUINEA

SIERRA LEONE

Freetown ○

LIBERIA

Monrovia ○

C. Palmas

O C E A N

Relief map copyright: Aero Service Corp., Philadelphia 20, Pa., a Division of Litton Industries

37

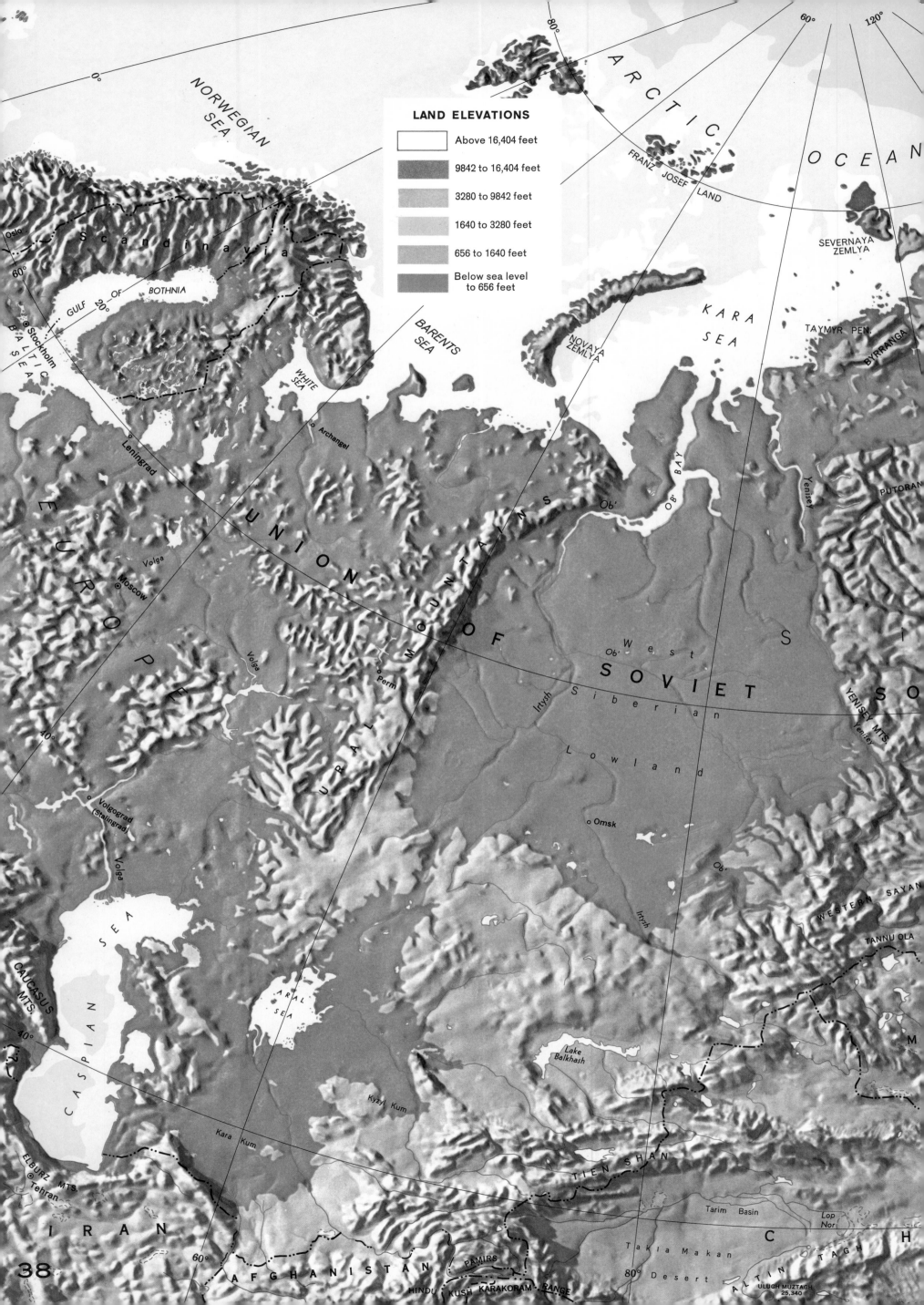

LAND ELEVATIONS

	Above 16,404 feet
	9842 to 16,404 feet
	3280 to 9842 feet
	1640 to 3280 feet
	656 to 1640 feet
	Below sea level to 656 feet

NORWEGIAN SEA

ARCTIC OCEAN

FRANZ JOSEF LAND

SEVERNAYA ZEMLYA

KARA SEA

NOVAYA ZEMLYA

TAYMYR PEN.

BYRRANGA

Oslo

Scandinavia

GULF OF BOTHNIA

Stockholm

BALTIC SEA

WHITE SEA

BARENTS SEA

Archangel

Leningrad

Volga

Moscow

UNION OF

Volga

Perm

URAL MOUNTAINS

Ob'

Ob' BAY

Yenisey

PUTORAN

West Ob'

SOVIET

Irtysh

Siberian

Lowland

YENISEY MTS.

Yenisey

S

Volgograd (Stalingrad)

Volga

Omsk

Ob'

Irtysh

WESTERN SAYAN

CAUCASUS MTS.

CASPIAN SEA

ARAL SEA

Lake Balkhash

TANNU OLA

Kyzyl Kum

ELBURZ MTS.

Tehran

Kara Kum

TIEN SHAN

Tarim Basin

Lop Nor

IRAN

AFGHANISTAN

PAMIRS

HINDU KUSH KARAKORAM RANGE

Takla Makan Desert

ALTIN TAGH

ULUGH MUZTAGH 25,340

C H

38

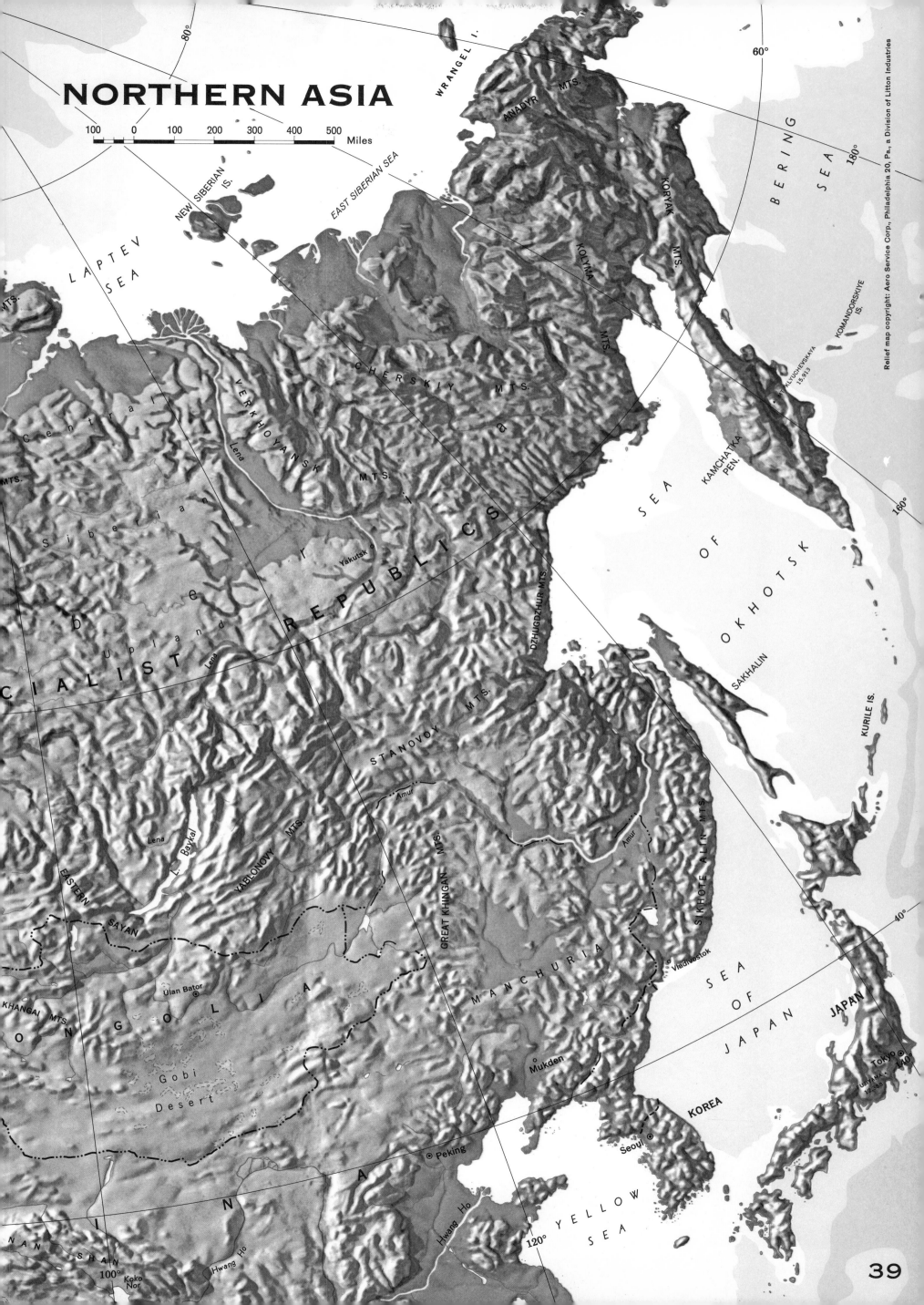

NORTHERN ASIA

100   0   100   200   300   400   500
Miles

WRANGEL I.

LAPTEV
SEA

NEW SIBERIAN
IS.

EAST SIBERIAN SEA

ANADYR MTS.

KORYAK
MTS.

KOLYMA
MTS.

BERING
SEA

Central

Siberian

Upland

VERKHOYANSK

Lena

Yakutsk

CHERSKIY   MTS.

KAMCHATKA
PEN.

MT. KLYUCHEVSKAYA
15,913

KOMANDORSKIYE
IS.

SEA

OF

OKHOTSK

SAKHALIN

DZHUGDZHUR MTS.

CIALIST   REPUBLICS

Lena

STANOVOY   MTS.

Amur

Lena

L. Baykal

YABLONOVY

MTS.

Amur

Amur

SIKHOTE ALIN MTS.

KURILE IS.

EASTERN
SAYAN

GREAT KHINGAN   MTS.

MANCHURIA

Vladivostok

SEA

OF

JAPAN

JAPAN

KHANGAI MTS.

ONGOLIA

Ulan Bator

Gobi

Desert

Mukden

KOREA

Seoul

Tokyo

FUJIYAMA
12,388

INA

Peking

Hwang Ho

YELLOW

SEA

NAN   SHAN

Koko
Nor

Hwang Ho

Relief map copyright: Aero Service Corp., Philadelphia 20, Pa., a Division of Litton Industries

80°

60°

180°

160°

40°

120°

100°

140°

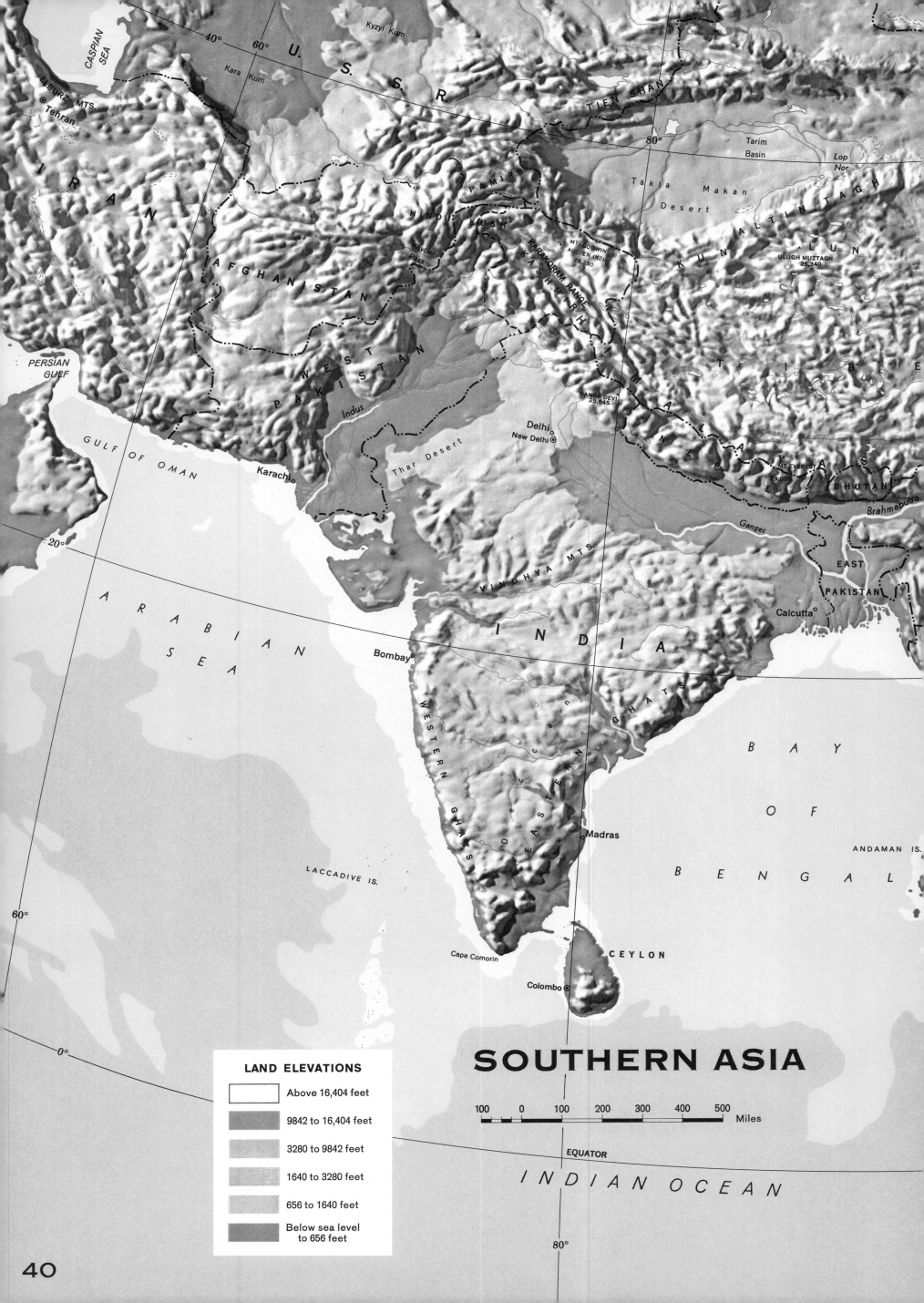

SOUTHERN ASIA

LAND ELEVATIONS

Above 16,404 feet

9842 to 16,404 feet

3280 to 9842 feet

1640 to 3280 feet

656 to 1640 feet

Below sea level to 656 feet

100 0 100 200 300 400 500

Miles

EQUATOR

INDIAN OCEAN

CASPIAN SEA

ELBURZ MTS.

Tehran

PERSIAN GULF

IRAN

GULF OF OMAN

Karachi

ARABIAN SEA

LACCADIVE IS.

Kyzyl Kum

Kara Kum

U. S. S. R.

TIEN SHAN

80°

Tarim Basin

Lop Nor

Takla Makan Desert

ALTINTAGH

KUN LUN

ULUGH MUZTAGH 25,340

PAMIRS

HINDU KUSH

Khyber Pass

AFGHANISTAN

KARAKORAM RANGE

MT. GODWIN AUSTEN (K2) 28,250

KASHMIR

WEST PAKISTAN

Indus

Thar Desert

NANDA DEVI 25,645

Delhi
New Delhi

NEPAL

MT. EVEREST 29,028

BHUTAN

Brahmaputra

Ganges

EAST PAKISTAN

Calcutta

VINDHYA MTS.

I N D I A

TIBET

Bombay

WESTERN GHATS

DECCAN

EASTERN GHATS

Madras

BAY OF BENGAL

ANDAMAN IS.

Cape Comorin

CEYLON

Colombo

40°   60°

20°

60°

0°

80°

MONGOLIA
Gobi Desert

NAN SHAN
SHAN
Koko Nor
Hwang Ho

120°

Peking

40°

Hwang Ho

Seoul

KOREA

SEA OF JAPAN

JAPAN

YELLOW
SEA

C H I N A

CHIN LING SHAN

Yangtze

Shanghai

EAST
CHINA
SEA

RYUKYU IS.

T

MINYA
KONKE
24,900

Chungking

Wuhan

NAGA HILLS

20°

TAIWAN

Canton

Hong Kong

BURMA

Irrawaddy

GULF OF TONKING

PHILIPPINES

Manila

VIETNAM

SOUTH

THAILAND

LAOS

CHINA

ANDAMAN
SEA

Bangkok

CAMBODIA

GULF
OF
SIAM

SEA

CELEBES

NICOBAR IS.

CELEBES
SEA

0°

MALAYA

EQUATOR

Singapore

BORNEO

CELEBES

SUMATRA

JAVA SEA

INDONESIA

BANDA SEA

120°

100°

JAVA

Djakarta

Relief map copyright: Aero Service Corp., Philadelphia 20, Pa., a Division of Litton Industries

41

THE GREAT OCEANS

THE OCEANS of our planet are still largely unexplored. Oceanography, the fascinating study of oceans, has developed only in the past fifty years. The resources of a number of sciences, particularly engineering, are required to plumb the three-to-seven-mile deeps of the great ocean beds. Until recently the equipment for such research has not been available. The ocean bottoms, once believed to be almost level, have mountains greater than the highest on land, this new study has revealed, and depths in which Mount Everest would sink more than 5000 feet beneath the surface.

Two of the most dramatic experiments in this field have been the "Mohole Project" and the descents of Auguste Piccard and his son by bathyscaphe. In 1960 Jacques Piccard reached the Pacific bottom in the Marianas Trench with the bathyscaphe *Trieste* at 36,198 feet. The Mohole Project, financed by the United States government, is learning much of scientific value about the oceans and the earth beneath them in a series of experimental Atlantic and Pacific drillings. Its ultimate aim is to bore past the "Moho" or Mohorovičić Discontinuity; this marks the transition between the Earth's crust and the dense rock of its mantle, which man has never penetrated. At sea, the crust averages only three miles in thickness, on land about 25 miles. (See "The Earth's Structure," page 138.)

The continents, which sit on the crust, are surrounded by CONTINENTAL SHELVES, or the shallow edges of the ancient land masses, edges later drowned by the rising sea. Most of these end quite abruptly at the steep CONTINENTAL SLOPES, which are cut by deep-sea canyons, continuing riverbeds of present-day rivers—for example, the Hudson Canyon off the east coast of the United States. The transition from the sharp slopes to the more gradual inclines marks the beginning of the CONTINENTAL RISE, ending in the OCEAN BASINS. In the centers of the ocean basins are often found the flat ABYSSAL PLAINS.

Much of the scenery of the ocean floor is craggy, irregular and complex. The DEEPS (beginning at 18,000 feet below sea level) are the lowest points of oceanic depressions. TRENCHES often occur along mountainous coastal regions or on the convex side of an arc-shaped ridge, whose uppermost points may comprise an island chain. It is in the trenches of the Pacific that the greatest deeps have been found. RIDGES with steep, irregular sides may occur independently of trenches. SEAMOUNTS are isolated sea mountains.

SEASCARPS are long, steep slopes or escarpments. A FRACTURE ZONE is an area of geological cracking, as in the Northeast Pacific, related to the upthrust of mountains on land. Most ISLANDS are volcanic in origin; on the tops of some submerged islands, calcareous animals and plants have built coral ATOLLS and REEFS. Volcanoes under the sea erupt as readily as those on land, often causing whole islands to disappear. In the valleys of the ocean the silt of rivers, the shells and remains of sea creatures, volcanic ash and other debris form a thick layer of SEDIMENT.

The tides and currents of the great oceans are not the least of their marvels. Tides are governed by the gravitational pull of the Moon and, to a lesser extent, of the Sun. Currents are determined by the position of land masses, the ceaseless revolutions of the Earth, and by the winds and the heat of the Sun. The Atlantic and Pacific each have two great current systems; it is the Earth's rotation that causes the currents north of the Equator to flow generally clockwise and those south of it to move in a counterclockwise direction. The Sargasso Sea, part of the West Atlantic, is an area of floating plankton, almost devoid of current. Currents strongly influence the local climate on land and provide swimmers with unexpected contrasts, such as that between the chill waters off the coast of Maine (from the Labrador Current) and the comfortable seas around the more northerly Nova Scotia (tempered by the Gulf Stream).

THE NORTH ATLANTIC

The legend of the lost Atlantis appears to have been fable, but the dark abysses of the Atlantic Ocean (shown at the right) are dramatic in their own right. Here are the bold and jagged mountains of the Mid-Atlantic Ridge—a range outstripping the Rockies in height and as majestic as the Himalayas. A 10,000-mile stretch, it is now thought to be only a part of a 40,000-mile Earth-girdling chain. The trench that has been discovered to run along its uppermost ridge is almost exactly the midpoint between the bordering continents, which are believed to have "drifted" apart or to have been separated by the gradual expansion of the Earth,

leaving the yawning chasms of the oceans between the land masses. (See "The Earth's Structure," p. 138.)

There is only one break in this Ridge, one link between its eastern and western valleys—that of the Romanche Trench on the Equator. The Atlantic has only three other small trenches, two in the West Indies and one in the Antarctic. The Milwaukee Deep near Puerto Rico is its deepest point—30,180 feet. The North Atlantic is characterized by its great basins, ridges, plateaus, deep-sea channels and relatively few seamounts. Only 4150 miles wide at its broadest, the Atlantic has the heaviest shipping of any ocean.

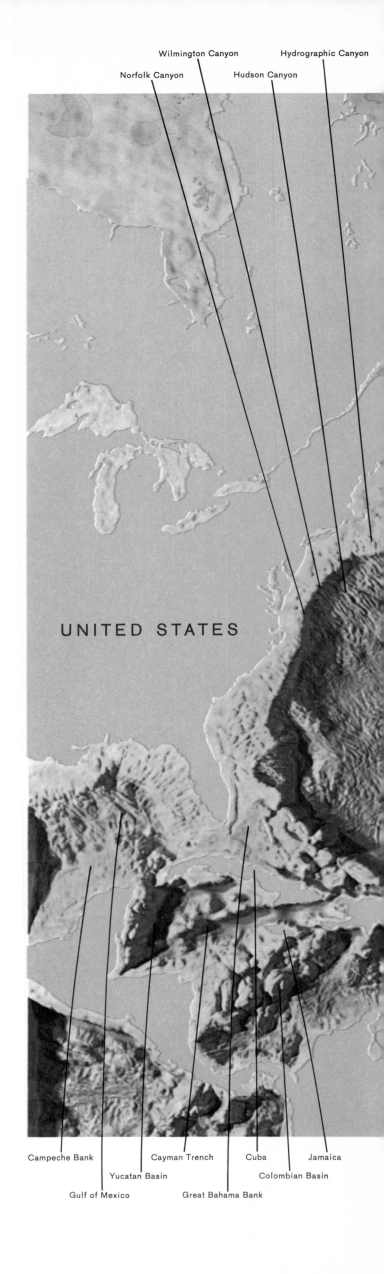

Norfolk Canyon — Wilmington Canyon — Hudson Canyon — Hydrographic Canyon

UNITED STATES

Campeche Bank — Cayman Trench — Cuba — Jamaica
Yucatan Basin — Colombian Basin
Gulf of Mexico — Great Bahama Bank

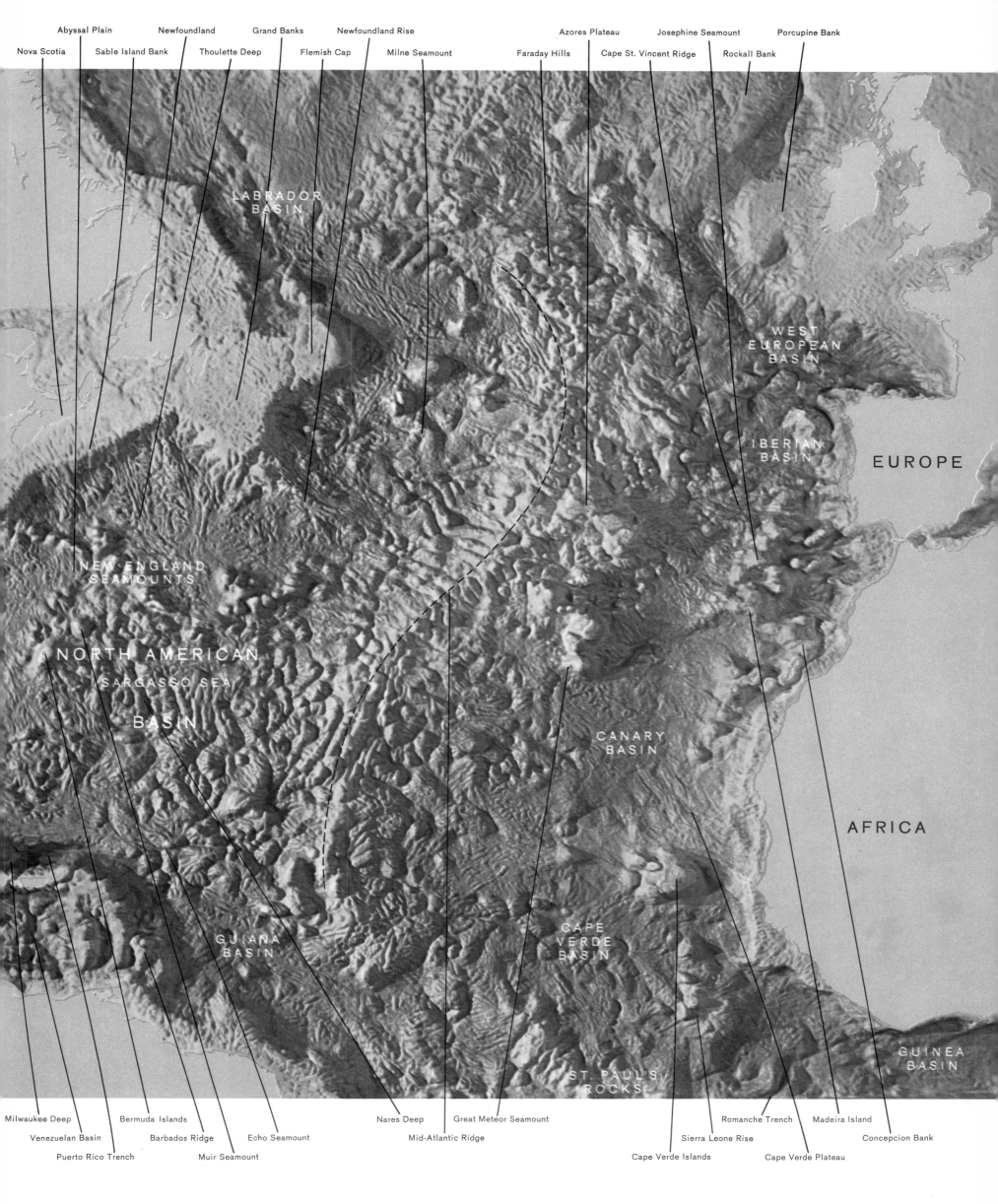

Nova Scotia
Abyssal Plain
Sable Island Bank
Newfoundland
Thoulette Deep
Grand Banks
Flemish Cap
Newfoundland Rise
Milne Seamount
Faraday Hills
Azores Plateau
Cape St. Vincent Ridge
Josephine Seamount
Rockall Bank
Porcupine Bank

LABRADOR
BASIN

WEST
EUROPEAN
BASIN

IBERIAN
BASIN

EUROPE

NEW ENGLAND
SEAMOUNTS

NORTH AMERICAN

SARGASSO SEA

BASIN

CANARY
BASIN

AFRICA

GUIANA
BASIN

CAPE
VERDE
BASIN

ST. PAUL'S
ROCKS

GUINEA
BASIN

Milwaukee Deep
Venezuelan Basin
Puerto Rico Trench
Bermuda Islands
Barbados Ridge
Muir Seamount
Echo Seamount
Nares Deep
Mid-Atlantic Ridge
Great Meteor Seamount
Cape Verde Islands
Sierra Leone Rise
Romanche Trench
Cape Verde Plateau
Madeira Island
Concepcion Bank

Martha's Vineyard
Azores
Gibraltar

© 1963 The Reader's Digest Association, Inc.

This section of the sea bed between Martha's Vineyard, off Massachusetts, and Gibraltar magnifies vertical distances about 40 times in relation to horizontal distances, to highlight the steepness of slopes. It shows the continental shelves and slopes which fringe the land masses, the deep ocean floors and interrupting seamounts.

43

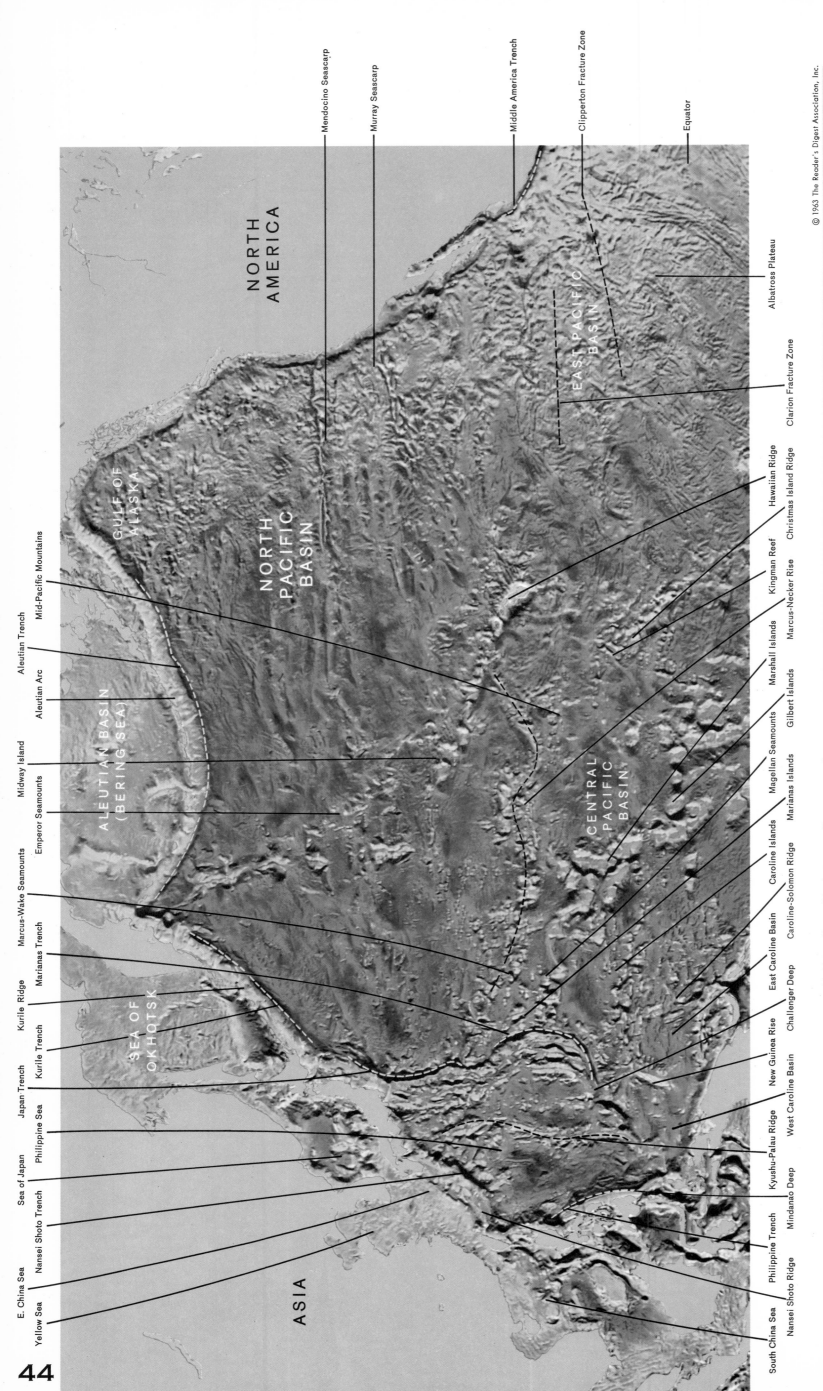

© 1963 The Reader's Digest Association, Inc.

ASIA

NORTH
AMERICA

GULF OF
ALASKA

ALEUTIAN BASIN
(BERING SEA)

SEA OF
OKHOTSK

NORTH PACIFIC
BASIN

CENTRAL
PACIFIC
BASIN

EAST
PACIFIC
BASIN

Mendocino Seascarp
Murray Seascarp
Middle America Trench
Clipperton Fracture Zone
Equator

Mid-Pacific Mountains
Aleutian Trench
Aleutian Arc
Midway Island
Emperor Seamounts
Marcus-Wake Seamounts
Kurile Ridge
Marianas Trench
Kurile Trench
Japan Trench
Sea of Japan
Philippine Sea
Nansei Shoto Trench
E. China Sea
Yellow Sea

Kyushu-Palau Ridge
New Guinea Rise
Challenger Deep
East Caroline Basin
Caroline Islands
Caroline-Solomon Ridge
Marianas Islands
Magellan Seamounts
Gilbert Islands
Marshall Islands
Marcus-Necker Rise
Kingman Reef
Christmas Island Ridge
Hawaiian Ridge

West Caroline Basin
Mindanao Deep
Philippine Trench
Nansei Shoto Ridge
South China Sea

Albatross Plateau
Clarion Fracture Zone

Cape Mendocino

Mendocino Seascarp

Bikini
Marcus-Necker Rise
Hawaiian Ridge
Hawaii

This section of the sea bed between Bikini, in the Marshall Islands, and Cape Mendocino, California, magnifies vertical distances about 40 times in relation to horizontal distances to highlight the steepness of the slopes. It shows the rough and irregular floor of the Pacific, which contains mountains and deep trenches. The island of Hawaii is not on a line with Bikini and Cape Mendocino, but is included to show the highest land point of the Pacific in comparison with its depths.

THE PACIFIC OCEAN—11,000 miles wide between Panama and the China Sea—has a border of volcanic activity of which the ridge-trench arcs of islands are part. This border is sometimes called the "Ring of Fire." It also possesses great depths. In 1960 the U.S. bathyscaphe *Trieste* touched bottom at 36,198 feet in the Marianas Trench. The Pacific is characterized by its volcanic activity; its island chains, many of them coral; its trenches with their great deeps; and its many seamounts. Peculiar to the Northeast are the four regular extensions of seascarps and fracture zones. The mid-Pacific islands are the peaks of the globe-encircling mountain range, thought to connect with the Mid-Atlantic Ridge via the Arctic and Indian Oceans.

THE
NORTH
PACIFIC

PART TWO

THE COUNTRIES
OF THE WORLD

UNITED STATES
OF AMERICA

EXCEPT ALASKA AND HAWAII

SCALE: 1 INCH TO 142 MILES
1:9,000,000

SEE PAGE 72 FOR STATE OF HAWAII
AND PAGES 76-77 FOR STATE OF ALASKA

© JOHN BARTHOLOMEW & SON LTD.

47

LEGEND AND INDEX TO UNITED STATES MAPS

International Boundaries ⎯⎯⎯⎯
State Boundaries ⎯⎯⎯⎯
State Capitals are underlined ⎯⎯⎯⎯
Spot Heights in Feet ▲20,320

Special Highways ⎯⎯⎯⎯
U.S. Highways ⎯ ⎯ ⎯
State Highways and Other Main Roads ⎯⎯⎯
Trails ⎯ ⎯ ⎯

Railroads ⎯|⎯|⎯
Canals ⎯⎯⎯⎯
Main Civil Airports Ⓐ Ⓐ
Swamp and Flood Areas

Deserts and Salt Flats
Salt Marshes
Glaciers and Ice Caps
Lagoons, Reefs and Banks

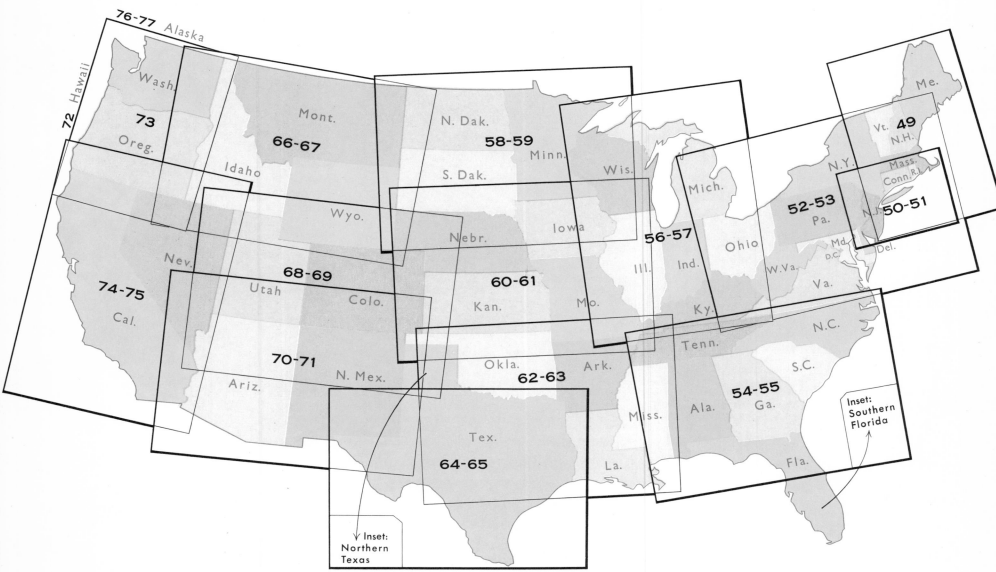

The frames outline the geographical areas mapped on the pages indicated.

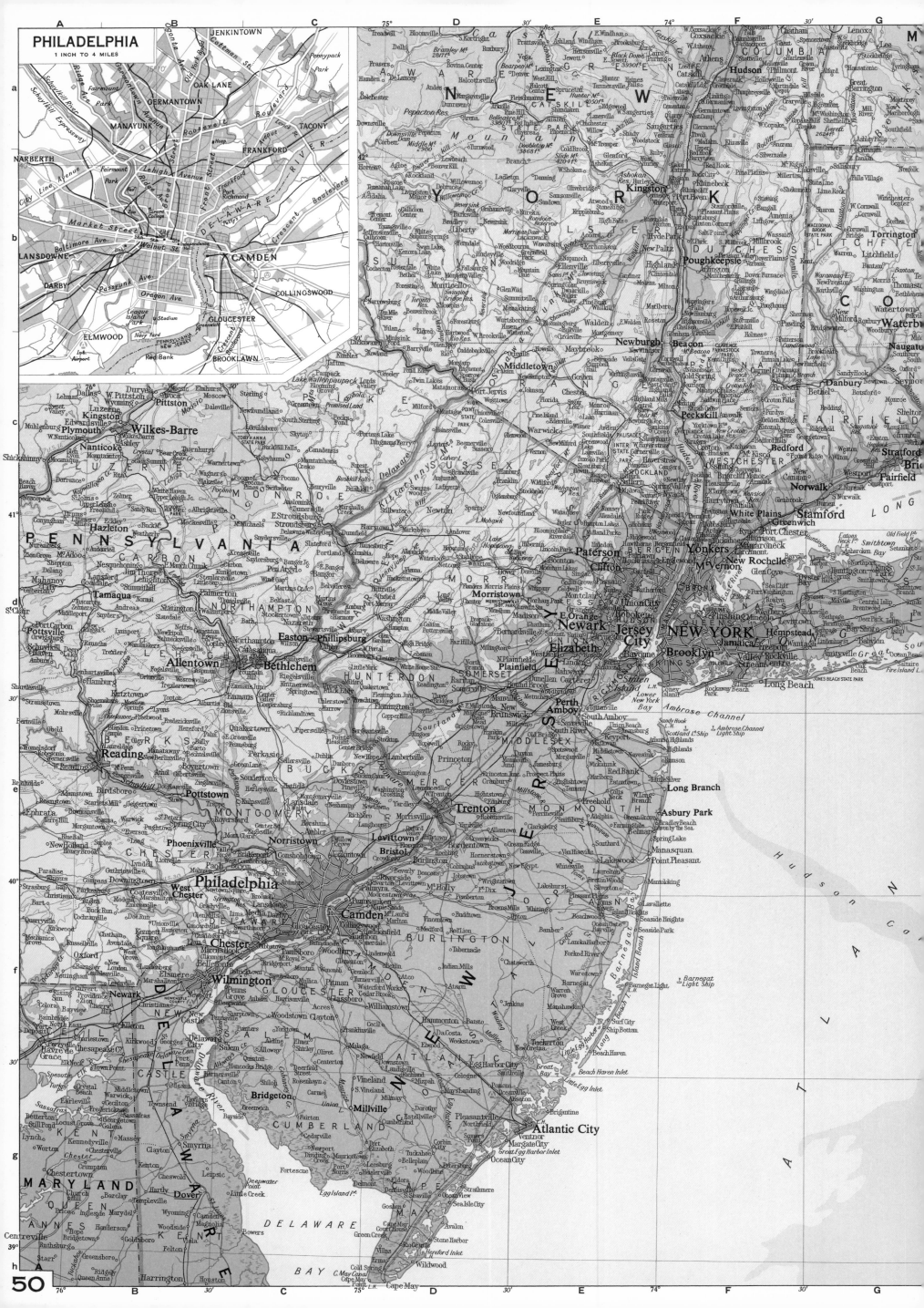

MIDDLE ATLANTIC SEABOARD

SCALE: 1 INCH TO 16 MILES

1 : 1,000,000

10   5   0   5   10   20   30 Miles

Feet   656   164   0   300   600 1500 3000 Feet

SEE LEGEND ON PAGE 48   © JOHN BARTHOLOMEW & SON LTD.

NEW YORK
AND ENVIRONS

1 INCH TO 4 MILES

0   1   2   3 Miles

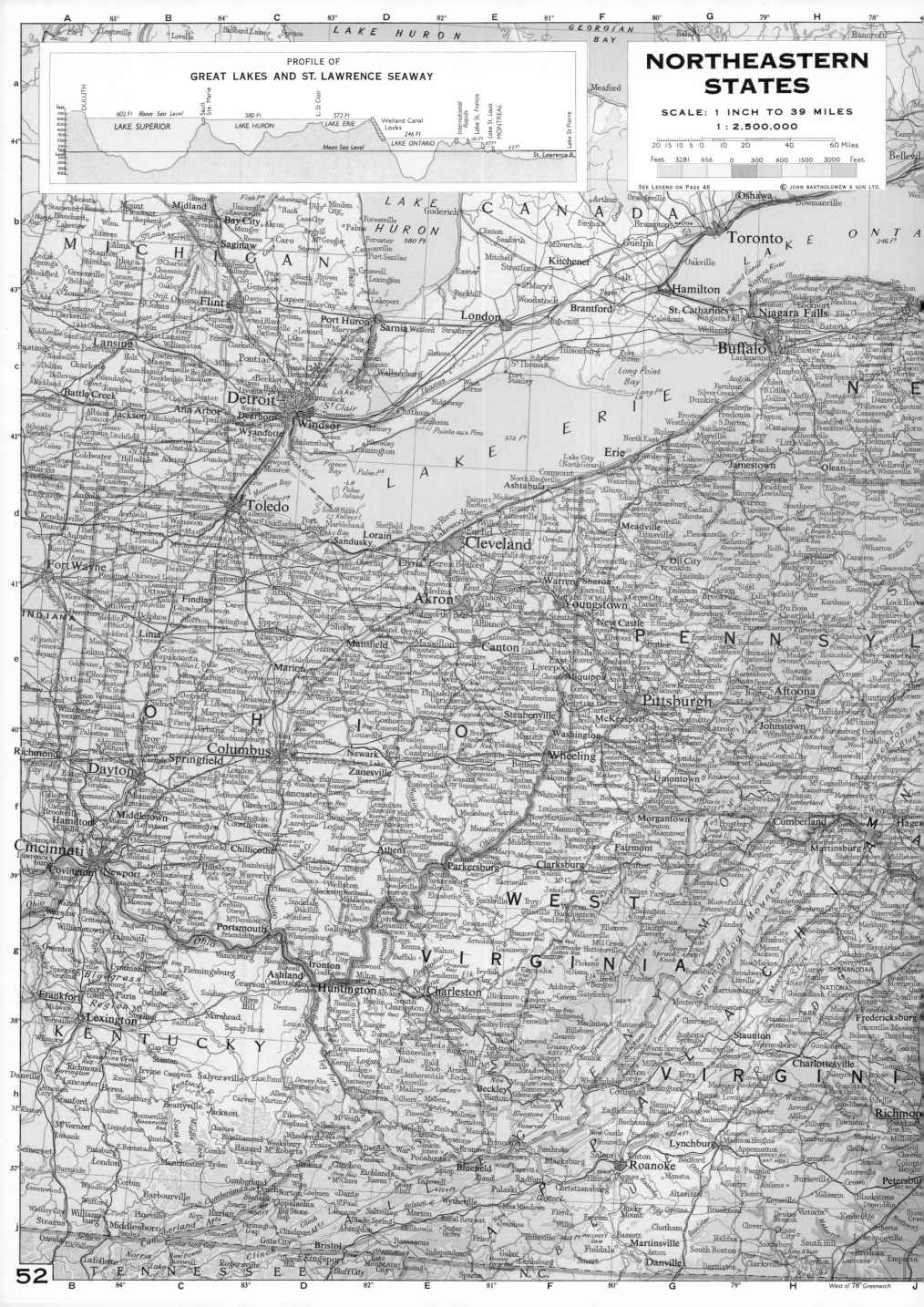

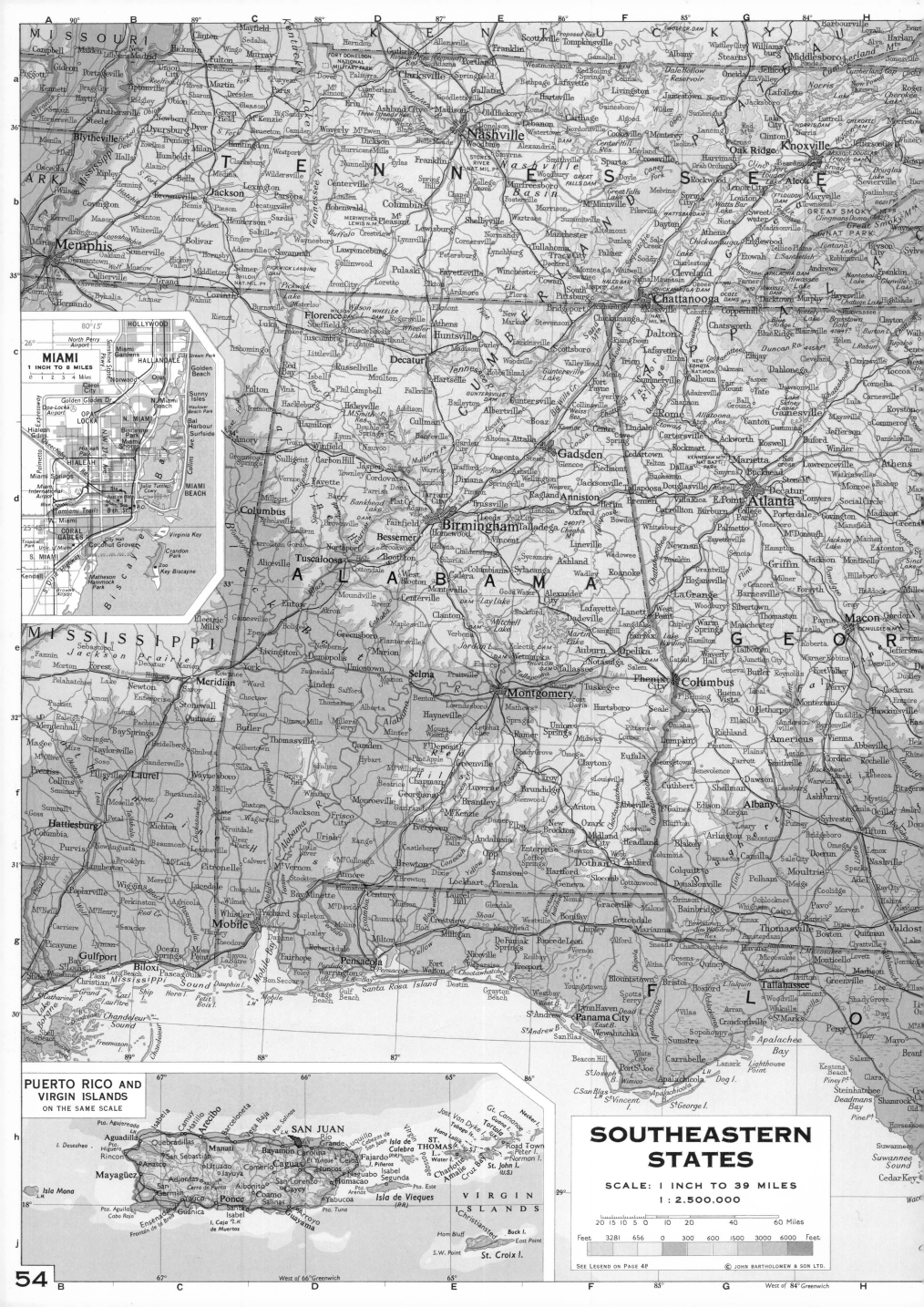

SOUTHEASTERN STATES

SCALE: 1 INCH TO 39 MILES
1 : 2.500.000

SEE LEGEND ON PAGE 42

© JOHN BARTHOLOMEW & SON LTD.

MIAMI
1 INCH TO 8 MILES

PUERTO RICO AND VIRGIN ISLANDS
ON THE SAME SCALE

54

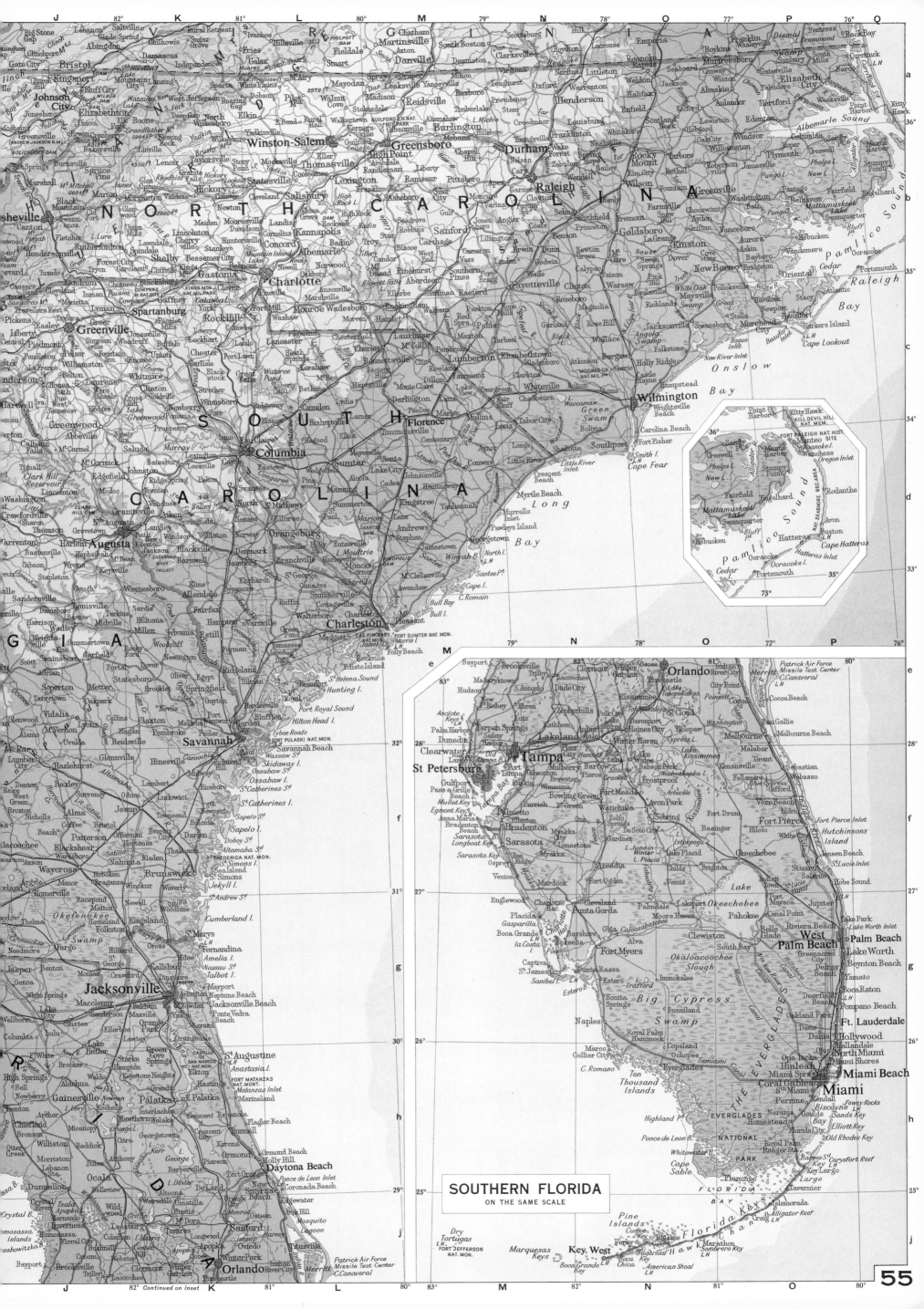

SOUTHERN FLORIDA
ON THE SAME SCALE

55

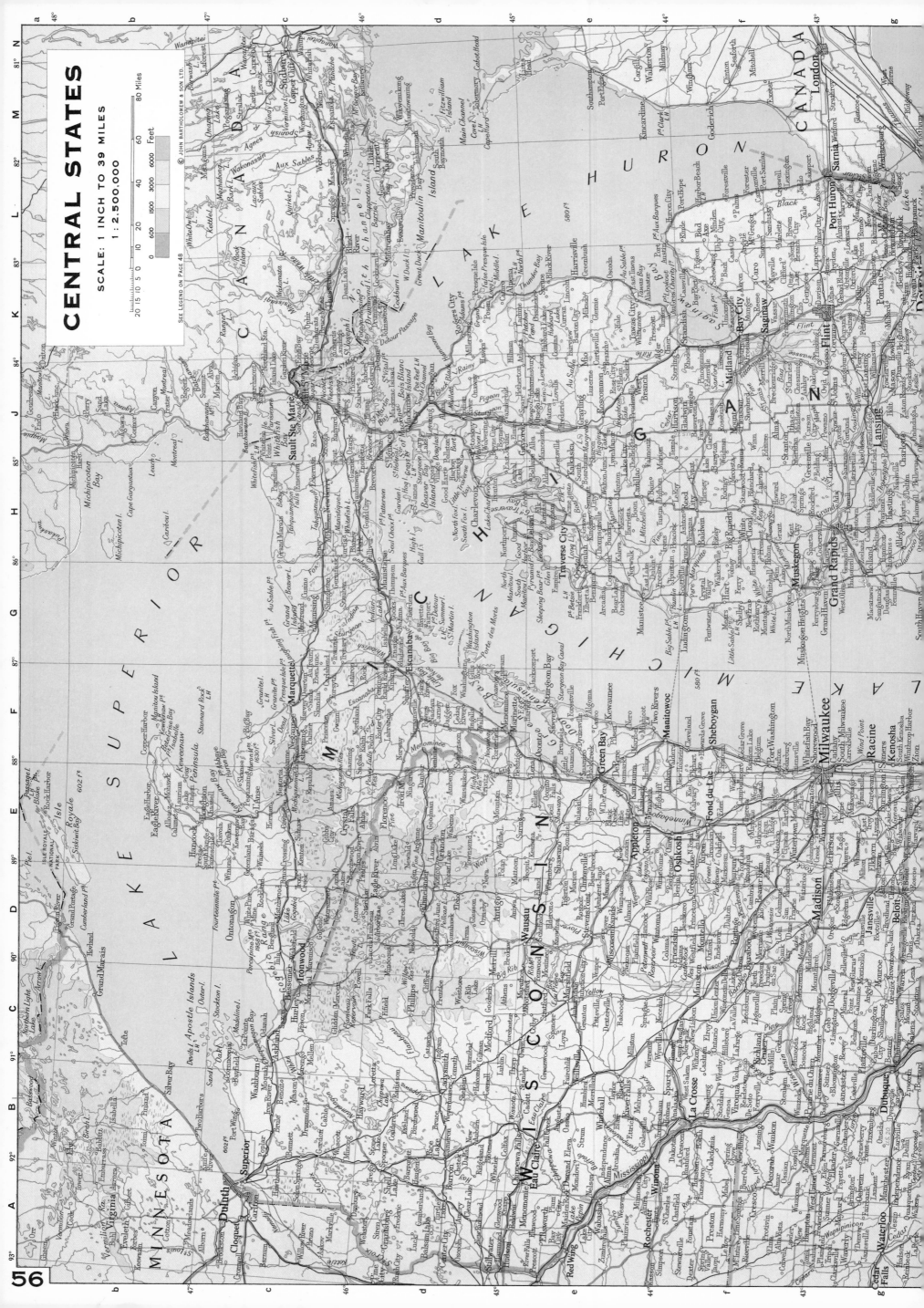

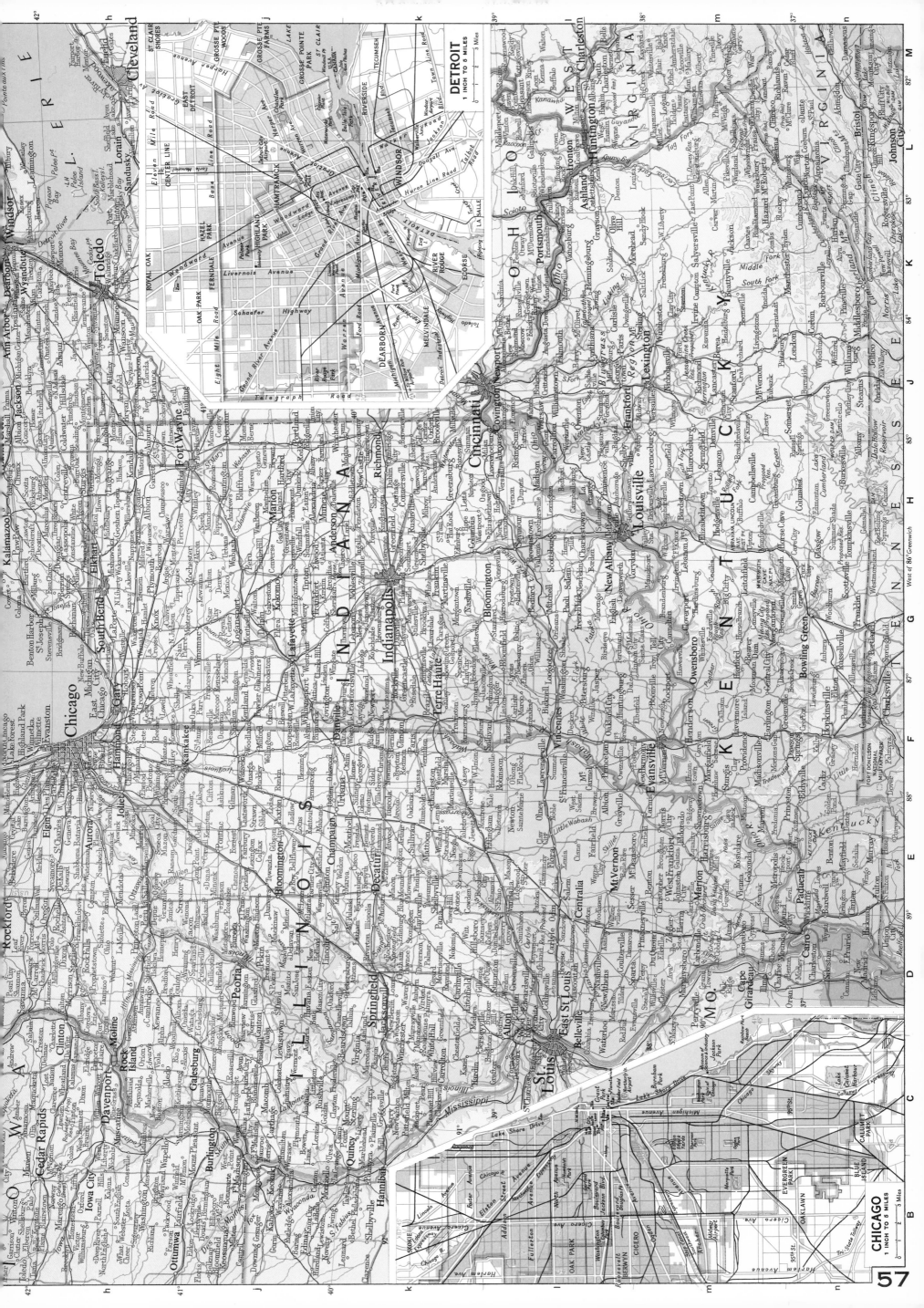

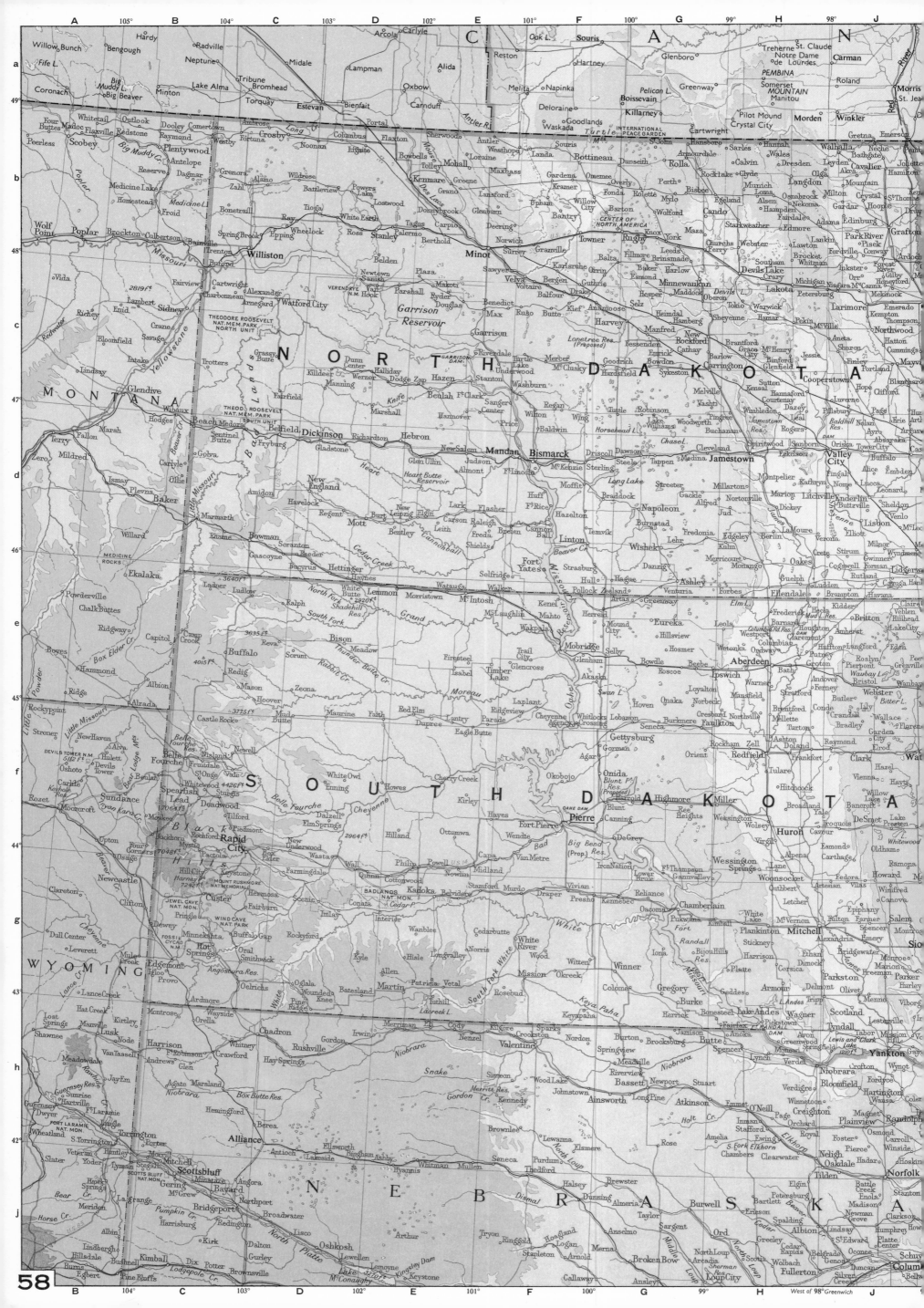

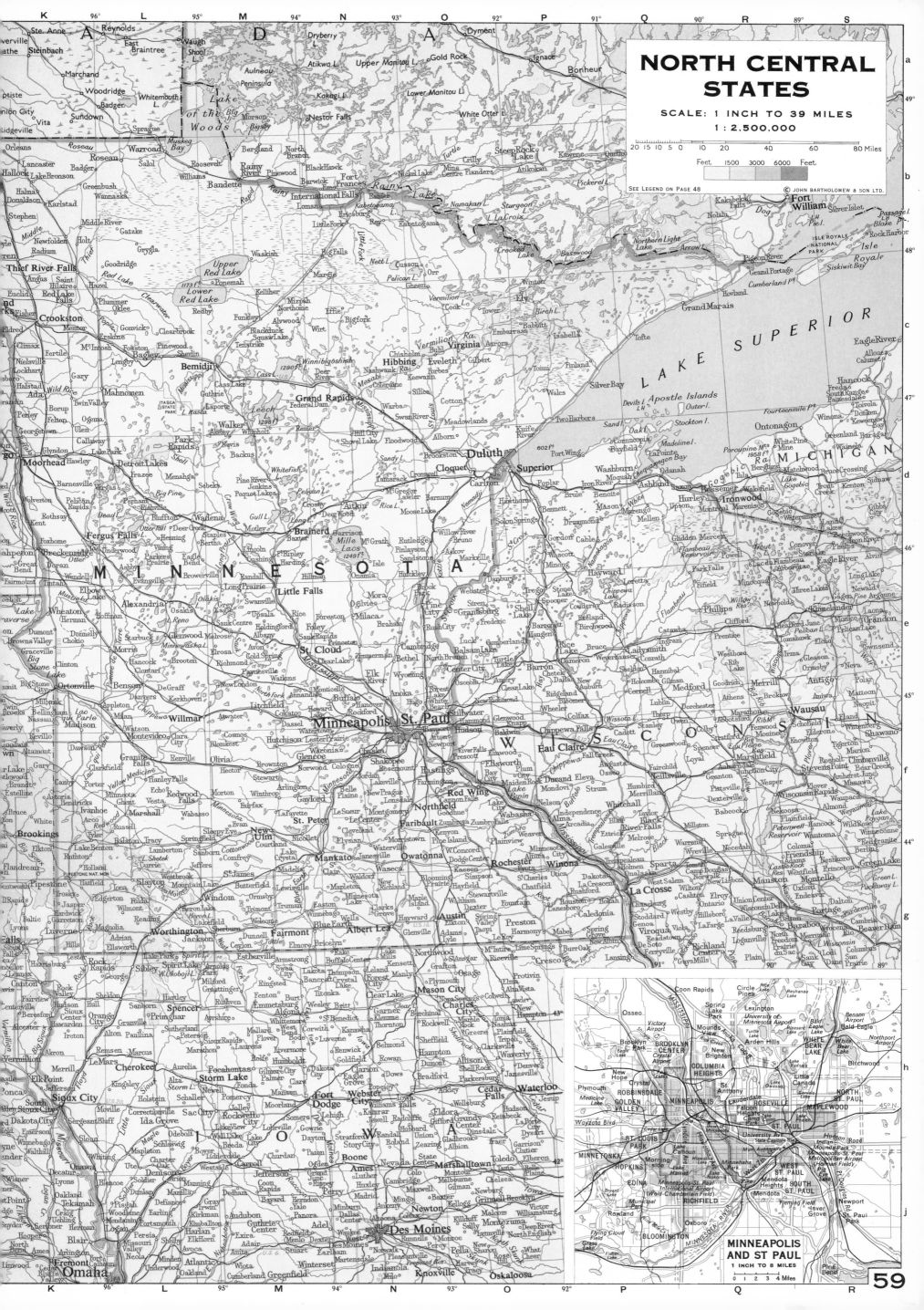

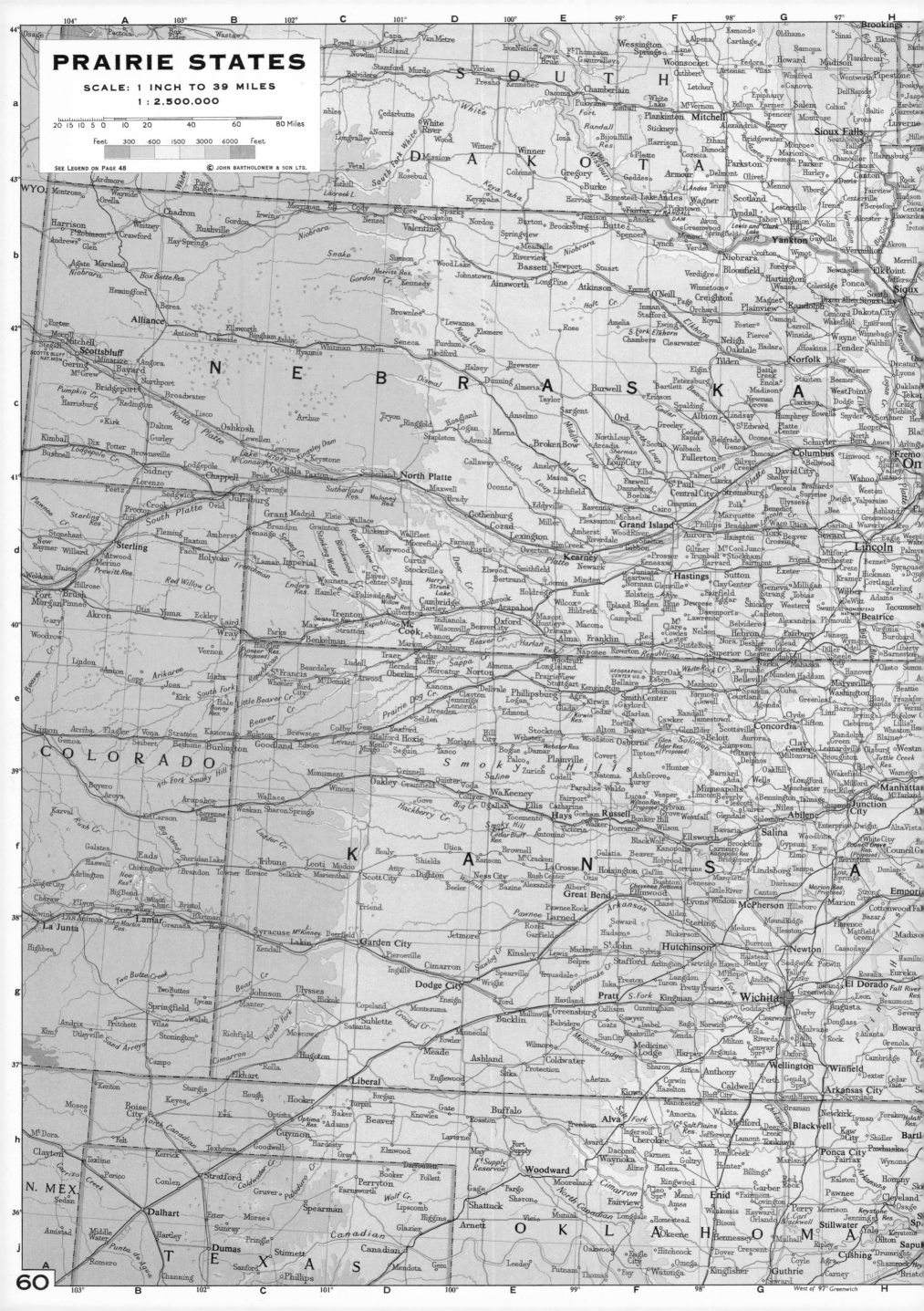

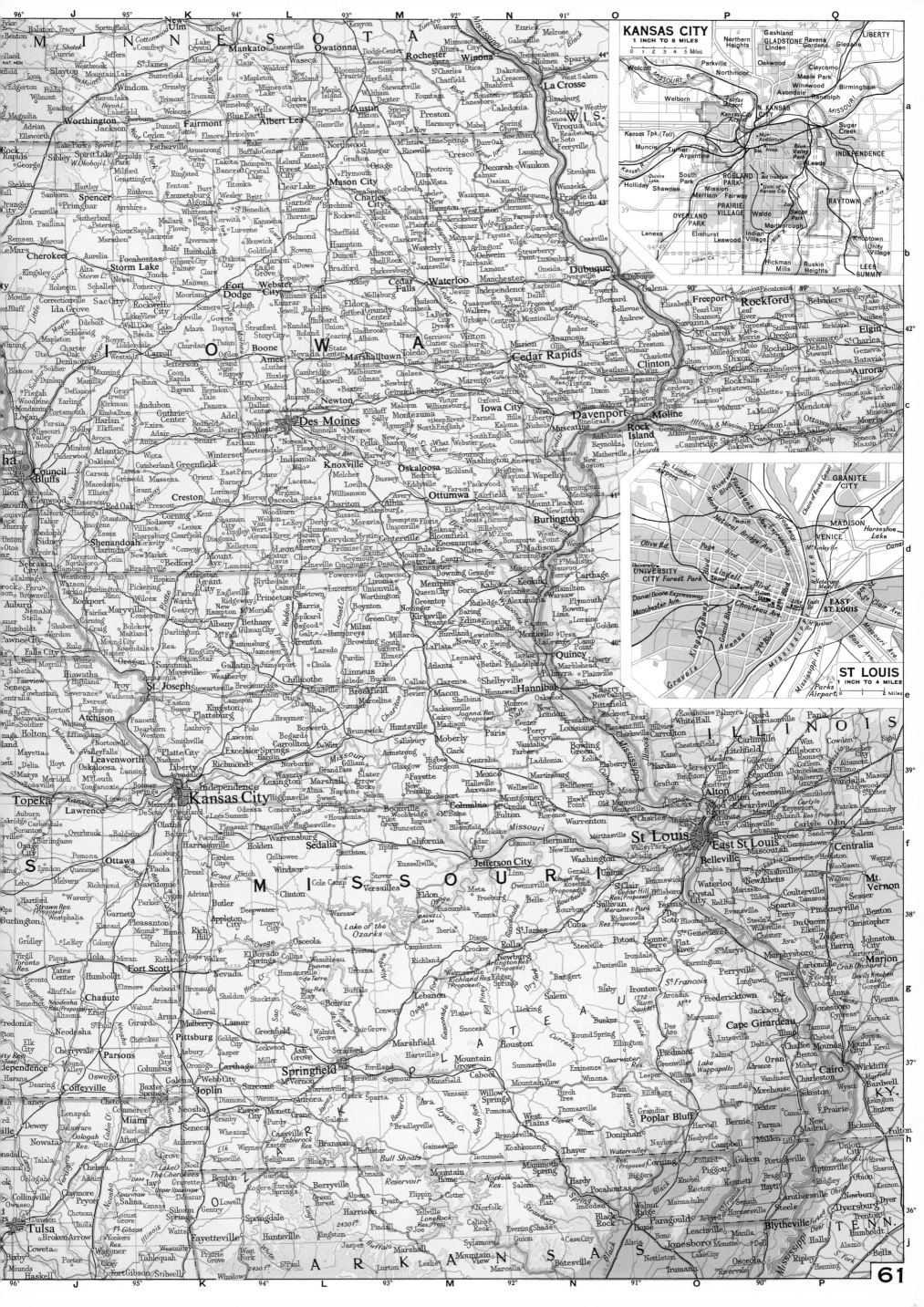

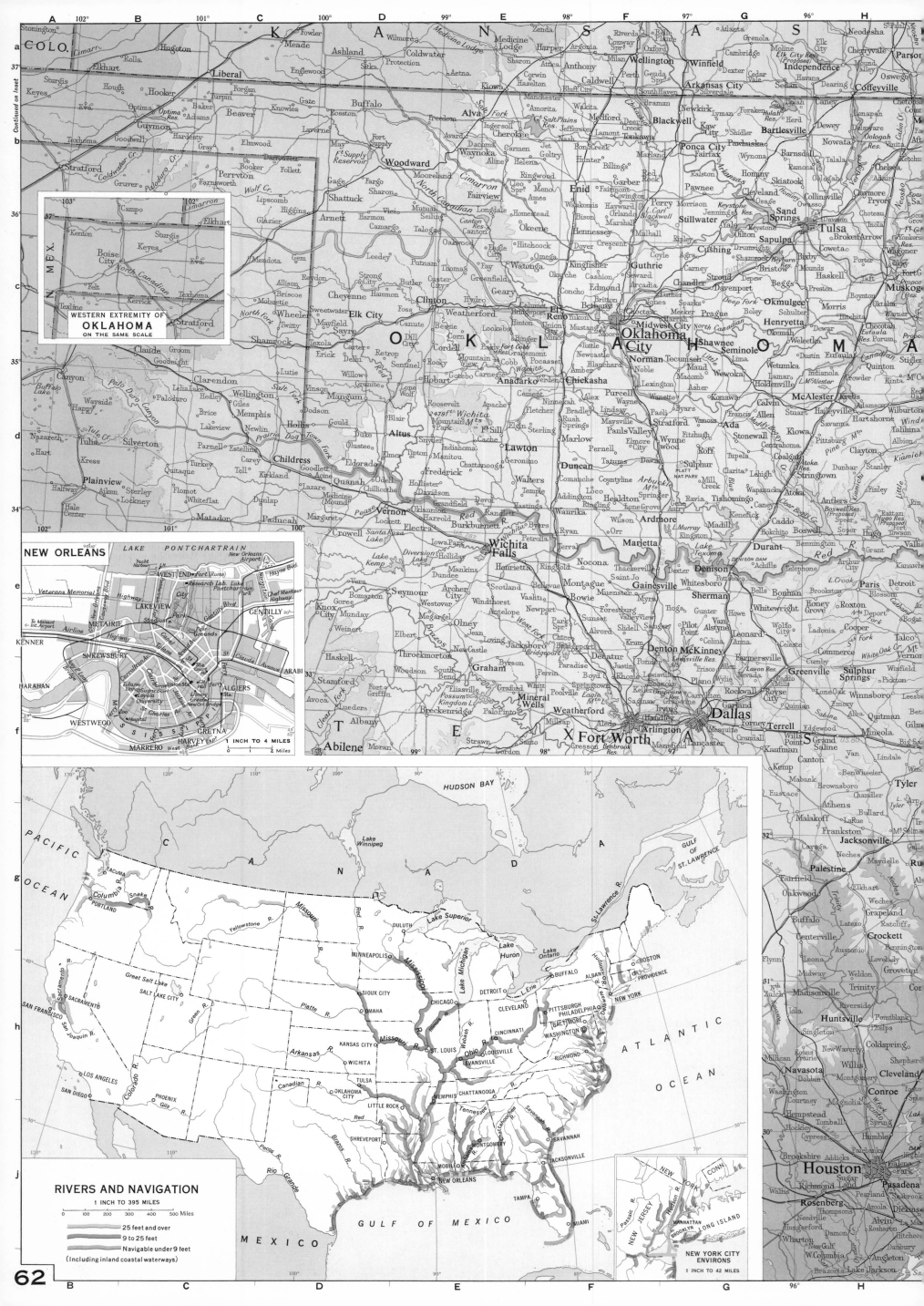

WESTERN EXTREMITY OF OKLAHOMA
ON THE SAME SCALE

NEW ORLEANS
1 INCH TO 4 MILES
0 — 1 — 2 Miles

RIVERS AND NAVIGATION
1 INCH TO 395 MILES
0 100 200 300 400 500 Miles

___ 25 feet and over
___ 9 to 25 feet
___ Navigable under 9 feet
(Including inland coastal waterways)

NEW YORK CITY ENVIRONS
1 INCH TO 42 MILES

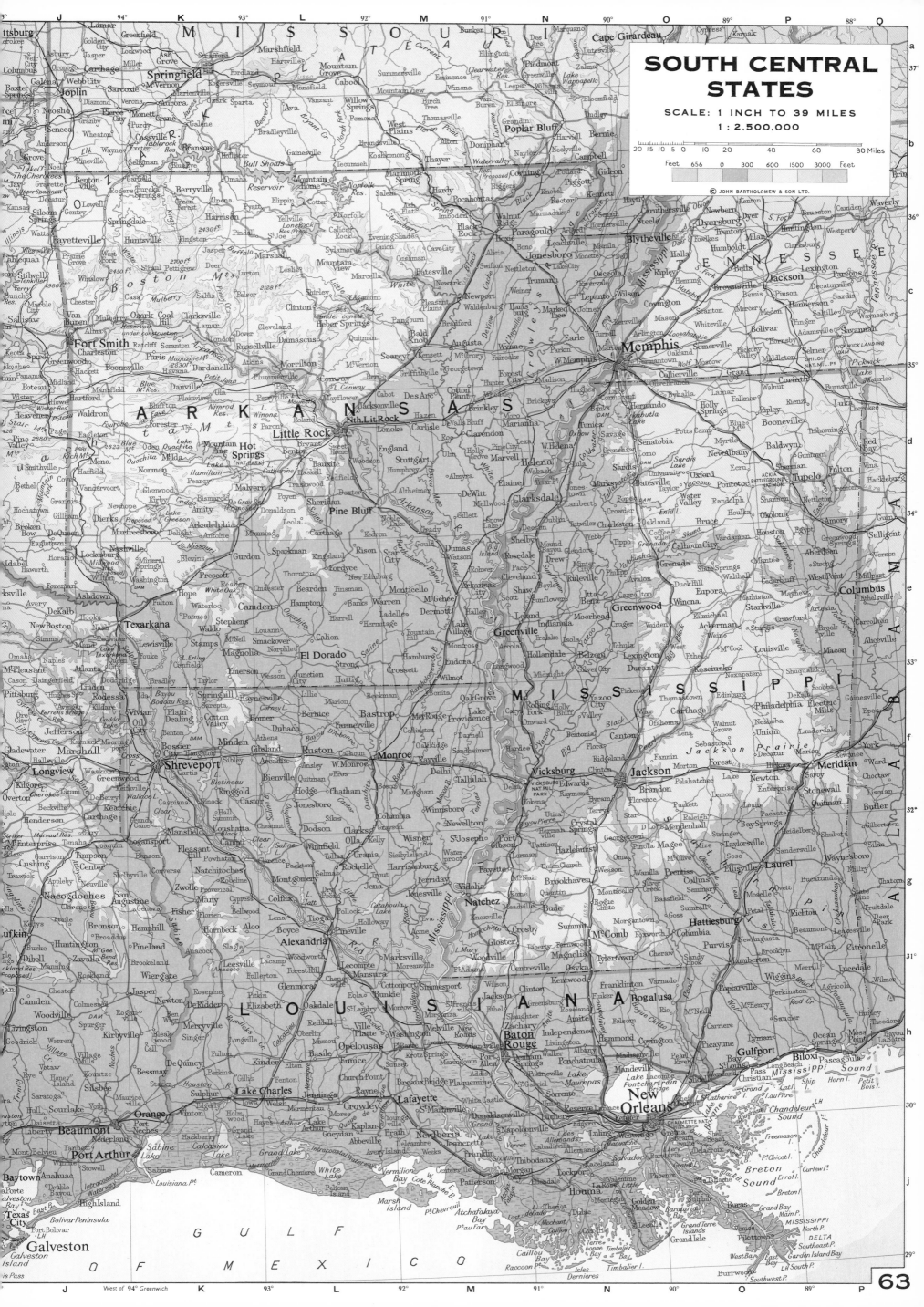

SOUTH CENTRAL STATES

SCALE: 1 INCH TO 39 MILES
1 : 2,500,000

20 15 10 5 0   10   20   40   60   80 Miles

Feet 656   0   300 600 1500 3000 Feet

© JOHN BARTHOLOMEW & SON LTD.

MISSOURI

Springfield
Joplin

Cape Girardeau

Poplar Bluff

ARKANSAS

Fort Smith

Little Rock
Hot Springs

Paragould
Jonesboro
Blytheville

Memphis
W. Memphis

TENNESSEE

Jackson

Texarkana

El Dorado

Pine Bluff

Greenville

MISSISSIPPI

Greenwood

Columbus

ALABAMA

Shreveport

Longview
Marshall

Monroe

Vicksburg
Jackson

Meridian

Natchez

Alexandria

Nacogdoches

Hattiesburg

LOUISIANA

Lake Charles
Lafayette

Baton Rouge

Gulfport
Biloxi

Beaumont
Port Arthur

New
Orleans

Texas
City
Galveston

GULF   OF   MEXICO

Mississippi Sound

Chandeleur
Sound

Breton
Sound

63

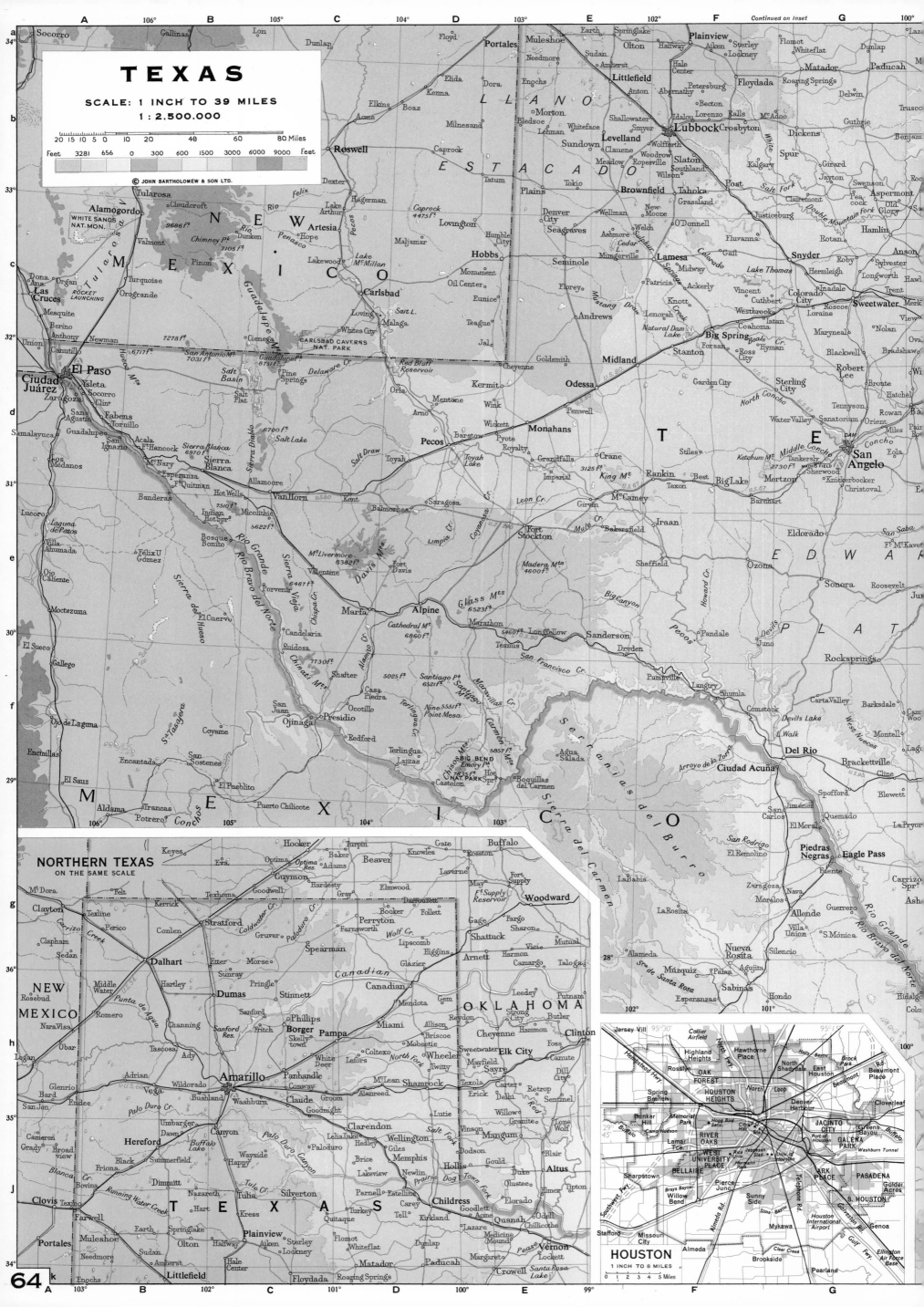

FORT WORTH — DALLAS

1 INCH TO 9½ MILES

0 1 2 3 4 5 6 7 8 9 10 Miles

65

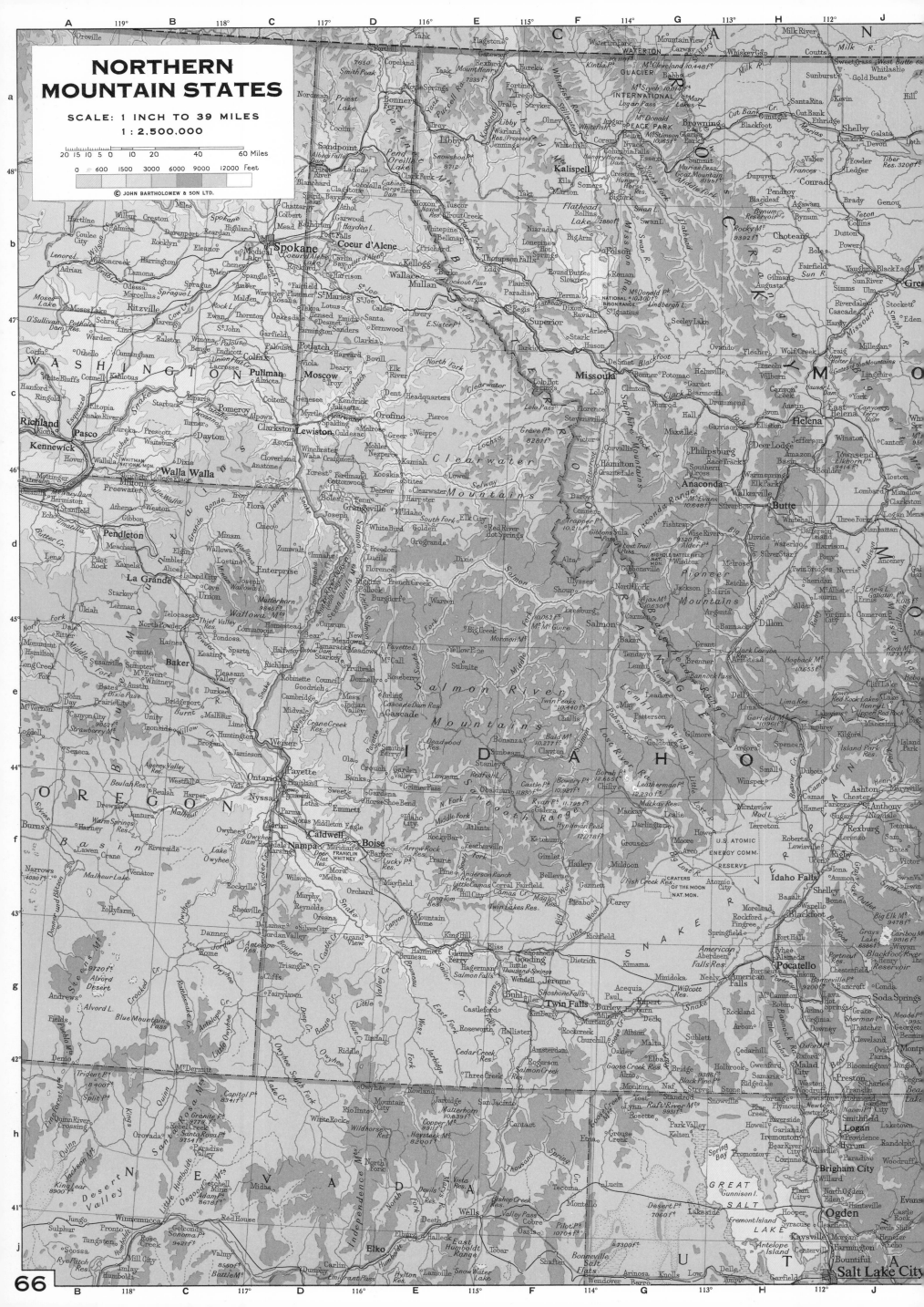

NORTHERN MOUNTAIN STATES

SCALE: 1 INCH TO 39 MILES

1 : 2,500,000

20 15 10 5 0   10   20   40   60 Miles

0   600   1500   3000   6000   9000   12000 Feet

© JOHN BARTHOLOMEW & SON LTD.

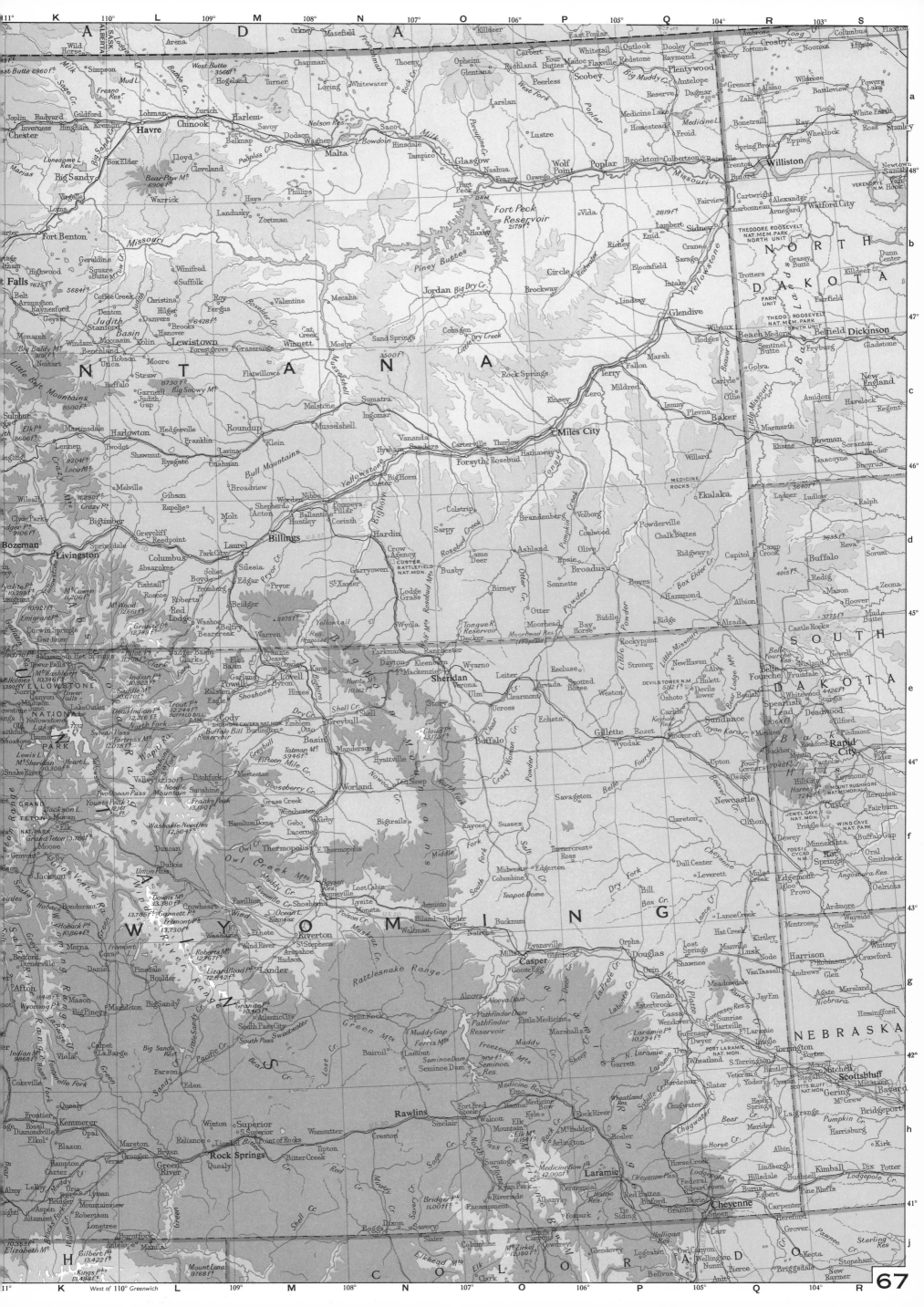

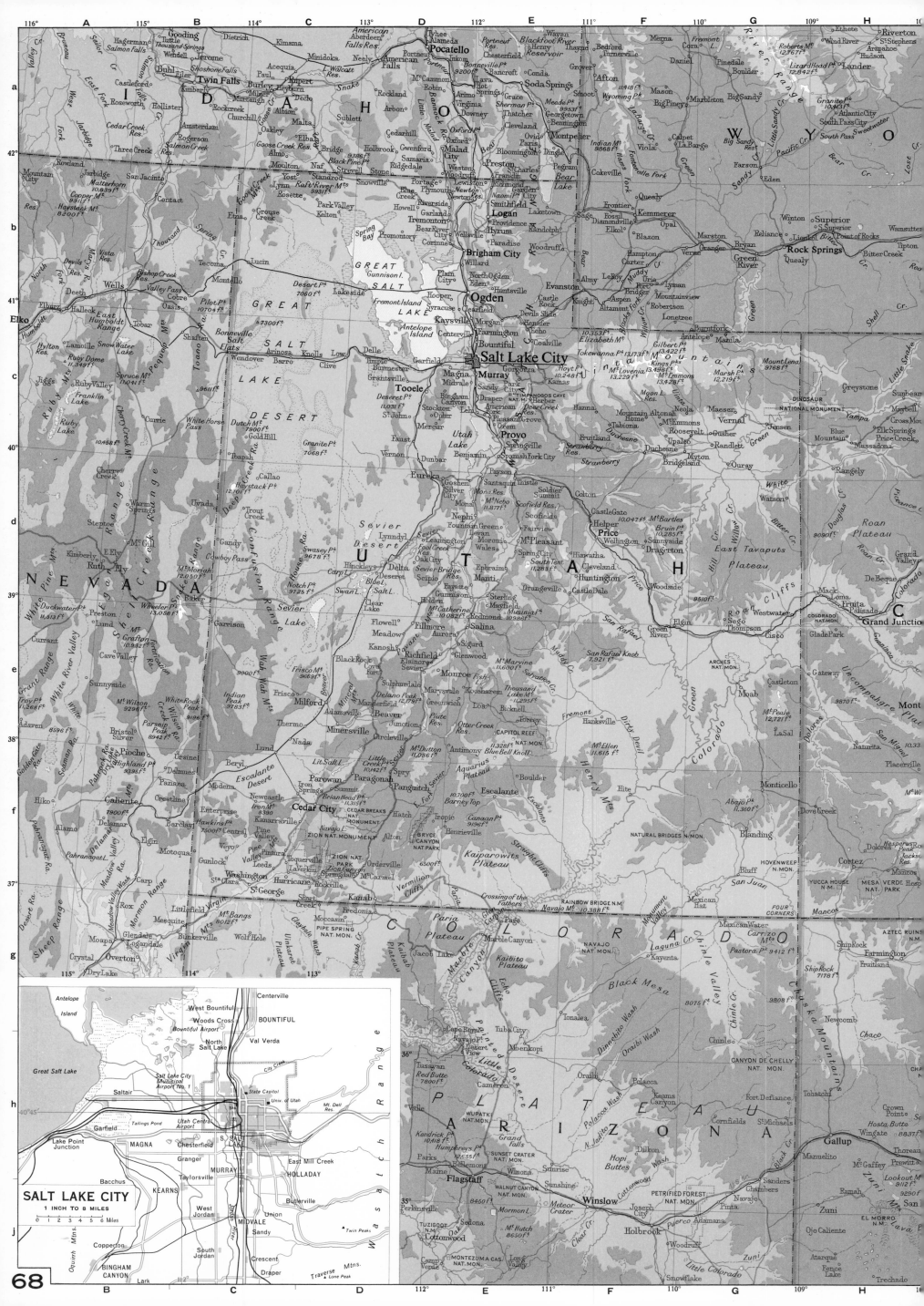

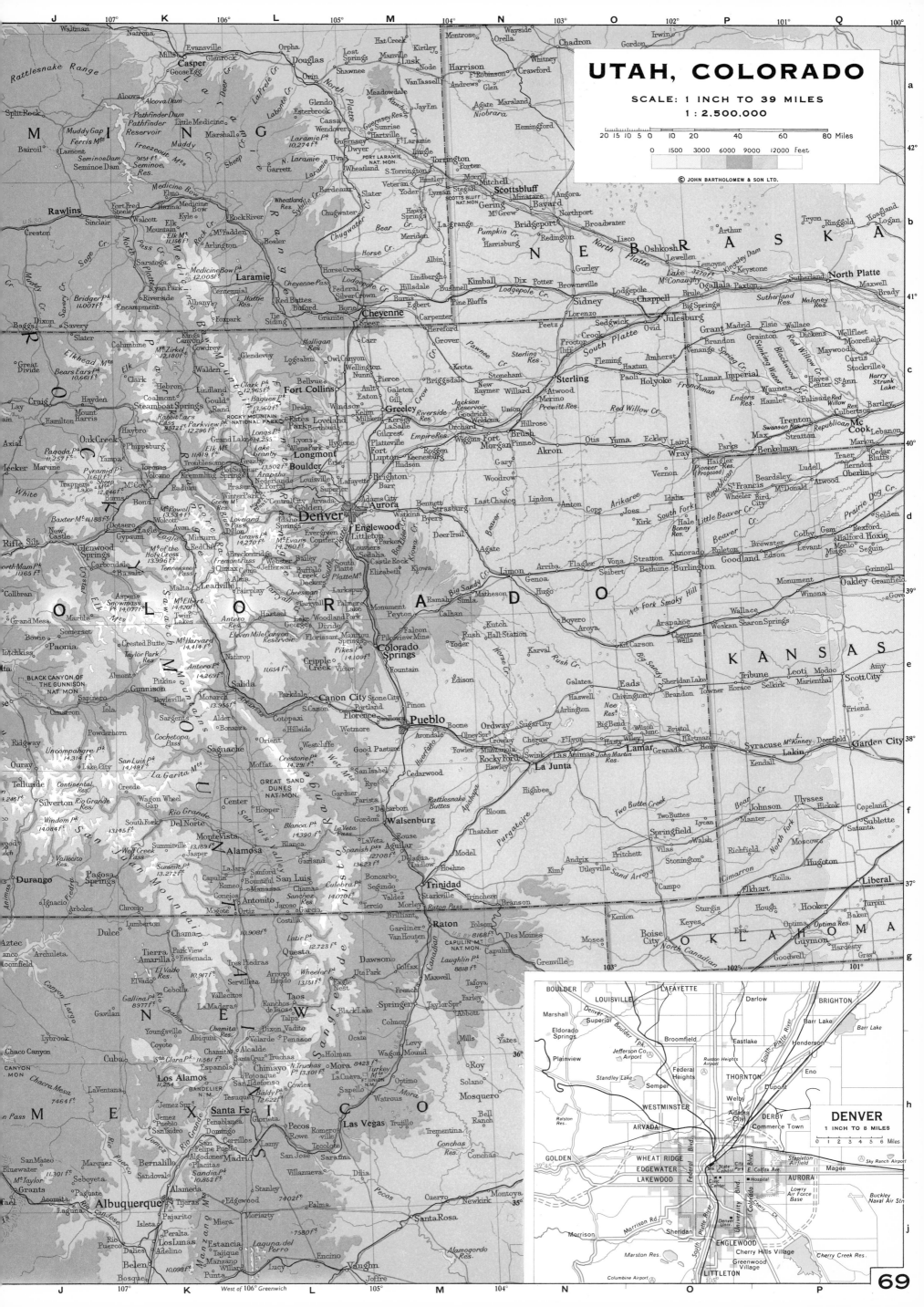

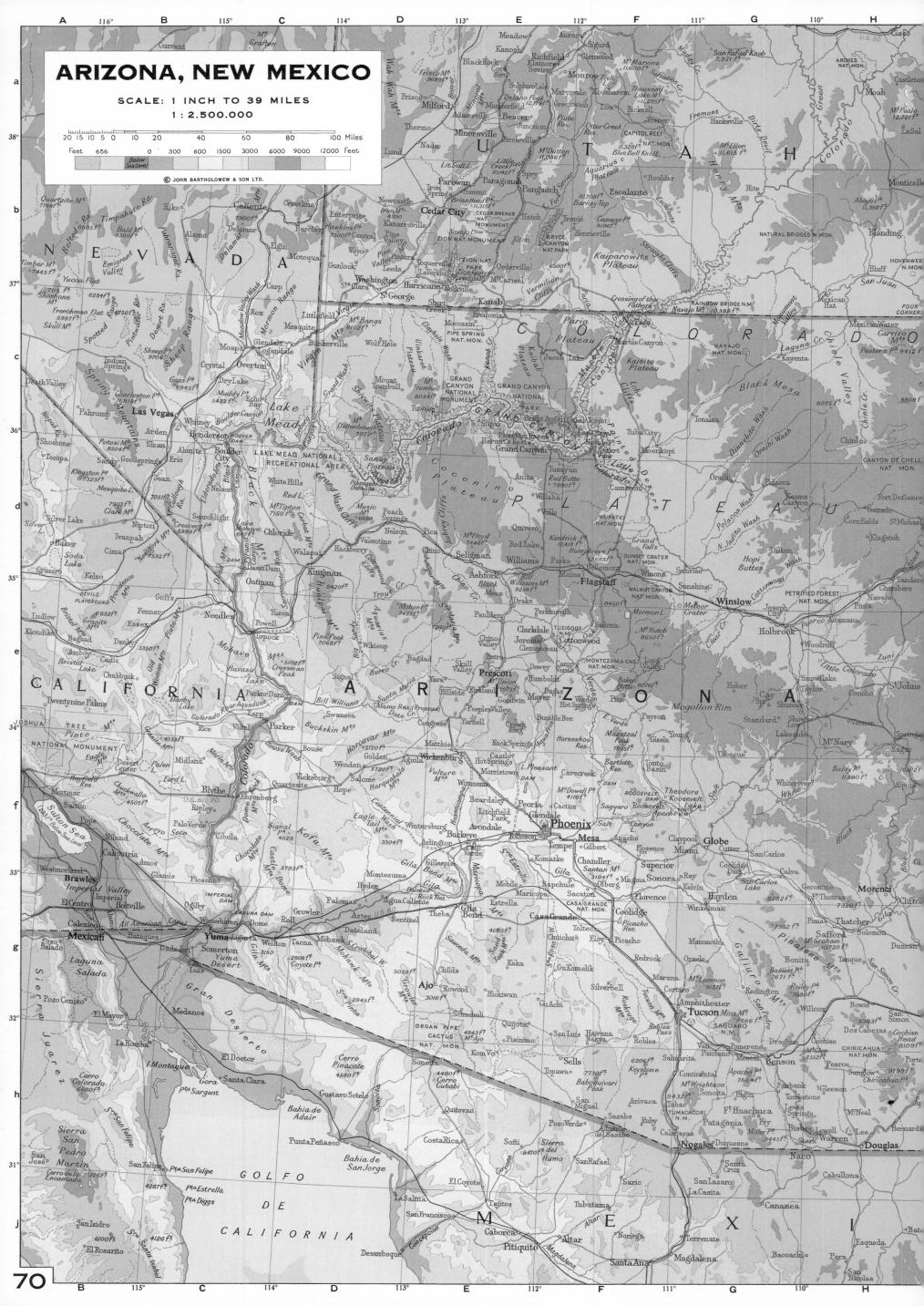

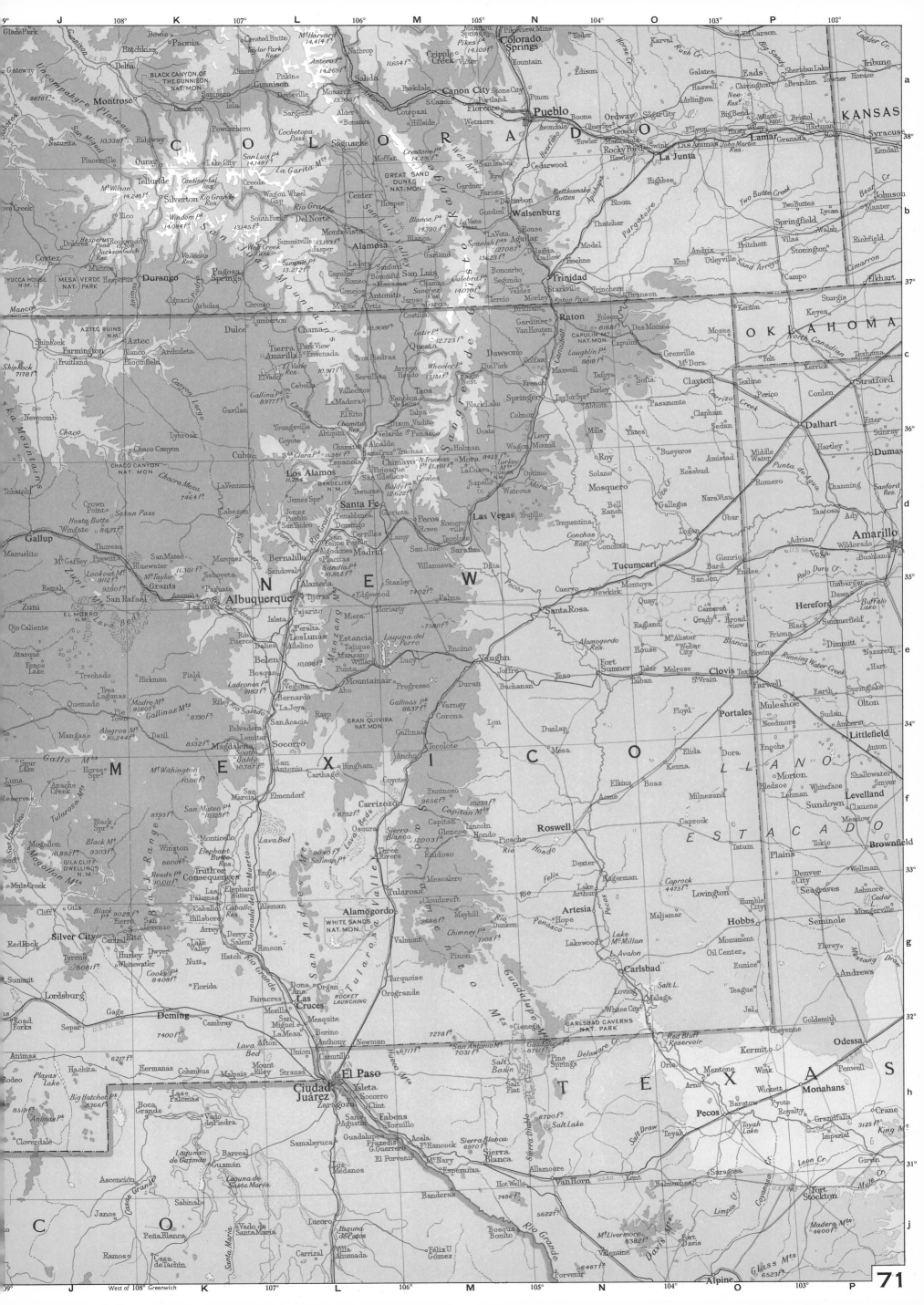

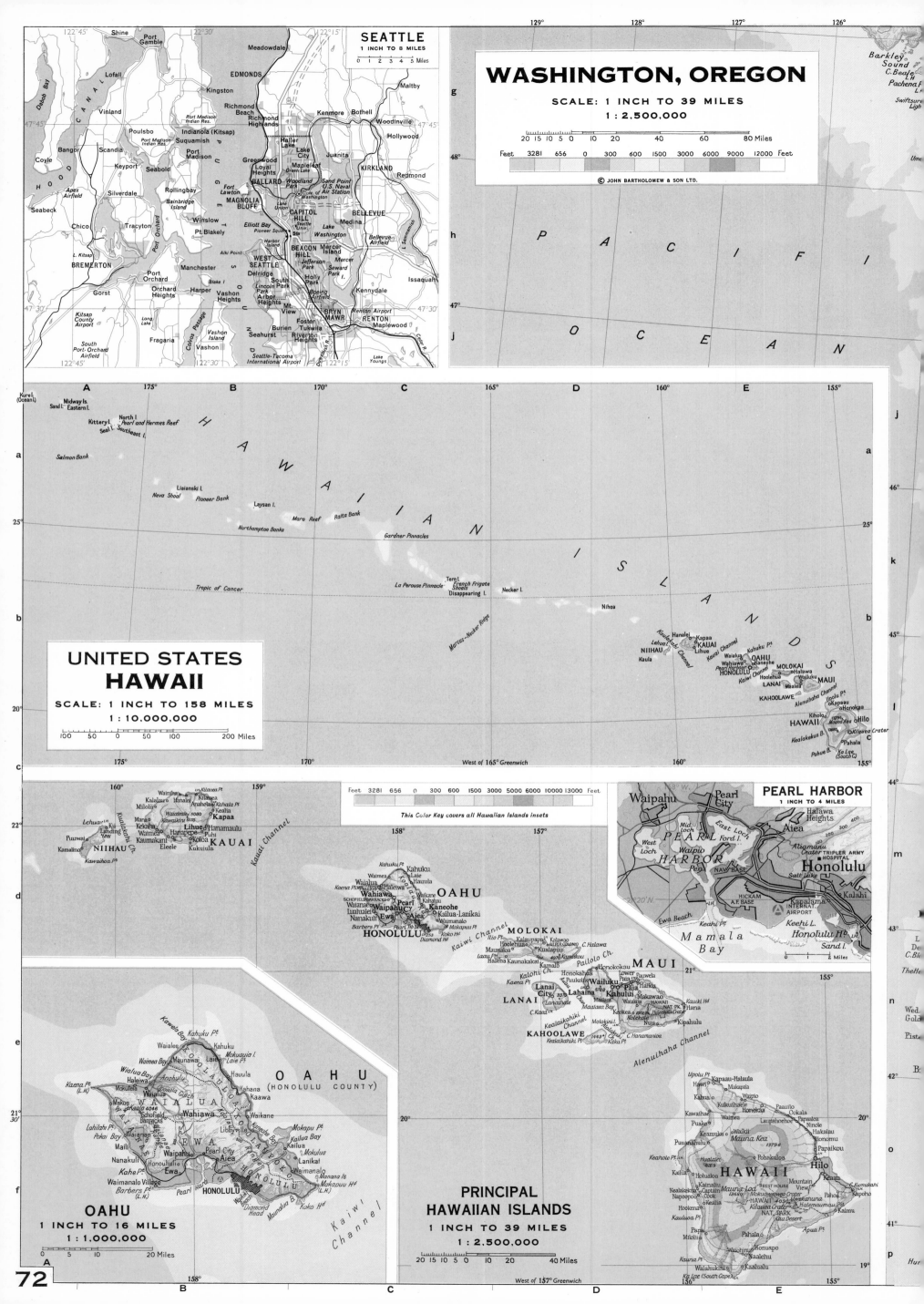

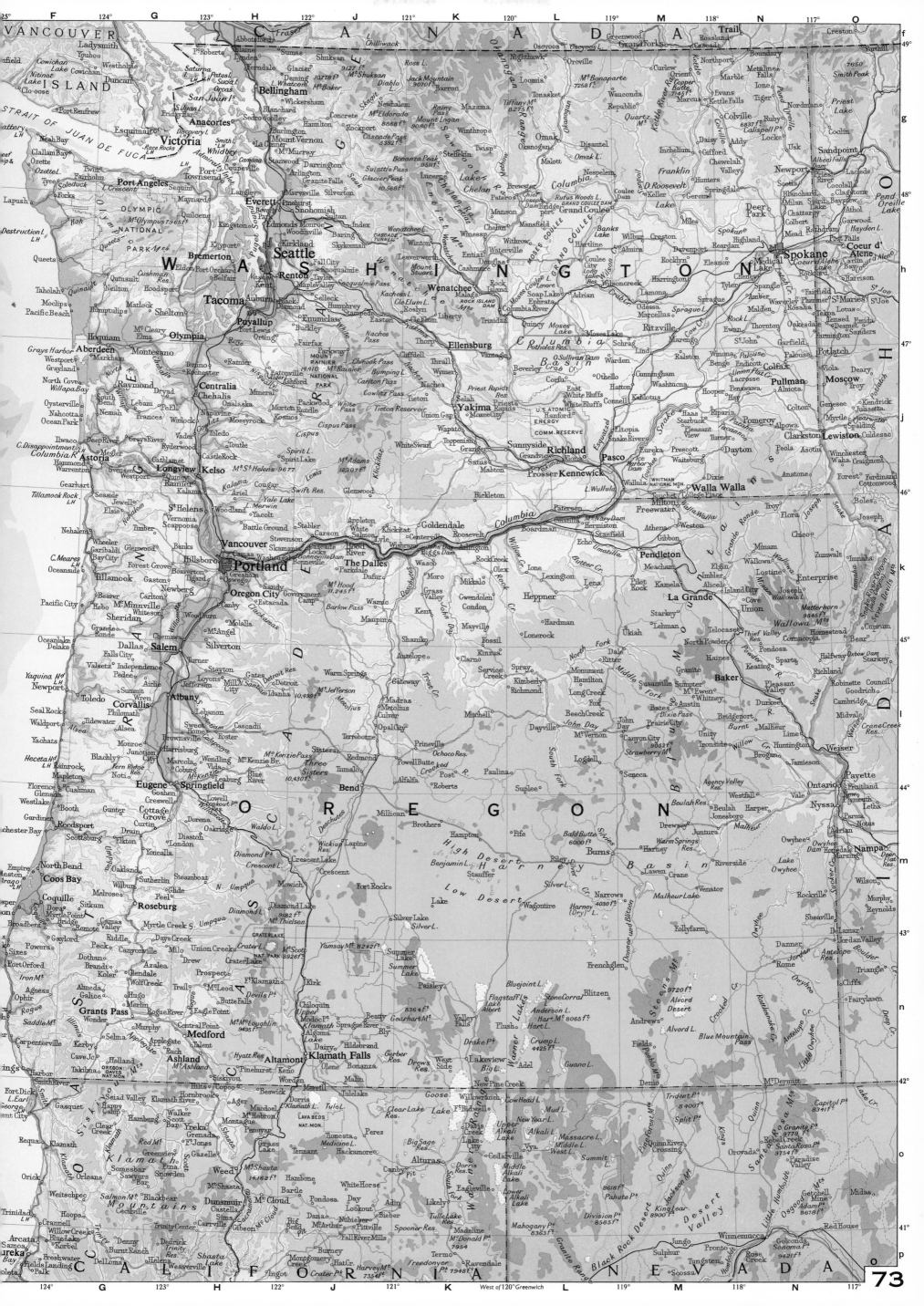

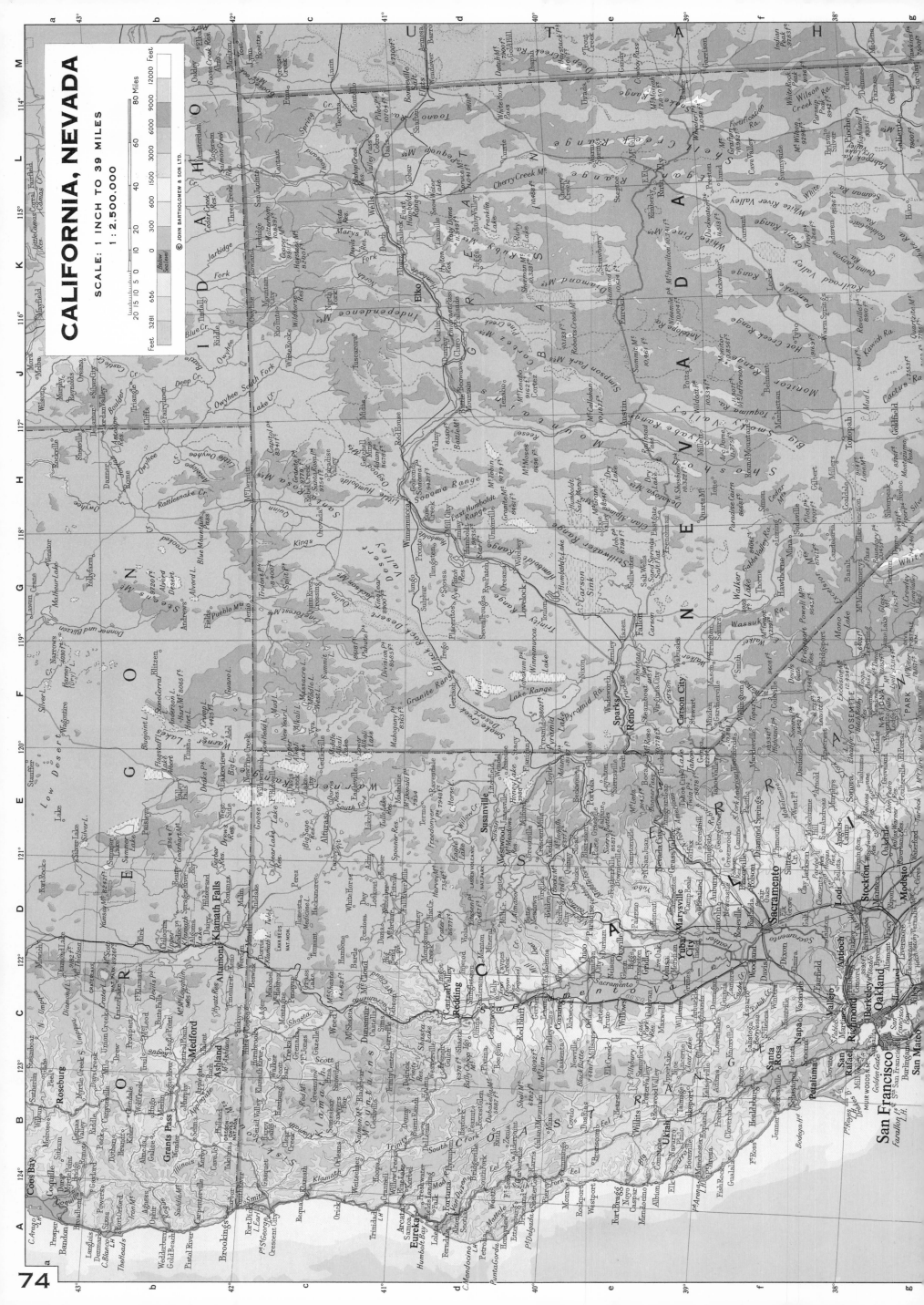

CALIFORNIA, NEVADA

SCALE: 1 INCH TO 39 MILES

1 : 2,500,000

© JOHN BARTHOLOMEW & SON LTD.

74

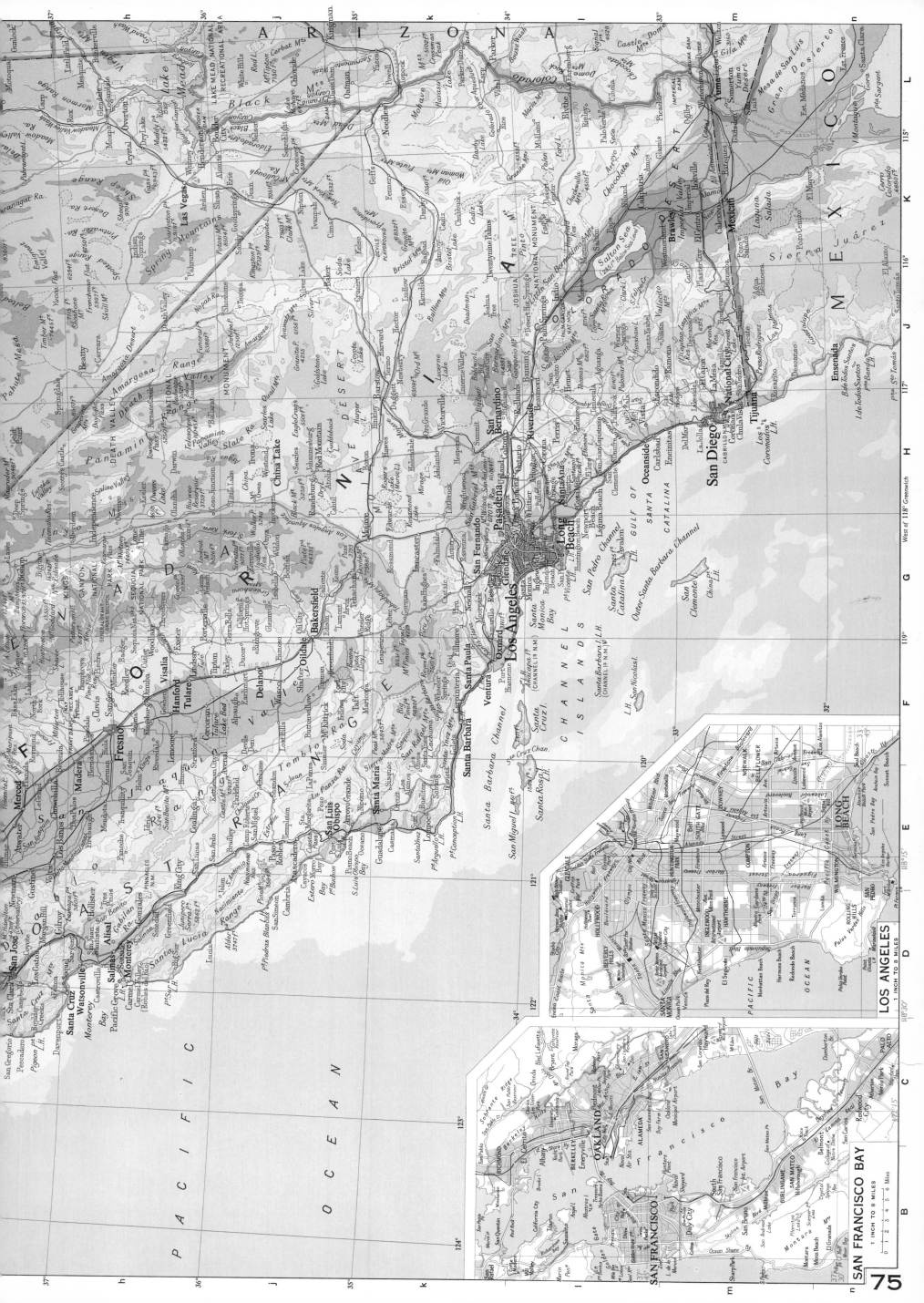

UNITED STATES
ALASKA

SCALE: 1 INCH TO 79 MILES

1 : 5,000,000

40 30 20 10 0 10 20   40   60   80   100 Statute Miles

Feet 6562 656 0 600 1500 3000 6000 9000 12000 Feet

© JOHN BARTHOLOMEW & SON LTD.

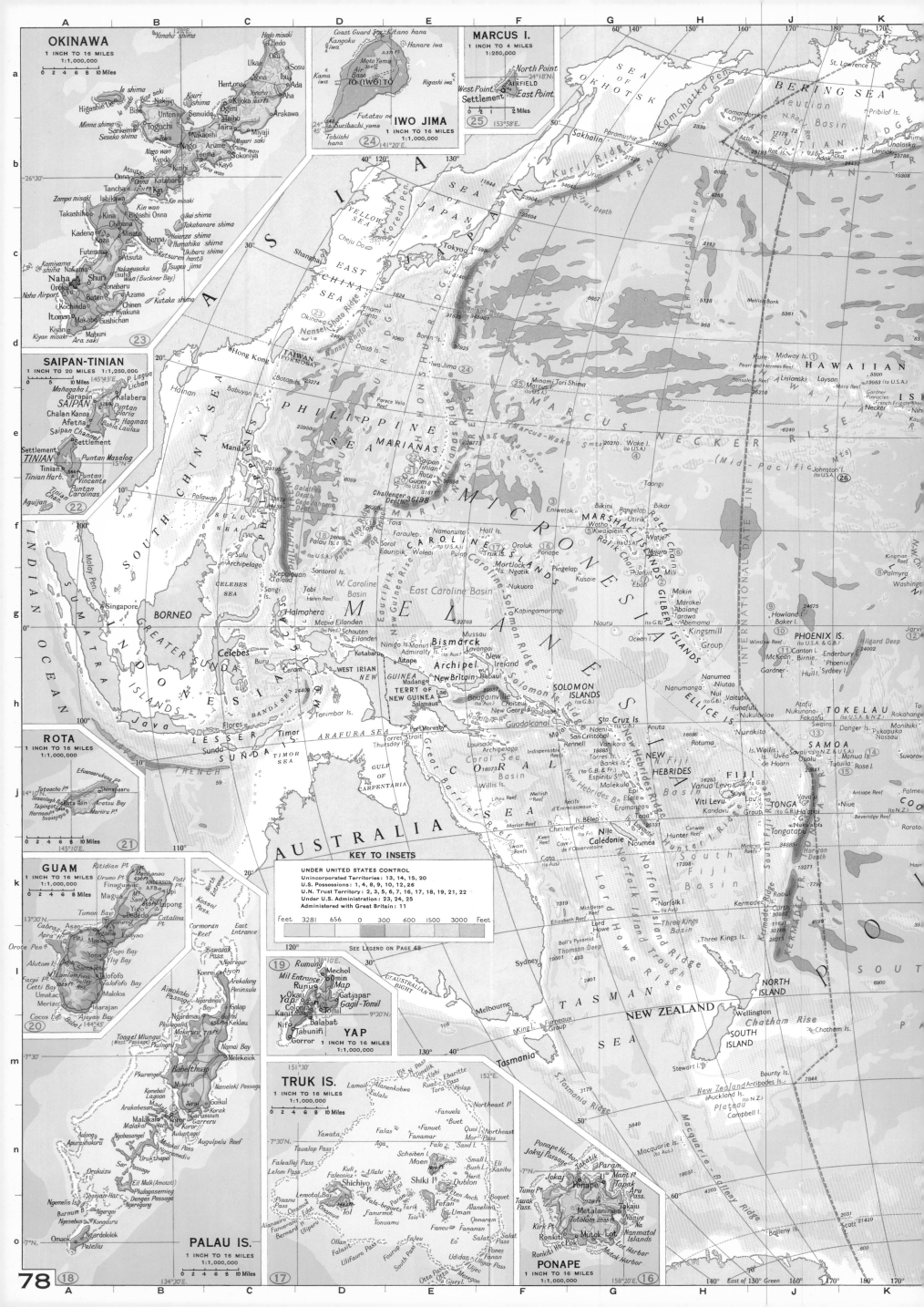

CANADA

AREA: 3,851,809 sq. mi. POP: 18,238,247 CAP: Ottawa
Canada, the world's largest country after the U.S.S.R., 5780 miles

HEIGHTS
IN FEET

12.000
10000
6000
3000
1500
600

SEA LEVEL

3000

DEPTHS
IN FEET

80

CHAMBERLIN TRIMETRIC PROJECTION

SCALE: 1:12,500,000 OR 1 INCH TO 197 MILES
(Approximately)

MAIN HIGHWAYS   CANALS
RAILWAYS   OIL PIPE LINES

at its widest and bordering the United States for 3986 miles, comprises a massive central upland or great Shield, surrounded by inner flanking lowlands and outer marginal mountains. The Shield covers nearly half the country and is a growing source of mineral wealth.

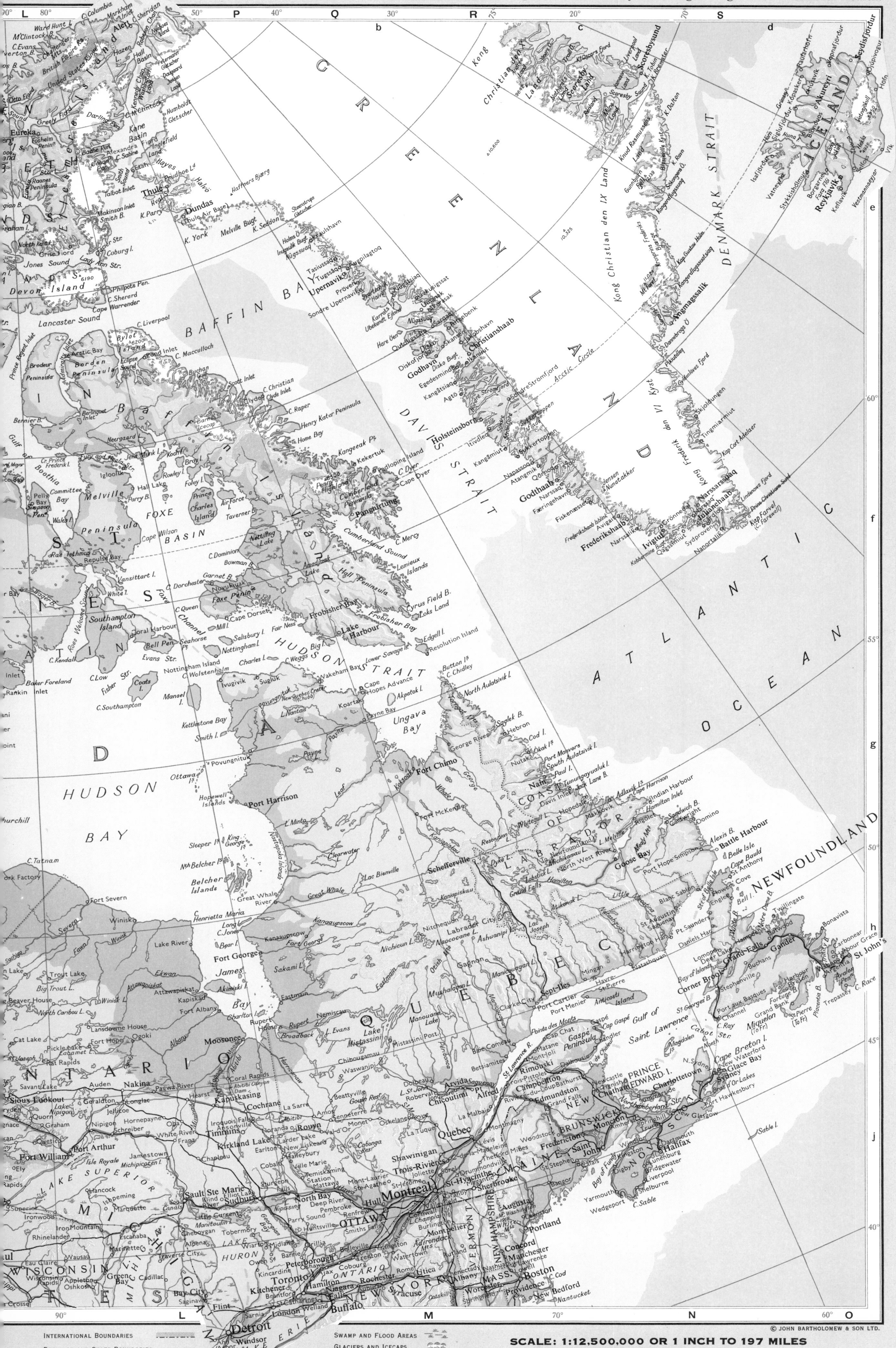

GREENLAND

ICELAND
Reykjavik

BAFFIN BAY

DAVIS STRAIT

DENMARK STRAIT

ATLANTIC OCEAN

Arctic Circle

Baffin Island

FOXE BASIN

Foxe Peninsula

Hudson Strait

Ungava Bay

HUDSON BAY

Southampton Island

Belcher Islands

James Bay

LABRADOR

QUEBEC

NEWFOUNDLAND

Fort Chimo
Port Harrison
Great Whale River
Fort George
Moosonee
Schefferville
Labrador City
Goose Bay
Gander
St. John's
Corner Brook
Grand Falls

ONTARIO

LAKE SUPERIOR
LAKE HURON
LAKE MICHIGAN
LAKE ERIE
LAKE ONTARIO

Fort William
Fort Arthur
Sudbury
North Bay
Ottawa
Montreal
Quebec
Trois-Rivières
Shawinigan
Chicoutimi
Arvida

NEW BRUNSWICK
NOVA SCOTIA
PRINCE EDWARD I.
Charlottetown
Halifax
Sydney
Saint John
Fredericton

MAINE
NEW HAMPSHIRE
VERMONT
NEW YORK
MASS.

Detroit
Windsor
Toronto
Hamilton
Buffalo
Boston
Portland

Gulf of Saint Lawrence
Gaspé Peninsula
Anticosti Island
Cape Breton I.

© JOHN BARTHOLOMEW & SON LTD.

SCALE IN MILES
100
200
300
400
500
600
700
800
900
1000
1100
1200
1300
1400
1500
1600
1700
1800
1900
2000

INTERNATIONAL BOUNDARIES
PROVINCE AND STATE BOUNDARIES
SWAMP AND FLOOD AREAS
GLACIERS AND ICECAPS
SPOT HEIGHTS IN FEET

SCALE: 1:12,500,000 OR 1 INCH TO 197 MILES
(Approximately)

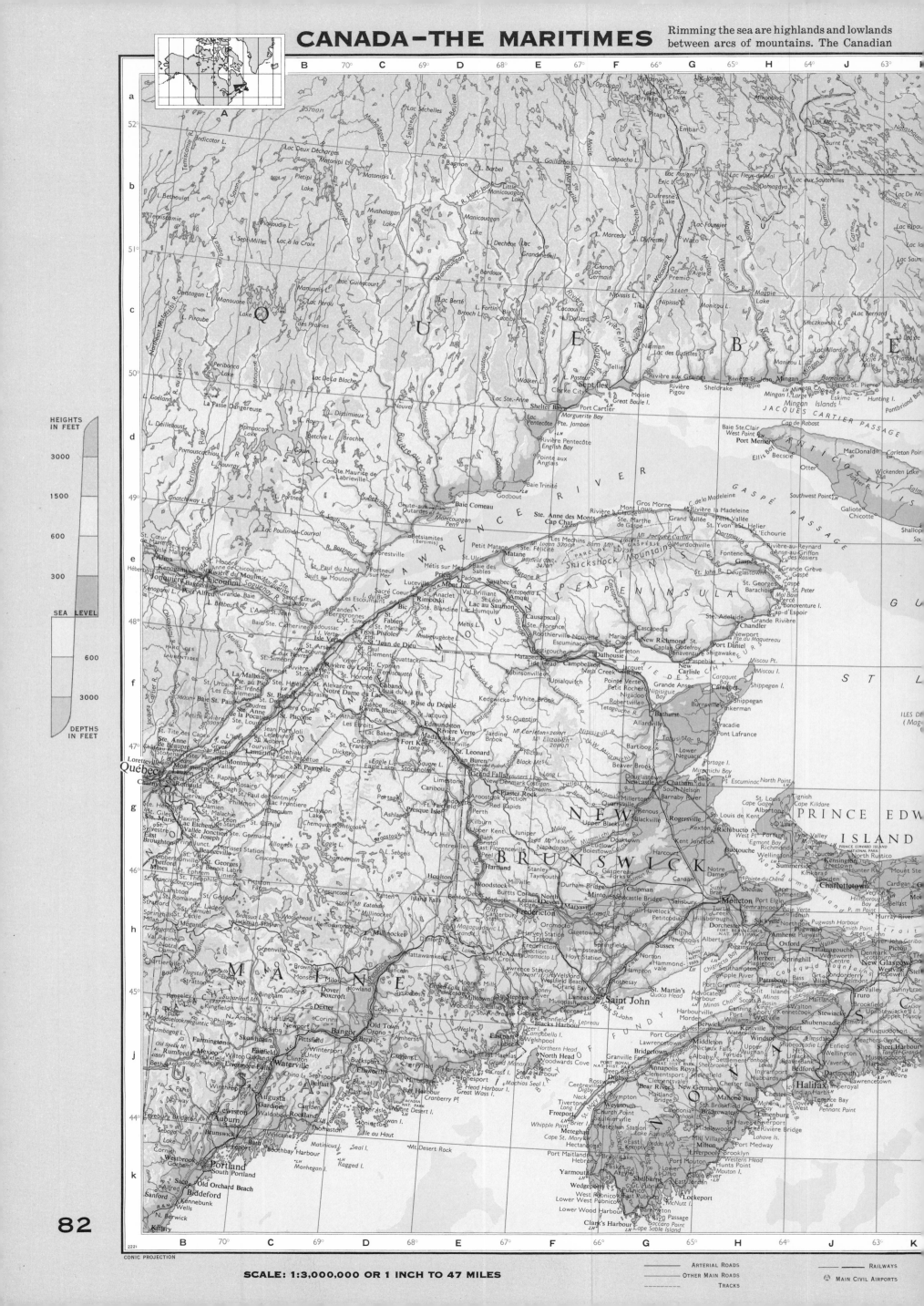

HEIGHTS IN FEET

3000
1500
600
300

SEA LEVEL

600
3000

DEPTHS IN FEET

82

CONIC PROJECTION

SCALE: 1:3,000,000 OR 1 INCH TO 47 MILES

——— ARTERIAL ROADS
——— OTHER MAIN ROADS
--------- TRACKS
——— RAILWAYS
✈ MAIN CIVIL AIRPORTS

Appalachians comprise an outer chain—Newfoundland's Avalon Peninsula, the Cape Breton
highlands and Nova Scotia uplands—and an
inner chain—Newfoundland's Long Range, the
Shickshock Mountains of the Gaspé, the Notre
Dame Mountains and Eastern Quebec uplands.

SCALE IN MILES

COAST OF LABRADOR

ATLANTIC OCEAN

NEWFOUNDLAND

STRAIT OF BELLE ISLE

White Bay

Notre Dame Bay

Fogo Island

Gander Lake

Gander

Grand Falls

Deer Lake

Corner Brook

Bay of Islands

St. George's Bay

Port aux Basques

Channel

LONG RANGE MOUNTAINS

St. Anthony

St. John's

AVALON PENINSULA

PLACENTIA BAY

Burin Peninsula

St. Pierre (To France)

Miquelon (To France)

GULF OF ST. LAWRENCE

CABOT STRAIT

CAPE BRETON ISLAND

CAPE BRETON HIGHLANDS NATIONAL PARK

Sydney

Glace Bay

Louisburg

ATLANTIC OCEAN

SABLE ISLAND

SABLE ISLAND BANK

MADELEINE (Islands)

Havre Aubert

West 62° of Greenwich

83

© JOHN BARTHOLOMEW & SON LTD.

INTERNATIONAL BOUNDARIES
PROVINCIAL BOUNDARIES
SWAMP AND FLOOD AREAS
SPOT HEIGHTS IN FEET

SCALE: 1:3,000,000 OR 1 INCH TO 47 MILES

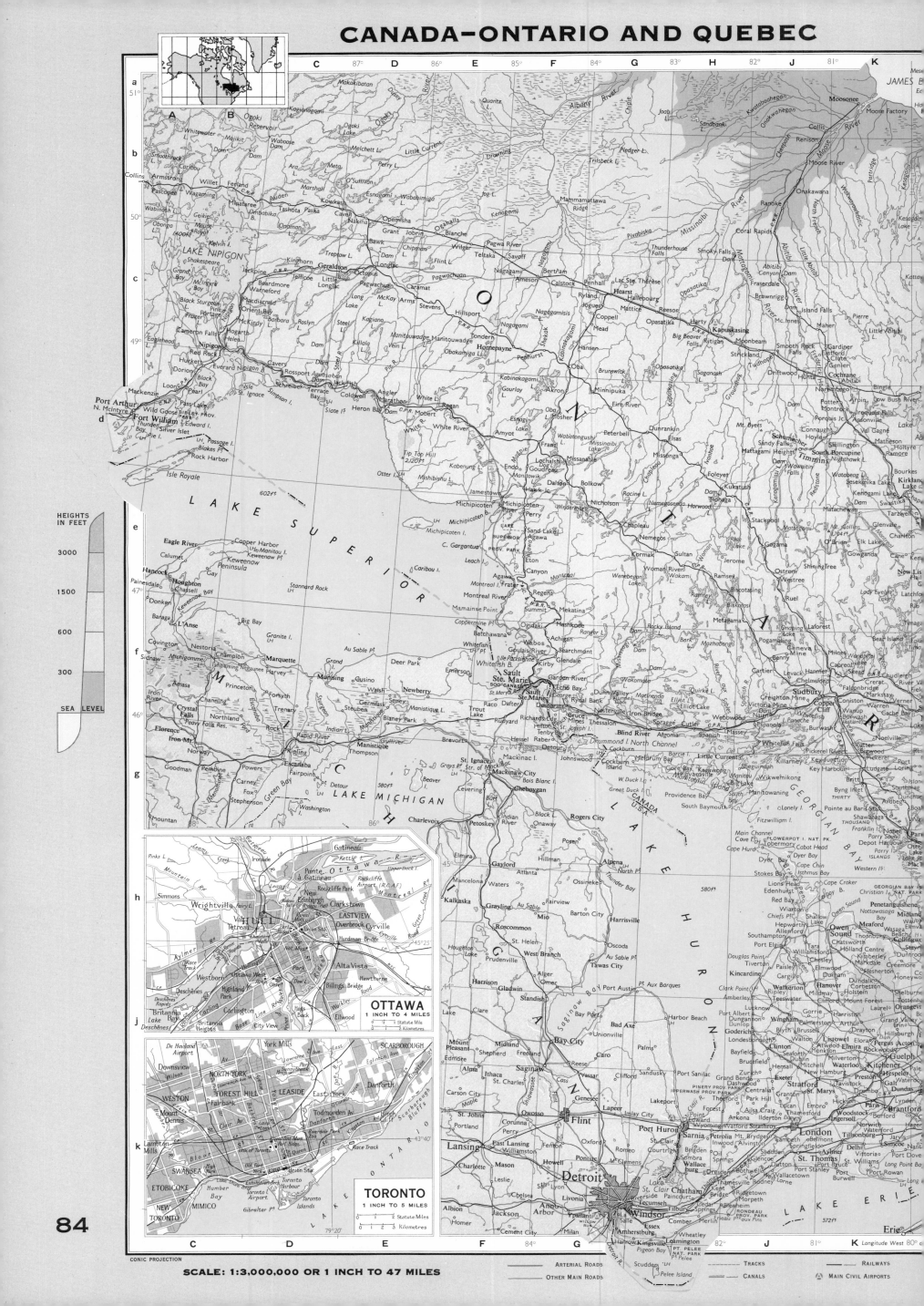

CANADA—ONTARIO AND QUEBEC

84

SCALE: 1:3,000,000 OR 1 INCH TO 47 MILES

CONIC PROJECTION

The Great Lakes-St. Lawrence lowlands form the economic heartland of Canada. This region is one of the smallest geographic units in the country, but contains 60 percent of the population. It is probably the most productive area in Canada.

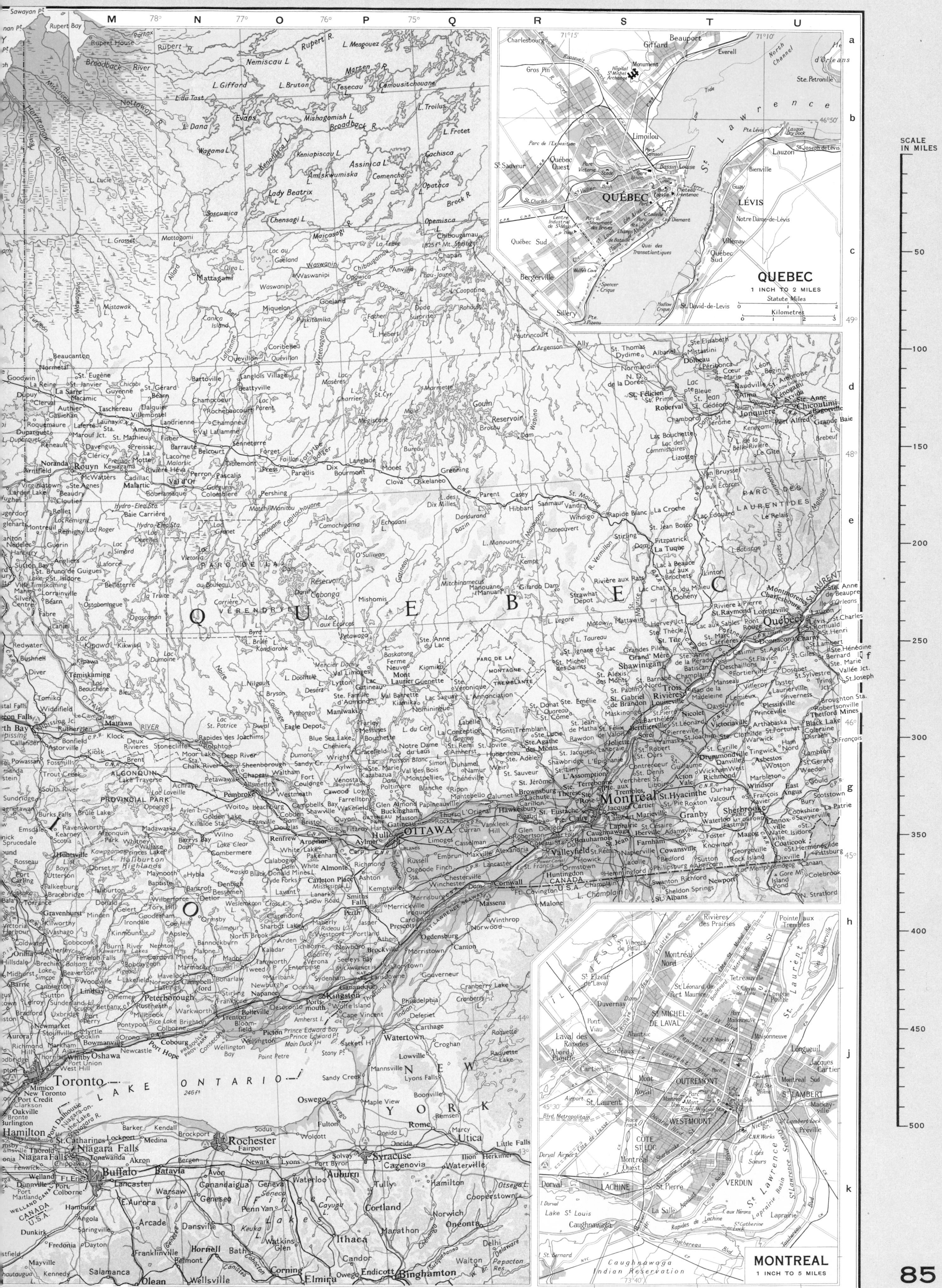

QUEBEC
1 INCH TO 2 MILES
Statute Miles
Kilometres

MONTREAL
1 INCH TO 5 MILES

SCALE IN MILES

50
100
150
200
250
300
350
400
450
500

85

INTERNATIONAL BOUNDARIES
PROVINCIAL BOUNDARIES
SWAMP AND FLOOD AREAS
SPOT HEIGHTS IN FEET △ 2,120 ft

© JOHN BARTHOLOMEW & SON LTD.

SCALE: 1:3,000,000 OR 1 INCH TO 47 MILES

CANADA–PRAIRIES

Canada's prairies, taking in large areas of three provinces, were formed by deposits from the Pre-Cambrian Shield and from marginal mountains (the

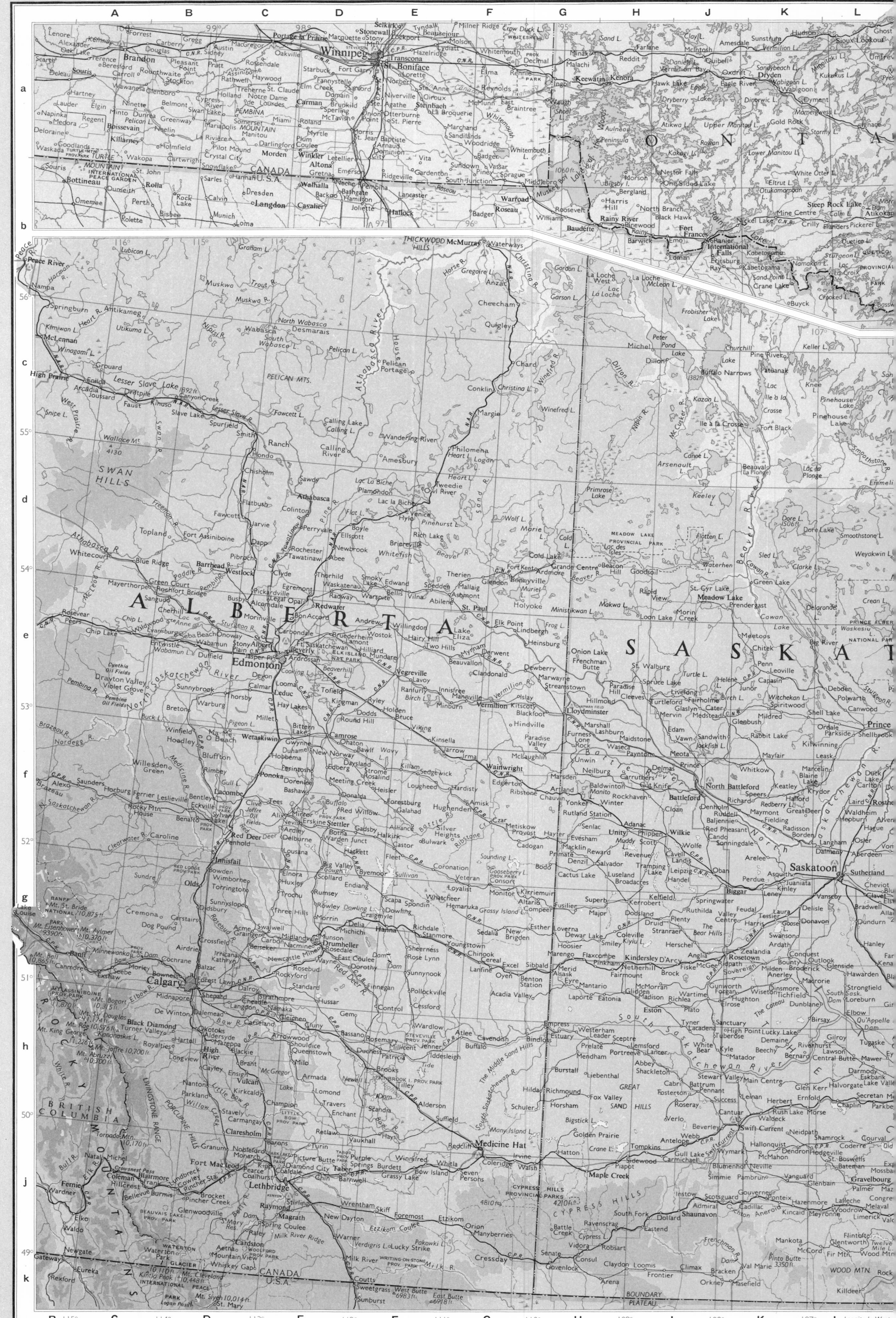

HEIGHTS IN FEET

9000

6000

3000

1500

600

SEA LEVEL

CONIC PROJECTION

SCALE: 1:3,000,000 OR 1 INCH TO 47 MILES

Arterial Roads | Tracks | Railways
Other Main Roads | Canals | Main Civil Airports

Rockies) laid down in shallow seas. Their sweeping, fertile expanses have made them the breadbasket of the country for the past half century. They have also recently become a major source of oil and gas.

SCALE IN MILES

SCALE: 1:3,000,000 OR 1 INCH TO 47 MILES

© JOHN BARTHOLOMEW & SON LTD.

INTERNATIONAL BOUNDARIES
PROVINCIAL BOUNDARIES
SWAMP AND FLOOD AREAS
SPOT HEIGHTS IN FEET ○11,870ᶠᵗ

WESTERN CANADA

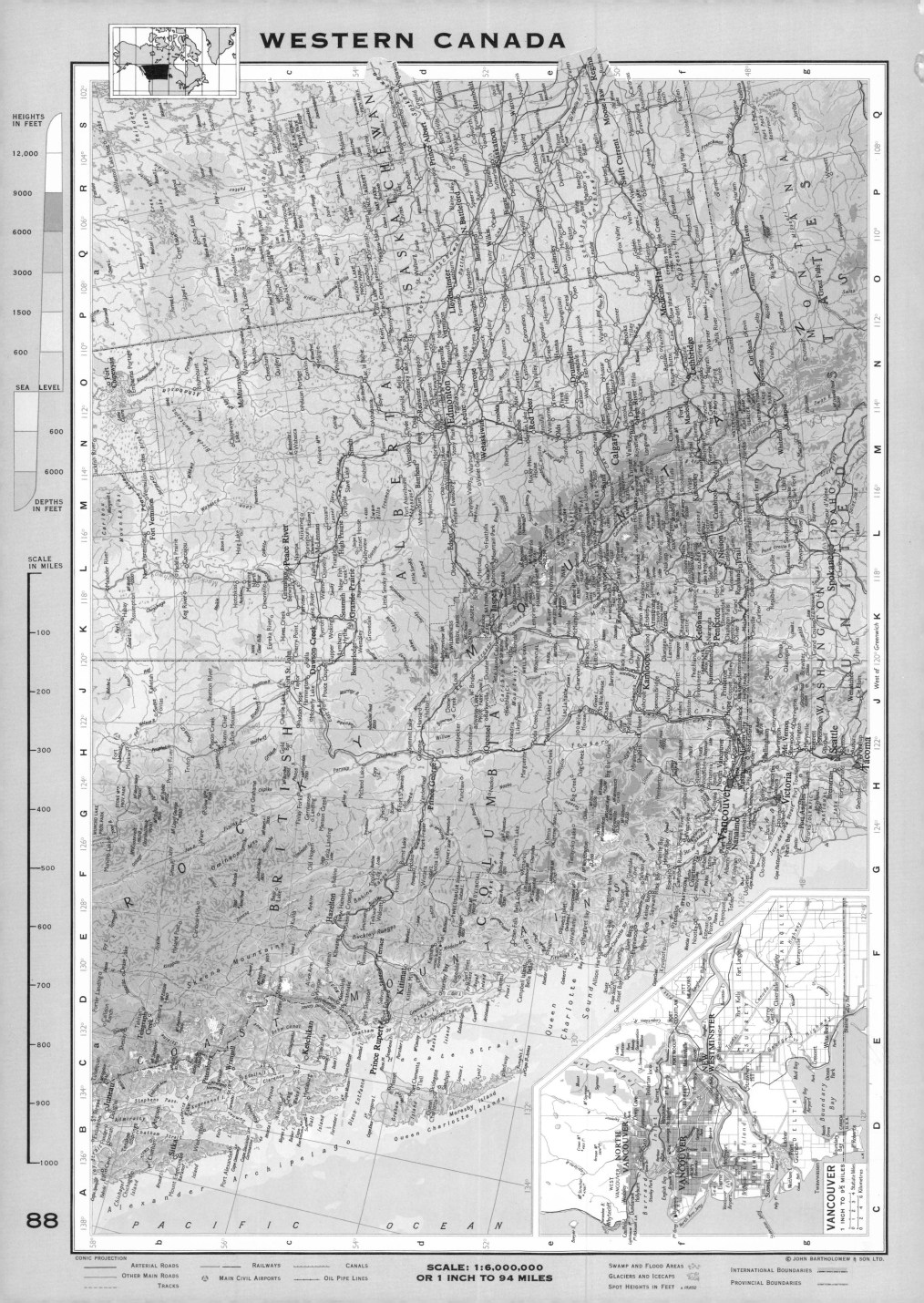

HEIGHTS IN FEET

12,000
9000
6000
3000
1500
600
SEA LEVEL
600
6000
DEPTHS IN FEET

SCALE IN MILES

100
200
300
400
500
600
700
800
900
1000

88

CONIC PROJECTION

ARTERIAL ROADS
OTHER MAIN ROADS
TRACKS
RAILWAYS
MAIN CIVIL AIRPORTS
CANALS
OIL PIPE LINES
SWAMP AND FLOOD AREAS
GLACIERS AND ICECAPS
SPOT HEIGHTS IN FEET
INTERNATIONAL BOUNDARIES
PROVINCIAL BOUNDARIES

© JOHN BARTHOLOMEW & SON LTD.

SCALE: 1:6,000,000
OR 1 INCH TO 94 MILES

VANCOUVER
1 INCH TO 9½ MILES

PACIFIC OCEAN

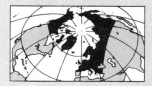

The Asian and North American continents almost meet at the narrow and shallow Bering Strait, only 45 miles across. Between them lies the Arctic Ocean, nearly enclosed and always covered with drifting ice. The high plateau of Greenland is covered with ice up to 11,000 feet thick, yet reaches down to the same latitude as Oslo and Leningrad.

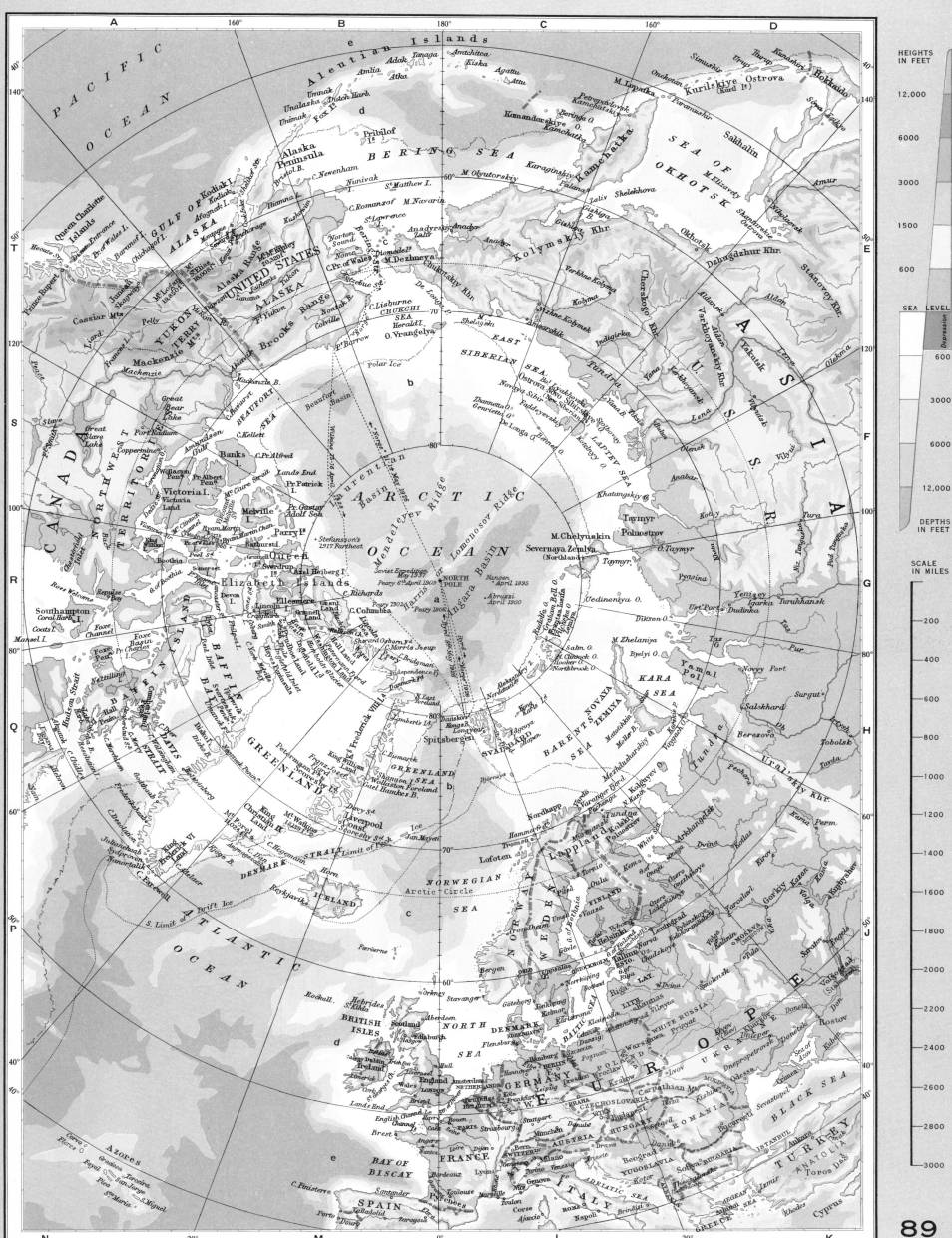

HEIGHTS IN FEET

12,000
6000
3000
1500
600

SEA LEVEL

Depression

600
3000
6000
12,000

DEPTHS IN FEET

SCALE IN MILES

200
400
600
800
1000
1200
1400
1600
1800
2000
2200
2400
2600
2800
3000

89

LAMBERT'S AZIMUTHAL EQUAL-AREA PROJECTION

INTERNATIONAL BOUNDARIES

© JOHN BARTHOLOMEW & SON LTD.

SCALE: 1:30,000,000 OR 1 INCH TO 474 MILES
(Approximately)

MEXICO

GUATEMALA, HONDURAS,
BRITISH HONDURAS, EL SALVADOR

MEXICO AREA: 760,336 sq. mi. POP: 34,923,129 CAP: *Mexico City*
GUATEMALA AREA: 42,042 sq. mi. POP: 3,868,000 CAP: *Guatemala City*
HONDURAS AREA: 43,277 sq. mi. POP: 1,883,173 CAP: *Tegucigalpa*
BRITISH HONDURAS AREA: 8867 sq. mi. POP: 90,381 CAP: *Belize*
EL SALVADOR AREA: 8260 sq. mi. POP: 2,501,278 CAP: *San Salvador*

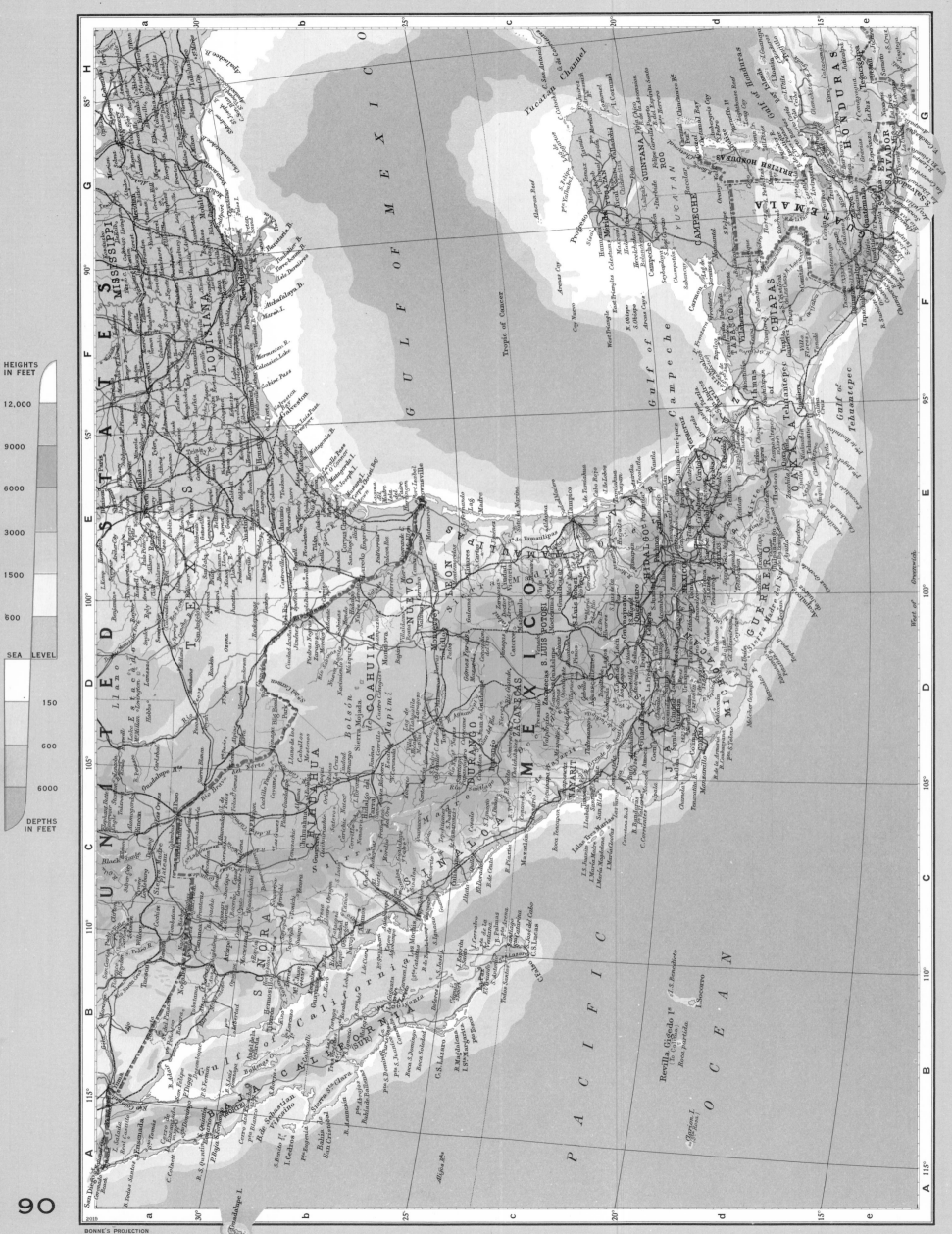

HEIGHTS IN FEET

12,000
9000
6000
3000
1500
600
SEA LEVEL
150
600
6000

DEPTHS IN FEET

90

BONNE'S PROJECTION

SCALE: 1:10,000,000 OR 1 INCH TO 158 MILES

INTERNATIONAL BOUNDARIES
STATE BOUNDARIES

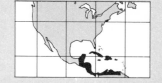

NICARAGUA AREA: *57,143 sq. mi.* POP: *1,477,000* CAP: *Managua*
COSTA RICA AREA: *19,695 sq. mi.* POP: *1,224,000* CAP: *San José*
PANAMA AREA: *28,575 sq. mi.* POP: *1,075,541* CAP: *Panama City*
CUBA AREA: *44,218 sq. mi.* POP: *6,933,000* CAP: *Havana*
JAMAICA AREA: *4411 sq. mi.* POP: *1,613,880* CAP: *Kingston*

THE CARIBBEAN
WEST INDIES, CUBA, PANAMA CANAL, NICARAGUA, COSTA RICA
(Continuation of Map on Facing Page)

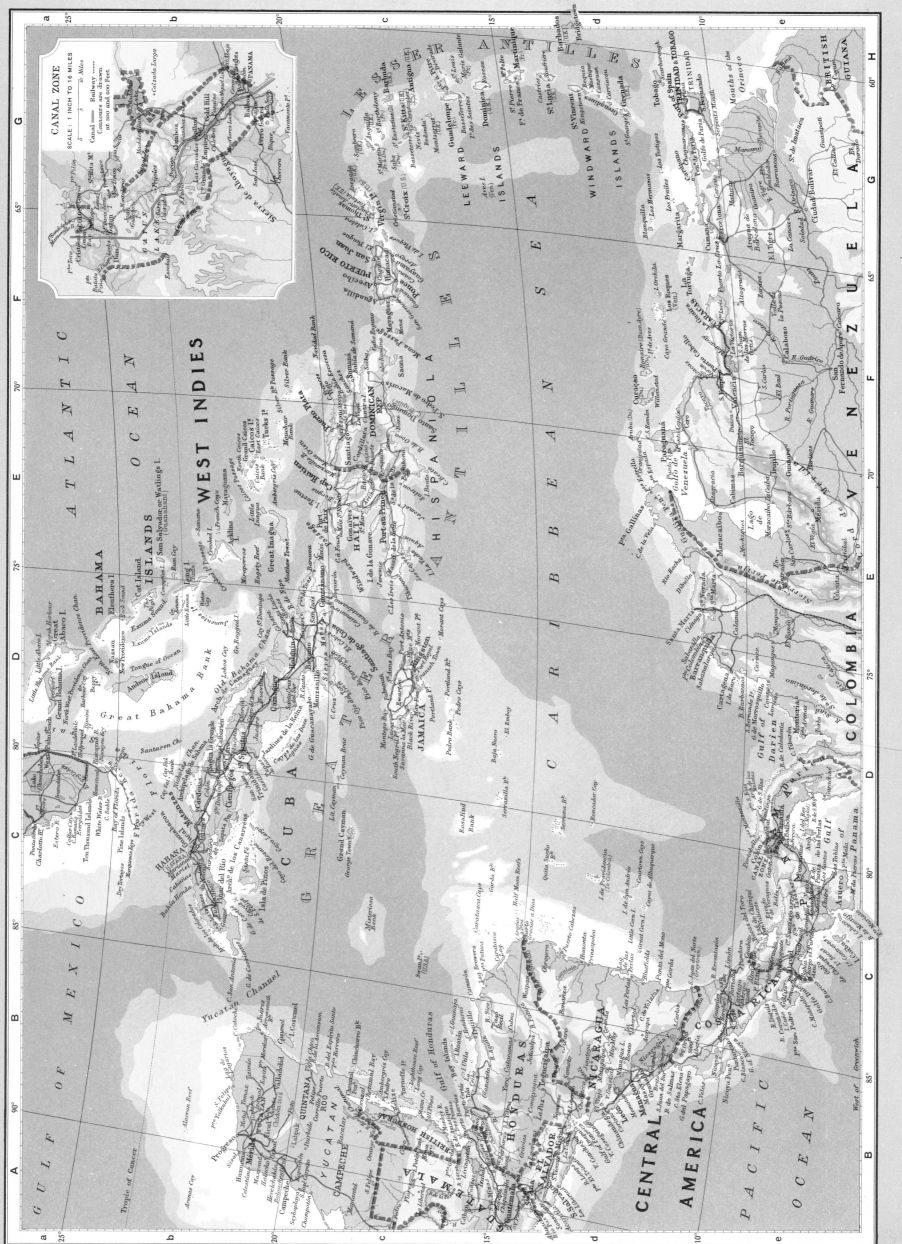

SCALE IN MILES

MAIN ROADS
RAILWAYS

© JOHN BARTHOLOMEW & SON LTD.

SCALE: 1:10,000,000 OR 1 INCH TO 158 MILES

SOUTH AMERICA (NORTH)

BRAZIL, BOLIVIA, PERU, ECUADOR, COLOMBIA, VENEZUELA, BRITISH GUIANA, SURINAM, FRENCH GUIANA

BRAZIL AREA: 3,288,000 sq. mi.
POP: 70,799,352 CAP: Brasilia
BOLIVIA AREA: 424,163 sq. mi.
POP: 3,509,000 CAP: La Paz

HEIGHTS IN FEET

16,000
12,000
10,000
6000
3000
1500
600

SEA LEVEL

150
600
6000

DEPTHS IN FEET

92

LAMBERT'S AZIMUTHAL EQUAL-AREA PROJECTION

SCALE: 1:12,500,000 OR 1 INCH TO 197 MILES
(Approximately)

MAIN ROADS
RAILWAYS

PERU AREA: *482,259 sq. mi.*
POP: *10,714,620* CAP: *Lima*
ECUADOR AREA: *105,685 sq. mi.*
POP: *4,455,000* CAP: *Quito*

COLOMBIA AREA: *439,513 sq. mi.*
POP: *14,447,000* CAP: *Bogotá*
VENEZUELA AREA: *352,143 sq. mi.*
POP: *7,523,999* CAP: *Caracas*

BRITISH GUIANA AREA: *83,000 sq. mi.*
POP: *560,620* CAP: *Georgetown*
SURINAM AREA: *54,144 sq. mi.*
POP: *308,000* CAP: *Paramaribo*

FRENCH GUIANA
AREA: *35,000 sq. mi.*
POP: *31,000* CAP: *Cayenne*

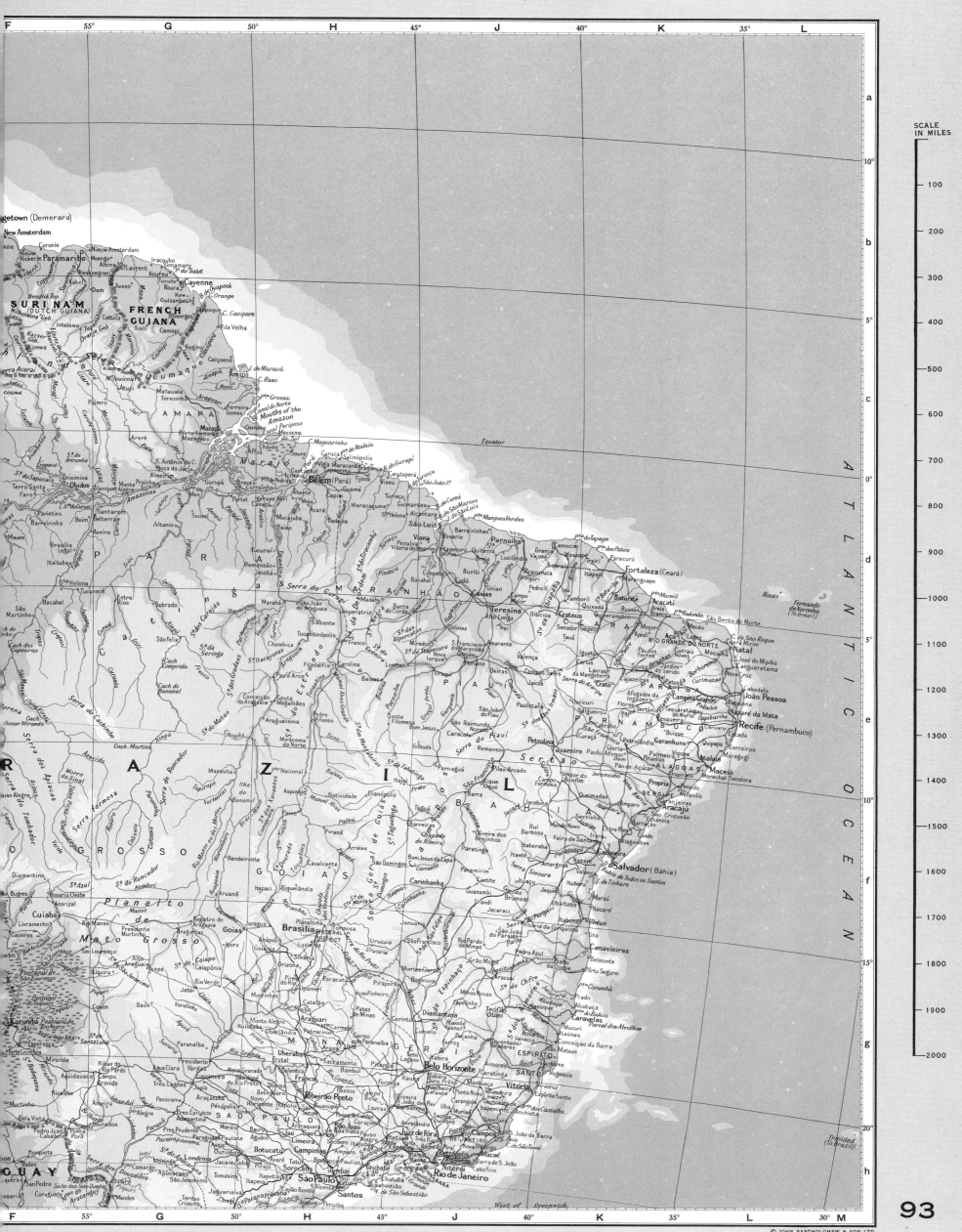

93

© JOHN BARTHOLOMEW & SON LTD.

INTERNATIONAL BOUNDARIES

STATE AND PROVINCIAL BOUNDARIES

SCALE: 1:12,500,000 OR 1 INCH TO 197 MILES
(Approximately)

SCALE IN MILES

SOUTH AMERICA (SOUTH) ARGENTINA, CHILE, PARAGUAY, URUGUAY

ARGENTINA AREA: *1,072,646 sq. mi.*   CHILE AREA: *286,397 sq. mi.*   PARAGUAY AREA: *157,047 sq. mi.*   URUGUAY AREA: *72,172 sq. mi.*

POP: *20,008,945*   POP: *7,339,546*   POP: *1,812,000*   POP: *2,827,000*

CAP: *Buenos Aires*   CAP: *Santiago*   CAP: *Asunción*   CAP: *Montevideo*

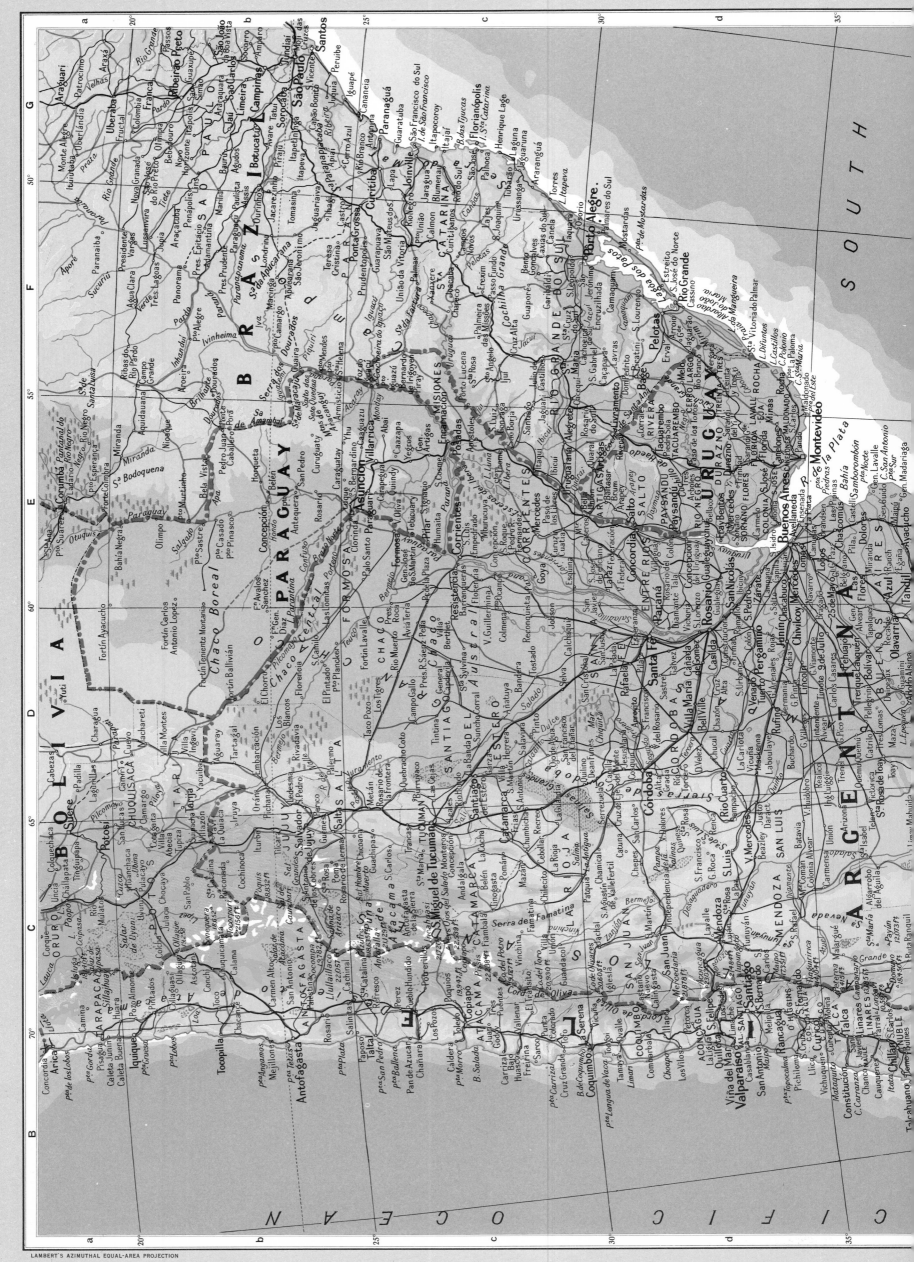

HEIGHTS IN FEET

16,000
12,000
10,000
6000
3000
1500
600

SEA LEVEL

150
600
6000

DEPTHS IN FEET

LAMBERT'S AZIMUTHAL EQUAL-AREA PROJECTION

SCALE: 1:9,000,000 OR 1 INCH TO 142 MILES

—————— MAIN ROADS

———————— RAILWAYS

South America, shown here and on the two pages preceding, is the fourth largest continent. It has the second highest mountain range in the world and the longest—the An- des, which follow the western coast for more than 4000 miles. Many of the majestic peaks rise over 20,000 feet. The Amazon River system is the world's largest. The broad Ama- zon basin, with its moist jungles, cuts between the Brazilian and Guiana highlands to meet the great central lowland, which runs south to the fertile pampas of Argentina.

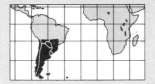

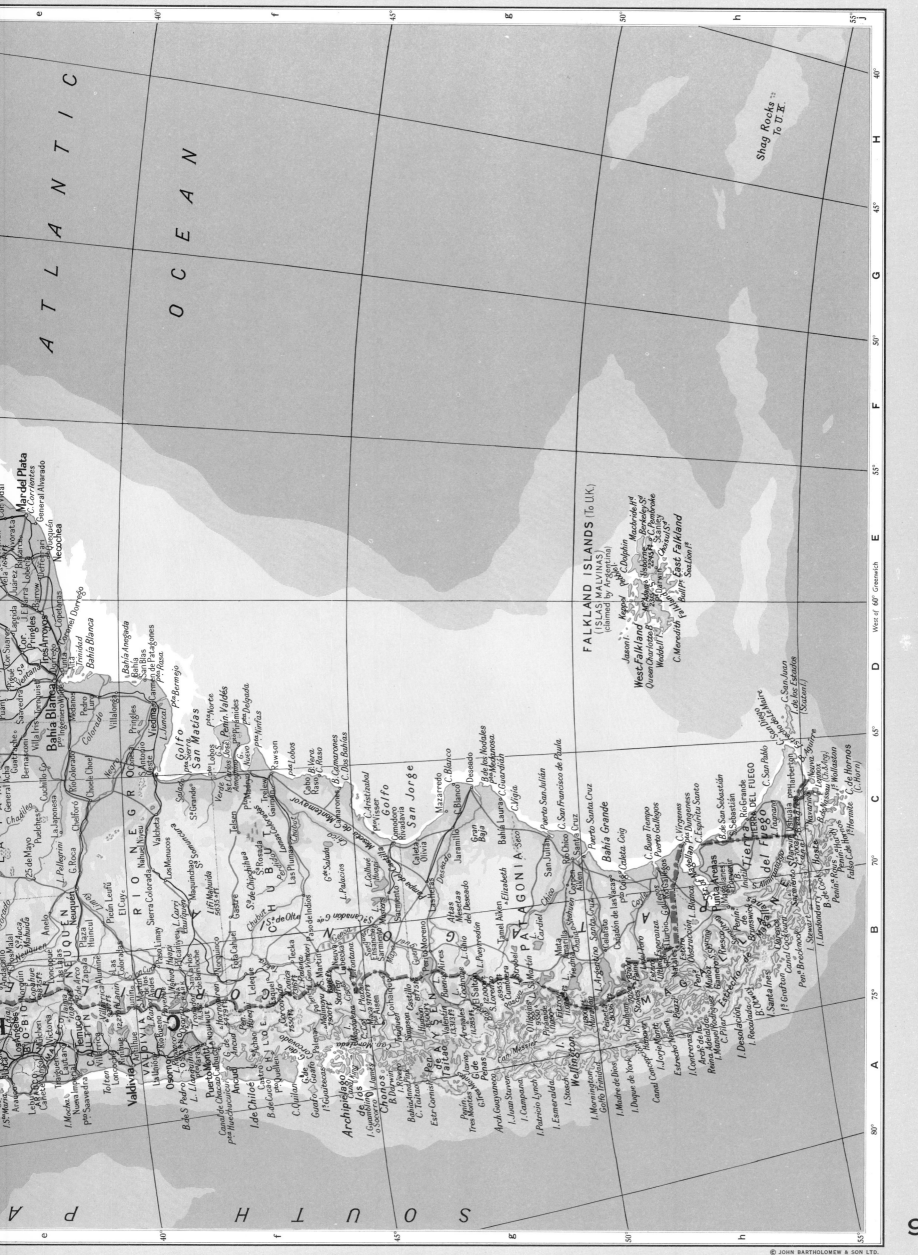

SCALE IN MILES

— 100
— 200
— 300
— 400
— 500
— 600
— 700
— 800
— 900
— 1000
— 1100
— 1200
— 1300
— 1400
— 1500

© JOHN BARTHOLOMEW & SON LTD.

INTERNATIONAL BOUNDARIES

STATE AND PROVINCIAL BOUNDARIES

SCALE: 1:9,000,000 OR 1 INCH TO 142 MILES

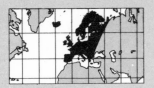

EUROPE

Itself a peninsula of Asia, Europe is made up of smaller peninsulas such as Scandinavia, Iberia, Italy and Greece. Characteristic of these countries are north-south backbones of mountains, some of them offshoots of the great chain of fold mountains extending from the Pyrenees to the Black Sea. This east-west axis separates the broad North European

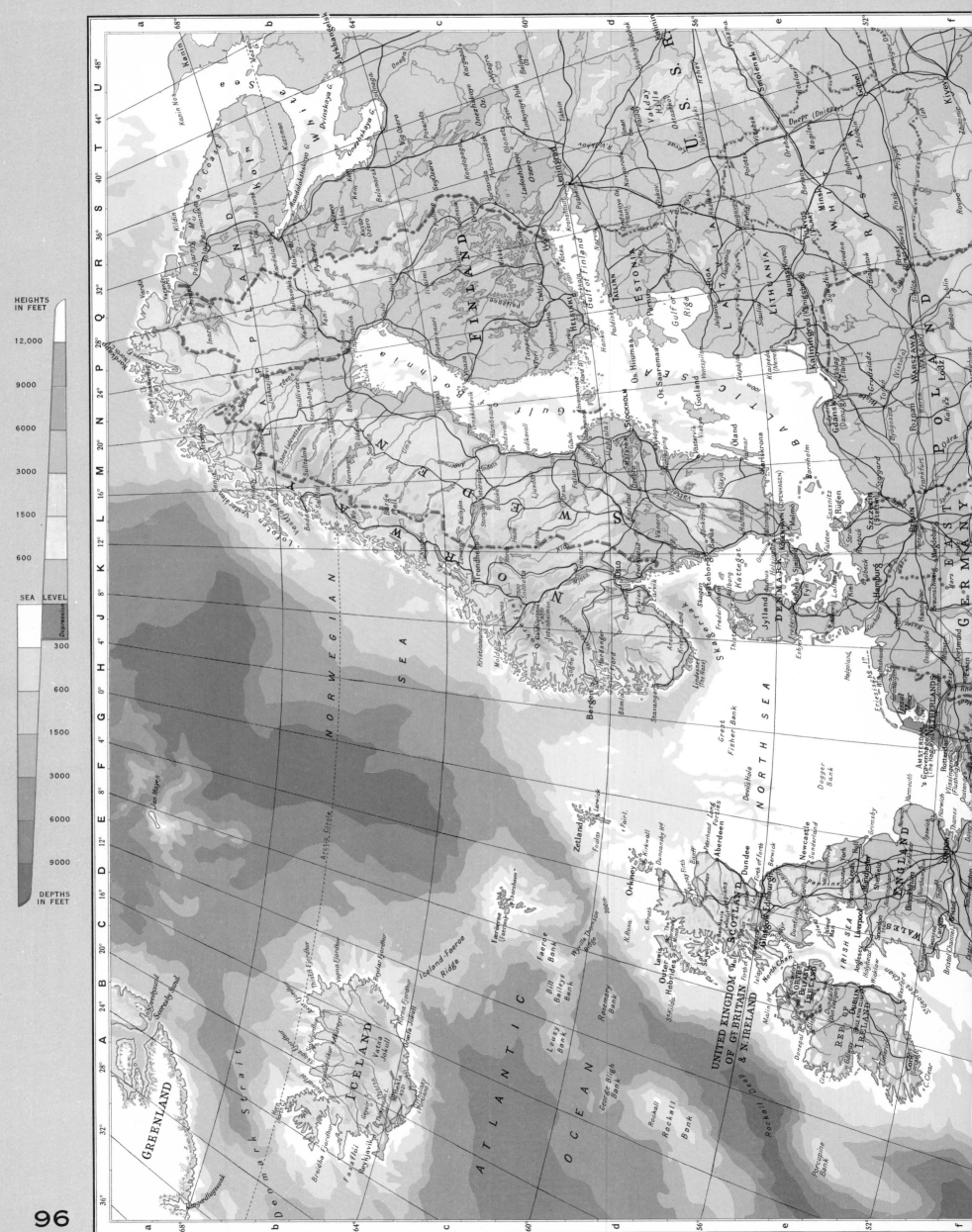

HEIGHTS IN FEET

12,000
9000
6000
3000
1500
600

SEA LEVEL

Depression

300
600
1500
3000
6000
9000

DEPTHS IN FEET

BONNE'S PROJECTION

SCALE: 1:10,000,000 OR 1 INCH TO 158 MILES

————— MAIN ROADS
————— RAILWAYS

Plain stretching from Ireland to Russia, and the two basins of the Mediterranean, each as deep as the mountains are high.

This relatively small continent contains many striking geographical contrasts—paralleled by the diversity of its peoples and cultures, which once included the great ancient Greek and Roman civilizations. The maritime outlook prevalent in the western areas of Europe led to the great explorations that took these people and their cultures to the farthest corners of the Earth.

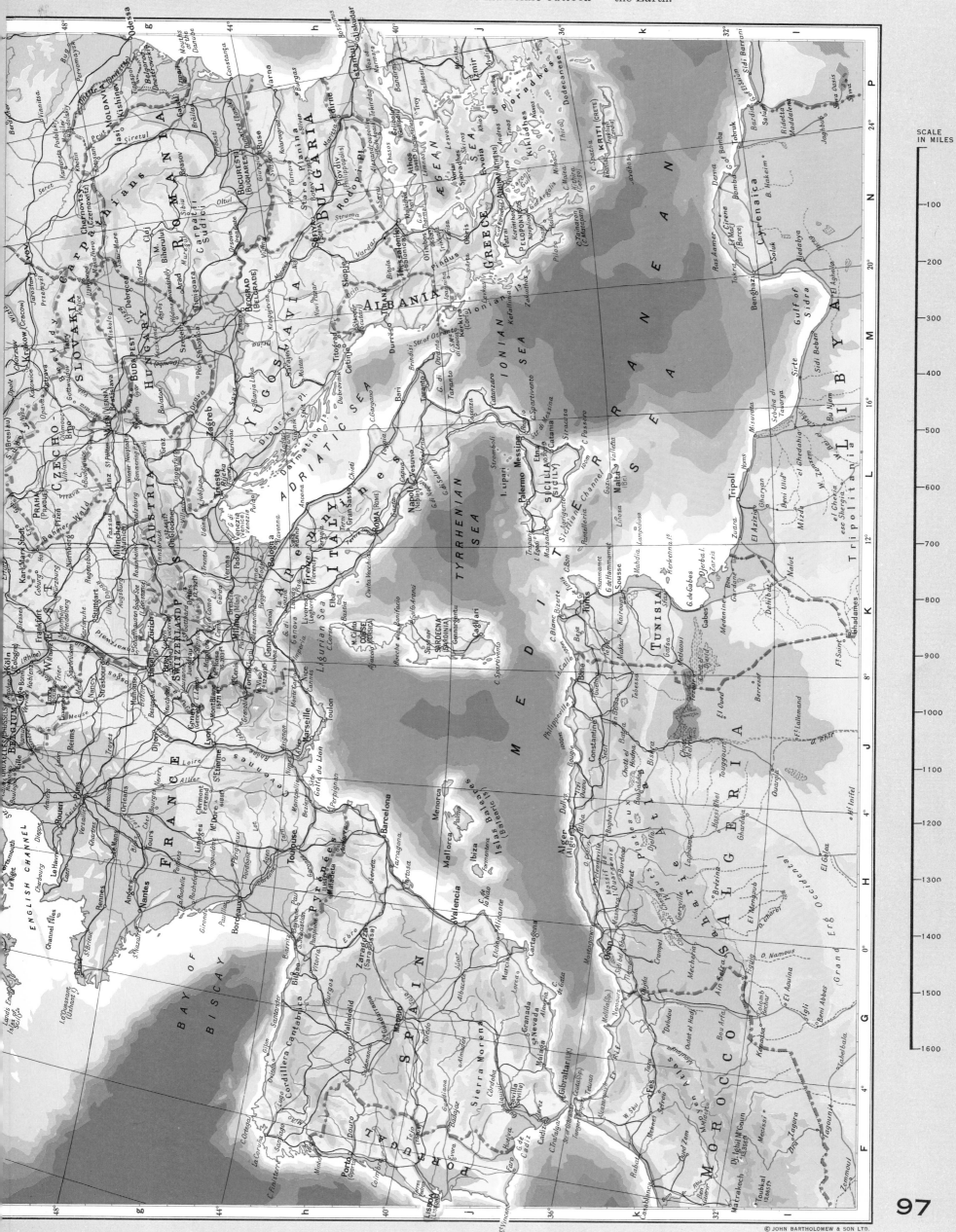

SCALE
IN MILES

— 100
— 200
— 300
— 400
— 500
— 600
— 700
— 800
— 900
— 1000
— 1100
— 1200
— 1300
— 1400
— 1500
— 1600

© JOHN BARTHOLOMEW & SON LTD.

97

INTERNATIONAL BOUNDARIES
STATE BOUNDARIES
BOUNDARY NOT PERMANENTLY ESTABLISHED

SCALE: 1:10,000,000 OR 1 INCH TO 158 MILES

THE BRITISH ISLES

UNITED KINGDOM (England, Scotland, Wales, N. Ireland)
AREA: *94,207 sq. mi.* POP: *52,675,556* CAP: *London*
REPUBLIC OF IRELAND
AREA: *26,600 sq. mi.* POP: *2,814,703* CAP: *Dublin*

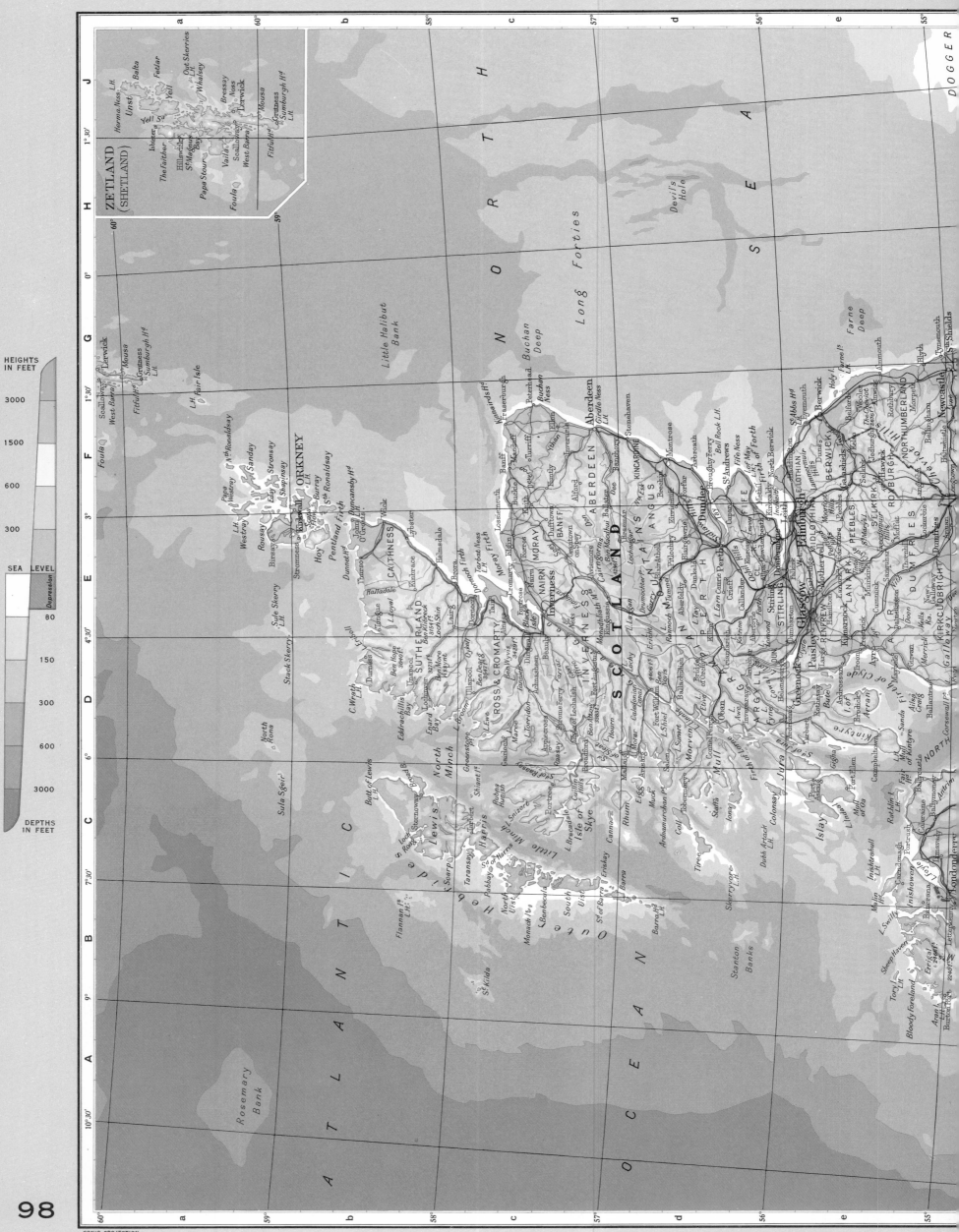

HEIGHTS IN FEET

3000
1500
600
300

SEA LEVEL

Depression
80
150
300
600
3000

DEPTHS IN FEET

ZETLAND (SHETLAND)

98

CONIC PROJECTION

SCALE: 1:2,500,000 OR 1 INCH TO 39 MILES

MAIN ROADS
RAILWAYS

The British Isles, in their relatively small area, show great structural variety. Scotland's Ben Nevis (4406 feet) is their highest point. A line drawn northeastward from Exmouth in Devon to the south Durham coast roughly separates Great Britain's ancient uplands from the gentler hills of southeast England. Signs of a onetime connection with the Continent are also evident in the south. Ireland is edged almost entirely by uplands, which often rise sheer from the sea. Inside is an extensive lowland area covered with lakes, moors, low-lying boglands and groups of hills.

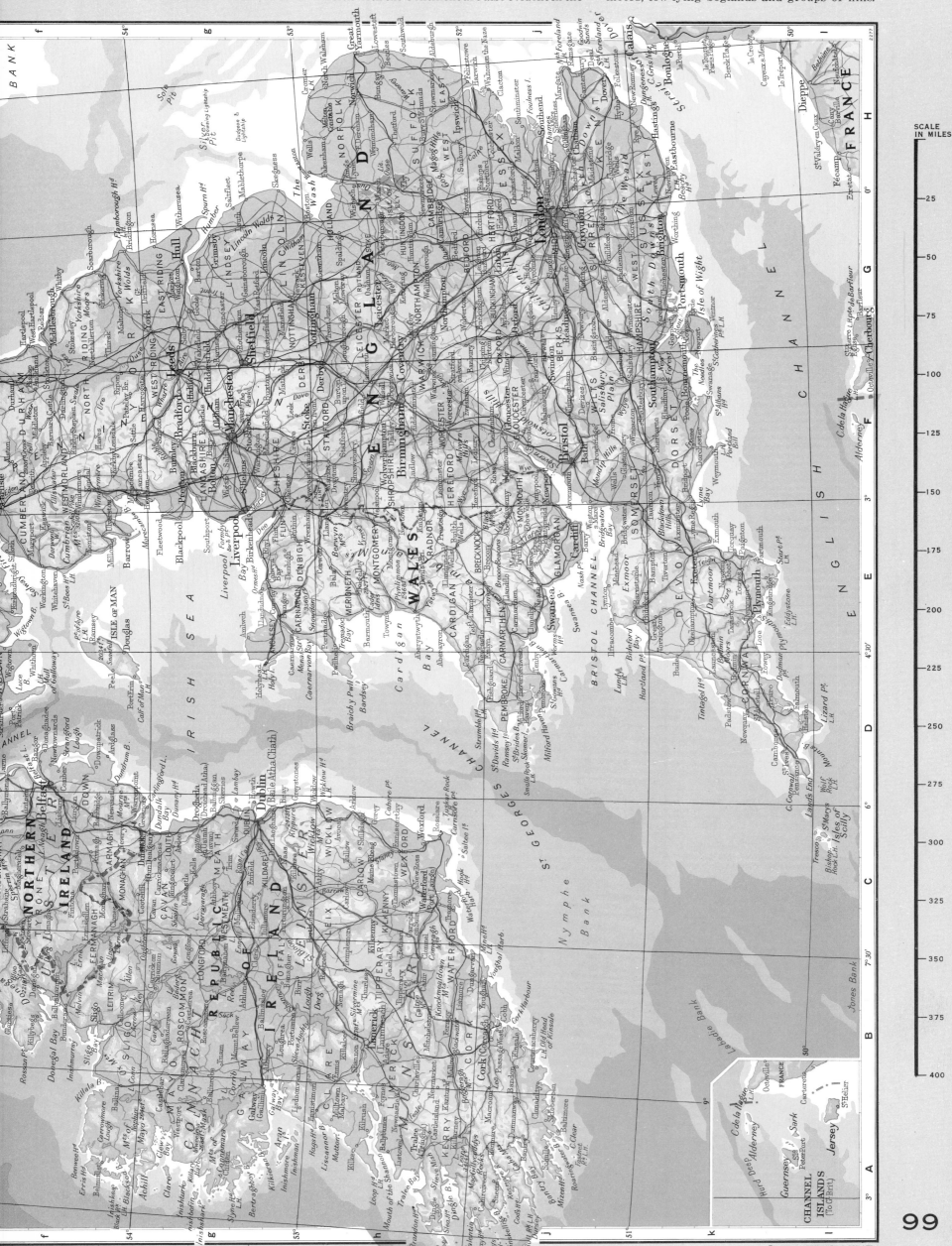

SCALE
IN MILES

STATE BOUNDARY

SCALE: 1:2,500,000 OR 1 INCH TO 39 MILES

© JOHN BARTHOLOMEW & SON LTD.

99

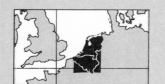

THE LOW COUNTRIES
BELGIUM, NETHERLANDS, LUXEMBOURG

BELGIUM AREA: *11,779 sq. mi.*
POP: *9,153,000*
CAP: *Brussels*

NETHERLANDS AREA: *12,746 sq. mi.*
POP: *11,637,000*
CAP: *Amsterdam* GOVT: *The Hague*

LUXEMBOURG AREA: *998 sq. mi.*
POP: *314,889*
CAP: *Luxembourg*

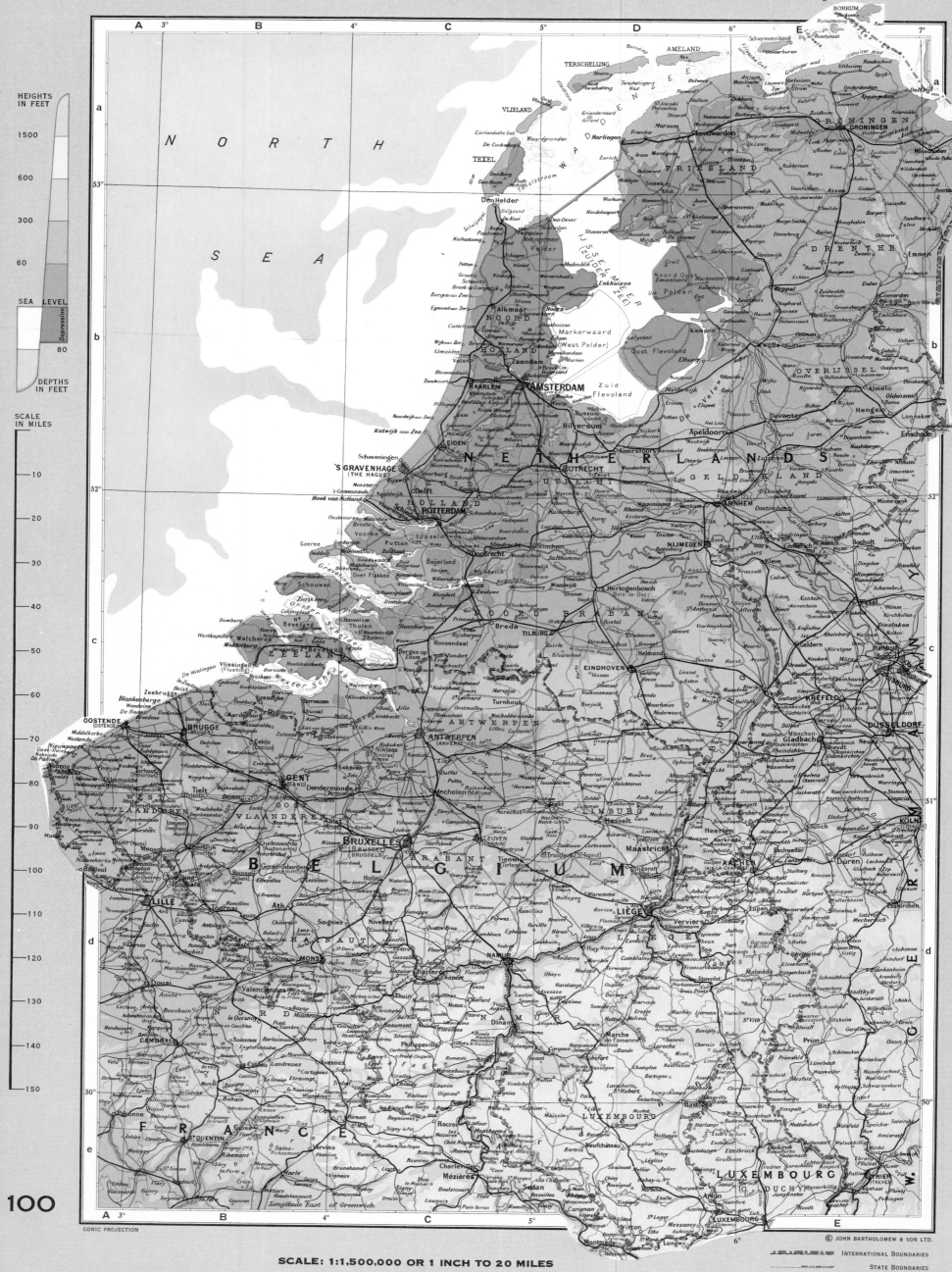

HEIGHTS
IN FEET

1500
600
300
60

SEA LEVEL
Depression

80

DEPTHS
IN FEET

SCALE
IN MILES

10
20
30
40
50
60
70
80
90
100
110
120
130
140
150

100

CONIC PROJECTION

© JOHN BARTHOLOMEW & SON LTD.

INTERNATIONAL BOUNDARIES

STATE BOUNDARIES

SCALE: 1:1,500,000 OR 1 INCH TO 20 MILES

SWITZERLAND

AREA: *15,941 sq. mi.* **POP**: *5,429,061* **CAP**: *Berne*

The Swiss Alps, rising to 15,203 feet (Monte Rosa), cover more than half of Switzerland, making it the most mountainous country in Europe. The country is divided into three belts, running northeast to southwest, by the broad valley of the Aar and the narrower one of the Upper Rhine and Upper Rhône.

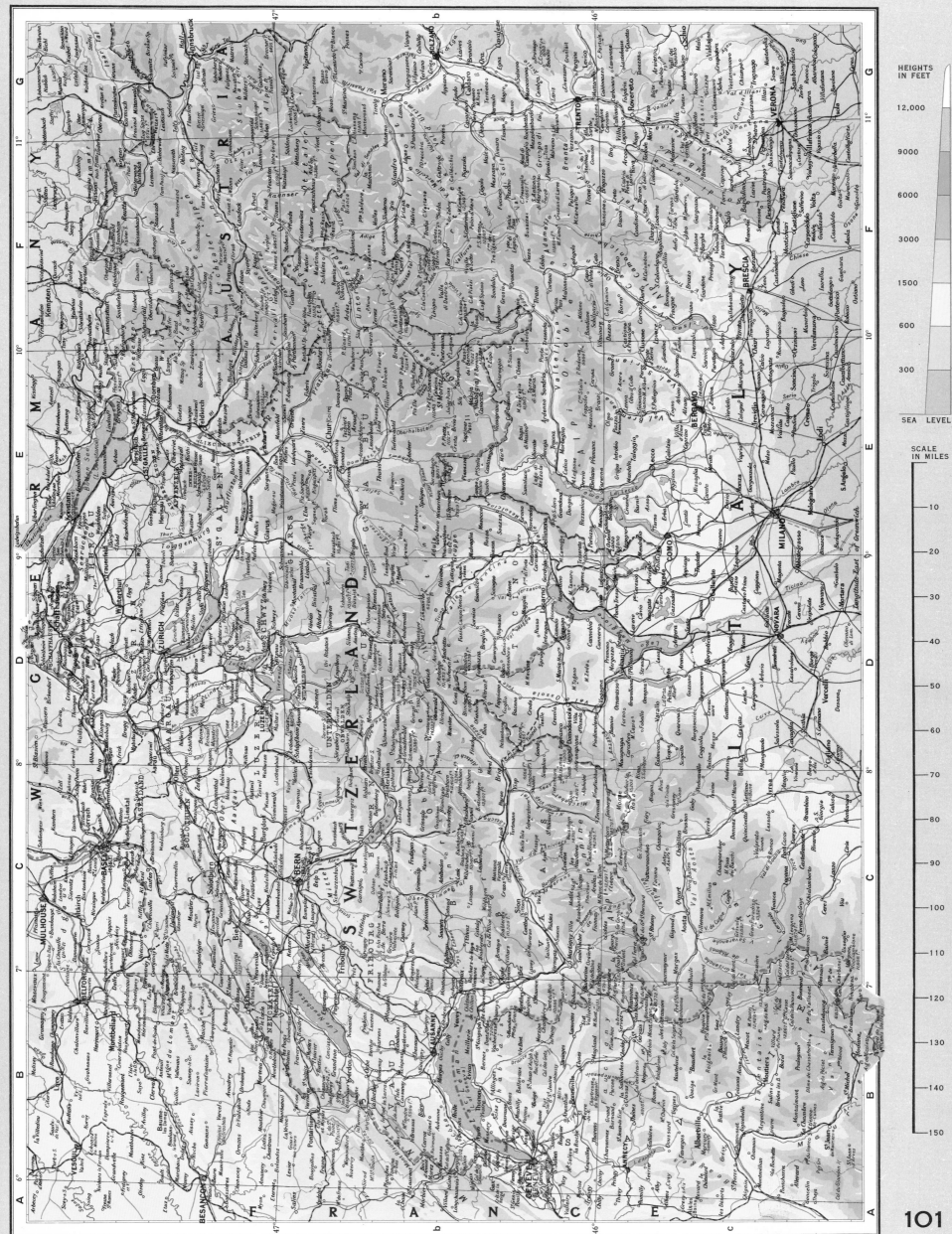

HEIGHTS
IN FEET

12,000

9000

6000

3000

1500

600

300

SEA LEVEL

SCALE
IN MILES

10

20

30

40

50

60

70

80

90

100

110

120

130

140

150

CONIC PROJECTION

MAIN ROADS ————

RAILWAYS ————

© JOHN BARTHOLOMEW & SON LTD.

SCALE: 1:1,500,000 OR 1 INCH TO 20 MILES

SCANDINAVIA AND FINLAND

NORWAY, SWEDEN, DENMARK, ICELAND, FINLAND

NORWAY AREA: *125,065 sq. mi.* POP: *3,611,000* CAP: *Oslo*
SWEDEN AREA: *173,624 sq. mi.* POP: *7,495,129* CAP: *Stockholm*
From the backbone of mountains shared by Norway and Sweden come rivers that feed the many lakes on both sides. Norway continues as a high, rugged plateau, falling abruptly to a coastline broken by fjords

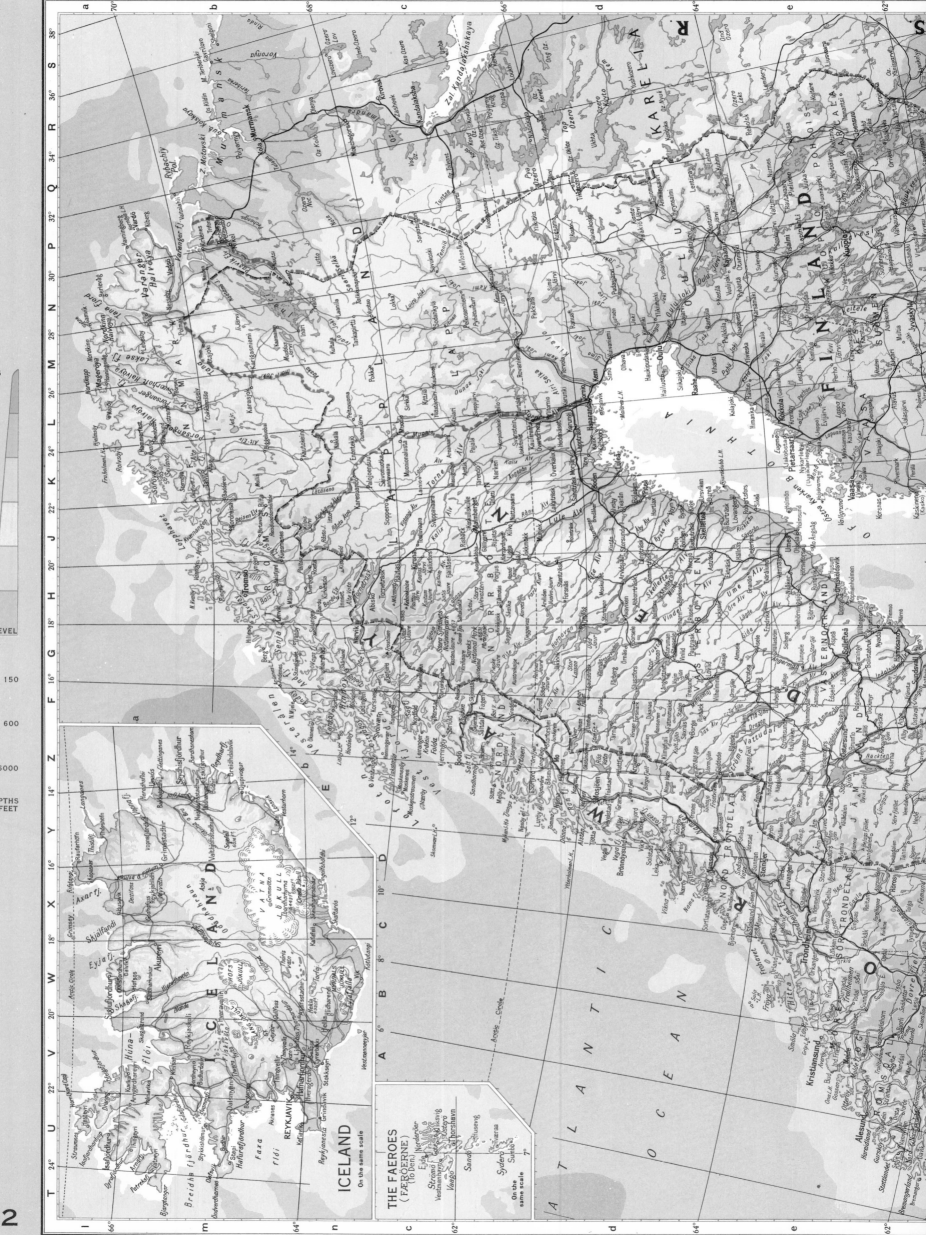

HEIGHTS
IN FEET

6000

3000

1500

600

300

SEA LEVEL

150

600

6000

DEPTHS
IN FEET

ICELAND
On the same scale

THE FAEROES
(FÆRÖERNE)
(To Den.)
On the
same scale

102

CONIC PROJECTION

SCALE: 1:4.500.000 OR 1 INCH TO 71 MILES

MAIN ROADS
RAILWAYS

and islands. Sweden, low-lying in the south, is better suited to cultivation and settlement.

DENMARK AREA: *16,619 sq. mi.*
POP: *4,581,000* CAP: *Copenhagen*

Smallest and lowest-lying of the Scandinavian countries, Denmark rarely rises more than 500 feet above sea level. Besides the peninsula of Jutland, it comprises the four main islands of

Zealand, Fünen, Lolland and Falster.
ICELAND AREA: *39,768 sq. mi.*
POP: *176,000* CAP: *Reykjavik*
FINLAND AREA: *130,119 sq. mi.*
POP: *4,449,000* CAP: *Helsinki*

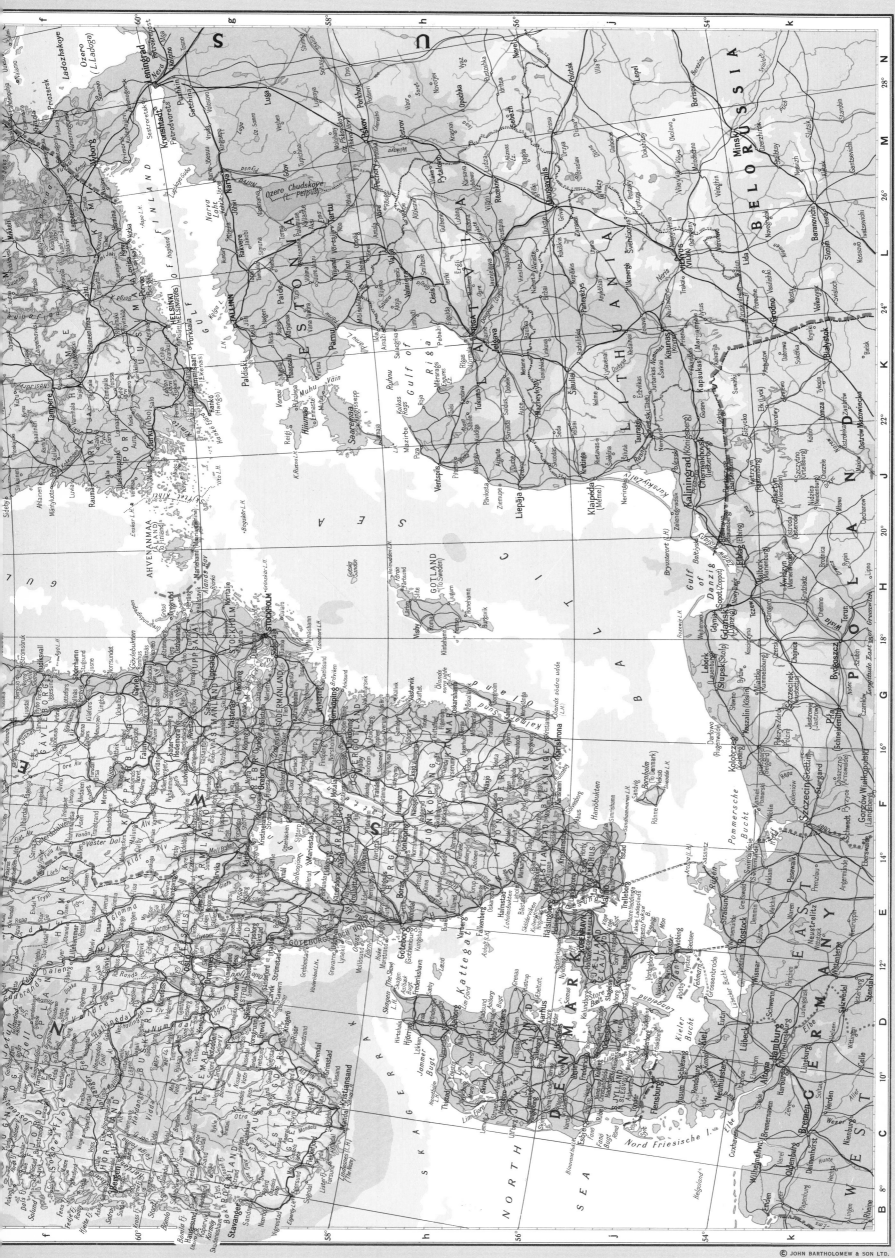

SCALE IN MILES

© JOHN BARTHOLOMEW & SON LTD.

INTERNATIONAL BOUNDARIES
STATE BOUNDARIES
BOUNDARY NOT PERMANENTLY ESTABLISHED

SCALE: 1:4,500,000 OR 1 INCH TO 71 MILES

103

CENTRAL EUROPE
GERMANY, POLAND, CZECHOSLOVAKIA, AUSTRIA, HUNGARY

GERMANY (Fed. Republic) AREA: 95,913 sq. mi.
POP: 54,214,000 CAP: *Bonn*
EAST GERMANY AREA: 41,634 sq. mi. POP: 16,164,000
CAP: *East Berlin*

HEIGHTS
IN FEET

12,000
9000
6000
3000
1500
600
300

SEA LEVEL
Depression
100

DEPTHS
IN FEET

104

CONIC PROJECTION

SCALE: 1:3,000,000 OR 1 INCH TO 47 MILES

———— MAIN ROADS
...... RAILWAYS

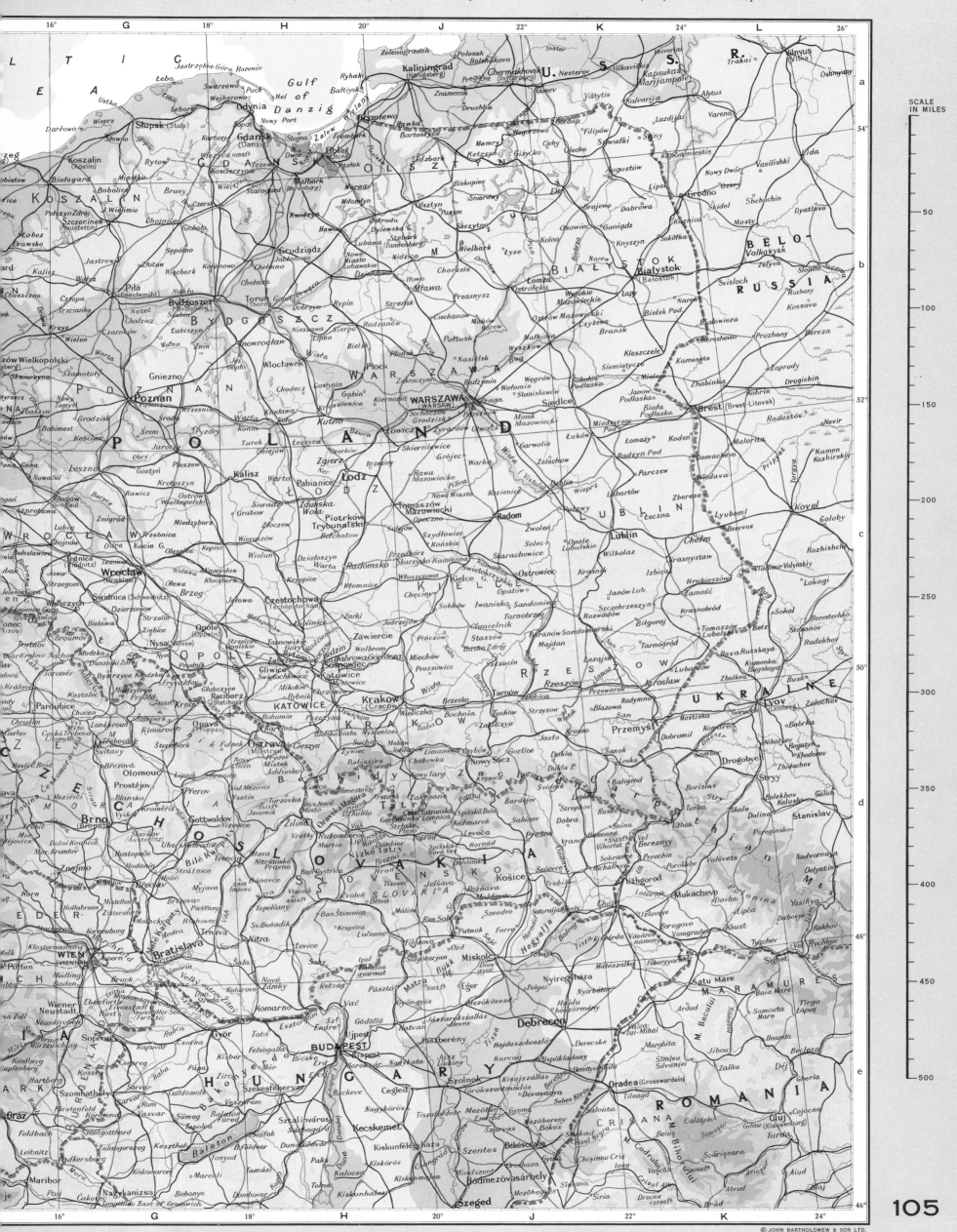

In the south of Germany the Bavarian Alps form
a boundary with Austria. Lower mountains in
the center give way to the North German Plain,
now divided between East and West Germany.

POLAND AREA: 120,359 sq. mi.
POP: 29,731,009 CAP: Warsaw
CZECHOSLOVAKIA AREA: 49,354 sq. mi.
POP: 13,741,529 CAP: Prague

AUSTRIA AREA: 32,374 sq. mi.
POP: 7,067,432 CAP: Vienna
HUNGARY AREA: 35,919 sq. mi.
POP: 9,976,530 CAP: Budapest

SCALE
IN MILES

105

© JOHN BARTHOLOMEW & SON LTD.

INTERNATIONAL BOUNDARIES
STATE BOUNDARIES
BOUNDARY NOT PERMANENTLY ESTABLISHED

SCALE: 1:3,000,000 OR 1 INCH TO 47 MILES

SPAIN and PORTUGAL

SPAIN AREA: 194,419 sq. mi. POP: 30,430,698 CAP: Madrid
PORTUGAL AREA: 35,453 sq. mi. POP: 8,920,787
CAP: Lisbon
Roughly pentagonal in shape, the Iberian peninsula is di-

HEIGHTS
IN FEET

9000
6000
3000
1500
600
300
SEA LEVEL
Depression
150
600
6000
DEPTHS
IN FEET

106

CONIC PROJECTION

SCALE: 1:3,000,000 OR 1 INCH TO 47 MILES

MAIN ROADS
RAILWAYS

vided between Spain, Portugal and the small state of Andorra. Seven eighths of it is bordered by sea, the remainder by the high wall of the Pyrenees, which separates it from France and the land mass of Europe. Southward, only eight and a half miles away at its nearest point, lies the continent of Africa. More than half the peninsula is covered by the Meseta, a high central plateau which is surrounded and traversed by mountain ranges. The rivers, notably the Tagus, flow mainly westward. The four main islands of the Balearic group form a province of Spain.

© JOHN BARTHOLOMEW & SON LTD.

INTERNATIONAL BOUNDARIES
STATE BOUNDARIES

SCALE: 1:3,000,000 OR 1 INCH TO 47 MILES

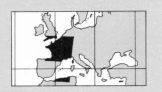

FRANCE and
NORTHERN ALGERIA

FRANCE AREA: 212,974 sq. mi.
POP: 45,960,000 CAP: Paris
France is bordered by three seas, into
which flow the four great French

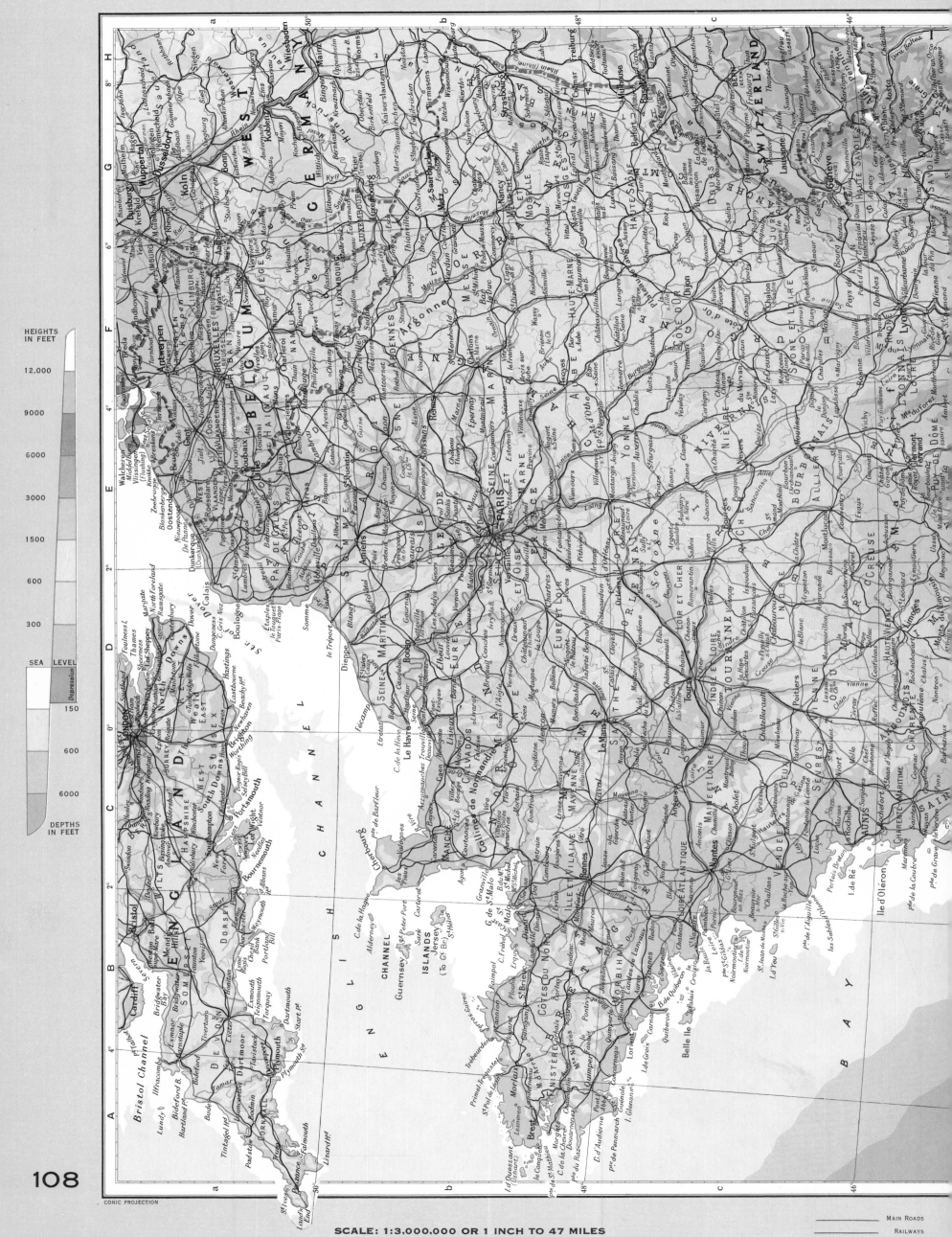

HEIGHTS
IN FEET

12,000

9000

6000

3000

1500

600

300

SEA LEVEL

150

600

6000

DEPTHS
IN FEET

CONIC PROJECTION

SCALE: 1:3,000,000 OR 1 INCH TO 47 MILES

MAIN ROADS

RAILWAYS

rivers: the Seine into the English Channel, the Loire and Garonne into the Atlantic, and the Rhône into the Mediterranean. This maritime outlook provides a mild, even climate. Northwestern France is mainly low-lying. On the eastern border rise the high mountains of the Vosges, the Jura and the Alps (Mont Blanc, 15,771 feet, is the highest peak in Europe). Running southward from the center is the Massif Central, while the Pyrenees in the southwest form a natural barrier between France and Spain. ALGERIA: see page 118.

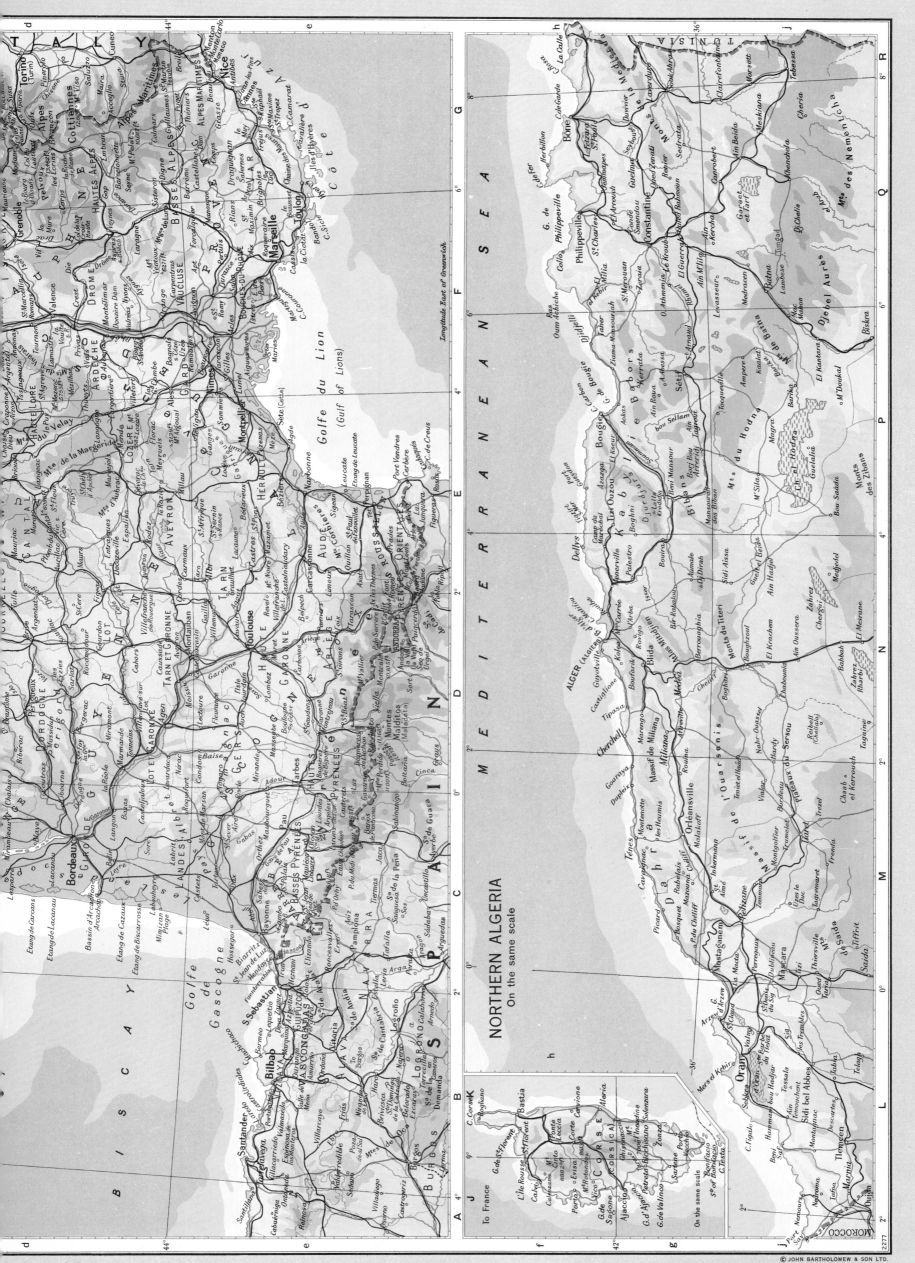

NORTHERN ALGERIA
On the same scale

SCALE IN MILES

© JOHN BARTHOLOMEW & SON LTD.

INTERNATIONAL BOUNDARIES
DEPARTMENT BOUNDARIES

SCALE: 1:3,000,000 OR 1 INCH TO 47 MILES

ITALY

AREA : 116,286 sq. mi.
POP : 50,463,762 CAP : Rome

Italy owes its bootlike shape to the Apennines, which reach down its whole length and culminate, across the Straits of Messina, in the island of Sicily. To the north, the Italian Alps encircle the peninsula like the head of a mushroom, while east of the Alps are the strange-shaped Dolomites. This mountain barrier makes the country difficult to approach, and

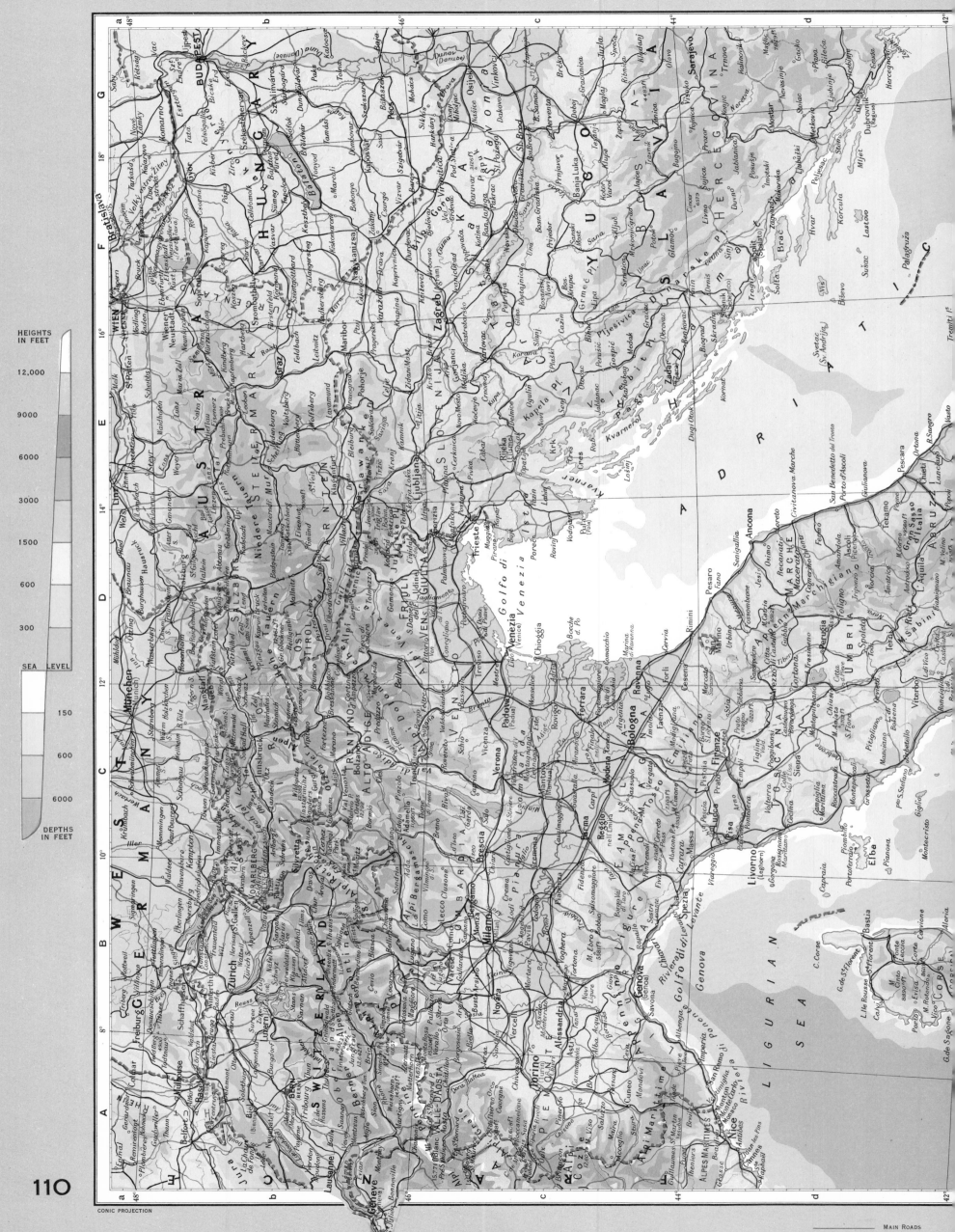

HEIGHTS
IN FEET

12,000
9000
6000
3000
1500
600
300
SEA LEVEL
150
600
6000
DEPTHS
IN FEET

SCALE: 1:3,000,000 OR 1 INCH TO 47 MILES

MAIN ROADS
RAILWAYS

CONIC PROJECTION

110

the names of the principal passes—the Simplon and St. Gotthard from Switzerland, and the Brenner from Austria—have become household words among travelers all over Europe.

Italy contains the only active volcanoes in Europe, notably Etna (the highest, 10,705 feet) in Sicily, and Vesuvius near Naples. Of the rivers, most of which are unnavigable, the long-

est is the Po (420 miles), which waters the fertile plain of Lombardy before entering the Adriatic between Venice and Ravenna. Other important rivers are the Tiber and the Arno.

SCALE IN MILES

© JOHN BARTHOLOMEW & SON LTD.

INTERNATIONAL BOUNDARIES
REGIONAL BOUNDARIES

SCALE: 1:3,000,000 OR 1 INCH TO 47 MILES

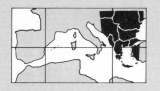

THE BALKANS
ROMANIA, YUGOSLAVIA, BULGARIA, ALBANIA, GREECE

ROMANIA AREA: 91,699 sq. mi.
POP: 10,028,000 CAP: *Bucharest*
YUGOSLAVIA AREA: 98,766 sq. mi.
POP: 18,538,150 CAP: *Belgrade*

HEIGHTS
IN FEET

6000
3000
1500
600
300

SEA LEVEL

150
600
6000

112

CONIC PROJECTION

SCALE: 1:3,000,000 OR 1 INCH TO 47 MILES

MAIN ROADS
RAILWAYS

BULGARIA AREA: *42,796 sq. mi.*
POP: *7,867,000* CAP: *Sofia*
ALBANIA AREA: *10,629 sq. mi.*
POP: *1,625,378* CAP: *Tirana*

GREECE AREA: *51,182 sq. mi.*
POP: *8,387,201* CAP: *Athens*
The Balkan peninsula, with its
broken coastline and many off-

shore islands, is separated from
the rest of Europe by the river
Danube (1770 miles long and
western Europe's longest river),

which flows eastward from Hungary, through a gorge between
the Carpathians and Dinaric Alps,
to the Black Sea.

© JOHN BARTHOLOMEW & SON LTD.

INTERNATIONAL BOUNDARIES

PROVINCIAL BOUNDARIES

SCALE: 1:3,000,000 OR 1 INCH TO 47 MILES

SCALE
IN MILES

U.S.S.R.

AREA : 8,603,852 sq. mi. POP : 208,826,650
CAP : *Moscow*
The vast area of the U.S.S.R., straddling all
Asia and half of Europe, shares its im-

mense boundaries with many countries in
both continents. It is divided structurally
into three regions from west to east: two
enormous plains, separated by the Urals (a

CONIC PROJECTION

SCALE: 1:17,500,000 OR 1 INCH TO 276 MILES
(Approximately)

———— MAIN ROADS
———— RAILWAYS

useful dividing line between Asia and Europe) and a vast region of hazardous country ending in the remote peninsula of Kamchatka. On the north-south axis there are also three zones. The frozen tundra of the Arctic merges into forests and fertile plains, which end at the borders of the great desert belt stretching from Mongolia to the Caspian. In fact, the U.S.S.R. is hemmed in on three fronts by hot or cold deserts or mountains, so that access is easy only in the west, through Europe.

SCALE IN MILES

100
200
300
400
500
600
700
800
900
1000
1100
1200
1300
1400
1500
1600
1700
1800
1900
2000
2100
2200
2300
2400
2500
2600
2700
2800
2900
3000

INTERNATIONAL BOUNDARIES
STATE BOUNDARIES

SCALE: 1:17,500,000 OR 1 INCH TO 276 MILES
(Approximately)

© JOHN BARTHOLOMEW & SON LTD.

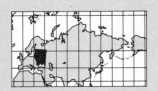

WEST EUROPEAN RUSSIA

The area between the Baltic and the Black Sea is part of the enormous Russian Plain west of the Urals. The low level of this land is indicated by the meandering rivers and the lakes and marshes of the Pripyat region. To the south, the mild undulations of the Ukrainian steppe interrupt the monotony of the northern plain.

HEIGHTS
IN FEET

6000

3000

1500

600

300

SEA LEVEL

Depression

160

600

DEPTHS
IN FEET

116

CONIC PROJECTION

SCALE: 1:6,000,000 OR 1 INCH TO 94 MILES

© John Bartholomew & Son Ltd.

INTERNATIONAL BOUNDARIES

STATE BOUNDARIES

This map shows the highest and the lowest parts of European Russia, from the Urals, up to 5500 feet high, to the northern end of the Caspian, 50 feet below sea level. The two main rivers are the Don and the 2293-mile Volga, which flows through several immense artificial lakes, recently created. A huge, low-lying plain circles the northern end of the Caspian.

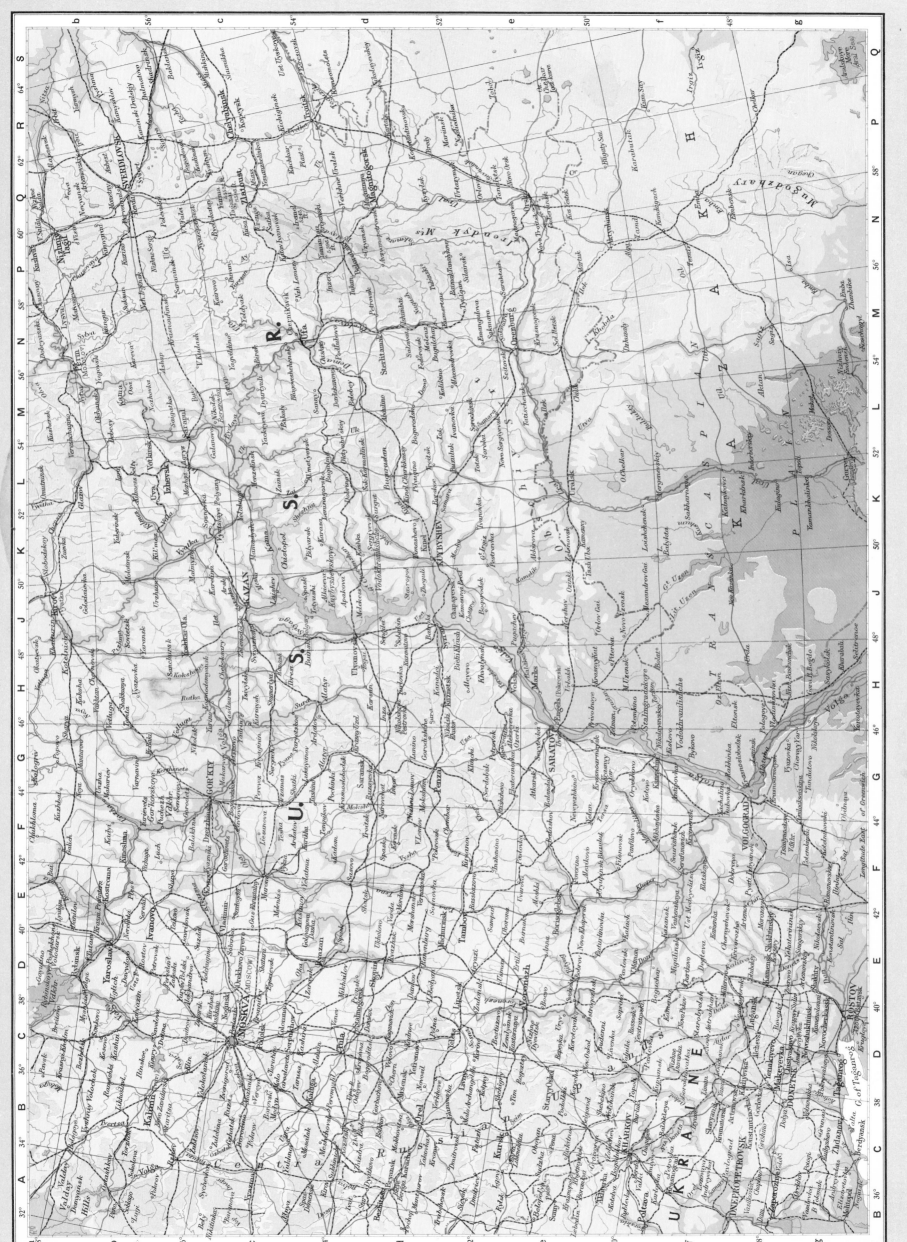

SCALE IN MILES

© JOHN BARTHOLOMEW & SON LTD.

MAIN ROADS ————

RAILWAYS ----------

CONIC PROJECTION

SCALE: 1:6,000,000 OR 1 INCH TO 94 MILES

NORTHERN AFRICA

MOROCCO AREA: *c. 160,000 sq. mi.* POP: *11,626,000* CAP: *Rabat*
ALGERIA AREA: *846,124 sq. mi.* POP: *11,020,000* CAP: *Algiers*
TUNISIA AREA: *c. 48,300 sq. mi.* POP: *4,168,000* CAP: *Tunis*
LIBYA AREA: *c. 680,000 sq. mi.* POP: *1,216,000* CAPS: *Benghazi, Tripoli*
UNITED ARAB REPUBLIC (EGYPT)
  AREA: *386,198 sq. mi.* POP: *25,929,000* CAP: *Cairo*

HEIGHTS IN FEET

12,000
9000
6000
3000
1500
600
SEA LEVEL

DEPTHS IN FEET

Depression
150
600
6000

118

LAMBERT'S AZIMUTHAL EQUAL-AREA PROJECTION

SCALE: 1:12,500,000 OR 1 INCH TO 197 MILES
(Approximately)

MAIN ROADS
RAILWAYS

NIGER AREA: *449,400 sq. mi.* POP: *2,870,000* CAP: *Niamey*
MALI AREA: *c. 448,200 sq. mi.* POP: *4,100,000* CAP: *Bamako*
UPPER VOLTA AREA: *c. 113,100 sq. mi.* POP: *4,400,000* CAP: *Ouagadougou*
MAURITANIA AREA: *418,810 sq. mi.* POP: *640,000* CAP: *Nouakchott*
SENEGAL AREA: *76,000 sq. mi.* POP: *2,980,000* CAP: *Dakar*
GUINEA AREA: *96,865 sq. mi.* POP: *3,000,000* CAP: *Conakry*

SIERRA LEONE AREA: *27,925 sq. mi.* POP: *2,450,000* CAP: *Freetown*
LIBERIA AREA: *43,000 sq. mi.* POP: *1,290,000* CAP: *Monrovia*
IVORY COAST AREA: *127,520 sq. mi.* POP: *3,300,000* CAP: *Abidjan*
GHANA AREA: *92,100 sq. mi.* POP: *6,943,000* CAP: *Accra*
TOGO AREA (est.): *21,893 sq. mi.* POP: *1,440,000* CAP: *Lomé*
DAHOMEY AREA: *44,290 sq. mi.* POP: *2,050,000* CAP: *Porto Novo*

© JOHN BARTHOLOMEW & SON LTD.

INTERNATIONAL BOUNDARIES

STATE BOUNDARIES

SCALE: 1:12,500,000 OR 1 INCH TO 197 MILES
(Approximately)

SCALE IN MILES

CENTRAL AFRICA

NIGERIA AREA: *356,669 sq. mi.* POP: *35,752,000* CAP: *Lagos*
REP. OF CHAD AREA: *485,750 sq. mi.* POP: *2,639,000* CAP: *Fort Lamy*
CAMEROON AREA: *193,681 sq. mi.* POP: *4,097,000* CAP: *Yaoundé*
CENT. AFRICAN REP. AREA: *238,220 sq. mi.* POP: *1,227,000* CAP: *Bangui*
SUDAN AREA: *967,500 sq. mi.* POP: *12,109,000* CAP: *Khartoum*
ETHIOPIA AREA: *c. 395,000 sq. mi.* POP: *c. 20,000,000* CAP: *Addis Ababa*

HEIGHTS IN FEET

12,000
9000
6000
3000
1500
600
SEA LEVEL
150
600
6000

DEPTHS IN FEET

120

LAMBERT'S AZIMUTHAL EQUAL-AREA PROJECTION

SCALE: 1:12,500,000 OR 1 INCH TO 197 MILES
(Approximately)

MAIN ROADS
RAILWAYS

SOMALI REP. AREA: c.262,000 sq.mi. POP: 1,990,000 CAP: Mogadiscio
KENYA AREA: 224,960 sq. mi. POP: 7,287,000 CAP: Nairobi
UGANDA AREA: 93,981 sq. mi. POP: 6,845,000 CAP: Entebbe
TANGANYIKA AREA: 362,688 sq.mi. POP: 9,404,000 CAP: Dar es Salaam
RWANDA AREA: 10,069 sq. mi. POP: 2,694,749 CAP: Kigali
BURUNDI AREA: 10,747 sq.mi. POP: 2,234,141 CAP: Usumbura

REP. OF THE CONGO AREA: 904,754 sq.mi. POP: 14,150,000 CAP: Léopoldville
CONGO REPUB. AREA: 139,000 sq. mi. POP: 900,000 CAP: Brazzaville
REP. OF GABON AREA: 103,089 sq. mi. POP: 450,000 CAP: Libreville
ANGOLA AREA: 481,351 sq. mi. POP: 4,642,000 CAP: Luanda
MALAGASY REP. AREA: 227,602 sq.mi. POP: 5,393,000 CAP: Tananarive

121

INTERNATIONAL BOUNDARIES

STATE BOUNDARIES

SCALE: 1:12,500,000 OR 1 INCH TO 197 MILES
(Approximately)

SCALE IN MILES

SOUTHERN AFRICA

N. RHODESIA AREA: *288,130 sq. mi.* POP: *2,480,000* CAP: *Lusaka*
S. RHODESIA AREA: *150,333 sq. mi.* POP: *3,140,000* CAP: *Salisbury*
NYASALAND AREA: *49,177 sq. mi.* POP: *2,890,000* CAP: *Zomba*
S. WEST AFRICA AREA: *317,887 sq. mi.* POP: *522,000* CAP: *Windhoek*
REP. OF S. AFRICA AREA: *472,685 sq. mi.* POP: *16,122,000*

CAPS: *Cape Town, Pretoria*
BECHUANALAND AREA: *275,000 sq. mi.*
POP: *288,000* CAP: *Mafeking*
MOZAMBIQUE AREA: *297,731 sq. mi.*
POP: *6,482,000* CAP: *Lourenço Marques*

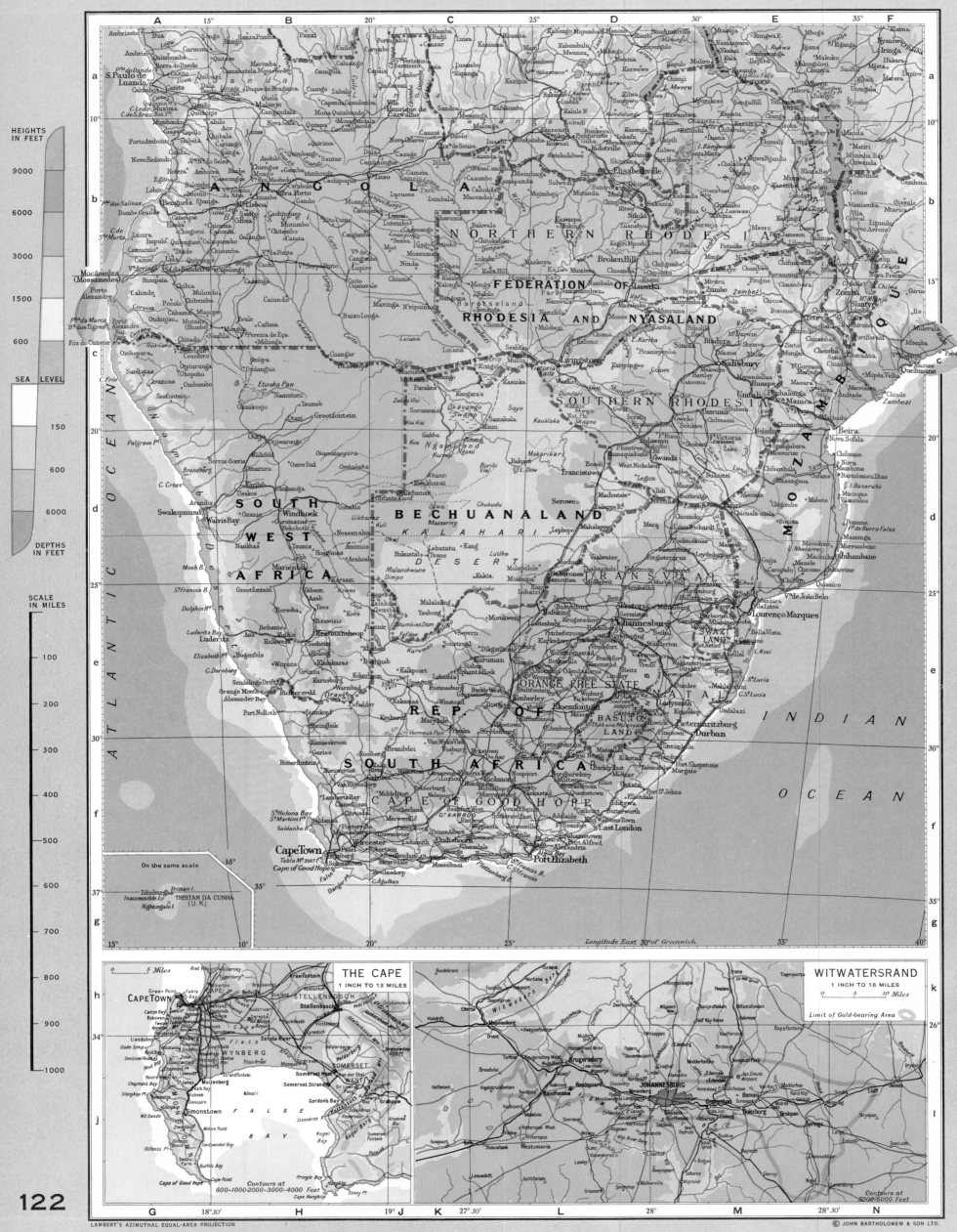

HEIGHTS IN FEET

9000
6000
3000
1500
600
SEA LEVEL
150
600
6000
DEPTHS IN FEET

SCALE IN MILES

100
200
300
400
500
600
700
800
900
1000

THE CAPE
1 INCH TO 13 MILES

WITWATERSRAND
1 INCH TO 16 MILES
0   5   10 Miles
Limit of Gold-bearing Area

122

LAMBERT'S AZIMUTHAL EQUAL-AREA PROJECTION

© JOHN BARTHOLOMEW & SON LTD.

SCALE: 1:12,500,000 OR 1 INCH TO 197 MILES
(Approximately)

MAIN ROADS
RAILWAYS

THE LEVANT

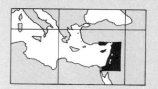

SYRIA AREA: 71,398 sq. mi. LEBANON AREA: 4000 sq. mi. ISRAEL AREA: 7992 sq. mi. JORDAN AREA: 37,302 sq. mi.
POP: 4,555,267 POP: 1,646,000 POP: 2,170,082 POP: 1,690,123
CAP: *Damascus* CAP: *Beirut* CAP: *Jerusalem* CAP: *Amman*

HEIGHTS IN FEET

9000
6000
3000
1500
600
300
SEA LEVEL
Depression
150
600
6000
DEPTHS IN FEET

SCALE IN MILES
25
50
75
100
125
150
175
200
225
250

123

CONIC PROJECTION

INTERNATIONAL BOUNDARIES
STATE BOUNDARIES

SCALE: 1:2,500,000 OR 1 INCH TO 39 MILES

© JOHN BARTHOLOMEW & SON LTD.

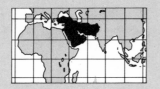

THE MIDDLE EAST

TURKEY, IRAQ, IRAN, AFGHANISTAN, SAUDI ARABIA

TURKEY AREA: 296,185 sq. mi. POP: 27,829,198
CAP: Ankara
IRAQ AREA: 171,599 sq. mi. POP: 7,085,000
CAP: Baghdad

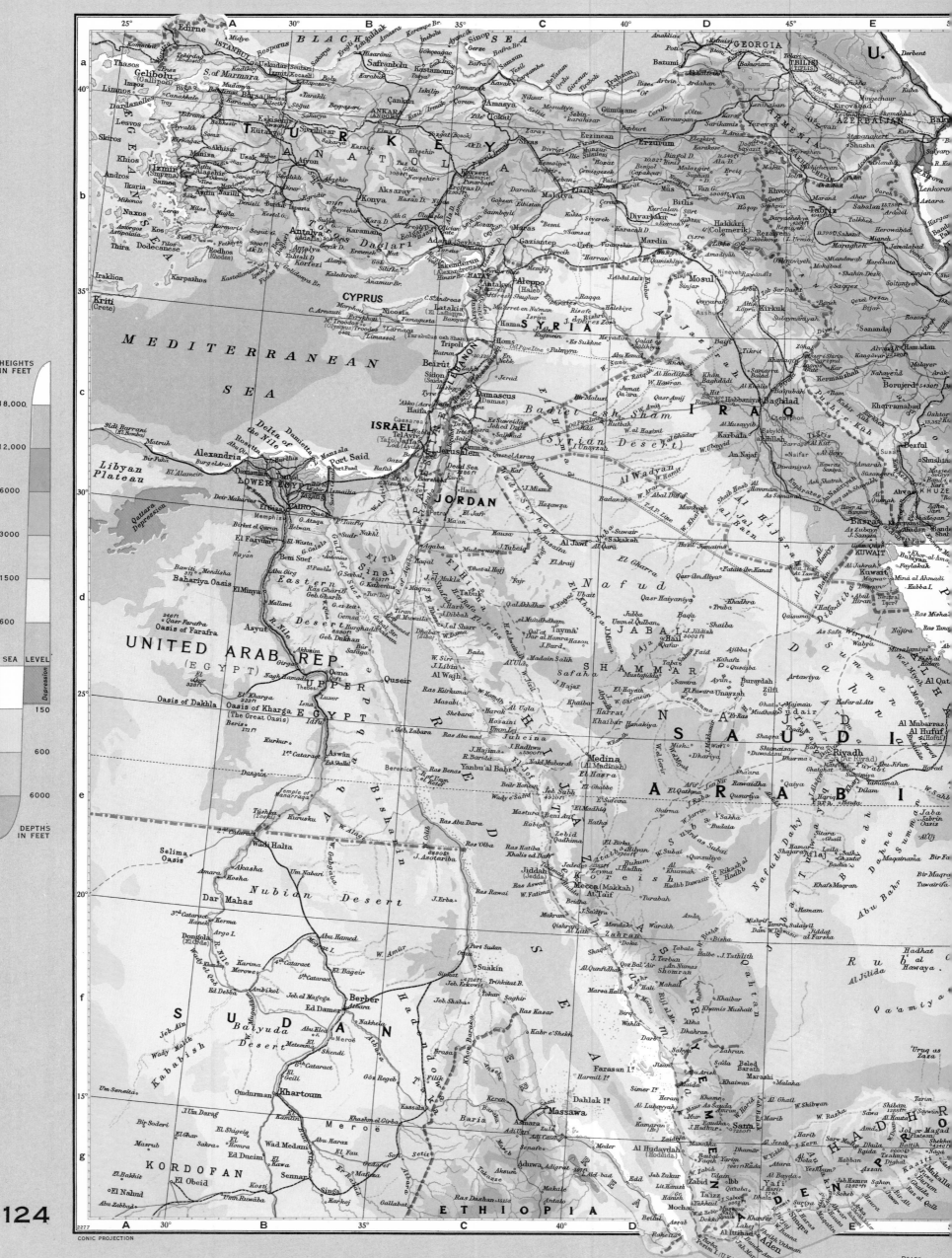

124

CONIC PROJECTION

SCALE: 1:10,000,000 OR 1 INCH TO 158 MILES

ROADS
RAILWAYS

IRAN AREA: 634,400 sq. mi.
POP: 20,678,000 CAP: *Tehran*
AFGHANISTAN AREA: 250,000 sq. mi.
POP: 13,800,000 CAP: *Kabul*

SAUDI ARABIA AREA: c. 618,000 sq. mi.
POP: c. 7,000,000 CAP: *Riyadh*
The map shows the fold mountain belt widening
from the Georgian Caucasus into the broad plateau

of Iran, and narrowing at the heights of the Hindu
Kush. The deep rift of the Jordan and the Dead
Sea broadens into the Red Sea, and continues south
as the Great Rift Valley of Africa.

125

© JOHN BARTHOLOMEW & SON LTD.

INTERNATIONAL BOUNDARIES
STATE BOUNDARIES

SCALE: 1:10,000,000 OR 1 INCH TO 158 MILES

SCALE
IN MILES

INDIA, PAKISTAN, CEYLON. BURMA

INDIA AREA: 1,173,828 sq. mi.
POP: 434,807,245 CAP: New Delhi
PAKISTAN AREA: 365,037 sq. mi.
POP: 93,831,982 GOVT: Rawalpindi

CEYLON AREA: 25,332 sq. mi.
POP: 10,167,000 CAP: Colombo
BURMA AREA: 261,789 sq. mi.
POP: 21,527,000 CAP: Rangoon

HEIGHTS IN FEET

18,000
12,000
6000
3000
1500
600
SEA LEVEL
150
600
6000
DEPTHS IN FEET

126

CONIC PROJECTION

SCALE: 1:10,000,000 OR 1 INCH TO 158 MILES

————— MAIN ROADS
----------- RAILWAYS

NEPAL AREA: 54,362 sq. mi.
POP: 9,407,127 CAP: *Katmandu*
BHUTAN AREA: 19,305 sq. mi.
POP: 670,000 CAP: *Punakha*

The Indian peninsula falls into three main regions: the Himalayas, the great plains of the Indus and the Ganges, and the Deccan plateau. The mountains to the north virtually seal off the peninsula from the rest of Asia.

Along the coast, from the Gulf of Cambay down to Cape Comorin, runs the long mountain range of the Western Ghats. The high mountains of Burma are separated by the valley of the Irrawaddy and Sittang rivers.

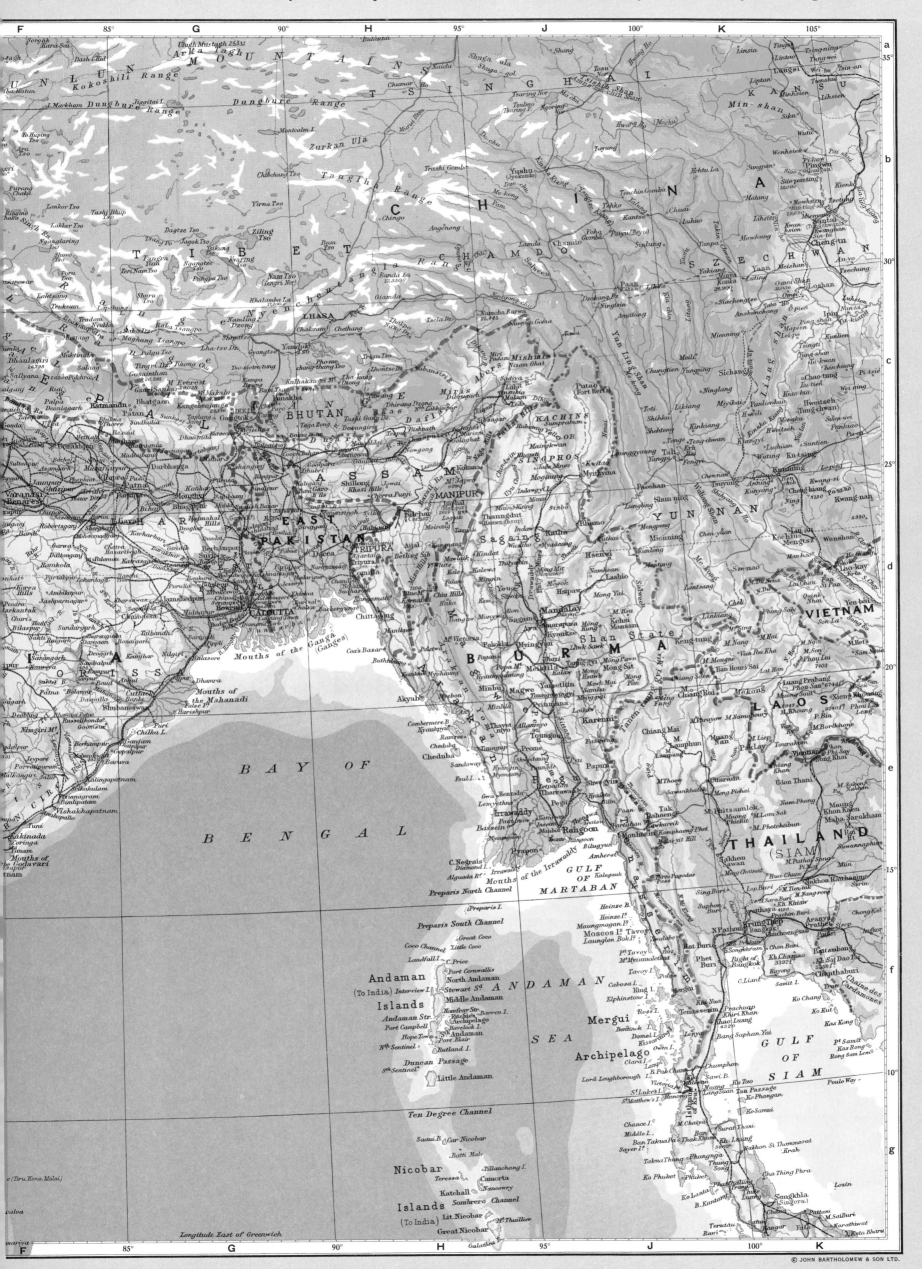

SCALE IN MILES

127

© JOHN BARTHOLOMEW & SON LTD.

INTERNATIONAL BOUNDARIES

STATE BOUNDARIES

SCALE: 1:10,000,000 OR 1 INCH TO 158 MILES

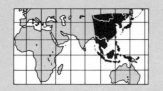

THE FAR EAST
NORTH KOREA, SOUTH KOREA, PHILIPPINES, INDONESIA

NORTH KOREA AREA: 46,814 sq. mi. POP: 9,418,000
CAP: *Pyongyang*
SOUTH KOREA AREA: 38,452 sq. mi. POP: 24,994,117 CAP: *Seoul*
PHILIPPINES AREA: 115,707 sq. mi. POP: 27,455,799 CAP: *Manila*

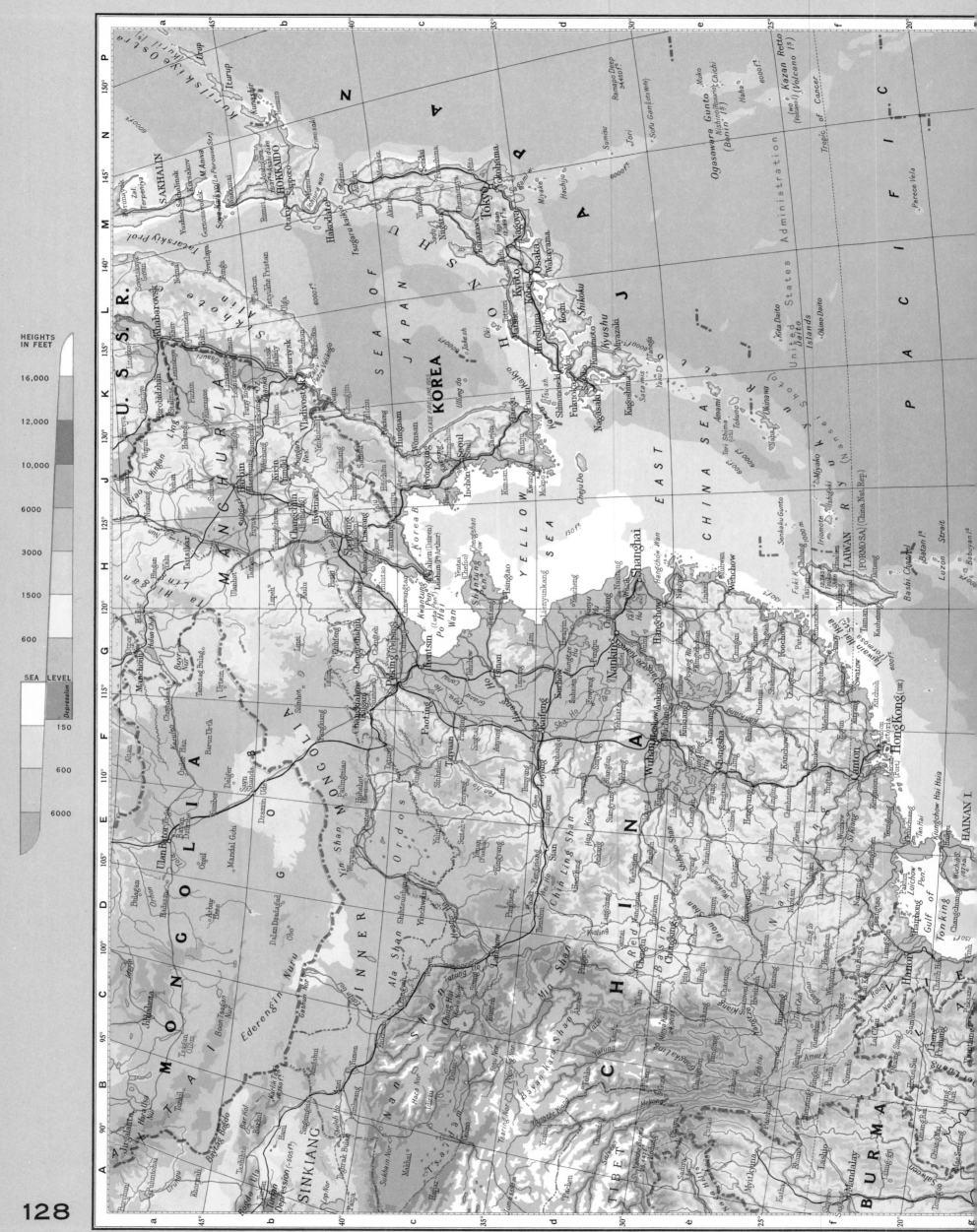

HEIGHTS
IN FEET

16,000
12,000
10,000
6000
3000
1500
600
SEA LEVEL
Depression
150
600
6000

128

BONNE'S PROJECTION

SCALE: 1:15,000,000 OR 1 INCH TO 237 MILES
(Approximately)

MAIN ROADS
RAILWAYS

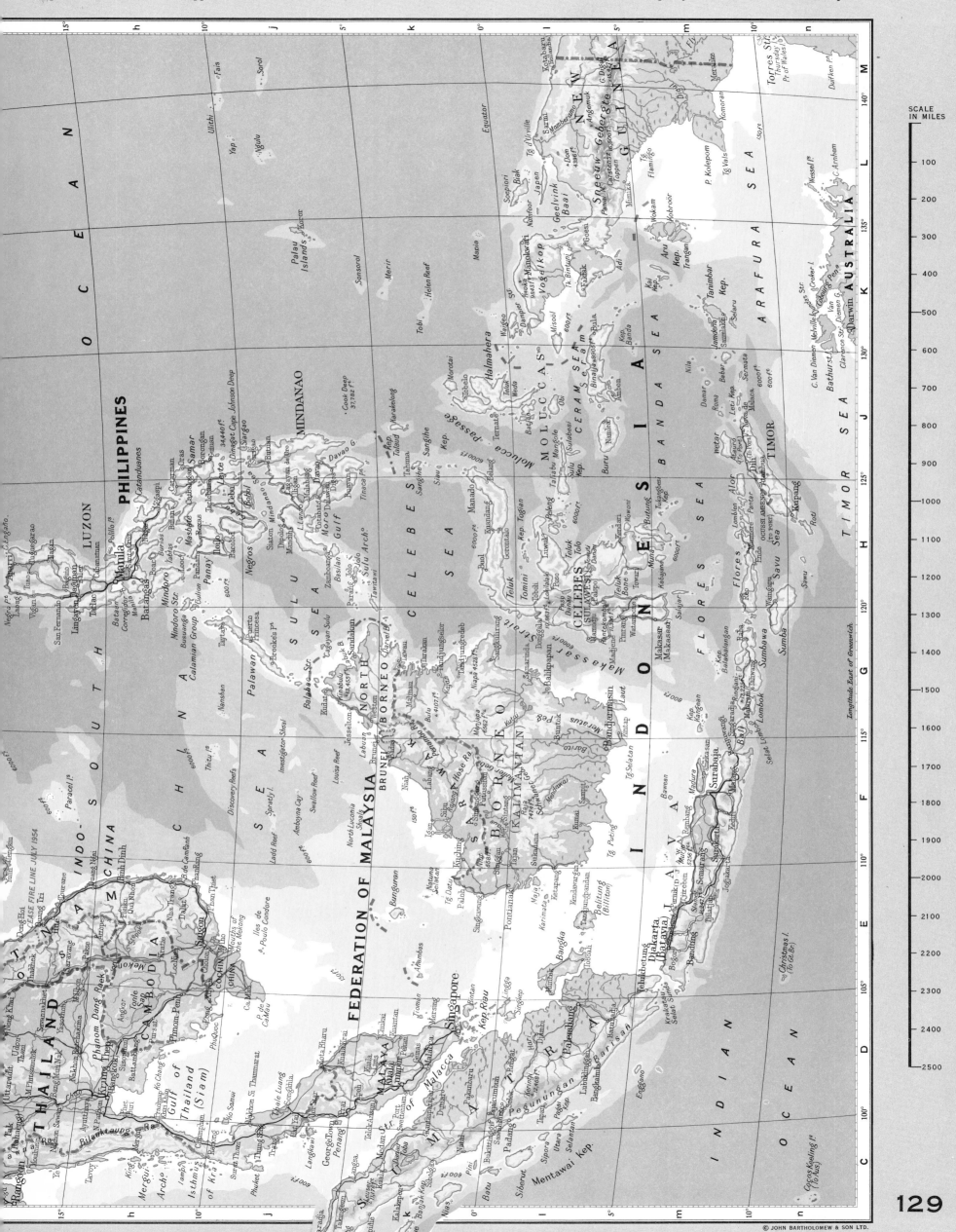

INDONESIA AREA: *575,895 sq. mi.*
POP: *95,189,000* CAP: *Djakarta*
From the high Tibetan plateau to the deep ocean bed off the Philippines is a drop of nearly 50,000 feet. The shallow seas of the Indonesian Archipelago and the mainly volcanic formation of the mountainous islands curving round Malaya to New Guinea are a marked contrast to the Himalayan fold mountains. The Philippines, comprising some 7000 islands, form the apex of a triangle based on Indonesia and pointing north to the equally mountainous islands of Japan.

SCALE
IN MILES

INTERNATIONAL BOUNDARIES
STATE BOUNDARIES

© JOHN BARTHOLOMEW & SON LTD.

129

SCALE: 1:15,000,000 OR 1 INCH TO 237 MILES
(Approximately)

EAST CHINA

CHINA AREA: *3,759,000 sq. mi.*
POP: *646,530,000* CAP: *Peking*
Though half covered by mountains, China
has the largest population of any country

in the world, and also the largest area of
fertile land. In the east is a semicircle of
low-lying land dotted with lakes, testify-
ing to inadequate river drainage. This

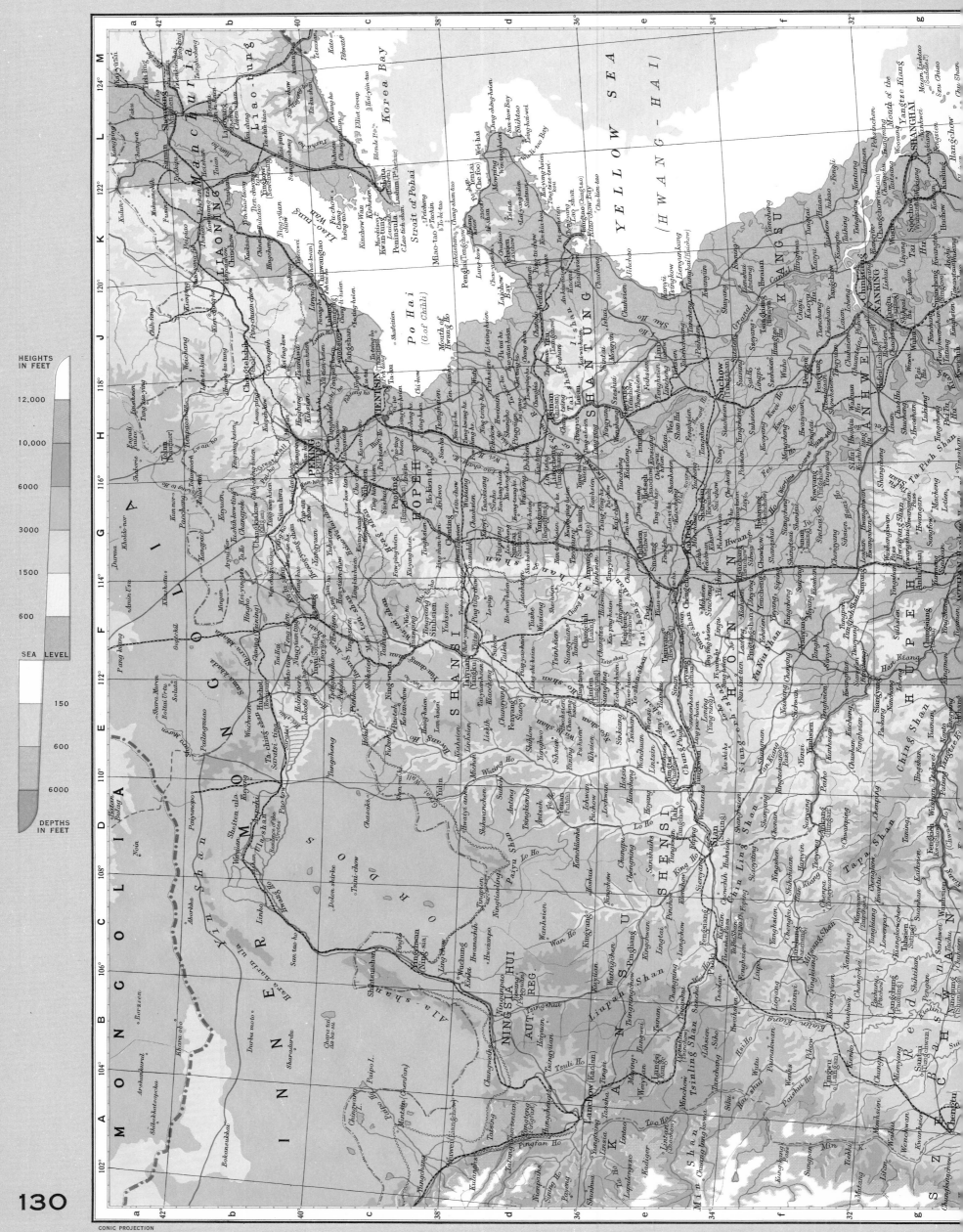

HEIGHTS
IN FEET

12,000
10,000
6000
3000
1500
600
SEA LEVEL
150
600
6000

DEPTHS
IN FEET

CONIC PROJECTION

SCALE: 1:6,000,000 OR 1 INCH TO 94 MILES

————————— MAIN ROADS
- - - - - - - - - RAILWAYS

area is backed by vast mountain ranges running northeast to Siberia, and cut up by mountainous tracts on a south-east axis reaching down to the coast of Chekiang. Each of the three main rivers, the Hwang Ho (Yellow River), the Yangtze Kiang and the Si Kiang, has a broad, well-watered valley, and together these valleys contain more than two thirds of China's inhabitants. Sinkiang, the largest province, is mostly desert. Another desert, the Gobi, which separates northern China from Outer Mongolia, covers nearly one third of China's total area.

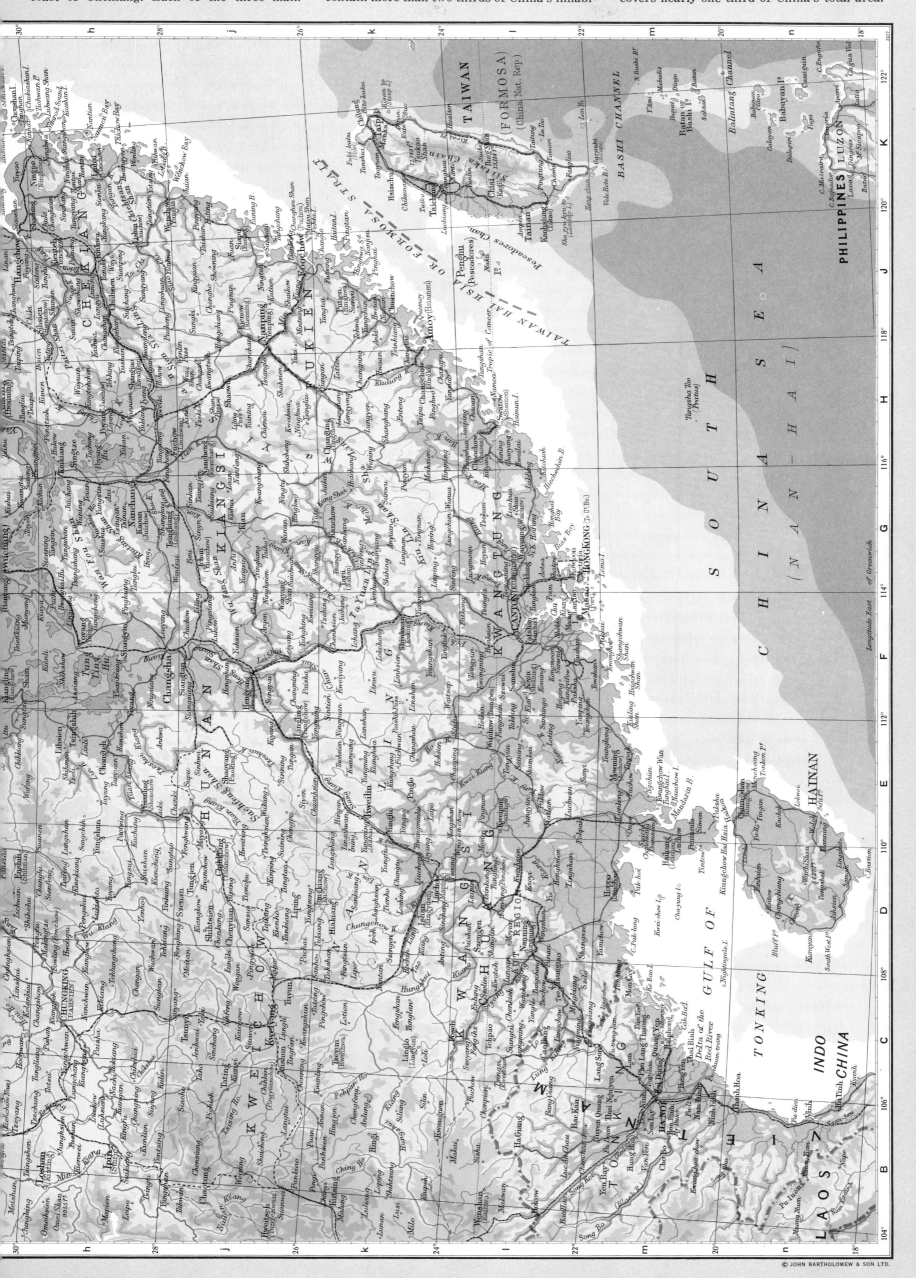

© JOHN BARTHOLOMEW & SON LTD.

INTERNATIONAL BOUNDARIES
PROVINCIAL BOUNDARIES

SCALE: 1:6,000,000 OR 1 INCH TO 94 MILES

SCALE IN MILES

SOUTHEAST ASIA

THAILAND AREA : *198,270 sq. mi.*
POP: *26,257,848* CAP: *Bangkok*
MALAYA AREA : *50,690 sq. mi.*
POP: *6,909,000* CAP: *Kuala Lumpur*

NORTH VIETNAM AREA : *63,360 sq. mi.*
POP: *15,916,955* CAP: *Hanoi*
SOUTH VIETNAM AREA : *65,726 sq. mi.*
POP: *14,100,000* CAP: *Saigon*

LAOS AREA : *91,400 sq. mi.* POP: *1,850,000*
CAP: *Luang Prabang* GOVT: *Vientiane*
CAMBODIA AREA : *69,900 sq. mi.*
POP: *4,845,000* CAP: *Phnom-Penh*

HEIGHTS
IN FEET

18,000
12,000
6000
3000
1500
600
SEA LEVEL
150
600
6000

DEPTHS
IN FEET

SCALE
IN MILES

100
200
300
400
500
600
700
800
900
1000

132

CONIC PROJECTION

© JOHN BARTHOLOMEW & SON LTD.

SCALE: 1:10,000,000 OR 1 INCH TO 158 MILES

MAIN ROADS

RAILWAYS

JAPAN

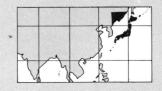

AREA: *142,719 sq. mi.* POP: *93,418,501*
CAP: *Tokyo*

Japan consists of a group of four large islands and many smaller ones, stretching from north to south over a thousand miles and separated from China by the shallow Sea of Japan. The main island is Honshu, which is approximately the same size as Great Britain.

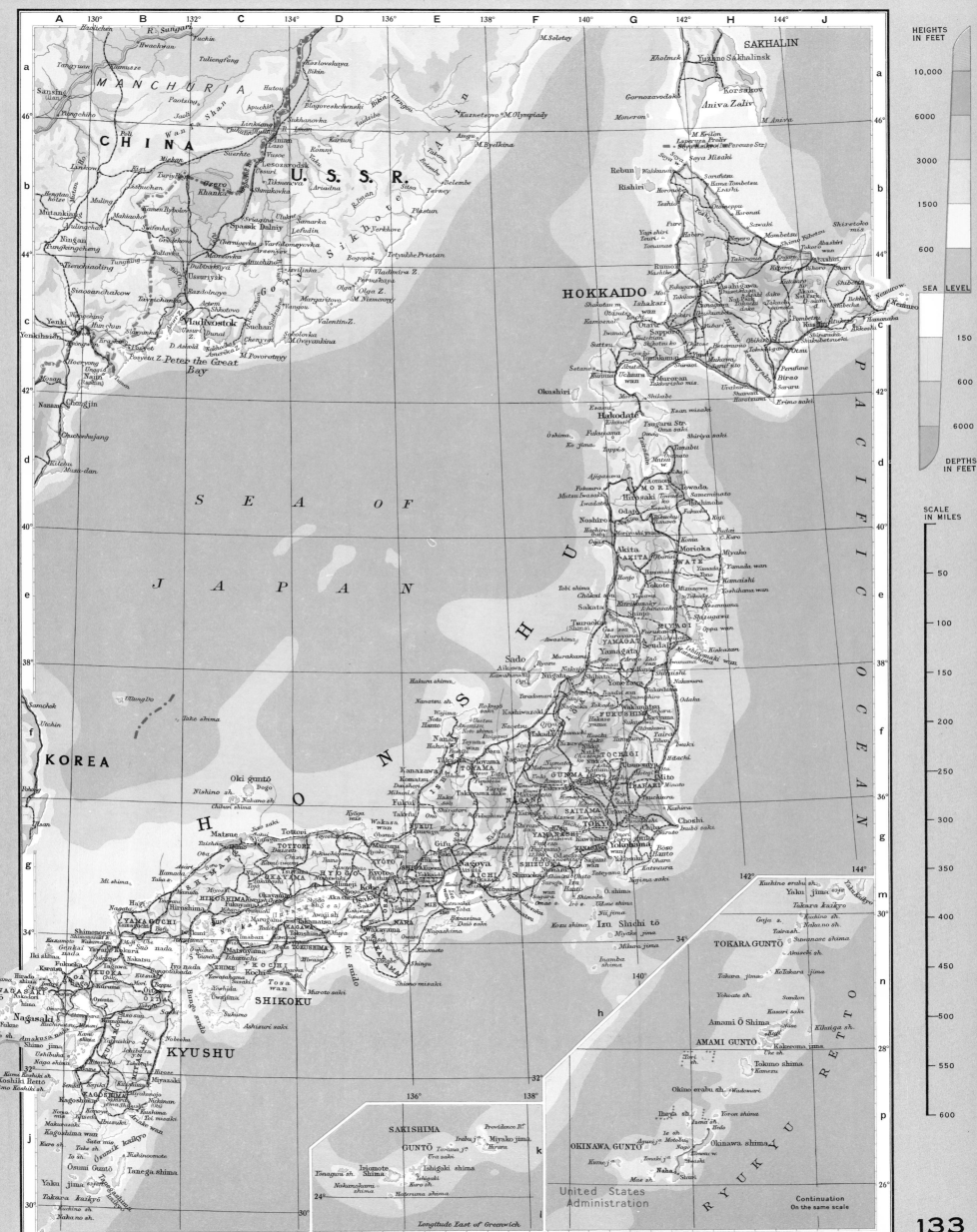

CONIC PROJECTION

INTERNATIONAL BOUNDARIES
PROVINCIAL BOUNDARIES

SCALE: 1:10,000,000 OR 1 INCH TO 158 MILES

© JOHN BARTHOLOMEW & SON LTD.

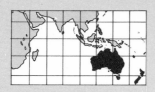

AUSTRALIA AND NEW ZEALAND

AUSTRALIA
AREA: *2,971,081 sq. mi.*
POP: *10,508,191* CAP: *Canberra*
Australia is the largest island

in the world. The Great Dividing Range of
mountains reaches from Melbourne in the south
right up to Cape York peninsula. It divides the
fertile coastland from a fertile tableland, which

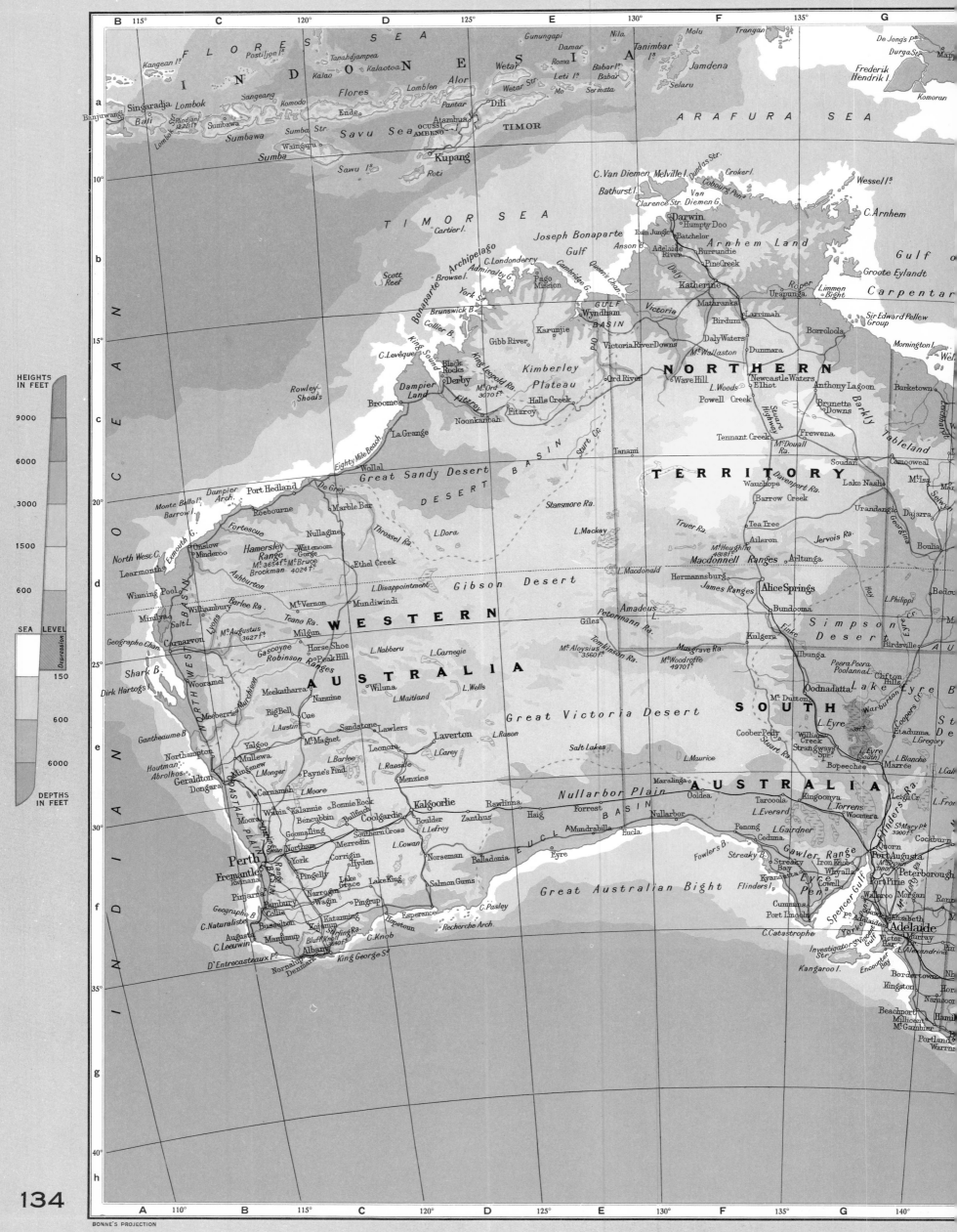

BONNE'S PROJECTION

SCALE: 1:12,500,000 OR 1 INCH TO 197 MILES

MAIN ROADS ——————

ARTESIAN BASINS   RAILWAYS

is flanked on the west by an extensive inland plain. The Lake Eyre Basin, partly below sea level, drains the rivers of the eastern plateau. Farther westward, poorly watered plains give way to enormous deserts—and a fertile strip to the extreme southwest.

NEW ZEALAND AREA: *103,736 sq. mi.*
POP: *2,414,984* CAP: *Wellington*

New Zealand includes North Island, South Island and several minor islands. The main islands are mountainous with rich coastal plains.

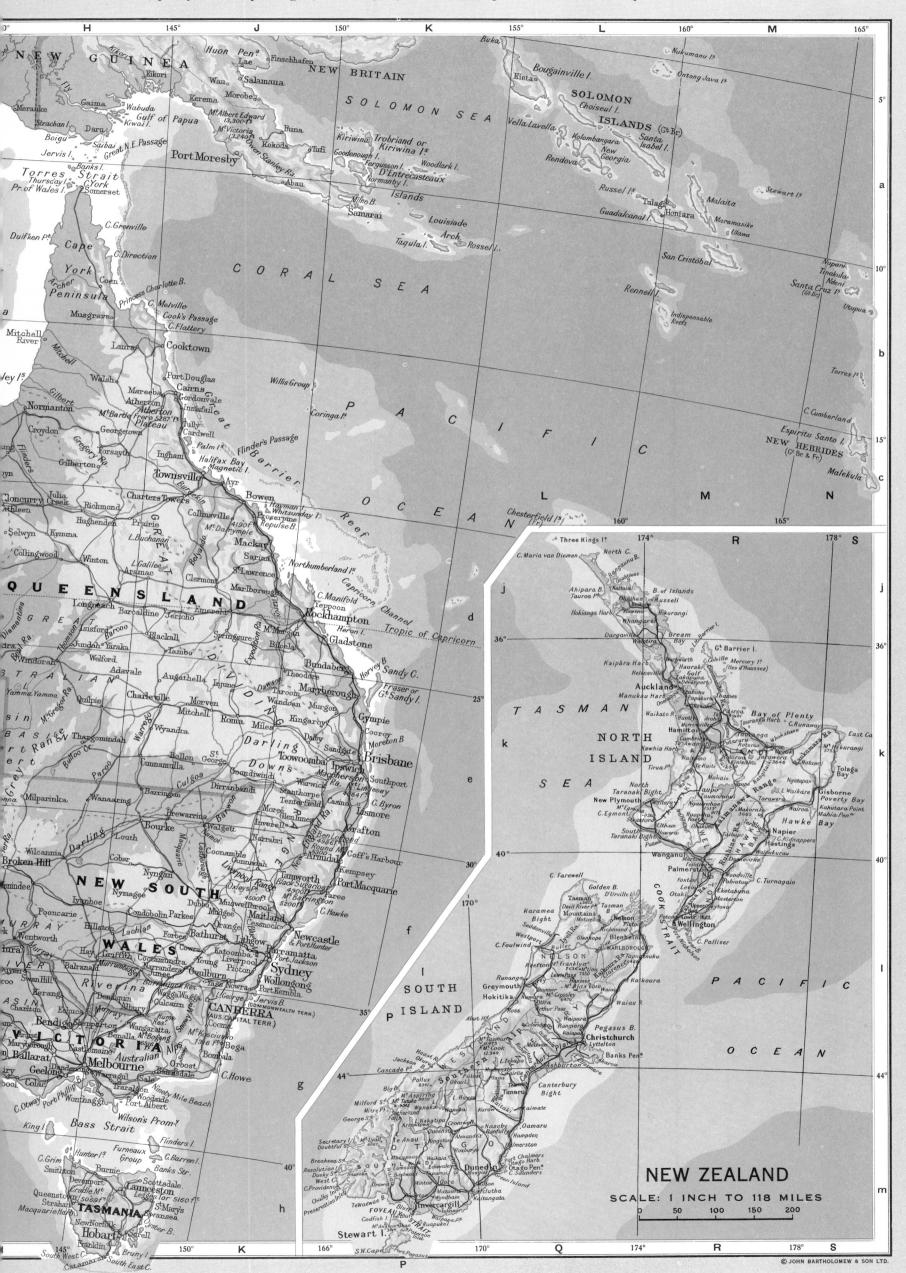

SCALE IN MILES

NEW ZEALAND

SCALE: 1 INCH TO 118 MILES

0   50   100   150   200

© JOHN BARTHOLOMEW & SON LTD.

INTERNATIONAL BOUNDARIES
STATE BOUNDARIES

SCALE: 1:12,500,000 OR 1 INCH TO 197 MILES

THE ANTARCTIC

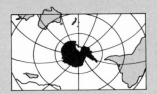

The Antarctic comprises those seas and lands around the South Pole within the Antarctic Circle at 66° 33′ S., a total area of about five million square miles. This continent is uniquely isolated, and is covered by an ice cap thousands of feet thick. Much of the rock surface beneath the ice is below sea level. About 35°F. colder than the Arctic, it is uninhabited.

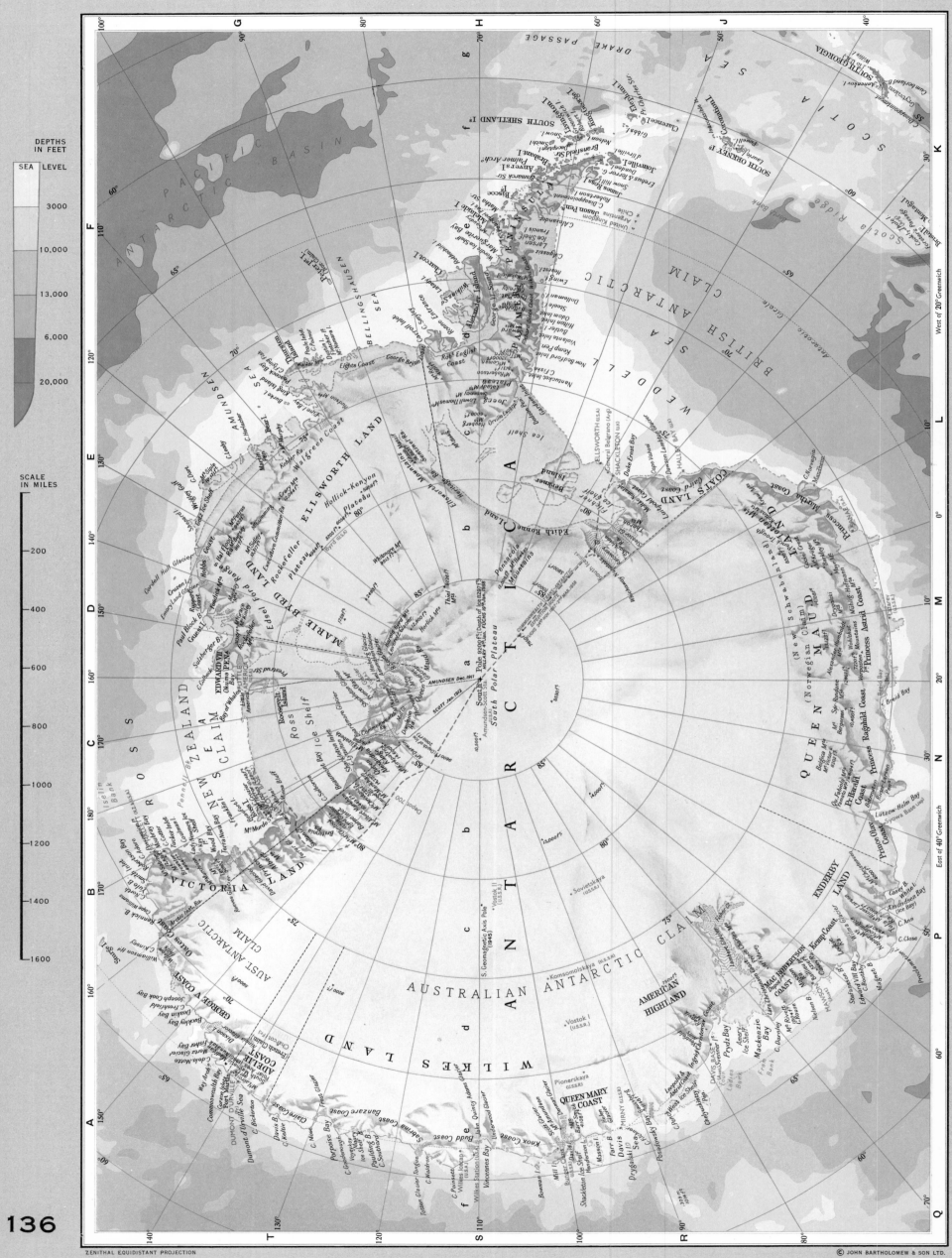

DEPTHS IN FEET

SEA LEVEL
3000
10,000
13,000
6,000
20,000

SCALE IN MILES

200
400
600
800
1000
1200
1400
1600

ZENITHAL EQUIDISTANT PROJECTION

© JOHN BARTHOLOMEW & SON LTD.

SCALE: 1:20,000,000 OR 1 INCH TO 316 MILES   BASES AND STATIONS SHOWN IN RED   GLACIERS   ICE SHELF

PART THREE

THE WORLD ABOUT US

THE EARTH'S STRUCTURE

OUR PLANET EARTH is about four and a half billion years old. It is customary to imagine the origin of the Earth in a rotating cloud of hot interstellar gas, along with other planets of our Solar System. A highly favored recent explanation indicates a union of cold "dust" materials whose size grew and whose gravitational force increased. The dust, probably born from an exploding star, was made up of all the elements now found on Earth, including certain radioactive elements which provided heat energy. The Earth's interior thus gradually warmed up, and since rock is a poor heat conductor, the temperature in the interior rapidly rose, approaching 7200°F. As the entire planet heated up, its surface shell became warmed from within. Lighter mineral elements and gases erupted to the surface, forming the first land, ocean and atmosphere.

Many kinds of rock, of the density and character of granite, became welded together to form the continental granitic and gneissic "shields" as we know them today. Each continent retains this ancient shell (indicated on the map in lavender).

The Wegener Theory of 1912 states that originally the continents fractured and gradually drifted apart, sliding over a molten zone in the Mantle. However, earthquake data prove that no such molten layer in the Mantle exists.

It has also long been thought that an initially hot Earth must be steadily shrinking as it cools. But Einstein's theory of relativity has provided us with the idea of an expanding universe. This suggests a slow reduction in the force of gravity which would cause each of the planets to expand. The Hungarian geophysicist Egyed calculated a rate of expansion for the diameter of the Earth at one yard every thousand years. Radioactive heat would provide further expansive energy.

The concept of an expanding globe would allow the ancient continents to separate slowly without a molten layer. Instead, periodic cracks in the ocean floor would open to become sealed by volcanic material (basaltic). The presence of a volcanic submarine ridge has been discovered to extend for 40,000 miles around the world, more or less across the middle of every ocean basin (green lines). Note how the land-filled north seems to split open into an oceanic southern hemisphere.

Gradually such great forces led to the opening of cracks and hollows in the ancient crust, particularly along the shores of the early continents. The cracks permitted volcanoes to rise from molten chambers in the basaltic crust; then sediment, washed off the land, settled in depressions or trenches on the floor of the sea. Periodically a critical imbalance of weight resulted. Large

masses of rock became detached and slid along thrust faults into the trenches. Violent shifting produced great heat in the Earth, melting the rock. Liquids and gases concentrated near the surface further produced light molten "granitic" rock material. These new zones rose to form mountains.

This process of cracking, sedimentation and rising has been repeated many times. The older mountain belts, formed 250 to 500 million years ago (marked in purple), may be traced in each of the continents today, though they have long since worn down. The younger mountain fold belts, formed over the last 200 million years, partly effaced the older ranges and so are more impressive (marked in blue). Deep fractures still cause the eruption of active volcanoes (red dots).

The Earth's crust never becomes quite stable: within the shield, sags have created broad basins. The earliest basins, 200 to 600 million years old, underlie many of the world's great interior plains (solid dark green), as in the American midwest. The younger ones, less than 200 million years of age, are more often in coastal areas (yellow).

The younger mountains follow the margins of the Pacific and separate Eurasia from Africa-India-Australia. These are the principal volcanic and earthquake regions of today (see map). The rim of the Pacific is known as the "Ring of Fire."

DIAGRAMMATIC SECTION THROUGH THE CRUST

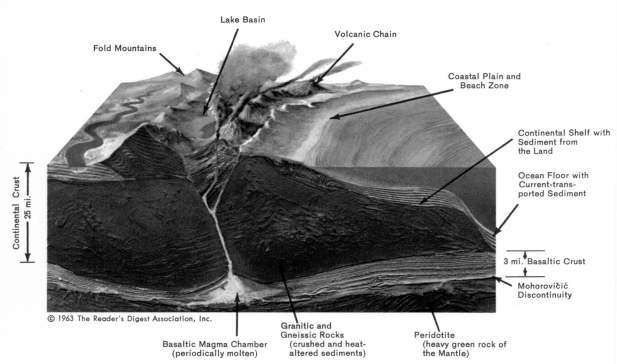

Fold Mountains

Lake Basin

Volcanic Chain

Coastal Plain and Beach Zone

Continental Shelf with Sediment from the Land

Ocean Floor with Current-transported Sediment

Continental Crust 25 mi.

3 mi. Basaltic Crust

Mohorovičić Discontinuity

© 1963 The Reader's Digest Association, Inc.

Basaltic Magma Chamber (periodically molten)

Granitic and Gneissic Rocks (crushed and heat-altered sediments)

Peridotite (heavy green rock of the Mantle)

CROSS SECTION OF THE EARTH

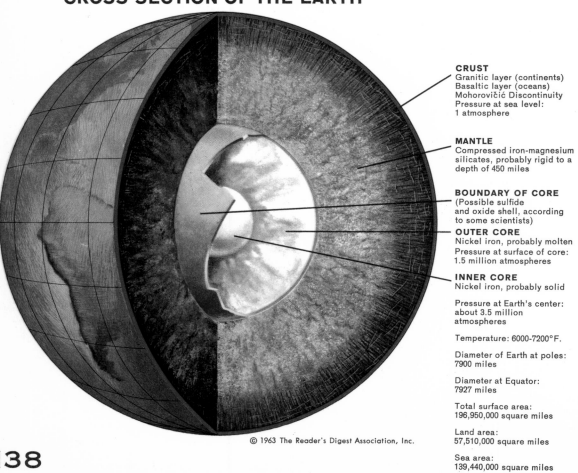

CRUST
Granitic layer (continents)
Basaltic layer (oceans)
Mohorovičić Discontinuity
Pressure at sea level:
1 atmosphere

MANTLE
Compressed iron-magnesium silicates, probably rigid to a depth of 450 miles

BOUNDARY OF CORE
(Possible sulfide and oxide shell, according to some scientists)

OUTER CORE
Nickel iron, probably molten
Pressure at surface of core:
1.5 million atmospheres

INNER CORE
Nickel iron, probably solid

Pressure at Earth's center:
about 3.5 million atmospheres

Temperature: 6000-7200°F.

Diameter of Earth at poles:
7900 miles

Diameter at Equator:
7927 miles

Total surface area:
196,950,000 square miles

Land area:
57,510,000 square miles

Sea area:
139,440,000 square miles

© 1963 The Reader's Digest Association, Inc.

THE EARTH'S INTERIOR

THE CRUST OF THE EARTH under the continents is quite different from that below the ocean. The continental crust is about 20-30 miles thick, made of relatively light materials often called "granitic," as granite is a typical continental rock. The oceanic crust, beneath its layer of water and about 1000 feet of accumulated muddy sediments, is of denser material. It is generally called "basaltic" after the basalt lava so often seen erupting from oceanic island volcanoes. In contrast to the continents, the ocean crust is only about three miles thick.

The interior of the Earth is known mainly from

EXPANSION OF THE EARTH

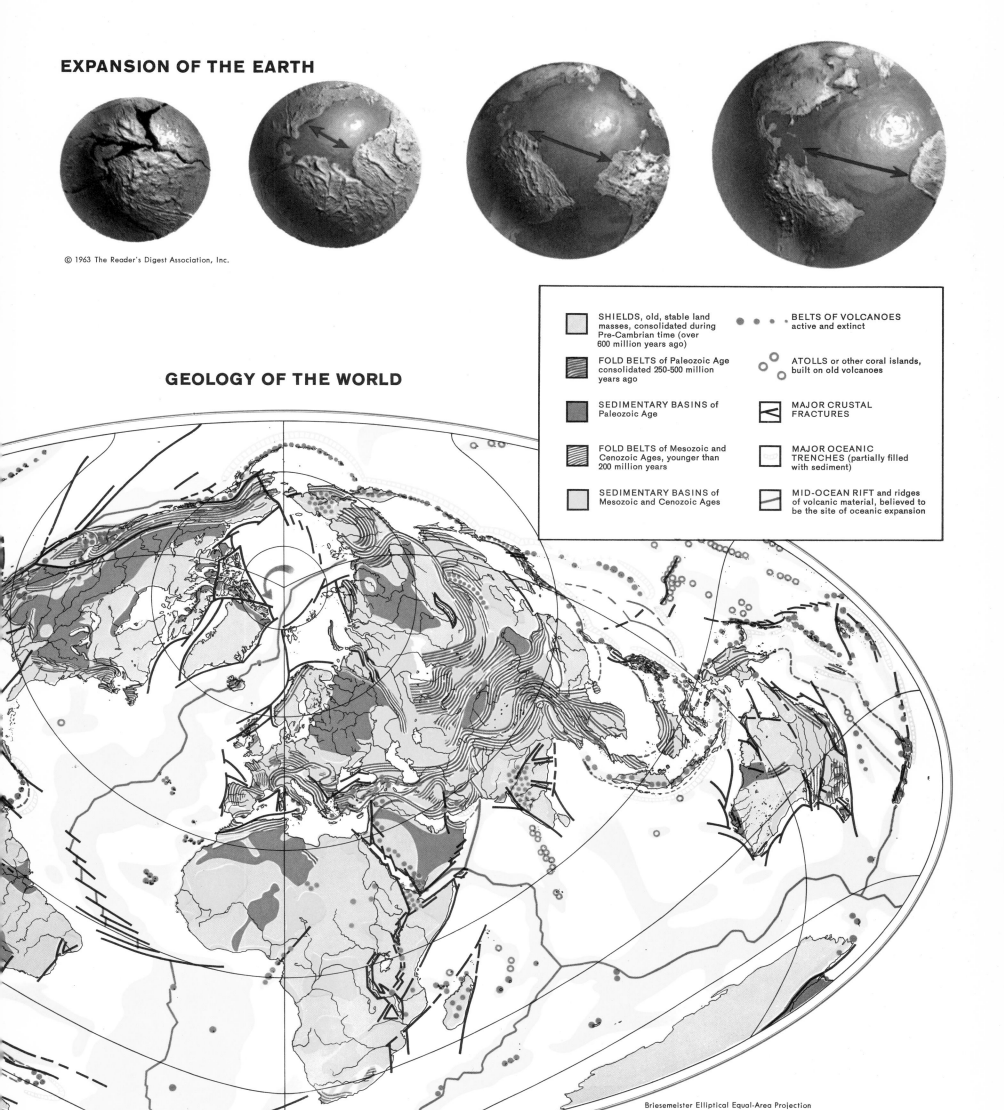

© 1963 The Reader's Digest Association, Inc.

GEOLOGY OF THE WORLD

SHIELDS, old, stable land masses, consolidated during Pre-Cambrian time (over 600 million years ago)

FOLD BELTS of Paleozoic Age consolidated 250-500 million years ago

SEDIMENTARY BASINS of Paleozoic Age

FOLD BELTS of Mesozoic and Cenozoic Ages, younger than 200 million years

SEDIMENTARY BASINS of Mesozoic and Cenozoic Ages

BELTS OF VOLCANOES active and extinct

ATOLLS or other coral islands, built on old volcanoes

MAJOR CRUSTAL FRACTURES

MAJOR OCEANIC TRENCHES (partially filled with sediment)

MID-OCEAN RIFT and ridges of volcanic material, believed to be the site of oceanic expansion

Briesemeister Elliptical Equal-Area Projection

© 1963 Rhodes W. Fairbridge

earthquake records. These vibrations pass quickly through rock of high density and more slowly through the lighter material. The shock waves change their direction and speed at certain levels which are known as discontinuities. The first major discontinuity is at the base of the crust. This is named the "Mohorovičić Discontinuity" (Moho for short), after the famous Yugoslav scientist who discovered it. Attempts have been and are being made to drill down to the Moho level. Below it is the Mantle, a deep section which probably consists of a dense greenish rock, "peridotite," to a depth of 1800 miles.

At the base of the Mantle another major discontinuity marks the beginning of the Outer Core of the Earth. The Outer Core, 1310 miles thick, is a "dead" zone for certain earthquake waves, which indicates that it may be liquid. It has been much discussed. Perhaps it is iron with a certain alloy of nickel, resembling a type of meteorite that is believed to have originated at the same time as our Solar System. Such a core in the Earth would be magnetic and would account for the strong magnetic field that prevents the Earth from being dangerously bombarded by cosmic rays.

Beneath the molten layer lies the Inner Core,

850 miles in radius, so dense that it has become solid again. Pressure at the center may approach 3.5 million atmospheres.

The solid nucleus of the Earth is said to possess a momentum of its own, and to spin in the liquid bath of the Outer Core, lagging behind the rotation of the Mantle and the crust of the Earth. From time to time the position of the outer Earth (Mantle and crust) has shifted in relation to the Inner Core, and there has been a reversal in the magnetic field. Magnetic rocks show that the last "flip-over" occurred a million years ago when the North Pole became positive and the South negative.

THE AGES
OF THE EARTH

FOR ITS first billion and a half years the Earth was probably without life. The Earth's earliest crust may have been volcanic; the most ancient rocks have dominantly greenish colors, an indication of old lavas and their products. The early atmosphere was probably without oxygen, consisting, it is thought, of hydrogen, water vapor, methane and ammonia. An atmosphere rich in oxygen must have evolved at least three billion years ago; in rocks of that age we find fossils of primitive plants which used carbon dioxide and liberated oxygen. Sediments were washed into the ocean, shifting the weight of the crust, producing violent heat changes and creating numerous mountain systems. Widespread ice ages alternated with warmer times.

Seaweeds and probably bacteria were the only forms of plant life. Certain species of algae (*Collenia, Cryptozoon*) fixed lime around themselves, and their extensive fossil remains are found on every continent.

Forms of animal life appeared in the tropical seas — worms, jellyfish, sponges as well as other soft-bodied (invertebrate) forms. Fossil imprints of these organisms are rare, but some were perfectly preserved. The land was apparently lifeless, without soil or plants. All of the above occurred in what geologists call the Pre-Cambrian Era.

Geological time is divided into named periods, each shorter than the one before. The later the stage, the greater its variety of land formations and life, and the more abundant the fossils. The major divisions are the Eras. The first, Pre-Cambrian, including the Proterozoic and Archean, is the time before 600 million years ago, when only primitive soft organisms lived. During the Paleozoic, 225-600 million years ago, fishes and simple reptiles became the greatest creatures on Earth, and plants came to clothe the dry land and create soil. The Mesozoic, 70-225 million years ago, produced giant reptiles and primitive mammals on the land. In the Cenozoic, 70 million years ago till the present, mammals became ascendant and, in the last million years, man's ancestors emerged.

These Eras are in turn subdivided into Periods, as shown in the column on the opposite page.

GEOLOGY OF THE UNITED STATES

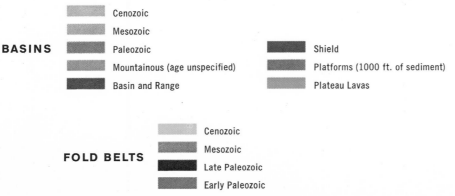

BASINS	
	Cenozoic
	Mesozoic
	Paleozoic
	Mountainous (age unspecified)
	Basin and Range
	Shield
	Platforms (1000 ft. of sediment)
	Plateau Lavas

FOLD BELTS	
	Cenozoic
	Mesozoic
	Late Paleozoic
	Early Paleozoic

PALEOZOIC (Ancient Life)

Cambrian Period (from about 500 to 600 million years ago). The great Pre-Cambrian ice melted. Shallow seas spread across half the land area of the world. Around the borders of the Canadian Shield, the typical rocks laid down were first yellow-red sandstones, then limestones and shales. Great sedimentary basins began to form in the belt from New England to Alabama and in the far west. Climatic conditions were moderately warm.

Lime-secreting plants in the sea, such as *Collenia*, continued to be the only vegetation of which there is evidence. They were restricted to warm, shallow water, where light penetrated. Land was still without life.

Mysterious chemical changes in the seas enabled animals to build skeletons or shells of lime. Advanced groups such as the trilobites (similar to king crabs of today) emerged.

Ordovician Period (from about 440 to 500 million years ago). Shallow seas extended over most of North America, save for some large islands in northern Canada. Climates seem to have remained warm and equable. Over much of the midwest the deposits of the receding seas were limestone or dolomite (magnesium-rich limestone), but in the deep trenches of the east and west coasts thick shales accumulated. Their greatly increased weight began to fold the Earth's crust into mountains from the Carolinas to New England and in the far west.

Plant life was still restricted to the shallow oceans, and widespread limestone suggests the growth of floating algae. Reeflike constructions of algae built up in shallow waters.

In the ocean the ostracoderms — horny-armored, ancestral fish — were the first animals with backbones (vertebrates). Floating

MESOZOIC (Middle Life)

Triassic Period (from about 180 to 225 million years ago). Conditions in the midwest were similar to the Rocky Mountain area in many ways. The seas withdrew further, the climate became even drier and the prevailing colors of the rocks were reds, yellows and white, as we can see today in the Grand Canyon and Painted Desert. The recently formed Appalachians settled; enormous fracture zones produced basins (quickly filled with red-hued sediment) and created volcanoes all along the mountain range.

Arid conditions over much of the Northern Hemisphere discouraged plant life; in southern lands, especially in Africa, India and Australia, a great variety of pines, cycads (similar to the palm) and ferns appeared.

The "Age of Reptiles" dominated most of the Mesozoic Era. Dinosaurs, at first no more than six inches long, appeared in this period. The first mammals—warm-blooded creatures—also very small, evolved from the reptiles. In the insect world the earliest flies and termites arrived.

CENOZOIC (Modern Life)

Eocene Period (from about 40 to 70 million years ago). Late in the Cretaceous Period and continuing in the Eocene, great mountains were emerging from Alaska to South America. Around the margin of the Pacific and from the Alps to Indonesia the present mountain belts began to lift up. Seas remained in the eastern and southern U.S., and interior plains enjoyed a subtropical climate.

On land, flowering plants and deciduous trees dominated, but warm belts permitted tropical species to flourish up to Canada and palms as far north as Greenland.

The giant reptiles became extinct. On land, crocodiles and turtles came and all the groups of insects. A "vacuum" was left by the dinosaurs' eclipse, and an enormous variety of mammals took their place: the pygmy elephant, rhinoceros, dog-sized horse, pig, primitive cattle and the earliest monkey. Life in the sea became much as we know it today.

Oligocene Period (from about 25 to 40 million years ago). Seas retreated slowly from eastern North America and the Gulf coast. In the Rockies massive fracturing helped form interior basins. Sediment from mountain ranges poured out over the great plains in vast alluvial fans. New marine trenches appeared only along the Pacific seaboard, where new deep deposits of sediment were accumulating and mountain-building pressures were rising. Warm conditions continued, but some areas experienced a cycle of cooler winters.

Emergence of broad plains encouraged the spread of extensive grasslands. Tropical coal swamps occurred in low-lying areas.

The new plains favored rapid growth of the grass-eating mammals. The early dog, cat and bear also appeared. A tailless, primitive ape forecast a possible ancestor of man.

far and wide were the graptolites, relatives of the coral. No life on land.

Silurian Period (from about 400 to 440 million years ago). Across the midwest a more distinct pattern of long ridges and broad basins began to emerge. Mountains of both coasts eroded, providing sediments to help fill trenches of the bordering seas.

Vegetation, still leafless, began to evolve further in lakes and swamps—the oldest known fossils are found in Australia. No life known on land. Simple marine invertebrates achieved great variety. Coral reefs grew to a grand scale. Giant-clawed sea scorpions up to nine feet long terrorized the waters.

Devonian Period (from about 350 to 400 million years ago). As Earth's crust sank into basins in the midwest, coral-type reefs formed around them in shallow seas from Iowa to New York. In New England the Cambrian basins became folded, melted, granitized and rose to form the Acadian Mountains. Sediments washed from the existing mountains, forming great deltas, such as one seen today in the Catskills and eastern Pennsylvania.

Vigorous plant life emerged on land everywhere, including horse-tails and ferns, some 40 feet tall. In the Catskill region of New York, fossil trunks of these ancient ferns are over three feet in diameter.

Called the "Age of Fish." Fish evolved rapidly in all modern groups, including early sharks up to 20 feet long. The first amphibians began to exploit favorable land; also spiders, millipedes and wingless insects.

Carboniferous Period (from about 270 to 350 million years ago). The "Great Age of Coal."

The shallow interior seas generally silted up, becoming steamy tropical swamps. Coal seams alternated with layers of sandstones, limestones and shales. In Australia a great ice age was in progress, and its fluctuations caused frequent rise and fall of sea level, leaving lakes and swamps. This worldwide effect caused layering of coal seams. The Northern Hemisphere was largely tropical.

Development of great fresh-water swamps favored evolution of tropical tree ferns, horsetails and the earliest conifers (notably pines) up to 100 feet tall. These, when buried, were converted to coal.

Swamps and coastal plains encouraged rapid evolution of amphibians, including a salamander 15 feet long, and the first reptiles. Insects developed wings; giant dragonflies grew to the size of eagles.

Permian Period (from about 225 to 270 million years ago). The seas retreated forever from the midwest, but new basins forming seas developed in the Rocky Mountain area and Texas. Abundant life in warm waters favored the creation of great oilfields. Climate on land in the Northern Hemisphere became more arid, and extensive sand-dune deposits appeared (as in Colorado). The Appalachians reached their greatest height.

During the great ice age of the Southern Hemisphere, strongly marked seasons emerged. Plants adapted to arid and cold conditions, especially deciduous trees, which drop their leaves to withstand frost.

In the ocean many Paleozoic invertebrate types, such as the trilobites and graptolites, died out. On land the reptiles increased slowly, but insects multiplied greatly (lacking natural enemies).

Jurassic Period (from about 135 to 180 million years ago). Often considered by geologists as the ideal "quiet time"; warm seas from the south returned to lap the southern Appalachians, forming the ancestral Gulf of Mexico, and filled many basins in the Rockies. Along the Pacific seaboard the deep Paleozoic trenches gradually filled and pressures began to fold the great Rocky Mountains.

With subtropical conditions returning almost everywhere, land and swamp plants evolved in profusion, including pines, ferns and the cycad with cones which were forerunners of flowers. Some coal swamps developed.

Reptiles reached fantastic dimensions (extremely weak in brain-power), the heavier ones in lakes where their weight (up to 35 tons) could be supported by water. Flying reptiles dominated the air, and swimming reptiles (ichthyosaurs) the ocean. Mammals remained small, no bigger than rats.

Cretaceous Period (from about 70 to 135 million years ago). The "Age of Chalk" began with a general lowering of sea level, probably due to trenches forming in the Mediterranean and around the Pacific. Soon the sea, successively rising and falling, advanced into the interior of America. At its maximum almost 90 percent of the Earth's surface was water-covered. The climate was almost universally temperate to subtropical.

Tropical and subtropical climates favored the development of fleshy-leaved and other deciduous trees—fig, magnolia, poplar and plane. The evolution of insects permitted dissemination of pollen from flowering plants. In temperate belts, vegetation showed a well-marked seasonal control, with growth rings.

Giant reptiles still dominated land, sea and air, but warm-blooded birds were already developing. Mammals remained inconspicuous. A new arrival was the pouched marsupial (ancestor of the kangaroo). By the end of the period, dinosaurs and many other of the earlier animals became totally extinct. Fish were forming in the species familiar today.

Miocene Period (from 11 million to 25 million years ago). Tremendous forces lifted up the Rockies; new local basins were formed by extensive fractures. Marginal seas appeared from New Jersey to the Gulf of Mexico, and on the west coast. Climates became universally warmer and wetter: subtropical in U.S., temperate in Canada. In Eurasia a series of thrusts occurred from the Alps to the Himalayas, and on to the Pacific border.

Favorable climate stimulated deciduous forests (maple, oak, poplar) throughout Europe and North America as well as grasslands on the great North American plains. Coal swamps and tropical forests appeared around the Gulf of Mexico.

Bony fish continued to develop, with sharks 60 feet long. Anthropoid apes were evolving in Africa, Asia and Europe. Elephants, increasing in size, spread from Africa through Siberia to North America. Ducks, pelicans and great penguins appeared.

Pliocene Period (from 1 million to 11 million years ago). Warm humid climates of North America cooled, and present desert areas began to dry. At first, because there were no ice caps, the sea level was over 500 feet above that of today, but continents were assuming their present outlines. The water level fell as the Antarctic Ice Age set in, building its cap, and as the smaller oceanic basins sank and the mountain chains rose.

Oceans gradually cooled. As continents grew drier, grasslands spread out over the great plains in many parts of the world where subtropical plant life had existed.

Giant sharks died out, and many of the species of the ocean became identical to present forms. In contrast, on land the mammals were fast evolving, the horse and giraffe adapting to grasslands. Manlike apes thrived

in forests and also, in open country, a species that walked upright.

Pleistocene Period (started 1 million years ago). The "Great Ice Age," still continuing today, passed through warm and cold cycles of 20,000 to 90,000 years. Continental ice advanced over large tracts of North America and Eurasia. Warm periods with melting ice formed the great lakes of North America. Temperatures were higher than today and wet tropics spread. Desert areas expanded during cold periods.

Many plants survived in America and Asia by migrating south during the ice ages, but perished in Europe where sea and mountain areas cut them off. Pines developed.

Shifting climates forced tremendous migrations upon ancestral man and animals. Modern elephant, horse and cattle evolved. Ape-like creatures began to use stones as weapons and tools, marking the dawn of human intelligence.

Holocene Period (started 10,000 years ago). Our present epoch is an interglacial period. At its beginning the sea rose 330 feet because of the partial melting of glaciers of the Northern Hemisphere, creating the shorelines that we know today. World climates were cool at first, rising to a peak of warmth 5000 years ago, then cooling again.

With the arrival of warm seasons, trees advanced northward, first pines, later birch and hazel, then oak and elder. Forest margins are now retreating again.

Paleolithic man attained fire and practical arts at the close of the last ice phase. Then Mesolithic and Neolithic men became farmers and house-builders and learned to domesticate animals. About 5000 B.C. metal-working ushered in the age of cultivated man.

EVOLUTION OF LIFE

GEOLOGICAL DIVISIONS

Holocene
started 10,000 years ago

Pleistocene
started 1 million years ago

Pliocene
from 1 million to 11 million years ago

Miocene
from 11 million to 25 million years ago

Oligocene
from about 25 to 40 million years ago

Eocene
from about 40 to 70 million years ago

Cretaceous
from about 70 to 135 million years ago

Jurassic
from about 135 to 180 million years ago

Triassic
from about 180 to 225 million years ago

Permian
from 225 to 270 million years ago

Carboniferous
from 270 to 350 million years ago

Devonian
from about 350 to 400 million years ago

Silurian
from about 400 to 440 million years ago

Ordovician
from about 440 to 500 million years ago

Cambrian
from about 500 to 600 million years ago

Proterozoic
and
Archean

© 1963 The Reader's Digest Association, Inc.

FROM THE PRIZED FLINTS of the Stone Age to the uranium ores of the Atomic Age, minerals have contributed vitally to the growth of civilization. Man has long recognized the importance of precious metals and precious stones, and of base metals such as copper, lead and zinc. Tomb paintings made in the Nile Valley nearly 5000 years ago show craftsmen weighing fine metals, smelting mineral ores and carving emeralds into gems.

Rocks are made up of minerals, and minerals themselves are composed of one or more of the 90-odd natural elements in the Earth's crust. While a few elements, such as gold, are found in the pure state, the majority occur in chemical combination with other elements. Thus, oxides are produced when metals combine with oxygen, and sulfides when metals combine

GALENA

Sulfide and chief ore of lead. Lead is used in storage batteries, cable coverings, pigments, ammunition, solder and as a safety shield with radioactive material. *Broken Hill, Australia*

FLUORSPAR

Calcium fluoride. Ornamental stone in Victorian days. Used in steel, ceramic and aluminum industries. *Illinois*

URANIUM MINERALS

Atomic-energy developments are based on uranium. Uranium does not occur in the free state, but is present in over 100 minerals.

SPHALERITE

Sulfide and chief ore of zinc. Zinc is used in castings, galvanizing iron, in brasses, paints, ceramics, rubber, cosmetics. *Sullivan Mine, British Columbia*

ASBESTOS

A group of fire-resisting fibrous minerals, most of which can be spun into fabrics. *Quebec, Canada*

PITCHBLENDE

Uranium oxides with other components. A variety of uraninite, the most important ore. *Shinkolobwe, Katanga, Congo*

TORBERNITE

Hydrated copper-uranium phosphate. Green plates resemble a mica. *Cornwall, England*

CASSITERITE

Oxide and chief ore of tin. Alloyed with copper, it was the basis of Bronze Age implements. Used in tin plating, solders, bronzes, pewter and silk stockings. *Malaya*

TOPAZ

Silicate of fluorine and aluminum. Used as gemstone and in refractories. *Ouro Preto, Brazil*

OLIVINE

Magnesium-iron silicate. A common rock-forming mineral. Peridot is the gem variety. *Zebirget, Egypt*

ALUMINA MINERALS

The most abundant metal, aluminum, does not occur in the free state, and commercial production did not start until the present century. Alloys are used in automobiles and airplanes, aluminum in electric transmission lines. Ruby and sapphire are gem varieties of corundum, a natural aluminum oxide.

CORUNDUM

Hardness only exceeded by diamond. Used as an abrasive in grinding-wheels. *Transvaal, South Africa*

SAPPHIRE

Corundum gemstones of whatever color are sapphires with the exception of red (ruby). *Ceylon*

RUBY

"Pigeon-blood" red variety. Large rubies are among the most precious of stones. *Mogok, Burma*

BAUXITE

A rock rich in aluminum oxides. Ore of aluminum. Used in making abrasives, refractories, chemicals, high-alumina cement. *Jamaica*

CINNABAR

Sulfide and chief ore of mercury (quicksilver). Used in scientific instruments, detonators, the metal, chemical and electrical industries. *Almaden, Spain*

COPPER MINERALS

Copper was probably the first metal used by man. Used extensively in the electrical industry, also in bronzes, brasses and other alloys. At least 240 minerals are known to contain copper.

IRON MINERALS

Iron is industry's indispensable metal. Although iron minerals occur abundantly, pure iron is too soft for use, so man learned to harden it by adding carbon. Thus the Iron Age followed the Bronze Age. A moderate amount of carbon produces steel, an excess produces cast iron.

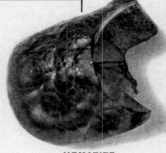

AZURITE

Hydrated copper carbonate. *Katanga, Congo*

CHALCOPYRITE

Copper-iron sulfide. Crystals of chalcopyrite and quartz are shown. Most widespread and important ore of copper. *Northern Rhodesia*

MALACHITE

Hydrated copper carbonate. An ornamental stone as well as a valuable ore. *Katanga, Congo*

MAGNETITE

Magnetic iron oxide. Crystals show octahedral form. Lodestone (leading stone), a variety with magnetic polarity, was used in primitive compasses. *Kiruna, Sweden*

HEMATITE

Oxide of iron. The "kidney-ore" variety is shown. *Minnesota*

Sullivan Mine, *British Columbia* Sphalerite
Minnesota: *Hematite* Quebec, *Asbestos*
U.S.A., *Garnet* Sudbury, Ontario, *Pentlandite*
Illinois, *Fluorspar*
W. Virginia, *Coal*
Texas, *Sulfur*

United
Coal, *Kaolin*

Almaden

Mexico, *Silver*

Jamaica, *Bauxite*

Colombia, *Emerald*

Equator

Brazil, *Quartz*

Minas Gerais, *Aquamarine*
Ouro Preto, *Topaz*

Oil

TREASURES

EARTH'S CRUST

with sulfur. Minerals are formed in various ways—for example, by crystallization from molten lava, just as ice crystals form when water freezes, and by crystallization from vapors, as in the formation of sulfur crystals by the cooling of sulfur-bearing gases around active volcanoes.

Some 2000 minerals have been recorded so far. At depths below those of the present deepest mine, we may one day find new minerals that are stable at the high pressures and temperatures nearer the center of the Earth. And the advent of space travel opens up the possibility of the discovery of unknown minerals on other planets.

This small selection of the Earth's minerals shows the variety of their natural forms and colors. Commercially important deposits are indicated on the map.

APATITE
Calcium phosphate. A massive form is the chief constituent of phosphate rock. Used in manufacture of fertilizers.
Kola Peninsula, Russia

PENTLANDITE
Nickel-iron sulfide. Used extensively in steels and alloys, nickel is alloyed with copper to make the United States "nickel" and Britain's "silver" coins.
Sudbury, Ontario

BERYLLIUM MINERALS
Beryllium is unusually light and has valuable metallurgical properties. Used in alloys with copper and nickel, also in X-ray tubes. Beryllium-mineral deposits are rare. Beryl is the most common; aquamarine and emerald are varieties with similar composition.

KAOLIN (CHINA CLAY)
Hydrated aluminum silicate. Used in paper, pottery, rubber, textiles and insecticides.
Cornwall, England

ZIRCON
Zirconium silicate. Besides being a gemstone, zircon provides the zirconium oxide used in refractories and ceramics. Zirconium metal is used in steel alloys and radio tubes.

BERYL
Can occur in very large crystals up to 25 tons in weight. *Mozambique*

EMERALD
Grass-green, unflawed stones exceeding six carats command high prices. Ranks with diamond and ruby as the most precious stone. *Colombia*

AQUAMARINE
Sea-green variety.
Minas Gerais, Brazil

CARBON MINERALS
Native carbon occurs as two important minerals, diamond and graphite. Coals consist largely of noncrystalline carbon. Combination with oxygen and hydrogen produces the natural hydrocarbons which constitute petroleums and bitumens.

DIAMOND
Hardest known mineral. Crystallized deep down at high temperature and pressure. Photograph shows a crystal in kimberlite. Most diamonds are used in industry, for cutting or abrasive purposes. *Kimberley, South Africa*

COAL
Bituminous coal showing banded structure.
United Kingdom

GRAPHITE
One of the softest minerals. The "lead" in lead pencils. Used in refractory crucibles, electrical equipment, lubricants, pigments and in atomic piles.
Korea

SILVER
Specimen carries some milky-white quartz. Used as alloy with copper in coinage, plate and jewelry. Used in the electrical, photographic and chemical industries and in brazing solders.
Mexico

SULFUR (BRIMSTONE)
Essential to modern industry, used in manufacture of sulfuric acid, paper, insecticides and vulcanizing rubber goods. *Texas*

GOLD
Man used gold for decoration from early times. Pure gold is too soft for use, and is hardened by alloying with copper, silver, palladium or nickel.
The Rand, South Africa

PLATINUM
Natural platinum usually contains variable amounts of the other platinum-group metals—palladium, iridium, osmium, rhodium and ruthenium. Hardened with iridium or ruthenium, it is used in jewelry and laboratory equipment, the electrical industry, dentistry, several important industrial processes.
Urals

SILICA MINERALS
Silicon does not occur in the free state, but its components are abundant. The oxide, quartz, and the great group of silicates are the most important rock-forming minerals. Opal is a hydrated noncrystalline form of silica; chalcedony, a cryptocrystalline variety of quartz, mixed with opal and other constituents; flint, a variety of chalcedonic silica; white onyx, chrysoprase, carnelian and agate are precious varieties.

GARNET
Photograph shows crystal in a metamorphic rock. Garnet is the name of a group of silicates, and is used as a gemstone. The iron-aluminum garnet, almandine, is used as an abrasive.
Connecticut

OPAL
A beautiful mineral showing a variegated play of colors or "fire."
New South Wales, Australia

QUARTZ
One of the commonest minerals. High-grade rock crystal is used for electrical and optical purposes. *Brazil*

VARIETIES OF CHALCEDONY

SALT
Sodium chloride. Man requires 12 pounds of salt a year. Apart from its use in food seasoning and preserving, salt is used predominantly by the chemical industry. *Cheshire, England*

ONYX
An agate with regular bands in sharply contrasted colors.

CHRYSOPRASE
Apple-green variety colored by nickel oxide.

CARNELIAN
Reddish or yellowish-red variety.

AGATE
Grayish variety in which irregular bands conform to shape of original cavity. Easily stained and used for umbrella handles, brooches, etc., also in laboratory equipment.

Kola Peninsula, *Apatite*
Kiruna, *Magnetite*
...gdom
...lt, *Torbernite*
...nabar
Urals, *Platinum*
Zebirget, *Olivine*
Korea, *Graphite*
Mogok, *Ruby*
Ceylon, *Sapphire*
Malaya, *Cassiterite*
Katanga,
...itchblende, *Azurite, Malachite*
Northern Rhodesia, *Chalcopyrite*
Mozambique, *Beryl*
Transvaal, *Corundum*
Kimberley, *Diamond*
The Rand, *Gold*
Broken Hill, *Galena*
New South Wales, *Zircon, Opal*

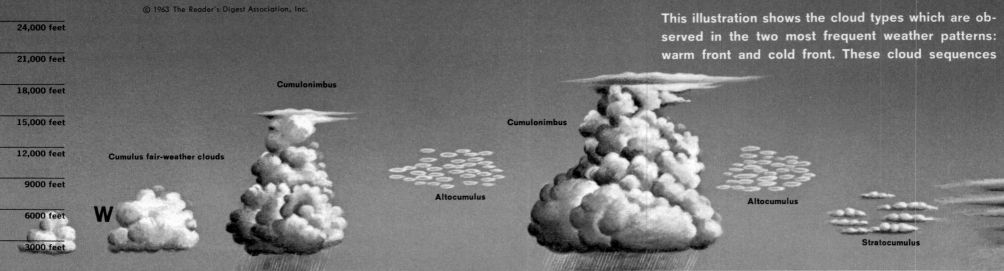

© 1963 The Reader's Digest Association, Inc.

This illustration shows the cloud types which are observed in the two most frequent weather patterns: warm front and cold front. These cloud sequences

24,000 feet	
21,000 feet	
18,000 feet	Cumulonimbus
15,000 feet	
12,000 feet	Cumulus fair-weather clouds
9000 feet	
6000 feet	W
3000 feet	

Cumulonimbus
Altocumulus
Cumulonimbus
Altocumulus
Stratocumulus

THUNDERSTORMS,   INTERMITTENT RAIN SQUALLS   ADVANCING COLD FRONT   WARM AIR MASS

PRESSURE ZONES (January)

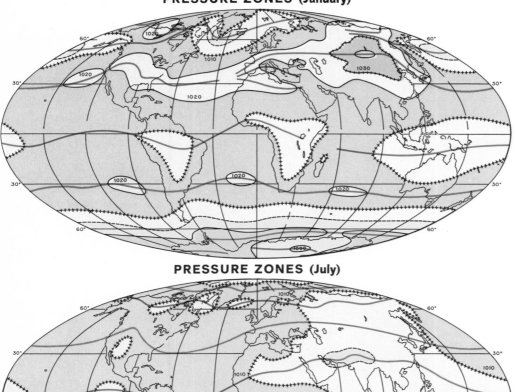

PRESSURE ZONES (July)

© 1963 The Reader's Digest Association, Inc.

Average U.S. pressure at sea level: 1015 millibars
(29.9 inches of barometric pressure)
Yellow and green areas: high-pressure areas

Shades of pink: low-pressure areas
Red lines: join minimum-pressure points of longitude
Blue lines: join maximum-pressure points of longitude

© 1963 The Reader's Digest Association, Inc.

Canadian Blizzards
Ice-Cap Blizzards
Chinook Winds
Helm Winds
Norther Winds
Mistral Winds
Levanter Winds
Sirocco Winds
Norte Winds
Harmattan Winds
Pampero Winds
Polar Winds

CHART OF TROPICAL CYC

Many local atmospheric phenomena exist which are brought about by particular local conditions. In the low latitudes where there are high temperatures and great humidity, whirling movements are produced which create violent storms known as tropical cyclones (see circled areas). Then there are the hot dry winds that descend from mountains — the Chinook in the Rockies, the Foehn in Switzerland, the Berg Winds in Africa. In contrast are the cold mountain winds — in Europe the Helms,

HOW HOT IS IT?

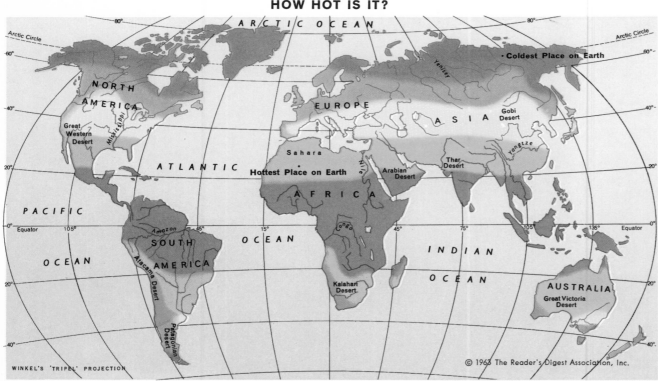

WINKEL'S 'TRIPEL' PROJECTION

© 1963 The Reader's Digest Association, Inc.

■	ALWAYS COLD
■	WARM SUMMER, COLD WINTER
■	HOT SUMMER, COLD WINTER
■	ALWAYS WARM
■	HOT SUMMER, WARM WINTER
■	ALWAYS HOT

Almost all of our heat comes from the Sun. Therefore the more vertical the Sun's position, the more heat we receive. Air is warmed chiefly by contact with the Earth's surface. The sea both warms and parts with its heat more slowly, so that climates near oceans are more equable than those inland. The highest tempera-

tures have been recorded in the Sahara, the lowest in Siberia and the Antarctic.
The heat of the Tropics is somewhat distributed by ocean currents and winds. Thanks to the Gulf Stream and prevailing southeasterly winds, the average temperature of the British Isles is 50°F.; Labrador, in the same latitude, averages 32°F.

PATTERNS

THE CLIMATES OF THE WORLD vary mostly according to latitude. Within the Tropics the climate remains fairly stable, but elsewhere climates are seasonal because of the twice-yearly swing of the Sun across the Equator.

From the strength of the winds, we know that the atmosphere has weight; where the atmosphere has piled up, it tends to flow outward on the surface of the Earth, just as water would do, and so becomes a wind. The principal pressure zones on the Earth (see *Pressure Zones* maps) are responsible for a continuous flow of air toward the Equator and toward the Poles, but these flows are not due south or due north, because of the rotation of the Earth. This eastward rotation deflects winds toward the right in the Northern Hemisphere and toward the left south of the Equator. As a result, the Trade Winds in the Northern Hemisphere blow from the northeast and the southern Trades from the southeast (see *Dominant Winds* maps). In higher latitudes, however, the winds flow from the west and are known as the Prevailing Westerlies.

The flow of winds is also influenced by the distribution of lands and seas, for in summer temperatures are higher and

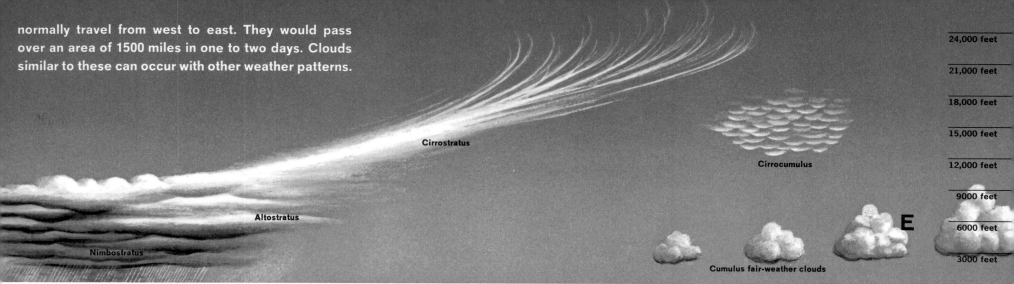

normally travel from west to east. They would pass over an area of 1500 miles in one to two days. Clouds similar to these can occur with other weather patterns.

Cirrostratus

Cirrocumulus

Altostratus

Nimbostratus

Cumulus fair-weather clouds

24,000 feet
21,000 feet
18,000 feet
15,000 feet
12,000 feet
9000 feet
6000 feet
3000 feet

PROLONGED WARM-FRONT RAIN   ADVANCING WARM FRONT   COLD AIR MASS

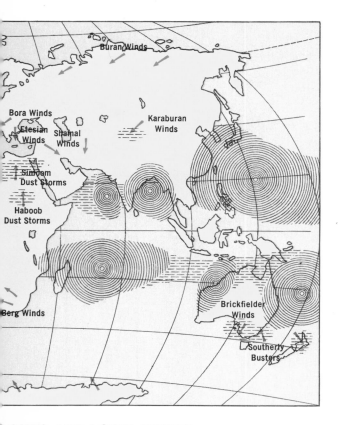

LONES AND LOCAL WINDS

Bora, Mistral, Etesians and Levanters; in Asia the Buran and Karaburan; in the Middle East the Shamal; in South America the Pampero; and in Australia the Southerly Busters. Other cold winds are the American Nortes and Northers. Local winds with snow include blizzards and Polar winds; hot winds originating in desert areas include the African Harmattan, Simoom, Haboob and Sirocco (the latter blowing from North Africa across to Italy) and the Australian Brickfielders.

DOMINANT WINDS (January)

DOMINANT WINDS (July)

© 1963 The Reader's Digest Association, Inc.

→ Northeast and Southeast Trade Winds
→ Monsoons (dry in January, wet in July)
→ Prevailing Westerlies
→ Other major winds
━━ Predominant path of Jet Streams
━━ Boundaries of Trade Winds

OF CLIMATE

pressures are lower on land, and the reverse is true in winter. In summer the air above the land tends to rise, and surface winds flow in to take its place. This can be seen on a large scale in the Asiatic Monsoons: a wet Monsoon blows in from sea toward land in summer, and a dry Monsoon blows from land toward sea in winter (see *Dominant Winds* maps).

Although winds are almost horizontal, the air also tends to rise and fall. As air rises, its humidity is condensed, leading to the formation of clouds and, finally, to rain and snow. On the other hand, when the wind is directed downward, the descending air heats and cannot produce either clouds or rain, as in the desert regions near the Tropics and in the Polar regions (see *How Wet Is It?* map). In the temperate zones these descending movements have the additional effect of bringing masses of air coming from the north into contact with masses from the south, the characteristics of which are very different. At 30,000 to 40,000 feet, an altitude where the relative differences of pressure are greater, the winds resulting from this contact are greater. They are called Jet Streams and may reach speeds of 300 miles an hour (see *Dominant Winds* maps).

HOW WET IS IT?

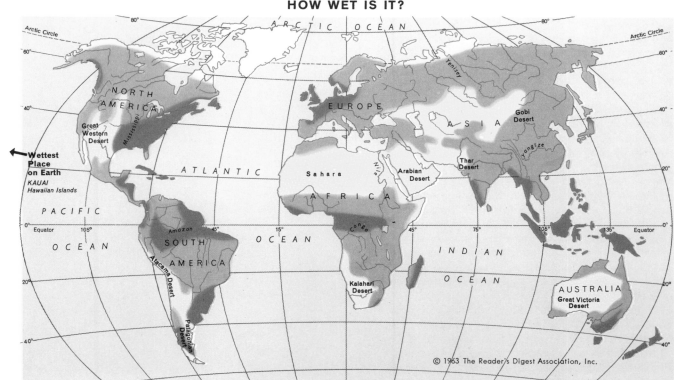

© 1963 The Reader's Digest Association, Inc.

LIGHT SNOW
SELDOM RAINY
LIGHT SEASONAL RAIN
HEAVY SEASONAL RAIN
RAINFALL IN EVERY MONTH

Air is most likely to be moist over the sea and where temperatures are high. The wettest places are in the Tropics, where moist sea air rises on the windward slopes of high mountains. Rainfall belts move northward and southward with the Sun, so that some places, such as the Mediterranean, have most of their rain in winter,

while others, such as the Monsoon areas, have more in summer.

The driest areas on Earth are where winds have blown for long distances over heated land, or, more locally, where a range of mountains extracts all the rain on its windward side, leaving what is called a rain shadow on its leeward side.

FRONTIERS OF VEGETATION

ABOUT ONE TENTH of the world's land surface is now under cultivation, little more than one acre per person. The rest, except for areas where nothing grows—such as the permanent ice fields—presents a vast pattern of grassland, woodland, forest and other types of natural vegetation.

This worldwide pattern of vegetation is closely keyed to another pattern—that of climate. Where similar plant cover grows, regardless of continent or hemisphere, a similar climate is usually found.

The world's heaviest and most vigorous growth of natural vegetation is in the rain forests of the tropics. Here thousands of species of trees and other plants flourish in wild, colorful profusion. As there is little seasonal change in this hot moist region, each plant has its own individual time schedule, so that there is continuous shedding of leaves, budding, flowering and fruit bearing.

In contrast are the trees of the seasonal forest (Nos. 3, 4, 5, 6, 13 and 14 on map) which extends from the tropics to the temperate and polar zones, both north and south. These provide the major supply of the world's soft timber—spruce, pine, fir. Trees of the seasonal forest become dormant during part of each year and, in the case of the deciduous species, lose all their leaves in one season.

Twenty percent of our world's land surface is covered by the dry lands we call deserts. Few of them are actually rainless, although some have to wait a year or so between showers. Despite popular belief, a desert is not an endless stretch of sand completely devoid of vegetation. Shrubs and grasses are part of the desert scene, and there are large areas of oasis, some covering hundreds of square miles, where land is extremely fertile.

A region frequently referred to as the cold desert lies far to the north (but not in the Antarctic). This is the tundra, which covers a great strip across Alaska, northern Canada and northern Eurasia. With long cold winters and short cool summers, the climate of the tundra is much too harsh for trees. The natural vegetation is a ground covering of grass, lichens and—sometimes—stunted brush. Similar conditions are found above the tree line in mountain ranges. The limitations that high latitude and high altitude place on vegetation are much alike. In the Rockies of the United States, trees do not grow above 11,000 feet; in Canada few trees grow above the latitude of the Arctic Circle.

Great grasslands stretch across the inland basins of the temperate lands—in the United States and Canada, Australia, Argentina, South Africa and the Soviet Union (Nos. 8 and 9 on map). These have long provided for generations of grazing animals, from buffalo and wild cattle to domesticated cattle and sheep.

Primitive man first demonstrated intelligence by taking direct advantage of the natural vegetation around him, as well as the wildlife it supported. He made use of leaves and wood for fire, and of reeds and saplings to build shelters. He satisfied his appetite first by collecting fruits and nuts, then learned to cultivate wild rice, yams, sugar cane and grains. He tapped trees for their juices and used barks and herbs to treat his ills. The seasonal changes of vegetation and the consequent movements of animal herds caused migrations of hunting tribes. In earliest historic times, areas of rich natural vegetation gave rise to industries such as lumbering and shipbuilding and to the founding of cities such as Tyre.

Man has misused the bounty of Earth's vegetation, too. In prehistoric time great sections of woodland and forest were laid waste by fire. Many of these areas were replaced by grasslands, changing the original pattern of the Earth's vegetation. Little of the "natural" vegetation of the world was left unchanged by primitive man.

Through ignorance and neglect, the land has been scarred and mutilated. Poor farming, including the removal of all trees in large areas, destroyed the natural structure of the soil, reducing it to dust, as in the great Dust Bowl, or creating new man-made deserts. Too often the soil has been washed off unprotected slopes by rain, leaving behind bare unproductive subsoil.

In the areas of yearly crops the maintenance of soil fertility is of the first importance. In North America and parts of South America, Europe, the U.S.S.R., South Africa and Australia, cultivation with machinery is pursued on a grand commercial scale. But in South and East Asia, where good land is scarce and precious and the crops must support some of the densest rural populations in the world, much of the work is done with simple hand tools.

Subsistence farming with crude tools and rudimentary techniques still predominates in many countries of Asia, Africa and Central America. Food is raised largely for home consumption, though some crops, such as cacao, oil palm and peanuts, are grown for sale in local markets.

Areas of shifting cultivation are found near and among the tropical rain forests. Here land is generally cleared indiscriminately for individual needs and, after being wastefully denuded of its fertility by primitive farming methods, is abandoned. Where land in tropical rain forests is successfully cleared and maintained, it is fertile and suitable for such plantation crops as rubber, tobacco, sugar, tea, oil palm and cacao.

Patterns of cultivation vary from country to country according to economic and social development. In the highly developed countries a relatively small number of workers can provide the entire community with enough of the right kinds of food. In the United States, 5,700,000 people (8 percent of the working population) are employed in cul-

© John Bartholomew & Son Ltd.

tivation. In India 95,000,000 people (almost 70 percent of the working population) engage in producing barely enough food for the population of that country.

Scientific and improved technical methods have been constantly applied throughout the world to improve the quality and yield of crops. Irrigation and water conservation in the American west have transformed land once infertile and semi-arid. Cotton is now grown extensively in the irrigated areas of southern California and other parts of the southwest. Forest conservation and reforestation are practiced in many lands, and silviculture, a new type of forest industry in which trees are grown on a crop basis, is vigorously pursued.

By such methods man is not only working to protect natural vegetation and rebuild depleted areas; he is also extending the frontiers of all cultivation. Because of the growing acceptance of scientific agriculture, the raising of food will probably prove no serious problem even in the face of the dramatic population explosion.

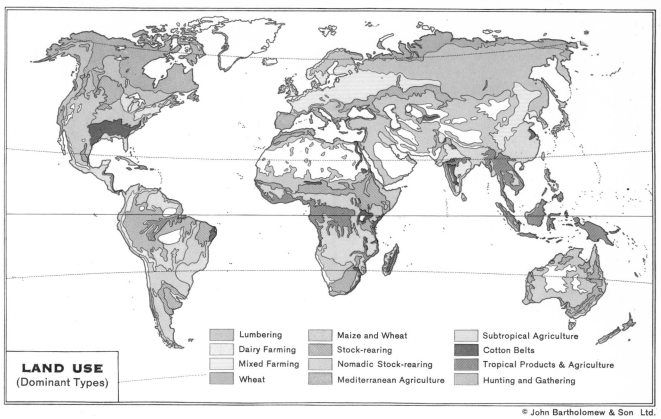

LAND USE
(Dominant Types)

Lumbering	Maize and Wheat	Subtropical Agriculture
Dairy Farming	Stock-rearing	Cotton Belts
Mixed Farming	Nomadic Stock-rearing	Tropical Products & Agriculture
Wheat	Mediterranean Agriculture	Hunting and Gathering

© John Bartholomew & Son Ltd.

TYPES OF NATURAL VEGETATION

1 Mountain Vegetation	**6** Broadleaf Forest *(Deciduous)*	**11** Tropical Rain Forest
2 Tundra *(Moss and Lichen)*	**7** Mediterranean Scrub *(Citrus, Olive, Agave, etc.)*	**12** Monsoon Forest *(Moist Deciduous)*
3 Northern Forest *("Taiga"—Spruce, Larch)*	**8** Prairie *(Long Grass)*	**13** Dry Tropical Forest *(Semi-Deciduous)*
4 Conifer Forest *(Pine)*	**9** Steppe *(Short Grass)*	**14** Subtropical Forest *(Broadleaf Evergreen)*
5 Mixed Forest (Mid-Latitudes) *(Broadleaf and Conifer)*	**10** Savanna *(Grass and Scrub)*	**15** Dry Tropical Scrub & Thorn Forest

16 Desert Vegetation *(Drought-resistant plants)*

(?) Natural Type uncertain

Sand
Stone } Desert *(No Vegetation)*
Salt

— — Mangroves

Swamps

SOUTHERN LIMIT OF PALMS

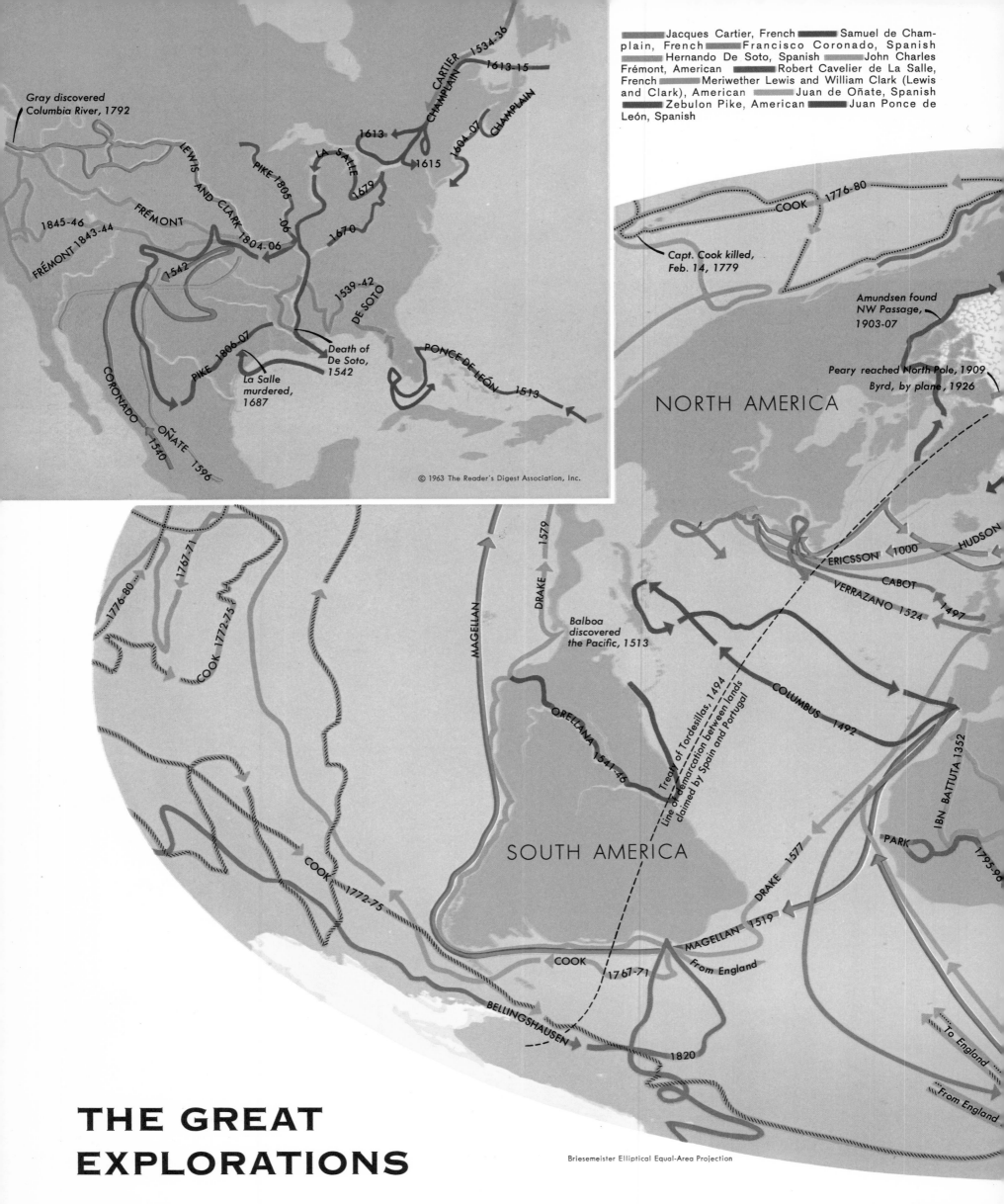

Gray discovered
Columbia River, 1792

LEWIS AND CLARK

PIKE 1805

FRÉMONT

1845-46

FRÉMONT 1843-44

-06

1804-06

1542

PIKE 1806-07

CORONADO 1540

OÑATE 1596

CARTIER 1534-36

CHAMPLAIN

1613-15

1613

1604-07 CHAMPLAIN

LA SALLE

1679

1615

1670

1539-42

DE SOTO

Death of
De Soto,
1542

La Salle
murdered,
1687

PONCE DE LEÓN

PONCE DE LEÓN 1513

© 1963 The Reader's Digest Association, Inc.

COOK 1776-80

Capt. Cook killed,
Feb. 14, 1779

Amundsen found
NW Passage,
1903-07

Peary reached North Pole, 1909
Byrd, by plane, 1926

NORTH AMERICA

Jacques Cartier, French   Samuel de Champlain, French   Francisco Coronado, Spanish   Hernando De Soto, Spanish   John Charles Frémont, American   Robert Cavelier de La Salle, French   Meriwether Lewis and William Clark (Lewis and Clark), American   Juan de Oñate, Spanish   Zebulon Pike, American   Juan Ponce de León, Spanish

1767-71

1776-80

COOK 1772-75

COOK 1772-75

MAGELLAN

DRAKE 1579

Balboa
discovered
the Pacific, 1513

ORELLANA 1541-46

Treaty of Tordesillas, 1494
Line of demarcation between lands
claimed by Spain and Portugal

COLUMBUS 1492

ERICSSON 1000

HUDSON

CABOT 1497

VERRAZANO 1524

IBN BATTUTA 1352

SOUTH AMERICA

DRAKE 1577

PARK

1795-96

COOK 1767-71

MAGELLAN 1519

From England

BELLINGSHAUSEN

1820

To England

From England

THE GREAT EXPLORATIONS

Briesemeister Elliptical Equal-Area Projection

MAN'S CURIOSITY and his delight in widening his world — for adventure or gain — have throughout history drawn him to its remotest regions.

As early as 700 B.C., Phoenician traders ventured down the west coast of Africa. Alexander the Great reached India about 330 B.C.; the Greeks and Romans knew the Baltic by the time of Christ; a thousand years later Ericsson, the Norseman, was probably the first European to set foot on North America. In the thirteenth century the Italian Marco Polo, the greatest traveler of his era, made his journeys to the Far East.

But it was in the 1400s that the great Age of Discovery began. Within 30 years all the known oceans were crossed. Columbus voyaged to America in 1492, and Da Gama reached India in 1498. Early in the sixteenth century Balboa discovered the Pacific Ocean, and Magellan's ship sailed around the whole world. In succeeding years many intrepid European explorers, under the flags of many countries, laid claim to land in the Americas and explored some of the New World's mightiest rivers: the St. Lawrence, Mississippi and Amazon.

Then came the Age of Scientific Discovery, an

era not yet ended. In the quest for knowledge Captain Cook made three great voyages at the time of the American Revolution.

Exploration by land was slower. It was not till the 1800s that men such as Lewis and Clark, Pike and Frémont opened the American West. The nineteenth century also saw the penetration of Africa by explorers including Nachtigal, Stanley and the remarkable Livingstone. The long-sought Northeast and Northwest Passages through the Arctic seas were found at last — the latter by Amundsen in 1905.

In the early twentieth century the polar regions

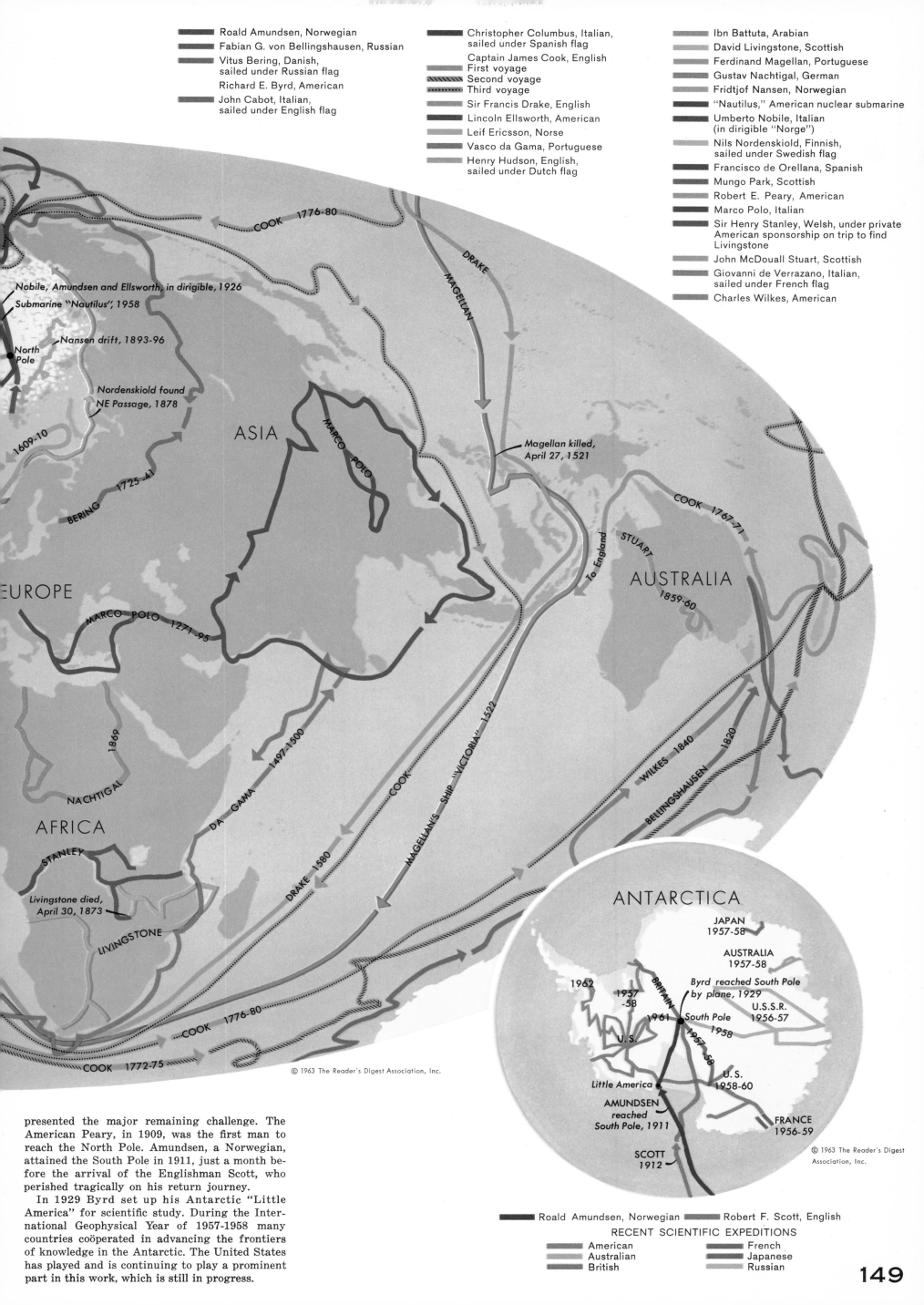

Roald Amundsen, Norwegian
Fabian G. von Bellingshausen, Russian
Vitus Bering, Danish,
sailed under Russian flag
Richard E. Byrd, American
John Cabot, Italian,
sailed under English flag

Christopher Columbus, Italian,
sailed under Spanish flag
Captain James Cook, English
First voyage
Second voyage
Third voyage
Sir Francis Drake, English
Lincoln Ellsworth, American
Leif Ericsson, Norse
Vasco da Gama, Portuguese
Henry Hudson, English,
sailed under Dutch flag

Ibn Battuta, Arabian
David Livingstone, Scottish
Ferdinand Magellan, Portuguese
Gustav Nachtigal, German
Fridtjof Nansen, Norwegian
"Nautilus," American nuclear submarine
Umberto Nobile, Italian
(in dirigible "Norge")
Nils Nordenskiold, Finnish,
sailed under Swedish flag
Francisco de Orellana, Spanish
Mungo Park, Scottish
Robert E. Peary, American
Marco Polo, Italian
Sir Henry Stanley, Welsh, under private
American sponsorship on trip to find
Livingstone
John McDouall Stuart, Scottish
Giovanni de Verrazano, Italian,
sailed under French flag
Charles Wilkes, American

Nobile, Amundsen and Ellsworth, in dirigible, 1926
Submarine "Nautilus", 1958
North Pole
Nansen drift, 1893-96
Nordenskiold found NE Passage, 1878
1609-10
COOK 1776-80
DRAKE
MAGELLAN
ASIA
MARCO POLO
BERING 1725-41
Magellan killed, April 27, 1521
EUROPE
MARCO POLO 1271-95
1869
NACHTIGAL
AFRICA
STANLEY
Livingstone died, April 30, 1873
LIVINGSTONE
DA GAMA 1497-1500
COOK
DRAKE 1580
MAGELLAN'S SHIP "VICTORIA" 1522
To England
STUART
COOK 1767-71
AUSTRALIA
1859-60
WILKES 1840
BELLINGSHAUSEN 1820
COOK 1776-80
COOK 1772-75

© 1963 The Reader's Digest Association, Inc.

ANTARCTICA
JAPAN 1957-58
AUSTRALIA 1957-58
Byrd reached South Pole by plane, 1929
1962
1957-58
BRITAIN
1961
South Pole
U.S.S.R. 1956-57
1958
U.S.
1957-58
Little America
U.S. 1958-60
AMUNDSEN reached South Pole, 1911
FRANCE 1956-59
SCOTT 1912

© 1963 The Reader's Digest Association, Inc.

presented the major remaining challenge. The American Peary, in 1909, was the first man to reach the North Pole. Amundsen, a Norwegian, attained the South Pole in 1911, just a month before the arrival of the Englishman Scott, who perished tragically on his return journey.

In 1929 Byrd set up his Antarctic "Little America" for scientific study. During the International Geophysical Year of 1957-1958 many countries coöperated in advancing the frontiers of knowledge in the Antarctic. The United States has played and is continuing to play a prominent part in this work, which is still in progress.

Roald Amundsen, Norwegian   Robert F. Scott, English
RECENT SCIENTIFIC EXPEDITIONS
American   French
Australian   Japanese
British   Russian

149

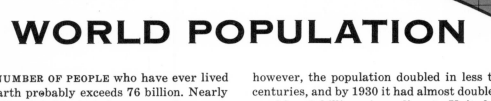

| Australasia 29 million | Africa 517 million | Central and S. America 592 million | N. America 312 million | U.S.S.R. 379 million | Europe 568 million |

2000 A.D. — 2 Billion   1 Billion

1960

1950

WORLD POPULATION

THE NUMBER OF PEOPLE who have ever lived on earth probably exceeds 76 billion. Nearly 3 billion inhabit it today, more than ever before at any one time. Throughout most of history, world population increased very slowly. Poverty, disease and disorder permitted growth from perhaps 300 million people at the beginning of the Christian era to only 550 million by 1650. Then, however, the population doubled in less than two centuries, and by 1930 it had almost doubled again, reaching 2 billion. According to United Nations forecasts, from today's figure it will grow to more than 6 billion by the year 2000. This phenomenal expansion, the result of widespread improvements in food production and increased medical knowledge, is shown on the graph at the right.

MIGRATIONS SINCE 1650 A.D.

1900

1850

© 1963 The Reader's Digest Association, Inc.

MOVEMENTS OF POPULATIONS occur mainly for political, religious and economic reasons. The more important migrations of the past 300 years are shown above. The arrows mark the areas of origin and the destinations but are not intended to indicate the routes.

Europeans to U.S.A. During the 17th century about 500,000 people emigrated from Great Britain to settle principally in New England and Virginia (although some settled in the West Indies). They were followed in the 18th century by three times that number (mainly Irish and Scots). In the 19th century Germans, Italians, Austro-Hungarians and Scandinavians helped to increase the flow. From 1900 to 1920 a total of 14,500,000 from many countries were admitted (1,042,000 in 1907 — a peak for any one year). In the next 30 years the tide slackened (only 5,500,000 were admitted), but from 1951 to 1959 the rate of immigration accelerated to reach a total of 2,250,000.

Europeans to Canada During the 18th century Quebec Province was settled by the French, but later the majority of immigrants to Canada came from Great Britain. Until 1900 settlement was slow, but from 1900 to 1920 about 2,250,000 people entered the country, to be followed by 1,500,000 in the next 30 years. Thereafter immigration greatly increased, with more than 1,500,000 people settling in Canada in the period from 1951 to 1959.

Europeans to South and Central America Spaniards, Portuguese and Italians have predominated among the nearly 20,000,000 Europeans who have migrated to Central and South America during the last three centuries, with Argentina, Brazil and Panama as their principal goals. Immigration was slow until the 1890s, but reached its peak before 1914. From 1900 to 1920 about 3,000,000 settled in Argentina, about 1,500,000 in Brazil.

The Slave Trade Traffic in slaves from West Africa began in the 16th century, reaching its peak in the late 18th and early 19th centuries. About 20,000,000 slaves were taken, chiefly to the tobacco, sugar and coffee plantations of the Caribbean and Brazil. Many, perhaps a million, were moved on to the cotton fields of the southern United States.

Europeans to Africa In the 16th century the French established trading posts in Algeria, but large-scale settlement did not begin there until French rule was established in 1830. Today about 15 percent of the population of this newly independent nation is of European ancestry. Few Europeans settled in Central Africa before 1880, when diamond deposits were discovered in Rhodesia. Since then the British (nearly 300,000) have settled in Rhodesia and the Belgians in the Congo in large numbers. In East Africa, which received settlers from 1906 on, nearly 100,000 Europeans have made permanent residence, principally in Kenya, Uganda and Tanganyika. In South Africa the first Europeans to settle were the Dutch in 1652. By the end of the 18th century emigrants from the British Isles began arriving in great numbers, and in the 19th century the establishment of British rule in Cape Colony was followed by the revolt of the Dutch farmers (Boers) and their Great Trek to the Transvaal. In this century there have been mass movements of South Africans into mining and industrial areas.

Europeans to Australia and New Zealand The first Europeans settled in Australia in 1788, but immigration was slow until the Gold Rush period between 1850 and 1860. After 1860 it slowed down again until the turn of the century. Between 1901 and 1920 about 400,000 emigrated to Australia, principally from the United Kingdom, but since 1945 more than a million people from many European countries have settled in Australia. Emigration to New Zealand has followed much the same pattern but on a smaller scale.

Chinese Migration From the middle of the 19th century onward the Chinese migrated in large numbers, chiefly to Malaya, Burma and the East Indies. In the 1920s there were mass movements to Mongolia, Manchuria and Asiatic Russia. More than 9,500,000 were abroad in 1948, mostly in Asia; more than 100,000 were in the United States.

Jewish Migration Intermittent migrations of Jews from many countries into Palestine took place after the First World War, but since the formation of the State of Israel in 1948 almost a million European Jews have been admitted.

Internal Migration in the U.S.A. From the end of the 18th century, when pioneers started the movement westward, migration to the west has continued, as well as movement on the Atlantic seaboard to the south. California is now the nation's most populous state. The population of Florida has increased by more than 75 percent. Many Negroes have moved northward from the southern states, and Puerto Ricans have come to the continental U.S. to settle in cities in the eastern states.

Internal Migration in the U.S.S.R. Since 1918 great movements of European Russians to the east of the Urals have taken place. The Second World War accelerated industrial growth beyond the Urals, and a feature of the recent Five Year Plans has been the movement to and the settling of people in Kazakhstan and farther east.

1800

1750

1700

150

1650 A.D.

© 1963 The Reader's Digest Association, Inc.

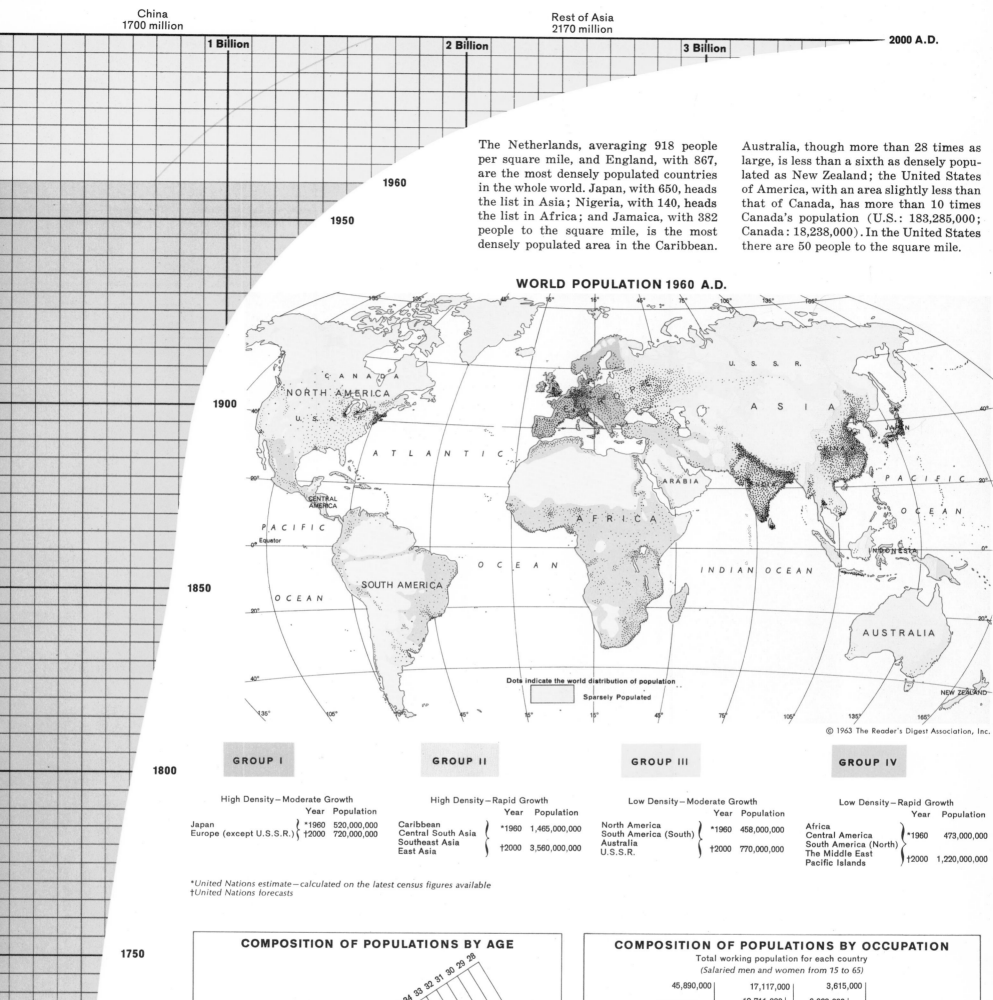

China
1700 million

Rest of Asia
2170 million

1 Billion   2 Billion   3 Billion   2000 A.D.

1960
1950
1900
1850
1800
1750
1700

The Netherlands, averaging 918 people per square mile, and England, with 867, are the most densely populated countries in the whole world. Japan, with 650, heads the list in Asia; Nigeria, with 140, heads the list in Africa; and Jamaica, with 382 people to the square mile, is the most densely populated area in the Caribbean.

Australia, though more than 28 times as large, is less than a sixth as densely populated as New Zealand; the United States of America, with an area slightly less than that of Canada, has more than 10 times Canada's population (U.S.: 183,285,000; Canada: 18,238,000). In the United States there are 50 people to the square mile.

WORLD POPULATION 1960 A.D.

Dots indicate the world distribution of population

Sparsely Populated

© 1963 The Reader's Digest Association, Inc.

GROUP I	GROUP II	GROUP III	GROUP IV
High Density—Moderate Growth	High Density—Rapid Growth	Low Density—Moderate Growth	Low Density—Rapid Growth

GROUP I — High Density—Moderate Growth

	Year	Population
Japan	*1960	520,000,000
Europe (except U.S.S.R.)	†2000	720,000,000

GROUP II — High Density—Rapid Growth

	Year	Population
Caribbean, Central South Asia, Southeast Asia, East Asia	*1960	1,465,000,000
	†2000	3,560,000,000

GROUP III — Low Density—Moderate Growth

	Year	Population
North America, South America (South), Australia, U.S.S.R.	*1960	458,000,000
	†2000	770,000,000

GROUP IV — Low Density—Rapid Growth

	Year	Population
Africa, Central America, South America (North), The Middle East, Pacific Islands	*1960	473,000,000
	†2000	1,220,000,000

*United Nations estimate—calculated on the latest census figures available
†United Nations forecasts

COMPOSITION OF POPULATIONS BY AGE

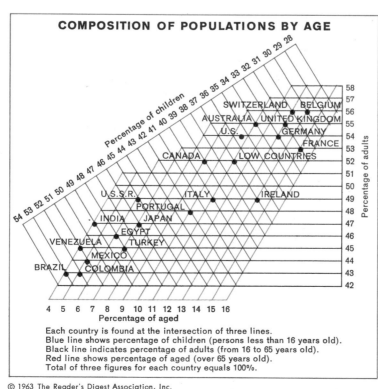

Percentage of children
28 29 30 31 32 33 34 35 36 37 38 39 40 41 42 43 44 45 46 47 48 49 50 51 52 53 54

Percentage of adults
42 43 44 45 46 47 48 49 50 51 52 53 54 55 56 57 58

SWITZERLAND BELGIUM
AUSTRALIA UNITED KINGDOM
U.S. GERMANY
FRANCE
CANADA LOW COUNTRIES
U.S.S.R. ITALY IRELAND
PORTUGAL
INDIA JAPAN
VENEZUELA EGYPT
TURKEY
MEXICO
BRAZIL COLOMBIA

Percentage of aged
4 5 6 7 8 9 10 11 12 13 14 15 16

Each country is found at the intersection of three lines.
Blue line shows percentage of children (persons less than 16 years old).
Black line indicates percentage of adults (from 16 to 65 years old).
Red line shows percentage of aged (over 65 years old).
Total of three figures for each country equals 100%.

© 1963 The Reader's Digest Association, Inc.

COMPOSITION OF POPULATIONS BY OCCUPATION

Total working population for each country
(Salaried men and women from 15 to 65)

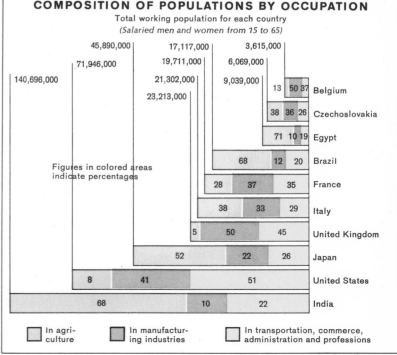

Country	In agriculture	In manufacturing industries	In transportation, commerce, administration and professions	Total
Belgium	13	50	37	3,615,000
Czechoslovakia	38	36	26	6,069,000
Egypt	71	10	19	9,039,000
Brazil	68	12	20	17,117,000
France	28	37	35	19,711,000
Italy	38	33	29	21,302,000
United Kingdom	5	50	45	23,213,000
Japan	52	22	26	45,890,000
United States	8	41	51	71,946,000
India	68	10	22	140,696,000

Figures in colored areas indicate percentages

☐ In agriculture   ☐ In manufacturing industries   ☐ In transportation, commerce, administration and professions

© 1963 The Reader's Digest Association, Inc.

1650 A.D.

FACTS ABOUT THE EARTH

Estimated age . . . at least 4,500,000,000 years
Area . . . . 196,950,769 sq. miles
Land surface . . . . . 57,469,928 sq. miles
Water surface (71% of
   total area) . . . . . . 139,480,841 sq. miles

Equatorial circumference . . . . . 24,902 miles
Polar circumference . . . . . . 24,860 miles
Volume of the Earth . 260,000,000,000 cubic miles
Mass or weight 5,887,613,230,000,000,000,000 tons
Highest point—Mount Everest . . . 29,028 feet

Lowest point—Shores of the Dead Sea,
   Israel . . . . . . 1286 feet below sea level
Greatest ocean depth—
   Marianas Trench off the
   Philippines . . . . 36,198 feet below sea level

CONTINENTS

	Area (square miles)	Mean Elevation (feet)	Highest Elevation (feet)	Lowest Elevation (feet)	Highest Recorded Temperature	Lowest Recorded Temperature
AFRICA	11,699,000	1900	Mt. Kilimanjaro, Tanganyika 19,340	Qattara Depression, Egypt 436 below sea level	el Azizia, Libya 136.4°F.	Semrir, Morocco − 11.4°F.
ANTARCTICA	5,100,000	6000	Vinson Massif 16,863	Sea level	Esperanza, Palmer Peninsula 58.3°F.	Vostok − 126.9°F.
ASIA	18,685,000	3000	Mt. Everest, Nepal—Tibet 29,028	Dead Sea, Israel 1286 below sea level	Jacobabad, Pakistan 127.1°F.	Oymyakon, U.S.S.R. − 89.9°F.
AUSTRALIA	3,201,000	1000	Mt. Kosciusko, N.S. Wales 7316	Lake Eyre, South Australia 39 below sea level	Cloncurry, Queensland 127.5°F.	Charlotte Pass, N.S. Wales − 8°F.
EUROPE	2,085,000	980	Mt. El'brus, U.S.S.R. 18,482	Caspian Sea, U.S.S.R. 92 below sea level	Seville, Spain 122°F.	Ust' Shchugor, U.S.S.R. − 67.0°F.
NORTH AMERICA	9,420,000	2000	Mt. McKinley, Alaska 20,320	Death Valley, California 282 below sea level	Death Valley, California 137°F.	Snag, Yukon − 81.0°F.
SOUTH AMERICA	6,860,000	1800	Mt. Aconcagua, Argentina 23,035	Salinas Grandes, Argentina 131 below sea level	Rivadavia, Argentina 120.0°F.	Colonia Sarmiento, Argentina − 27.4°F.

HIGHEST MOUNTAINS OF THE WORLD

	Feet
AFRICA	
Kilimanjaro, *Tanganyika*	19,340
Kenya, *Kenya*	17,058
Margherita, *Congo–Uganda*	16,795
Ruwenzori, *Congo–Uganda*	16,794
Rasdajan, *Ethiopia*	15,158
ANTARCTICA	
Vinson Massif	16,863
Elizabeth	14,698
Kirkpatrick	14,600
Markham	14,270
Andrew Jackson	13,747

	Feet
ASIA	
Everest, *Nepal–Tibet*	29,028
Godwin Austen (K2), *Kashmir*	28,250
Kanchenjunga, *Nepal–India*	28,146
Makalu, *Tibet–Nepal*	27,827
Dhaulagiri, *Nepal*	26,795
EUROPE	
El'brus, *U.S.S.R.*	18,482
Shkhara, *U.S.S.R.*	17,059
Dykh-Tau, *U.S.S.R.*	17,054
Kashtan-Tau, *U.S.S.R.*	16,877

	Feet
Dzhangi Tau, *U.S.S.R.*	16,565
Kazbek, *U.S.S.R.*	16,554
Mont Blanc, *France*	15,771
Monte Rosa, *Switzerland*	15,203
Dom, *Switzerland*	14,912
Weisshorn, *Switzerland*	14,781
NORTH AMERICA	
McKinley, *Alaska, U.S.*	20,320
Logan, *Canada*	19,850
Citlaltepetl, *Mexico*	18,700
St. Elias, *Alaska, U.S.*	18,008
Popocatepetl, *Mexico*	17,887

	Feet
Foraker, *Alaska, U.S.*	17,400
Ixtaccihuatl, *Mexico*	17,343
Lucania, *Canada*	17,150
King, *Canada*	17,130
Blackburn, *Alaska, U.S.*	16,523
SOUTH AMERICA	
Aconcagua, *Argentina*	23,035
Ancohuma, *Bolivia*	23,012
Bonete, *Argentina*	22,546
Ojos del Salado, *Argentina*	22,539
Tupungato, *Argentina–Chile*	22,310

GREATEST OCEANS AND SEAS OF THE WORLD

	Area (sq. miles)	Average Depth (feet)	Greatest Depth (feet)
Pacific Ocean	63,985,000	14,040	36,198
Atlantic Ocean	31,529,000	12,880	30,180
Indian Ocean	28,357,000	13,000	24,444
Arctic Ocean	5,541,600	4200	17,500
Mediterranean Sea	1,145,000	4500	15,564
South China Sea	895,000	5400	16,456

	Area (sq. miles)	Average Depth (feet)	Greatest Depth (feet)
Bering Sea	878,000	1665	13,420
Caribbean Sea	750,000	8400	23,750
Gulf of Mexico	700,000	4700	12,426
Okhotsk, Sea of	582,000	3000	12,621
East China Sea	480,000	610	8920
Yellow Sea	480,000	160	348

	Area (sq. miles)	Average Depth (feet)	Greatest Depth (feet)
Hudson Bay	472,000	440	846
Japan, Sea of	405,000	4835	13,241
North Sea	221,000	180	2165
Red Sea	178,000	1490	9301
Black Sea	168,000	4300	7362
Baltic Sea	158,000	221	1400

LONGEST RIVERS OF THE WORLD

	Miles
Nile, *Africa*	4132
Amazon, *South America*	3900
Mississippi–Missouri–Red Rock, *U.S.A.*	3860
Ob-Irtysh, *Asia*	3461
Yangtze, *China*	3430
Hwang Ho (Yellow), *China*	2903
Congo, *Africa*	2900

	Miles
Amur, *Asia*	2802
Lena, *U.S.S.R.*	2653
Mackenzie, *Canada*	2635
Mekong, *Asia*	2600
Niger, *Africa*	2590
Yenisey, *U.S.S.R.*	2566
Paraná, *South America*	2450

	Miles
Murray–Darling, *Australia*	2310
Volga, *U.S.S.R.*	2293
Madeira, *South America*	2060
Indus, *Asia*	1980
Purus, *South America*	1900
St. Lawrence, *Canada*	1900
Rio Grande, *U.S.A.*	1885

	Miles
Brahmaputra, *Asia*	1800
Orinoco, *South America*	1800
São Francisco, *S. America*	1800
Yukon, *Alaska, U.S.A.*	1800
Danube, *Europe*	1770
Salween, *Burma–China*	1730
Euphrates, *Asia*	1675

LARGEST LAKES OF THE WORLD

	Sq. Miles
Caspian Sea, *U.S.S.R.–Iran (salt)*	151,123
Superior, *U.S.A.–Canada*	31,820
Victoria, *Africa*	26,828
Aral, *U.S.S.R. (salt)*	26,525
Huron, *U.S.A.–Canada*	23,010
Michigan, *U.S.A.*	22,400
Tanganyika, *Africa*	12,355

	Sq. Miles
Baykal, *U.S.S.R.*	12,162
Great Bear, *Canada*	12,000
Great Slave, *Canada*	11,170
Nyasa, *Africa*	10,900
Erie, *U.S.A.–Canada*	9940
Winnipeg, *Canada*	9094
Chad, *Africa*	8000

	Sq. Miles
Ontario, *U.S.A.–Canada*	7540
Ladoga, *U.S.S.R.*	7104
Balkhash, *U.S.S.R.*	6680
Onega, *U.S.S.R.*	3822
Eyre, *Australia (salt)*	3700
Rudolf, *Kenya (salt)*	3500
Titicaca, *Peru–Bolivia*	3261

	Sq. Miles
Nicaragua, *Nicaragua*	3060
Athabasca, *Canada*	3058
Reindeer, *Canada*	2440
Torrens, *Australia (salt)*	2400
Koko Nor, *China (salt)*	2300
Issyk-Kul', *U.S.S.R.*	2200
Vänern, *Sweden*	2150

PART FOUR

INDEXES

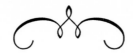

INDEX TO
THE UNITED STATES
OF AMERICA

LIST OF ABBREVIATIONS

Arch. Archipelago
B. Bay
Batt. Battle
B.C. British Columbia
C. Cape
Can. Canal
Chan. Channel
Cr. Creek
Des. Desert
G. Gulf
Harb. Harbor
Hd. Head
Hist. Historical
I. Island, Isle, Ile
Is. Islands, Isles
L. Lake, Lac
Mil. Military
Mon. Monument
Mt. Mountain, Mount
Nat. National
Pen. Peninsula
Pk. Peak
Plat. Plateau
Prom. Promontory
Pt., Pte. Point, Pointe
R. River
Ra. Range
Res. Reservoir
Sd. Sound
St., Ste. Saint, Sainte
Str. Strait
Val. Valley
Vol. Volcano

(Population figures for towns over 25,000 are from the United States census, 1960)

Alta Vista, Iowa 61 M a
Alta Vista, Kansas 60 H f
Altavista, Virginia 52 G h
Altha, Florida 54 F g
Altheimer, Arkansas 63 M d
Alto, Texas 65 M d
Alton, California 74 A d
Alton, Illinois (43,047) 57 C l
Alton, Iowa 61 H b
Alton, Kansas 60 F e
Alton, Missouri 61 N h
Alton, New Hampshire 49 D e
Alton, New York 53 K b
Alton, Utah 68 D f
Altona, Illinois 57 C h
Altona, New York 53 N a
Altonah, Utah 68 F c
Altoona, Alabama 54 E c
Altoona, Florida 55 K h
Altoona, Iowa 61 L c
Altoona, Kansas 61 J g
Altoona, Pennsylvania (69,407) 52 H e
Altura, Minnesota 59 P f
Alturas, California 74 E c
Alturas, Florida 55 N f
Altus, Oklahoma 62 D d
Alunite, Nevada 75 L j
Alva, Florida 55 N g
Alva, Kentucky 57 K n
Alva, Oklahoma 62 E b
Alva, Wyoming 67 Q e
Alvarado, Texas 65 K c
Alvin, Illinois 57 F j
Alvin, Texas 65 M f
Alvin, Wisconsin 56 E d
Alvo, Nebraska 60 H d
Alvord, Texas 65 K b
Alvord Des., Oregon 73 M n
Alvord L., Oregon 73 M n
Alvwood, Minnesota 59 M c
Aly, Arkansas 63 K d
Alzada, Montana 67 Q d
Amagansett, New York 51 J d
Amak I., Alaska 76 F j
Amanda, Ohio 52 D f
Amargosa Des., Nevada 75 J h
Amargosa R., California 75 J j
Amargosa Ra., California 75 J h
Amarillo, Texas (137,969) 64 C h
Amasa, Michigan 56 E c
Amatignak I., Alaska 77 N j
Amawalk, New York 50 F c
Amazon, Montana 66 H c
Amazonia, Missouri 61 K e
Amber, Iowa 61 N b
Amber, Oklahoma 62 F c
Amber, Washington 73 N h
Amber B., Alaska 76 J h
Amberg, Wisconsin 56 F d
Ambler, Pennsylvania 50 C e
Ambler R., Alaska 76 J c
Amboy, California 75 K k
Amboy, Illinois 57 D h
Ambridge, Pennsylvania 52 F e
Ambrose, Georgia 54 H f
Ambrose, North Dakota 58 C b
Ambrose Chan., New Jersey-New York 50 F e
Amchitka I., Alaska 76 M j
Amchitka Pass, Alaska 76 M j
Amedee, California 74 E d
Amelia, Nebraska 60 F b
Amelia, Virginia 52 J h
Amelia I., Florida 55 K g
Amenia, New York 53 N d
American Falls, Idaho 66 H g
American Falls Res., Idaho 66 H g
Americus, Georgia 54 G e
Amery, Wisconsin 56 A d
Ames, Iowa (27,003) 61 L b
Ames, Nebraska 60 H c
Ames, Oklahoma 62 E b
Amesbury, Massachusetts 49 E f
Amesville, Ohio 52 E f
Amherst, Colorado 69 O c
Amherst, Maine 49 G d
Amherst, Massachusetts 49 C f
Amherst, Nebraska 60 E d
Amherst, New Hampshire 49 D f
Amherst, Ohio 52 D d
Amherst, South Dakota 58 J e
Amherst, Texas 64 E a
Amherst, Virginia 52 G h
Amherstdale, West Virginia 52 E h
Amherst Junction, Wisconsin 56 D e
Amidon, North Dakota 58 C d
Amite, Louisiana 63 N h
Amite R., Louisiana 63 N h
Amity, Arkansas 63 K d
Amityville, New York 50 G d
Amlia I., Alaska 77 Q j
Ammon, Idaho 66 J f
Amorita, Oklahoma 62 E b
Amory, Mississippi 63 P e
Amos, California 75 K l
Amphitheater, Arizona 70 G g
Amsterdam, Georgia 54 G g
Amsterdam, Idaho 66 F g
Amsterdam, New York (28,772) 53 M c
Amsterdam, Ohio 52 F e
Amston, Connecticut 51 J b
Amukta Pass, Alaska 77 R j
Amy, Kansas 60 D f
Anacapa Is., California 75 F l
Anacoco, Louisiana 63 K g
Anacoco L., Louisiana 63 K g
Anaconda, Montana 66 H c
Anaconda Ra., Montana 66 G d
Anacortes, Washington 73 H g
Anacostia, District of Columbia 53 Q h
Anadarko, Oklahoma 62 E c
Anaheim, California (104,184) 75 H l
Anaheim B., California 75 F n
Anahuac, Texas 65 N f
Anaktuk, Alaska 76 H a
Anaktuvuk Pass, Alaska 76 M b
Anaktuvuk R., Alaska 76 M b
Analomink, Pennsylvania 50 C c
Anamoose, North Dakota 58 F c
Anamosa, Iowa 61 N b
Anastasia I., Florida 55 K h
Anatone, Washington 73 N j
Anceney, Montana 66 J d
Ancho, New Mexico 71 M f
Anchorage, Alaska (44,237) 76 N f
Anchorage, Kentucky 57 H l
Anchor B., Michigan 56 L g
Anchor Point, Alaska 76 M g
Anclote Keys, Florida 55 M e
Ancram, New York 50 F a
Andale, Kansas 60 G g
Andalusia, Alabama 54 E f
Andalusia, Illinois 57 C h
Anderson, California 74 C d
Anderson, Indiana (49,061) 57 H j
Anderson, Missouri 61 K h
Anderson, South Carolina (41,316) 55 J c
Anderson L., Oregon 73 L n
Anderson Ranch Res., Idaho 66 E f
Andersonville, Georgia 54 G e
Andersonville, Indiana 57 H k
Andes, L., South Dakota 58 H g
Andes, New York 50 D a
Andover, Connecticut 51 J b
Andover, Maine 49 E d
Andover, New Hampshire 49 D e
Andover, New Jersey 50 D d
Andover, New York 52 J c
Andover, Ohio 52 F d
Andover, South Dakota 58 J e
Andreafsky, Alaska 76 F e
Andreafsky R., Alaska 76 F e
Andreanof Is., Alaska 77 O j
Andreas, Pennsylvania 50 B d
Andrew, Iowa 61 O b
Andrew Jackson Nat. Mon., Tennessee 55 J a
Andrews, Indiana 57 H j
Andrews, Nebraska 60 A b
Andrews, North Carolina 54 H b
Andrews, Oregon 73 M n
Andrews, South Carolina 55 M d
Andrews, Texas 64 E c
Andrix, Colorado 69 N f
Andronica I., Alaska 76 G j
Androscoggin R., Maine 49 E d
Aneta, North Dakota 58 J c
Angel I., California 75 B l
Angelica, New York 52 H c
Angelina R., Texas 65 N d
Angels Camp, California 74 E f
Angier, North Carolina 55 N b
Angleton, Texas 65 M f
Angola, Indiana 57 J h
Angola, New York 52 G c
Angola Swamp, North Carolina 55 O c
Angoon, Alaska 77 U h
Angora, Nebraska 60 A c
Angostura Res., South Dakota 58 C g
Angus, Minnesota 59 K b
Aniakchak Vol. Crater, Alaska 76 H h
Aniak R., Alaska 76 H f
Animas, New Mexico 71 J h
Animas Pk., New Mexico 71 J h
Animas R., Colorado 69 J f
Anita, Arizona 70 E d
Anita, Iowa 61 K c
Aniuk R., Alaska 76 J b
Aniwa, Wisconsin 56 D d
Ankeny, Iowa 61 L c
Ann, C., Massachusetts 49 E f
Anna, Illinois 57 D m
Anna, Ohio 52 B e
Anna, Texas 65 L b
Anna Maria, Florida 55 M f
Annandale, Minnesota 59 M e
Annapolis, Maryland 53 K g
Ann Arbor, Michigan (67,340) 57 K g
Annawan, Illinois 57 D h
Annette, Alaska 77 W j
Anniston, Alabama (33,657) 54 F d
Annona, Texas 65 N b
Annville, Pennsylvania 53 K e
Anoka, Minnesota 59 N e
Anoka, Nebraska 60 F b
Anselmo, Nebraska 60 E c
Ansley, Louisiana 63 L f
Ansley, Nebraska 60 E c
Anson, Texas 64 H c
Ansonia, Connecticut 51 G c
Ansonia, Ohio 52 B e
Ansonville, North Carolina 55 L b
Ansted, West Virginia 52 E g
Antelope, Montana 67 Q a
Antelope, Oregon 73 K l
Antelope, Texas 65 J b
Antelope, Utah 68 G c
Antelope Cr., Oregon 73 N n
Antelope I., Utah 68 A g
Antelope Ra., Nevada 74 J e
Antelope Res., Oregon 73 N n
Antero Pk., Colorado 69 K e
Antero Res., Colorado 69 L e
Anthony, Florida 55 J h
Anthony, Kansas 60 F g
Anthony, New Mexico 71 L g
Anthony, Rhode Island 51 K b
Antigo, Wisconsin 56 D d
Antimony, Utah 68 E e
Antioch, California 74 D f
Antioch, Illinois 56 E g
Antioch, Nebraska 60 B b
Antler, North Dakota 58 E b
Antlers, Oklahoma 62 H d
Antoine, Arkansas 63 K d
Anton, Colorado 69 N d
Anton, Texas 64 E b
Antonino, Kansas 60 E f
Antonito, Colorado 69 L f
Antrim, New Hampshire 49 C e
Antrim, Pennsylvania 53 J d
Antwerp, New York 53 L a
Antwerp, Ohio 52 B d
Anvik, Alaska 76 G e
Anvik R., Alaska 76 G e
Anvil Pk., Alaska 76 M j
Anxvasse, Missouri 61 N e
Apache, Arizona 70 H h
Apache, Oklahoma 62 E d
Apache Creek, New Mexico 71 J f
Apache Junction, Arizona 70 F f
Apache L., Arizona 70 F f
Apache Pk., Arizona 70 G h
Apahola, Hawaii 72 B c
Apalachee B., Florida 54 G g
Apalachia Dam, North Carolina 54 G b
Apalachicola, Florida 54 F h
Apalachicola B., Florida 54 G h
Apalachicola R., Florida 54 F g
Apalachin, New York 53 K c
Apex, North Carolina 55 N b
Apgar, Montana 66 F a
Aphrewn R., Alaska 76 E f
Apishapa R., Colorado 69 M f
Apopka, Florida 55 K j
Apopka, L., Florida 55 K j
Apostle Is., Wisconsin 56 C b
Appalachia, Virginia 52 D j
Appalachian Mts., Pennsylvania, etc. 47 K c
Appleby, Texas 65 N d
Applegate, California 74 E f
Applegate, Oregon 73 G n
Applegate R., Oregon 73 G n
Apple Springs, Texas 65 N d
Appleton, Maine 49 F d
Appleton, Minnesota 59 L e
Appleton, Washington 73 J k
Appleton, Wisconsin (48,411) 56 E e
Appleton City, Missouri 61 K f
Appomattox, Virginia 52 H h
Appomattox Court House Nat. Mon., Virginia 52 H h
Apua Pt., Hawaii 72 E f
Aquarius Mts., Arizona 70 D e
Aquarius Plateau, Utah 68 E f
Aquebogue, New York 51 H d
Aquilla, Texas 65 K d
Arabi, Georgia 54 H f
Arago, C., Oregon 73 F m
Aransas B., Texas 65 K h
Aransas Pass, Texas 65 K h
Arapaho, Mt., Colorado 69 L c
Arapahoe, Colorado 69 O e
Arapahoe, Nebraska 60 E d
Arapahoe, Wyoming 67 M g
Arboles, Colorado 69 J f
Arbon, Idaho 66 H g
Arbor Heights, Washington 72 B j
Arbor Vitae, Wisconsin 56 D d
Arbuckle, California 74 C e
Arbuckle, L., Florida 55 N f
Arbuckle Mts., Oklahoma 62 F d
Arbutus, Maryland 53 P f
Arbyrd, Missouri 61 O h
Arcade, New York 52 H c
Arcadia, California (41,005), vicinity of Los Angeles
Arcadia, Florida 55 N f
Arcadia, Indiana 57 G j
Arcadia, Kansas 61 K g
Arcadia, Louisiana 63 L f
Arcadia, Michigan 56 G e
Arcadia, Missouri 61 O g
Arcadia, Nebraska 60 F c
Arcadia, Ohio 52 C d
Arcadia, Oklahoma 62 F c
Arcadia, Rhode Island 51 K b
Arcadia, Wisconsin 56 B e
Arcanum, Ohio 52 B f
Arcata, California 74 A d
Arc Dome, Nevada 74 H f
Archbald, Pennsylvania 53 L d
Archbold, Ohio 52 B d
Archer, Florida 55 J h
Archer City, Texas 65 J b
Arches Nat. Mon., Utah 68 G e
Archie, Missouri 61 K f
Archuleta, New Mexico 71 K c
Arco, Idaho 66 G f
Arco, Minnesota 59 K f
Arcola, Illinois 57 E k
Arcola, Mississippi 63 N e
Arcola, Texas 65 M f
Arctic Lagoon, Alaska 76 D d
Arctic Village, Alaska 77 O b
Arden, Nevada 75 K h
Arden, New York 50 E c
Arden Hills, Minnesota 59 Q h
Ardmore, Oklahoma 62 F d
Ardmore, Pennsylvania 50 C e
Ardmore, South Dakota 58 C g
Ardmore, Tennessee 54 E b
Ardoch, North Dakota 58 J b
Ardsley, New York 50 F d
Arena, New York 50 D a
Arena, Pt., California 74 B f
Arendale, North Carolina 55 M b
Argenta, Montana 66 H d
Argentine, Kansas 61 P a
Argonia, Kansas 60 G g
Argonne, Wisconsin 56 D d
Argora, Idaho 66 H e
Argos, Indiana 57 G h
Arguello, Pt., California 75 E k
Argus Ra., California 75 H j
Argusville, North Dakota 58 J c
Argyle, Georgia 55 J f
Argyle, Michigan 56 L f
Argyle, Minnesota 59 K b
Argyle, Wisconsin 56 D g
Ariel, Washington 73 H k
Arion, Iowa 61 J c
Arikaree R., Colorado 69 O d
Arimo, Idaho 66 H g
Arinosa, Utah 68 C c
Ariton, Alabama 54 F f
Arivaca, Arizona 70 F h
Ariyak R., Alaska 76 L b
Arizona 70
Arkabutla L., Mississippi 63 O n
Arkadelphia, Arkansas 63 K d
Arkansas 63
Arkansas City, Arkansas 63 M e
Arkansas City, Kansas 60 G g
Arkansas R., Arkansas, etc. 47 H c
Arkport, New York 52 J c
Arkville, New York 50 D a
Arlee, Montana 66 F b
Arling, Idaho 66 D e
Arlington, Arizona 70 E f
Arlington, California 75 H l
Arlington, Colorado 69 N e
Arlington, Florida 55 K g
Arlington, Georgia 54 G f
Arlington, Iowa 61 N b
Arlington, Kansas 60 F g
Arlington, Kentucky 57 D n
Arlington, Maryland 53 P g
Arlington, Massachusetts (49,953) 49 F h
Arlington, Minnesota 59 M f
Arlington, Nebraska 60 H c
Arlington, Ohio 52 C e
Arlington, Oregon 73 K k
Arlington, South Dakota 58 J f
Arlington, Tennessee 54 B b
Arlington, Texas (44,775) 65 M j
Arlington, Vermont 49 B e
Arlington, Virginia (163,401) 53 O h
Arlington, Washington 73 H g
Arlington, Wyoming 67 O h
Arlington Heights, Illinois (27,878) 57 E g
Arlington Res., Missouri 61 M g
Armington, Montana 67 K b
Arminto, Wyoming 67 N f
Armonk, New York 50 F d
Armour, South Dakota 58 H g
Armourdale, North Dakota 58 G b
Armstead, Montana 66 H e
Armstrong, Illinois 57 F j
Armstrong, Iowa 61 K a
Armstrong, Missouri 61 M e
Armstrong, Texas 65 K j
Arnegard, North Dakota 58 C c
Arnett, Oklahoma 62 D b
Arnett, West Virginia 52 E h
Arnia, Kansas 61 K g
Arno, Texas 64 D d
Arnold, California 74 E f
Arnold, Nebraska 60 D c
Arnold, Pennsylvania 52 G e
Arnoldsburg, West Virginia 52 E g
Arnolds Park, Iowa 61 K a
Aroostook R., Maine 49 G b
Aropuk L., Alaska 76 F f
Aroya, Colorado 69 N e
Arp, Texas 65 M c
Arran, Florida 54 G g
Arrey, New Mexico 71 K g
Arriba, Colorado 69 N d
Arrow Cr., Montana 67 L b
Arrow Rock, Missouri 61 M e
Arrow Rock Res., Idaho 66 E f
Arroyo Grande, California 75 E j
Arroyo Hondo, New Mexico 71 M c
Arroyo Seco, California 75 K l
Artas, South Dakota 58 G e
Artesia, California 75 F m
Artesia, Mississippi 63 P e
Artesia, New Mexico 71 N g
Artesian, South Dakota 58 J g
Artesia Wells, Texas 65 H g
Arthur, Illinois 57 E k
Arthur, L., Louisiana 63 L h
Arthur, Nebraska 60 C c
Arthur, North Dakota 58 J c
Arthur City, Texas 65 M b
Arthur Kill, New Jersey 51 J g
Arthursburg, New York 50 F b
Artois, California 74 C e
Arvada, Colorado 69 O h
Arvada, Wyoming 67 O e
Arvin, California 75 G j
Arvonia, Virginia 52 H h
Asbury, Kansas 61 K g
Asbury, New Jersey 50 C d
Asbury Park, New Jersey 50 F e
Asharoken, New York 50 G d
Ashaway, Rhode Island 51 K c
Ashburn, Georgia 54 H f
Ashby, Minnesota 59 L d
Ashby, Nebraska 60 C b
Ashdown, Arkansas 63 J e
Asheboro, North Carolina 55 M b
Asher, Oklahoma 62 G c
Asherton, Texas 65 H g
Asheville, North Carolina (60,192) 55 J b
Ash Flat, Arkansas 63 M b
Ashford, Alabama 54 F f
Ashford, Connecticut 51 J b
Ashford, Washington 73 H j
Ashfork, Arizona 70 E d
Ash Grove, Kansas 60 F e
Ash Grove, Missouri 61 L g
Ashkum, Illinois 57 F j
Ashland, Alabama 54 F d
Ashland, Illinois 57 C k
Ashland, Kansas 60 E g
Ashland, Kentucky (31,283) 57 L l
Ashland, Maine 49 G b
Ashland, Montana 67 O d
Ashland, Mt., Oregon 73 H n
Ashland, Nebraska 60 H c
Ashland, New Hampshire 49 D e
Ashland, New York 50 E a
Ashland, Ohio 52 D e
Ashland, Oregon 73 H n
Ashland, Pennsylvania 53 K e
Ashland, Virginia 52 J h
Ashland, Wisconsin 56 C c
Ashland City, Tennessee 54 D a
Ashley, Illinois 57 D l
Ashley, Michigan 56 J f
Ashley, North Dakota 58 G d
Ashley, Pennsylvania 50 B c
Ashley Falls, Massachusetts 50 G a
Ashmore, Texas 64 E c
Ashokan, New York 50 E b
Ashokan Res., New York 50 E b
Ashtabula, Ohio 52 F d
Ashton, Idaho 66 J e
Ashton, Illinois 57 D h
Ashton, Michigan 56 H f
Ashton, Rhode Island 51 L b
Ashton, South Dakota 58 H f
Ashville, Alabama 54 E d
Askin, North Carolina 55 O b
Askov, Minnesota 59 O d
Asotin, Washington 73 N j
Aspen, Colorado 69 K d
Aspen, Wyoming 67 K h
Aspermont, Texas 64 G b
Aspid, Mt., Alaska 76 D k
Aspinwall, Pennsylvania 53 Q a
Assateague I., Virginia 53 L g
Assawompset Pond, Massachusetts 51 M b
Assonet, Massachusetts 51 L b
Assumption, Illinois 57 D k
Astoria, Illinois 57 C j
Astoria, Oregon 73 G j
Astoria, South Dakota 59 K f
Atanik, Alaska 76 H a
Atarque, New Mexico 71 J e
Atascadero, California 75 J f
Atascosa R., Texas 65 J f
Atchafalaya B., Louisiana 63 M j
Atchafalaya R., Louisiana 63 M l
Atchison, Kansas 61 J e
Atchueelinguk R., Alaska 76 G e
Atco, Georgia 54 G c
Atco, New Jersey 50 D f
Atglen, Pennsylvania 50 A f
Athelstan, Iowa 61 K d
Athena, Oregon 73 M k
Athens, Alabama 54 E c
Athens, Georgia (31,355) 54 H d
Athens, New York 50 F a
Athens, Illinois 57 D k
Athens, Louisiana 63 K f
Athens, Maine 49 F d
Athens, Michigan 57 H g
Athens, Ohio 52 D f
Athens, Pennsylvania 53 K d
Athens, Tennessee 54 G b
Athens, Texas 65 M c
Athens, Wisconsin 56 C d
Atherton, California 75 C n
Athol, Idaho 66 D b
Athol, Massachusetts 49 C f
Athol, Pennsylvania 50 B e
Atka, Alaska 77 Q j
Atkasuk, Alaska 76 J a
Atkins, Arkansas 63 L c
Atkinson, Illinois 57 C h
Atkinson, Nebraska 60 F b
Atkinson, North Carolina 55 N c
Atlanta, Georgia (487,455) 54 G d
Atlanta, Idaho 66 E f
Atlanta, Illinois 57 D j
Atlanta, Indiana 57 G j
Atlanta, Kansas 60 H g
Atlanta, Michigan 56 J d
Atlanta, Missouri 61 M e
Atlanta, New York 53 J c
Atlanta, Texas 65 N b
Atlantic, Iowa 61 J c
Atlantic, North Carolina 55 P c
Atlantic Beach, New York 50 F d
Atlantic City, New Jersey (59,544) 50 E g
Atlantic City, Wyoming 67 M g
Atlantic Highlands, New Jersey 50 E e
Atlas, Michigan 56 K g
Atmore, Alabama 54 D f
Atoka, Oklahoma 62 G d
Atoka Res., Oklahoma 62 G d
Atolia, California 75 H j
Atomic City, Idaho 66 H f
Atsion, New Jersey 50 D f
Attalla, Alabama 54 E c
Attica, Indiana 57 F j
Attica, Kansas 60 F g
Attica, Michigan 56 K f
Attica, New York 52 H c
Attica, Ohio 52 D d
Attleboro, Massachusetts (27,118) 51 L b
Attoya Bayou, Texas 65 N d
Attu, Alaska 76 J j
Attu I., Alaska 76 J j
Atwater, California 75 E g
Atwater, Minnesota 59 M e
Atwood, Colorado 69 N c
Atwood, Illinois 57 E k
Atwood, Kansas 60 C e
Atwood, New York 50 E b
Atwood Res., Ohio 52 E e
Auau Chan., Hawaii 72 D e
Aubry Cliffs, Arizona 70 E d
Auburn, Alabama 54 F e
Auburn, California 74 D f
Auburn, Indiana 57 H h
Auburn, Illinois 57 D k
Auburn, Kansas 61 J f
Auburn, Kentucky 57 G n
Auburn, Maine 49 E d
Auburn, Massachusetts 51 K a
Auburn, Michigan 56 J f
Auburn, Nebraska 61 J d
Auburn, New Jersey 50 C f
Auburn, New York (35,249) 53 K c
Auburn, Pennsylvania 50 A d
Auburn, Washington 73 H h
Auburndale, Florida 55 N e
Auburndale, Wisconsin 56 D e
Aucilla R., Florida 54 H g
Audenried, Pennsylvania 50 B d
Audubon, Iowa 61 K c
Audubon, New Jersey 50 C f
Au Gres, Michigan 56 K e
Augusta, Arkansas 63 M c
Augusta, Georgia (70,626) 55 J d
Augusta, Illinois 57 C j
Augusta, Kansas 60 H g
Augusta, Kentucky 57 J l
Augusta, Maine 49 F d
Augusta, Michigan 57 H g
Augusta, Montana 66 H b
Augusta, New Jersey 50 D c
Augusta, Wisconsin 56 B e
Augusta Springs, Virginia 52 G g
Augustine I., Alaska 76 L g
Auke Bay, Alaska 77 U g
Aulander, North Carolina 55 O a
Ault, Colorado 69 M c
Aurelia, Iowa 61 J b
Aurora, Colorado (48,548) 69 P h
Aurora, Illinois (63,715) 57 E h
Aurora, Indiana 57 J k
Aurora, Kansas 60 G e
Aurora, Minnesota 59 O c
Aurora, Missouri 61 L h
Aurora, Nebraska 60 F d
Aurora, New York 53 K c
Aurora, North Carolina 55 P b
Aurora, Utah 68 E d
Aurora Lodge, Alaska 77 O d
Ausable Forks, New York 53 N a
Au Sable Pt., Michigan 56 G c
Au Sable Pt., Michigan 56 K e
Au Sable R., Michigan 56 J e
Ausable R., New York 53 N a
Austell, Georgia 54 G d
Austerlitz, New York 50 G a
Austin, Minnesota (27,908) 59 O g
Austin, Montana 66 H c
Austin, Nevada 74 H e
Austin, Oregon 73 M l
Austin, Pennsylvania 52 H d
Austin, Texas (186,545) 65 K e
Austonio, Texas 65 M d
Austwell, Texas 65 L g
Au Train, Michigan 56 G c
Aux Barques, Pt., Michigan 56 G d
Aux Barques, Pt., Michigan 56 L e
Ava, Illinois 57 D m
Ava, Missouri 61 M h
Avalik R., Alaska 76 H a
Avalon, California 75 G l
Avalon, L., New Mexico 71 N g
Avalon, Mississippi 63 N e
Avalon, New Jersey 50 D g
Avalon, Pennsylvania 53 O a
Avard, Oklahoma 62 E b
Avatanak I., Alaska 76 E j
Avawatz Mts., California 75 J j
Avella, Pennsylvania 52 F e
Avenal, California 75 E j
Avery, Idaho 66 E b
Avery, Iowa 61 M c
Avery, Texas 65 N b
Avery Island, Louisiana 63 M j
Avinger, Texas 65 N c
Avis, Pennsylvania 53 J d

Berkeley Springs, West Virginia 52 H f
Berkley, Massachusetts 51 L b
Berkley, Michigan 56 K g
Berkshire Hills, Massachusetts 49 B f
Berlin, Maryland 53 L g
Berlin, New Hampshire 49 D d
Berlin, New Jersey 50 D f
Berlin, North Dakota 58 H d
Berlin, Pennsylvania 52 H f
Berlin, Wisconsin 56 E f
Berlin Res., Ohio 52 F e
Bern, Kansas 61 J e
Bernalillo, New Mexico 71 L d
Bernard, Iowa 61 O b
Bernardino, Arizona 70 H h
Bernardo, New Mexico 71 L e
Bernardsville, New Jersey 50 D d
Berne, Indiana 57 J j
Bernice, Louisiana 63 L f
Bernie, Missouri 61 P h
Bernville, Pennsylvania 50 A e
Berrien Springs, Michigan 57 G g
Berry, Alabama 54 D d
Berry, Kentucky 57 J l
Berry, Maine 49 H d
Berryessa, L., California 74 C f
Berryville, Arkansas 63 K b
Berryville, Virginia 52 H f
Bertha, Minnesota 59 L d
Berthold, North Dakota 58 E b
Berthoud, Colorado 69 L c
Bertram, Texas 65 J e
Bertrand, Nebraska 60 E d
Berwick, Maine 49 E e
Berwick, Pennsylvania 53 K d
Berwyn, Illinois (54,224) 57 A l
Berwyn, Pennsylvania 50 B e
Beryl, Utah 68 C f
Besboro I., Alaska 76 G d
Bessemer, Alabama (33,054) 54 E d
Bessemer, Michigan 56 C c
Bessemer, Pennsylvania 52 F e
Bessemer City, North Carolina 55 K b
Bessie, Oklahoma 62 E c
Bessmay, Texas 65 O e
Best, Texas 64 F d
Beswick, California 74 C c
Bete Grise B., Michigan 56 F b
Bethany, Connecticut 51 H c
Bethany, Missouri 61 K d
Bethany, Oklahoma 62 F c
Bethany Beach, Delaware 53 L g
Bethel, Alaska 76 G f
Bethel, Connecticut 50 G c
Bethel, Delaware 53 L g
Bethel, Missouri 61 M e
Bethel, New York 50 D b
Bethel, North Carolina 55 O b
Bethel, Ohio 52 B g
Bethel, Oklahoma 63 J d
Bethel, Minnesota 59 N e
Bethel, Vermont 49 C e
Bethel Park, Pennsylvania 53 O c
Bethesda, Maryland (56,527) 53 J f
Bethesda, Ohio 52 E e
Bethlehem, Connecticut 50 G b
Bethlehem, New Hampshire 49 D d
Bethlehem, Pennsylvania (75,408) 50 C d
Bethpage, New York 50 G d
Bethpage, Tennessee 54 E a
Bethpage Junction, New York 50 G d
Bethune, Colorado 69 O d
Bethune, South Carolina 55 L c
Betsie, Pt., Michigan 56 G e
Betsy, Michigan 56 H c
Betterton, Maryland 50 A g
Bettie, Texas 65 N c
Bettles, Alaska 76 M c
Bettles Field, Alaska 76 M c
Bettsville, Ohio 52 C d
Beulah, Michigan 56 G e
Beulah, North Dakota 58 E c
Beulah, Oregon 73 M m
Beulah, Wyoming 67 Q e
Beulah Res., Oregon 73 M m
Beulaville, North Carolina 55 O c
Beverley, Washington 73 L j
Beverly, Alaska 60 G e
Beverly, L., Alaska 76 H g
Beverly, Massachusetts (36,108) 49 E f
Beverly, New Jersey 50 D e
Beverly, Ohio 52 E f
Beverly, West Virginia 52 G g
Beverly Hills, California (30,817) 75 D l
Beverly Park, Washington 73 H h
Bevier, Missouri 61 M e
Bexley, Ohio 52 D f
Bickleton, Washington 73 K k
Bickmore, West Virginia 52 E g
Bicknell, Indiana 57 F l
Bicknell, Utah 68 E e
Biddle, Montana 67 P d
Biddleford, Maine 49 E e
Bidwell, Ohio 52 D g
Bieber, California 74 D c
Bienville, Louisiana 63 L f
Big Arm, Montana 66 F b
Big Baldy Mt., Montana 67 K b
Big Bay, Michigan 56 F c
Big Bear City, California 75 J k
Big Bear Cr., Texas 65 M h
Big Bear L., California 75 H k
Big Belt Mts., Montana 66 J c
Big Bend, California 74 D c
Big Bend, Colorado 69 O e
Big Bend Nat. Park, Texas 64 D f
Big Bend Res., South Dakota 58 F f
Big Black Cr., South Carolina 55 L c
Big Black Mt., Virginia 52 D j
Big Black R., Mississippi 63 O e
Big Blue R., Nebraska 60 H d
Big Canyon, Texas 64 E e
Big Clifty, Kentucky 57 G m
Big Cr., Kansas 60 D f
Big Creek, Idaho 66 E d
Big Creek, West Virginia 52 D g
Big Cypress Swamp, Florida 55 N g
Big Delta, Alaska 77 O d
Big Dry Cr., Montana 67 O b
Big Eau Pleine Res., Wisconsin 56 C e
Big Elk Mt., Idaho 66 J f
Bigelow, Kansas 60 H e
Big Falls, Minnesota 59 N b
Bigfork, Minnesota 59 N c
Bigfork, Montana 66 F a
Big Fossil Cr., Texas 65 L j
Biggers, Arkansas 63 N b
Biggs, California 74 D e
Biggs, Oregon 73 K k
Biggsville, Illinois 57 C j
Big Hatchet Pk., New Mexico 71 J h
Big Hole Battlefield Nat. Mon., Montana 66 G d
Big Hole R., Montana 66 H d
Big Horn, Montana 67 N c
Big Horn Mts., Wyoming 67 N e
Bighorn R., Montana-Wyoming 67 N d
Big I., Arkansas 63 M e
Big Indian, New York 50 E a
Big Island, Virginia 52 G h
Big Koniuji I., Alaska 76 H j
Big L., Maine 49 H c
Big L., Oregon 73 K n
Big Lake, Alaska 76 N c
Big Lake, Texas 64 F d
Biglerville, Pennsylvania 53 J f
Big Lost R., Idaho 66 G f
Big Moose, New York 53 L b
Big Muddy Cr., Montana 67 Q a
Big Muddy R., Illinois 57 D m
Bigpine, California 75 G g
Big Pine, Florida 55 N j
Big Pine L., Minnesota 59 L d
Big Pine Pk., California 75 F k
Big Piney, Wyoming 67 K g
Big Piney R., Missouri 61 M g
Big R., Alaska 76 K e
Big R., California 74 B e
Big Rapids, Michigan 56 H f
Big Rib R., Wisconsin 56 D d
Big Rice L., Minnesota 59 N d
Big Sable Pt., Michigan 56 G e
Big Sage Res., California 74 E c
Big Sandy, Montana 67 K a
Big Sandy, Tennessee 54 C a
Big Sandy, Texas 65 M c
Big Sandy, Wyoming 67 L g
Big Sandy Cr., Colorado 69 M d
Big Sandy Cr., Montana 67 K a
Big Sandy R., Arizona 70 D e
Big Sandy R., West Virginia 52 D g
Big Sandy Res., Wyoming 67 L g
Big Sioux R., South Dakota 59 K h
Big Smoky Val., Nevada 74 H f
Big Snowy Mt., Montana 67 L c
Big Spring, Texas (31,230) 64 F c
Big Springs, Idaho 66 J e
Big Springs, Nebraska 60 B c
Big Stone City, South Dakota 59 K e
Big Stone Gap, Virginia 52 D j
Big Stone L., Minnesota 59 K e
Big Sur, California 75 D h
Bigtimber, Montana 67 L d
Bigtrails, Wyoming 67 N f
Big Wells, Texas 65 H g
Big Wills Cr., Alabama 54 F c
Big Wood R., Idaho 66 F f
Bijou Hills, South Dakota 58 G g
Bill, Wyoming 67 P f
Billings, Montana (52,851) 67 M d
Billings, New York 50 F b
Billings, Oklahoma 62 F b
Bill Williams Mt., Arizona 70 E d
Bill Williams R., Arizona 70 D e
Biloxi, Mississippi (44,053) 63 P h
Binford, North Dakota 58 H c
Binger, Oklahoma 62 E c
Bingham, Maine 49 F c
Bingham, Michigan 56 H e
Bingham, Nebraska 60 B b
Bingham, New Mexico 71 L f
Bingham Canyon, Utah 68 B j
Binghamton, New York (75,941) 53 L c
Biola, California 75 F h
Bippus, Indiana 57 H j
Birch Cr., Alaska 77 P c
Birch Creek, Alaska 77 P c
Birches, Alaska 76 L d
Birch L., Minnesota 59 P c
Birch Tree, Missouri 61 N h
Birchwood, Minnesota 59 R h
Birchwood, Wisconsin 56 B d
Bird Cape, Alaska 76 M j
Bird City, Kansas 60 C e
Bird I., Alaska 76 H j
Birdsboro, Pennsylvania 50 B e
Birdseye, Indiana 57 G l
Birmingham, Alabama (340,887) 54 E d
Birmingham, Iowa 61 N d
Birmingham, Michigan (25,525) 56 K g
Birmingham, Missouri 61 Q a
Birney, Montana 67 O d
Birthday Pass, Alaska 76 J b
Bisbee, Arizona 70 H h
Bisbee, North Dakota 58 G b
Biscayne B., Florida 54 B e
Biscoe, North Carolina 55 M b
Bishop, California 75 G g
Bishop, Georgia 54 H d
Bishop, Maryland 53 L g
Bishop, Texas 65 K h
Bishop Creek Res., Nevada 74 L c
Bishopville, South Carolina 55 L c
Bismarck, Arkansas 63 K d
Bismarck, Illinois 57 F j
Bismarck, Missouri 61 O g
Bismarck, North Dakota (27,670) 58 F d
Bison, Oklahoma 62 F b
Bison, South Dakota 58 D e
Bistineau, L., Louisiana 63 K f
Bitely, Michigan 56 H f
Bitter Cr., Utah 68 G d
Bitter Cr., Wyoming 67 M h
Bitter Creek, Wyoming 67 M h
Bitter L., South Dakota 58 J e
Bitterroot R., Montana 66 F c
Bitterroot Ra., Idaho 66 G e
Bixby, Missouri 61 N g
Bixby, Oklahoma 62 H c
Blachly, Oregon 73 G l
Black, Alaska 76 E e
Black, Texas 64 B j
Black B., Louisiana 63 O j
Blackbear, California 74 B c
Blackburn, Mt., Alaska 77 Q f
Black Butte, California 74 C e
Black Canyon, Nevada-Arizona 75 L j
Black Canyon of the Gunnison Nat. Mon., Colorado 69 J e
Black Cr., Arizona 70 H d
Black Creek, Wisconsin 56 E e
Black Diamond, Washington 73 H h
Black Dome, mt., New York 50 E a
Blackduck, Minnesota 59 M c
Black Eagle, Montana 66 J b
Blackey, Kentucky 57 K l
Blackfoot, Idaho 66 H f
Blackfoot, Montana 66 H a
Blackfoot R., Idaho 66 J f
Blackfoot R., Montana 66 G c
Blackfoot River Res., Idaho 66 J g
Black Hills, South Dakota 58 C f
Black L., Alaska 76 H h
Black L., Louisiana 63 K f
Black L., Michigan 56 J d
Black L., New York 53 L a
Black L., North Carolina 55 N c
Black Lake, New Mexico 71 M c
Blackleaf, Montana 66 H a
Black Lick, Pennsylvania 52 G e
Black Mesa, Arizona 70 G c
Black Mesa, Arizona 70 E d
Black Mountain, North Carolina 55 J b
Black Mt., California 75 H j
Black Mt., New Mexico 71 J f
Black Mts., Arizona 70 C d
Black Pine Pk., Idaho 66 G g
Black Pk., New Mexico 71 J g
Black R., Alabama 54 D d
Black R., Alaska 77 Q c
Black R., Arizona 70 H f
Black R., Arkansas, etc. 63 M c
Black R., Louisiana 63 M g
Black R., Michigan 56 J d
Black R., Michigan 56 L f
Black R., Mississippi 63 P h
Black R., North Carolina 55 N c
Black R., South Carolina 55 M d
Black R., Wisconsin 56 C e
Black Ra., New Mexico 71 K f
Black Rapids, Alaska 76 P e
Black River, Michigan 56 K e
Black River Falls, Wisconsin 56 C e
Black Rock, Arkansas 63 M b
Black Rock, Utah 68 D e
Black Rock Des., Nevada 74 F d
Blacksburg, South Carolina 55 K b
Blacksburg, Virginia 52 F h
Blackshear, Georgia 55 J f
Blackshear, L., Georgia 54 H f
Black Springs, New Mexico 71 J f
Blackstock, South Carolina 55 K c
Blackstone, Massachusetts 51 K a
Blackstone, Virginia 52 J h
Blackston R., Rhode Island 51 L b
Blacksville, West Virginia 52 F f
Blackville, South Carolina 55 K d
Blackwater, Missouri 61 L f
Blackwater R., Florida 54 E g
Blackwater R., Missouri 61 L f
Blackwater R., Virginia 53 J h
Blackwell, Oklahoma 62 F b
Blackwell, Texas 64 G c
Black Wolf, Kansas 60 F f
Blackwood Cr., Nebraska 60 C d
Bladen, Georgia 55 K f
Bladen, Nebraska 60 F d
Bladenboro, North Carolina 55 N c
Blain, Pennsylvania 52 J e
Blaine, Kansas 60 H e
Blaine, Washington 73 H g
Blaine, West Virginia 52 G f
Blair, Nebraska 61 H c
Blair, Okahoma 62 D d
Blair, West Virginia 52 E h
Blair, Wisconsin 56 B e
Blair Junction, Nevada 74 H g
Blairsden, California 74 E e
Blairstown, Iowa 61 M c
Blairstown, New Jersey 50 D d
Blairsville, Georgia 54 H c
Blairsville, Pennsylvania 52 G e
Blake I., Washington 72 B h
Blakely, Georgia 54 G f
Blake Pt., Michigan 56 E a
Blakesburg, Iowa 61 M d
Blakeslee, Pennsylvania 50 B c
Blakes Pt., Minnesota 59 S b
Blanca, Colorado 69 L f
Blanca Cr., New Mexico 71 O e
Blanca Pk., Colorado 69 L f
Blanchard, Idaho 66 D a
Blanchard, Michigan 56 H f
Blanchard, North Dakota 58 J c
Blanchard, Oklahoma 62 F c
Blanchard, Washington 73 H g
Blanchester, Ohio 52 C f
Blanco, C., Oregon 73 F n
Blanco, New Mexico 71 K c
Blanco, Texas 65 J e
Bland, Virginia 52 E h
Blandford, Massachusetts 51 H a
Blanding, Utah 68 G f
Blandinsville, Illinois 57 C j
Blandon, Pennsylvania 50 B e
Blaney, South Carolina 55 L c
Blaney Park, Michigan 56 H c
Blanket, Texas 65 J d
Blasdell, New York 52 H c
Blawnox, Pennsylvania 53 Q a
Blazon, Wyoming 67 K h
Bleakwood, Texas 65 O e
Bledsoe, Texas 64 E b
Blencoe, Iowa 61 H c
Blessing, Texas 65 L g
Blevins, Arkansas 63 K e
Blewett, Texas 64 G f
Blewett Falls L., North Carolina 55 M b
Bligh I., Alaska 77 O f
Bliss, Idaho 66 F g
Blissfield, Michigan 57 K h
Blitzen, Oregon 73 L n
Block I., Rhode Island 51 K c
Block Island, Rhode Island 51 K c
Block Island Sd., Rhode Island 51 K c
Blomkest, Minnesota 59 M f
Bloodworth I., Maryland 53 K g
Bloom, Colorado 69 N f
Bloomer, Wisconsin 56 B d
Bloomfield, Connecticut 51 H b
Bloomfield, Indiana 57 G k
Bloomfield, Iowa 61 M d
Bloomfield, Kentucky 57 H m
Bloomfield, Missouri 61 P h
Bloomfield, Montana 67 Q b
Bloomfield, Nebraska 60 G b
Bloomfield, New Jersey (51,867) 51 K e
Bloomfield, New Mexico 71 K c
Bloomfield, Vermont 49 D d
Bloomingburg, New York 50 E b
Bloomingdale, New Jersey 50 E d
Blooming Grove, Pennsylvania 50 C c
Blooming Grove, Texas 65 L c
Bloomington, Minnesota (50,498) 59 Q j
Bloomington, Texas 65 L g
Bloomsdale, Missouri 61 O f
Blooming Prairie, Minnesota 59 N g
Bloomington, Idaho 66 J g
Bloomington, Illinois (36,271) 57 E g
Bloomington, Indiana (31,357) 57 G k
Bloomington, Wisconsin 56 C g
Bloomsburg, Pennsylvania 53 K d
Bloomsbury, New Jersey 50 C d
Bloomville, New York 50 D a
Bloomville, Ohio 52 C d
Blossburg, Pennsylvania 53 J d
Blossom, Texas 65 M b
Blountstown, Florida 54 F g
Blowing Rock, North Carolina 55 K a
Bloxom, Virginia 53 L h
Blue Ball, Pennsylvania 50 A e
Blue Bell Knoll, Utah 68 E e
Blue Cr., Idaho 66 D g
Blue Creek, Utah 68 D b
Blue Cypress L., Florida 55 O f
Blue Diamond, Kentucky 57 K m
Blue Earth, Minnesota 59 M g
Blue Earth R., Minnesota 59 M g
Blue Eye, Missouri 61 L h
Bluefield, West Virginia 52 E h
Blue Grass, Iowa 61 O c
Blue Hill, Maine 49 G d
Blue Hill, Nebraska 60 F d
Blue Hill B., Maine 49 G d
Blue I., Illinois 57 F h
Blue Island, Illinois 57 B n
Bluejoint L., Oregon 73 L n
Blue Knob, mt., Pennsylvania 52 H e
Blue L., Utah 68 D d
Blue Lagoon, Florida 54 B d
Blue Lake, California 74 B d
Bluemont, Virginia 52 J f
Blue Mound, Illinois 57 D k
Blue Mountain, Colorado 68 H c
Blue Mountain, Mississippi 63 O d
Blue Mountain Lake, New York 53 M b
Blue Mountain Pass, Oregon 73 N n
Blue Mt., Arkansas 63 K d
Blue Mt., Pennsylvania 53 K e
Blue Mt. Res., Arkansas 63 K c
Blue Mts., Oregon 73 M l
Blue Point, New York 51 G d
Blue R., Arizona 70 H f
Blue R., Colorado 69 K d
Blue R., Missouri 61 P b
Blue R., Oklahoma 62 G d
Blue Rapids, Kansas 60 H e
Blue Ridge, Georgia 54 G c
Blue Ridge L., Georgia 54 G c
Blue River, Oregon 73 H l
Bluestone Res., West Virginia 52 F h
Bluewater, New Mexico 71 K d
Bluff, Utah 68 G f
Bluff City, Kansas 60 G g
Bluff City, Tennessee 55 J a
Bluffdale, Texas 65 J c
Bluff Pt., North Carolina 55 P b
Bluffs, Illinois 57 C k
Bluffton, Arkansas 63 K d
Bluffton, Georgia 54 G f
Bluffton, Indiana 57 H j
Bluffton, Minnesota 59 L d
Bluffton, Ohio 52 C e
Bluffton, South Carolina 55 L e
Blum, Texas 65 K c
Blunt, South Dakota 58 G f
Blunt Point Res., South Dakota 58 F f
Bly, Oregon 73 J n
Blying Sd., Alaska 77 N g
Blythe, California 75 L l
Blythedale, Missouri 61 L d
Blytheville, Arkansas 63 O c
Boardman, Oregon 73 L k
Boardman R., Michigan 56 H e
Boaz, Alabama 54 E c
Boaz, New Mexico 71 O f
Bobrof I., Alaska 77 O j
Boca, California 74 E e
Boca Chica, Florida 55 N j
Boca Grande, Florida 55 M g
Boca Grande Key, Florida 55 N j
Boca Raton, Florida 55 O g
Bode, Iowa 61 K b
Bodega Hd., California 74 B f
Bodfish, California 75 G j
Boelus, Nebraska 60 F c
Boerne, Texas 65 J f
Boeuf R., Arkansas-Louisiana 63 M f
Bogalusa, Louisiana 63 O h
Bogard, Missouri 61 L e
Bogata, Texas 65 M b
Bogoslof I., Alaska 76 C k
Bogue, Kansas 60 E e
Bogue Chitto, Mississippi 63 N g
Bogue Chitto R., Louisiana 63 N h
Bogue Inlet, North Carolina 55 O c
Bois Blanc I., Michigan 56 J d
Boise, Idaho (34,481) 66 D f
Boise City, Oklahoma 62 B c
Boise R., Idaho 66 D f
Bokchito, Oklahoma 62 G d
Bokeelia, Florida 55 M g
Bokoshe, Oklahoma 63 J c
Bolckow, Missouri 61 K d
Bole, Montana 66 H b
Boles, Idaho 66 D d
Boley, Oklahoma 62 G c
Boligee, Alabama 54 C e
Bolivar, Missouri 61 L g
Bolivar, New York 52 H c
Bolivar, Tennessee 54 C b
Bolivar Pen., Texas 65 N f
Bolivia, North Carolina 55 N c
Bolton, North Carolina 55 N c
Bomarton, Texas 65 H b
Bona, Mt., Alaska 77 R f
Bon Air, Virginia 52 J h
Bonanza, Colorado 69 K e
Bonanza, Idaho 66 F e
Bonanza, Oregon 73 J n
Bonanza Pk., Washington 73 K g
Bonaparte, Iowa 61 N d
Bonaparte, Mt., Washington 73 L g
Bonasila Dome, mt., Alaska 76 G e
Boncarbo, Colorado 69 M f
Bond, Colorado 69 K d
Bondsville, Massachusetts 51 J a
Bonduel, Wisconsin 56 E e
Bondurant, Wyoming 67 K f
Bone, Idaho 66 J f
Bonesteel, South Dakota 58 H g
Bonetraill, North Dakota 58 C b
Bonhan, Texas 65 L b
Bonifay, Florida 54 F g
Bonita, Arizona 70 G g
Bonita, Louisiana 63 M f
Bonita, Pt., California 75 B l
Bonita Springs, Florida 55 N g
Bonner, Montana 66 G c
Bonners Ferry, Idaho 66 D a
Bonner Springs, Kansas 61 K e
Bonne Terre, Missouri 61 O g
Bonneville, Oregon 73 J k
Bonneville, Wyoming 67 M f
Bonneville Dam, Oregon 73 J k
Bonneville Pk., Idaho 66 J g
Bonneville Salt Flats, Utah 68 C c
Bonny Res., Colorado 69 O d
Bono, Arkansas 63 N c
Bon Secour, Alabama 54 D g
Booker, Texas 64 D g
Boon, Michigan 56 H e
Boone, Colorado 69 M e
Boone, Iowa 61 L b
Boone, North Carolina 55 K a
Boones Mill, Virginia 52 G h
Boonesboro, Maryland 52 J f
Booneville, Arkansas 63 K c
Booneville, California 74 B e
Booneville, Kentucky 57 K m
Booneville, Mississippi 63 P d
Booneville Res., Kentucky 57 K m
Boonton, New Jersey 50 E d
Boonville, Indiana 57 F l
Boonville, Missouri 61 M f
Boonville, New York 53 L b
Booth, Oregon 73 F m
Boothbay Harbor, Maine 49 F e
Boothton, Alabama 54 E d
Borah Pk., Idaho 66 G e
Bordeaux, Wyoming 67 Q h
Borden, Indiana 57 H l
Bordentown, New Jersey 50 D e
Borger, Texas 64 C h
Borgne, L., Louisiana 63 O h
Borie, Wyoming 67 Q h
Boron, California 75 H j
Borup, Minnesota 59 K c
Boscawen, New Hampshire 49 D e
Bosco, Louisiana 63 L f
Boscobel, Wisconsin 56 C f
Bosler, Wyoming 67 P h
Bosque, New Mexico 71 L e
Bossier City, Louisiana (32,776) 63 K f
Boston, Georgia 54 H g
Boston, Massachusetts (697,197) 49 E f
Boston B., Massachusetts 49 H h
Boston Corners, New York 50 F a
Boston Harb., Massachusetts 49 H j
Boston Mts., Arkansas 63 K c
Boswell, Indiana 57 F j
Boswell, Oklahoma 62 H d
Boswell, Pennsylvania 52 G e
Boswell Res., Oklahoma 62 H d
Bosworth, Missouri 61 L e
Bothell, Washington 72 C g
Botkins, Ohio 52 B e
Botsford, Connecticut 50 G c
Bottineau, North Dakota 58 F b
Boudreau, B., Louisiana 63 O j
Boulder, Colorado (37,718) 69 L c
Boulder, Montana 66 H c
Boulder, Utah 68 E f
Boulder, Wyoming 67 L g
Boulder Canyon, Nevada 75 L h
Boulder City, Nevada 75 L j
Boulder Cr., Idaho 66 D g
Boulder Creek, California 75 C g
Boulevard, California 75 J m
Boundary, Washington 73 N g
Boundary Pk., Nevada 74 G g
Bound Brook, New Jersey 50 D d
Bountiful, Colorado 69 L f
Bountiful, Utah 68 C g
Bourbeuse R., Missouri 61 N f
Bourbon, Indiana 57 G h
Bourbon, Missouri 61 N f
Bourne, Massachusetts 51 M b
Bouse, Arizona 70 D f
Bouse Wash., Arizona 70 C f
Bovill, Idaho 66 D c
Bovina, Texas 64 B j
Bovina Center, New York 50 D a
Bowbells, North Dakota 58 D b
Bowden, Florida 55 K g
Bowdle, South Dakota 98 G e
Bowdoin, L., Montana 67 N a
Bowdon, Alabama 54 F d
Bowdon, North Dakota 58 G c
Bowen, Illinois 57 B j
Bowers, Delaware 50 B g
Bowersville, Ohio 52 C f
Bowery Pk., Idaho 66 F e
Bowie, Arizona 70 H g
Bowie, Colorado 69 J e
Bowie, Texas 65 K b
Bowling Green, Florida 55 N f
Bowling Green, Indiana 57 F k
Bowling Green, Kentucky (28,338) 57 G m
Bowling Green, Missouri 61 N e
Bowling Green, Ohio 52 C d
Bowling Green, Virginia 52 J g
Bowman, Georgia 54 H c
Bowman, North Dakota 58 C d
Bowmansville, Pennsylvania 50 A e
Boyce, Louisiana 63 L g
Boyce, Virginia 52 H f
Boyd, Montana 67 L d
Boyd, Texas 65 K b
Boydton, Virginia 52 H j
Boyer, Iowa 61 J b
Boyero, Colorado 69 N e
Boyer R., Iowa 61 J b
Boyertown, Pennsylvania 50 B e
Boyes, Montana 67 P d
Boykins, Virginia 53 J j
Boyle, Mississippi 63 N e
Boyne City, Michigan 56 J d
Boyne Falls, Michigan 56 J d
Boynton, Missouri 61 L d
Boynton, Oklahoma 62 H c
Boynton Beach, Florida 55 O g

Charlotte, Michigan 56 J g
Charlotte, North Carolina (201,564) 55 L b
Charlotte, Texas 65 J g
Charlottesville, Virginia (29,427) 52 H h
Charlton City, Massachusetts 51 K a
Charlotte Harb., Florida 55 M g
Charlotte Harbor, Florida 55 M g
Charter Oak, Iowa 61 J b
Chartiers Cr., Pennsylvania 53 O b
Chase, Kansas 60 F f
Chaseburg, Wisconsin 56 B f
Chase City, Virginia 52 H j
Chase L., North Dakota 58 G d
Chaska, Minnesota 59 N f
Chassahowitzka B., Florida 55 J j
Chassell, Michigan 56 E b
Chatanika, Alaska 77 O d
Chatanika R., Alaska 77 O d
Chateaugay, New York 53 M a
Chatfield, Minnesota 59 O g
Chatham, Alaska 77 U h
Chatham, Illinois 57 D k
Chatham, Louisiana 63 L f
Chatham, Massachusetts 51 N b
Chatham, New Jersey 50 E d
Chatham, New York 50 F a
Chatham, Pennsylvania 50 B f
Chatham, Virginia 52 G j
Chatham Str., Alaska 77 U h
Chatom, Alabama 54 C f
Chatooga R., Alabama 54 F c
Chatsworth, Georgia 54 G c
Chatsworth, Illinois 57 E j
Chatsworth, New Jersey 50 D f
Chattahoochee, Florida 54 G g
Chattahoochie R., Alabama 54 F f
Chattanooga, Oklahoma 62 E d
Chattanooga, Tennessee (130,009) 54 F b
Chattaroy, Washington 73 N h
Chattaroy, West Virginia 52 D h
Chattooga R., South Carolina 54 H c
Chatuga L., North Carolina 54 H b
Chaubunagungamaug, L., Massachusetts 51 K a
Chauekuktuli L., Alaska 76 H f
Chaumont, New York 53 K a
Chauncey, Ohio 52 D f
Chautauqua, New York 52 G c
Chautauqua L., New York 52 G c
Chavies, Kentucky 57 K m
Chazy, New York 53 N a
Cheaha Mt., Alabama 54 F d
Cheat R., West Virginia 52 G f
Cheboygan, Michigan 56 J d
Checotah, Oklahoma 62 H c
Cheeching, Alaska 76 E f
Cheektowaga-Northwest, New York (52,362), vicinity of Buffalo
Cheesman L., Colorado 69 L d
Chef Menteur, Louisiana 63 O h
Chefornak, Alaska 76 E f
Chehalis, Washington 73 H j
Chehalis R., Washington 73 G j
Chelan, L., Washington 73 K g
Chelan, Washington 73 K h
Chelan Ra., Washington 73 K g
Chelatna L., Alaska 76 L e
Chelsea, Iowa 61 M c
Chelsea, Massachusetts (33,749) 49 G h
Chelsea, Michigan 57 J g
Chelsea, New York 50 F b
Chelsea, Oklahoma 62 H b
Chelsea, Pennsylvania 50 B f
Chelsea, Vermont 49 C e
Chelyan, West Virginia 52 E g
Chemawa, Oregon 73 H k
Chemquasabamticook L., Maine 49 F b
Chemung R., New York 53 K c
Chena Hot Springs, Alaska 77 O d
Chenango R., New York 53 L c
Chena R., Alaska 77 O d
Chenega, Alaska 77 N f
Cheney, Kansas 60 G g
Cheney, Washington 73 N h
Cheneyville, Louisiana 63 L g
Chenik, Alaska 76 K g
Chenoa, Illinois 57 E j
Chepachet, Rhode Island 51 K b
Chequamegon B., Wisconsin 56 C c
Cheraw, Colorado 69 N e
Cheraw, Mississippi 63 O g
Cheraw, South Carolina 55 M c
Chernabura I., Alaska 76 H j
Cherni I., Alaska 76 E j
Cherokee, Alabama 54 D c
Cherokee, Iowa 61 J b
Cherokee, Oklahoma 62 E b
Cherokee, Texas 65 J d
Cherokee Dam, Tennessee 54 H a
Cherokee L., Tennessee 54 H a
Cherokee L., Texas 65 N c
Cherokees, L. o' the, Oklahoma 63 J b
Cherry Creek, Colorado 69 P h
Cherry Creek, Nevada 74 L e
Cherry Creek, New York 52 G c
Cherry Creek, South Dakota 58 E f
Cherry Creek Mt., Nevada 74 L d
Cherry Creek Res., Colorado 69 P j
Cherrydale, Virginia 53 O h
Cherryfield, Maine 49 H d
Cherry Grove, New York 51 G d
Cherry Hill, Maryland 50 A f
Cherry Hills Village, Colorado 69 O j
Cherryvale, Kansas 61 J g
Cherry Valley, New York 53 M c
Cherryville, North Carolina 55 K b
Chesaning, Michigan 56 J f
Chesapeake, Ohio 52 D g
Chesapeake, Maryland 53 L f
Chesapeake B., Maryland 53 K f
Chesapeake Beach, Maryland 53 K g
Chesapeake City, Maryland 50 B f
Chesapeake Delaware Can., Delaware 50 B f
Cheshire, Connecticut 51 H b
Cheshire, Massachusetts 49 B f
Chesnee, South Carolina 55 K b
Chester, Arkansas 63 J c
Chester, California 74 D d
Chester, Connecticut 51 J c
Chester, Idaho 66 J e
Chester, Illinois 57 D m
Chester, Massachusetts 51 H a
Chester, Montana 67 K a
Chester, Nebraska 60 G d
Chester, New Jersey 50 D d
Chester, New York 50 E c
Chester, Ohio 52 F e
Chester, Pennsylvania 50 B f
Chester, South Carolina 55 K c
Chester, Pennsylvania (63,658) 53 L f
Chester, Vermont 49 C e
Chester, Texas 65 N e
Chester, Virginia 52 J h
Chesterfield, Connecticut 51 J c
Chesterfield, Idaho 66 J g
Chesterfield, Illinois 57 C k
Chesterfield, New Hampshire 49 C f
Chesterfield, South Carolina 55 L c
Chesterfield, Utah 68 C h
Chesterfield, Virginia 52 J h
Chesterhill, Ohio 52 E f
Chester Pen., Maryland 53 K f
Chester R., Maryland 50 A g
Chesterton, Indiana 57 F h
Chestertown, Maryland 50 A g
Chestertown, New York 53 N b
Chesterville, Maryland 50 A g
Chestnut, Louisiana 63 K f
Chestnut Ridge, Pennsylvania 52 G e
Chesuncook, Maine 49 F b
Chesuncook L., Maine 49 F b
Cheswold, Delaware 50 B g
Chetek, Wisconsin 56 B d
Chetopa, Kansas 61 K g
Chevak, Alaska 76 E f
Cheverly, Maryland 53 R h
Chevreuil, Pt., Louisiana 63 M j
Chevy Chase, Maryland 53 P g
Chewelah Valley, Washington 73 N g
Cheyenne, Oklahoma 62 D c
Cheyenne, Texas 64 D d
Cheyenne, Wyoming (43,505) 67 Q h
Cheyenne Agency, South Dakota 58 F e
Cheyenne Bottoms, Kansas 60 F f
Cheyenne Pass, Wyoming 67 P h
Cheyenne R., South Dakota 58 D f
Cheyenne R., Wyoming 67 Q f
Cheyenne Wells, Colorado 69 O e
Chiachi I., Alaska 76 H j
Chibukak Pt., Alaska 76 B e
Chicago, Illinois (3,550,404) 57 F h
Chicago Heights, Illinois (34,331) 57 F h
Chicago R., Illinois 57 A k
Chichagof, Alaska 77 T h
Chichagof I., Alaska 77 U h
Chichester, New York 50 E a
Chickahominy R., Virginia 53 J h
Chickaloon, Alaska 77 N f
Chickamauga, Georgia 54 F c
Chicamauga Dam, Tennessee 54 F b
Chickamauga L., Tennessee 54 G b
Chickasawhay R., Mississippi 63 P g
Chickasha, Oklahoma 62 F c
Chicken, Alaska 77 R d
Chico, California 74 D e
Chico, Oregon 73 N k
Chico, Texas 65 K b
Chico, Washington 72 A h
Chicopee, Massachusetts (61,553) 51 H a
Chidester, Arkansas 63 K e
Chief Joseph Dam, Washington 73 L g
Chiefland, Florida 55 J h
Chiftak, Alaska 76 E f
Chicago Ship Can., Illinois 57 E h
Chiginigak, Mt., Alaska 76 J h
Chigmit Mts., Alaska 76 L f
Chignik, Alaska 76 H h
Chignik B., Alaska 76 H h
Chignik L., Alaska 76 H h
Chikaskia R., Oklahoma 62 F b
Chikuminuk L., Alaska 76 H f
Chilcoot, California 74 E e
Childersburg, Alabama 54 E d
Childress, Texas 64 D j
Childs, Arizona 70 E g
Childs, Florida 55 N f
Chilhowee, Missouri 61 L f
Chilhowie, Virginia 52 E j
Chilikadrotna R., Alaska 76 K f
Chilkat R., Alaska 77 U g
Chillicothe, Illinois 57 D j
Chillicothe, Missouri 61 L e
Chillicothe, Ohio 52 C f
Chillicothe, Texas 65 H a
Chilly, Idaho 66 G e
Chilmark, Massachusetts 51 M c
Chiloquin, Oregon 73 J n
Chilton, Wisconsin 56 E e
Chimayo, New Mexico 71 M d
Chimney Pk., New Mexico 71 M g
China, Maine 49 F d
China Grove, North Carolina 55 L b
China L., California 75 H j
China L., Maine 49 F d
China L., California 75 H j
China Pt., California 75 G m
China Spring, Texas 65 K d
Chinati Mts., Texas 64 C f
Chincoteague, Virginia 53 L h
Chincoteague B., Virginia 53 L g
Chiniak, C., Alaska 76 L h
Chinitna B., Alaska 76 L g
Chinle, Arizona 70 H c
Chinle Cr., Arizona 70 H c
Chinle Valley, Arizona 70 H c
Chino, Arizona 70 E d
Chino Cr., Arizona 70 E d
Chinook, Montana 67 L a
Chinook Pass, Washington 73 J j
Chino Valley, Arizona 70 E e
Chipley, Georgia 54 G e
Chipley, Florida 54 F g
Chipola R., Florida 54 F g
Chippewa Falls, Wisconsin 56 B e
Chippewa L., Wisconsin 56 B d
Chippewa R., Minnesota 59 L e
Chippewa R., Wisconsin 56 B e
Chippewa Res., Wisconsin 56 B d
Chireno, Texas 65 N d
Chiricahua Nat. Mon., Arizona 70 H g
Chiricahua Pk., Arizona 70 H h
Chirikof I., Alaska 76 K j
Chisana, Alaska 77 Q e
Chisana Glacier, Alaska 77 Q f
Chisana R., Alaska 77 R e
Chisholm, Maine 49 E d
Chisholm, Minnesota 59 O c
Chisos Mts., Texas 64 D f
Chispa Cr., Texas 64 C e
Chistochina, Alaska 77 P e
Chitanana R., Alaska 76 L d
Chitina, Alaska 77 P f
Chitina R., Alaska 77 Q f
Chivington, Colorado 69 O e
Chloride, Arizona 70 C d
Chocolate Mts., Arizona 70 C f
Chocolate Mts., California 75 K l
Chocorua, New Hampshire 49 D e
Chocowinity, North Carolina 55 O b
Choctaw, Alabama 54 C e
Choctaw, Oklahoma 62 F c
Choctawhatchee B., Florida 54 E g
Choctawhatchee R., Alabama 54 F f
Choctawhatchee R., Florida 54 F g
Chokio, Minnesota 59 K e
Cholame, California 75 E j
Cholame Cr., California 75 E j
Choptank R., Maryland 53 L g
Choteau, Montana 66 H b
Choteau, Oklahoma 62 H b
Chowan R., North Carolina 55 P a
Chowchilla, California 75 E g
Chowhoctolik, Alaska 76 F f
Chowiet I., Alaska 76 J h
Chrisman, Illinois 57 F k
Christian, Alaska 77 P c
Christiana, Delaware 50 B f
Christiana, Pennsylvania 50 A f
Christiansburg, Ohio 52 C e
Christiansburg, Virginia 52 F h
Christian Sd., Alaska 77 U h
Christina, Montana 67 L b
Christine, Texas 65 J g
Christopher, Illinois 57 D m
Christoval, Texas 64 G d
Chromo, Colorado 69 K f
Chubbuck, California 75 K k
Chuckatuck, Virginia 53 K j
Chuckwalla Mts., California 75 K l
Chugach Is., Alaska 76 M g
Chugach Mts., Alaska 77 O f
Chuginadak I., Alaska 77 T h
Chugul I., Alaska 77 P j
Chugwater, Wyoming 67 Q h
Chugwater Cr., Wyoming 67 P h
Chuichu, Arizona 70 F g
Chuilnuk Mts., Alaska 76 J f
Chukchi Sea, Alaska 76 C c
Chukfaktoolik, Alaska 76 F f
Chula, Georgia 54 H f
Chula, Missouri 61 L e
Chula, Virginia 52 J h
Chula Vista, California (42,034) 75 H m
Chulitna, Alaska 76 N e
Chulitna R., Alaska 76 N e
Chumuckla, Florida 54 D g
Chunchila, Alabama 54 C g
Church Creek, Maryland 53 K g
Church Hill, Maryland 50 A g
Church Hill, Tennessee 55 J a
Churchill, Idaho 66 G g
Churchill L., Maine 49 F b
Church Point, Louisiana 63 L h
Churchs Ferry, North Dakota 58 G b
Churchville, New York 52 J b
Churchville, Virginia 52 G g
Churdan, Iowa 61 K b
Churubusco, Indiana 57 H h
Chuska Mts., New Mexico 71 J c
Cibecue, Arizona 70 G e
Cibola, Arizona 70 C f
Cicero, Illinois (69,130) 57 B l
Cicero, Indiana 57 G j
Cicero, New York 53 K b
Cienega, New Mexico 71 M g
Cima, California 75 K j
Cimarron, Kansas 60 D g
Cimarron R., Kansas 60 C g
Cimarron R., Oklahoma 62 E b
Cincinnati, Iowa 61 M d
Cincinnati, Ohio (502,550) 52 B f
Cincinnatus, New York 53 L c
Cinder R., Alaska 76 H h
Circle, Alaska 77 Q d
Circle, Montana 67 P b
Circle Hot Springs, Alaska 76 P d
Circle Pines, Minnesota 59 Q h
Circleville, New York 50 E c
Circleville, Ohio 52 C f
Circleville, Utah 68 D e
Cisco, Illinois 57 E k
Cisco, Texas 65 J c
Cisco, Utah 68 G e
Cisne, Illinois 57 E l
Cispus Pass, Washington 73 J j
Cispus R., Washington 73 J j
Cistern, Texas 65 K f
Citra, Florida 55 J h
Citronelle, Alabama 54 C f
City I., New York 51 N e
City Point, Florida 55 L j
Clackamas R., Oregon 73 H k
Claflin, Kansas 60 F f
Clagstone, Idaho 66 D a
Claire City, South Dakota 58 J e
Clairemont, Texas 64 G b
Clairton, Pennsylvania 52 G e
Clallam Bay, Washington 73 F g
Clan Alpine Mts., Nevada 74 H e
Clanton, Alabama 54 E e
Clapham, New Mexico 71 O c
Clara, Florida 54 H h
Clara City, Minnesota 59 L f
Clare, Iowa 61 K b
Clare, Michigan 56 J f
Claremont, New Hampshire 49 C e
Claremont, South Dakota 58 H e
Clarence, Iowa 61 N c
Clarence, Louisiana 63 K g
Clarence, Missouri 61 M e
Clarence Fahnestock Park, New York 50 F c
Clarence Str., Alaska 77 V j
Clarendon, Arkansas 63 M d
Clarendon, Pennsylvania 52 G d
Clarendon, Texas 64 D j
Clarendon, Virginia 53 O h
Clareton, Wyoming 67 Q f
Clarinda, Iowa 61 J d
Clarington, Ohio 52 F f
Clarington, Pennsylvania 52 G d
Clarion, Iowa 61 L b
Clarion R., Pennsylvania 52 G d
Clarita, Oklahoma 62 G d
Clark, Colorado 69 K c
Clark, L., Alaska 76 K f
Clark, Missouri 61 M e
Clark, South Dakota 58 J f
Clark, Wyoming 67 L e
Clark Canyon Res., Montana 66 H e
Clarkdale, Arizona 70 E e
Clarkfield, Minnesota 59 L f
Clark Fork, Idaho 66 D a
Clark Fork, Montana 66 G c
Clark Fork, Wyoming 67 L e
Clark Fork R., Montana 66 E b
Clark Hill Dam, Georgia 55 J d
Clark Hill Res., South Carolina-Georgia 55 J d
Clarkia, Idaho 66 D b
Clark L., California 75 J l
Clark Mt., California 75 J j
Clark Pk., Colorado 69 L c
Clarks, Louisiana 63 L f
Clarks, Nebraska 60 G c
Clarksburg, New Jersey 50 E e
Clarksburg, West Virginia (28,112) 52 F f
Clarksburg, Tennessee 54 C b
Clarksdale, Mississippi 63 N d
Clarks Grove, Minnesota 59 N g
Clarks Hill, Indiana 57 G j
Clarkson, Nebraska 60 G c
Clarks Point, Alaska 76 H g
Clarkston, Michigan 56 K g
Clarkston, Montana 66 J c
Clarkston, Washington 73 N j
Clarksville, Arkansas 63 K c
Clarkesville, Georgia 54 H c
Clarkesville, Iowa 61 M b
Clarksville, Maryland 53 K f
Clarksville, Michigan 56 H g
Clarksville, Missouri 61 O e
Clarksville, Tennessee 54 D a
Clarksville, Texas 65 M b
Clarksville, Virginia 52 H j
Clarkton, North Carolina 55 N c
Clarkwood, Texas 65 K h
Clarno, Oregon 73 K l
Claryville, New York 50 D b
Claude, Texas 64 C h
Clauene, Texas 64 E b
Claverack, New York 50 F a
Clay, California 74 D f
Clay, Kentucky 57 F m
Clay, West Virginia 52 E g
Clay, Texas 65 L e
Clay Center, Kansas 60 G e
Clay Center, Nebraska 60 F d
Clay City, Illinois 57 E l
Clay City, Indiana 57 F k
Clay City, Kentucky 57 K m
Claycomo, Missouri 61 Q a
Clayhole Wash, Arizona 70 D c
Claymont, Delaware 50 B f
Claymore, Oklahoma 62 H b
Claypool, Arizona 70 G f
Clay Springs, Arizona 70 G e
Claysville, Pennsylvania 52 F e
Clayton, Alabama 54 F f
Clayton, Delaware 50 B g
Clayton, Georgia 54 H c
Clayton, Idaho 66 F e
Clayton, Indiana 57 G k
Clayton, Kansas 60 D e
Clayton, New Jersey 50 C f
Clayton, New Mexico 71 O c
Clayton, New York 53 K a
Clayton, North Carolina 55 N b
Clayton, Oklahoma 62 H d
Claytor L., Virginia 52 F h
Clayville, New York 53 L c
Clayville, Rhode Island 51 K b
Claxton, Georgia 55 K e
Clear Boggy Cr., Oklahoma 62 G d
Clearbrook, Minnesota 59 L c
Clearco, West Virginia 52 F g
Clear Cr., Arizona 70 G e
Clear Cr., Texas 64 G j
Clear Cr., Wyoming 67 O e
Clear Creek, California 74 B c
Cleare, C., Alaska 76 O g
Clearfield, Iowa 61 K d
Clearfield, Pennsylvania 52 H d
Clearfield, Utah 68 D b
Clear L., California 74 C e
Clear L., Iowa 61 L a
Clear L., Louisiana 63 K f
Clear Lake, Iowa 61 L a
Clear Lake, Minnesota 59 N e
Clear Lake, South Dakota 59 K f
Clear Lake, Wisconsin 56 A d
Clear Lake, Utah 68 D d
Clear Lake Highlands, California 74 C f
Clear Lake Res., California 74 D c
Clearmont, Wyoming 67 O e
Clearview, Washington 72 C g
Clearwater, Florida (34,653) 55 M f
Clearwater, Idaho 66 E c
Clearwater, Kansas 60 G g
Clearwater, Nebraska 60 F b
Clearwater Mts., Idaho 66 E c
Clearwater R., Idaho 66 D c
Clearwater R., Minnesota 59 L c
Clearwater Res., Missouri 61 O g
Cleburne, Kansas 60 H e
Cleburne, Texas 65 K c
Cle Elum, Washington 73 K h
Cle Elum L., Washington 73 J h
Clegg, Texas 65 J g
Clemenceau, Arizona 70 E e
Clementon, New Jersey 50 C f
Clements, California 74 D f
Clendenin, West Virginia 52 E g
Clendening Res., Ohio 52 E e
Cleo Springs, Oklahoma 62 E b
Clermont, Florida 55 K j
Clermont, Iowa 61 N a
Clermont, New York 50 F a
Clermont, Pennsylvania 52 H d
Cleveland, Arkansas 63 L c
Cleveland, Florida 55 N g
Cleveland, Georgia 54 H c
Cleveland, Idaho 66 J g
Cleveland, Minnesota 59 N f
Cleveland, Mississippi 63 N e
Cleveland, Montana 67 L a
Cleveland, Mt., Alaska 77 T h
Cleveland, Mt., Montana 66 G a
Cleveland, New York 53 L b
Cleveland, North Carolina 55 L b
Cleveland, North Dakota 58 G d
Cleveland, Ohio (876,050) 52 E d
Cleveland, Oklahoma 62 G b
Cleveland, South Carolina 55 J b
Cleveland, Tennessee 54 G b
Cleveland, Texas 65 M e
Cleveland, Utah 68 F d
Cleveland, Wisconsin 56 F f
Cleveland Heights, Ohio (61,813), vicinity of Cleveland
Clewiston, Florida 55 O g
Clichy R., Tennessee 54 H a
Clietry R., Tennessee 54 H a
Cliff, New Mexico 71 J g
Cliffdell, Washington 73 J j
Cliff Lake, Montana 66 J e
Clifford, Massachusetts 51 M b
Clifford, Michigan 56 K f
Clifford, North Dakota 58 J c
Clifford, Virginia 52 G h
Clifford, Wisconsin 56 C d
Cliffs, Idaho 66 D g
Cliffside, North Carolina 55 K b
Cliffside Park, New Jersey 51 L e
Clifton, Arizona 70 H f
Clifton, Illinois 57 F j
Clifton, Kansas 60 G e
Clifton, New Jersey (82,084) 51 K e
Clifton, Texas 65 K d
Clifton, Wyoming 67 Q f
Clifton Forge, Virginia 52 G h
Climax, Colorado 69 K d
Climax, Georgia 54 G g
Climax, Michigan 57 H g
Climax, Minnesota 59 K c
Clinch Mts., Tennessee-Virginia 52 D j
Clincho, Virginia 52 D h
Clinchport, Virginia 52 D j
Clinch R., Tennessee-Virginia 54 G b
Cline, Texas 64 G f
Clingmans Dome, mt., Tennessee 54 H b
Clint, Texas 64 A d
Clinton, Arkansas 63 L c
Clinton, Connecticut 51 H c
Clinton, Illinois 57 E j
Clinton, Indiana 57 F k
Clinton, Iowa (33,589) 61 O c
Clinton, Louisiana 63 M h
Clinton, Maine 49 F d
Clinton, Massachusetts 49 D f
Clinton, Michigan 57 K g
Clinton, Minnesota 59 K e
Clinton, Mississippi 63 N f
Clinton, Missouri 61 L f
Clinton, Montana 66 G c
Clinton, New Jersey 50 D d
Clinton, New York 53 L b
Clinton, North Carolina 55 N b
Clinton, Oklahoma 62 D c
Clinton, South Carolina 55 K c
Clinton, Tennessee 54 G a
Clinton, Wisconsin 56 E g
Clinton Corners, New York 50 F b
Clintondale, New York 50 E b
Clintonville, Wisconsin 56 E e
Clio, Alabama 54 F f
Clio, Iowa 61 L d
Clio, Michigan 56 K f
Clio, South Carolina 55 M c
Clive, Utah 68 C c
Clontarf, Minnesota 59 L e
Cloquet, Minnesota 59 O d
Closter, New Jersey 50 E d
Cloudcroft, New Mexico 71 M g
Cloud Pk., Wyoming 67 N e
Cloudy Mt., Alaska 76 J e
Clover, South Carolina 55 K b
Clover, Virginia 52 H j
Cloverdale, California 74 B f
Cloverdale, Indiana 57 G k
Cloverdale, New Mexico 71 J h
Cloverleaf, Texas 64 G h
Cloverport, Kentucky 57 G m
Clovis, California 75 F h
Clovis, New Mexico 71 O e
Cluro, Nevada 74 J d
Clutier, Iowa 61 M b
Clyattville, Georgia 54 H g
Clyde, Kansas 60 G e
Clyde, New York 53 K b
Clyde, North Dakota 58 H b
Clyde, Ohio 52 D d
Clyde, Texas 65 H c
Clyde Park, Montana 67 K d
Clyman, Wisconsin 56 E f
Clymer, Pennsylvania 52 H e
Coahoma, Texas 64 F c
Coal City, Illinois 57 E h
Coaldale, Nevada 74 H f
Coaldale, Pennsylvania 50 B d
Coalgate, Oklahoma 62 G d
Coal Grove, Ohio 52 D g
Coal Hill, Arkansas 63 K c
Coalinga, California 75 E h
Coalmont, Colorado 69 K c
Coalport, Pennsylvania 52 H e
Coal R., West Virginia 52 E g
Coalton, Ohio 52 D f
Coalville, Utah 68 E c
Coalwood, Montana 67 P d
Coast Ra., California 74 B d
Coast Ra., California 75 D g
Coats, Kansas 60 F g
Coats, North Carolina 55 N b
Coatsville, Missouri 61 M d
Coatesville, Pennsylvania 50 B f
Cobb, I., Virginia 53 L h
Cobb, Wisconsin 56 C g
Cobble Mountain Res., Massachusetts 51 H a
Cobden, Illinois 57 D m
Cobleskill, New York 53 M c
Cobol, Alaska 77 U h
Cobre, Nevada 74 L c
Coburg, Oregon 73 G l
Coburn, Pennsylvania 53 J e
Cochecton, New York 50 C b
Cochetopa Pass, Colorado 69 K e
Cochise, Arizona 70 H g
Cochise Head, mt., Arizona 70 H g
Cochituate, Massachusetts 51 L a
Cochran, Georgia 54 H e
Cochranton, Pennsylvania 52 G d
Cochranville, Pennsylvania 50 A f
Cockeysville, Maryland 53 K f
Cockrell Hill, Texas 65 N j
Cocoa, Florida 55 O e
Cocoa Beach, Florida 55 O e
Cocodrie, Louisiana 63 N j
Cocolalla, Idaho 66 D a
Coconino Plateau, Arizona 70 E d
Coconut Grove, Florida 54 B d
Cod, C., Massachusetts 51 N b
Codell, Kansas 60 E e
Cody, Nebraska 60 C b
Cody, Wyoming 67 L e
Coeburn, Virginia 52 D j
Coeur d'Alene, Idaho 66 D b

Fruitdale, South Dakota 58 C f
Fruitdale, Texas 65 N j
Fruitland, Idaho 66 D e
Fruitland, New Mexico 71 J c
Fruitland, Utah 68 F c
Fruitvale, Idaho 66 D e
Fruto, California 74 C e
Fry, Arizona 70 G h
Fryburg, Maine 49 E d
Fryburg, North Dakota 58 C d
Fulda, Minnesota 59 L g
Fullerton, California (56,180) 75 H l
Fullerton, Kentucky 57 K l
Fullerton, Louisiana 63 L g
Fullerton, Nebraska 60 G e
Fulton, Alabama 54 D f
Fulton, Arkansas 63 K e
Fulton, Illinois 57 C h
Fulton, Indiana 57 G j
Fulton, Kansas 61 K f
Fulton, Kentucky 57 E n
Fulton, Louisiana 63 K h
Fulton, Mississippi 63 P d
Fulton, Missouri 61 N f
Fulton, New York 53 K b
Fulton, Ohio 52 D e
Fulton, South Dakota 58 J g
Fultonham, New York 53 M c
Fultonville, New York 53 M c
Funeral Pk., California 75 J h
Funk, Nebraska 60 E d
Funkley, Minnesota 59 M c
Fuquay Springs, North Carolina 55 N b
Furman, South Carolina 55 K e
Furnace Creek, California 75 H h
Gabbs Valley Ra., Nevada 74 G f
Gabilan Ra., California 75 D h
Gabriels, New York 53 M a
Gackle, North Dakota 58 G d
Gadsden, Alabama 54 F d
Gadsden, Arizona 70 C g
Gaffney, South Carolina 55 K b
Gage, New Mexico 71 J g
Gage, Oklahoma 62 D b
Gagen, Wisconsin 56 D d
Gail, Texas 64 F c
Gaillard I., Connecticut 51 H c
Gaines, Michigan 56 K g
Gainesboro, Tennessee 54 F a
Gainesville, Alabama 54 C e
Gainesville, Florida (29,701) 55 J h
Gainesville, Georgia 54 H c
Gainesville, Missouri 61 M h
Gainesville, Texas 65 K b
Gaithersburg, Maryland 53 J f
Gakona, Alaska 77 P e
Galata, Montana 66 J a
Galatea, Colorado 69 N e
Galatia, Illinois 57 E m
Galatia, Kansas 60 F f
Galax, Virginia 52 F j
Galena, Alaska 76 J d
Galena, Illinois 56 C g
Galena, Kansas 61 K g
Galena, Maryland 50 B g
Galena Park, Texas 64 G j
Galene, Missouri 61 L h
Galera, Idaho 66 F f
Galera, Maryland 53 L f
Galesburg, Illinois (37,243) 57 G j
Galesburg, Michigan 57 H g
Galesville, Wisconsin 56 B e
Galeton, Colorado 69 M c
Galeton, Pennsylvania 52 J d
Galice, Oregon 73 G n
Galien, Michigan 57 G g
Galilee, Rhode Island 51 L c
Galion, Ohio 52 D e
Galiuro Mts., Arizona 70 G g
Gallatin, Missouri 61 L e
Gallatin, Tennessee 54 E a
Gallatin, Texas 65 M d
Gallatin Gateway, Montana 66 J d
Gallatin Pk., Montana 66 J d
Gallatin R., Montana 66 J d
Gallatin Ra., Montana 67 K d
Gallegos, New Mexico 71 O d
Gallina Pk., New Mexico 71 L c
Gallinas, New Mexico 71 M e
Gallinas Mts., New Mexico 71 K e
Gallinas Pk., New Mexico 71 M e
Gallipolis, Ohio 52 D g
Gallitzin, Pennsylvania 52 H e
Gallo Mts., New Mexico 71 J f
Galloo I., New York 53 K b
Gallup, New Mexico 71 J d
Galt, California 74 D f
Galt, Missouri 61 L d
Galva, Illinois 57 C h
Galveston, Indiana 57 G j
Galveston, Texas (67,175) 65 N f
Galveston B., Texas 65 N f
Galveston I., Texas 65 N f
Gamaliel, Kentucky 57 H n
Gambell, Alaska 76 B e
Gambier, Ohio 52 D e
Gammon, Pt., Massachusetts 51 N b
Ganado, Arizona 70 H d
Ganado, Texas 65 L f
Gandy, Utah 68 C d
Gannett, Idaho 66 F f
Gannett Pk., Wyoming 67 L f
Gannvalley, South Dakota 58 G f
Gap, Pennsylvania 50 A f
Garber, Oklahoma 62 F b
Garberville, California 74 B d
Garcia, Colorado 69 L f
Gardar, North Dakota 58 J b
Garden, Michigan 56 G d
Gardena, Idaho 66 D f
Gardena, North Dakota 58 F b
Garden City, Alabama 54 E c
Garden City, Georgia 55 K e
Garden City, Kansas 60 D g
Garden City, Michigan (38,017), vicinity of Detroit
Garden City, Missouri 61 K f
Garden City, South Dakota 58 J e
Garden City, Texas 64 F d
Garden City, Utah 68 E b
Gardendale, Texas 65 H g
Garden Grove, California (84,238), vicinity of Los Angeles
Garden Grove, Iowa 61 L d
Gardena, California 75 D m
Garden I., Michigan 56 H d
Garden Island B., Louisiana 63 O j
Garden Valley, Idaho 66 E e
Gardiner, Maine 49 F d
Gardiner, Montana 67 K d
Gardiner, New Mexico 71 N c
Gardiner, New York 50 E b
Gardiner, Oregon 73 F m
Gardiners B., New York 51 J c
Gardiners I., New York 51 J c
Gardner, Colorado 69 L f
Gardner, Florida 55 N f
Gardner, Illinois 57 E h
Gardner, Massachusetts 49 D f
Gardner L., Maine 49 H e
Gardner Pinnacles, Is., Hawaii 72 C a
Gardnerville, Nevada 74 F f
Gareloi I., Alaska 77 N j
Garfield, Arkansas 63 K b
Garfield, Georgia 55 J e
Garfield, Kansas 60 E f
Garfield, New Jersey (29,253) 50 E d
Garfield, Utah 68 B h
Garfield, Washington 73 N h
Garfield Heights, Ohio (38,455), vicinity of Cleveland
Garfield Mt., Montana 66 H e
Garibaldi, Oregon 73 G k
Garland, Kansas 61 K g
Garland, Nebraska 60 H d
Garland, North Carolina 55 N c
Garland, Pennsylvania 52 G d
Garland, Utah 68 D b
Garland, Texas (38,501) 65 O j
Garland, Wyoming 67 M e
Garlrand, Alabama 54 E f
Garnavillo, Iowa 61 N b
Garneill, Montana 67 L c
Garner, Iowa 61 L a
Garner, North Carolina 55 N b
Garnerville, New York 50 E c
Garnet, Michigan 56 H c
Garnet, Montana 66 G c
Garnett, Kansas 61 J f
Garrett, Indiana 57 H h
Garrett, Pennsylvania 52 G f
Garrett, Wyoming 67 P g
Garretson, South Dakota 59 K g
Garrettsville, Ohio 52 E d
Garrison, Iowa 61 M b
Garrison, Kentucky 57 K l
Garrison, Minnesota 59 N d
Garrison, Montana 66 H c
Garrison, New York 50 F c
Garrison, North Dakota 58 E c
Garrison, Texas 65 N d
Garrison, Utah 68 C e
Garrison Dam, North Dakota 58 E c
Garrison Res., North Dakota 58 D c
Garryowen, Montana 67 N d
Garwood, Idaho 66 D b
Garwood, Texas 65 L f
Gary, Colorado 69 N c
Gary, Indiana (178,320) 57 F h
Gary, Minnesota 59 K c
Gary, South Dakota 59 K f
Gary, Texas 65 N c
Gary, West Virginia 52 E h
Gas City, Indiana 57 H j
Gasconade R., Missouri 61 N f
Gascoyne, North Dakota 58 C d
Gashland, Missouri 61 P a
Gasparilla, I., Florida 55 M g
Gasquet, California 74 B c
Gassaway, West Virginia 52 F g
Gass Pk., Nevada 75 K h
Gaston, Oregon 73 G k
Gastonia, North Carolina (37,276) 55 K b
Gate, Oklahoma 62 C b
Gate City, Virginia 52 D j
Gates, Oregon 73 H l
Gates of the Mountains, Montana 66 J c
Gatesville, North Carolina 55 P a
Gatesville, Texas 65 K d
Gateway, Colorado 68 H e
Gateway, Montana 66 E a
Gateway, Oregon 73 J l
Gatlinburg, Tennessee 54 H b
Gatzke, Minnesota 59 L b
Gauley Bridge, West Virginia 52 E g
Gavilan, New Mexico 71 K c
Gaviota, California 75 E k
Gay, Michigan 56 E b
Gaylord, Kansas 60 F e
Gaylord, Michigan 56 J d
Gaylord, Minnesota 59 M f
Gaylord, Oregon 73 F n
Gays Mills, Wisconsin 56 C f
Gayville, South Dakota 58 J h
Gazelle, California 74 C c
Gearhart, Oregon 73 G j
Gearhart Mt., Oregon 73 K n
Geary, Oklahoma 62 E c
Gebo, Wyoming 67 M f
Geddes, South Dakota 58 H g
Geigertown, Pennsylvania 50 B e
Gem, Kansas 60 D e
Gem, Texas 64 D h
Gene Autry, Oklahoma 62 F d
Genesee, Idaho 66 D c
Genessee, Michigan 56 K f
Genesee R., New York 52 J c
Geneseo, Illinois 57 C h
Geneseo, Kansas 60 F f
Geneseo, New York 52 J c
Geneva, Alabama 54 F f
Geneva, Georgia 54 G e
Geneva, Illinois 57 E h
Geneva, Indiana 57 H j
Geneva, L., Wisconsin 56 E g
Geneva, Nebraska 60 G d
Geneva, New York 53 J c
Geneva, Ohio 52 F d
Geneva, Texas 65 O d
Genoa, Colorado 69 N d
Genoa, Florida 55 J g
Genoa, Illinois 57 E g
Genoa, Nebraska 60 G c
Genoa, Nevada 74 F e
Genoa, Ohio 52 C d
Genoa, Texas 64 G j
Genoa, Wisconsin 56 B f
Genoa City, Illinois 56 E g
Genou, Montana 66 J a
Gentilly, Louisiana 62 C e
Gentry, Arkansas 63 J b
Gentry, Missouri 61 K d
George, Iowa 61 H a
George, L., Alaska 77 N f
George, L., Alaska 77 P e
George, L., Florida 55 K h
George, L., New York 53 N b
George R., Alaska 76 J e
Georgetown, Arkansas 63 M c
Georgetown, California 74 E f
Georgetown, Connecticut 50 G c
Georgetown, Delaware 53 L g
Georgetown, Florida 55 K h
Georgetown, Georgia 54 F f
Georgetown, Idaho 66 J g
Georgetown, Illinois 57 F k
Georgetown, Kentucky 57 J l
Georgetown, Ohio 52 C g
Georgetown, Maryland 50 B g
Georgetown, Minnesota 59 K c
Georgetown, Mississippi 63 N g
Georgetown, South Carolina 55 M d
Georgetown, Texas 65 K e
George Washington Birthplace Nat. Mon., Virginia 53 J g
George West, Texas 65 J g
Georgia 54-55
Georgiana, Alabama 54 E f
Gerald, Missouri 61 N f
Geraldine, Montana 67 K b
Gerber, California 74 C d
Gerber Res., Oregon 73 J n
Gerdine, Mt., Alaska 76 L f
Gering, Nebraska 60 A c
Gerlach, Nevada 74 F d
Germantown, Illinois 57 D l
Germantown, Maryland 53 K f
Germantown, New York 53 N c
Germantown, Ohio 52 B f
Germantown, Pennsylvania 50 F f
Germantown, Tennessee 54 B b
Germfask, Michigan 56 G c
Gerome, Washington 73 M g
Geronimo, Arizona 70 G f
Geronimo, Oklahoma 62 E d
Gerstle R., Alaska 77 P e
Gervais L., Minnesota 59 R h
Getchell Mine, Nevada 74 H c
Gettysburg, Pennsylvania 52 J f
Gettysburg, South Dakota 58 G e
Geuda Springs, Kansas 60 G g
Geyser, Montana 67 K b
Gheen, Minnesota 59 O c
Ghent, Kentucky 57 H l
Ghent, Minnesota 59 L f
Ghent, New York 50 F a
Gibbon, Nebraska 60 F d
Gibbon, Oregon 73 M k
Gibbons Pass, Montana 66 F d
Gibbonsville, Idaho 66 G d
Gibbs City, Michigan 56 E c
Gibbstown, New Jersey 50 C f
Gibsland, Louisiana 63 K f
Gibson, California 74 C c
Gibson, Georgia 55 J d
Gibson, Montana 67 L c
Gibsonburg, Ohio 52 C d
Gibson City, Illinois 57 E j
Gibsonton, Florida 55 M f
Gibsonville, North Carolina 55 M a
Giddings, Texas 65 L e
Gideon, Missouri 61 P h
Gifford, Florida 55 O f
Gifford, Iowa 61 L b
Gifford, Washington 73 M g
Gila, New Mexico 71 J g
Gila Bend, Arizona 70 E g
Gila Bend Mts., Arizona 70 D f
Gila Cliff Dwellings Nat. Mon., New Mexico 71 J f
Gila Mts., Arizona 70 C g
Gila R., Arizona 70 F f
Gilbert, Arizona 70 F f
Gilbert, Minnesota 59 O c
Gilbert, Mt., Alaska 77 N f
Gilbert, Nevada 74 H f
Gilbert, West Virginia 52 E h
Gilberton, Pennsylvania 50 A d
Gilbertown, Alabama 54 C f
Gilbert Pk., Utah 68 F c
Gilbertsville, Pennsylvania 50 B e
Gilbertville, Massachusetts 51 J a
Gilby, North Dakota 58 J b
Gilcrest, Colorado 69 M c
Gildford, Montana 67 K a
Gilead, Maine 49 E d
Gilead, Nebraska 60 G d
Giles, Texas 64 D j
Gill, Colorado 69 M c
Gillespie, Arizona 70 E f
Gillespie, Illinois 57 D k
Gillett, Arkansas 63 M d
Gillett, Pennsylvania 53 K d
Gillett, Texas 65 K f
Gillett, Wisconsin 56 E e
Gillette, Wyoming 67 P e
Gillham, Arkansas 63 J d
Gilliam, Missouri 61 L e
Gillis, Louisiana 63 K h
Gillon Pt., Alaska 76 J j
Gills Rock, Wisconsin 56 F d
Gilman, Illinois 57 E j
Gilman, Iowa 61 M c
Gilman, Montana 66 H b
Gilman, Wisconsin 56 C d
Gilman City, Missouri 61 L d
Gilmer, Texas 65 N c
Gilmore, Idaho 66 G e
Gilmore City, Iowa 61 K b
Gilroy, California 75 D g
Giltner, Nebraska 60 F d
Gimlet, Idaho 66 F f
Girard, Illinois 57 D k
Girard, Kansas 61 K g
Girard, Ohio 52 F d
Girard, Pennsylvania 52 F c
Girard, Texas 64 G b
Girdwood, Alaska 76 N f
Girvin, Texas 64 E d
Gisasa R., Alaska 76 H d
Gisela, Arizona 70 F e
Glacier, Washington 73 J g
Glacier Bay, Alaska 77 T g
Glacier Bay Nat. Mon., Alaska 77 T g
Glacier I., Alaska 77 O f
Glacier Mt., Alaska 77 Q d
Glacier Pk., Washington 73 J g
Gladbrook, Iowa 61 M b
Glade, Kansas 60 E e
Glade Park, Colorado 68 H e
Glade Spring, Virginia 52 E j
Gladewater, Texas 65 N c
Gladstone, Michigan 56 G d
Gladstone, Missouri 61 P a
Gladstone, New Jersey 50 D d
Gladstone, North Dakota 58 D d
Gladwin, Michigan 56 J f
Glady, West Virginia 52 G g
Gladys, Virginia 52 G h
Glamis, California 75 K l
Glasco, Kansas 60 G e
Glasco, New York 50 F a
Glasford, Illinois 57 D j
Glasgo, Connecticut 51 K b
Glasgow, Kentucky 57 H n
Glasgow, Missouri 61 M e
Glasgow, Montana 67 O a
Glasgow, Virginia 52 G h
Glassboro, New Jersey 50 C f
Glass Mt., California 74 G g
Glass Mts., Texas 64 D e
Glass Pen., Alaska 77 U h
Glassport, Pennsylvania 53 Q c
Glastonbury, Connecticut 51 H b
Glazier, Texas 64 D g
Gleason, Tennessee 54 C a
Gleason, Wisconsin 56 D d
Gleasonton, Pennsylvania 52 J d
Gleeson, Arizona 70 H h
Glen, Mt., Arizona 70 H g
Glen, Nebraska 60 A b
Glen, New Hampshire 49 D d
Glenada, Oregon 73 F m
Glenaire, Missouri 61 Q a
Glen Alpine, North Carolina 55 K b
Glenbrook, Connecticut 50 F c
Glenburn, North Dakota 58 E b
Glen Burnie, Maryland 53 K f
Glen Canyon, Arizona 70 F c
Glencoe, Alabama 54 F d
Glencoe, Minnesota 59 M f
Glencoe, New Mexico 71 M f
Glen Cove, New York 50 F d
Glencross, South Dakota 58 F e
Glendale, Arizona 70 E f
Glendale, California (119,442) 75 E l
Glendale, Florida 54 E g
Glendale, Kansas 60 G f
Glendale, Nevada 75 L h
Glendale, Ohio 52 B f
Glendale, Oregon 73 G n
Glendale, West Virginia 52 F f
Glendevey, Colorado 69 L c
Glendive, Montana 67 Q b
Glendo, Wyoming 67 P g
Glendora, Mississippi 63 N e
Glen Elder, Kansas 60 F e
Glen Elder Res., Kansas 60 F e
Glenfield, New York 53 L b
Glenfield, North Dakota 58 H c
Glen Flora, Texas 65 L f
Glenford, New York 50 E a
Glen Gardner, New Jersey 50 D d
Glenham, New York 50 F c
Glenham, South Dakota 58 F e
Glen L., Michigan 56 G e
Glen Lyon, Pennsylvania 50 A c
Glen Mills, Pennsylvania 50 B f
Glenmora, Louisiana 63 L h
Glenn, California 74 C e
Glennallen, Alaska 77 P e
Glenns Ferry, Idaho 66 E g
Glennie, Michigan 56 K e
Glennville, California 75 G j
Glennville, Georgia 55 K f
Glenrio, New Mexico 71 O d
Glen Rock, New Jersey 51 K d
Glen Rock, Pennsylvania 53 K f
Glenrock, Wyoming 67 P g
Glen Rose, Texas 65 K c
Glens Falls, New York 53 N b
Glenshaw, Pennsylvania 53 P a
Glen Spey, New York 50 D c
Glen Summit, Pennsylvania 50 B c
Glentana, Montana 67 O a
Glen Ullin, North Dakota 58 E d
Glenview, Illinois 57 F g
Glenville, Minnesota 59 N g
Glenville, Nebraska 60 F d
Glenville, West Virginia 52 F g
Glenville L., North Carolina 54 H b
Glen Wild, New York 50 D b
Glenwood, Alabama 54 E f
Glenwood, Arkansas 63 K d
Glenwood, Georgia 55 J e
Glenwood, Indiana 57 H k
Glenwood, Iowa 61 J c
Glenwood, Minnesota 59 L e
Glenwood, Missouri 61 M d
Glenwood, New Jersey 50 D c
Glenwood, New Mexico 71 J f
Glenwood, North Carolina 55 K b
Glenwood, Oregon 73 G k
Glenwood, Utah 68 E e
Glenwood, West Virginia 52 D g
Glenwood, Washington 73 J j
Glenwood, Wisconsin 56 A d
Glenwood Springs, Colorado 69 J d
Glidden, Wisconsin 56 C c
Glide, Oregon 73 G m
Globe, Arizona 70 G f
Glorieta, New Mexico 71 M d
Glory of Russia C., Alaska 76 A f
Gloster, Mississippi 63 M g
Gloucester, Massachusetts (25,789) 49 E f
Gloucester, New Jersey 50 G g
Gloucester, Virginia 53 K h
Gloucester City, New Jersey 50 C f
Glouster, Ohio 52 D f
Gloversville, New York 53 M b
Glyndon, Maryland 53 K f
Glyndon, Minnesota 59 K d
Gnadenhutten, Ohio 52 E e
Goat Mt., Montana 66 G a
Goddard, Kansas 60 G g
Goddard, Mt., California 75 J g
Godfrey, Illinois 57 C l
Godley, Texas 65 K c
Godwin, North Carolina 55 N b
Goff, Kansas 61 J e
Goffs, California 75 K k
Goffstown, New Hampshire 49 D e
Gogebic L., Michigan 56 D c
Gogebic Ra., Michigan 56 D c
Golconda, Illinois 57 E m
Golconda, Nevada 74 H d
Gold, Pennsylvania 52 J d
Gold Beach, Oregon 73 F n
Goldburg, Idaho 66 G e
Gold Butte, Montana 66 J a
Gold Creek, Alaska 76 N e
Golden, Arizona 70 D f
Golden, Colorado 69 L d
Golden, Idaho 66 E d
Golden, Illinois 57 B j
Golden Acres, Texas 64 G j
Golden Beach, Florida 54 C c
Golden Bridge, New York 50 F c
Golden City, Missouri 61 K g
Goldendale, Washington 73 K k
Golden Gate, California 75 B l
Golden Gate Ra., Nevada 74 K g
Golden Meadow, Louisiana 63 N j
Golden Pond, Kentucky 57 E n
Golden Valley, Minnesota 59 P h
Goldfield, Iowa 61 L b
Goldfield, Nevada 74 H g
Goldfinch, Texas 65 J g
Gold Hill, Utah 68 C c
Goldsboro, Maryland 50 B g
Goldsboro, North Carolina (28,873) 55 O b
Goldsmith, Texas 64 E c
Goldstone L., California 75 J j
Goldthwaite, Texas 65 J d
Goldville, South Carolina 55 K c
Goleta, California 75 F k
Goliad, Texas 65 K g
Golovin, Alaska 76 F d
Golovin B., Alaska 76 F d
Golsovia, Alaska 76 G e
Goltry, Oklahoma 62 E b
Golva, North Dakota 58 C d
Gonvick, Minnesota 59 L c
Gonzales, California 75 D h
Gonzales, Texas 65 K f
Goochland, Virginia 52 H h
Good Harbor B., Michigan 56 H d
Good Hart, Michigan 56 H d
Goodhope B., Alaska 76 F c
Goodhope R., Alaska 76 E d
Goodhue, Minnesota 59 O f
Gooding, Idaho 66 F g
Goodland, Kansas 60 C e
Goodlett, Texas 64 E j
Goodlettsville, Tennessee 54 E a
Goodman, Wisconsin 56 E d
Goodnews B., Alaska 76 G g
Goodnews Bay, Alaska 76 G g
Goodnews R., Alaska 76 G g
Goodnight, Texas 64 C h
Good Pasture, Colorado 69 M e
Goodpaster R., Alaska 77 P d
Goodrich, Colorado 69 M c
Goodrich, Idaho 66 D e
Goodrich, North Dakota 58 F c
Goodrich, Texas 65 N e
Goodrich, Wisconsin 56 C d
Goodridge, Minnesota 59 L b
Goodsprings, Nevada 75 K j
Good Water, Alabama 54 E d
Goodwell, Oklahoma 62 B b
Goodwin, Arizona 70 E e
Goodwin, South Dakota 59 K f
Gooseberry Cr., Wyoming 67 M e
Goose Cr., Idaho 66 G g
Goose Creek Res., Idaho 66 G g
Goose Egg, Wyoming 67 O g
Goose I., Alaska 76 F j
Goose L., California 74 E c
Gordo, Alabama 54 D d
Gordon, Alaska 77 R b
Gordon, Colorado 69 M f
Gordon, Georgia 54 H e
Gordon, Nebraska 60 B b
Gordon, Texas 65 J c
Gordon, Wisconsin 56 B c
Gordon Cr., Nebraska 60 C b
Gordonsville, Tennessee 54 F a
Gordonsville, Virginia 52 H g
Gore, Oklahoma 62 H c
Goree, Texas 65 H b
Gore Mt., Vermont 49 D d
Gore Pt., Alaska 76 M g
Gore Ra., Colorado 69 K d
Goreville, Illinois 57 E m
Gorgorza, Utah 68 E c
Gorham, Kansas 60 E f
Gorham, Maine 49 E e
Gorham, New Hampshire 49 D d
Gorham, New York 53 J c
Gorin, Missouri 61 M d
Gorman, California 75 G k
Gorman, South Dakota 58 F f
Gorman, Texas 65 J c
Gormania, Maryland 52 G f
Gorst, Washington 72 A j
Goshen, California 75 F h
Goshen, Connecticut 50 G b
Goshen, Indiana 57 H h
Goshen, New Jersey 50 D g
Goshen, New York 50 E c
Goshen, Oregon 73 H m
Goshen, Utah 68 E d
Goshen, Virginia 52 G h
Gosport, Indiana 57 G k
Goss, Mississippi 63 O g
Gotebo, Oklahoma 62 E c
Gotham, Wisconsin 56 C f
Gothenburg, Nebraska 60 D d
Gough, Georgia 55 J d
Gould, Arkansas 63 M e
Gould, Colorado 69 K c
Gould, Oklahoma 62 D d
Gould City, Michigan 56 H c
Goulds, Florida 55 O h
Gouldsboro, Pennsylvania 50 C c
Gouverneur, New York 53 L a
Gove, Kansas 60 D f
Government Camp, Oregon 73 J k
Governors I., New York 51 L f
Gowanda, New York 52 H c
Gower, Missouri 61 K e
Gowrie, Iowa 61 K b
Grace, Idaho 66 J g
Grace City, North Dakota 58 H c
Gracemont, Oklahoma 62 E c
Graceville, Florida 54 F g
Graceville, Minnesota 59 K e
Gracey, Kentucky 57 F n
Grady, Arkansas 63 M d
Grady, New Mexico 71 O e
Gradyville, Pennsylvania 50 B f
Graeagle, California 74 E e
Graettinger, Iowa 61 K a
Graford, Texas 65 J c
Grafton, Illinois 57 C l
Grafton, Iowa 61 L a
Grafton, Massachusetts 51 K a
Grafton, Mt., Nevada 74 L f
Grafton, New York 53 N c
Grafton, North Dakota 58 J b
Grafton, Ohio 52 D d
Grafton, West Virginia 52 G f
Grafton, Wisconsin 56 F f
Graham, New York 50 D c
Graham, Texas 65 J b
Graham L., Maine 49 G d
Graham Mt., Arizona 70 H g
Grahamsville, New York 50 D b
Grainfield, Kansas 60 D e
Grainton, Nebraska 60 C d
Granada, Colorado 69 O e

Hanley Falls, Minnesota 59 L f
Hanna, Utah 68 F c
Hanna, Wyoming 67 O h
Hannaford, North Dakota 58 H c
Hannah, North Dakota 58 H b
Hannibal, Missouri 61 N e
Hannibal, Wisconsin 56 C d
Hannover, North Dakota 58 E c
Hanover, Connecticut 51 J b
Hanover, Massachusetts 51 M a
Hanover, Minnesota 59 N e
Hanover, Montana 67 L b
Hanover, New Hampshire 49 C e
Hanover, Kansas 60 H e
Hanover, Pennsylvania 53 J f
Hansboro, North Dakota 58 G b
Hanson, Massachusetts 51 M a
Happy, Texas 64 C j
Happy Camp, California 74 B c
Harahan, Louisiana 62 B f
Harbor, Oregon 73 F n
Harbor Beach, Michigan 56 L f
Harbor I., Washington 72 B h
Harbor Springs, Michigan 56 J d
Harcuvar Mts., Arizona 70 D e
Hardee, Mississippi 63 N f
Hardeeville, South Carolina 55 K e
Hardesty, Oklahoma 62 B b
Hardin, Illinois 57 C k
Hardin, Missouri 61 L e
Hardin, Montana 67 N d
Harding, Minnesota 59 M d
Harding Icefield, Alaska 76 M f
Hardinsburg, Kentucky 57 G m
Hardman, Oregon 73 L k
Hardwick, Minnesota 59 K g
Hardwick, Vermont 49 C d
Hardy, Arkansas 63 M b
Hardy, Montana 66 J b
Hardy Res., Michigan 56 H f
Hargill, Texas 65 J j
Harkers Island, North Carolina 55 P c
Harlan, Iowa 61 J c
Harlan, Kansas 60 F e
Harlan, Kentucky 57 K n
Harlan Res., Nebraska 60 E d
Harlem, Georgia 55 J d
Harlem, Montana 67 M a
Harlemville, New York 50 F a
Harleysville, Pennsylvania 50 C e
Harleyville, South Carolina 55 L d
Harlingen, Texas (41,207) 65 K j
Harlow, North Dakota 58 G b
Harlowton, Montana 67 L c
Harman, West Virginia 52 G g
Harmarville, Pennsylvania 53 Q a
Harmersville, New Jersey 50 C g
Harmon, Oklahoma 62 D b
Harmony, Maine 49 F d
Harmony, Minnesota 59 O g
Harmony, New Jersey 50 C d
Harmony, Rhode Island 51 K b
Harney, L., Florida 55 K j
Harney, Oregon 73 M m
Harney Basin, Oregon 73 L m
Harney (Dry) L., Oregon 73 L m
Harney Pk., South Dakota 58 C g
Harpath R., Tennessee 54 D a
Harper, Kansas 60 F g
Harper, Mt., Alaska 77 Q d
Harper, Oregon 73 N m
Harper, Texas 65 H e
Harper, Washington 72 B j
Harper Bend, Alaska 76 M d
Harper L., California 75 H j
Harpers Ferry, West Virginia 52 J f
Harpster, Idaho 66 E d
Harquahala Mts., Arizona 70 D f
Harrah, Oklahoma 62 F c
Harrell, Arkansas 63 L e
Harriet, L., Minnesota 59 Q j
Harrietta, Michigan 56 H e
Harriman, New York 50 E c
Harriman, Tennessee 54 G b
Harrington, Delaware 50 B h
Harrington, Maine 49 H d
Harrington, Washington 73 M h
Harris, California 74 B d
Harris, L., Florida 55 K j
Harris, Missouri 61 L d
Harrisburg, Arkansas 63 N c
Harrisburg, Illinois 57 E m
Harrisburg, Nebraska 60 A c
Harrisburg, Ohio 52 C f
Harrisburg, Oregon 73 G l
Harrisburg, Pennsylvania (79,697) 53 J e
Harrisburg, South Dakota 59 K g
Harrison, Arkansas 63 K b
Harrison, Georgia 55 J e
Harrison, Idaho 66 D b
Harrison, Michigan 56 J e
Harrison, Montana 66 J d
Harrison, Nebraska 60 A b
Harrison, New Jersey 51 K f
Harrison, New York 50 F d
Harrison, South Dakota 58 H g
Harrison B., Alaska 76 L a
Harrisonburg, Louisiana 63 M g
Harrisonburg, Virginia 52 H g
Harrisonville, New Jersey 50 C f
Harrisonville, Missouri 61 K f
Harrisville, Michigan 56 K e
Harrisville, New York 53 L a
Harrisville, Rhode Island 51 K b
Harrisville, West Virginia 52 E f
Harrodsburg, Indiana 57 G k
Harrodsburg, Kentucky 57 J m
Harrold, South Dakota 58 G f
Harrold, Texas 65 H a
Harrow, Pennsylvania 50 C e
Harry Strunk L., Nebraska 60 D d
Hart, Michigan 56 G f
Hart, Texas 64 B j
Hartford, Arkansas 63 J c
Hartford, Alabama 54 F f
Hartford, Connecticut (162,178) 51 H b
Hartford, Ohio 52 D e
Hartford, Kansas 61 J f
Hartford, Kentucky 57 F m
Hartford, Michigan 57 G g
Hartford, Tennessee 54 H b
Hartford, Wisconsin 56 E f
Hartford City, Indiana 57 H j
Hartington, Nebraska 60 G b
Hart I., New York 51 N e
Hart L., Oregon 73 L n
Hartland, Maine 49 F d
Hartley, Iowa 61 J a
Hartley, Texas 64 B h
Hartline, Washington 73 L h
Hartly, Delaware 50 B g
Hartman, Colorado 69 O e
Hart Mt., Oregon 73 L n
Hartsdale, New York 50 F d
Hartsel, Colorado 69 L d
Hartselle, Alabama 54 E c
Hartshorne, Oklahoma 62 H d
Hartsville, South Carolina 55 L c
Hartsville, Tennessee 54 E a
Hartville, Missouri 61 M g
Hartville, Wyoming 67 Q g
Hartwell, Georgia 55 J c
Hartwell Res., South Carolina 55 J c
Hartwood, New York 50 D c
Harvard, California 75 J k
Harvard, Idaho 66 D c
Harvard, Illinois 56 E g
Harvard, Mt., Colorado 69 K e
Harvard, Nebraska 60 F d
Harvard Glacier, Alaska 77 O f
Harvey, Illinois (29,071) 57 F h
Harvey, Iowa 61 M c
Harvey, Louisiana 62 C f
Harvey, Michigan 56 F c
Harvey, North Dakota 58 F c
Harvey Mt., California 74 D d
Harveyville, Kansas 61 J f
Harviell, Missouri 61 O h
Harwich, Massachusetts 51 N b
Harwich Port, Massachusetts 51 N b
Harwinton, Connecticut 51 G b
Harwood, Texas 65 K f
Haskell, Arkansas 63 L d
Haskell, Oklahoma 62 H c
Haskell, Texas 65 H b
Haslet, Texas 65 L h
Hassayampa R., Arizona 70 E f
Hastings, Florida 55 K h
Hastings, Iowa 61 J c
Hastings, Michigan 56 H g
Hastings, Minnesota 59 O f
Hastings, Nebraska 60 F d
Hastings, Oklahoma 62 E d
Hastings, Pennsylvania 52 H e
Hastings-on-Hudson, New York 50 F d
Hasty, Colorado 69 O e
Haswell, Colorado 69 N e
Hatboro, Pennsylvania 53 L e
Hatch, New Mexico 71 K g
Hatch, Utah 68 D f
Hatchel, Texas 64 G d
Hatchie R., Tennessee 54 B b
Hatchville, Massachusetts 51 M b
Hat Creek, California 74 D d
Hat Creek, Wyoming 67 Q g
Hatfield, Arkansas 63 J d
Hatfield, Minnesota 59 K g
Hatfield, Pennsylvania 50 C e
Hathaway, Montana 67 O c
Hatteras, C., North Carolina 55 P d
Hatteras, North Carolina 55 P d
Hatteras Inlet, North Carolina 55 P d
Hattiesburg, Mississippi (34,989) 63 O g
Hatton, North Dakota 58 J c
Hatton, Washington 73 M j
Haugen, Wisconsin 56 B d
Haughton, Louisiana 63 K f
Haulover Beach Park, Florida 54 C c
Hauser Lake Dam, Montana 66 J c
Hauula, Hawaii 72 C d
Havana, Arkansas 63 K c
Havana, Florida 54 G g
Havana, Illinois 57 C j
Havana, Kansas 61 J g
Havana, North Dakota 58 J e
Havasu L., California 75 L k
Havelock, North Carolina 55 P c
Havelock, North Dakota 58 D d
Haven, Kansas 60 G g
Haven, New York 50 D b
Havensville, Kansas 61 H e
Haverhill, Massachusetts (46,346) 49 E f
Haverhill, New Hampshire 49 C d
Haverstraw, New York 50 F d
Haviland, Kansas 60 E g
Haviland, Ohio 52 B d
Havre, Montana 67 L a
Havre de Grace, Maryland 50 A f
Hawaii 72
Hawaii, I., Hawaii 72 E f
Hawaii Nat. Park, I. of Hawaii, Hawaii 72 E f
Hawaii Nat. Park, I. of Maui, Hawaii 72 D e
Hawarden, Iowa 60 H b
Hawes, California 75 H k
Hawesville, Kentucky 57 G m
Hawi, Hawaii 72 E e
Hawk Chan., Florida 55 O j
Hawk Inlet, Alaska 77 U g
Hawkins Pk., Utah 68 C f
Hawkinsville, Georgia 54 H e
Hawk Point, Missouri 61 N f
Hawks, Michigan 56 K d
Hawk Springs, Wyoming 67 Q h
Hawley, Colorado 69 N f
Hawley, Minnesota 59 K d
Hawley, Pennsylvania 53 L d
Hawley, Texas 65 H c
Haworth, Oklahoma 63 J e
Haw R., North Carolina 55 M b
Hawthorn, Florida 55 J h
Hawthorne, California (33,035) 75 D m
Hawthorne, Nevada 74 G f
Hawthorne, New Jersey 50 E d
Hawthorne, Wisconsin 56 B c
Hawthorne Place, Texas 64 F h
Hay, Washington 73 N j
Haybro, Colorado 69 K c
Haycock, Alaska 76 G d
Hayden, Arizona 70 G f
Hayden, Colorado 69 J c
Hayden L., Idaho 66 D b
Hayes, South Dakota 58 E f
Hayes Center, Nebraska 60 C d
Hayfield, Minnesota 59 O g
Hayfield Res., California 75 K l
Hayfork, California 74 B d
Hayes, Louisiana 63 L h
Hayes, Mt., Alaska 77 O e
Hayes Glaciers, Alaska 76 L f
Hayesville, North Carolina 54 H b
Haylow, Georgia 55 J g
Haymarket, Virginia 52 J g
Haynes, North Dakota 58 D e
Haynesville, Maine 49 G c
Haynesville, Louisiana 63 K f
Hayneville, Alabama 54 E e
Hay R., Wisconsin 56 B d
Hays, Kansas 60 E f
Hays, Montana 67 M a
Hays, Pennsylvania 53 Q b
Hay Springs, Nebraska 60 B b
Haystack Mt., Nevada 74 K c
Haystack Pk., Utah 68 C d
Hayti, Missouri 61 P h
Hayti, South Dakota 58 J f
Hayward, California (72,700) 75 C m
Hayward, Minnesota 59 N g
Hayward, Oklahoma 62 F b
Hayward, Wisconsin 56 B c
Haxby, Montana 67 O b
Haxtun, Colorado 69 O c
Hazard, Kentucky 57 K m
Hazardville, Connecticut 51 H b
Hazel, Kentucky 57 E n
Hazel, Minnesota 59 K e
Hazel, South Dakota 58 J f
Hazel Park, Michigan (25,631) 57 L j
Hazelton, Kansas 60 F g
Hazelton, North Dakota 58 F d
Hazelton, Pennsylvania 50 B d
Hazelwood, Pennsylvania 53 P b
Hazen, Arkansas 63 M d
Hazen, Nevada 74 G e
Hazen, North Dakota 58 E c
Hazen B., Alaska 76 E f
Hazewood, North Carolina 55 J b
Hazlehurst, Georgia 55 J f
Hazlehurst, Mississippi 63 N g
Hazleton, Pennsylvania (32,056) 53 L e
Headland, Alabama 54 F f
Head of Westport, Massachusetts 51 L b
Headquarters, Idaho 66 E c
Heads, The, Oregon 73 F n
Heafford Junction, Wisconsin 56 D d
Healdsburg, California 74 C f
Healdton, Oklahoma 62 F d
Healy, Alaska 76 N e
Healy, Kansas 60 D f
Healy L., Alaska 77 P e
Healy R., Alaska 77 P d
Hearne, Texas 65 L e
Hearst, California 74 B e
Heart Butte Res., North Dakota 58 E d
Heart L., Wyoming 67 K e
Heart R., North Dakota 58 D d
Heartwell, Nebraska 60 F d
Heath Springs, South Carolina 55 L c
Heathsville, Virginia 53 K h
Heavener, Oklahoma 63 J d
Hebbronville, Texas 65 J h
Heber, Arizona 70 G e
Heber Springs, Arkansas 63 L c
Hebgen L., Montana 66 J e
Hebo, Oregon 73 G k
Hebron, Connecticut 51 J b
Hebron, Colorado 69 K c
Hebron, Illinois 56 E g
Hebron, Indiana 57 F h
Hebron, Mt., California 74 C c
Hebron, Nebraska 60 G d
Hebron, North Dakota 58 D d
Hebron, Ohio 52 D f
Hebronville, Massachusetts 51 L b
Heceta Hd., Oregon 73 F l
Heceta I., Alaska 77 V j
Hecla, South Dakota 58 H e
Hector, California 75 J k
Hector, Minnesota 59 M f
Hedgesville, Montana 67 L c
Hedgesville, West Virginia 52 H f
Hedley, Texas 64 D j
Hedrick, Iowa 61 M c
Heflin, Alabama 54 F d
Heidelberg, Pennsylvania 53 O b
Heidelberg, Kentucky 57 J m
Heidelberg, Mississippi 63 P g
Heights, The, Michigan 56 J e
Heimdal, North Dakota 58 G e
Heine Creek, Alaska 77 N d
Heislerville, New Jersey 50 D g
Helen, Georgia 54 H c
Helen, Mt., Nevada 75 J g
Helena, Alabama 54 E d
Helena, Arkansas 63 N d
Helena, California 74 B d
Helena, Georgia 55 J e
Helena, Montana 66 H c
Helena, Oklahoma 62 E b
Helendale, California 75 H k
Hells Canyon, Idaho 66 D d
Helm, California 75 E h
Helmville, Montana 66 H c
Helotes, Texas 65 J f
Helper, Utah 68 F d
Heltonville, Indiana 57 G l
Hemet, California 75 J l
Hemingford, Nebraska 60 A b
Hemingway, South Carolina 55 M d
Hemlock Res., Connecticut 50 G c
Hemphill, Texas 65 O d
Hempstead, New York (34,641) 50 F d
Hempstead, Texas 65 L e
Henderson, Colorado 69 P h
Henderson, Kentucky 57 F m
Henderson, Maryland 50 B g
Henderson, Nevada 75 L h
Henderson, New York 53 K b
Henderson, North Carolina 55 N a
Henderson, Tennessee 54 C b
Henderson, Texas 65 N c
Henderson, West Virginia 52 D g
Hendersonville, North Carolina 55 J b
Hendricks, Minnesota 59 K f
Hendricks, West Virginia 52 G f
Henefer, Utah 68 E b
Henleyville, California 74 C e
Henlopen, C., Delaware 53 L g
Henly, Texas 65 J e
Hennepin, Illinois 57 D h
Hennessy, Oklahoma 62 F b
Henniker, New Hampshire 49 D e
Henning, Illinois 57 F j
Henning, Minnesota 59 L d
Henning, Tennessee 54 B b
Henrietta, Texas 65 J b
Henrieville, Utah 68 E f
Henry, C., Virginia 53 L j
Henry, Idaho 66 J g
Henry, Illinois 57 D h
Henry, Mt., Montana 66 E a
Henryetta, Oklahoma 62 G c
Henry L., Montana 66 J e
Henry Mts., Utah 68 E d
Henryville, Indiana 57 H l
Henryville, Pennsylvania 50 C c
Henshaw, Kentucky 57 E m
Henshaw L., California 75 J l
Hensonville, New York 50 E a
Hephzibah, Georgia 55 J d
Heppner, Oregon 73 L k
Herber, Utah 68 E c
Herbert I., Alaska 77 S j
Herd, Oklahoma 62 G b
Hereford, Colorado 69 M c
Hereford, Pennsylvania 50 B e
Hereford, Texas 64 B j
Hereford Inlet, New Jersey 50 D g
Herington, Kansas 60 H f
Herkimer, New York 53 M b
Herman, Michigan 56 E c
Herman, Minnesota 59 K e
Herman, Nebraska 60 H c
Hermanas, New Mexico 71 K h
Hermann, Missouri 61 N f
Hermansville, Michigan 56 F d
Hermansville, Mississippi 63 N g
Hermes Reef, Hawaii 72 A a
Hermiston, Oregon 73 L k
Hermitage, Arkansas 63 L e
Hermits Rest, Arizona 70 E c
Hermleigh, Texas 64 G c
Hermosa, South Dakota 58 C g
Hermosa Beach, California 75 D m
Hernando, Florida 55 J j
Hernando, Mississippi 63 O d
Herndon, California 75 E h
Herndon, Kansas 61 K c
Herndon, Iowa 60 D e
Herndon, Kentucky 57 F n
Herndon, Pennsylvania 53 K e
Herndon, Virginia 52 J f
Herndon, West Virginia 52 E h
Heron, Montana 66 E a
Heron L., Minnesota 59 L g
Heron Lake, Minnesota 59 L g
Herreid, South Dakota 58 F e
Herrick, South Dakota 58 G g
Herrin, Illinois 57 D m
Herrington L., Kentucky 57 J m
Herscher, Illinois 57 E h
Hersey, Michigan 56 H f
Hershey, Pennsylvania 53 K e
Hertford, North Carolina 55 P a
Hesper, North Dakota 58 G c
Hesperia, California 75 H k
Hesperia, Michigan 56 G f
Hesperus, Colorado 68 H f
Hesperus Pk., Colorado 68 H f
Hess Cr., Alaska 76 N d
Hessel, Michigan 56 J c
Hesston, Kansas 60 G f
Hetch Hetchy Res., California 74 F g
Hetherton, Michigan 56 J d
Hettinger, North Dakota 58 D d
Heuvelton, New York 53 L a
Hewitt, New Jersey 50 E c
Hewlett Point, New York 51 O e
Hext, Texas 65 H e
Heyburn, Idaho 66 G g
Heyburn Res., Oklahoma 62 G c
Hialeah, Florida (66,972) 54 B d
Hialeah Gardens, Florida 54 A d
Hialeah Park, Florida 54 B d
Hiawassee, Georgia 54 H c
Hiawatha, Kansas 61 J e
Hiawatha, Utah 68 F d
Hiawatha L., Minnesota 59 Q j
Hibbing, Minnesota 59 N c
Hibernia, New Jersey 50 E d
Hickewan, Arizona 70 E g
Hickman, Kentucky 57 D n
Hickman, Nebraska 60 H d
Hickman, New Mexico 71 K e
Hickman Mills, Missouri 61 P b
Hickok, Kansas 60 C g
Hickory, L., North Carolina 55 K b
Hickory, Mississippi 63 O f
Hickory, North Carolina 55 K b
Hickory Run State Park, Pennsylvania 50 B c
Hickory Valley, Tennessee 54 B b
Hicks, Texas 65 L h
Hicksville, New York (50,405) 50 G d
Hicksville, Ohio 52 B d
Hico, Texas 65 J d
Higbee, Missouri 61 M e
Higganum, Connecticut 51 H b
Higgins, Texas 64 D g
Higgins L., Michigan 56 J e
Higginsville, Missouri 61 L e
Highbee, Colorado 69 N f
High Bridge, New Jersey 50 D d
Highcliff, Wisconsin 56 E e
High Desert, Oregon 73 K m
High Falls, New York 50 E b
High Falls Res., Wisconsin 56 E d
High I., Michigan 56 H d
High Island, Texas 65 N f
Highland, California 75 H k
Highland, Illinois 57 D l
Highland, Kansas 61 J e
Highland, New York 50 F b
Highland, Washington 73 N h
Highland, Wisconsin 56 C f
Highland Falls, New York 50 E c
Highland Heights, Texas 64 F h
Highland L., Connecticut 51 H b
Highland Mills, New York 50 E c
Highland Park, Illinois (25,532) 57 F g
Highland Park, Michigan (38,063) 57 L j
Highland Park, Texas 65 N j
Highland Pk., California 74 F f
Highland Pk., Nevada 74 L g
Highland Pt., Florida 55 N h
Highlands, New Jersey 50 F e
Highlands, North Carolina 54 H b
Highlands, Texas 65 M f
Highland Springs, Virginia 53 J h
Highlandtown, Maryland 53 Q f
Highmore, South Dakota 58 G f
High Point, North Carolina (62,063) 55 M b
High Point State Park, New Jersey 50 D c
High Rock, North Carolina 55 L b
High Rock L., North Carolina 55 L b
High Springs, Florida 55 J h
Hightstown, New Jersey 50 D e
Highwood, Illinois 57 E g
Highwood, Montana 67 K b
Hiko, Nevada 74 K g
Hiland, Wyoming 67 N f
Hildebrand, Oregon 73 J n
Hildreth, Nebraska 60 E d
Hilger, Montana 67 L b
Hill, New Hampshire 49 D e
Hill, Montana 66 J a
Hilland, South Dakota 58 E f
Hillburn, New York 50 E c
Hill Cr., Utah 68 G d
Hill City, Idaho 66 E f
Hill City, Kansas 60 E e
Hill City, Minnesota 59 N d
Hill City, South Dakota 58 C g
Hillhead, South Dakota 58 J e
Hilliard, Florida 55 K g
Hillman, Michigan 56 K d
Hillman, Minnesota 59 N d
Hillrose, Colorado 69 N c
Hills, Iowa 61 N c
Hills, Minnesota 59 K g
Hillsboro, Georgia 54 H d
Hillsboro, Illinois 57 D k
Hillsboro, Iowa 61 N d
Hillsboro, Kansas 60 G f
Hillsboro, Missouri 61 O f
Hillsboro, New Hampshire 49 D e
Hillsboro, New Mexico 71 K g
Hillsboro, North Carolina 55 M a
Hillsboro, North Dakota 58 J c
Hillsboro, Ohio 52 C f
Hillsboro, Oregon 73 H k
Hillsboro, Texas 65 K c
Hillsboro, West Virginia 52 F g
Hillsboro, Wisconsin 56 C f
Hillsboro Canal, Florida 55 O g
Hillsborough, California 75 B m
Hillsdale, Michigan 57 J h
Hillsdale, New York 50 G a
Hillsdale, Wyoming 67 Q h
Hillside, Arizona 70 E e
Hillside, Colorado 69 L e
Hillside, New Jersey 51 J f
Hillsview, South Dakota 58 G e
Hillsville, Massachusetts 51 J a
Hillsville, Virginia 52 F j
Hilltonia, Georgia 55 K e
Hillview, Illinois 57 C k
Hilmar, California 75 E g
Hilo, Hawaii (25,966) 72 E f
Hilolo, Florida 55 O f
Hilton, New York 52 J b
Hilton Head I., South Carolina 55 L e
Hilts, California 74 C c
Himes, Wyoming 67 M e
Hinchinbrook Entrance, Alaska 77 O f
Hinchinbrook I., Alaska 77 O f
Hinckley, Minnesota 59 O d
Hinckley, Utah 68 D d
Hinckley Res., New York 53 M b
Hindes, Texas 65 J g
Hinesville, Georgia 55 K f
Hingham, Montana 67 K a
Hinesburg, Vermont 49 B d
Hinkley, California 75 H k
Hinsdale, Illinois 57 F h
Hinsdale, Massachusetts 49 C f
Hinsdale, Montana 67 N a
Hinsdale, New Hampshire 49 C f
Hinsdale, New York 52 H c
Hinton, Oklahoma 62 E c
Hinton, West Virginia 52 F h
Hiram, Maine 49 E e
Hisle, South Dakota 58 E g
Hitchcock, Oklahoma 62 E c
Hitchcock, South Dakota 58 H f
Hitchcock, Texas 65 M f
Hitchita, Oklahoma 62 H c
Hite, Utah 68 F f
Hither Hills State Park, New York 51 J c
Hiwassee Dam, North Carolina 54 G b
Hiwassee L., North Carolina 54 G b
Hiwassee R., Tennessee 54 G b
Hoagland, Nebraska 60 D c
Hoback Pk., Wyoming 67 K f
Hoback R., Wyoming 67 K f
Hobart, Indiana 57 F h
Hobart, Oklahoma 62 D c
Hobbs, New Mexico 71 O g
Hobbs Island, Alabama 54 E c
Hobe Sound, Florida 55 O f
Hobgood, North Carolina 55 O a
Hoboken, Georgia 55 J f
Hoboken, New Jersey (48,441) 50 E d
Hobson, Montana 67 L c
Hobucken, North Carolina 55 P b
Hochatown, Oklahoma 63 J d
Hochheim, Texas 65 K f
Hockingport, Ohio 52 E f
Hocking R., Ohio 52 D f
Hockley, Texas 65 M e
Hodge, Louisiana 63 L f
Hodgenville, Kentucky 57 H m
Hodges, L., California 75 H m
Hodges, Montana 67 Q c
Hodges, South Carolina 55 J c
Hodzana R., Alaska 77 N c
Hoehne, Colorado 69 M f
Hoffman, Minnesota 59 L e
Hoffman, North Carolina 55 M b
Hoffman I., New York 51 L g
Hogan Res., California 74 E f
Hogansville, Georgia 54 G d
Hogatzu R., Alaska 76 K c
Hogback Mt., Montana 66 H e
Hogeland, Montana 67 M a
Hog I., Michigan 56 H d
Hog I., Virginia 53 L h
Hog River, Alaska 76 K c
Hohenwald, Tennessee 54 D b
Hohokus, New Jersey 50 E c
Hoholitna R., Alaska 76 J f
Hoh R., Washington 73 F h
Hoisington, Kansas 60 F f
Hokah, Minnesota 59 P g
Holbrook, Arizona 70 G e
Holbrook, Idaho 66 H g
Holbrook, Massachusetts 51 L a
Holbrook, Nebraska 60 D d
Holcombe, Wisconsin 56 B d
Holden, Massachusetts 49 D f
Holden, Missouri 61 L f
Holden, Utah 68 D d
Holden, West Virginia 52 D h
Holdenville, Oklahoma 62 G c

Hold UNITED STATES INDEX Isle

Holdingford, Minnesota 59 M e
Holdrege, Nebraska 60 E d
Holgate, Ohio 52 B d
Holikachuk, Alaska 76 H e
Holitna R., Alaska 76 J f
Holladay, Utah 68 C h
Holland, Massachusetts 51 J a
Holland, New York 52 H c
Holland, Oregon 73 G n
Holland, Michigan 56 G g
Holland, Minnesota 59 K f
Holland, Texas 65 K e
Hollandale, Mississippi 63 N e
Holley, New York 52 H b
Holliday, Kansas 61 O a
Holliday, Texas 65 J b
Hollidaysburg, Pennsylvania 52 H e
Hollis, New York 51 N f
Hollister, California 75 D h
Hollister, Idaho 66 F g
Hollister, Missouri 61 L h
Hollister, Oklahoma 62 E d
Holliston, Massachusetts 51 L a
Hollowville, New York 50 F a
Holloway, Louisiana 63 L g
Holly, Colorado 69 O e
Holly, Michigan 56 K g
Holly Bluff, Mississippi 63 N f
Holly Grove, Arkansas 63 M d
Holly Hill, Florida 55 K h
Holly Hill, South Carolina 55 L d
Holly Ridge, North Carolina 55 O c
Holly Springs, Mississippi 63 O d
Hollywood, California 75 D l
Hollywood, Florida (35,237) 54 B c
Hollywood, Maryland 53 K g
Hollywood, Washington 72 C g
Holmes, New York 50 F c
Holopaw, Florida 55 N e
Holman, New Mexico 71 M c
Holmen, Wisconsin 56 B f
Holmes, Mt., Wyoming 67 K e
Holmwood, Louisiana 63 K h
Holstein, Iowa 61 J b
Holstein, Nebraska 60 F d
Holston Mt., Tennessee 55 J a
Holston R., Tennessee-Virginia 54 H a
Holt, Alabama 54 D d
Holt, Florida 54 E g
Holt, Michigan 56 J g
Holt, Minnesota 59 K b
Holt Cr., Nebraska 60 E b
Holter L., Montana 66 J c
Holton, Indiana 57 H k
Holton, Kansas 61 J e
Holton, Michigan 56 H f
Holtville, California 75 K m
Holvaloa, Hawaii 72 E f
Holy Cross, Alaska 76 H e
Holy Cross, Mt. of the, Colorado 69 K d
Holyoke, Colorado 69 O c
Holyoke, Massachusetts (52,689) 51 H a
Holyrood, Kansas 60 F f
Homedale, Idaho 66 D f
Homeland, Georgia 55 J g
Homer, Alaska 76 M g
Homer, Illinois 57 F j
Homer, Louisiana 63 K f
Homer, Michigan 57 J g
Homer, New York 53 K c
Homer City, Pennsylvania 52 G e
Homerville, Georgia 55 J f
Homestead, Florida 55 O h
Homestead, Iowa 61 N c
Homestead, Montana 67 Q a
Homestead, Oklahoma 62 E b
Homestead, Oregon 73 O k
Homestead, Pennsylvania 53 Q b
Homestead Nat. Mon., Nebraska 60 H d
Homewood, Alabama 54 E d
Hominy, Oklahoma 62 G b
Hominy R., Oklahoma 62 G b
Homochitto R., Mississippi 63 M g
Homosassa, Florida 55 J j
Homosassa Is., Florida 55 J j
Honcut, California 74 D e
Hondo, New Mexico 71 M f
Hondo, Texas 65 H f
Honea Path, South Carolina 55 J c
Honesdale, Pennsylvania 53 L d
Honey Brook, Pennsylvania 50 B e
Honeydew, California 74 A d
Honeyford, North Dakota 58 J b
Honey Grove, Texas 65 M b
Honey Island, Texas 65 N e
Honey L., California 74 E d
Honokaa, Hawaii 72 E e
Honokahua, Hawaii 72 D e
Honokokau, Hawaii 72 D d
Honolulu, Hawaii (294,194) 72 C d
Honomu, Hawaii 72 E f
Honuapo, Hawaii 72 E f
Hood, Mt., Oregon 73 J k
Hood Bay, Alaska 77 U h
Hood Can., Washington 72 A h
Hood River, Oregon 73 J k
Hoodsport, Washington 73 G h
Hookena, Hawaii 72 E f
Hooker, Oklahoma 62 B b
Hooks, Texas 65 N b
Hookset, New Hampshire 49 D e
Hoolehua, Hawaii 72 D d
Hoonah, Alaska 77 U g
Hoopa, California 74 B c
Hooper, Colorado 69 L f
Hooper, Nebraska 60 H c
Hooper, Utah 68 D b
Hooper, Washington 73 M j
Hooper B., Alaska 76 D f
Hooper Bay, Alaska 76 D f
Hooper I., Maryland 53 K g
Hoopeston, Illinois 57 F j
Hoople, North Dakota 58 J b
Hoosick Falls, New York 53 N c
Hoover, South Dakota 58 C e
Hoover Dam, Nevada-Arizona 75 L h
Hoover Res., Ohio 52 D e
Hooversville, Pennsylvania 52 H e
Hopatcong, L., New Jersey 50 D d
Hopatcong, New Jersey 50 D d
Hop Bottom, Pennsylvania 53 L d
Hope, Alaska 76 N f
Hope, Arizona 70 D f
Hope, Arkansas 63 K e
Hope, Indiana 57 H k
Hope, Kansas 60 G f
Hope, Maryland 50 A g
Hope, New Jersey 50 D d
Hope, New Mexico 71 N g
Hope, North Dakota 58 J c
Hope, Rhode Island 51 K b
Hopedale, Massachusetts 51 K a
Hope Mills, North Carolina 55 N c
Hope Valley, Rhode Island 51 K b
Hope Villa, Louisiana 63 M h
Hopewell, New Jersey 50 D e
Hopewell, Pennsylvania 52 H e
Hopewell, Virginia 53 J h
Hopewell Junction, New York 50 F b
Hopi Buttes, Arizona 70 G d
Hopkins, Michigan 56 H g
Hopkins, Minnesota 59 P j
Hopkins, Missouri 61 K d
Hopkinsville, Kentucky 57 F n
Hopkinton, Massachusetts 51 K a
Hopkinton, Rhode Island 51 K c
Hopland, California 74 B f
Hopwood, Pennsylvania 52 G f
Hoquiam, Washington 73 G j
Horace, Kansas 60 C f
Horatio, Arkansas 63 J e
Hords Creek Res., Texas 65 H d
Horicon, Wisconsin 56 E f
Hornbeck, Louisiana 63 K g
Hornbrook, California 74 C c
Hornell, New York 52 J c
Hornerstown, New Jersey 50 D e
Hornersville, Missouri 61 O h
Horn I., Mississippi 63 P h
Horn Mts., Alaska 76 H f
Hornsby, Tennessee 54 C b
Horse Branch, Kentucky 57 G m
Horse Cave, Kentucky 57 H m
Horse Cr., Colorado 69 N e
Horse Cr., Missouri 61 L g
Horse Cr., Wyoming 67 Q h
Horse Creek, Wyoming 67 P h
Horsehead L., North Dakota 58 G c
Horseheads, New York 53 K c
Horse L., California 74 E d
Horseneck Beach, Massachusetts 51 M b
Horseshoe, Florida 54 H h
Horse Shoe Bend, Idaho 66 D f
Horseshoe L., Illinois 61 Q d
Horseshoe Res., Arizona 70 F e
Horse Springs, New Mexico 71 J f
Horsham, Pennsylvania 50 C e
Hortense, Georgia 55 K f
Horton, Kansas 61 J e
Horton, New York 50 C b
Hortonville, New York 50 C b
Hosford, Florida 54 G g
Hoskins, Nebraska 60 G b
Hosmer, South Dakota 58 G e
Hosta Butte, New Mexico 71 J d
Hotchkiss, Colorado 69 J e
Hot Creek Ra., Nevada 74 J f
Hotham Inlet, Alaska 76 F c
Hot Springs, Arkansas (28,337), vicinity of Little Rock
Hot Springs, Montana 66 F b
Hot Springs, North Carolina 55 J b
Hot Springs, South Dakota 58 C g
Hot Springs, Texas 64 D f
Hot Springs, Virginia 52 G h
Hot Springs Nat. Park, Arkansas 63 K d
Hot Sulphur Springs, Colorado 69 K c
Hot Wells, Texas 64 B d
Hough, Oklahoma 62 B b
Houghton, Michigan 56 E b
Houghton, New York 52 H c
Houghton, South Dakota 58 H e
Houghton L., Michigan 56 J e
Houlka, Mississippi 63 O d
Houlton, Maine 49 H b
Houma, Louisiana 63 N j
Housatonic, Massachusetts 50 G a
Housatonic R., Connecticut 50 G b
Housatonic R., Massachusetts 50 G a
House, New Mexico 71 O e
House Ra., Utah 68 C d
Houston, Delaware 50 B h
Houston, L., Texas 65 M e
Houston, Minnesota 59 P g
Houston, Mississippi 63 O e
Houston, Missouri 61 N g
Houston, Texas (938,219) 65 M f
Houston Heights, Texas 64 F h
Houstonia, Missouri 61 L f
Houston R., Louisiana 63 K h
Houtzdale, Pennsylvania 52 H e
Hoven, North Dakota 58 G e
Hovenweep Nat. Mon., Utah 68 G f
Hovland, Minnesota 59 R c
Howard, Kansas 60 H g
Howard, Ohio 52 D e
Howard, Pennsylvania 52 J d
Howard, South Dakota 58 J f
Howard City, Michigan 56 H f
Howard Cr., Texas 64 F e
Howard Lake, Minnesota 59 M e
Howard Pass, Alaska 76 J b
Howards Grove, Wisconsin 56 F f
Howe, Idaho 66 G f
Howe, Indiana 57 H h
Howe, Oklahoma 63 J d
Howe, Texas 65 L b
Howell, Michigan 56 K g
Howell, Utah 68 D b
Howells, Nebraska 60 G c
Howells, New York 50 E c
Howes, South Dakota 58 D f
Howland, Maine 49 G c
Hoxie, Arkansas 63 N b
Hoxie, Kansas 60 D e
Hoyleton, Illinois 57 D l
Hoyt, Kansas 61 J e
Hoyt Pk., Utah 68 E c
Hualalei, Mt., Hawaii 72 E f
Hualpai Mts., Arizona 70 D e
Hubbard, Iowa 61 L b
Hubbard, Texas 65 L d
Hubbard L., Michigan 56 K e
Hubbard Lake, Michigan 56 K e
Hubbell, Nebraska 60 G d
Hudson, Colorado 69 M c
Hudson, Florida 55 M e
Hudson, Illinois 57 D j
Hudson, Indiana 57 H h
Hudson, Iowa 61 M b
Hudson, Michigan 57 J h
Hudson, Kansas 60 F f
Hudson, New Hampshire 49 D f
Hudson, New York 50 F a
Hudson, Ohio 52 E d
Hudson, South Dakota 59 K g
Hudson, Wisconsin 56 A d
Hudson, Wyoming 67 M g
Hudson Falls, New York 53 N b
Hudson Highlands, New York 50 E c
Hudson R., New York 50 F c
Hudsonville, Michigan 56 H g
Hueco Mts., Texas 64 A d
Huerfano R., Colorado 69 M e
Huff, North Dakota 58 F d
Huffton, South Dakota 58 H e
Huggins I., Alaska 76 K d
Hughes, Alaska 76 L c
Hughes, Arkansas 63 N d
Hughes Springs, Texas 65 N c
Hughesville, Missouri 61 L f
Hughsonville, New York 50 F b
Hugo, Colorado 69 N d
Hugo, Minnesota 59 N e
Hugo, Oklahoma 62 H d
Hugo, Oregon 73 G n
Hugo Res., Oklahoma 62 H d
Hugoton, Kansas 60 C g
Huguenot, New York 50 D c
Hulah, Oklahoma 62 G b
Hulah Res., Oklahoma 62 G b
Hulett, Wyoming 67 Q e
Hull, Illinois 57 B k
Hull, Massachusetts 51 M a
Hull, North Dakota 58 F d
Hull, Iowa 61 H a
Hull, Texas 65 N e
Humansville, Missouri 61 L g
Humbird, Wisconsin 56 C e
Humble, Texas 65 M f
Humble City, New Mexico 71 O g
Humboldt, Arizona 70 E e
Humboldt, Illinois 57 E k
Humboldt, Iowa 61 K b
Humboldt, Kansas 61 J g
Humboldt, Nebraska 61 J d
Humboldt, Nevada 74 G d
Humboldt, Tennessee 54 C b
Humboldt L., Nevada 74 G e
Humboldt R., Nevada 74 K d
Humboldt Ra., Nevada 74 G d
Humboldt Salt Marsh, Nevada 74 H e
Humbolt B., California 74 A d
Hume, Virginia 52 H g
Humeston, Iowa 61 L d
Hummelstown, Pennsylvania 53 K e
Humphrey, Arkansas 63 M d
Humphrey, Idaho 66 H e
Humphrey, Nebraska 60 G c
Humphrey, Washington 73 J h
Humphreys, California 75 F h
Humphreys, Missouri 61 L d
Humphreys, Mt., California 75 G g
Humphreys Pk., Arizona 70 F d
Humphreysville, New York 50 F a
Humptulips, Washington 73 G h
Hungerford, Texas 65 L f
Hungry Horse Dam, Montana 66 F a
Hungry Horse Res., Montana 66 G a
Hunnewell, Missouri 61 N e
Hunt, Texas 65 H e
Hunter, Arkansas 63 M c
Hunter, Kansas 60 F e
Hunter, Mt., Alaska 76 M e
Hunter, New York 50 E a
Hunter, North Dakota 58 J c
Hunter, Oklahoma 62 F b
Hunter, Texas 65 J f
Hunter, Mt., New York 50 E a
Hunters, Washington 73 M g
Hunters Point, California 75 B m
Hunterstown, Indiana 57 H h
Huntersville, North Carolina 55 L b
Huntersville, West Virginia 52 F g
Huntingburg, Indiana 57 F l
Huntingdon, Pennsylvania 52 J e
Huntingdon, Tennessee 54 C a
Hunting I., South Carolina 55 L e
Huntington, Indiana 57 H j
Huntington, Massachusetts 51 H a
Huntington, New York 50 G d
Huntington, Oregon 73 N l
Huntington, Texas 65 N d
Huntington, Utah 68 F d
Huntington, West Virginia (83,627) 52 D g
Huntington B., New York 50 G d
Huntington Beach, California 75 G l
Huntington L., California 75 F g
Huntington Park, California (29,920) 75 E l
Huntley, Montana 67 M d
Huntley, Nebraska 60 E d
Huntley, Wyoming 67 Q h
Hunts Mt., Wyoming 67 N e
Huntsville, Alabama (72,365) 54 E c
Huntsville, Arkansas 63 K b
Huntsville, Missouri 61 M e
Huntsville, Texas 65 M e
Huntsville, Utah 68 E b
Hurdland, Missouri 61 M d
Hurdsfield, North Dakota 58 G c
Hurley, Mississippi 63 P h
Hurley, New Mexico 71 J g
Hurley, New York 50 E b
Hurley, South Dakota 58 J g
Hurley, Wisconsin 56 C c
Hurleyville, New York 50 D b
Hurlock, Maryland 53 L g
Huron, California 75 E h
Huron, Kansas 61 J e
Huron, L., United States-Canada 47 K b
Huron, Ohio 52 D d
Huron, South Dakota 58 H f
Huron B., Michigan 56 E b
Huron City, Michigan 56 L e
Huron Mts., Michigan 56 F c
Hurricane, Utah 68 C f
Hurricane, West Virginia 52 D g
Hurricane Cr., Georgia 55 J f
Hurricane Mills, Tennessee 54 D b
Hurst, Texas 65 M j
Hurtsboro, Alabama 54 F e
Huslia, Alaska 76 J d
Huslia R., Alaska 76 J d
Huson, Montana 66 F b
Hutch, Mt., Arizona 70 F e
Hutchins, Texas 65 O k
Hutchinson, Kansas (37,574) 60 G f
Hutchinson, Minnesota 59 M f
Hutchinsons I., Florida 55 O f
Hutsonville, Illinois 57 F k
Huttig, Arkansas 63 L e
Hutto, Texas 65 K e
Huttonsville, West Virginia 52 F g
Huxley, Iowa 61 L c
Huxley, Mt., Alaska 77 R f
Hyalite Peak, Montana 67 K d
Hyampom, California 74 B d
Hyannis, Massachusetts 51 N b
Hyannis, Nebraska 60 C b
Hyannis Port, Massachusetts 51 N b
Hyatt Res., Oregon 73 H n
Hyattsville, Maryland 53 Q g
Hyattville, Wyoming 67 N e
Hybart, Alabama 54 D f
Hydaburg, Alaska 77 V j
Hyde Park, New York 50 E b
Hyden, Kentucky 57 K m
Hyder, Alaska 77 W j
Hyder, Arizona 70 D f
Hydro, Oklahoma 62 E c
Hye, Texas 65 J e
Hygiene, Colorado 69 L c
Hylton Res., Nevada 74 K d
Hyman, Texas 64 F c
Hymera, Indiana 57 F k
Hyndman, Pennsylvania 52 H f
Hyndman Pk., Idaho 66 F f
Hyner, Pennsylvania 52 J d
Hyrum, Utah 68 E b
Hysham, Montana 67 N c
Ia Costa I., Florida 55 M g
Iamonia, L., Florida 54 G g
Iatan, Texas 64 F c
Iatt, L., Louisiana 63 L g
Ibapah, Utah 68 C c
Iberia, Missouri 61 M f
Iceberg Canyon, Nevada-Arizona 75 L h
Ice Harbor Dam, Washington 73 M j
Icy B., Alaska 77 R g
Icy C., Alaska 76 F a
Icy Pt., Alaska 77 T g
Icy Str., Alaska 77 U g
Ida, Louisiana 63 K f
Ida, Michigan 57 K h
Idabel, Oklahoma 63 J e
Ida Grove, Iowa 61 J b
Idaho 66
Idaho City, Idaho 66 E f
Idaho Falls, Idaho (33,161) 66 H f
Idaho Springs, Colorado 69 L d
Idalia, Colorado 69 O d
Idalou, Texas 64 F b
Idanha, Oregon 73 H l
Ideal, Georgia 54 G e
Iditarod, Alaska 76 H e
Iditarod R., Alaska 76 H e
Idlewild (New York International Airport), New York 51 N f
Idria, California 75 E h
Igitkin I., Alaska 77 P j
Igiugig, Alaska 76 J g
Igloo, South Dakota 58 C g
Ignacio, Colorado 69 J f
Igo, California 74 C d
Igvak, C., Alaska 76 K h
Ikatan, Alaska 76 F j
Ikolik, C., Alaska 76 K h
Ikpikpuk R., Alaska 76 K a
Ilak I., Alaska 77 N j
Iliamna, Alaska 76 K g
Iliamna L., Alaska 76 K g
Iliamna Vol., Alaska 76 L f
Iliff, Colorado 69 N c
Ilion, New York 53 L b
Ilio Pt., Hawaii 72 D d
Ilivit Mts., Alaska 76 G e
Illinois 56-57
Illinois & Mississippi Can., Illinois 57 D h
Illinois R., Illinois 57 D j
Illinois R., Oklahoma 63 J b
Illinois R., Oregon 73 G n
Illiopolis, Illinois 57 D k
Illmo, Missouri 61 P g
Ilnik, Alaska 76 H h
Ilwaco, Washington 73 F j
Imbler, Oregon 73 N k
Imboden, Arkansas 63 M b
Imlay, Nevada 74 G d
Imlay, South Dakota 58 D g
Imlay City, Michigan 56 K f
Immaha, Oregon 73 O k
Immaha R., Oregon 73 O k
Immokalee, Florida 55 N g
Imogene, Iowa 61 J d
Imperial, California 75 K m
Imperial, Nebraska 60 C d
Imperial, Texas 64 E d
Imperial Dam, California 75 L m
Imperial Val., California 75 K m
Imuruk Basin, Alaska 76 D d
Imuruk L., Alaska 76 F d
Inadale, Texas 64 G c
Inanudak B., Alaska 76 C k
Inchelium, Washington 73 M g
Independence, California 75 G h
Independence, Iowa 61 N b
Independence, Kansas 61 J g
Independence, Louisiana 63 N h
Independence, Missouri (62,328) 61 K e
Independence, Oregon 73 G l
Independence, Virginia 52 E j
Independence, Wisconsin 56 B e
Independence Mts., Nevada 74 J c
Index, Washington 73 J h
Indiahoma, Oklahoma 62 E d
Indiana 57
Indiana, Pennsylvania 52 G e
Indianapolis, Indiana (476,258) 57 G k
Indian Cr., Kansas 61 P b
Indian Head, Maryland 53 J g
Indian L., Michigan 56 G c
Indian L., New York 53 M b
Indian L., Ohio 52 C e
Indian Mills, New Jersey 50 D f
Indian Mt., Wyoming 67 K g
Indianola, Iowa 61 L c
Indianola, Mississippi 63 N e
Indianola, Nebraska 60 D d
Indianola, Oklahoma 62 H c
Indianola, Washington 72 B g
Indian Pk., Utah 68 C e
Indian Pk., Wyoming 67 L e
Indian R., Florida 55 L j
Indian R., Michigan 56 G c
Indian R., New York 53 L a
Indian River, Michigan 56 J d
Indian River City, Florida 55 L j
Indian Springs, Nevada 75 K h
Indian Town, Florida 55 O f
Indian Valley, Idaho 66 D e
Indian Village, Missouri 61 P b
Indio, California 75 J l
Indrio, Florida 55 O f
Industry, Illinois 57 C j
Industry, Texas 65 L f
Inez, Texas 65 L g
Ingalls, Indiana 57 H k
Ingalls, Kansas 60 D g
Ingalls, Michigan 56 F d
Ingalls, Mt., California 74 E e
Ingersoll, Oklahoma 62 E b
Ingleside, Maryland 50 A g
Ingleside, Texas 65 K h
Inglewood, California (63,390) 75 D m
Inglutalik R., Alaska 76 G d
Ingomar, Montana 67 N c
Ingot, California 74 C d
Ingram, Pennsylvania 50 O b
Ingram, Texas 65 H e
Ingram, Wisconsin 56 C d
Iniakuk R., Alaska 76 L c
Inka, Kansas 60 F g
Inkom, Idaho 66 H g
Inkster, Michigan (39,097), vicinity of Detroit
Inkster, North Dakota 58 J b
Inland L., Alaska 76 H c
Inman, Nebraska 60 F b
Inman, New York 53 M a
Inman, South Carolina 55 J b
Inner Grove, Minnesota 59 R j
Innoko R., Alaska 76 H e
Inola, Oklahoma 62 H b
Intake, Montana 67 Q b
Interior, South Dakota 58 E g
Interlachen, Florida 55 K h
International Falls, Minnesota 59 N b
Inverness, Florida 55 J j
Inverness, Montana 67 K a
Inwood, California 74 D d
Inyan Kara Cr., Wyoming 67 Q e
Inyokern, California 75 G j
Inyo Mts., California 75 G g
Iola, Kansas 61 J g
Iola, Texas 65 L e
Iona, Idaho 66 J f
Iona, Minnesota 59 L g
Iona, South Dakota 58 G g
Ione, Nevada 74 H f
Ione, Oregon 73 L k
Ione, Washington 73 N g
Ionia, Iowa 61 M a
Ionia, Michigan 56 H g
Ionia, Missouri 61 L f
Iowa 60-61
Iowa, Louisiana 63 K h
Iowa City, Iowa (33,443) 61 N c
Iowa Falls, Iowa 61 L b
Iowa Park, Texas 65 J b
Iowa R., Iowa 61 M c
Ipava, Illinois 57 C j
Ipewik, Alaska 76 E b
Ipswich, Massachusetts 49 E f
Ipswich, South Dakota 58 G e
Iraan, Texas 64 F e
Irasburg, Vermont 49 C d
Iredell, Texas 65 K d
Ireland, Texas 65 K d
Irene, South Dakota 58 J g
Ireton, Iowa 60 H b
Irma, Wisconsin 56 D d
Irmo, South Carolina 55 K c
Iron Canyon Res., California 74 C d
Iron City, Tennessee 54 D b
Iron Creek, Alaska 76 E d
Irondale, Missouri 61 O g
Irondale, Ohio 52 F e
Iron Mt., Michigan 56 E d
Iron Mt., Oregon 73 F n
Iron Mt., Utah 68 C f
Iron Nation, South Dakota 58 G f
Iron Ridge, Wisconsin 56 E f
Iron River, Michigan 56 E c
Iron River, Wisconsin 56 B c
Irons, Michigan 56 H e
Ironside, Oregon 73 N l
Iron Springs, Utah 68 C f
Ironton, Michigan 56 H d
Ironton, Missouri 61 O g
Ironton, Ohio 52 D g
Ironwood, Michigan 56 D c
Ironwood, Wisconsin 56 C c
Iroquois, South Dakota 58 J f
Iroquois R., Illinois 57 F j
Irvine, Kentucky 57 K m
Irving, Kansas 60 H e
Irving, Texas (43,985) 65 L c
Irvington, Kentucky 57 G m
Irvington, New Jersey (59,379) 51 J f
Irvington, New York 50 F c
Irvington, Virginia 53 K h
Irvona, Pennsylvania 52 H e
Irwin, Idaho 66 J f
Irwin, Iowa 61 J c
Irwin, Nebraska 60 C b
Irwinton, Georgia 54 H e
Isabel, Kansas 60 F g
Isabel, South Dakota 58 E e
Isabella, California 75 G j
Isabella, Michigan 56 G d
Isabella, Minnesota 59 P c
Isabella Res., California 75 G j
Isabelle, Pt., Michigan 56 F b
Isbell, Alabama 54 D c
Ishpeming, Michigan 56 F c
Islamorada, Florida 55 O j
Island, Kentucky 57 F m
Island Beach, New Jersey 50 E f
Island City, Oregon 73 N k
Island Falls, Maine 49 G b
Island Heights, New Jersey 50 E f
Island Mountain, California 74 B d
Island Park, Idaho 66 J e
Island Park Res., Idaho 66 J e
Island Pond, Vermont 49 D d
Isle, Minnesota 59 N d
Isle au Haut, I., Maine 49 G d
Isle aux Pêches, Michigan 57 M k
Isle of Hope, Georgia 55 K f
Isle Royale, I., Michigan 56 E a
Isle Royale Nat. Pk., Michigan 56 E a
Islesboro, Maine 49 F d
Isles Dernieres, Louisiana 63 N j

Isle UNITED STATES INDEX Kiam

Isleta, New Mexico 71 L e
Isleton, California 74 D f
Islip, New York 50 G d
Ismay, Montana 67 Q c
Isola, Mississippi 63 N e
Isoline, Tennessee 54 F a
Issaquah, Washington 72 C h
Istokpoga, L., Florida 55 N f
Italy, Texas 65 L c
Itasca, L., Minnesota 59 L c
Itasca, Texas 65 K c
Itasca State Park, Minnesota 59 L c
Ithaca, Michigan 56 J f
Ithaca, New York (28,799) 53 K c
Itkilik R., Alaska 76 M b
Itta Bena, Mississippi 63 N e
Itulilik, Alaska 76 J f
Iuka, Illinois 57 E l
Iva, South Carolina 55 J c
Ivanhoe, Minnesota 59 K f
Ivanhoe, Virginia 52 F j
Ivanpah, California 75 K j
Ivesdale, Illinois 57 E k
Ivishak R., Alaska 77 N b
Ivor, Virginia 53 K j
Ivoryton, Connecticut 51 J c
Ivydale, West Virginia 52 E g
Izaviknek R., Alaska 76 F f
Izigan, C., Alaska 76 D k
Jacinto City, Texas 64 G h
Jackman, Maine 49 E c
Jack Mt., Pennsylvania 52 J e
Jack Mt., Washington 73 K g
Jacksboro, Tennessee 54 G a
Jacksboro, Texas 65 J b
Jackson, Alabama 54 D f
Jackson, California 74 E f
Jackson, Georgia 54 H d
Jackson, Kentucky 57 K m
Jackson, L., Florida 54 G g
Jackson, Louisiana 63 M h
Jackson, Michigan (50,720) 57 J g
Jackson, Minnesota 59 L g
Jackson, Mississippi (144,422) 63 N f
Jackson, Missouri 61 P g
Jackson, Montana 66 G d
Jackson, North Carolina 55 O a
Jackson, Ohio 52 D f
Jackson, South Carolina 55 K d
Jackson, Tennessee (34,376) 54 C b
Jackson, Wyoming 67 K f
Jackson Center, Ohio 52 C e
Jackson Gulch Res., Colorado 68 H f
Jackson Heights, New York 51 M f
Jackson L., Georgia 54 H d
Jackson L., Wyoming 67 K f
Jackson Mt., Nevada 74 G c
Jacksonport, Wisconsin 56 F e
Jackson Prairie, Mississippi 63 O f
Jackson Res., Colorado 69 M c
Jackson R., Virginia 52 G g
Jacksonville, Alabama 54 F d
Jacksonville, Arkansas 63 L d
Jacksonville, Florida (201,030) 55 K g
Jacksonville, Illinois 57 D k
Jacksonville, Missouri 61 M e
Jacksonville, North Carolina 55 O c
Jacksonville, Texas 65 M d
Jacksonville Beach, Florida 55 K g
Jack Wade, Alaska 77 R d
Jacob Lake, Arizona 70 E c
Jacobstown, New Jersey 50 D e
Jacumba, California 75 J m
Jaeger, West Virginia 52 E h
Jago R., Alaska 77 Q b
Jal, New Mexico 71 O g
Jamaica, New York 50 F d
Jamaica, Vermont 49 C e
Jamaica B., New York 51 M g
James, L., North Carolina 55 K b
Jamesburg, New Jersey 50 E e
James City, Pennsylvania 52 H d
Jameson, Missouri 61 L d
Jamesport, Missouri 61 L e
Jamesport, New York 51 H d
James R., Missouri 61 L h
James R., North-South Dakota 58 J g
James R., Virginia 53 K h
Jamestown, Indiana 57 G k
Jamestown, Kansas 60 G e
Jamestown, Michigan 56 H g
Jamestown, New York (41,818) 52 G c
Jamestown, North Dakota 58 H d
Jamestown, Ohio 52 C f
Jamestown, Pennsylvania 52 F d
Jamestown, Rhode Island 51 L b
Jamestown, South Carolina 55 M d
Jamestown, Tennessee 54 G a
Jamestown Nat. Hist. Site, Virginia 53 K h
Jamestown Res., North Dakota 58 H c
Jamesville, New York 53 K c
Jamesville, North Carolina 55 P b
Jamieson, Oregon 73 N l
Jamison, Nebraska 60 E b
Jamul, California 75 J m
Jane Lew, West Virginia 52 F f
Janesville, California 74 E d
Janesville, Iowa 61 M b
Janesville, Minnesota 59 N f
Janesville, Wisconsin (35,164) 56 D g
Jansen, Nebraska 60 G d
Jansen Kill, New York 50 F a
Jarbridge, Nevada 74 K c
Jarbridge R., Idaho 66 E g
Jaroso, Colorado 69 L f
Jarratt, Virginia 53 J j
Jarrell, Texas 65 K e
Jasonville, Indiana 57 F k
Jasper, Alabama 54 D d
Jasper, Arkansas 63 K c
Jasper, Colorado 69 K f
Jasper, Florida 55 J g
Jasper, Georgia 54 G c
Jasper, Indiana 57 G l
Jasper, Michigan 57 J h
Jasper, Minnesota 59 K g
Jasper, Missouri 61 K g
Jasper, New York 52 J c
Jasper, Tennessee 54 F b
Jasper, Texas 65 O c
Jay, Oklahoma 63 J b
Jay Em, Wyoming 67 Q g
Jayton, Texas 64 G b
Jean, Nevada 75 K j
Jean, Texas 65 J b
Jeanerette, Louisiana 63 M j
Jeannette, Pennsylvania 52 G e
Jeddo, Michigan 56 L f
Jeffers, Minnesota 59 L f
Jefferson, Colorado 69 L d
Jefferson, Georgia 54 H c
Jefferson, Iowa 61 K b
Jefferson, Maryland 52 J f
Jefferson, Montana 66 H c
Jefferson, Mt., Nevada 74 J f
Jefferson, Mt., Oregon 73 J l
Jefferson, Ohio 52 F d
Jefferson, Oklahoma 62 F b
Jefferson, Oregon 73 H l
Jefferson, South Dakota 59 K h
Jefferson, Texas 65 N c
Jefferson, Wisconsin 56 E f
Jefferson City, Missouri (28,228) 61 M f
Jefferson City, Tennessee 54 H a
Jefferson Island, Montana 66 J d
Jeffersontown, Kentucky 57 H l
Jeffersonville, Georgia 54 H e
Jeffersonville, New York 50 D b
Jeffersonville, Ohio 52 C f
Jeffersonville, Vermont 49 C d
Jekyll I., Georgia 55 K f
Jellico, Tennessee 54 G a
Jelly, California 74 C d
Jemez Pueblo, New Mexico 71 L d
Jemez R., New Mexico 71 L d
Jemez Springs, New Mexico 71 L d
Jena, Louisiana 63 L g
Jenkinjones, West Virginia 52 E h
Jenkins, Minnesota 59 M d
Jenkins, New Jersey 50 D f
Jenkintown, Pennsylvania 50 C e
Jenner, California 74 B f
Jennings, Florida 54 H g
Jennings, Kansas 60 D e
Jennings, Louisiana 63 L h
Jennings, Montana 66 E a
Jennings, Oklahoma 62 G b
Jennyjump Mt., New Jersey 50 D d
Jensen, Utah 68 G c
Jensen Beach, Florida 55 O f
Jerome, Arizona 70 E e
Jerome, Idaho 66 F g
Jersey City, New Jersey (276,101) 50 E d
Jersey Shore, Pennsylvania 52 J d
Jersey Village, Texas 64 E h
Jerseyville, Illinois 51 C k
Jessamine Creek Res., Kentucky 57 J m
Jessie, North Dakota 58 H c
Jessup, L., Florida 55 K j
Jesup, Georgia 55 K f
Jesup, Iowa 61 M b
Jet, Oklahoma 62 E b
Jetersville, Virginia 52 H h
Jetmore, Kansas 60 E f
Jewel Cave Nat. Mon., South Dakota 58 C g
Jewell, Iowa 61 L b
Jewell, Kansas 60 F e
Jewell, Oregon 73 G k
Jewett, Illinois 57 E k
Jewett, New York 50 E a
Jewett, Ohio 52 F e
Jewett, Texas 65 L d
Jewitt City, Connecticut 51 K b
Jiggs, Nevada 74 K d
Jim R., Alaska 76 M c
Jim Thorpe, Pennsylvania 50 B d
Jim Woodruff Res., Georgia 54 G g
Joanna, Pennsylvania 50 B e
Joanna Res., Missouri 61 N e
Joaquin, Texas 65 N d
Job Pk., Nevada 74 G e
Jobstown, New Jersey 50 D e
Joes, Colorado 69 O d
Joffre, New Mexico 71 M e
Johannesburg, California 75 H j
Johannesburg, Michigan 56 J d
John Day, Oregon 73 M l
John Day Dam, Oregon 73 K k
John Day R., Oregon 73 K k
John H. Kerr Res., Virginia 52 H j
John Martin Res., Colorado 69 O e
John R., Alaska 76 L c
Johnson, Kansas 60 C g
Johnson, Nebraska 61 H d
Johnson, New York 50 E c
Johnsonburg, Pennsylvania 52 H d
Johnson City, New York 53 L c
Johnson City, Tennessee (31,187) 55 J a
Johnson City, Texas 65 J e
Johnson Creek, Wisconsin 56 E f
Johnsonville, South Carolina 55 M d
Johnston, South Carolina 55 K d
Johnston City, Illinois 57 E m
Johnstown, Nebraska 60 D b
Johnstown, New York 53 M b
Johnstown, Ohio 52 D e
Johnstown, Pennsylvania (53,949) 52 H e
Johnswood, Michigan 56 K d
Joiner, Arkansas 63 N c
Joliet, Illinois (66,780) 57 E h
Joliet, Montana 67 L d
Joliette, North Dakota 58 J b
Jolley, Iowa 61 K b
Jolon, California 75 D j
Jones, Oklahoma 62 F c
Jones Beach State Park, New York 50 G d
Jonesboro, Arkansas 63 N c
Jonesboro, Georgia 54 G d
Jonesboro, Illinois 57 D m
Jonesboro, Louisiana 63 L f
Jonesboro, Maine 49 H d
Jonesboro, North Carolina 55 M b
Jonesboro, Tennessee 55 J a
Jonesboro, Texas 65 K d
Jones Is., Alaska 76 N a
Jonesport, Maine 49 H d
Jonestown, Mississippi 63 N d
Jonesville, Alaska 76 N f
Jonesville, Indiana 57 H k
Jonesville, Louisiana 63 M g
Jonesville, Michigan 57 J g
Jonesville, South Carolina 55 K c
Jonesville, Virginia 52 C j
Joplin, Missouri (38,958) 61 K g
Joplin, Montana 67 K a
Joppa, Illinois 57 E m
Jordan, Minnesota 59 N f
Jordan, Montana 67 O b
Jordan, New York 53 K b
Jordan L., Alabama 54 E e
Jordan R., Utah 68 C j
Jordan R., Oregon 73 N n
Jordan Valley, Oregon 73 N n
Jornada del Muerto, mts., New Mexico 71 K f
Joseph, Idaho 66 D d
Joseph, Oregon 73 N k
Joseph City, Arizona 70 G e
Joseph R., Oregon 73 N k
Joshua, Texas 65 K c
Joshua Tree, California 75 J k
Joshua Tree Nat. Mon., California 75 J k
Jourdanton, Texas 65 J g
Jualin, Alaska 77 U g
Juan, Texas 65 J j
Juan de Fuca, Str. of, United States-Canada 73 F g
Juanita, Washington 72 C h
Jubilee Pass, California 75 J j
Jud, North Dakota 58 H d
Juda, Wisconsin 56 D g
Judith, Pt., Rhode Island 51 L c
Judith Basin, Montana 67 K b
Judith Gap, Montana 67 L c
Judith R., Montana 67 L b
Judson, North Dakota 58 E d
Julesburg, Colorado 69 O c
Juliaetta, Idaho 66 D c
Julian, California 75 J l
Julius, Alaska 76 N d
Junction, Texas 65 H e
Junction, Utah 68 D e
Junction City, Arkansas 63 L e
Junction City, Georgia 54 G e
Junction City, Kansas 60 H e
Junction City, Kentucky 57 J m
Junction City, Oregon 73 G l
Junction City, Wisconsin 56 C e
Juneau, Alaska 77 U g
Juneau, Wisconsin 56 E f
June in Winter, L., Florida 55 N f
June L., California 74 F g
Jungo, Nevada 74 G d
Juniata, Nebraska 60 F d
Juniata R., Pennsylvania 53 J e
Junior, West Virginia 52 G g
Junior L., Maine 49 G c
Juniper Mts., Arizona 70 D d
Junipero Serra Pk., California 75 D h
Junjik R., Alaska 77 O b
Juno, Texas 64 F e
Juntura, Oregon 73 M m
Jupiter, Florida 55 O g
Justiceburg, Texas 64 F b
Justin, Texas 65 K b
Kaalualu, Hawaii 72 E f
Kabetogama, Minnesota 59 N b
Kabetogama L., Minnesota 59 N b
Kachemak B., Alaska 76 M g
Kachess L., Washington 73 J h
Kadoka, South Dakota 58 E g
Kaea, C., Hawaii 72 D e
Kaena Pt., I. of Lanai, Hawaii 72 D e
Kaena Pt., I. of Oahu, Hawaii 72 C d
Kagalaska I., Alaska 77 P j
Kagamil I., Alaska 77 T h
Kagati L., Alaska 76 G g
Kaguyak, Alaska 76 L h
Kahala Pt., Hawaii 72 B c
Kahaluu, Hawaii 72 C d
Kahiltna Glacier, Alaska 76 M e
Kahlotus, Washington 73 M j
Kahoka, Missouri 61 N d
Kahoolawe, I., Hawaii 72 D e
Kahua, Hawaii 72 E e
Kahuku, Hawaii 72 C d
Kahuku Pt., Hawaii 72 C d
Kahului, Hawaii 72 D e
Kaibab Cr., Arizona 70 E c
Kaibab Forest, Arizona 70 F c
Kaibib Plateau, Arizona 70 E c
Kaibito Plateau, Arizona 70 F c
Kailua, Hawaii 72 D f
Kailua-Lanikai, Hawaii (25,622) 72 C d
Kainaliu, Hawaii 72 E f
Kaiparowits Plateau, Utah 68 E f
Kaiser Pk., California 75 F g
Kaiwi Chan., Hawaii 72 C d
Kaiyuh Mts., Alaska 76 H e
Kaka, Arizona 70 E g
Kaka Pt., Hawaii 75 H h
Kakatovik, Alaska 77 Q a
Kake, Alaska 77 V h
Kakhonak, Alaska 76 K g
Kakhonak L., Alaska 76 K g
Ka Lae (South C.), Hawaii 72 E f
Kalalau, Hawaii 72 B c
Kalama, Washington 73 H j
Kalama R., Washington 73 H j
Kalamazoo, Michigan (82,089) 57 H g
Kalamazoo R., Michigan 56 H g
Kalaupapa, Hawaii 72 D d
Kalawao (Leper Colony), Hawaii 72 D d
Kaleva, Michigan 56 G e
Kalgary, Texas 64 F b
Kalgin I., Alaska 76 M f
Kalida, Ohio 52 B e
Kalispell, Montana 66 F a
Kalkaska, Michigan 56 H e
Kalona, Iowa 61 N c
Kaloni Chan., Hawaii 72 D e
Kalska, Alaska 76 G f
Kaltag, Alaska 76 H d
Kamakou, Mt., Hawaii 72 D d
Kamalino, Hawaii 72 A d
Kamalo, Hawaii 72 D d
Kamas, Utah 68 E c
Kamela, Oregon 73 M k
Kamiah, Idaho 66 E c
Kamishak B., Alaska 76 K g
Kamrar, Iowa 61 L b
Kanab, Utah 68 D f
Kanaga I., Alaska 77 O j
Kanakanak, Alaska 76 H g
Kanarraville, Utah 68 C f
Kanatak, Alaska 76 K h
Kanawha, Iowa 61 L b
Kanawha, Texas 65 M b
Kanawha R., West Virginia 52 D g
Kandik R., Alaska 77 R d
Kane, Illinois 57 C k
Kane, Pennsylvania 52 H d
Kane, Wyoming 67 M e
Kanektok R., Alaska 76 G g
Kaneohe, Hawaii 72 C d
Kangik, Alaska 76 H a
Kankakee, Illinois (27,666) 57 F h
Kankakee R., Illinois 57 E h
Kannapolis, North Carolina (34,647) 55 L b
Kanona, Kansas 60 D e
Kanopolis, Kansas 60 F f
Kanopolis Res., Kansas 60 F f
Kanorado, Colorado 69 O d
Kanorado, Kansas 60 C e
Kanosh, Utah 68 D e
Kansas 60-61
Kansas, Illinois 57 F k
Kansas, Oklahoma 63 J b
Kansas City, Kansas (121,901) 61 K e
Kansas City, Missouri (475,539) 61 K e
Kansas R., Kansas 61 J e
Kantishna, Alaska 76 M e
Kantishna R., Alaska 76 M d
Kanuti R., Alaska 76 M c
Kapaa, Hawaii 72 B c
Kapaau-Halaula, Hawaii 72 E e
Kaplan, Louisiana 63 L j
Kapoho, Hawaii 72 E f
Karlsruhe, North Dakota 58 F b
Karlstad, Minnesota 59 K b
Karluk, Alaska 76 K h
Karluk L., Alaska 76 K h
Karnack, Texas 65 N c
Karnak, Illinois 57 E m
Karnes City, Texas 65 K g
Karthaus, Pennsylvania 52 H d
Karval, Colorado 69 N e
Kasatochi I., Alaska 77 P j
Kasegaluk Lagoon, Alaska 76 F a
Kashega, Alaska 76 D k
Kashegelok, Alaska 76 J f
Kasigluk, Alaska 76 F f
Kasilof, Alaska 76 M f
Kaskaskia R., Illinois 57 D k
Kasson, Minnesota 59 O f
Katahdin, Mt., Maine 49 G c
Katakturak R., Alaska 77 P b
Katalla, Alaska 77 P f
Kateel R., Alaska 76 H d
Kathleen, Florida 55 M e
Kathryn, North Dakota 58 H d
Katmai, Mt., Alaska 76 K g
Katmai B., Alaska 76 K h
Katmai Nat. Mon., Alaska 76 K g
Katonah, New York 50 F c
Kauai, I., Hawaii 72 B d
Kauai Chan., Hawaii 72 B d
Kau Des., Hawaii 72 E f
Kaufman, Texas 65 L c
Kau I., Alaska 77 U h
Kauiki Hd., Hawaii 72 D e
Kaukauna, Wisconsin 56 E e
Kaula, I., Hawaii 72 D b
Kauluoa Pt., Hawaii 72 E f
Kaumakani, Hawaii 72 B d
Kaunakakai, Hawaii 72 D d
Kauna Pt., Hawaii 72 E f
Kavalga I., Alaska 77 N j
Kavik R., Alaska 77 O b
Kawaihae, Hawaii 72 E e
Kawaihoa Pt., Hawaii 72 A d
Kawaikini, Mt., Hawaii 72 B c
Kaw City, Oklahoma 62 G b
Kaweah R., California 75 F h
Kawich Ra., Nevada 74 J g
Kayak I., Alaska 77 P g
Kaycee, Wyoming 67 O f
Kayenta, Arizona 70 G c
Kayford, West Virginia 52 E g
Kaysville, Utah 68 E b
Keaau, Hawaii 72 E f
Keahole Pt., Hawaii 72 D f
Kealaikahiki Chan., Hawaii 72 D e
Kealaikahiki Pt., Hawaii 72 D e
Kealakekua, Hawaii 72 E f
Kealia, I. of Hawaii, Hawaii 72 E f
Kealia, I. of Kauai, Hawaii 72 B c
Keams Canyon, Arizona 70 G d
Keamuku, Hawaii 72 E f
Keansburg, New Jersey 50 E e
Kearns, Utah 68 B j
Kearny, New Jersey (37,472) 51 K f
Kearsarge Pass, California 75 G h
Keatchie, Louisiana 63 K f
Keating, Oregon 73 N l
Keating, Pennsylvania 52 H d
Keatons Beach, Florida 54 H h
Keddie, California 74 E d
Kedron, Arkansas 63 L d
Keeler, California 75 H h
Keene, California 75 G j
Keene, New Hampshire 49 C f
Keene, New York 53 N a
Keener, Alabama 54 F c
Keensburg, Colorado 69 M c
Keeseville, New York 53 N a
Keewatin, Minnesota 59 N c
Keithsburg, Illinois 57 C h
Keithville, Louisiana 63 K f
Kekaha, Hawaii 72 B d
Kelford, North Carolina 55 O a
Kelim, Colorado 69 M c
Keller, Texas 65 M h
Keller, Virginia 53 L h
Keller, Washington 73 M g
Kellerton, Iowa 61 K d
Kellettville, Pennsylvania 52 G d
Kelleys I., Ohio 52 D d
Kelliher, Minnesota 59 M c
Kellogg, Idaho 66 D b
Kellogg, Iowa 61 M c
Kelly, Kentucky 57 F n
Kelly, Louisiana 63 L g
Kelly, Wyoming 67 K f
Kelly R., Alaska 76 F b
Kelseyville, California 74 C f
Kelso, California 75 K j
Kelso, North Dakota 58 J c
Kelso, Washington 73 H j
Kelton, Utah 68 C b
Keltys, Texas 65 N d
Kelvin, Arizona 70 G f
Kemblesville, Pennsylvania 50 B f
Kemmerer, Wyoming 67 K h
Kemp, L., Texas 65 H b
Kemp, Texas 65 L c
Kempner, Texas 65 K d
Kempton, Illinois 57 E j
Kempton, North Dakota 58 J c
Kenai, Alaska 76 M f
Kenai L., Alaska 76 N f
Kenai Mts., Alaska 76 M g
Kenai Pen., Alaska 66 N f
Kenansville, Florida 55 O f
Kenbridge, Virginia 52 H j
Kendall, Florida 54 A e
Kendall, Kansas 60 C g
Kendall, New York 52 H b
Kendallville, Indiana 57 H h
Kendrick, Idaho 66 D c
Kendrick Pk., Arizona 70 F d
Kenedy, Texas 65 K g
Kenefick, Oklahoma 62 G d
Kenel, South Dakota 58 F e
Kenesaw, Nebraska 60 F d
Kenibuna L., Alaska 76 L f
Kenly, North Carolina 55 N b
Kenmare, North Dakota 58 E b
Kenmore, Washington 72 B g
Kenna, New Mexico 71 O f
Kenna, West Virginia 52 E g
Kennebago L., Maine 49 E c
Kennebec, South Dakota 58 G g
Kennebec R., Maine 49 F d
Kennebunk, Maine 49 E e
Kennebunkport, Maine 49 E e
Kennedy, Minnesota 59 K b
Kennedy, Nebraska 60 D b
Kennedy, New York 52 G c
Kennedyville, Maryland 50 A g
Kennendale, Texas 65 L k
Kenner, Louisiana 62 A e
Kennesaw Mountain Nat. Batt. Park, Georgia 54 G d
Kennett, Missouri 61 O h
Kennett Square, Pennsylvania 50 B f
Kennewick, Washington 73 L j
Keney, Illinois 57 D j
Kenney, Texas 65 L e
Kennydale, Washington 72 C h
Keno, Oregon 73 J n
Kenosha, Wisconsin (67,899) 56 F g
Kenova, Kentucky 57 L l
Kenoza Lake, New York 50 D b
Kensal, North Dakota 58 H c
Kensett, Arkansas 63 M c
Kensett, Iowa 61 L a
Kensico Res., New York 50 F c
Kensington, Connecticut 51 H b
Kensington, Kansas 60 E e
Kent, Connecticut 50 G b
Kent, Iowa 61 K d
Kent, Minnesota 59 K d
Kent, Ohio 52 E d
Kent, Oregon 73 K k
Kent, Texas 64 C d
Kent, Washington 73 H h
Kent City, Michigan 56 H f
Kent Cliffs, New York 50 F c
Kent Dam, Rhode Island 51 K b
Kentland, Indiana 57 F j
Kenton, Delaware 50 B g
Kenton, Michigan 56 E c
Kenton, Ohio 52 C e
Kenton, Oklahoma 62 B c
Kenton, Tennessee 54 B a
Kentucky 57
Kentucky Dam, Kentucky 57 E n
Kentucky L., Kentucky-Tennessee 54 C a
Kentucky R., Kentucky 57 J l
Kentwood, Louisiana 63 N h
Kenyon, Minnesota 59 O f
Kenyonville, Connecticut 51 J b
Keokea, Hawaii 72 D e
Keokuk, Iowa 61 N d
Keota, Colorado 69 M c
Keota, Iowa 61 N c
Keoto, Oklahoma 63 J c
Kerby, Oregon 73 G n
Kerens, Texas 65 L c
Kerhonkson, New York 50 E b
Kerkhoven, Minnesota 59 L e
Kerman, California 75 E h
Kermit, Texas 64 D d
Kermit, West Virginia 52 D h
Kernersville, North Carolina 55 L a
Kern R., California 75 G j
Kernville, California 75 G j
Kerr, L., Florida 55 K h
Kerrick, Texas 64 B g
Kerrs Creek, Virginia 52 G h
Kerrville, Tennessee 54 B b
Kerrville, Texas 65 H e
Kershaw, South Carolina 55 L c
Kersey, Colorado 69 M c
Keshena, Wisconsin 56 E e
Ketchikan, Alaska 77 W j
Ketchum, Idaho 66 F f
Ketchum, Oklahoma 62 H b
Ketchum Mt., Texas 64 F d
Ketik R., Alaska 76 H b
Kettering, Ohio (54,462), vicinity of Dayton
Kettle Cr., Pennsylvania 52 J d
Kettle Falls, Washington 73 M g
Kettleman City, California 75 E h
Kettle R., Minnesota 59 O d
Kettle R., Washington 73 M g
Kettle River Ra., Washington 73 M g
Keuka L., New York 53 J c
Kevil, Kentucky 57 E m
Kevin, Montana 66 J a
Kewanna, Indiana 57 G h
Kewanee, Illinois 57 D h
Kewanee, Mississippi 63 P f
Keweenaw B., Michigan 56 E c
Keweenaw Bay, Michigan 56 E c
Keweenaw Pen., Michigan 56 F b
Keweenaw Pt., Michigan 56 F b
Keyaluvik, Alaska 76 E f
Keyapaha, South Dakota 58 F g
Keya Paha R., South Dakota 58 F g
Key Biscayne, Florida 54 C e
Keyes, Oklahoma 62 A b
Keyesport, Illinois 57 D l
Keyhole Res., Wyoming 67 Q e
Key Largo, Florida 55 O h
Key Largo, town, Florida 55 O h
Keymar, Maryland 53 J f
Keyport, New Jersey 50 E e
Keyport, Washington 72 A h
Keyser, West Virginia 52 H f
Keystone, Iowa 61 M b
Keystone, Nebraska 60 C c
Keystone, Oklahoma 62 G b
Keystone, South Dakota 58 C g
Keystone, West Virginia 52 E h
Keystone Heights, Florida 55 J h
Keystone Park, Arizona 70 F h
Keystone Res., Oklahoma 62 G b
Keysville, Georgia 55 J d
Keysville, Virginia 52 H h
Key West, Florida (33,956) 55 N j
Kezar Falls, Maine 49 E e
Kezar L., Maine 49 E d
Kgun L., Alaska 76 F f
Khotol, Alaska 76 H d
Kiamichi Mts., Oklahoma 62 H d
Kiamichi R., Oklahoma 62 H d

Kiana, Alaska 76 G c
Kickaboo R., Wisconsin 56 C f
Kidder, South Dakota 58 J e
Kief, North Dakota 58 F c
Kiel, Wisconsin 56 E f
Kigalik R., Alaska 76 K b
Kigluaik Mts., Alaska 76 D d
Kii, Hawaii 72 A d
Kii Landing, Hawaii 72 A d
Kjik, Alaska 76 K f
Kikiakrorak R., Alaska 76 L b
Kila, Montana 66 F a
Kilauea, Hawaii 72 B c
Kilauea Crater, Hawaii 72 E f
Kilauea Pt., Hawaii 72 B c
Kilbuck Mts., Alaska 76 G f
Kildare, Texas 65 N c
Kilgore, Idaho 66 J e
Kilgore, Nebraska 60 D b
Kilgore, Texas 65 N c
Kiliuda B., Alaska 76 L h
Killdeer, North Dakota 58 D c
Kill Devil Hill Nat. Mon., North Carolina 55 P c
Killduff, Iowa 61 M c
Killeen, Texas 65 K d
Killik Bend, Alaska 76 K b
Killik R., Alaska 76 K b
Killingly, Connecticut 51 K b
Killingworth, Connecticut 51 H c
Kill Van Kull, New York-New Jersey 51 K g
Kilmarnook, Virginia 53 K h
Kilmichael, Mississippi 63 O e
Kim, Colorado 69 N f
Kimama, Idaho 66 G g
Kimball, Mt., Alaska 77 P e
Kimball, Nebraska 60 A c
Kimball, West Virginia 52 E h
Kimballton, Iowa 61 J c
Kimberly, Idaho 66 F g
Kimberly, Oregon 73 L l
Kimberly, Wisconsin 56 E e
Kimbles, Pennsylvania 50 C c
Kimmswick, Missouri 61 O f
Kincaid, Kansas 61 J f
Kinde, Michigan 56 L f
Kinder, Louisiana 63 L h
Kindred, North Dakota 58 J d
King City, California 75 D h
King City, Missouri 61 K d
King Cove, Alaska 76 F j
Kingfield, Maine 49 E d
Kingfisher, Oklahoma 62 F c
King Hill, Idaho 66 E f
King I., Alaska 76 C d
King Lear R., Nevada 74 G c
Kingman, Arizona 70 C d
Kingman, Kansas 60 F g
Kingman, Maine 49 G c
King Mt., Texas 64 E d
King Salmon, Alaska 76 J g
King Salmon R., Alaska 76 J g
Kingsburg, California 75 F h
Kingsbury, Texas 65 K f
Kings Canyon, Colorado 69 K c
Kings Canyon Nat. Park, California 75 G h
Kingsland, Arkansas 63 L e
Kingsland, Georgia 55 J g
Kingsley, Michigan 56 H e
Kingsley, Iowa 61 J b
Kingsley Dam, Nebraska 60 C c
Kings Mountain, North Carolina 55 K b
Kings Mountain Nat. Mil. Park, South Carolina 55 K b
Kings Park, New York 50 G d
King Solomon R., Alaska 76 H f
Kings Pk., Utah 68 F c
Kingsport, Tennessee (26,314) 55 J a
Kings R., Arkansas 63 K b
Kings R., California 75 E h
Kings R., Nevada 74 G c
Kingston, Arkansas 63 K b
Kingston, Massachusetts 51 M a
Kingston, Ohio 52 D f
Kingston, Missouri 61 K e
Kingston, New Hampshire 49 E f
Kingston, New York (29,260) 50 E b
Kingston, Oklahoma 62 G d
Kingston, Pennsylvania 50 B c
Kingston, Rhode Island 51 L c
Kingston, Washington 72 B g
Kingston, West Virginia 52 E g
Kingston Pk., California 75 K j
Kingston Point, New York 50 F b
Kingstree, South Carolina 55 M d
Kingsville, Ohio 52 F d
Kingsville, Texas (25,297) 65 K h
Kingwood, West Virginia 52 G f
Kinmundy, Illinois 57 E l
Kinnear, Wyoming 67 M f
Kinsale, Virginia 53 K g
Kinsey, Montana 67 P c
Kinsley, Kansas 60 E g
Kinsman, Ohio 52 F d
Kinston, North Carolina 55 O b
Kinta, Oklahoma 62 H c
Kintla Pk., Montana 66 F a
Kintnersville, Pennsylvania 50 C d
Kinzers, Pennsylvania 50 A e
Kinzua, Oregon 73 K l
Kinzua, Pennsylvania 52 G d
Kiona, Washington 73 L j
Kiowa, Colorado 69 M d
Kiowa, Kansas 60 F g
Kiowa, Oklahoma 62 H d
Kiowa Cr., Colorado 69 M d
Kipahulu, Hawaii 72 D e
Kipling, Michigan 56 F d
Kipnuk, Alaska 76 E g
Kiptopeke, Virginia 53 L h
Kirby, Arkansas 63 K d
Kirby, Wyoming 67 M f
Kirbyville, Texas 65 O e
Kirk, Colorado 69 O d
Kirk, Nebraska 60 A c
Kirk, Oregon 73 J n
Kirkland, Arizona 70 E e
Kirkland, Illinois 57 E g
Kirkland, Texas 64 D j
Kirkland, Washington 72 C h
Kirklin, Indiana 57 G j
Kirkman, Iowa 61 J c
Kirksville, Missouri 61 M d
Kirkwood, California 74 C e
Kirkwood, Delaware 50 B f
Kirkwood, Missouri (29,421), vicinity of St. Louis
Kirkwood, New York 53 L c
Kirkwood, Pennsylvania 50 A f
Kirley, South Dakota 58 E f
Kirtley, Wyoming 67 Q g
Kirwin, Kansas 60 E e
Kirwin Res., Kansas 60 E e
Kisaralik R., Alaska 76 G f
Kiska I., Alaska 76 L j
Kiska Vol., Alaska 76 L j
Kissimmee, Florida 55 N e
Kissimmee, L., Florida 55 N f
Kissimmee R., Florida 55 N f
Kit Carson, Colorado 69 O e
Kitchawan, New York 50 F c
Kitsap, Washington 72 B g
Kitsap, L., Washington 72 A h
Kittanning, Pennsylvania 52 G e
Kittatinny Mts., New Jersey 50 D c
Kite, Georgia 55 J e
Kittery, Maine 49 E e
Kittery I., Hawaii 72 A a
Kittery Point, Maine 49 E e
Kitty Hawk, North Carolina 55 P c
Kiukpalik I., Alaska 76 L g
Kivalina, Alaska 76 E c
Kivchak, Alaska 76 J g
Kivchak B., Alaska 76 J g
Kiwalik, Alaska 76 G c
Klagetoh, Arizona 70 H d
Klamath, California 74 A c
Klamath Falls, Oregon 73 J n
Klamath Mts., California 74 B c
Klamath R., California 74 B c
Klamath River, California 74 C c
Klawak, Alaska 77 V j
Kleenburn, Wyoming 67 N e
Klein, Montana 67 M c
Klemme, Iowa 61 L a
Klery Creek, Alaska 76 G c
Klickitat, Washington 73 J k
Klickitat R., Washington 73 J j
Kline, South Carolina 55 K d
Klondike, California 75 J k
Klukwan, Alaska 77 U g
Klutina L., Alaska 77 P f
Knapp, Wisconsin 56 A e
Knickerbocker, Texas 64 G d
Knife Pk., Alaska 76 K g
Knife R., North Dakota 58 D c
Knife River, Minnesota 59 P c
Knight, Wyoming 67 K h
Knight I., Alaska 77 O f
Knightstown, Indiana 57 H j
Knightsville, Indiana 57 F k
Knightville Res., Massachusetts 51 H a
Knik Arm, Alaska 76 N f
Knippa, Texas 65 H f
Knobel, Arkansas 63 N b
Knobtown, Missouri 61 Q b
Knolls, Utah 68 C c
Knott, Texas 64 F c
Knowles, Oklahoma 62 C b
Knowlton, Wisconsin 56 D e
Knox, Indiana 57 G h
Knox, North Dakota 58 G b
Knox, Pennsylvania 52 G d
Knox City, Missouri 61 M d
Knox City, Texas 65 H b
Knoxville, California 74 C f
Knoxville, Illinois 57 C j
Knoxville, Iowa 61 L c
Knoxville, Mississippi 63 M g
Knoxville, Pennsylvania 52 J d
Knoxville, Tennessee (111,827) 54 H b
Kobuk, Alaska 76 J c
Kobuk R., Alaska 76 H c
Koch Mt., Montana 66 J d
Kodiak, Alaska 76 L h
Kodiak I., Alaska 76 L h
Kofa Mts., Arizona 70 D f
Kogrukluk R., Alaska 76 H f
Kokadjo, Maine 49 F c
Koko Head, Hawaii 72 C d
Kokolik R., Alaska 76 F b
Kokomo, Indiana (47,197) 57 G j
Kokrine Hills, Alaska 76 K d
Kokrines, Alaska 76 K d
Kokwok R., Alaska 76 H g
Kolekole, mt., Hawaii 72 D e
Koler, Oregon 73 G n
Koliganek, Alaska 76 H g
Kolin, Montana 67 L b
Koloa, Hawaii 72 B d
Komatke, Arizona 70 E f
Kom Vo, Arizona 70 E h
Konawa, Oklahoma 62 G d
Kongakut R., Alaska 77 Q b
Koniuji I., Alaska 77 P j
Konomoc L., Connecticut 51 J c
Kontrashibuna L., Alaska 76 L f
Kookooligit Mts., Alaska 76 B e
Koolau Ra., Hawaii 72 C d
Koosauqua, Iowa 61 M d
Koosharem, Utah 68 E e
Kooskia, Idaho 66 D c
Kootenai R., Montana 66 E a
Koozata Lagoon, Alaska 76 B e
Koppel, Pennsylvania 52 F e
Kopperl, Texas 65 K c
Korbel, California 74 B d
Korona, Florida 55 K h
Korovin I., Alaska 76 G j
Korovin Vol., Alaska 77 Q j
Kosciusco, Mississippi 63 O e
Kosciusko I., Alaska 77 V h
Koshkonong, Missouri 61 N h
Kosmos, Washington 73 H j
Kosse, Texas 65 L d
Kotlik, Alaska 76 F e
Kotzebue, Alaska 76 F c
Kotzebue Sd., Alaska 76 E c
Kountze, Texas 65 N e
Koyuk, Alaska 76 G d
Koyuk R., Alaska 76 G d
Koyukuk, Alaska 76 H d
Koyukuk I., Alaska 76 J d
Koyukuk R., Alaska 76 J d
Koyukuk River, Alaska 76 J d
Kramer, Nebraska 60 H d
Kramer, North Dakota 58 F b
Krebs, Oklahoma 62 H d
Kresgeville, Pennsylvania 50 B d
Krekatok I., Alaska 76 D e
Kremlin, Montana 67 K a
Kremmling, Colorado 69 K c
Krenitzin Is., Alaska 76 D j
Kress, Texas 64 C j
Kripplebush, New York 50 E b
Krotz Springs, Louisiana 63 M h
Krugloi Pt., Alaska 76 K j
Krum, Texas 65 K b
Krusenstern, C., Alaska 76 F c
Kruzof I., Alaska 77 U h
Kualakahi Chan., Hawaii 72 B d
Kualapuu, Hawaii 72 D d
Kudiakof Is., Alaska 76 F j
Kudobin Is., Alaska 76 G j
Kugruk R., Alaska 76 F d
Kuk, Alaska 76 G a
Kukak, Alaska 76 K g
Kukaklek L., Alaska 76 K g
Kukaklik L., Alaska 76 G f
Kukpowruk R., Alaska 76 F b
Kukpuk, Alaska 76 E b
Kukuihaele, Hawaii 72 E e
Kukuiula, Hawaii 72 B d
Kulik, L., Alaska 76 H g
Kulik L., Alaska 76 K g
Kulm, North Dakota 58 H d
Kulpment, Pennsylvania 53 K e
Kulpsville, Pennsylvania 50 C e
Kumliun, C., Alaska 76 J h
Kumukahi, C., Hawaii 72 E f
Kuna R., Alaska 76 J b
Kunkletown, Pennsylvania 50 B d
Kuparuk R., Alaska 76 N b
Kupreanof I., Alaska 77 V h
Kupreanof Pt., Alaska 76 H j
Kupreanof Str., Alaska 76 L g
Kure I. (Ocean I.), Hawaii 72 A a
Kurupa Ls., Alaska 76 K b
Kurupa R., Alaska 76 K b
Kushtaka L., Alaska 77 P f
Kuskokwim B., Alaska 76 E g
Kuskokwim Mts., Alaska 76 H f
Kuskokwim R., Alaska 76 G f
Kustatan, Alaska 76 M f
Kutch, Colorado 69 N e
Kuttawa, Kentucky 57 E m
Kutztown, Pennsylvania 50 B d
Kuzitrin R., Alaska 76 F d
Kvichak R., Alaska 76 J g
Kwethluk, Alaska 76 G f
Kwethluk R., Alaska 76 G f
Kwigillingok, Alaska 76 F g
Kwiguk, Alaska 76 E e
Kwikpak, Alaska 76 E e
Kwinhagak, Alaska 76 G g
Kyle, South Dakota 58 D g
Kyle, Texas 65 K f
Kyle, Wyoming 67 O h
Laau Pt., Hawaii 72 D d
Labadie, Missouri 61 O f
Labadieville, Louisiana 63 N j
La Barge, Wyoming 67 K g
La Barge Cr., Wyoming 67 K g
La Belle, Missouri 61 N d
Labonte Cr., Wyoming 67 P g
Labranche, Michigan 56 F d
Lacamp, Louisiana 63 L g
Lac du Flambeau, Wisconsin 56 D d
Lachine, Michigan 56 K d
Lackawack, New York 50 E b
Lackawanna, New York (29,564) 52 H c
Lacawaxen, Pennsylvania 50 C c
Laclede, Idaho 66 D a
Laclede, Missouri 61 L e
Lacombe, Louisiana 63 O h
Lacon, Illinois 57 D h
Lacona, Iowa 61 L c
Lacona, New York 53 K b
Laconia, New Hampshire 49 D e
La Conner, Washington 73 H g
Lacoochee, Florida 55 J j
Lacoste, Texas 65 J f
Lac qui Parle, L., Minnesota 59 K e
Lac qui Parle R., Minnesota 59 K f
Lacreek L., South Dakota 58 E g
La Crescent, Minnesota 59 P g
La Crosse, Indiana 57 G h
La Crosse, Kansas 60 E f
Lacrosse, Virginia 52 H j
Lacrosse, Washington 73 N j
La Crosse, Wisconsin (47,575) 56 B f
La Cueva, New Mexico 71 M d
La Cygne, Kansas 61 K f
Ladd, Illinois 57 D h
Ladder Cr., Kansas 60 C f
Laddonia, Missouri 61 N e
Ladelle, Arkansas 63 M e
Ladleton, New York 50 D b
Ladner, South Dakota 58 C e
Ladoga, Indiana 57 G k
Ladonia, Texas 65 M b
Ladrones Pk., New Mexico 71 K e
Ladue R., Alaska 77 R e
Ladysmith, Wisconsin 56 B d
La Farge, Wisconsin 56 C f
La Fargeville, New York 53 K a
Lafayette, Alabama 54 F e
Lafayette, California 75 C l
Lafayette, Colorado 69 O g
Lafayette, Georgia 54 F c
Lafayette, Indiana (42,330) 57 G j
Lafayette, Louisiana (40,400) 63 M h
Lafayette, Minnesota 59 M f
Lafayette, Mt., New Hampshire 49 D d
Lafayette, New Jersey 50 D c
La Fayette, Rhode Island 51 K b
Lafayette, Tennessee 54 E a
Lafayette Res., California 75 C l
La Feria, Texas 65 K j
Lafferty Hill, Pennsylvania 53 P b
Lafollette, Tennessee 54 G a
Lafourche, Bayou, Louisiana 63 N j
La France, South Carolina 55 J c
La Garita Mts., Colorado 69 K f
La Grande, Oregon 73 M k
La Grange, Georgia 54 F d
La Grange, Indiana 57 H h
La Grange, Kentucky 57 H l
La Grange, Missouri 61 N d
La Grange, North Carolina 55 O b
Lagrange, Ohio 52 D d
La Grange, Texas 65 L f
Lagrange, Wyoming 67 Q h
Lagrangeville, New York 50 F b
La Guardia Airport, New York 51 M f
Laguna, New Mexico 71 K d
Laguna, Texas 64 G f
Laguna Beach, California 75 H l
Laguna Cr., Arizona 70 G c
Laguna Dam, Arizona 70 C g
Laguna del Perro, New Mexico 71 M e
Laguna Madre, Texas 65 K j
Laguna Mts., California 75 J m
La Habra, California (25,136), vicinity of Los Angeles
Lahaina, Hawaii 72 D e
La Harpe, Illinois 57 C j
Lahontan Res., Nevada 74 F e
Laie, Hawaii 72 C d
Laingsburg, Michigan 56 J g
Laird, Colorado 69 O c
La Jara, Colorado 69 K f
Lajitas, Texas 64 D f
La Jolla, California 75 H m
La Joya, New Mexico 71 L e
La Junta, Colorado 69 N f
Lake, Idaho 66 J e
Lake, Michigan 56 H f
Lake, Mississippi 63 O f
Lake, New York 50 E c
Lake, Oregon 73 K m
Lake Alfred, Florida 55 N e
Lake Arlington, Texas 65 M j
Lake Andes, South Dakota 58 H g
Lake Arthur, Louisiana 63 L h
Lake Arthur, New Mexico 71 N f
Lake Benton, Minnesota 59 K f
Lake Bronson, Minnesota 59 K b
Lake Butler, Florida 55 J g
Lake Calumet Harb., Illinois 57 C n
Lake Charles, Louisiana (63,392) 63 K h
Lake City, Arkansas 63 N c
Lake City, California 74 E c
Lake City, Colorado 69 J e
Lake City, Florida 55 J g
Lake City, Iowa 61 K b
Lake City, Michigan 56 H e
Lake City, Minnesota 59 O f
Lake City (North Girard), Pennsylvania 52 F c
Lake City, South Carolina 55 M d
Lake City, South Dakota 58 J e
Lake City, Tennessee 54 G a
Lake City, Washington 72 B h
Lake Cormorant, Mississippi 63 N d
Lake Cr., Nevada 74 J c
Lake Crystal, Minnesota 59 M f
Lake Denton, Wisconsin 56 D f
Lakefield, Minnesota 59 L g
Lake Forest, Illinois 57 F g
Lake Geneva, Wisconsin 56 E g
Lake George, Colorado 69 L e
Lake George, New York 53 N b
Lake Hattie Res., Wyoming 67 P h
Lake Hill, New York 50 E a
Lake Hughes, California 75 G k
Lakehurst, New Jersey 50 E e
Lake Jackson, Texas 65 M f
Lake Katrine, New York 50 F b
Lakeland, Florida (41,350) 55 N e
Lakeland, Georgia 54 H f
Lake Linden, Michigan 56 E b
Lake Mead Nat. Recreational Area, Arizona 70 C d
Lake Mills, Iowa 61 L a
Lake Milton, Ohio 52 E d
Lake Minchumina, Alaska 76 L e
Lake Moxie, Maine 49 F c
Lake Mundelein, Illinois 57 E g
Lake Odessa, Michigan 56 H g
Lake Orion, Michigan 56 K g
Lake Outlet, Wyoming 67 K e
Lake Park, Florida 55 O g
Lake Park, Georgia 54 H g
Lake Park, Iowa 61 J a
Lake Park, Minnesota 59 K d
Lake Placid, Florida 55 N f
Lake Placid, New York 53 N a
Lake Point Junction, Utah 68 B h
Lakeport, California 74 C e
Lakeport, Florida 55 N g
Lakeport, Michigan 56 L f
Lake Preston, South Dakota 58 J f
Lake Providence, Louisiana 63 M f
Lake Ra., Nevada 74 F d
Lakeshore, California 75 F g
Lakeside, Arizona 70 G e
Lakeside, California 75 J m
Lakeside, Nebraska 60 B b
Lakeside, Utah 68 D b
Lake Texoma, Oklahoma 62 G e
Laketown, Utah 68 E b
Lake Toxaway, North Carolina 55 J b
Lake Valley, New Mexico 71 K g
Lake Victor, Texas 65 J e
Lake View, Iowa 61 J b
Lakeview, Louisiana 62 B e
Lakeview, Michigan 56 H f
Lakeview, Montana 66 J e
Lakeview, Oregon 73 K n
Lake View, South Carolina 55 M c
Lakeview, Texas 65 M j
Lake Village, Arkansas 63 M e
Lakeville, Connecticut 50 G b
Lakeville, Indiana 57 G h
Lakeville, Massachusetts 51 M b
Lakeville, Minnesota 59 N f
Lakeville, New York 50 E c
Lakeville, New York 52 J c
Lake Wales, Florida 55 N f
Lake Williams, North Dakota 58 G c
Lakewood, California (67,126) 75 E m
Lakewood, Colorado 69 O h
Lakewood, New Jersey 50 E e
Lakewood, New Mexico 71 N g
Lakewood, New York 52 G c
Lakewood, Ohio (66,154) 52 E d
Lakewood, Rhode Island 51 L b
Lake Worth, Florida 55 O g
Lake Worth Inlet, Florida 55 O g
Lake Worth Village, Texas 65 L j
Lakin, Kansas 60 C g
Lakota, Iowa 61 K a
Lakota, North Dakota 58 H b
La Madera, New Mexico 71 L c
Lamar, Arkansas 63 K c
Lamar, Colorado 69 O e
Lamar, Mississippi 63 O d
Lamar, Missouri 61 K g
Lamar, Nebraska 60 C d
Lamar, Oklahoma 62 G c
Lamar, South Carolina 55 L c
La Marque, Texas 65 N f
Lamar R., Wyoming 67 K e
Lamar Terrace, Texas 64 F j
Lambert, Georgia 55 K f
Lambert, Mississippi 63 N d
Lambert, Montana 67 Q b
Lamberton, Minnesota 59 L f
Lambertville, New Jersey 50 D e
Lambsburg, Virginia 52 F j
Lame Deer, Montana 67 O d
La Mesa, California (30,441) 75 J m
La Mesa, New Mexico 71 L g
Lamesa, Texas 64 F c
Lamkin, Texas 65 J d
La Moile, Illinois 57 D h
Lamoille, Nevada 74 K d
Lamoille R., Vermont 49 C e
La Moine R., Illinois 57 C j
Lamona, Washington 73 M h
Lamoni, Iowa 61 L d
Lamont, California 75 G j
Lamont, Florida 54 H g
Lamont, Idaho 66 J f
Lamont, Iowa 61 N b
Lamont, Oklahoma 62 F b
Lamont, Wyoming 67 N g
La Moure, North Dakota 58 H d
Lampasas, Texas 65 J d
Lampasas R., Texas 65 K e
Lamy, New Mexico 71 M d
Lanai, I., Hawaii 72 D e
Lanai City, Hawaii 72 D e
Lanaihale, mt., Hawaii 72 D e
Lanark, Florida 54 G h
Lanark, Illinois 57 D g
Lancaster, California (26,012) 75 G k
Lancaster, Kentucky 57 J m
Lancaster, Minnesota 59 K b
Lancaster, Missouri 61 M d
Lancaster, New Hampshire 49 D d
Lancaster, New York 52 H c
Lancaster, Ohio (29,916) 52 D f
Lancaster, Pennsylvania (61,055) 53 K e
Lancaster, South Carolina 55 L c
Lancaster, Texas 65 N k
Lancaster, Virginia 53 K h
Lancaster, Wisconsin 56 C g
Lance Cr., Wyoming 67 Q f
Lance Creek, Wyoming 67 Q f
Lancing, Tennessee 54 G a
Landa, North Dakota 58 F b
Landenberg, Pennsylvania 50 B f
Lander, Wyoming 67 M g
Landes, West Virginia 52 G g
Landis, North Carolina 55 L b
Landisville, New Jersey 50 D f
Lando, South Carolina 55 K c
Land o' Lakes, Wisconsin 56 D c
Landrum, South Carolina 55 J b
Landusky, Montana 67 M b
Lane, South Carolina 55 M d
Lane, South Dakota 58 H f
Lane City, Texas 65 L f
Lanesboro, Minnesota 59 P g
Lanesville, New York 50 E a
Lanett, Alabama 54 F e
Langdale, Alabama 54 F e
Langdon, Kansas 60 F g
Langdon, North Dakota 58 H b
Langford, South Dakota 58 J e
Langhorne, Pennsylvania 53 M e
Langley, South Carolina 55 K d
Langley, Washington 73 H g
Langlois, Oregon 73 F n
Lango, Florida 55 M f
Langtry, Texas 64 F f
L'Anguille R., Arkansas 63 N c
Lankin, North Dakota 58 H b
Lanoka Harbor, New Jersey 50 E f
Lansdale, Pennsylvania 50 C e
Lansdowne, Maryland 53 P f
Lansdowne, Pennsylvania 50 F g
Lansford, North Dakota 58 E b
Lansford, Pennsylvania 50 B d
L'Anse, Michigan 56 E c
Lansing, Iowa 61 N a
Lansing, Kansas 61 K e
Lansing, Michigan (107,807) 56 J g
Lansing, North Carolina 55 K a
Lantry, South Dakota 58 E e
Laona, Wisconsin 56 E d
La Panza, California 75 E j
La Panza Ra., California 75 E j
Lapaz, Indiana 57 G h
Lapel, Indiana 57 H j
Lapeer, Michigan 56 K f
La Perouse Pinnacle, Hawaii 72 C b
Lapine, Oregon 73 J m
Laplace, Louisiana 63 N h
Laplant, South Dakota 58 F e
La Plata, Maryland 53 K g
La Plata, Missouri 61 M d
La Pointe, Wisconsin 56 C c
La Porte, California 74 E e
La Porte, Indiana 57 G h
Laporte, Minnesota 59 M c
Laporte, Pennsylvania 53 K d
La Porte, Texas 65 M f
La Porte City, Iowa 61 M b
La Prele Cr., Wyoming 67 P g
La Pryor, Texas 64 G g
Lapush, Washington 73 F h
Laramie, Wyoming 67 P h
Laramie Pk., Wyoming 67 P g
Laramie R., Wyoming 67 P g
Laramie Ra., Wyoming 67 P g
Larchmont, New York 51 N d
Laredo, Missouri 61 L d
Laredo, Texas (60,678) 65 H h
Largo R., New Mexico 71 K c
Larimore, North Dakota 58 J c
Lark, North Dakota 58 E d
Lark, Utah 68 B j
Larkspur, Colorado 69 M d
Larman, Mississippi 63 M g
Larned, Kansas 60 E f
La Rose, Louisiana 63 N j
Larsen Bay, Alaska 76 L h
Larslan, Montana 67 O a
La Rue, Texas 65 M c
La Salle, Michigan 57 L k
Las Animas, Colorado 69 N e
Las Cruces, New Mexico (29,367) 71 L g
Las Palomas, New Mexico 71 K f
La Sal, Utah 68 G e
La Salle, Colorado 69 M c
La Salle, Illinois 57 D h
Lassen Pk., California 74 D d
Lassen Volcanic Nat. Park, California 74 D d
Last Chance, Colorado 69 N d
Las Vegas, Nevada (64,405) 75 K h
Las Vegas, New Mexico 71 M d
Latah Cr., Washington 73 N h
Latexo, Texas 65 M d
Latham, Illinois 57 D k
Lathrop, Michigan 56 F c
Lathrop, Missouri 61 K e
Latimer Mines, Pennsylvania 50 B d
Latir Pk., New Mexico 71 M c
Latouche, Alaska 77 O f
Latrobe, Pennsylvania 52 G e
Latta, South Carolina 55 M c

Latty, Ohio 52 B d
Lauderdale, Minnesota 59 Q h
Lauderdale, Mississippi 63 P f
Laughing Fish Pt., Michigan 56 G c
Laughlin Pk., New Mexico 71 N c
Laupahoehoe, Hawaii 72 E f
Laurel, Delaware 53 L g
Laurel, Indiana 57 H k
Laurel, Maryland 53 K f
Laurel, Mississippi (27,889) 63 O g
Laurel, Montana 67 M d
Laureldale, Pennsylvania 50 B e
Laurel Hill, Florida 54 E g
Laurel Hill, Pennsylvania 52 G f
Laurelton, New Jersey 50 E e
Laurelville, Ohio 52 D f
Laurens, Iowa 61 K b
Laurens, New York 53 L c
Laurens, South Carolina 55 J c
Laurin, Montana 66 H d
Laurinburg, North Carolina 55 M c
Laurium, Michigan 56 E b
Lava Beds Nat. Mon., California 74 D c
Lavaca B., Texas 65 L g
Lavaca R., Texas 65 L f
Lava Hot Springs, Idaho 66 J g
La Valle, Wisconsin 56 C f
Lavallette, New Jersey 50 E f
Laveaga Pk., California 75 D h
Lavenia, Georgia 54 H c
La Ventana, New Mexico 71 K d
La Verkin, Utah 68 C f
Laverne, Oklahoma 62 D b
La Vernia, Texas 65 J f
La Veta, Colorado 69 L f
La Veta Pass, Colorado 69 L f
Lavina, Montana 67 M c
Lavon Res., Texas 65 L b
Laward, Texas 65 L g
Lawen, Oregon 73 M m
Lawler, Iowa 61 M a
Lawler, Minnesota 59 N d
Lawn, Texas 65 H c
Lawndale, North Carolina 55 K b
Lawrence, Indiana 57 G k
Lawrence, Kansas (32,858) 61 J f
Lawrence, Massachusetts (70,933) 49 D f
Lawrence, Nebraska 60 F d
Lawrenceburg, Indiana 57 J k
Lawrenceburg, Kentucky 57 J l
Lawrenceburg, Tennessee 54 D b
Lawrenceville, Georgia 54 H d
Lawrenceville, Illinois 57 E l
Lawrenceville, New Jersey 50 D e
Lawrenceville, Pennsylvania 53 P a
Lawrenceville, Virginia 52 J j
Laws, California 75 G g
Lawson, Missouri 61 K e
Lawtey, Florida 55 J g
Lawton, Michigan 57 H g
Lawton, North Dakota 58 H b
Lawton, Oklahoma (61,697) 62 E d
Lawton, Pennsylvania 53 K d
Lay, Colorado 69 J c
Lay L., Alabama 54 E e
Laysan I., Hawaii 72 B a
Laysville, Connecticut 51 J c
Layton, New Jersey 50 D c
Lazare, Texas 64 H a
Leaburg, Oregon 73 H l
Leachville, Arkansas 63 N c
Lead, South Dakota 58 C f
Leadore, Idaho 66 G e
Leadville, Colorado 69 K d
Leaf River, Illinois 57 D g
Leakesville, Mississippi 63 P g
Leakey, Texas 65 H f
Leaksville, North Carolina 55 M a
Leal, North Dakota 58 H c
Leal R., Mississippi 63 O g
Leamington, Utah 68 D d
Leander, Texas 65 J e
Leary, Georgia 54 G f
Leatherman Pk., Idaho 66 G e
Leavenworth, Indiana 57 G l
Leavenworth, Kansas 61 K e
Leavenworth, Washington 73 K h
Leavitt Pk., California 74 F f
Leawood, Kansas 61 P b
Lebam, Washington 73 G j
Lebanon, Connecticut 51 J b
Lebanon, Illinois 57 D l
Lebanon, Indiana 57 G j
Lebanon, Kansas 60 F e
Lebanon, Kentucky 57 H m
Lebanon, Missouri 61 M g
Lebanon, Nebraska 60 D d
Lebanon, New Hampshire 49 C e
Lebanon, New Jersey 50 D d
Lebanon, Ohio 52 B f
Lebanon, Oregon 73 H l
Lebanon, Pennsylvania (30,045) 53 K e
Lebanon, South Dakota 58 G e
Lebanon, Tennessee 54 E a
Lebanon, Virginia 52 D j
Lebanon Junction, Kentucky 57 H m
Lebanon Station, Florida 55 J h
Lebec, California 75 G k
Lebo, Kansas 61 J f
Le Center, Minnesota 59 N f
Le Claire, Iowa 61 O c
Lecompte, Louisiana 63 L g
Ledger, Montana 66 J a
Ledyard, Connecticut 51 J c
Lee, Arizona 70 H h
Lee, Florida 54 H g
Lee, Illinois 57 E h
Lee, Massachusetts 50 G a
Leechburg, Pennsylvania 52 G e
Leech L., Minnesota 59 M c
Leedey, Oklahoma 62 D c
Leeds, Alabama 54 E d
Leeds, Massachusetts 51 H a
Leeds, Missouri 61 Q a
Leeds, New York 50 F a
Leeds, North Dakota 58 G b
Leeds, Utah 68 C f
Leeds Junction, Maine 49 E d
Leenanau L., Michigan 56 H e
Leeper, Missouri 61 O g
Leeper, Pennsylvania 52 G d
Leesburg, Florida 55 K j
Leesburg, Georgia 54 G f
Leesburg, Idaho 66 F d
Leesburg, New Jersey 50 D g
Leesburg, Ohio 52 C f
Leesburg, Texas 65 M c
Leesburg, Virginia 52 J f
Lees Summit, Missouri 61 Q b
Leesville, Louisiana 63 K g
Leesville, South Carolina 55 K d
Leesville, Texas 65 K f
Leesville Res., Ohio 52 E e
Leetonia, Ohio 52 F e
Leetsville, Michigan 56 H e
Leeville, Louisiana 63 N j
Leevining, California 74 F g
Lefors, Texas 64 D h
Le Grand, California 75 E g
Lehi, Utah 68 E c
Lehigh, Iowa 61 K b
Lehigh, Oklahoma 62 G d
Lehigh R., Pennsylvania 50 B d
Lehighton, Pennsylvania 50 B d
Lehman, Oregon 73 M k
Lehman, Pennsylvania 50 A c
Lehman, Texas 64 E b
Lehr, North Dakota 58 G d
Lehua, I., Hawaii 72 A c
Leicester, Massachusetts 51 K a
Leighton, Alabama 54 D c
Leipsic, Delaware 50 B g
Leipsic, Ohio 52 C d
Leitchfield, Kentucky 57 G m
Leiter, Wyoming 67 O e
Leith, North Dakota 58 E d
Leland, Iowa 61 L a
Leland, Michigan 56 H d
Leland, Mississippi 63 N e
Lelia Lake, Texas 64 D j
Le Mars, Iowa 61 H b
Lemasters, Pennsylvania 52 J f
Lemhi, Idaho 66 G e
Lemhi R., Idaho 66 G e
Lemhi Ra., Idaho 66 G e
Lemitar, New Mexico 71 K e
Lemmon, South Dakota 58 D e
Lemmon Mt., Arizona 70 G g
Lemon, Mississippi 63 O f
Lemoore, California 75 F h
Lemoyne, Nebraska 60 C c
Lena, Illinois 56 D g
Lena, Louisiana 63 L g
Lena, Mississippi 63 O f
Lena, Oregon 73 L k
Lenapah, Oklahoma 62 H b
Lenexa, Kansas 61 O b
Lengby, Minnesota 59 L c
Lenhartsville, Pennsylvania 50 B d
Lennep, Montana 67 K c
Lennox, California (31,224) vicinity of Los Angeles
Lennox, South Dakota 59 K g
Lenoir, North Carolina 55 K b
Lenoir City, Tennessee 54 G b
Lenora, Kansas 60 D e
Lenorah, Texas 64 F c
Lenore L., Washington 73 L h
Lenox, Georgia 54 H f
Lenox, Iowa 61 K d
Lenox, Massachusetts 50 G a
Leola, Arkansas 63 L d
Leola, South Dakota 58 H e
Leominster, Massachusetts (27,929) 49 D f
Leon, Iowa 61 L d
Leon, Kansas 60 H g
Leon, West Virginia 52 E g
Leona, Texas 65 M d
Leona R., Texas 65 H g
Leonard, Michigan 56 K g
Leonard, Missouri 61 M e
Leonard, North Dakota 58 J d
Leonard, Texas 65 L b
Leonardville, Kansas 60 H e
Leon Cr., Texas 64 E d
Leon R., Texas 65 K d
Leon Springs, Texas 65 J f
Leontovitch C., Alaska 76 F j
Leoti, Kansas 60 C f
Lepanto, Arkansas 63 N c
Le Raysville, Pennsylvania 53 K d
Lerna, Illinois 57 E k
Le Roy, Illinois 57 E j
Le Roy, Iowa 61 L d
Le Roy, Kansas 61 J f
Leroy, Michigan 56 H e
Le Roy, Minnesota 59 O g
Le Roy, New York 52 H c
Le Roy, Wyoming 67 K h
Lery, L., Louisiana 63 O j
Leslie, Arkansas 63 L c
Leslie, Georgia 54 G f
Leslie, Idaho 66 G f
Leslie, Michigan 56 J g
Leslie Prairie, Minnesota 59 M f
Lester, Iowa 60 H a
Lester, Nebraska 60 F d
Lester, West Virginia 52 E h
Lesterville, South Dakota 58 J g
Le Sueur, Minnesota 59 N f
Letcher, South Dakota 58 H g
Letha, Idaho 66 D f
Letohatchee, Alabama 54 E e
Letts, Indiana 57 H k
Levan, Utah 68 E d
Levant, Kansas 60 C e
Levelland, Texas 64 E b
Levelock, Alaska 76 J g
Leverett, Wyoming 67 Q f
Levering, Michigan 56 J d
Levittown, New Jersey 50 D e
Levittown, New York (65,276) 50 F d
Levittown, Pennsylvania 50 D e
Levy, L., Florida 55 J h
Levy, New Mexico 71 N c
Lewanna, Nebraska 60 D b
Lewbeach, New York 50 D a
Lewellen, Nebraska 60 B c
Lewes, Delaware 53 L g
Lewis, Iowa 61 J c
Lewis, Kansas 60 E g
Lewis & Clark L., South Dakota 58 J h
Lewisburg, Kentucky 57 G n
Lewisburg, Ohio 52 B f
Lewisburg, Pennsylvania 53 J e
Lewisburg, Tennessee 54 E b
Lewisburg, West Virginia 52 F h
Lewis L., Wyoming 67 K e
Lewis R., Washington 73 J j
Lewis Ra., Montana 66 G a
Lewis Run, Pennsylvania 52 H d
Lewis Springs, Arizona 70 G h
Lewiston, Idaho 66 D c
Lewiston, Maine (40,804) 49 E d
Lewiston, Michigan 56 J e
Lewiston, Missouri 61 N d
Lewiston, New York 52 H b
Lewiston, North Carolina 55 O a
Lewiston, Utah 68 E b
Lewistown, Illinois 57 C j
Lewistown, Montana 67 L b
Lewistown, Pennsylvania 52 J e
Lewisville, Arkansas 63 K e
Lewisville, Idaho 66 H f
Lewisville, Minnesota 59 M g
Lewisville, Pennsylvania 50 B f
Lewisville, Texas 65 L b
Lewisville Res., Texas 65 K b
Lexa, Arkansas 63 N d
Lexington, Illinois 57 E j
Lexington, Indiana 57 H l
Lexington, Kentucky (62,810) 57 J l
Lexington, Massachusetts (27,691) 49 E h
Lexington, Michigan 56 L f
Lexington, Minnesota 59 Q h
Lexington, Mississippi 63 N e
Lexington, Missouri 61 L e
Lexington, Nebraska 60 E d
Lexington, New York 50 E a
Lexington, North Carolina 55 L b
Lexington, Oklahoma 62 F c
Lexington, Oregon 73 L k
Lexington, South Carolina 55 K d
Lexington, Tennessee 54 C b
Lexington, Texas 65 L e
Lexington, Virginia 52 G h
Leyden, North Dakota 58 J b
Libby, Montana 66 E a
Libby Res., Montana 66 E a
Liberal, Kansas 60 D g
Liberal, Missouri 61 K g
Liberator L., Alaska 76 H b
Liberty, Alaska 77 R d
Liberty, Illinois 57 B k
Liberty, Indiana 57 J k
Liberty, Kentucky 57 J m
Liberty, Mississippi 63 N g
Liberty, Missouri 61 Q a
Liberty, Nebraska 60 H d
Liberty, New York 50 D b
Liberty, North Carolina 55 M b
Liberty, Pennsylvania 53 J d
Liberty, South Carolina 55 J c
Liberty, Texas 65 N e
Liberty, Washington 73 K h
Liberty Center, Ohio 52 B d
Liberty Hill, South Carolina 55 L c
Liberty Hill, Texas 65 J e
Liberty I., New York 51 L f
Libertytown, Maryland 53 J f
Libertyville, Iowa 61 M d
Libertyville, New York 50 E b
Licking, Missouri 61 N g
Licking R., Kentucky 57 K l
Licking R., Ohio 52 D e
Lida, Nevada 75 H g
Lidderdale, Iowa 61 K b
Lidgerwood, North Dakota 58 J d
Light, Texas 65 H g
Lighthouse Pt., Florida 54 G h
Lignite, North Dakota 58 D b
Lignum, Virginia 52 J g
Ligonier, Indiana 57 H h
Ligonier, Pennsylvania 52 G e
Ligurta, Arizona 70 C g
Lihue, Hawaii 72 B d
Likely, California 74 E c
Lilbourn, Missouri 61 P h
Lillie, Louisiana 63 L f
Lillington, North Carolina 55 N b
Lillis, Kansas 60 H e
Lilly, Pennsylvania 52 H e
Lily, South Dakota 58 J e
Lima, Illinois 57 B j
Lima, Montana 66 H e
Lima, New York 52 J c
Lima, Ohio (51,037) 52 B e
Lima, Oklahoma 62 G c
Lima, Pennsylvania 50 B f
Lima Res., Montana 66 H e
Lime, Oregon 73 N l
Lime Hills, Alaska 76 K f
Limerick, Maine 49 E e
Lime Rock, Connecticut 50 G b
Lime Springs, Iowa 61 M a
Limestone, Florida 55 N f
Limestone, Maine 49 H b
Limestone, New York 52 H c
Lime Village (Hungry), Alaska 76 K f
Limon, Colorado 69 N d
Limpia Cr., Texas 64 D e
Lincoln, Alabama 54 E d
Lincoln, California 74 D f
Lincoln, Delaware 53 L g
Lincoln, Illinois 57 D j
Lincoln, Kansas 60 F e
Lincoln, Maine 49 G c
Lincoln, Michigan 56 K e
Lincoln, Minnesota 59 M d
Lincoln, Montana 66 H c
Lincoln, Nebraska (128,521) 60 H d
Lincoln, New Hampshire 49 D d
Lincoln, New Mexico 71 M f
Lincoln City, Indiana 57 G l
Lincoln Cr., Nebraska 60 G d
Lincoln Park, New Jersey 50 E d
Lincoln Park, Michigan (53,933) vicinity of Detroit
Lincoln Place, Pennsylvania 53 Q b
Lincolnton, Georgia 55 J d
Lincolnton, North Carolina 55 K b
Lincolnville, Maine 49 F d
Lind, Washington 73 M j
Lindale, Georgia 54 F c
Lindale, Texas 65 M c
Lindbergh, Wyoming 67 Q h
Lindbergh L., Montana 66 G b
Linden, Alabama 54 D e
Linden, Indiana 57 G j
Linden, Missouri 61 P a
Linden, New Jersey (39,931) 50 E d
Linden, New York 52 H c
Linden, North Carolina 55 N b
Linden, Tennessee 54 D b
Linden, Texas 65 N b
Lindenhurst, New York 50 G d
Lindenwold, New Jersey 50 D f
Lindland, Colorado 69 K c
Lindon, Colorado 69 N d
Lindsay, California 75 F h
Lindsay, Montana 67 P b
Lindsay, Oklahoma 62 F d
Lindsay, Nebraska 60 G c
Lindsborg, Kansas 60 G f
Lindsey, Ohio 52 C d
Linesville, Pennsylvania 52 F d
Lineville, Alabama 54 F d
Lineville, Iowa 61 L d
Lingle, Wyoming 67 Q g
Lingshire, Montana 66 J c
Linlithgo, New York 50 F a
Linn, Kansas 60 G e
Linn, Missouri 61 N f
Linn, Mt., California 74 C d
Linn, Texas 65 J j
Linneus, Maine 49 H b
Linneus, Missouri 61 L e
Linthicum Heights, Maryland 53 P g
Linton, Indiana 57 F k
Linton, North Dakota 58 F d
Linville, North Carolina 55 K a
Linville, Virginia 52 H g
Linwood, Kansas 61 J e
Linwood, Michigan 56 K f
Linwood, Nebraska 60 H c
Lionkol, Wyoming 67 L h
Lionville, Pennsylvania 50 B e
Lipan, Texas 65 J c
Lipscomb, Texas 64 D g
Lisbon, Illinois 57 E h
Lisbon, New Hampshire 49 D d
Lisbon, New York 53 L a
Lisbon, North Dakota 58 J d
Lisbon, Ohio 52 F e
Lisbon Falls, Maine 49 E e
Lisburne, C., Alaska 76 D b
Lisco, Nebraska 60 B c
Lisianski I., Hawaii 72 B a
Lisle, New York 53 K c
Lisman, Alabama 54 C e
Litchfield, California 74 E d
Litchfield, Connecticut 50 G b
Litchfield, Illinois 57 D k
Litchfield, Michigan 57 J g
Litchfield, Minnesota 59 M e
Litchfield, Nebraska 60 E c
Litchfield Park, Arizona 70 E f
Litchville, North Dakota 58 H d
Lithgow, New York 50 F b
Lititz, Pennsylvania 53 K e
Little Beaver Cr., Kansas 60 C e
Little Belt Mts., Montana 67 K c
Little B. de Noc, Michigan 56 F d
Little Black R., Alaska 77 Q c
Little Blue R., Missouri 61 Q b
Little Camas Res., Idaho 66 E f
Little Canada, Minnesota 59 R h
Little Chute, Wisconsin 56 E e
Little Colorado R., Arizona 70 F d
Little Compton Commons, Rhode Island 51 L c
Little Creek Pk., Utah 68 D f
Little Creek, Delaware 50 B g
Little Cypress Cr., Texas 65 N c
Little Diomede I., Alaska 76 C d
Little Dry Cr., Montana 67 O b
Little Egg Harbor, New Jersey 50 E f
Little Egg Inlet, New Jersey 50 E g
Little Falls, Minnesota 59 M e
Little Falls, New Jersey 51 K e
Little Falls, New York 53 M b
Littlefield, Arizona 70 D c
Littlefield, Texas 64 E b
Little Fork, Minnesota 59 N b
Little Gap, Pennsylvania 50 B d
Little Grassy L., Illinois 57 D m
Little Humboldt R., Nevada 74 H c
Little Kanawha R., West Virginia 52 E f
Little Kiska I., Alaska 76 L j
Little Koniuji I., Alaska 76 H j
Little L., Louisiana 63 N j
Little Lake, California 75 H j
Little Lost R., Idaho 66 G f
Little Malad R., Idaho 66 H g
Little Meadows, Pennsylvania 53 K d
Little Medicine, Wyoming 67 P g
Little Miami R., Ohio 52 B f
Little Missouri R., Arkansas 63 K e
Little Missouri R., North Dakota-Wyoming 58 C d
Little Neck B., New York 51 N e
Little Osage R., Missouri 61 K g
Little Owyhee R., Oregon 73 N n
Little Peconic B., New York 51 J c
Little Pee Dee R., South Carolina 55 M c
Little Powder R., Wyoming 67 P e
Little R., Georgia 55 J d
Little R., Georgia 54 H f
Little R., Kentucky 57 F n
Little R., Louisiana 63 L g
Little R., North Carolina 55 M b
Little R., North Carolina 55 N b
Little R., Oklahoma 62 H d
Little R., Oklahoma 62 G c
Little R., Texas 65 L e
Little Red R., Arkansas 63 L c
Little River, Alabama 54 D f
Little River, Kansas 60 F f
Little River, South Carolina 55 N d
Little River Inlet, North Carolina 55 N d
Little Rock, Arkansas (107,813) 63 L d
Littlerock, California 75 H k
Little Sable Pt., Michigan 56 G f
Little Sac R., Missouri 61 L g
Little Salmon R., Idaho 66 D d
Little Salt L., Utah 68 D f
Little San Bernardino Mts., California 75 J l
Little Sandy Cr., Wyoming 67 L g
Little Satilla R., Georgia 55 J f
Little Silver, New Jersey 50 E e
Little Sioux R., Iowa 61 J b
Little Sitkin I., Alaska 76 M j
Little Snake R., Colorado 68 H c
Littlestown, Pennsylvania 53 J f
Little Suamico, Wisconsin 56 F e
Little Tanaga I., Alaska 77 P j
Little Tennessee R., Tennessee 54 G b
Littleton, Colorado 69 O j
Littleton, Illinois 57 C j
Littleton, New Hampshire 49 D d
Littleton, North Carolina 55 O a
Littleton, West Virginia 52 F f
Little Traverse B., Michigan 56 H d
Little Tupper L., New York 53 M a
Little Valley, New York 52 H c
Little Valley Cr., Idaho 66 D g
Littleville, Alabama 54 D c
Little Wabash R., Illinois 57 E l
Little Wood R., Idaho 66 F f
Little York, New Jersey 50 C d
Lituya B., Alaska 77 T g
Livengood, Alaska 77 N d
Lovenia, Mt., Utah 68 F c
Live Oak, California 74 D e
Live Oak, Florida 55 J g
Livermore, California 74 D g
Livermore, Iowa 61 K b
Livermore, Kentucky 57 F m
Livermore Falls, Maine 49 E d
Livermore, Mt., Texas 64 C e
Liverpool, New York 53 K b
Livingston, Alabama 54 C e
Livingston, Louisiana 63 N h
Livingston, Montana 67 K d
Livingston, New York 50 F a
Livingston, Tennessee 54 F a
Livingston, Texas 65 N e
Livingston, Wisconsin 56 C g
Livingstone, Kentucky 57 J m
Livingston Manor, New York 50 D b
Livonia, Louisiana 63 M h
Livonia, Michigan (66,702) 56 K g
Livonia, Missouri 61 M d
Lizard Head Pk., Wyoming 67 L g
Lizella, Georgia 54 H e
Lizemores, West Virginia 52 E g
Lizton, Indiana 57 G k
Llano, Texas 65 J e
Llano Estacado, New Mexico-Texas 64 E b
Llano R., Texas 65 H e
Lloyd, Montana 67 L a
Lloyd Harbor, New York 50 G d
L. M. Smith Res., Alabama 54 D c
Loa, Utah 68 E e
Loag, Pennsylvania 50 B e
Loami, Illinois 57 D k
Lobo Hot Springs, Montana 66 F c
Lobos, Pt., California 75 B l
Lochsa R., Idaho 66 E c
Locke, New York 53 K c
Locke, Washington 73 N g
Locker, Texas 65 J d
Lockes, Nevada 74 K f
Lockesburg, Arkansas 63 J e
Lockett, Texas 65 H a
Lockhart, Alabama 54 E f
Lockhart, Minnesota 59 K c
Lockhart, South Carolina 55 K c
Lockhart, Texas 65 K f
Lock Haven, Pennsylvania 52 J d
Lockney, Texas 64 F a
Lockport, Illinois 57 E h
Lockport, Louisiana 63 N j
Lockport, New York (26,443) 52 H b
Lockridge, Iowa 61 N d
Lockwood, Missouri 61 L g
Lockwood Hills, Alaska 76 J c
Loco, Oklahoma 62 F d
Loco Mt., Montana 67 K c
Locust Cr., Missouri 61 L d
Locust Grove, Maryland 50 A g
Locust Grove, Ohio 52 C g
Locust Grove, Oklahoma 62 H b
Loda, Illinois 57 E j
Lodge Grass, Montana 67 N d
Lodge, Mt., Alaska 77 T g
Lodgepole, Nebraska 60 B c
Lodgepole Cr., Nebraska 60 A c
Lodgepole Cr., Wyoming 67 Q h
Lodi, California 74 D f
Lodi, Ohio 52 E d
Lodi, Wisconsin 56 D f
Lofall, Washington 72 A g
Logan, Iowa 61 J c
Logan, Kansas 60 E e
Logan, Montana 66 J d
Logan, Mt., Washington 73 K g
Logan, Nebraska 60 D c
Logan, New Mexico 71 O d
Logan, Ohio 52 D f
Logan, Utah 68 E b
Logan, West Virginia 52 D h
Logan Cr., Nebraska 60 H c
Logandale, Nevada 75 L h
Logan Glacier, Alaska 77 R f
Logan Pass, Montana 66 G a
Logan Res., Ohio 52 D f
Logansport, Indiana 57 G j
Logansport, Louisiana 63 K g
Loganton, Pennsylvania 53 J d
Loganville, Wisconsin 56 C f
Logcabin, Colorado 69 L c
Logdell, Oregon 73 L l
Lohman, Montana 67 L a
Lohn, Texas 65 H d
Lohrville, Iowa 61 K b
Lola, Colorado 69 J e
Lola, Mt., California 74 E
Loleta, California 74 A d
Lolo, Montana 66 F c
Lolo Pass, Idaho 66 F c
Loma, Colorado 68 H d
Loma, Montana 67 K b
Loma, North Dakota 58 H b
Loman, Minnesota 59 N b
Lombard, Montana 66 J c
Lometa, Texas 65 J d
Lomira, Wisconsin 56 E f
Lomita, California 75 D m
Lompoc, California 75 E k
Lon, New Mexico 71 M e
Lonaconing, Maryland 52 H f
London, Arkansas 63 K c
London, Kentucky 57 J m
London, Ohio 52 C f
London, Oregon 73 G m
London, Texas 65 H e
Londonderry, New Hampshire 49 D f
Londonderry, Vermont 49 C e
Lone Grove, Oklahoma 62 F d
Lone Mt., Nevada 74 H g
Lone Oak, Texas 65 M c
Lone Pine, California 75 G h
Lonepine, Montana 66 F b
Lone Pk., Utah 68 D j
Lonerock, Oregon 73 L k
Lone Rock, Wisconsin 56 C f
Lone Rock Res., Arkansas 63 L b
Lonesome Lake Res., Montana 67 K a
Lonetree, Wyoming 67 K h
Lonetree Res., North Dakota 58 F c
Lone Wolf, Oklahoma 62 D d
Long, Alaska 76 K d
Long B., South Carolina 55 N d
Long Beach, California (344,168) 75 G l
Long Beach, Mississippi 63 O h
Long Beach, New York (26,473) 50 F d
Long Beach I., New Jersey 50 E f
Longboat Key, Florida 55 M f
Long Branch, New Jersey (26,228) 50 F e
Long Cr., North Dakota 58 C b

Long Creek, Oregon 73 L l
Longdale, Oklahoma 62 E b
Long Eddy, New York 53 L d
Long Falls Dam, Maine 49 E c
Longfellow, Texas 64 E e
Longford, Kansas 60 G e
Long Hill, Connecticut 50 G c
Longhurst, North Carolina 55 N a
Long I., Massachusetts 49 H j
Long I., New York 50 F d
Long Island, Kansas 60 E e
Long Island City, New York 51 M f
Long Island Sd., New York-Connecticut 50 G d
Long L., Alaska 76 K f
Long L., Maine 49 G a
Long L., Michigan 56 H e
Long L., Michigan 56 K d
Long L., Minnesota 59 M d
Long L., New York 53 M a
Long L., North Dakota 58 F d
Long L., Washington 72 A j
Long Lake, New York 53 M b
Long Lake, Wisconsin 56 E d
Long Lake Res., Washington 73 L h
Longmeadow, Massachusetts 51 H a
Longmont, Colorado 69 L c
Long Pine, Nebraska 60 E b
Long Point, Illinois 57 E h
Long Pond, Massachusetts 51 L b
Long Prairie, Minnesota 59 M e
Long Prairie R., Minnesota 59 M d
Longs, South Carolina 55 N d
Longs Pk., Colorado 69 L c
Long Tom Res., Idaho 66 E f
Longton, Kansas 61 H g
Longtown, Missouri 61 P g
Long Valley, Arizona 70 F e
Long Valley, New Jersey 50 D d
Longvalley, South Dakota 58 E g
Long Valley Res., California 74 G g
Longview, Texas (40,050) 65 N c
Longview, Washington 73 H j
Longville, Louisiana 63 K h
Longwood, Florida 55 K j
Longwood, Mississippi 63 M e
Longworth, Texas 64 G c
Lonoke, Arkansas 63 M d
Lonsdale, Minnesota 59 N f
Lonsdale, Rhode Island 51 L b
Loogootee, Indiana 57 G l
Lookeba, Oklahoma 62 E c
Lookingglass R., Michigan 56 J g
Lookout, California 74 D c
Lookout, C., North Carolina 55 P c
Lookout Pt., Michigan 56 K e
Lookout Mt., Alaska 76 H e
Lookout Mt., California 75 G h
Lookout Mt., Georgia 54 F c
Lookout Mt., New Mexico 71 J d
Lookout Pass, Montana 66 E b
Lookout Point Res., Oregon 73 H m
Lookout Ridge, Alaska 76 H b
Lookout Shoals L., North Carolina 55 K b
Loomis, Nebraska 60 E d
Loomis, Washington 73 L g
Loon L., Maine 49 F b
Loosahatchie R., Tennessee 54 B b
Lopez, Pennsylvania 53 K d
Lorain, Ohio (68,932) 52 D d
Loraine, Illinois 57 B j
Loraine, North Dakota 58 E b
Loraine, Texas 64 G c
Lordsburg, New Mexico 71 J g
Lorena, Texas 65 K d
Lorenzo, Idaho 66 J f
Lorenzo, Nebraska 60 A c
Lorenzo, Texas 64 F b
Loretta, Wisconsin 56 C d
Loretto, Kentucky 57 H m
Loretto, Tennessee 54 D b
Loring, Montana 67 N a
Lorimor, Iowa 61 K c
Loris, South Carolina 55 N c
Lords Valley, Pennsylvania 50 C c
Lorraine, Kansas 60 F f
Los Alamitos, California 75 F m
Los Alamos, California 75 E k
Los Alamos, New Mexico 71 L d
Los Angeles, California (2,479,015) 75 G k
Los Angeles, Texas 65 H g
Los Angeles Harb., California 75 E n
Los Banos, California 75 E g
Los Ebanos, Texas 65 J j
Los Fresnos, Texas 65 K j
Los Gatos, California 75 D g
Los Indios, Texas 65 K j
Los Lunas, New Mexico 71 L e
Los Molinos, California 74 C d
Los Olivos, California 75 E k
Los Cabin, Wyoming 67 N f
Los City, West Virginia 52 H g
Lost Cr., Wyoming 67 M g
Lost Hills, California 75 F j
Lostine, Oregon 73 N k
Lost L., Louisiana 63 M j
Lost Nation, Iowa 61 O c
Lost River, West Virginia 52 H g
Lost River Ra., Idaho 66 G e
Lost Springs, Kansas 60 H f
Lost Springs, Wyoming 67 Q g
Lost Trail Pass, Montana 66 G d
Lostwood, North Dakota 58 D b
Lothair, Montana 66 J a
Lott, Texas 65 K d
Lotts Cr., Georgia 55 K e
Lotus, Idaho 66 D b
Lotus, Illinois 57 E j
Louann, Arkansas 63 L e
Loudon, New Hampshire 49 D e
Loudon, Tennessee 54 G b
Loudonville, Ohio 52 D e
Louin, Mississippi 63 O f
Louisa, Kentucky 57 L l
Louisa, Virginia 52 H g
Louisburg, Kansas 61 K f
Louisburg, North Carolina 55 N a
Louise, L., Alaska 77 O e
Louise, Texas 65 L f
Louisiana 63
Louisiana, Missouri 61 N e
Louisiana Pt., Texas-Louisiana 65 O f
Louisville, Alabama 54 F f
Louisville, Colorado 69 O g
Louisville, Georgia 55 J d
Louisville, Kentucky (390,639) 57 H l
Louisville, Mississippi 63 O e
Louisville, Nebraska 61 H d
Louisville, Ohio 52 E e
Loup City, Nebraska 60 F c
Loup R., Nebraska 60 F c
Louviers, Colorado 69 M d
Lovelady, Texas 65 M d
Loveland, Colorado 69 L c
Loveland, Ohio 52 B f
Loveland Pass, Colorado 69 L d
Lovell, Wyoming 67 M e
Lovells, Michigan 56 J e
Lovelock, Nevada 74 G d
Love Point, Maryland 53 K f
Lovett, Florida 54 H g
Lovilia, Iowa 61 M c
Loving, New Mexico 71 N g
Loving, Texas 65 J b
Lovingston, Virginia 52 H h
Lovington, Illinois 57 E k
Lovington, New Mexico 71 O g
Low, Utah 68 C c
Lowden, Iowa 61 N c
Low Des., Oregon 73 K m
Lowell, Arizona 70 H h
Lowell, Arkansas 63 J b
Lowell, Idaho 66 E c
Lowell, Indiana 57 F h
Lowell, Massachusetts (92,107) 49 D f
Lowell, Michigan 56 H g
Lowell, Ohio 52 E f
Lowell, Oregon 73 H m
Lower Alkali L., California 74 E c
Lower Brule, South Dakota 58 G f
Lower Falls, Wyoming 67 K e
Lower Klamath L., California 74 D c
Lower Lake, California 74 C f
Lower New York B., New York 51 L g
Lower Paia, Hawaii 72 D e
Lower Red L., Minnesota 59 L c
Lower Red Rock Ls., Montana 66 J e
Lowes, Kentucky 57 E n
Lowman, Idaho 66 E e
Lowndesboro, Alabama 54 E e
Lowry City, Missouri 61 L f
Lowrys, South Carolina 55 K c
Lowville, New York 53 L b
Loxley, Alabama 54 D g
Loyal, Wisconsin 56 C e
Loyal Heights, Washington 72 B h
Loyall, Kentucky 57 K n
Loyalsock Cr., Pennsylvania 53 K d
Loyalton, California 74 E e
Loyalton, South Dakota 58 G e
Loyons, Oregon 73 H l
Lualualei, Hawaii 72 C d
Lubbock, Texas (128,691) 64 F b
Lubec, Maine 49 H e
Lublin, Wisconsin 56 C d
Lucas, Iowa 61 L c
Lucas, Kansas 60 F e
Lucas, Ohio 52 D e
Lucca, North Dakota 58 J d
Lucedale, Mississippi 63 P h
Lucerne, California 74 C e
Lucerne, Missouri 61 L d
Lucerne, Washington 73 K g
Lucerne, Wyoming 67 M f
Lucerne L., California 75 J k
Lucerne Valley, California 75 J k
Lucher, Louisiana 63 N h
Lucia, California 75 D h
Lucile, Idaho 66 D d
Lucin, Utah 68 C b
Lucinda, Pennsylvania 52 G d
Luck, Wisconsin 56 A d
Lucky Peak Res., Idaho 66 E f
Lucy, New Mexico 71 M e
Ludden, North Dakota 58 H d
Ludell, Kansas 60 D e
Ludington, Michigan 56 G f
Ludlow, California 75 J k
Ludlow, Colorado 69 M f
Ludlow, Illinois 57 E j
Ludlow, Massachusetts 51 J a
Ludlow, Pennsylvania 52 H d
Ludlow, South Dakota 58 C e
Ludlow, Vermont 49 C e
Ludowici, Georgia 55 K f
Lueders, Texas 65 H c
Lufkin, Texas 65 N d
Luka, Mississippi 63 P d
Lula, Georgia 54 H c
Lula, Mississippi 63 N d
Luling, Louisiana 63 N j
Luling, Texas 65 K f
Lulu, Florida 55 J g
Lumber City, Georgia 55 J f
Lumber City, Pennsylvania 52 H e
Lumberport, West Virginia 52 F f
Lumber R., North Carolina 55 M c
Lumberton, Mississippi 63 O g
Lumberton, New Mexico 71 L c
Lumberton, North Carolina 55 M c
Lumpkin, Georgia 54 G e
Luna, New Mexico 71 J f
Lund, Nevada 74 K f
Lund, Utah 68 C e
Lunenburg, Vermont 49 D d
Luning, Nevada 74 G f
Lupus, Missouri 61 M f
Luray, Kansas 60 F e
Luray, Virginia 52 H g
Lure, L., North Carolina 55 J b
Lurton, Arkansas 63 K c
Lusk, Wyoming 67 Q g
Lustre, Montana 67 P a
Lutesville, Missouri 61 P g
Luther, Iowa 61 L c
Luther, Oklahoma 62 F c
Lutie, Texas 64 D h
Luttrell, Tennessee 54 H a
Lutz, Florida 55 M e
Luverne, Alabama 54 E f
Luverne, Iowa 61 K b
Luverne, Minnesota 59 K g
Luverne, North Dakota 58 J c
Luxapalila R., Alabama 54 D d
Luxemburg, Iowa 61 N b
Luzerne, Michigan 56 J e
Luzerne, New York 53 N b
Luzerne, Pennsylvania 50 B c
Lybrook, New Mexico 71 K c
Lycan, Colorado 69 O f
Lydia, South Carolina 55 L c
Lyell, Mt., California 74 F g
Lyerly, Georgia 54 F c
Lyford, Texas 65 K j
Lykens, Pennsylvania 53 K e
Lyle, Minnesota 59 O g
Lyle, Washington 73 J k
Lyles, Tennessee 54 D b
Lyman, Mississippi 63 O h
Lyman, Oklahoma 62 G b
Lyman, South Carolina 55 J c
Lyman, Nebraska 60 A c
Lyman, Wyoming 67 K h
Lyme, New Hampshire 49 C e
Lyn, Indiana 57 J j
Lynch, Kentucky 57 L n
Lynch, Maryland 50 A g
Lynch, Nebraska 60 F b
Lynchburg, Ohio 52 C f
Lynchburg, Tennessee 54 E b
Lynchburg, Virginia (54,790) 52 G h
Lynches R., South Carolina 55 M d
Lynchville, Maine 49 E d
Lyndell, Pennsylvania 50 B e
Lynden, Washington 73 H g
Lyndhurst, New Jersey 51 K e
Lyndon, Kansas 61 J f
Lyndon, Vermont 49 C d
Lyndonville, New York 52 H b
Lyndonville, Vermont 49 C d
Lynn, Alabama 54 D c
Lynn, Massachusetts (94,478) 49 H g
Lynn, Utah 68 C b
Lynn Can., Alaska 77 U g
Lynndyl, Utah 68 D d
Lynn Harb., Massachusetts 49 H h
Lynn Haven, Florida 54 F g
Lynnport, Pennsylvania 50 B d
Lynnville, Iowa 61 M c
Lynnville, Tennessee 54 D b
Lynwood, California (31,614) 75 E m
Lyon Manor, Michigan 56 J e
Lyon Mountain, New York 53 N a
Lyons, Colorado 69 L c
Lyons, Georgia 55 J e
Lyons, Indiana 57 F l
Lyons, Kansas 60 F f
Lyons, Michigan 56 J g
Lyons, Nebraska 60 H c
Lyons, New York 53 J b
Lyons, Ohio 52 B d
Lyons, Pennsylvania 50 B e
Lyons, South Dakota 59 K g
Lyons, Texas 65 L e
Lyons, Wisconsin 56 E g
Lyons Falls, New York 53 L b
Lysite, Wyoming 67 N f
Lytle, Texas 65 J f
Lytton, California 74 C f
Maalaea, Hawaii 72 D e
Maalaea B., Hawaii 72 D e
Mabank, Texas 65 L c
Mabel, Minnesota 59 P g
Maben, West Virginia 52 E h
Mabton, Washington 73 K j
McAdoo, Pennsylvania 50 A d
McAdoo, Texas 64 F b
McAlester, L., Oklahoma 62 H c
McAlester, Oklahoma 62 H d
McAlister, New Mexico 71 O e
McAllen, Texas (32,728) 65 J j
McAllister, Montana 66 J d
McAlpin, Florida 55 J g
McArthur, California 74 D c
McArthur, Ohio 52 D f
Macatawa, Michigan 56 G g
McBain, Michigan 56 H e
McBaine, Missouri 61 M f
McBean, Georgia 55 K d
McBee, South Carolina 55 L c
McCall, Idaho 66 D e
McCamey, Texas 64 E d
McCammon, Idaho 66 H g
McCanna, North Dakota 58 J b
McCarthy, Alaska 77 Q f
McCleary, Washington 73 G h
Macclenny, Florida 55 J g
McClellanville, South Carolina 55 M d
McCloud, California 74 C c
McCloud R., California 74 C c
McClure, L., California 74 E g
McClure, Ohio 52 C d
McClure, Pennsylvania 53 J e
McClure, Virginia 52 D h
McClusky, North Dakota 58 F c
McColl, South Carolina 55 M c
McComb, Mississippi 63 N g
McComb, Ohio 52 C d
Macomb, Oklahoma 62 F c
McConaughy, L., Nebraska 60 C c
McConnellsburg, Pennsylvania 52 H f
McCook, Nebraska 60 D d
McCool, Mississippi 63 O e
McCool Junction, Nebraska 60 G d
McCormick, South Carolina 55 J d
McCoy, Colorado 69 K d
McCracken, Kansas 60 E f
McCredie, Missouri 61 N f
McCrory, Arkansas 63 M c
McCullough, Alabama 54 D f
McCullough Ra., Nevada 75 K j
McCurtain, Oklahoma 63 J c
McDade, Texas 65 K e
McDavid, Florida 54 D g
McDermitt, Nevada 74 H c
McDermitt, Oregon 73 N n
McDermott, Ohio 52 C g
Macdoel, California 74 C c
McDonald, Kansas 60 C e
McDonald, L., Montana 66 G a
McDonald, Pennsylvania 52 F e
McDonald Pk., California 74 E d
McDonald Pk., Montana 66 G b
McDonough, Georgia 54 G d
McDowell Pk., Arizona 70 F f
Macedon, New York 52 J b
Macedonia, Iowa 61 J c
Macedonia Brook State Park, Connecticut 50 G b
McEwen, Oregon 73 M l
McEwen, Tennessee 54 D a
McFadden, Wyoming 67 O h
McFall, Missouri 61 K d
McFarland, Kansas 60 H e
McGaffey, New Mexico 71 J d
McGee Bend Res., Texas 65 N d
McGehee, Arkansas 63 M e
McGill, Nevada 74 L e
McGrath, Alaska 76 K e
McGrath, Minnesota 59 N d
McGraw, New York 53 K c
McGregor, Michigan 56 L f
McGregor, Minnesota 59 N d
McGregor, Texas 65 K d
McGrew, Nebraska 60 A c
McGuire, Mt., Idaho 66 F d
Machen, Georgia 54 H d
McHenry, Illinois 56 E g
McHenry, Mississippi 63 O h
McHenry, North Dakota 58 H c
Machias, Maine 49 H d
Machias B., Maine 49 H d
Machias R., Maine 49 G b
Machias Seal I., Maine 49 H d
McIntire, Iowa 61 M a
McIntosh, Minnesota 59 L c
McIntosh, South Dakota 58 E e
Mack, Colorado 68 H d
Mackay, Idaho 66 G f
Mackay Res., Idaho 66 G f
McKeesport, Pennsylvania (45,489) 53 Q c
McKees' Rocks, Pennsylvania 53 O a
McKenzie, Alabama 54 E f
McKenzie, North Dakota 58 F d
McKenzie, Tennessee 54 C a
McKenzie Bridge, Oregon 73 H l
McKenzie Pass, Oregon 73 H l
McKenzie R., Oregon 73 H l
Mackinac, Str. of, Michigan 56 J d
Mackinac Island, Michigan 56 J d
Mackinaw, Illinois 57 D j
Mackinaw City, Michigan 56 J d
Mackinaw R., Illinois 57 D j
McKinley, Mt., Alaska 76 M e
McKinley Park, Alaska 77 N e
McKinney, Kentucky 57 J m
McKinney, L., Kansas 60 C f
McKinney, Texas 65 L b
McKinnon, Tennessee 54 D a
McKittrick, California 75 F j
Macksburg, Ohio 52 E f
Macks Inn, Idaho 66 J e
Macksville, Kansas 60 F g
McLain, Mississippi 63 P g
MacLaren R., Alaska 77 O e
McLaughlin, South Dakota 58 F e
McLean, Illinois 57 D j
McLean, Texas 64 D h
McLean, Virginia 53 J g
McLeansboro, Illinois 57 E l
McLeod, North Dakota 58 J d
McLeod, Oregon 73 H n
McLoughlin, Mt., Oregon 73 H n
McLouth, Kansas 61 J e
McMechen, West Virginia 52 F e
McMichaels, Pennsylvania 50 C c
McMillan, L., New Mexico 71 N g
McMillan, Michigan 56 H c
McMinnville, Oregon 73 G k
McMinnville, Tennessee 54 F b
McMurray, Washington 73 H g
McNair, Mississippi 63 M g
McNary, Arizona 70 H e
McNary, Texas 64 B d
McNary Dam, Oregon 73 L k
McNeal, Arizona 70 H h
McNeil, Arkansas 63 K e
McNeil, Texas 65 K e
McNeill, Mississippi 63 O h
Macomb, Illinois 57 C j
Macon, Georgia (69,764) 54 H e
Macon, Illinois 57 E k
Macon, Mississippi 63 P e
Macon, Missouri 61 M e
Macon, Nebraska 60 F d
Macon Bayou, Louisiana 63 M f
McPherson, Kansas 60 G f
McRae, Georgia 55 J e
McRoberts, Kentucky 57 L m
Macungie, Pennsylvania 53 L e
McVeigh, Kentucky 57 L m
McVille, North Dakota 58 H c
Macwahoc, Maine 49 G c
McWilliams, Alabama 54 D f
Madalin, New York 50 F a
Maddock, North Dakota 58 G c
Madelia, Minnesota 59 M f
Madeline, California 74 E c
Madeline I., Wisconsin 56 C c
Madera, California 75 E h
Madera, Mt., Texas 64 E e
Madera, Pennsylvania 52 H e
Madill, Oklahoma 62 G d
Madison, Alabama 54 E c
Madison, Arkansas 63 N c
Madison, Connecticut 51 H c
Madison, Florida 54 H g
Madison, Georgia 54 H d
Madison, Illinois 61 Q d
Madison, Indiana 57 H l
Madison, Kansas 60 H f
Madison, Maine 49 F d
Madison, Minnesota 59 K e
Madison, Missouri 61 M e
Madison, Nebraska 60 G c
Madison, New Jersey 50 E d
Madison, North Carolina 55 M a
Madison, Ohio 52 E d
Madison, South Dakota 58 J f
Madison, Tennessee 54 E a
Madison, Virginia 52 H g
Madison, West Virginia 52 E g
Madison, Wisconsin (126,706) 56 D f
Madison Heights, Michigan (33,343), vicinity of Detroit
Madison Heights, Virginia 52 G h
Madison Junction, Wyoming 67 K e
Madison R., Montana 66 J d
Madison Ra., Montana 66 J d
Madisonville, Kentucky 57 F m
Madisonville, Louisiana 63 N h
Madisonville, Tennessee 54 G b
Madisonville, Texas 65 M e
Madoc, Montana 67 P a
Mad R., California 74 B d
Madras, Oregon 73 J l
Madre Mt., New Mexico 71 K e
Madrid, Iowa 61 L c
Madrid, Nebraska 60 C d
Madrid, New Mexico 71 L d
Madrid, New York 53 L a
Maeser, Utah 68 G c
Magazine Mt., Arkansas 63 K c
Magdalena, New Mexico 71 K e
Magee, Colorado 69 P h
Magee, Mississippi 63 O g
Mageik Vol., Alaska 76 K g
Magic Res., Idaho 66 F f
Magma, Arizona 70 F f
Magna, Utah 68 B h
Magnet, Nebraska 60 G b
Magnolia, Arkansas 63 K e
Magnolia, Delaware 50 B g
Magnolia, Minnesota 59 K g
Magnolia, Mississippi 63 N g
Magnolia, North Carolina 55 N c
Magnolia, Texas 65 M e
Magnolia Bluff, Washington 72 B h
Magnum, Oklahoma 62 D d
Magruder Mt., Nevada 75 H g
Mahaffy, Pennsylvania 52 H e
Mahanoy City, Pennsylvania 50 A d
Mahaska, Kansas 60 G e
Mahnomen, Minnesota 59 L c
Mahogany Pk., Nevada 74 F e
Mahomet, Illinois 57 E j
Mahopac, New York 50 F c
Mahopac Falls, New York 50 F c
Mahto, South Dakota 58 F e
Maiden, North Carolina 55 K b
Maiden Cr., Pennsylvania 50 B d
Maiden Rock, Wisconsin 56 A e
Maine 49
Maine, Arizona 70 F d
Maine, New York 53 K c
Maineville, Ohio 52 B f
Main Pt., Louisiana 63 O j
Maitland, Missouri 61 J d
Makapala, Hawaii 72 E e
Makapuu Pt., Hawaii 72 C d
Makawao, Hawaii 72 D e
Makoti, North Dakota 58 E c
Makushin B., Alaska 76 D k
Makushin Vol., Alaska 76 D k
Malabar, Florida 55 O e
Malad City, Idaho 66 H g
Malaga, New Jersey 50 C f
Malaga, New Mexico 71 N g
Malaga, Washington 73 K h
Malakoff, Texas 65 L c
Malaspina Glacier, Alaska 77 R g
Malcom, Iowa 61 M c
Malden, Massachusetts (57,676) 49 G h
Malden, Missouri 61 P h
Malden, Washington 73 N h
Malden, West Virginia 52 E g
Malheur, Oregon 73 N l
Malheur L., Oregon 73 M m
Malheur R., Oregon 73 N m
Malin, Oregon 73 J n
Maljamar, New Mexico 71 O g
Mallard, Iowa 61 K b
Mallory, West Virginia 52 E h
Malone, Florida 54 F g
Malone, New York 53 M a
Malone, Texas 65 L d
Maloney Res., Nebraska 60 D c
Malott, Washington 73 L g
Malpais, New Mexico 71 K h
Malta, Colorado 69 K d
Malta, Idaho 66 G g
Malta, Montana 67 N a
Malta, Ohio 52 E f
Maltby, Washington 72 C g
Malvern, Arkansas 63 L d
Malvern, Iowa 61 J c
Malvern, Ohio 52 E e
Malvern, Pennsylvania 50 B e
Mamakating, New York 50 E b
Mamaroneck, New York 50 F d
Mammoth, Arizona 70 G g
Mammoth, West Virginia 52 E g
Mammoth Cave, Kentucky 57 G m
Mammoth Cave Nat. Park, Kentucky 57 G m
Mammoth Hot Springs, Wyoming 67 K e
Mammoth Spring, Arkansas 63 M b
Mamou, Louisiana 63 L h
Mamtou, New York 50 F c
Man, West Virginia 52 E h
Mana, Hawaii 72 B c
Manahawkin, New Jersey 50 E f
Manakin, Virginia 52 J h
Manasquan, New Jersey 50 E e
Manasquan R., New Jersey 50 E e
Manassa, Colorado 69 L f
Manassas, Virginia 53 J g
Manatawny, Pennsylvania 50 B e
Manawa, Wisconsin 56 D e
Manayunk, Pennsylvania 50 F f
Mancelona, Michigan 56 H e
Manchaug, Massachusetts 51 K a
Manchaug Pond, Massachusetts 51 K a
Manchester, California 75 D m
Manchester, Connecticut (42,102) 51 H b
Manchester, Georgia 54 G e
Manchester, Illinois 57 C k
Manchester, Iowa 61 N b
Manchester, Kansas 60 G e
Manchester, Kentucky 57 K m
Manchester, Michigan 57 K g
Manchester, New Hampshire (88,282) 49 D f
Manchester, New York 53 J c
Manchester, Ohio 52 C g
Manchester, Oklahoma 62 E b
Manchester, Pennsylvania 53 K e
Manchester, Tennessee 54 E b
Manchester, Vermont 49 B e
Manchester, Washington 72 B h
Manchester Bridge, New York 50 F b
Mancos R., Colorado 68 H f
Mandan, North Dakota 58 E d
Manderfield, Utah 68 D e
Manderson, Wyoming 67 N e
Mandeville, Louisiana 63 N h
Manfred, North Dakota 58 G c
Mangas, New Mexico 71 J e
Mangham, Louisiana 63 M f
Mangum, Oklahoma 62 D d
Manhan R., Massachusetts 51 H a
Manhattan, Illinois 57 F h
Manhattan, Kansas 60 H e
Manhattan, Montana 66 J d
Manhattan, Nevada 74 H f
Manhattan, New York 50 F d
Manhattan Beach, California (33,934) 75 D m
Manhattan I., New York 51 M e
Manila, Arkansas 63 N c
Manila, Utah 68 G c
Manilla, Iowa 61 J c
Manistee, Michigan 56 G e
Manistee R., Michigan 56 H e
Manistique, Michigan 56 G d
Manistique L., Michigan 56 H c
Manistique R., Michigan 56 G c
Manito, Illinois 57 D j
Manitou, Oklahoma 62 E d
Manitou I., Michigan 56 F b
Manitou Springs, Colorado 69 L e
Manitowoc, Wisconsin (32,275) 56 F e

Mankato, Kansas 60 F e
Mankato, Minnesota 59 N f
Mankins, Texas 65 J b
Manley Hot Springs, Alaska 76 M d
Manlius, New York 53 L b
Manly, Iowa 61 L a
Manning, Arkansas 63 L d
Manning, Iowa 61 J c
Manning, North Dakota 58 D c
Manning, South Carolina 55 L d
Manning, Texas 65 N d
Mannington, West Virginia 52 F f
Manns Harbor, North Carolina 55 Q b
Mannsville, New York 53 K b
Manokotak, Alaska 76 H g
Manor, Georgia 55 J f
Manor, Texas 65 K e
Manorville, New York 51 H d
Mansfield, Arkansas 63 J c
Mansfield, Connecticut 51 J b
Mansfield, Georgia 54 H d
Mansfield, Illinois 57 E j
Mansfield, Louisiana 63 K f
Mansfield, Massachusetts 51 L a
Mansfield, Missouri 61 M g
Mansfield, Mt., Vermont 49 C d
Mansfield, Ohio (47,325) 52 D e
Mansfield, Pennsylvania 53 K d
Mansfield, South Dakota 58 H e
Mansfield, Texas 65 K c
Mansfield, Washington 73 L h
Manson, Iowa 61 K b
Manson, Washington 73 K h
Mansura, Louisiana 63 L g
Manteca, California 74 D g
Mantee, Mississippi 63 O e
Manteno, Illinois 57 F h
Manteo, North Carolina 55 P d
Manter, Kansas 60 C g
Manti, Utah 68 E d
Mantoloking, New Jersey 50 E e
Manton, California 74 D d
Manton, Michigan 56 H e
Mantua, New Jersey 50 C f
Mantua, Ohio 52 E d
Manuelito, New Mexico 71 J d
Manvel, North Dakota 58 J b
Manville, New Jersey 50 D d
Manville, Rhode Island 51 L b
Manville, Wyoming 67 Q g
Many, Louisiana 63 K g
Manzano, New Mexico 71 L e
Manzanola, Colorado 69 N e
Manzano Mts., New Mexico 71 L e
Maple Heights, Ohio (31,667), vicinity of Cleveland
Maple Island, Minnesota 59 N g
Mapleleaf, Washington 72 B h
Maple Park, Missouri 61 Q a
Maple R., Iowa 61 J b
Maple R., Michigan 56 J f
Maple Shade, New Jersey 50 D f
Maplesville, Alabama 54 E e
Mapleton, Iowa 61 J b
Mapleton, Maine 49 G b
Mapleton, Minnesota 59 N g
Mapleton, Oregon 73 G l
Maple Valley, Washington 73 H h
Maple View, New York 53 K b
Maplewood, Minnesota 59 R h
Maplewood, New Jersey 51 J f
Maplewood, Washington 72 C j
Maquoketa, Iowa 61 O b
Maquoketa R., Iowa 61 O b
Maquon, Illinois 57 D j
Marais des Cygnes R., Kansas 61 K f
Marana, Arizona 70 F g
Marathon, Iowa 61 K b
Marathon, New York 53 K c
Marathon, Texas 64 D e
Marathon, Wisconsin 56 C e
Maravillas Cr., Texas 64 D f
Marble, Colorado 69 J d
Marble, Washington 73 N g
Marble Canyon, Arizona 70 F c
Marble City, Oklahoma 63 J c
Marble Falls, Texas 65 J e
Marblehead, Illinois 57 B k
Marblehead, Massachusetts 49 E f
Marblehead, Ohio 52 D d
Marble Rock, Iowa 61 M b
Marbleton, Wyoming 67 K g
Marbury, Maryland 53 J g
Marceline, Missouri 61 M e
Marcella, Arkansas 63 M c
Marcellus, Michigan 57 H g
Marcellus, Washington 73 M h
Marco, Florida 55 N h
Marcola, Oregon 73 H l
Marco, Indiana 57 F l
Marcus, Iowa 61 J b
Marcus, Washington 73 M g
Marcus Baker, Mt., Alaska 77 O f
Marcus Hook, Pennsylvania 50 C f
Marcy, Mt., New York 53 M a
Marcy, New York 53 L b
Marengo, Indiana 57 G l
Marengo, Illinois 57 E g
Marengo, Iowa 61 M c
Marengo, Ohio 52 D e
Marengo, Washington 73 M h
Marengo, Wisconsin 56 C c
Marenisco, Michigan 56 D c
Margaret, Texas 65 H a
Margaretville, New York 50 D a
Margate City, New Jersey 50 E g
Margie, Minnesota 59 N b
Margrethe, L., Michigan 56 J e
Maria, Texas 64 C e
Maria Mts., California 75 L h
Marian, L., South Carolina 55 L d
Marianna, Arkansas 63 N d
Marianna, Florida 54 F g
Marias Pass, Montana 66 G a
Marias R., Montana 66 H a
Maribel, Wisconsin 56 F e
Maricopa, Arizona 70 E f
Maricopa, California 75 F j
Maricopa Mts., Arizona 70 E f
Marienthal, Kansas 60 C f
Marienville, Pennsylvania 52 G d
Marietta, Georgia (25,565) 54 G d
Marietta, Ohio 52 E f
Marietta, Oklahoma 62 F e
Marietta, Pennsylvania 53 K e
Marietta, South Carolina 55 J b
Marine, Illinois 57 D l
Marine City, Michigan 56 L g
Marineland, Florida 55 K h
Marinette, Wisconsin 56 F d
Maringouin, Louisiana 63 M h
Marin Is., California 75 B k
Marin Pen., California 75 B l
Marion, Alabama 54 D e
Marion, Arkansas 63 N c
Marion, Illinois 57 E m
Marion, Indiana (37,854) 57 H j
Marion, Iowa 61 N b
Marion, Kansas 60 G f
Marion, Kentucky 57 E m
Marion, Louisiana 63 L f
Marion, Maine 49 H e
Marion, Massachusetts 51 M b
Marion, Michigan 56 H e
Marion, Mississippi 63 P f
Marion, Montana 66 F a
Marion, Nebraska 60 D d
Marion, North Carolina 55 J b
Marion, North Dakota 58 H d
Marion, Ohio (37,079) 52 C e
Marion, South Carolina 55 M c
Marion, South Dakota 58 J g
Marion, Texas 65 J f
Marion, Virginia 52 E j
Marion, Wisconsin 56 E e
Marion Junction, Alabama 54 D e
Marion Res., Kansas 60 G f
Marionville, Missouri 61 L g
Mariposa, California 75 F g
Mariposa R., California 75 E g
Mariposa Res., California 75 F g
Marissa, Illinois 57 D l
Marked Tree, Arkansas 63 N c
Markesan, Wisconsin 56 E f
Markham, Texas 65 L g
Markham, Virginia 52 J g
Markham, Washington 73 G J
Markleville, California 74 F f
Marks, Mississippi 63 N d
Marksboro, New Jersey 50 D d
Marksville, Louisiana 63 L g
Markville, Minnesota 59 O d
Marland, Oklahoma 62 F b
Marlboro, Massachusetts 49 D f
Marlboro, New Jersey 50 E e
Marlboro, New Hampshire 49 C f
Marlboro, New York 50 F b
Marlborough, Connecticut 51 J b
Marlborough, Missouri 61 P b
Marlette, Michigan 56 K f
Marlin, Texas 65 L d
Marlington, West Virginia 52 F g
Marlow, New Hampshire 49 C e
Marlow, Oklahoma 62 F d
Marlton, New Jersey 50 D f
Marmaduke, Arkansas 63 N b
Marmarth, North Dakota 58 C d
Marmet, West Virginia 52 E g
Marmot B., Alaska 76 L g
Marmot I., Alaska 76 L g
Marne, Michigan 56 H f
Maroa, Illinois 57 E j
Maro Reef, Hawaii 72 B a
Marquand, Missouri 61 O g
Marquesas Keys, Florida 55 M j
Marquette, Iowa 61 N a
Marquette, Kansas 60 G f
Marquette, Michigan 56 F c
Marquette, Nebraska 60 F c
Marquez, New Mexico 71 K d
Marquez, Texas 65 L d
Marrero, Louisiana 62 B f
Mars, Pennsylvania 52 G e
Marseilles, Illinois 57 E h
Marseilles, Ohio 52 C e
Marsh, Montana 67 Q c
Marshall, Alaska 76 F f
Marshall, Arkansas 63 L c
Marshall, Colorado 69 N g
Marshall, Illinois 57 F k
Marshall, Michigan 57 J g
Marshall, Minnesota 59 L f
Marshall, Missouri 61 L e
Marshall, North Carolina 55 J b
Marshall, North Dakota 58 D c
Marshall, Oklahoma 62 F b
Marshall, Texas 65 N c
Marshall, Virginia 52 J g
Marshall, Wyoming 67 P g
Marshalls Cr., Pennsylvania 50 C c
Marshallton, Delaware 50 B f
Marshallton, Pennsylvania 50 B f
Marshalltown, Iowa 61 L b
Marshfield, Massachusetts 51 M a
Marshfield, Missouri 61 M g
Marshfield, Wisconsin 56 C e
Marshfield Hills, Massachusetts 51 M a
Mars Hill, Maine 49 G b
Marsh Hill, Pennsylvania 53 K d
Marsh I., Louisiana 63 L j
Marsh Pk., Utah 68 G c
Marshville, North Carolina 55 L c
Marsing, Idaho 66 D f
Marsland, Nebraska 60 A b
Marston, Wyoming 67 L h
Marston Res., Colorado 69 O j
Mart, Texas 65 L d
Martensdale, Iowa 61 L c
Marthasville, Missouri 61 N f
Martha's Vineyard, Massachusetts 51 M c
Martin, Alaska 77 N d
Martin, Kentucky 57 L m
Martin, Michigan 56 H g
Martin, South Dakota 58 E g
Martin, Tennessee 54 C a
Martindale, Texas 65 K f
Martindale Depot, New York 50 F a
Martinez, California 74 C f
Martin L., Alabama 54 F e
Martin Pt., Alaska 77 Q a
Martinsburg, Missouri 61 N e
Martinsburg, Ohio 52 D e
Martinsburg, Pennsylvania 52 H e
Martinsburg, New York 53 L b
Martinsburg, West Virginia 52 H f
Martins Creek, Pennsylvania 50 C d
Martins Creek Junction, Pennsylvania 50 C d
Martinsdale, Montana 67 K c
Martins Ferry, Ohio 52 F e
Martinsville, Illinois 57 F k
Martinsville, Indiana 57 G k
Martinsville, Virginia 52 G j
Marvell, Arkansas 63 N d
Marvin, South Dakota 59 K e
Marvine, Colorado 69 J c
Marvine, Mt., Utah 68 E e
Mary, L., Mississippi 63 M g
Marydel, Maryland 50 B g
Maryland 52-53
Maryneal, Texas 64 G c
Marys R., Nevada 74 K c
Marysvale, Utah 68 D e
Marysville, California 74 D e
Marysville, Idaho 66 J e
Marysville, Kansas 60 H e
Marysville, Michigan 56 L g
Marysville, Ohio 52 C e
Marysville, Washington 73 H g
Maryville, Missouri 61 K d
Maryville, Tennessee 54 H b
Masardis, Maine 49 G b
Masaryktown, Florida 55 J j
Mascot, Nebraska 60 E d
Mascot, Tennessee 54 H a
Mascouta, Illinois 57 D l
Mashpee, Massachusetts 51 N b
Mason, Illinois 57 E l
Mason, Ohio 52 B f
Mason, Michigan 56 J g
Mason, Nebraska 60 E c
Mason, Nevada 74 F f
Mason, South Dakota 58 C e
Mason, Tennessee 54 B b
Mason, Texas 65 H e
Mason, West Virginia 52 E g
Mason, Wisconsin 56 B c
Mason, Wyoming 67 K g
Mason City, Illinois 57 D j
Mason City, Iowa (30,642) 61 L a
Masontown, Pennsylvania 52 G f
Masontown, West Virginia 52 G f
Massachusetts 49
Massachusetts B., Massachusetts 51 M a
Massacre L., Nevada 74 F c
Massadona, Colorado 68 H c
Massanutten Mt., Virginia 52 H g
Massapequa, New York (32,900), vicinity of New York City
Massaponax, Virginia 52 J g
Massena, Iowa 61 K c
Massena, New York 53 M a
Massey, Maryland 50 B g
Massies Mill, Virginia 52 G h
Massillon, Ohio (31,236) 52 E e
Mastic Beach, New York 51 H d
Matador, Texas 64 G a
Matagorda, Texas 65 M g
Matagorda B., Texas 65 L g
Matagorda I., Texas 65 L g
Matagorda Pen., Texas 65 M g
Matamoras, Pennsylvania 50 D c
Matanuska, Alaska 77 N f
Matanuska R., Alaska 77 N f
Matanzas Inlet, Florida 55 K h
Matawan, New Jersey 50 E e
Matchwood, Michigan 56 D c
Matewan, West Virginia 52 D h
Matfield Green, Kansas 60 H f
Mather, California 74 F g
Mather, Pennsylvania 52 F f
Matherville, Illinois 57 C h
Matheson, Colorado 69 N d
Mathews, Alabama 54 E e
Mathews, Virginia 53 K h
Mathis, Texas 65 K g
Mathiston, Mississippi 63 O e
Matinicus I., Maine 49 G e
Matlock, Washington 73 G h
Matoaka, West Virginia 52 E h
Mattamuskeet L., North Carolina 55 P b
Mattapoisett, Massachusetts 51 M b
Mattaponi R., Virginia 53 K h
Mattawamkeag, Maine 49 G c
Matterhorn, Nevada 74 K c
Matterhorn, Oregon 73 N k
Matthie, Arizona 70 E e
Mattituck, New York 51 H d
Mattole R., California 74 A d
Mattoon, Illinois 57 E k
Mattoon, Kentucky 57 E m
Mattoon, Wisconsin 56 D d
Matunuck, Rhode Island 51 K c
Maud, Oklahoma 62 G c
Maud, Texas 65 N b
Maudlow, Montana 66 J c
Mauganville, Maryland 52 J f
Maui, I., Hawaii 72 D e
Maukport, Indiana 57 G l
Maumee, Ohio 52 C d
Maumee B., Michigan 57 K h
Maumee B., Ohio 52 C d
Maumee R., Ohio 52 C d
Maumelle, L., Arkansas 63 L d
Mauna Kea, mt., Hawaii 72 E f
Maunaloa, Hawaii 72 D d
Mauna Loa, mt., Hawaii 72 E f
Mauneluk R., Alaska 76 J c
Maupin, Oregon 73 J k
Maurepas, L., Louisiana 63 N h
Maurice R., New Jersey 50 C g
Mauricetown, New Jersey 50 C g
Mauriceville, Texas 65 O e
Maurine, South Dakota 58 D e
Mauston, Wisconsin 56 C f
Mawah, New Jersey 50 E c
Max, Nebraska 60 C d
Max, North Dakota 58 E c
Maxbass, North Dakota 58 E b
Maxeys, Georgia 54 H d
Max Meadows, Virginia 52 F j
Maxton, North Carolina 55 M c
Maxville, Florida 55 J g
Maxville, Montana 66 G c
Maxwell, California 74 C e
Maxwell, Iowa 61 L c
Maxwell, Nebraska 60 D c
Maxwell, New Mexico 71 N c
May, C., New Jersey 50 D g
May, Idaho 66 G e
May, Oklahoma 62 D b
May, Texas 65 J d
Maybee, Michigan 57 K g
Maybell, Colorado 68 H c
Maybrook, New York 50 E c
Maydelle, Texas 65 M d
Mayer, Arizona 70 E e
Mayesville, South Carolina 55 L d
Mayetta, Kansas 61 J e
Mayfield, Idaho 66 E f
Mayfield, Oklahoma 62 D c
Mayfield, Pennsylvania 53 L d
Mayfield, Utah 68 E d
Mayfield Cr., Kentucky 57 E n
Mayflower, Arkansas 63 L d
Mayhew, Mississippi 63 P e
Mayhill, New Mexico 71 M g
Mayland, Tennessee 54 F a
Maynard, Iowa 61 N b
Maynard, Washington 73 H h
Mayo, Florida 54 H g
Mayo, Maryland 53 K g
Mayodan, North Carolina 55 M a
Mayport, Florida 55 K g
Mays Landing, New Jersey 50 D g
Maysville, Georgia 54 H c
Maysville, Kentucky 57 K l
Maysville, Missouri 61 K e
Maysville, North Carolina 55 O c
Maysville, Oklahoma 62 F d
Mayville, Michigan 56 K f
Mayville, New York 52 G c
Mayville, North Dakota 58 J c
Mayville, Oregon 73 K k
Mayville, Wisconsin 56 E f
Maywood, California 75 E m
Maywood, Illinois (27,330), vicinity of Chicago
Maywood, Nebraska 60 D d
Maza, North Dakota 58 G b
Mazama, Washington 73 K g
Mazatzal Pk., Arizona 70 F e
Mazomanie, Wisconsin 56 D f
Mazon, Illinois 57 E h
Meacham, Oregon 73 M k
Mead, L., Nevada 75 L h
Mead, Washington 73 N h
Meade, Kansas 60 D g
Meade Pk., Idaho 66 J g
Meade R., Alaska 76 J a
Meade River, Alaska 76 J a
Meadow, South Dakota 58 D e
Meadow, Texas 64 E b
Meadow, Utah 68 D e
Meadow Bridge, West Virginia 52 F h
Meadowbrook, Texas 65 M j
Meadow Creek, West Virginia 52 F h
Meadowdale, Washington 72 B g
Meadowdale, Wyoming 67 Q g
Meadowlands, Minnesota 59 O c
Meadows, Idaho 66 D e
Meadow Valley Ra., Nevada 75 L g
Meadow Valley Wash, Nevada 75 L h
Meadville, Mississippi 63 N g
Meadville, Missouri 61 L e
Meadville, Nebraska 60 E b
Meadville, Pennsylvania 52 F d
Meares, C., Oregon 73 G k
Mears, Michigan 56 G f
Mebane, North Carolina 55 M a
Mecaha, Montana 67 N b
Mecca, California 75 J l
Mechanic Falls, Maine 49 E d
Mechanicsburg, Ohio 52 C e
Mechanicsburg, Pennsylvania 53 J e
Mechanics Grove, Pennsylvania 50 A f
Mechanicsville, Maryland 53 K g
Mechanicville, New York 53 N c
Mechant Caillou L., Louisiana 63 N j
Meckesville, Pennsylvania 50 B d
Mecosta, Michigan 56 H f
Medaryville, Indiana 57 G h
Meddybemps L., Maine 49 H c
Medfield, Massachusetts 51 L a
Medford, Massachusetts (64,971) 49 G h
Medford, New Jersey 50 D f
Medford, Oklahoma 62 F b
Medford, Oregon 73 H n
Medford, Wisconsin 56 C d
Medford Station, New York 51 H d
Medfra, Alaska 76 K e
Media, Pennsylvania 50 C f
Mediapolis, Iowa 61 N c
Medical Lake, Washington 73 N h
Medicine Bow, Wyoming 67 O h
Medicine Bow Mts., Wyoming-Colorado 67 O h
Medicine Bow Pk., Wyoming 67 O h
Medicine Bow R., Wyoming 67 O h
Medicine L., California 74 D c
Medicine L., Minnesota 59 P h
Medicine L., Montana 67 Q a
Medicine Lake, Montana 67 Q a
Medicine Lodge, Kansas 60 F g
Medicine Lodge R., Kansas 60 F g
Medicine Mound, Texas 65 H a
Medicine Rocks, Montana 67 Q c
Medina, Ohio 52 E d
Medina, New York 52 H b
Medina, North Dakota 58 G d
Medina, Tennessee 54 C b
Medina, Texas 65 H f
Medina, Washington 72 C h
Medina L., Texas 65 J f
Medina R., Texas 65 H f
Medon, Tennessee 54 C b
Medora, Illinois 57 C k
Medora, Kansas 60 G f
Medora, North Dakota 58 C d
Medway, Maine 49 G c
Medway, Massachusetts 51 L a
Meeker, Colorado 69 J c
Meeker, Oklahoma 62 G c
Meeteetse, Wyoming 67 M e
Megargel, Texas 65 J b
Meggett, South Carolina 55 L e
Megler, Washington 73 G j
Meherrin, Virginia 52 H h
Meherrin R., Virginia 52 H j
Meigs, Georgia 54 G f
Mekinock, North Dakota 58 J b
Mekoryuk, Alaska 76 D f
Melba, Idaho 66 D f
Melbourne, Florida 54 O e
Melbourne, Iowa 61 L c
Melbourne Beach, Florida 55 O e
Melcher, Iowa 61 L c
Meldrim, Georgia 55 K e
Melfa, Virginia 53 L h
Mellen, Wisconsin 56 C c
Mellenville, New York 50 F a
Mellette, South Dakota 58 H e
Mellwood, Arkansas 63 N d
Melones Res., California 74 E g
Melozitna, Alaska 76 K d
Melrose, Idaho 66 D c
Melrose, Massachusetts (29,619) 49 G g
Melrose, Minnesota 59 M e
Melrose, Montana 66 H d
Melrose, New Mexico 71 O e
Melrose, Oregon 73 G m
Melrose, Wisconsin 56 B e
Melstone, Montana 67 N c
Melstrand, Michigan 56 G c
Melvern, Kansas 61 J f
Melville, Louisiana 63 M h
Melville, Montana 67 L c
Melville, New York 50 G d
Melvin, Texas 65 H d
Melvindale, Michigan 57 K k
Melvine, Tennessee 54 F b
Memphis, Missouri 61 M d
Memphis, Tennessee (497,524) 54 A b
Memphis, Texas 64 D j
Mena, Arkansas 63 J d
Menahga, Minnesota 59 L d
Menard, Montana 66 J d
Menard, Texas 65 H e
Menasha, Wisconsin 56 E e
Mendenhall, C., Alaska 76 D g
Mendenhall, Mississippi 63 O g
Mendham, New Jersey 50 D d
Mendocino, California 74 B e
Mendocino, C., California 74 A d
Mendon, Massachusetts 51 K a
Mendon, Michigan 57 H g
Mendon, Ohio 52 B e
Mendota, California 75 E h
Mendota, Illinois 57 D h
Mendota, L., Wisconsin 56 D f
Mendota, Minnesota 59 R j
Mendota, Texas 64 D h
Mendota Heights, Minnesota 59 R j
Menlo, Georgia 54 F c
Menlo, Iowa 61 K c
Menlo, Kansas 60 D e
Menlo Park, California (26,957) 75 C n
Menno, South Dakota 58 J g
Meno, Oklahoma 62 E b
Menominee, Michigan 56 F d
Menominee R., Michigan 56 F d
Menomonee Falls, Wisconsin 56 E f
Menomonie, Wisconsin 56 B e
Mentanontli L., Alaska 76 L c
Mentasta Mts., Alaska 77 Q e
Mentasta Village, Alaska 77 P e
Mentone, Indiana 57 G h
Mentone, Texas 64 D d
Mentor, Minnesota 59 K c
Mentor, Ohio 52 E d
Meramec Park, Missouri 61 O f
Merced, California 75 E g
Merced, L. de la, California 75 B m
Mercedes, Texas 65 K j
Merced R., California 75 E g
Mercer, Missouri 61 L d
Mercer, North Dakota 58 F c
Mercer, Pennsylvania 52 F d
Mercer, Tennessee 54 B b
Mercer, Washington 72 C h
Mercer, Wisconsin 56 C c
Mercer I., Washington 72 C h
Mercersburg, Pennsylvania 52 H f
Mercur, Utah 68 D c
Mercury, Texas 65 H d
Meredith, New Hampshire 49 D e
Meredosia, Illinois 57 C k
Meriden, Connecticut (51,850) 51 H b
Meriden, Kansas 61 J e
Meriden, New Hampshire 49 C e
Meriden, Wyoming 67 Q h
Meridian, California 74 D e
Meridian, Idaho 66 D f
Meridian, Mississippi (49,374) 63 P f
Meridian, New York 53 K b
Meridian, Texas 65 K d
Merino, Colorado 69 N c
Meriwether Lewis Nat. Mon., Tennessee 54 D b
Merkel, Texas 64 G c
Merlin, Oregon 73 G n
Mermentau, Louisiana 63 L h
Mermentau R., Louisiana 63 L j
Merna, Nebraska 60 E c
Merna, Wyoming 67 K g
Merriam, Kansas 61 P b
Merricourt, North Dakota 58 H d
Merrill, Iowa 60 H b
Merrill, Michigan 56 J f
Merrill, Mississippi 63 P h
Merrill, Oregon 73 J n
Merrill, Wisconsin 56 D d
Merrillan, Wisconsin 56 C e
Merrimac, Wisconsin 56 D f
Merrimack R., New Hampshire 49 D e
Merriman, Nebraska 60 C b
Merriman Dam, New York 50 E b
Merritt, L., California 75 C l
Merritt I., Florida 55 L j
Merritt Res., Nebraska 60 D b
Mer Rouge, Louisiana 63 M f
Merryville, Louisiana 63 K h
Mertzon, Texas 64 G d
Merwin, L., Washington 73 H k
Mesa, Arizona (33,772) 70 F f
Mesa, Idaho 66 D e
Mesa, New Mexico 71 N f
Mesabi Ra., Minnesota 59 N c
Mesa Mts., Alaska 76 K f
Mesa Verde Nat. Park, Colorado 68 H f
Mescal, Arizona 70 G h
Mescalero, New Mexico 71 M f
Mesick, Michigan 56 H e
Mesilla, New Mexico 71 L g
Mesquite, Nevada 75 L h
Mesquite, New Mexico 71 L g
Mesquite, Texas (27,526) 65 O j
Mesquite L., California 75 K j
Messick (Poquoson), Virginia 53 K h
Meta, Missouri 61 M f
Metairie, Louisiana 62 B e
Metaline Falls, Washington 73 N g
Metamora, Illinois 57 D j
Methow R., Washington 73 K g
Methuen, Massachusetts (28,114) 49 D f
Metlakatla, Alaska 77 W j
Meto, Bayou, Arkansas 63 M d
Metolius, Oregon 73 J l
Metolius R., Oregon 73 J l
Metropolis, Illinois 57 E m
Metter, Georgia 55 J e
Metuchen, New Jersey 50 E d
Meville, North Dakota 58 G c
Mexia, Texas 65 L d
Mexico, Indiana 57 G j
Mexico, Maine 49 E d
Mexico, Missouri 61 N e
Mexico, New York 53 K b
Mexican Hat, Utah 68 G f

177

Odan UNITED STATES INDEX Park

Odanah, *Wisconsin* 56 C c
Odebolt, *Iowa* 61 J b
Odell, *Illinois* 57 E h
Odell, *Nebraska* 60 H d
Odell, *Texas* 64 E j
Odem, *Texas* 65 K h
Oden, *Arkansas* 63 K d
Odessa, *Delaware* 50 B g
Odessa, *Missouri* 61 L f
Odessa, *New York* 53 K c
Odessa, *Texas (80,338)* 64 E d
Odessa, *Washington* 73 M h
Odin, *Illinois* 57 D l
Odon, *Indiana* 57 G l
O'Donnell, *Texas* 64 F c
Odum, *Georgia* 55 J f
Oelrichs, *South Dakota* 58 C g
Oelwein, *Iowa* 61 N b
Ofahoma, *Mississippi* 63 O f
Offerman, *Georgia* 55 J f
Ogallah, *Kansas* 60 E f
Ogallala, *Nebraska* 60 C c
Ogden, *Illinois* 57 E j
Ogden, *Iowa* 61 K b
Ogden, *Kansas* 60 H e
Ogden, *Utah (70,197)* 68 E b
Ogdensberg, *New Jersey* 50 D c
Ogdensburg, *New York* 53 L a
Ogeechee R., *Georgia* 55 K e
Ogema, *Minnesota* 59 L c
Ogilby, *California* 75 L m
Ogilvie, *Minnesota* 59 N e
Oglala, *South Dakota* 58 D g
Oglala Pass, *Alaska* 76 M j
Oglesby, *Illinois* 57 E h
Oglesby, *Texas* 65 K d
Oglethorpe, *Georgia* 54 G e
Ogliuga Is., *Alaska* 77 N j
Ogunquit, *Maine* 49 E e
Ohio 52
Ohio, *Illinois* 57 D h
Ohio City, *Ohio* 52 B e
Ohio R., *Illinois, etc.* 47 J c
Ohogamiut, *Alaska* 76 G f
Ohoopee R., *Georgia* 55 J e
Oil Center, *New Mexico* 71 O g
Oil City, *California* 75 G j
Oil City, *Louisiana* 63 K f
Oil City, *Pennsylvania* 52 G d
Oildale, *California* 75 F j
Oil Pt., *Alaska* 76 L g
Oilton, *Oklahoma* 62 G b
Oilton, *Texas* 65 J h
Oilville, *Virginia* 52 J h
Ojai, *California* 75 F k
Ojo Caliente, *New Mexico* 71 J e
Ojus, *Florida* 54 B c
Okaloacoochee Slough, *Florida* 55 N g
Okanogan, *Washington* 73 L g
Okanogan R., *Washington* 73 L g
Okarche, *Oklahoma* 62 F c
Okatoma R., *Mississippi* 63 O g
Okawville, *Illinois* 57 D l
Okay, *Oklahoma* 62 H c
Okeechobee, *Florida* 55 O f
Okeechobee, L., *Florida* 55 O g
Okeene, *Oklahoma* 62 E b
Okefenokee Swamp, *Georgia* 55 J g
Okemah, *Oklahoma* 62 G c
Oketo, *Kansas* 60 H e
Oklahoma 62-63
Oklahoma City, *Oklahoma (324,253)* 62 F c
Oklaunion, *Texas* 65 H a
Oklawaha R., *Florida* 55 K h
Oklee, *Minnesota* 59 L c
Okmok Vol., *Alaska* 76 C k
Okmulgee, *Oklahoma* 62 G c
Okobojo, *South Dakota* 58 F f
Okolona, *Mississippi* 63 P d
Okonogan Ra., *Washington* 73 L g
Okreek, *South Dakota* 58 F g
Oktaha, *Oklahoma* 62 H c
Ola, *Arkansas* 63 K c
Ola, *Idaho* 66 D e
Olamon, *Maine* 49 G c
Olancha, *California* 75 H h
Olancha Pk., *California* 75 G h
Olanta, *South Carolina* 55 M d
Olathe, *Kansas* 61 K f
Olberg, *Arizona* 70 F f
Olcott, *New York* 52 H b
Old Bridge, *New Jersey* 50 E e
Olden, *Texas* 65 J c
Old Faithful, *Wyoming* 67 K e
Old Field Pt., *New York* 50 G d
Old Forge, *New York* 53 L b
Old Forge, *Pennsylvania* 53 L d
Old Fort, *North Carolina* 55 J b
Old Glory, *Texas* 64 G b
Oldham, *South Dakota* 58 J f
Old Harbor, *Alaska* 76 L h
Old Hickory, *Tennessee* 54 E a
Old John L., *Alaska* 77 P b
Old Lyme, *Connecticut* 51 J c
Old Monroe, *Missouri* 61 O f
Old Mystic, *Connecticut* 51 K c
Old Orchard Beach, *Maine* 49 E e
Old Rampart, *Alaska* 77 Q c
Old Rhodes Key, *Florida* 55 O h
Old Saybrook, *Connecticut* 51 J c
Old Spekle Mt., *Maine* 49 E d
Old Tampa B., *Florida* 55 M f
Old Town, *Florida* 55 J h
Old Towne, *Maine* 49 G d
Old Woman Mts., *California* 75 K k
Old Woman R., *Alaska* 76 G e
Old Zionsville, *Pennsylvania* 50 B e
Olean, *New York* 52 H c
Olene, *Oregon* 73 J n
Olex, *Oregon* 73 K k
Oley, *Pennsylvania* 50 B e
Olga, *Florida* 55 N g
Olga, *North Dakota* 58 H b
Olga B., *Alaska* 76 K h
Olin, *Iowa* 61 N b
Olinda, *California* 74 C d
Olive, *Montana* 67 P d
Olive Branch, *Mississippi* 63 O d
Olivebridge, *New York* 50 E b
Olive Hill, *Kentucky* 57 K l
Oliver, *Georgia* 55 K e
Oliverea, *New York* 50 E a
Olivet, *Michigan* 56 J g
Olivet, Mt., *Kentucky* 57 J l
Olivet, *New Jersey* 50 C f
Olivet, *South Dakota* 58 J g
Olivia, *Minnesota* 59 M f
Olivia, *Texas* 65 L g
Olla, *Louisiana* 63 L g
Ollie, *Montana* 67 Q c
Olney, *Illinois* 57 E l
Olney, *Montana* 66 F a
Olney, *Texas* 65 J b
Olney Springs, *Colorado* 69 N e
Olpe, *Kansas* 61 H f
Olsburg, *Kansas* 60 H e
Olton, *Texas* 64 E a
Olustee, *Florida* 55 J g
Olustee, *Oklahoma* 62 D d
Olympia, *Washington* 73 H h
Olympic Mts., *Washington* 73 G h
Olympic Nat. Park, *Washington* 73 G h
Olympus, Mt., *Washington* 73 G h
Olyphant, *Pennsylvania* 53 L d
Oma, *Mississippi* 63 N g
Omaha, *Arkansas* 63 K b
Omaha, *Georgia* 54 G e
Omaha, *Nebraska (301,598)* 61 J c
Omaha, *Texas* 65 N b
Omak, *Washington* 73 L g
Omak L., *Washington* 73 L g
Omar, *West Virginia* 52 D h
Omega, *Alabama* 54 F f
Omega, *Georgia* 54 H f
Omega, *Oklahoma* 62 E c
Omemee, *North Dakota* 58 F b
Omena, *Michigan* 56 H d
Omer, *Michigan* 56 K e
Ommaney, C., *Alaska* 77 U h
Omro, *Wisconsin* 56 E e
Ona, *Florida* 55 N f
Onaga, *Kansas* 60 H e
Onaka, *North Dakota* 58 G e
Onalaska, *Washington* 73 H j
Onalaska, *Wisconsin* 56 B f
Onamia, *Minnesota* 59 N d
Onancock, *Virginia* 53 L h
Onarga, *Illinois* 57 F j
Onawa, *Iowa* 61 H b
Onaway, *Michigan* 56 J d
Oneco, *Florida* 55 M f
Oneida, *Illinois* 57 C h
Oneida, *Iowa* 61 N b
Oneida, *Kentucky* 57 K m
Oneida, *New York* 53 L b
Oneida, *Tennessee* 54 G a
Oneida L., *New York* 53 L b
O'Neill, *Nebraska* 60 F b
Onekama, *Michigan* 56 G e
Oneonta, *Alabama* 54 E d
Oneonta, *New York* 53 L c
Onida, *South Dakota* 58 F f
Onley, *Virginia* 53 L h
Onondaga, *Michigan* 56 J g
Onset, *Massachusetts* 51 M b
Onslow B., *North Carolina* 55 O c
Onsted, *Michigan* 57 J g
Ontario, *California (46,617)* 75 H k
Ontario, L., *New York* 52 H b
Ontario, L., *United States-Canada* 47 L b
Ontario, *Oregon* 73 O l
Ontario, *Wisconsin* 56 C f
Ontelaunee, L., *Pennsylvania* 50 B e
Ontonagon, *Michigan* 56 D c
Onward, *Mississippi* 63 N f
Onyx, *California* 75 G j
Ookala, *Hawaii* 72 E e
Oolitic, *Indiana* 57 G l
Oologah, *Oklahoma* 62 H b
Oologah Res., *Oklahoma* 62 H b
Oostanaula R., *Georgia* 54 F c
Opal, *Wyoming* 67 K h
Opal City, *Oregon* 73 J l
Opa-Locka, *Florida* 54 B d
Opelika, *Alabama* 54 F e
Opelousas, *Louisiana* 63 L h
Opheim, *Montana* 67 O a
Ophir, *Alaska* 76 J e
Ophir, *Oregon* 73 F n
Ophur, *Utah* 68 D c
Opp, *Alabama* 54 E f
Optima, *Oklahoma* 62 B b
Optima Res., *Oklahoma* 62 B b
Optimo, *New Mexico* 71 N d
Oquawka, *Illinois* 57 C j
Oquirrh Mts., *Utah* 68 B j
Oquossoc, *Maine* 49 E d
Oracle, *Arizona* 70 G g
Oraibi, *Arizona* 70 G d
Oraibi Wash, *Arizona* 70 G c
Oral, *South Dakota* 58 C g
Oran, *Missouri* 61 P g
Orange, *California (26,444)* 75 H l
Orange, *Connecticut* 51 G c
Orange, *Massachusetts* 49 C f
Orange, *New Jersey (35,789)* 50 E d
Orange, *Texas (25,605)* 65 O e
Orange Beach, *Alabama* 54 D g
Orangeburg, *South Carolina* 55 L d
Orange City, *Florida* 55 K j
Orange City, *Iowa* 61 H b
Orange Cr., *Alaska* 77 Q c
Orangedale, *Florida* 55 K g
Orange Grove, *Texas* 65 K h
Orange L., *Florida* 55 J h
Orange Park, *Florida* 55 K g
Orangeville, *Illinois* 56 D g
Orangeville, *Utah* 68 E d
Orbisonia, *Pennsylvania* 52 J e
Orca B., *Alaska* 77 O f
Orcas I., *Washington* 73 H g
Orchard, *Colorado* 69 M c
Orchard, *Idaho* 66 D f
Orchard, *Nebraska* 60 F b
Orchard Heights, *Washington* 72 A j
Orchard Park, *New York* 52 H c
Orcutt, *California* 75 E k
Ord, *Nebraska* 60 F c
Orderville, *Utah* 68 D f
Ord Mt., *California* 75 J k
Ordway, *Colorado* 69 N e
Ordway, *South Dakota* 58 H e
Oreana, *Idaho* 66 D f
Oreana, *Nevada* 74 G d
Ore City, *Texas* 65 N c
Oregon, *Illinois* 57 D g
Oregon 73
Oregon, *Missouri* 61 J e
Oregon, *Wisconsin* 56 D g
Oregon Caves Nat. Mon., *Oregon* 73 G n
Oregon City, *Oregon* 73 H k
Oregon Inlet, *North Carolina* 55 P d
Orella, *Nebraska* 60 A b
Orem, *Utah* 68 E c
Orford, *New Hampshire* 49 C e
Organ, *New Mexico* 71 L g
Organ Pipe Cactus Nat. Mon., *Arizona* 70 E g
Orick, *California* 74 A c
Orient, *Colorado* 69 L e
Orient, *Iowa* 61 K c
Orient, *Maine* 49 H c
Orient, *New York* 51 J c
Orient, *South Dakota* 58 G f
Orient, *Texas* 64 G d
Orient, *Washington* 73 M g
Oriental, *North Carolina* 55 P b
Orient I., *New York* 53 O d
Orient Pt., *New York* 51 J c
Orin, *Wyoming* 67 P g
Orinda, *California* 75 C l
Orion, *Illinois* 57 C h
Oriska, *North Dakota* 58 J d
Oriskany Falls, *New York* 53 L c
Oritz, *Colorado* 69 K f
Orla, *Texas* 64 D d
Orland, *California* 74 C e
Orland, *Indiana* 57 H h
Orland, *Maine* 49 G d
Orlando, *Florida (88,135)* 55 K j
Orlando, *Oklahoma* 62 F b
Orleans, *California* 74 B c
Orleans, *Indiana* 57 G l
Orleans, *Massachusetts* 51 N b
Orleans, *Minnesota* 59 K b
Orleans, *Nebraska* 60 E d
Orleans, *Vermont* 49 C d
Ormond, *Florida* 55 K h
Ormond Beach, *Florida* 55 K h
Ormsby, *Minnesota* 59 M g
Ormsby, *Wisconsin* 56 D d
Orofino, *Idaho* 66 D c
Oro Grande, *California* 75 H k
Orogrande, *Idaho* 66 E d
Orogrande, *New Mexico* 71 M g
Orono, *Maine* 49 G d
Oronogo, *Missouri* 61 K g
Orovada, *Nevada* 74 H c
Oroville, *Washington* 73 L g
Orpha, *Wyoming* 67 P g
Orr, *Minnesota* 59 O b
Orr, *North Dakota* 58 J b
Orr, *Oklahoma* 62 F d
Orrin, *North Dakota* 58 F b
Orrstown, *Pennsylvania* 52 J e
Orrville, *Ohio* 52 E e
Orting, *Washington* 73 H h
Ortonville, *Michigan* 56 K g
Orviston, *Pennsylvania* 52 J d
Orwell, *New York* 53 L b
Orwell, *Ohio* 52 F d
Orwell, *Vermont* 49 B e
Orwigsburg, *Pennsylvania* 50 A d
Osage, *Iowa* 61 M a
Osage, *Oklahoma* 62 G b
Osage, *Wyoming* 67 Q f
Osage City, *Kansas* 61 J f
Osage R., *Missouri* 61 M f
Osakis, *Minnesota* 59 L e
Osakis L., *Minnesota* 59 L e
Osawatomie, *Kansas* 61 K f
Osborne, *Kansas* 60 F e
Osceola, *Arkansas* 63 O c
Osceola, *Iowa* 61 L c
Osceola, *Missouri* 61 L f
Osceola, *Nebraska* 60 G c
Osceola, *Pennsylvania* 52 H e
Osceola, *Wisconsin* 56 A d
Oscoda, *Michigan* 56 K e
Oscura, *New Mexico* 71 L f
Osgood, *Indiana* 57 H k
Osgood, *Missouri* 61 L d
Osgood Mts., *Nevada* 74 H c
Oshkosh, *Nebraska* 60 B c
Oshkosh, *Wisconsin (45,110)* 56 E f
Oshoto, *Wyoming* 67 Q e
Oskaloosa, *Iowa* 61 M c
Oskaloosa, *Kansas* 61 J e
Osmond, *Nebraska* 60 G b
Osnabrock, *North Dakota* 58 H b
Osprey, *Florida* 55 M f
Ossabaw I., *Georgia* 55 K f
Ossabaw Sd., *Georgia* 55 K f
Osseo, *Minnesota* 59 P h
Osseo, *Wisconsin* 56 B e
Ossian, *Iowa* 61 N a
Ossineke, *Michigan* 56 K e
Ossining, *New York* 50 F c
Ossipee L., *New Hampshire* 49 D e
Osteen, *Florida* 55 K j
Osterburg, *Pennsylvania* 52 H e
Osterville, *Massachusetts* 51 N b
Ostrander, *Ohio* 52 C e
O'Sullivan Dam, *Washington* 73 L j
Oswayo, *Pennsylvania* 52 J d
Oswegatchie R., *New York* 53 L a
Oswego, *Illinois* 57 E h
Oswego, *Kansas* 61 J g
Oswego, *Montana* 67 P a
Oswego, *New York* 53 K b
Oswego, *Oregon* 73 H k
Oswego R., *New York* 53 K b
Osyka, *Mississippi* 63 N g
Otego, *New York* 53 L c
Othello, *Washington* 73 L j
Otis, *Colorado* 69 O c
Otis, *Kansas* 60 E f
Otis, *Massachusetts* 49 B f
Otisco L., *New York* 53 K c
Otis Res., *Massachusetts* 51 G a
Otisville, *New York* 50 D c
Otoe, *Nebraska* 61 H d
Otsego, *Michigan* 56 H g
Otsego L., *Michigan* 56 J e
Otsego L., *New York* 53 M c
Otsego Lake, *Michigan* 56 J e
Ottawa, *Illinois* 57 E h
Ottawa, *Kansas* 61 J f
Ottawa, *Ohio* 52 B d
Otter, *Montana* 67 O d
Otterbein, *Indiana* 57 F j
Otter Cr., *Montana* 67 O d
Otter Creek, *Florida* 55 J h
Otter Creek Res., *Utah* 68 E e
Otter I., *Alaska* 76 B h
Otter Lake, *Michigan* 56 K f
Otter R., *Virginia* 52 G h
Otter Tail L., *Minnesota* 59 L d
Otter Tail R., *Minnesota* 59 K d
Otto, *Texas* 65 L d
Otto, *Wyoming* 67 M e
Ottoville, *Ohio* 52 B e
Ottumwa, *Iowa (33,871)* 61 M c
Ottumwa, *South Dakota* 58 E f
Otway, *Ohio* 52 C g
Ouachita, L., *Arkansas* 63 K d
Ouachita Mts., *Arkansas* 63 K d
Ouachita Mts., *Oklahoma-Arkansas* 63 J d
Ouachita R., *Arkansas* 63 L e
Ouachita R., *Louisiana* 63 L f
Ouray, *Colorado* 69 J e
Ouray, *Utah* 68 G c
Outer I., *Wisconsin* 56 C b
Outer Santa Barbara Chan., *California* 75 G l
Outlook, *Montana* 67 Q a
Ouzinkie, *Alaska* 76 L h
Ovalo, *Texas* 65 H c
Ovando, *Montana* 66 G b
Overbrook, *Kansas* 61 J f
Overbrook, *Pennsylvania* 53 P b
Overland Park, *Kansas* 61 P b
Overle, *Maryland* 53 R e
Overly, *North Dakota* 58 F b
Overton, *Nebraska* 60 E d
Overton, *Nevada* 75 L h
Overton, *Texas* 65 N c
Ovett, *Mississippi* 63 O g
Ovid, *Colorado* 69 O c
Ovid, *Idaho* 66 J g
Ovid, *Michigan* 56 J g
Ovid, *New York* 53 K c
Oviedo, *Florida* 55 K j
Owasco L., *New York* 53 K c
Owasso L., *Minnesota* 59 Q h
Owasso, *Oklahoma* 62 H b
Owatonna, *Minnesota* 59 N f
Owego, *New York* 53 K c
Owen, *Wisconsin* 56 C e
Owens, *West Virginia* 52 E g
Owensboro, *Kentucky (42,471)* 57 F m
Owens L., *California* 75 H h
Owens R., *California* 75 G g
Owensville, *Indiana* 57 F l
Owensville, *Missouri* 61 N f
Owenton, *Kentucky* 57 J l
Owingsville, *Kentucky* 57 K l
Owl Canyon, *Colorado* 69 L c
Owl Cr., *Wyoming* 67 M f
Owl Creek Mts., *Wyoming* 67 M f
Owosso, *Michigan* 56 J f
Owyhee, L., *Oregon* 73 N m
Owyhee, *Nevada* 74 J c
Owyhee, *Oregon* 73 N m
Owyhee Dam, *Oregon* 73 N m
Owyhee R., *Idaho* 66 D g
Owyhee R., *Oregon* 73 N m
Oxboro, *Minnesota* 59 Q j
Oxbow Dam, *Idaho* 66 D e
Oxbow L., *Mississippi* 63 N d
Oxford, *Alabama* 54 F d
Oxford, *Connecticut* 50 G c
Oxford, *Idaho* 66 H g
Oxford, *Indiana* 57 F j
Oxford, *Iowa* 61 N c
Oxford, *Kansas* 60 G g
Oxford, *Maine* 49 E d
Oxford, *Maryland* 53 K g
Oxford, *Massachusetts* 51 K a
Oxford, *Michigan* 56 K g
Oxford, *Mississippi* 63 O d
Oxford, *Nebraska* 60 E d
Oxford, *New Jersey* 50 D d
Oxford, *New York* 53 L c
Oxford, *North Carolina* 55 N a
Oxford, *Ohio* 52 B f
Oxford, *Pennsylvania* 50 A f
Oxford, *Wisconsin* 56 D f
Oxford Pk., *Idaho* 66 H g
Oxford Valley, *Pennsylvania* 50 D e
Oxnard, *California (40,265)* 75 F k
Oyster Bay, *New York* 50 F d
Oyster Cr., *Texas* 65 M f
Oysterville, *Washington* 73 F j
Ozark, *Alabama* 54 F f
Ozark, *Arkansas* 63 K c
Ozark, *Michigan* 56 J c
Ozark, *Missouri* 61 L g
Ozark Plateau, *Missouri* 61 N g
Ozarks, L. of The, *Missouri* 61 M f
Ozette, *Washington* 73 F g
Ozette I., *Washington* 73 F g
Ozone, *Texas* 64 F e
Paauilo, *Hawaii* 72 E e
Pace, *Mississippi* 63 N e
Pachaug, *Connecticut* 51 K b
Pachaug L., *Connecticut* 51 K b
Pachuta, *Mississippi* 63 P f
Pacific, *California* 74 E f
Pacific, *Missouri* 61 O f
Pacific Beach, *Washington* 73 F h
Pacific City, *Oregon* 73 G k
Pacific Cr., *Wyoming* 67 L g
Pacific Grove, *California* 75 D h
Pack, *Oregon* 73 D h
Packton, *Louisiana* 63 L g
Packwood, *Iowa* 61 M c
Packwood, *Washington* 73 J j
Pacolet Mills, *South Carolina* 55 K c
Pacolet R., *South Carolina* 55 J b
Pacotopaug L., *Connecticut* 51 H b
Pactola, *South Dakota* 58 C f
Paden City, *West Virginia* 52 F f
Padre I., *Texas* 65 K h
Paducah, *Kentucky (34,479)* 57 E m
Paducah, *Texas* 64 G a
Page, *Arizona* 70 F c
Page, C., *Massachusetts* 51 N c
Page, *Nebraska* 60 F b
Page, *North Dakota* 58 J c
Page, *Oklahoma* 63 J d
Page, *West Virginia* 52 E g
Pageland, *South Carolina* 55 L c
Pagoda Pk., *Colorado* 69 J c
Pagosa Springs, *Colorado* 69 J f
Paguate, *New Mexico* 71 K d
Pahala, *Hawaii* 72 E f
Pahoa, *Hawaii* 72 E f
Pahokee, *Florida* 55 O g
Pah R., *Alaska* 76 K c
Pahranagat L., *Nevada* 75 K g
Pahranagat Ra., *Nevada* 75 K g
Pahrock Ra., *Nevada* 74 L g
Pahrump, *Nevada* 75 K h
Pahsimeroi R., *Idaho* 66 G e
Pahute Mesa, *Nevada* 75 J g
Pahute Pk., *Nevada* 74 F c
Paia, *Hawaii* 72 D e
Paige, *Texas* 65 K e
Pailolo Chan., *Hawaii* 72 D d
Paimiut, *Alaska* 76 G e
Painesdale, *Michigan* 56 E b
Painesville, *Ohio* 52 E d
Painted Des., *Arizona* 70 F c
Painted Rock Res., *Arizona* 70 E g
Paint Rock, *Texas* 64 H d
Paisley, *Oregon* 73 K n
Pajarito, *New Mexico* 71 L e
Pala, *California* 75 H l
Palacios, *Texas* 65 L g
Palatka, *Florida* 55 K h
Palco, *Kansas* 60 E e
Palen L., *California* 75 K l
Palenville, *New York* 50 F a
Palermo, *California* 74 D e
Palermo, *North Dakota* 58 D b
Palestine, *Illinois* 57 E l
Palestine, *Ohio* 52 B e
Palestine, *Texas* 65 M d
Paliner, *Tennessee* 54 F b
Palisade, *Colorado* 68 H d
Palisade, *Nebraska* 60 C d
Palisade, *Nevada* 74 J d
Palisades Interstate Park, *New Jersey* 51 M c
Palisades Res., *Idaho* 66 J f
Palito Blanco, *Texas* 65 J h
Palm, *Pennsylvania* 50 B e
Palma, *New Mexico* 71 M d
Palm Beach, *Florida* 55 O g
Palm Canyon Nat. Mon., *California* 75 J l
Palmdale, *California* 75 G k
Palmdale, *Florida* 55 N g
Palmer, *Alaska* 77 N f
Palmer, *Illinois* 57 D k
Palmer, *Iowa* 61 K b
Palmer, *Massachusetts* 51 J a
Palmer, *Michigan* 56 F c
Palmer, *Nebraska* 60 F c
Palmer, *Texas* 65 L c
Palmer Lake, *Colorado* 69 M d
Palmerton, *Pennsylvania* 50 B d
Palmetto, *Florida* 55 M f
Palmetto, *Georgia* 54 G d
Palm Harbor, *Florida* 55 M e
Palms, *Michigan* 56 L f
Palm Springs, *California* 75 J l
Palmyra, *Illinois* 57 D k
Palmyra, *Missouri* 61 N e
Palmyra, *Nebraska* 60 H d
Palmyra, *New Jersey* 50 D e
Palmyra, *New York* 53 J b
Palmyra, *Pennsylvania* 53 K e
Palmyra, *Tennessee* 54 D a
Palmyra, *Virginia* 52 H h
Palmyra, *Wisconsin* 56 E g
Palo, *Iowa* 61 N b
Palo Alto, *California (52,287)* 75 C n
Paloduro, *Texas* 64 C j
Palo Duro Canyon, *Texas* 64 C j
Palo Duro Cr., *Texas* 64 B h
Paloduro Cr., *Texas* 64 C g
Palomar Mt., *California* 75 J l
Palomas, *Arizona* 70 D g
Palo Pinto, *Texas* 65 J c
Palos Verdes Hills, *California* 75 D n
Palos Verdes Pt., *California* 75 D n
Palouse, *Washington* 73 N j
Palouse R., *Washington* 73 N j
Palo Verde, *Arizona* 70 E f
Palo Verde, *California* 75 L l
Pamlico R., *North Carolina* 55 P b
Pamlico Sd., *North Carolina* 55 P b
Pampa, *Texas* 64 D h
Pamplin City, *Virginia* 52 H h
Pamunkey R., *Virginia* 53 J h
Pana, *Illinois* 57 D k
Panaca, *Nevada* 74 L g
Panama, *New York* 52 G c
Panama, *Oklahoma* 63 J c
Panama City, *Florida (33,275)* 54 F g
Panamint Ra., *California* 75 H h
Panamint Val., *California* 75 H h
Pancake Ra., *Nevada* 74 J f
Pandale, *Texas* 64 F e
Pangburn, *Arkansas* 63 M c
Panguitch, *Utah* 68 D f
Panhandle, *Texas* 64 C h
Pankof, C., *Alaska* 76 F j
Panoche, *California* 75 E h
Panora, *Iowa* 61 K c
Pantano, *Arizona* 70 G h
Pantego, *North Carolina* 55 P b
Pantego, *Texas* 65 M j
Panther R., *Kentucky* 57 F m
Paola, *Kansas* 61 K f
Paoli, *Colorado* 69 O c
Paoli, *Indiana* 57 G l
Paoli, *Oklahoma* 62 F d
Paoli, *Pennsylvania* 50 B e
Paonia, *Colorado* 69 J e
Papa, *Hawaii* 72 E f
Papaaloa, *Hawaii* 72 E f
Papaikou, *Hawaii* 72 E f
Papillion, *Nebraska* 61 H c
Parade, *South Dakota* 58 E e
Paradise, *California* 74 D e
Paradise, *Kansas* 60 F e
Paradise, *Michigan* 56 H c
Paradise, *Montana* 66 F b
Paradise, *Pennsylvania* 50 A e
Paradise, *Texas* 65 K b
Paradise, *Utah* 68 E b
Paradise Cairn, *Nevada* 74 H f
Paradise Valley, *Nevada* 74 H c
Paragon, *Indiana* 57 G k
Paragonah, *Utah* 68 D f
Paragould, *Arkansas* 63 N b
Paramount, *California (27,249), vicinity of Los Angeles*
Pardee Res., *California* 74 E f
Pardeeville, *Wisconsin* 56 D f
Paria Plateau, *Arizona* 70 F c
Paria R., *Utah* 68 E f
Paris, *Arkansas* 63 K c
Paris, *Idaho* 66 J g
Paris, *Illinois* 57 F k
Paris, *Kentucky* 57 J l
Paris, *Missouri* 61 N e
Paris, *Tennessee* 54 C a
Paris, *Texas* 65 M b
Parish, *New York* 53 K b
Park City, *Kentucky* 57 G m
Park City, *Montana* 67 M d
Park City, *Utah* 68 E c
Parkdale, *Colorado* 69 L e
Parkdale, *Oregon* 73 J k
Parker, *Arizona* 70 C e
Parker, *Colorado* 69 M d
Parker, *Idaho* 66 J f
Parker, *Kansas* 61 K f
Parker, *South Dakota* 58 J g
Parker City, *Indiana* 57 H j
Parker City, *Pennsylvania* 52 G d
Parker Dam, *California* 75 L k
Parkersburg, *Iowa* 61 M b
Parkersburg, *West Virginia (44,797)* 52 E f

Sanford Res., *Texas* 64 C h
San Francisco, *California* *(740,316)* 74 C g
San Francisco B., *California* 74 C g
San Francisco Cr., *Texas* 64 E f
San Francisco R., *New Mexico* 71 J f
San Gabriel Mts., *California* 75 H k
Sangamon R., *Illinois* 57 C j
Sanger, *California* 75 F h
Sanger, *North Dakota* 58 E c
Sanger, *Texas* 65 K b
San Gorgonio Mt., *California* 75 J k
Sangre de Cristo Mts., *Colorado-New Mexico* 46 E c
Sangre de Cristo Ra., *New Mexico* 71 M c
San Gregorio, *California* 75 C g
Sanibel I., *Florida* 55 M g
San Ildefonso, *New Mexico* 71 M d
San Isabel, *Colorado* 69 L f
Sanish, *North Dakota* 58 D c
San Jacinto, *California* 75 J l
San Jacinto, *Nevada* 74 L c
San Jacinto Mts., *California* 75 J l
San Jacinto R., *Texas* 65 M e
San Joaquin, *California* 75 E h
San Joaquin R., *California* 75 E g
San Joaquin Val., *California* 75 E h
San Jon, *New Mexico* 71 O d
San Jose, *California (204,196)* 75 D g
San Jose, *Illinois* 57 D j
San Jose, *New Mexico* 71 M d
San Juan Bautista, *California* 75 D h
San Juan Capistrano, *California* 75 H l
San Juan I., *Washington* 73 G g
San Juan Is., *Washington* 73 H g
San Juan Mts., *Colorado* 69 J f
San Juan Mts., *New Mexico* 71 L c
San Juan R., *California* 75 E j
San Juan R., *Utah* 68 G f
San Leandro Res., *California* 75 C l
San Leandro, *California* *(65,962)* 75 C l
San Leandro B., *California* 75 C m
San Lorenzo, *California* 75 C m
San Lorenzo, *New Mexico* 71 K g
San Lucas, *California* 75 D h
Santa Lucia Ra., *California* 75 D h
San Luis, *Arizona* 70 C g
San Luis, *Arizona* 70 F g
San Luis, *Colorado* 69 L f
San Luis Obispo, *California* 75 E j
San Luis Obispo B., *California* 75 D j
San Luis Pass, *Texas* 65 M f
San Luis Pk., *Colorado* 69 K e
San Luis Rey R., *California* 75 H l
San Luis Val., *Colorado* 69 L f
San Marcial, *New Mexico* 71 K f
San Marcos, *Texas* 65 J f
San Mateo, *California* *(69,870)* 75 B m
San Mateo, *New Mexico* 71 K d
San Mateo Pk., *New Mexico* 71 K f
San Mateo Pt., *California* 75 B m
San Miguel, *Arizona* 70 F h
San Miguel, *California* 75 E j
San Miguel, *New Mexico* 71 L g
San Miguel Cr., *Texas* 65 J g
San Miguel I., *California* 75 E k
San Miguel R., *Colorado* 68 H e
San Nicolas I., *California* 75 F l
San Onofre, *California* 75 H l
San Pablo, *California* 75 B k
San Pablo B., *California* 74 C f
San Pablo Cr., *California* 75 C k
San Pablo Pt., *California* 75 B k
San Pablo Res., *California* 75 C k
San Pedro, *California* 75 E n
San Pedro B., *California* 75 E n
San Pedro Chan., *California* 75 G l
San Pedro Pt., *California* 75 B m
San Pedro R., *Arizona* 70 G g
San Pierre, *Indiana* 57 G h
Sanpoil R., *Washington* 73 M g
San Quentin, *California* 75 B k
San Raphael, *California* 75 B k
San Rafael, *New Mexico* 71 K d
San Rafael Knob, *Utah* 68 F d
San Rafael R., *Utah* 68 F d
San Rafael Mts., *California* 75 F k
San Saba, *Texas* 65 J d
San Saba R., *Texas* 64 G e
San Simeon, *California* 75 D j
San Simon, *Arizona* 70 H g
San Simon Cr., *Arizona* 70 H g
San Souci, *Michigan* 56 L g
Santa, *Idaho* 66 D b
Santa Ana, *California* *(100,350)* 75 H l
Santa Ana Mts., *California* 75 H l
Santa Ana R., *California* 75 H l
Santa Anna, *Texas* 65 H d
Santa Barbara, *California* *(58,768)* 75 F k
Santa Barbara Chan., *California* 75 E k
Santa Barbara I., *California* 75 F l
Santa Barbara Res., *California* 75 F k
Santa Catalina, Gulf of, *California* 75 G l
Santa Catalina I., *California* 75 G l
Santa Clara, *California* *(58,880)* 75 D g
Santa Clara, *New York* 53 M a
Santa Clara, *Utah* 68 C f
Santa Clara Pk., *New Mexico* 71 L c
Santa Clara R., *California* 75 F k
Santa Claus, *Indiana* 57 G l
Santa Cruz, *California* *(25,596)* 75 C h
Santa Cruz, *New Mexico* 71 M c
Santa Cruz Chan., *California* 75 F k
Santa Cruz I., *California* 75 F l
Santa Cruz Mts., *California* 75 C g
Santa Elena, *Texas* 65 J j
Santa Fe, *New Mexico* *(33,394)* 71 L d
Santa Fe R., *Florida* 55 J h
Santa Fe L., *Florida* 55 J h
Santa Margarita, *California* 75 E j
Santa Margarita R., *California* 75 H l
Santa Maria, *California* 75 E k
Santa Maria Mts., *Arizona* 70 E e
Santa Maria R., *Arizona* 70 D e
Santa Monica, *California* *(83,249)* 76 D l
Santa Monica B., *California* 75 G l
Santa Monica Mts., *California* 75 D l
Santan Mt., *Arizona* 70 F f
Santa Paula, *California* 75 F k
Santaquin, *Utah* 68 E d
Santa Rita, *Montana* 66 H a
Santa Rosa, *California* *(31,027)* 74 C f
Santa Rosa, *New Mexico* 71 N e
Santa Rosa I., *California* 75 E k
Santa Rosa I., *Florida* 54 D g
Santa Rosa L., *Texas* 65 H b
Santa Rosa Mts., *California* 75 J l
Santa Rosa Mts., *Nevada* 74 H c
Santa Rosa Pk., *Nevada* 74 H c
Santa Rosa R., *Arizona* 70 F g
Santa Ynez, *California* 75 E k
Santa Ynez Mts., *California* 75 F k
Santa Ynez R., *California* 75 J j
Santa Ysabel, *California* 75 J l
Santee Dam, *South Carolina* 55 L d
Santee Pt., *South Carolina* 55 M d
Santee R., *South Carolina* 55 M d
Santeetlah, L., *North Carolina* 54 H b
Santiago Mts., *Texas* 64 D f
Santiago Pk., *California* 75 H l
Santiago Pk., *Texas* 64 D f
Santo, *Texas* 65 J c
San Ygnacio, *Texas* 65 H h
San Ysidro, *California* 75 J m
San Ysidro, *New Mexico* 71 L d
Sapello, *New Mexico* 71 M d
Sapelo I., *Georgia* 55 K f
Sapelo Sd., *Georgia* 55 K f
Sapinero, *Colorado* 69 J e
Sappa Cr., *Kansas* 60 D e
Sapphire Mts., *Montana* 66 G c
Sapulpa, *Oklahoma* 62 G b
Sarafina, *New Mexico* 71 M d
Saragosa, *Texas* 64 D d
Sarana B., *Alaska* 76 J j
Saranac, *Michigan* 56 H g
Saranac Lake, *New York* 53 M a
Saranac R., *New York* 53 N a
Sarasota, *Florida (34,083)* 55 M f
Sarasota B., *Florida* 55 M f
Sarasota Key, *Florida* 55 M f
Saratoga, *Texas* 65 N e
Saratoga, *Wyoming* 67 O h
Saratoga L., *New York* 53 N b
Saratoga Springs, *New York* 53 N b
Sarcoxie, *Missouri* 61 K g
Sardinia, *Ohio* 52 C f
Sardis, *Georgia* 55 K e
Sardis, *Mississippi* 63 O d
Sardis, *Ohio* 52 E f
Sardis, *Tennessee* 54 C b
Sardis L., *Mississippi* 63 O d
Sarepta, *Louisiana* 63 K f
Sargent, *California* 75 D h
Sargent, *Nebraska* 60 E c
Sargent Icefield, *Alaska* 77 N f
Sargents, *Colorado* 69 K e
Sarichef, C., *Alaska* 76 E j
Sarita, *Texas* 65 K h
Sarles, *North Dakota* 58 H b
Sarpy, *Montana* 67 O d
Sasabe, *Arizona* 70 F h
Sasmik, C., *Alaska* 77 O j
Saspamco, *Texas* 65 J f
Sassafras, *Maryland* 50 B g
Sassafras Mt., *South Carolina* 55 J b
Sassafras R., *Maryland* 50 A g
Satan Pass, *New Mexico* 71 K d
Satanta, *Kansas* 60 D g
Satilla R., *Georgia* 55 K g
Satus, *Washington* 73 K j
Sauceda Mts., *Arizona* 70 E g
Saucier, *Mississippi* 63 O h
Saugatuck, *Michigan* 56 G g
Saugatuck Res., *Connecticut* 50 G c
Saugerties, *New York* 50 F a
Sauk Centre, *Minnesota* 59 M e
Sauk City, *Wisconsin* 56 D f
Sauk R., *Minnesota* 59 M e
Sauk R., *Washington* 73 J g
Sauk Rapids, *Minnesota* 59 M e
Sault Ste. Marie, *Michigan* 56 J c
Sauderstown, *Rhode Island* 51 L b
Sausalito, *California* 75 B l
Savage, *Maryland* 53 K f
Savage, *Mississippi* 63 N d
Savage, *Montana* 67 Q b
Savageton, *Wyoming* 67 P f
Savanna, *Illinois* 57 C g
Savanna, *Oklahoma* 62 H d
Savannah, *Georgia (149,245)* 55 K e
Savannah, *Missouri* 61 K e
Savannah, *Ohio* 52 D e
Savannah, *Tennessee* 54 C b
Savannah Beach, *Georgia* 55 K f
Savannah R., *South Carolina* 55 K e
Savannah River Project, *South Carolina* 55 K d
Savery, *Wyoming* 67 N h
Savery Cr., *Wyoming* 67 N h
Saville Dam, *Connecticut* 51 H b
Savona, *New York* 53 J c
Savoonga, *Alaska* 76 B e
Savoy, *Mississippi* 63 P f
Savoy, *Montana* 67 M a
Sawatch Mts., *Colorado* 69 K d
Sawlog Cr., *Kansas* 60 E g
Sawtooth Mt., *Alaska* 77 N d
Sawtooth Mts., *Idaho* 66 E f
Sawtooth Ra., *Idaho* 66 F f
Sawtooth Ra., *Washington* 73 K g
Sawyer, *Kansas* 60 F g
Sawyer, *North Dakota* 58 E b
Sawyer, *Wisconsin* 56 F e
Sawyers Bar, *California* 74 B c
Saxis, *Virginia* 53 L h
Saxman, *Alaska* 77 W j
Saxon, *Wisconsin* 56 C c
Saxton, *Pennsylvania* 52 H e
Saybrook, *Connecticut.* *See Old Saybrook.*
Saylorsburg, *Pennsylvania* 50 C d
Sayre, *Oklahoma* 62 D c
Sayre, *Pennsylvania* 53 K d
Sayreville, *New Jersey* 50 E e
Sayville, *New York* 51 G d
Scales Mound, *Illinois* 56 C g
Scammon Bay, *Alaska* 76 E f
Scandia, *Kansas* 60 G e
Scandia, *Washington* 72 A h
Scantic, *Connecticut* 51 H b
Scappoose, *Oregon* 73 H k
Scarlets Mill, *Pennsylvania* 50 B e
Scarper Pk., *California* 75 B m
Scenic, *South Dakota* 58 D g
Schaffer, *Michigan* 56 F d
Schaller, *Iowa* 61 J b
Schenectady, *New York* *(81,682)* 53 M c
Schertz, *Texas* 65 J f
Schickshinny, *Pennsylvania* 50 A c
Schleswig, *Iowa* 61 J b
Schnecksville, *Pennsylvania* 50 B d
Schofield, *Wisconsin* 56 D e
Schoharie, *New York* 53 M c
Schoharie Cr., *New York* 50 E a
Schoodic L., *Maine* 49 F c
Schoodic Pt., *Maine* 49 H d
Schoolcraft, *Michigan* 57 H g
Schrag, *Washington* 73 M h
Schroon L., *New York* 53 N b
Schroon Lake, *New York* 53 N b
Schuchuli, *Arizona* 70 E g
Schulenburg, *Texas* 65 L f
Schulter, *Oklahoma* 62 G c
Schurz, *Nevada* 74 G f
Schuyler, *Nebraska* 60 G c
Schuyler, *Virginia* 52 H h
Schuylerville, *New York* 53 N b
Schuylkill Haven, *Pennsylvania* 50 A d
Schuylkill R., *Pennsylvania* 50 B e
Schwatka Mts., *Alaska* 76 J c
Scio, *New York* 52 J c
Scio, *Ohio* 52 E e
Scioto R., *Ohio* 52 D g
Sciotoville, *Ohio* 52 D g
Scipio, *Utah* 68 D d
Scituate, *Massachusetts* 51 M a
Scituate Res., *Rhode Island* 51 K b
Scobey, *Montana* 67 P a
Scofield, *Utah* 68 E d
Scofield Res., *Utah* 68 E d
Scooba, *Mississippi* 63 P f
Scossa, *Nevada* 74 G d
Scotch Cap I., *Alaska* 76 F j
Scotia, *California* 74 A d
Scotia, *Nebraska* 60 F c
Scotia, *Washington* 73 N g
Scotland, *South Dakota* 58 J g
Scotland, *Texas* 65 J b
Scotland Neck, *North Carolina* 55 O a
Scotlandville, *Louisiana* 63 M h
Scott, *Georgia* 55 J e
Scott, *Mississippi* 63 M e
Scott, Mt., *Oregon* 73 H n
Scott, *Ohio* 52 B e
Scott Bar, *California* 74 B c
Scott City, *Kansas* 60 D f
Scottdale, *Pennsylvania* 52 G e
Scott R., *California* 74 C c
Scotts, *Michigan* 57 H g
Scottsbluff, *Nebraska* 60 A c
Scotts Bluff Nat. Mon., *Nebraska* 60 A c
Scottsboro, *Alabama* 54 E c
Scottsburg, *Indiana* 57 H l
Scottsburg, *Oregon* 73 G m
Scottsburg, *Virginia* 52 H j
Scotts Ferry, *Florida* 54 F g
Scottsville, *Kansas* 60 G e
Scottsville, *Kentucky* 57 G n
Scottsville, *Virginia* 52 H h
Scottville, *Michigan* 56 G f
Scotty's Castle, *California* 75 H g
Scranton, *Arkansas* 63 K c
Scranton, *Kansas* 61 J f
Scranton, *North Dakota* 58 C d
Scranton, *Pennsylvania* *(111,443)* 53 L d
Scriba, *New York* 53 K b
Scribner, *Nebraska* 60 H c
Seabeck, *Washington* 72 A h
Seaboard, *North Carolina* 55 O a
Seabold, *Washington* 72 A h
Seabrook, *Texas* 65 M f
Sea Cliff, *New York* 50 F d
Seadrift, *Texas* 65 L g
Seaford, *Delaware* 53 L g
Seagraves, *Texas* 64 E c
Seagrove, *North Carolina* 55 M b
Seahurst, *Washington* 72 B j
Sea Island, *Georgia* 55 K f
Sea Isle City, *New Jersey* 50 D g
Seal Beach, *California* 75 F n
Seal C., *Alaska* 76 H h
Seale, *Alabama* 54 F e
Seal I., *Hawaii* 72 A a
Seal I., *Maine* 49 G e
Seal Rock, *Oregon* 73 F l
Seal Rocks, *California* 75 B l
Sealy, *Texas* 65 L f
Seaman Ra., *Nevada* 74 K g
Searchlight, *Nevada* 75 L j
Searcy, *Arkansas* 63 M c
Searles, *California* 75 H j
Searles L., *California* 75 H j
Searsport, *Maine* 49 F d
Seaside, *California* 75 D h
Seaside, *Oregon* 73 G k
Seaside Heights, *New Jersey* 50 E f
Seaside Park, *New Jersey* 50 E f
Seattle, *Washington (557,087)* 73 H h
Sebago L., *Maine* 49 E e
Sebastian, *Florida* 55 O f
Sebastian, *Texas* 65 K j
Sebasticook L., *Maine* 49 F d
Sebasticook R., *Maine* 49 F d
Sebastopol, *California* 74 C f
Sebastopol, *Mississippi* 63 O f
Sebeka, *Minnesota* 59 L d
Sebewaing, *Michigan* 56 K f
Seboeis L., *Maine* 49 G c
Seboomook L., *Maine* 49 F c
Seboyeta, *New Mexico* 71 K d
Sebree, *Kentucky* 57 F m
Sebrell, *Virginia* 53 J j
Sebring, *Florida* 55 N f
Sebring, *Ohio* 52 F e
Secaucus, *New Jersey* 51 L e
Secession L., *South Carolina* 55 J c
Second L., *New Hampshire* 49 D c
Sedalia, *Colorado* 69 M d
Sedalia, *Kentucky* 57 E n
Sedalia, *Missouri* 61 L f
Sedalia, *Ohio* 52 C f
Sedan, *Kansas* 60 H g
Sedan, *New Mexico* 71 O c
Sedanka I., *Alaska* 76 D k
Sedgwick, *Colorado* 69 O c
Sedgwick, *Kansas* 60 G g
Sedgwick, *Maine* 49 G d
Sedona, *Arizona* 70 F e
Sedro Woolley, *Washington* 73 H g
Seekonk, *Massachusetts* 51 L b
Seeley Lake, *Montana* 66 G b
Sego, *Utah* 68 G d
Segovia, *Texas* 65 H e
Seguan I., *Alaska* 77 R j
Seguan Pass., *Alaska* 77 R j
Seguin, *Kansas* 60 D e
Seguin, *Texas* 65 K f
Segula I., *Alaska* 76 M h
Segundo, *Colorado* 69 M f
Seiad Valley, *California* 74 B c
Seibert, *Colorado* 69 O d
Seiling, *Oklahoma* 62 E b
Selah, *Washington* 73 K j
Selawik, *Alaska* 76 H c
Selawik L., *Alaska* 76 G c
Selawik R., *Alaska* 76 H c
Selby, L., *Alaska* 76 K c
Selby, *South Dakota* 58 F e
Selbyville, *Delaware* 53 L g
Selden, *Kansas* 60 D e
Selden, *New York* 51 G d
Seldovia, *Alaska* 76 M g
Selfridge, *North Dakota* 58 F d
Seligman, *Arizona* 70 E d
Seligman, *Missouri* 61 L h
Selinsgrove, *Pennsylvania* 53 K e
Selkirk, *Kansas* 60 C f
Selkirk, *Michigan* 56 J e
Selleck, *Washington* 73 J h
Sellersburg, *Indiana* 57 H l
Sellersville, *Pennsylvania* 50 C e
Sells, *Arizona* 70 F h
Selma, *Alabama (28,385)* 54 D e
Selma, *California* 75 F h
Selma, *Louisiana* 63 L g
Selma, *North Carolina* 55 N b
Selma, *Oregon* 73 G n
Selmer, *Tennessee* 54 C b
Selway R., *Idaho* 66 E c
Selz, *North Dakota* 58 G c
Semichi Is., *Alaska* 76 K j
Semidi Is., *Alaska* 76 J h
Seminary, *Mississippi* 63 O g
Seminoe Dam, town, *Wyoming* 67 N g
Seminoe Dam, *Wyoming* 67 N g
Seminoe Res., *Wyoming* 67 O g
Seminole, *Oklahoma* 62 G c
Seminole, *Texas* 64 E c
Semisopochnoi I., *Alaska* 76 M j
Semper, *Colorado* 69 O h
Senath, *Missouri* 61 O h
Senatobia, *Mississippi* 63 O d
Seneca, *Illinois* 57 E h
Seneca, *Kansas* 61 H e
Seneca, *Missouri* 61 K h
Seneca, *Nebraska* 60 D b
Seneca, *Oregon* 73 M l
Seneca, *South Carolina* 55 J c
Seneca, *South Dakota* 58 G e
Seneca Falls, *New York* 53 K c
Seneca L., *New York* 53 K c
Senecaville, *Ohio* 52 E f
Senecaville Res., *Ohio* 52 E f
Seney, *Michigan* 56 H c
Senoia, *Georgia* 54 G d
Sentinel, *Arizona* 70 D g
Sentinel, *Oklahoma* 62 D c
Sentinel Butte, *North Dakota* 58 C d
Separ, *New Mexico* 71 J g
Sequatchie R., *Tennessee* 54 F b
Sequim, *Washington* 73 G g
Sequoia Nat. Park, *California* 75 G h
Sergeant Bluff, *Iowa* 60 H b
Sergeantsville, *New Jersey* 50 D e
Serpentine Hot Springs, *Alaska* 76 E d
Service Creek, *Oregon* 73 K l
Servilleta, *New Mexico* 71 M c
Sesser, *Illinois* 57 D l
Setauket, *New York* 50 G d
Seth, *West Virginia* 52 E g
Seul Choix Pt., *Michigan* 56 H d
Seven Devils Mt., *Idaho* 66 D d
Seven Sisters, *Texas* 65 J g
Seven Springs, *North Carolina* 55 O b
Seven Troughs, *Nevada* 74 G d
Severance, *Kansas* 61 J e
Severy, *Kansas* 60 H g
Sevier, *Utah* 68 D e
Sevier Bridge Res., *Utah* 68 D d
Sevier Des., *Utah* 68 D d
Sevier L., *Utah* 68 C d
Sevier R., *Utah* 68 D e
Sevierville, *Tennessee* 54 H b
Sewanee, *Tennessee* 54 F b
Seward, *Alaska* 76 N f
Seward, *Kansas* 60 F f
Seward, *Nebraska* 60 G d
Seward, *Pennsylvania* 52 H e
Seward Pen., *Alaska* 76 D d
Sewickley, *Pennsylvania* 52 F e
Seymour, *Connecticut* 50 G c
Seymour, *Iowa* 61 L d
Seymour, *Missouri* 61 M g
Seymour, *Texas* 65 H b
Seymour, *Wisconsin* 56 E e
Shabbona, *Illinois* 57 E h
Shadehill Res., *South Dakota* 58 D e
Shady, *New York* 50 E a
Shady Grove, *Alabama* 54 E f
Shady Grove, *Florida* 54 H g
Shadyside, *Ohio* 52 F f
Shafter, *California* 75 F j
Shafter, *Nevada* 74 L d
Shafter, *Texas* 64 C f
Shageluk, *Alaska* 76 H e
Shaker Heights, *Ohio (36,460), vicinity of Cleveland*
Shakopee, *Minnesota* 59 N f
Shaktoolik, *Alaska* 76 G d
Shaktoolik R., *Alaska* 76 G d
Shallotte, *North Carolina* 55 N d
Shallowater, *Texas* 64 E b
Shamokin, *Pennsylvania* 53 K e
Shamrock, *Florida* 54 H h
Shamrock, *Oklahoma* 62 G c
Shamrock, *Texas* 64 D h
Shandaken, *New York* 50 E a
Shandon, *California* 75 E j
Shanksville, *Pennsylvania* 52 H e
Shaniko, *Oregon* 73 K k
Shannock, *Rhode Island* 51 K c
Shannon, *Georgia* 54 F c
Shannon, *Illinois* 57 D g
Shannon, *Mississippi* 63 P d
Shannon City, *Iowa* 61 K d
Sharon, *Connecticut* 50 G b
Sharon, *Georgia* 55 J d
Sharon, *Kansas* 60 F g
Sharon, *Massachusetts* 51 L a
Sharon, *Michigan* 56 H e
Sharon, *North Dakota* 58 J c
Sharon, *Oklahoma* 62 D b
Sharon, *Pennsylvania (25,267)* 52 F d
Sharon, *Tennessee* 54 C a
Sharon, *Vermont* 49 C e
Sharon, *Wisconsin* 56 E g
Sharon Springs, *Kansas* 60 C f
Sharp Park, *California* 75 B m
Sharps, *Virginia* 53 K h
Sharpsburg, *Iowa* 61 K d
Sharpsburg, *Maryland* 52 J f
Sharpsburg, *Pennsylvania* 53 Q a
Sharpstown, *Texas* 64 F j
Sharpsville, *Indiana* 57 G j
Sharptown, *Maryland* 53 L g
Sharptown, *New Jersey* 50 C f
Shartlesville, *Pennsylvania* 50 A d
Shasta, Mt., *California* 74 C c
Shasta L., *California* 74 C d
Shattuck, *Oklahoma* 62 D b
Shaver L., *California* 75 F g
Shavers Fork, *West Virginia* 52 G g
Shaw, *Mississippi* 63 N e
Shawangunk Kill, *New York* 50 E b
Shawangunk Mts., *New York* 50 D c
Shawano, *Wisconsin* 56 E e
Shawano L., *Wisconsin* 56 E e
Shawmut, *Montana* 67 L c
Shawnee, *Kansas* 61 O a
Shawnee, *Ohio* 52 D f
Shawnee, *Oklahoma* 62 G c
Shawnee, *Wyoming* 67 Q g
Shawneetown, *Illinois* 57 E m
Sheaville, *Oregon* 73 N m
Sheboygan, *Wisconsin* *(45,747)* 56 F f
Sheenjek R., *Alaska* 77 Q b
Sheep Cr., *Wyoming* 67 P g
Sheep Mt., *Colorado* 69 J d
Sheep Pk., *Nevada* 75 K h
Sheep Range, *Nevada* 75 K h
Sheepshead Bay, *New York* 51 M g
Sheffield, *Alabama* 54 D c
Sheffield, *Illinois* 57 D h
Sheffield, *Iowa* 61 L b
Sheffield, *Massachusetts* 50 G a
Sheffield, *Pennsylvania* 52 G d
Sheffield, *Texas* 64 F e
Sheffield Lake, *Ohio* 52 D d
Shekomiko, *New York* 50 F b
Shelbiana, *Kentucky* 57 L m
Shelbina, *Missouri* 61 M e
Shelburn, *Indiana* 57 F k
Shelburne, *Vermont* 49 B d
Shelburne Falls, *Massachusetts* 49 C f
Shelby, *Indiana* 57 F h
Shelby, *Iowa* 61 J c
Shelby, *Michigan* 56 G f
Shelby, *Mississippi* 63 N e
Shelby, *Montana* 66 J a
Shelby, *Nebraska* 60 G c
Shelby, *North Carolina* 55 K b
Shelby, *Ohio* 52 D e
Shelbyville, *Illinois* 57 E k
Shelbyville, *Indiana* 57 G k
Shelbyville, *Kentucky* 57 H l
Shelbyville, *Missouri* 61 M e
Shelbyville, *Tennessee* 54 E b
Shelbyville, *Texas* 65 N d
Sheldon, *Illinois* 57 F j
Sheldon, *Iowa* 61 J a
Sheldon, *Missouri* 61 K g
Sheldon, *North Dakota* 58 J d
Sheldon, *Wisconsin* 56 C d
Sheldons Point, *Alaska* 76 E e
Sheldon Springs, *Vermont* 49 C d
Sheldonville, *Massachusetts* 51 L a
Shelikof Str., *Alaska* 76 K h
Shell, *Wyoming* 67 N e
Shell Beach, *Louisiana* 63 O j
Shell Cr., *Wyoming* 67 M h
Shell Cr., *Wyoming* 67 N e
Shell Creek Ra., *Nevada* 74 L e
Shelley, *Idaho* 66 H f
Shell Lake, *Wisconsin* 56 B d
Shellman, *Georgia* 54 G f
Shell Mt., *California* 74 B d
Shell R., *Minnesota* 59 L d
Shell Rock, *Iowa* 61 M b
Shellrock R., *Iowa* 61 M b
Shellsburg, *Iowa* 61 N b
Shelter Cove, *California* 74 A d
Shelter I., *New York* 51 J c
Shelter Island, *New York* 51 J c
Shelton, *Connecticut* 50 G c
Shelton, *Nebraska* 60 F d
Shelton, *Washington* 73 G h
Shemya I., *Alaska* 76 K j
Shenandoah, *Iowa* 61 J d
Shenandoah, *Pennsylvania* 53 K e
Shenandoah, *Virginia* 52 H g
Shenandoah Junction, *West Virginia* 52 J f
Shenandoah Mts., *West Virginia* 52 G g
Shenandoah Nat. Park, *Virginia* 52 H g
Shenandoah R., *Virginia* 52 J f
Shenango R., *Pennsylvania* 52 F d
Shepherd, *Michigan* 56 J f
Shepherd, *Montana* 67 M d
Shepherd, *Texas* 65 M e
Shepherdstown, *West Virginia* 52 J f
Shepherdsville, *Kentucky* 57 H m
Sheppton, *Pennsylvania* 50 A d
Sherborn, *Massachusetts* 51 L a
Sherburne, *New York* 53 L c
Sheridan, *Arkansas* 63 L d
Sheridan, *Colorado* 69 O j
Sheridan, *Indiana* 57 G j
Sheridan, *Michigan* 56 H f
Sheridan, *Montana* 66 H d
Sheridan, Mt., *Wyoming* 67 K e
Sheridan, *Oregon* 73 G k
Sheridan, *Wyoming* 67 O e
Sheridan Lake, *Colorado* 69 O e
Sherman, *Connecticut* 50 G b
Sherman, *Mississippi* 63 P d
Sherman, *New York* 52 G c
Sherman, *Texas* 65 L b
Sherman Mills, *Maine* 49 G c
Sherman Mt., *Nevada* 74 K d
Sherman Pk., *Idaho* 66 J g
Sherman Res., *Nebraska* 60 F c
Sherrill, *New York* 53 L b
Sherwood, *North Dakota* 58 E b
Sherwood, *Texas* 64 G d

Spri UNITED STATES INDEX Tama

Springfield, Pennsylvania (26,733), vicinity of Philadelphia
Springfield, South Carolina 55 K d
Springfield, South Dakota 58 J h
Springfield, Tennessee 54 E a
Springfield, Vermont 49 C e
Spring Glen, New York 50 E b
Spring Green, Wisconsin 56 C f
Spring Grove, Minnesota 59 P g
Spring Grove, Pennsylvania 53 K f
Springhill, Louisiana 63 K f
Spring Hill, Tennessee 54 E b
Spring Hope, North Carolina 55 N b
Spring Lake, Michigan 56 G f
Spring Lake, New Jersey 50 E e
Springlake, Texas 64 E a
Spring Lake Park, Minnesota 59 Q h
Spring Mts., Nevada 75 K h
Spring R., Arkansas 63 M b
Spring R., Oklahoma 63 J b
Springs, New York 51 J c
Springton Res., Pennsylvania 50 B f
Springtown, Pennsylvania 50 C d
Springtown, Texas 65 K c
Springvale, Maine 49 E e
Spring Valley, Minnesota 59 O g
Spring Valley, New York 50 E c
Springview, Nebraska 60 E b
Springville, Alabama 54 E d
Springville, New York 52 H c
Springville, Utah 68 E c
Springwater, New York 52 J c
Spruce, Michigan 56 K e
Spruce Knob, West Virginia 52 G g
Spruce Pine, North Carolina 55 J b
Spruce Mt., Nevada 74 L d
Spruceton, New York 50 E a
Spry, Utah 68 D f
Spur, Texas 64 G b
Spurger, Texas 65 N e
Spur Lake, New Mexico 71 J f
Spurr, Mt., Alaska 76 L f
Squam L., New Hampshire 49 D e
Squantum, Massachusetts 49 H j
Squapan L., Maine 49 G b
Square Butte, Montana 67 K b
Square L., Maine 49 G a
Squaw Lake, Minnesota 59 M c
Squibnocket Pt., Massachusetts 51 M c
Squirrel R., Alaska 76 G c
Squirrel R., Alaska 77 Q d
Stattsburg, New York 50 F b
Stabler, Washington 73 J k
Stacy, California 74 E d
Stacy, North Carolina 55 P c
Stafford, Connecticut 51 J b
Stafford, Kansas 60 F g
Stafford, Nebraska 60 F b
Stafford, Texas 64 E j
Stafford, Virginia 52 J g
Stafford Springs, Connecticut 51 J b
Stalwart, Michigan 56 J c
Stamford, Connecticut (92,713) 50 F c
Stamford, New York 53 M c
Stamford, South Dakota 58 E g
Stamford, Texas 65 H c
Stampede, Washington 73 J h
Stamping Ground, Kentucky 57 J l
Stamps, Arkansas 63 K e
Stanardsville, Virginia 52 H g
Stanberry, Missouri 61 K d
Standard, Arizona 70 G e
Standish, Michigan 56 K f
Standley L., Colorado 69 O h
Standrod, Utah 68 C b
Stanfield, Oregon 73 L k
Stanford, Indiana 57 G k
Stanford, Kentucky 57 J m
Stanford, Montana 67 K b
Stanfordville, New York 50 F b
Stanhope, New Jersey 50 D d
Stanislaus R., California 74 E g
Stanley, Idaho 66 F e
Stanley, New Mexico 71 M d
Stanley, North Carolina 55 K b
Stanley, North Dakota 58 D b
Stanley, Oklahoma 62 H d
Stanley, Virginia 52 H g
Stanley, Wisconsin 56 C e
Stannard Rock, Michigan 56 F b
Stanton, Iowa 61 J d
Stanton, Kentucky 57 K m
Stanton, Michigan 56 H f
Stanton, Nebraska 60 G c
Stanton, North Dakota 58 E c
Stanton, Tennessee 54 B b
Stanton, Texas 64 F c
Stanwood, Michigan 56 H f
Stanwood, Washington 73 H g
Staples, Minnesota 59 M d
Stapleton, Alabama 54 D g
Stapleton, Georgia 55 J d
Stapleton, Nebraska 60 D c
Stapleton, New York 51 L g
Star, Mississippi 63 N f
Star, North Carolina 55 M b
Star, Texas 65 J d
Starbuck, Minnesota 59 L e
Starbuck, Washington 73 M j
Star City, Arkansas 63 M e
Star City, Indiana 57 G j
Star City, West Virginia 52 F f
Stark, Arizona 70 G h
Stark, Montana 66 F b
Stark, New Hampshire 49 D d
Starke, Florida 55 J h
Starkey, Idaho 66 D e
Starkey, Oregon 73 M k
Starks, Louisiana 63 K h
Starkville, Colorado 69 M f
Starkville, Mississippi 63 P e
Starkweather, North Dakota 58 H b
Starlake, Wisconsin 56 D c
Star Pk., Nevada 74 G d
Starr, Maryland 50 A h
State Center, Iowa 61 L b
State College, Pennsylvania 52 J e
State Line, Mississippi 63 P g
State Line, New York 50 G b
Staten I., New York 51 K g
Statesboro, Georgia 55 K e
Statesville, North Carolina 55 L b
Stauffer, Oregon 73 K m
Staunton, Illinois 57 D k
Staunton, Virginia 52 G g
Stayton, Oregon 73 H l
Steamboat, Nevada 74 F e
Steamboat, Oregon 73 H m
Steamboat Springs, Colorado 69 K c
Stearns, Kentucky 57 J n
Stebbins, Alaska 76 F e
Steel Creek, Alaska 77 R d
Steele, Alabama 54 E d
Steele, Missouri 61 P h
Steele, North Dakota 58 G d
Steele City, Nebraska 60 G d
Steele Valley, Illinois 57 D l
Steelton, Pennsylvania 53 K e
Steelville, Missouri 61 N g
Steens Mt., Oregon 73 M n
Stegall, Nebraska 60 A c
Steger, Illinois 57 F h
Steinauer, Nebraska 60 H d
Steinhatchee, Florida 54 H h
Steins, New Mexico 71 J g
Steliekin, Washington 73 K g
Stella, Nebraska 61 J d
Stella, North Carolina 55 O c
Steller, Mt., Alaska 77 Q f
Stem, North Carolina 55 N a
Stemplersville, Pennsylvania 50 B d
Stephen, Minnesota 59 K b
Stephens, Arkansas 63 K e
Stephens City, Virginia 52 H f
Stephenson, Michigan 56 F d
Stephens Pass, Alaska 77 V h
Stephenville, Texas 65 J c
Stepovak B., Alaska 76 H j
Steptoe, Nevada 74 L e
Sterley, Texas 64 F a
Sterling, Alaska 76 M f
Sterling, Colorado 69 N c
Sterling, Connecticut 51 K b
Sterling, Illinois 57 D h
Sterling, Kansas 60 F f
Sterling, Michigan 56 J e
Sterling, Mt., Kentucky 57 K l
Sterling, Nebraska 60 H d
Sterling, North Dakota 58 F d
Sterling, Oklahoma 62 E d
Sterling, Pennsylvania 50 C c
Sterling, Utah 68 E d
Sterling City, Texas 64 G d
Sterling Landing, Alaska 76 K e
Sterling Res., Colorado 69 N c
Steuben, Michigan 56 G c
Steuben, Wisconsin 56 C f
Steubenville, Ohio (32,495) 52 F e
Stevenson, Alabama 54 F c
Stevenson, Washington 73 J k
Stevens Pt., Wisconsin 56 D e
Stevens Village, Alaska 76 N c
Stevensville, Michigan 57 G g
Stevensville, Montana 66 F c
Steward, Illinois 57 E h
Stewardson, Illinois 57 E k
Stewart, Minnesota 59 M f
Stewart, Nevada 74 F e
Stewartstown, Pennsylvania 53 K f
Stewartsville, Missouri 61 K e
Stewartsville, New Jersey 50 C d
Stewartville, Minnesota 59 O g
Stibnite, Idaho 66 E e
Stickney, South Dakota 58 H g
Stigler, Oklahoma 62 H c
Stikine Str., Alaska 77 V h
Stiles, Texas 64 F d
Stilesville, Indiana 57 G k
Stillman Valley, Illinois 57 D g
Still Pond, Maryland 50 A g
Stillwater, Minnesota 59 O e
Stillwater, New Jersey 50 D c
Stillwater, Oklahoma 62 F b
Stillwater, Wisconsin 56 A d
Stillwater, Nevada 74 G e
Stillwater R., Montana 66 F a
Stillwater Ra., Nevada 74 G e
Stilwell, Oklahoma 63 J c
Stimson, Mt., Montana 66 G a
Stinnett, Texas 64 C h
Stirling City, California 74 D e
Stirum, North Dakota 58 J d
Stissing, New York 50 F b
Stites, Idaho 66 E c
Stitzer, Wisconsin 56 C g
Stockbridge, Massachusetts 50 G a
Stockbridge, Michigan 56 J g
Stockdale, Ohio 52 D g
Stockdale, Texas 65 K f
Stockertown, Pennsylvania 50 C d
Stockett, Montana 66 J b
Stockham, Nebraska 60 F d
Stockholm, Maine 49 G a
Stockholm, New Jersey 50 E c
Stockport, New York 50 F a
Stockport, Ohio 52 E f
Stockton, Alabama 54 D g
Stockton, California (86,321) 74 D g
Stockton, Illinois 56 C g
Stockton, Kansas 60 E e
Stockton, Maryland 53 L g
Stockton, Missouri 61 L g
Stockton, New Jersey 50 D e
Stockton, Utah 68 D c
Stockton I., Wisconsin 56 C c
Stockton Is., Alaska 77 O a
Stockton Springs, Maine 49 G d
Stockville, Nebraska 60 D d
Stoddard, Wisconsin 56 B f
Stokesdale, North Carolina 55 M a
Stone, Idaho 66 H g
Stoneboro, Pennsylvania 52 F d
Stone City, Colorado 69 M e
Stone Corral L., Oregon 73 L n
Stoneham, Colorado 69 N c
Stone Harbor, New Jersey 50 D g
Stone Lake, Wisconsin 56 B d
Stone Mountain, Georgia 54 G d
Stone Ridge, New York 50 E b
Stonersville, Pennsylvania 50 B e
Stones River Nat. Mil. Park, Tennessee 54 E b
Stoneville, Massachusetts 51 K a
Stonewall, Mississippi 63 P f
Stonewall, Oklahoma 62 G d
Stonewall, Texas 65 J e
Stonington, Colorado 69 O f
Stonington, Connecticut 51 K c
Stonington, Illinois 57 D k
Stonington, Maine 49 G d
Stony Brook, New York 50 G d
Stony Creek, Connecticut 51 H c
Stony Creek, Virginia 52 J j
Stonyford, California 74 C e
Stony Point, New York 50 E c
Stony Point, North Carolina 55 K b
Stony Pt., New York 53 K b
Stony R., Alaska 76 K f
Stony River, Alaska 76 J f
Storm L., Iowa 61 J b
Storm Lake, Iowa 61 J b
Stormville, New York 50 F b
Story, Wyoming 67 O e
Story City, Iowa 61 L b
Stotttville, New York 50 F a
Stoughton, Massachusetts 51 L a
Stoughton, Wisconsin 56 D g
Stoutsville, Ohio 52 D f
Stover, Missouri 61 M f
Stowe, Pennsylvania 53 O a
Stowe, Vermont 49 C d
Stowell, Texas 65 N f
Strafford, Missouri 61 L g
Straight Cliffs, Utah 68 E f
Strang, Nebraska 60 G d
Strasburg, Colorado 69 M d
Strasburg, Illinois 57 E k
Strasburg, North Dakota 58 F d
Strasburg, Ohio 52 E e
Strasburg, Pennsylvania 50 A f
Strasburg, Virginia 52 H g
Stratford, California 75 F h
Stratford, Connecticut (45,012) 50 G c
Stratford, New Hampshire 49 D d
Stratford, Iowa 61 L b
Stratford, Oklahoma 62 G d
Stratford, South Dakota 58 H e
Stratford, Texas 64 B g
Stratford, Wisconsin 56 C e
Stratford Pt., Connecticut 51 G c
Strathmere, New Jersey 50 D g
Stratton, Colorado 69 O d
Stratton, Maine 49 E c
Stratton, Nebraska 60 C d
Strauss, New Mexico 71 L h
Strausstown, Pennsylvania 50 A d
Straw, Montana 67 L c
Strawberry, Arkansas 63 M b
Strawberry, Nevada 74 K e
Strawberry Mt., Oregon 73 M l
Strawberry Point, Iowa 61 N b
Strawberry R., Utah 68 F c
Strawberry Res., Utah 68 E c
Strawn, Illinois 57 E j
Strawn, Texas 65 J c
Strawn Res., Kansas 61 J f
Streator, Illinois 57 E h
Streeter, North Dakota 58 G d
Streeter, Texas 65 H e
Streetman, Texas 65 L d
Strevell, Idaho 66 G g
Striker Creek Res., Texas 65 N d
Stringer, Mississippi 63 O g
Stringtown, Oklahoma 62 G d
Stromsburg, Nebraska 60 G c
Stroner, Wyoming 67 P e
Strong, Arkansas 63 L e
Strong, Maine 49 E d
Strong, Mississippi 63 P e
Strong City, Kansas 60 H f
Strong City, Oklahoma 62 D c
Stronghurst, Illinois 57 C j
Strongs, Michigan 56 J c
Strongsville, Ohio 52 E d
Strother, South Carolina 55 K c
Stroud, Oklahoma 62 G c
Stroudsburg, Pennsylvania 50 C d
Strum, Wisconsin 56 B e
Struthers, Ohio 52 F d
Stryker, Montana 66 F a
Stryker, Ohio 52 B d
Stuart, Florida 55 O f
Stuart, Iowa 61 K c
Stuart, Mt., Washington 73 K h
Stuart, Nebraska 60 E b
Stuart, Oklahoma 62 G d
Stuart, Virginia 52 F j
Stuart I., Alaska 76 F e
Studio City, California 75 D l
Stumpy Point, North Carolina 55 Q b
Sturbridge, Massachusetts 51 J a
Sturgeon, Missouri 61 M e
Sturgeon B., Michigan 56 H d
Sturgeon Bay, Wisconsin 56 F e
Sturgeon Bay Can., Wisconsin 56 F e
Sturgeon R., Michigan 56 G c
Sturgis, Kentucky 57 F m
Sturgis, Michigan 57 H h
Sturgis, Mississippi 63 O e
Sturgis, Oklahoma 62 A a
Sturgis, South Dakota 58 C f
Sturtevant, Wisconsin 56 E g
Stuttgart, Arkansas 63 M d
Stuttgart, Kansas 60 E e
Stuyvesant Falls, New York 50 F a
Suamico, Wisconsin 56 E e
Sublett, Idaho 66 G g
Sublette, Illinois 57 D h
Sublette, Kansas 60 D g
Sublime, Texas 65 L f
Success, Missouri 61 M g
Sucia I., Washington 73 H g
Sucker Cr., Oregon 73 N m
Suckling, C., Alaska 77 Q g
Sudan, Texas 64 E a
Sudbury Res., Massachusetts 51 K a
Suemez I., Alaska 77 V j
Sue Pk., Texas 64 D f
Suffern, New York 50 E c
Suffield, Connecticut 51 H b
Suffolk, Montana 67 L b
Suffolk, Virginia 53 K j
Sugar, Idaho 66 J f
Sugar City, Colorado 69 N e
Sugar Creek, Missouri 61 Q a
Sugar Grove, Pennsylvania 52 G d
Sugar Grove, Virginia 52 E j
Sugar I., Michigan 56 J c
Sugar Land, Texas 65 M f
Sugar Loaf, New York 50 E c
Sugarloaf Key, Florida 55 N j
Sugar R., Wisconsin 56 D g
Suiattle Pass, Washington 73 J g
Suitland, Maryland 53 K g
Sula, Montana 66 G d
Sulatna R., Alaska 76 K d
Sulligent, Alabama 54 C d
Sullivan, Illinois 57 E k
Sullivan, Indiana 57 F k
Sullivan, Missouri 61 N f
Sully, Iowa 61 M c
Sulphur, Louisiana 63 K h
Sulphur, Montana 67 K c
Sulphur, Nevada 74 G d
Sulphur, Oklahoma 62 G d
Sulphurdale, Utah 68 D e
Sulphur R., Arkansas 63 K e
Sulphur Springs, Texas 65 M b
Sulphur Springs Cr., Texas 64 F c
Sultan, Washington 73 J h
Sulukna R., Alaska 76 K e
Sulzer, Mt., Alaska 77 R f
Sumas, Washington 73 H g
Sumatra, Florida 54 G g
Sumatra, Montana 67 N c
Sumiton, Alabama 54 D d
Summerfield, Kansas 60 H e
Summerfield, Ohio 52 E f
Summerfield, Texas 64 B j
Summer I., Michigan 56 G d
Summer L., Oregon 73 K n
Summer Lake, Oregon 73 K n
Summer Shade, Kentucky 57 H n
Summer Str., Alaska 77 V h
Summersville, Missouri 61 N g
Summersville, West Virginia 52 F g
Summerton, South Carolina 55 L d
Summertown, Georgia 55 J e
Summerville, Georgia 54 F c
Summerville, Pennsylvania 52 G d
Summerville, South Carolina 55 L d
Summit, Alaska 76 N e
Summit, California 75 H k
Summit, Mississippi 63 N g
Summit, Montana 66 G a
Summit, New Jersey 50 E d
Summit, New Mexico 71 J g
Summit, Oregon 73 G l
Summit, South Dakota 59 K e
Summit, Utah 68 D f
Summit City, Michigan 56 H e
Summithill, Pennsylvania 50 B d
Summit L., Alaska 77 P e
Summit L., Nevada 74 F c
Summit Mt., Nevada 74 J e
Summit Pk., Colorado 69 K f
Summitville, Colorado 69 K f
Summitville, Indiana 57 H j
Summitville, New York 50 E b
Summitville, Tennessee 54 F b
Sumner, Illinois 57 E l
Sumner, Missouri 61 L e
Sumner, Iowa 61 M b
Sumpter, Oregon 73 M l
Sumrall, Mississippi 63 O g
Sumter, South Carolina 55 L d
Sunbeam, Colorado 68 H c
Sunbeam, Idaho 66 F e
Sunbright, Tennessee 54 G a
Sunburst, Montana 66 J a
Sunbury, North Carolina 55 P a
Sunbury, Ohio 52 D e
Sunbury, Pennsylvania 53 K e
Sun City, Kansas 60 F g
Suncook, New Hampshire 49 D e
Sundance, Wyoming 67 Q e
Sunderland, Massachusetts 49 C f
Sundown, New York 50 E b
Sundown, Texas 64 E b
Sunfield, Michigan 56 J g
Sunflower, Mississippi 63 N e
Sunflower R., Mississippi 63 N e
Sunglow, Arizona 70 H h
Sunman, Indiana 57 H k
Sunniland, Florida 55 N g
Sunny Isles, Florida 54 C c
Sunnyside, Nevada 74 K f
Sunny Side, Texas 64 F j
Sunnyside, Utah 68 F d
Sunnyside, Washington 73 L j
Sunnyvale, California (52,898), vicinity of San Francisco
Sun Prairie, Wisconsin 56 D f
Sun R., Montana 66 H b
Sunray, Texas 64 C g
Sunrise, Alaska 76 N f
Sunrise, Arizona 70 G d
Sunrise, Wyoming 67 Q g
Sun River, Montana 66 J b
Sunset, Louisiana 63 L h
Sunset, Texas 65 K b
Sunset Beach, California 75 F n
Sunset Crater Nat. Mon., Arizona 70 F d
Sunshine, Arizona 70 F d
Sunshine, Wyoming 67 L e
Suntrana, Alaska 77 N e
Sunup Plateau, Arizona 70 D d
Supai, Arizona 70 E c
Superior, Arizona 70 F f
Superior, Colorado 69 N g
Superior, L., United States-Canada 47 J a
Superior, Montana 66 F b
Superior, Nebraska 60 F d
Superior, Wisconsin (33,563) 56 A b
Superior, Wyoming 67 M h
Suplee, Oregon 73 L l
Suplee, Pennsylvania 50 B e
Suquamish, Washington 72 B h
Sur, Pt., California 75 D h
Surf, California 75 E k
Surf City, New Jersey 50 E f
Surfside, Florida 54 C d
Suring, Wisconsin 56 E d
Surprise, Nebraska 60 G c
Surrency, Georgia 55 J f
Surrey, North Dakota 58 E b
Surry, Virginia 53 K h
Survey Pass, Alaska 76 K c
Susan R., California 74 E d
Susanville, California 74 E d
Susanville, Oregon 73 M l
Susitna, Alaska 76 M f
Susitna L., Alaska 77 O e
Susitna R., Alaska 76 M e
Susquehanna, Pennsylvania 53 L d
Susquehanna R., New York 53 L c
Susquehanna R., Pennsylvania 53 K e
Sussex, New Jersey 50 D c
Sussex, Wyoming 67 O f
Susulatna R., Alaska 76 K e
Sutherland, Iowa 61 J b
Sutherland, Nebraska 60 C c
Sutherland Res., Nebraska 60 C c
Sutherlin, Oregon 73 G m
Sutter Creek, California 74 E f
Sutton, Massachusetts 51 K a
Sutton, Nebraska 60 G d
Sutton, North Dakota 58 H c
Sutton Res., West Virginia 52 F g
Sutwik I., Alaska 76 J h
Suwannee, Florida 54 H h
Suwannee R., Georgia 55 J g
Suwannee R., Florida 54 H h
Suwannee Sd., Florida 54 H h
Suwanoochee Cr., Georgia 55 J g
Svensen, Oregon 73 G j
Swainsboro, Georgia 55 J e
Swallows, Colorado 69 M e
Swan L., Montana 66 G b
Swan L., South Dakota 58 G e
Swan L., Utah 68 D d
Swan Lake, Montana 66 G b
Swan Lake, New York 50 D b
Swannanoa, North Carolina 55 J b
Swanquarter, North Carolina 55 P b
Swan R., Montana 66 G b
Swan River, Minnesota 59 N c
Swansboro, North Carolina 55 O c
Swansea, Arizona 70 D e
Swansea, Massachusetts 51 L b
Swansea, South Carolina 55 K d
Swans I., Maine 49 G d
Swanson Res., Nebraska 60 C d
Swanton, Nebraska 60 G d
Swanton, Ohio 52 C d
Swanton, Vermont 49 B d
Swan Valley, Idaho 66 J f
Swanville, Minnesota 59 M e
Swarthmore, Pennsylvania 50 C f
Swartswood, New Jersey 50 D c
Swasey Pk., Utah 68 C d
Swea City, Iowa 61 K a
Swedesboro, New Jersey 50 C f
Sweeny, Texas 65 M f
Sweet, Idaho 66 D f
Sweetgrass, Montana 66 J a
Sweet Home, Arkansas 63 L d
Sweet Home, Oregon 73 H l
Sweet Home, Texas 65 L f
Sweet Springs, Missouri 61 L f
Sweet Valley, Pennsylvania 50 A c
Sweetwater, Oklahoma 62 D c
Sweetwater, Tennessee 54 G b
Sweetwater, Texas 64 G c
Sweetwater R., Wyoming 67 M g
Swenson, Texas 64 G b
Swifton, Arkansas 63 M c
Swift R., Alaska 76 K f
Swift R., Maine 49 E d
Swift Res., Washington 73 H j
Swiftwater, Pennsylvania 50 C c
Swinburne I., New York 51 L g
Swinging Bridge Res., New York 50 D b
Swink, Colorado 69 N e
Swissvale, Pennsylvania 53 Q b
Sybille Cr., Wyoming 67 P h
Sycamore, Alabama 54 E d
Sycamore, Illinois 57 E h
Sycamore, Ohio 52 C e
Sycamore, South Carolina 55 K d
Sykeston, North Dakota 58 G c
Sykesville, Maryland 53 K f
Sykesville, Pennsylvania 52 H d
Sylacanga, Alabama 54 E d
Sylamore, Arkansas 63 L c
Sylva, North Carolina 54 H b
Sylvan, Pennsylvania 52 H f
Sylvan Grove, Kansas 60 F e
Sylvania, Georgia 55 K e
Sylvania, Ohio 52 C d
Sylvan Pass, Wyoming 67 L e
Sylvester, Georgia 54 H f
Sylvester, Texas 64 G c
Sylvia, Kansas 60 F g
Syosset, New York 50 G d
Syracuse, Indiana 57 H h
Syracuse, Kansas 60 C g
Syracuse, Nebraska 60 H d
Syracuse, New York (216,038) 53 K b
Syracuse, Utah 68 D b
Sysladobsis L., Maine 49 G c
Tabernacle, New Jersey 50 D f
Tabiona, Utah 68 F c
Table Mt., Alaska 77 Q b
Tablerock Res., Missouri 61 L h
Tabor, Iowa 61 J d
Tabor, South Dakota 58 J h
Tabor City, North Carolina 55 N c
Tacna, Arizona 70 D g
Tacoma, Washington (147,979) 73 H h
Tafoya, New Mexico 71 N c
Taft, California 75 F j
Taft, Oklahoma 62 H c
Taft, Texas 65 K h
Tafton, Pennsylvania 50 C c
Taftville, Connecticut 51 J b
Tagagawik R., Alaska 76 H d
Tagalak I., Alaska 77 P j
Tagus, North Dakota 58 E b
Tahlequah, Oklahoma 63 J c
Tahoe, L., California-Nevada 74 E e
Tahoe City, California 74 E e
Tahoe Valley, California 74 E f
Tahoka, Texas 64 F b
Taholah, Washington 73 F h
Tahquamenon Falls, Michigan 56 H c
Tahquamenon R., Michigan 56 H c
Taiban, New Mexico 71 O e
Tailings Pond, Utah 68 B h
Tajique, New Mexico 71 L e
Takilma, Oregon 73 G n
Takoma Park, Maryland 53 Q g
Takotna, Alaska 76 J e
Takslesluk, Alaska 76 F f
Taku Glacier, Alaska 77 U g
Taku Harbor, Alaska 77 V g
Talala, Oklahoma 62 H b
Talbot I., Florida 55 K g
Talbotton, Georgia 54 G e
Talco, Texas 65 M b
Talcott, West Virginia 52 F h
Talent, Oregon 73 H n
Talihina, Oklahoma 62 H d
Talkeetna, Alaska 76 N e
Talkeetna Mts., Alaska 77 N e
Talkeetna R., Alaska 77 N e
Talladega, Alabama 54 E d
Tallahala R., Mississippi 63 O g
Tallahassee, Florida (48,174) 54 G g
Tallahatchie R., Mississippi 63 N d
Tallapoosa, Georgia 54 F d
Tallapoosa R., Alabama 54 E e
Tallassee, Alabama 54 F e
Tallula, Illinois 57 D k
Tallulah, Louisiana 63 M f
Talmage, California 74 B e
Talmage, Kansas 60 G e
Talmage, Nebraska 61 H d
Taloga, Oklahoma 62 E b
Talpa, New Mexico 71 M c
Talpa, Texas 65 H d
Talquin, L., Florida 54 G g
Tama, Iowa 61 M c
Tamaqua, Pennsylvania 50 B d
Tamarack, Idaho 66 D e
Tamarack, Minnesota 59 N d
Tamarack Landing, Alaska 76 K d
Tamaroa, Illinois 57 D l

Tulsa, Oklahoma (261,685) 62 H b
Tuluksak, Alaska 76 G f
Tumacacori Nat. Mon., Arizona 70 G h
Tumalo, Oregon 73 J l
Tumbledown Mt., Maine 49 E c
Tungsten, Nevada 74 G d
Tunica, Mississippi 63 N d
Tunkhannock, Pennsylvania 53 K d
Tunnelton, West Virginia 52 G f
Tuntatuliag, Alaska 76 F f
Tuolumne Meadows, California 74 F g
Tuolumne R., California 74 E g
Tupelo, Mississippi 63 P d
Tupelo, Oklahoma 62 G d
Tupman, California 75 F j
Tupper L., New York 53 M a
Tupper Lake, New York 53 M a
Turin, New York 53 L b
Turkey, Texas 64 D j
Turkey Cr., Michigan 57 L k
Turkey Mts., New Mexico 71 N d
Turkey Pt., Maryland 50 A g
Turkey R., Iowa 61 N b
Turlock, California 74 E g
Turlock L., California 74 E g
Turner, Kansas 61 O a
Turner, Maine 49 E d
Turner, Michigan 56 K e
Turner, Montana 67 M a
Turner, Oregon 73 H l
Turner, Washington 37 N j
Turnercrest, Wyoming 67 P f
Turners Falls, Massachusetts 49 C f
Turnerville, New Jersey 50 C f
Turnerville, Wyoming 67 K g
Turnwood, New York 50 D a
Turon, Kansas 60 F g
Turpin, Oklahoma 62 C b
Turquoise, New Mexico 71 M g
Turquoise L., Alaska 76 K f
Turrell, Arkansas 63 N c
Turtle Creek, Pennsylvania 53 R b
Turtle L., Minnesota 59 Q h
Turtle Lake, North Dakota 58 F c
Turtle Lake, Wisconsin 56 A d
Turton, South Dakota 58 H e
Tusayan, Arizona 70 E d
Tuscaloosa, Alabama (63,370) 54 D d
Tuscarawas R., Ohio 52 E e
Tuscarora, Nevada 74 J c
Tuscarora, Pennsylvania 50 A d
Tuscarora Mt., Pennsylvania 52 J e
Tuscola, Illinois 57 E k
Tuscola, Texas 65 H c
Tuscor, Montana 66 E b
Tuscumbia, Alabama 54 D c
Tuscumbia, Missouri 61 M f
Tuskegee, Alabama 54 F e
Tussey Mt., Pennsylvania 52 H e
Tustin, California 75 H l
Tustin, Michigan 56 H e
Tustumena I., Alaska 76 M f
Tuthill, South Dakota 58 E g
Tuttle, Idaho 66 F g
Tuttle, North Dakota 58 F c
Tuttle, Oklahoma 62 F c
Tuttle Creek Res., Kansas 60 H e
Tuttle L., Minnesota 59 M g
Tutwiler, Mississippi 63 N d
Tuweep, Arizona 70 D c
Tuxedni B., Alaska 76 L f
Tuxedo, North Carolina 55 J b
Tuxedo Park, New York 50 E c
Tuzigoot Nat. Mon., Arizona 70 F e
Twelvemile Summit, Alaska 77 P d
Twentynine Palms, California 75 K k
Twin, Washington 73 G g
Twin Bridges, Montana 66 H d
Twin Brooks, South Dakota 59 K e
Twin Falls, Idaho 66 F g
Twin L., Michigan 56 J e
Twin Lake, Michigan 56 G f
Twin Lakes, Colorado 69 K d
Twin Lakes, Pennsylvania 50 D c
Twin Lakes Res., Idaho 66 F f
Twin Ls., Alaska 76 K f
Twin Mountain, New Hampshire 49 D d
Twin Pk., California 74 E e
Twin Pks., California 75 B l
Twin Pks., Idaho 66 F e
Twin Pks., Utah 68 D j
Twin Valley, Minnesota 59 K c
Twisp, Washington 73 K g
Twitty, Texas 64 D h
Two Buttes, Colorado 69 O f
Two Butte Cr., Colorado 69 O f
Twodot, Montana 67 K c
Two Harbors, Minnesota 59 P c
Two Headed I., Alaska 76 L h
Two Ocean Pass, Wyoming 67 K e
Two Rivers, Wisconsin 56 F e
Tybee Roads, South Carolina 55 L e
Tybo, Nevada 74 J f
Tyee, Washington 73 F g
Tye River, Virginia 52 H h
Tygart, R., West Virginia 52 G g
Tygart Res., West Virginia 52 G f
Tyhee, Idaho 66 H g
Tyler, L., Texas 65 M c
Tyler, Minnesota 59 K f
Tyler, Pennsylvania 52 H d
Tyler, Texas (51,230) 65 M c
Tyler, Washington 73 N h
Tylertown, Mississippi 63 N g
Tyndall, South Dakota 58 J g
Tyonek, Alaska 76 M f
Tyone R., Alaska 77 O e
Tyringham, Massachusetts 50 G a
Tyrone, New Mexico 71 J g
Tyrone, Pennsylvania 52 H e
Ualik, L., Alaska 76 H g
Ubly, Michigan 56 L f
Ucon, Idaho 66 J f
Ucross, Wyoming 67 O e
Uehling, Nebraska 60 H c
Ugaiushak I., Alaska 76 J h
Ugak B., Alaska 76 L h
Ugak I., Alaska 76 L h
Ugamak I., Alaska 76 E j
Uganik I., Alaska 76 L h
Ugashik, Alaska 76 J h
Ugashik B., Alaska 76 J h
Ugashik Ls., Alaska 76 J h
Uhlerstown, Pennsylvania 50 C d
Uhrichsville, Ohio 52 E e
Uinkaret Plateau, Arizona 70 D c
Uinta Mts., Utah 68 F c
Ukiah, California 74 B e
Ukiah, Oregon 73 M k
Ulak I., Alaska 77 N j
Ulen, Minnesota 59 K c
Uliaga I., Alaska 77 T h
Ullin, Illinois 57 D m
Ulm, Arkansas 63 M c
Ulm, Montana 66 J b
Ulm, Wyoming 67 O e
Ulster, Pennsylvania 53 K d
Ulster Park, New York 50 F b
Ulysses, Idaho 66 F d
Ulysses, Kansas 60 C g
Ulysses, Nebraska 60 G c
Umak I., Alaska 77 P j
Umatilla, Florida 55 K j
Umatilla, Oregon 73 L k
Umatilla R., Oregon 73 L k
Umatilla Reef, Washington 73 F g
Umbagog L., New Hampshire 49 D d
Umbarger, Texas 64 B j
Umiat, Alaska 76 L b
Umnak I., Alaska 76 C k
Umnak Pass, Alaska 76 D k
Umpqua R., Oregon 73 G m
Unadilla, Georgia 54 H e
Unadilla, New York 53 L c
Unadilla R., New York 53 L c
Unalakleet, Alaska 76 G e
Unalakleet R., Alaska 76 G e
Unalaska, Alaska 76 D k
Unalaska I., Alaska 76 D k
Unalga I., Alaska 76 D k
Unalga I., Alaska 77 N j
Uncasville, Connecticut 51 J c
Uncompahgre Pk., Colorado 69 J e
Uncompahgre Plateau, Colorado 68 H e
Underwood, Iowa 61 J c
Underwood, Minnesota 59 L d
Underwood, North Dakota 58 E c
Unga, Alaska 76 G j
Ungalik, Alaska 76 G d
Ungalik R., Alaska 76 G d
Unicoi, Tennessee 55 J a
Unimak, Alaska 76 E j
Unimak B., Alaska 76 E j
Unimak I., Alaska 76 E j
Unimak Pass, Alaska 76 E j
Union, Colorado 69 N c
Union, Connecticut 51 J b
Union, Iowa 61 L b
Union, Louisiana 63 N h
Union, Maine 49 F d
Union, Mississippi 63 O f
Union, Missouri 61 N f
Union, Mt., Arizona 70 E e
Union, Nebraska 61 J d
Union, New Jersey (51,499) 50 E d
Union, New Mexico 71 L h
Union, Oregon 73 N k
Union, South Carolina 55 K c
Union, Utah 68 C j
Union, West Virginia 52 F h
Union Beach, New Jersey 50 E e
Union Bridge, Maryland 53 J f
Union Center, Wisconsin 56 C f
Union Church, Mississippi 63 N g
Union City, Michigan 57 H g
Union City, New Jersey (52,180) 50 E d
Union City, Oklahoma 62 F c
Union City, Ohio 52 B e
Union City, Pennsylvania 52 G d
Union City, Tennessee 54 B a
Union Creek, Oregon 73 H n
Uniondale, Pennsylvania 53 L d
Union Flat Cr., Washington 73 N j
Union Gap, Washington 73 K j
Union L., New Jersey 50 C g
Union L., Washington 72 B h
Union Mills, North Carolina 55 K b
Union Pass, Wyoming 67 L f
Union Point, Georgia 54 H d
Union Res., Missouri 61 N f
Union Springs, Alabama 54 F e
Union Springs, New York 53 K c
Union Star, Missouri 61 K e
Uniontown, Alabama 54 D e
Uniontown, Kentucky 57 F m
Uniontown, Pennsylvania 52 G f
Unionville, Connecticut 51 H b
Unionville, Iowa 61 M d
Unionville, Michigan 56 K f
Unionville, Missouri 61 L d
Unionville, Nevada 74 G d
Unionville, Pennsylvania 50 B f
Unionville, Virginia 52 J g
Unita R., Utah 68 F c
U. S. Atomic Energy Commission Reserve, Idaho 66 H f
U. S. Atomic Energy Commission Reserve, Washington 73 L j
Unity, Maine 49 F d
Unity, Oregon 73 M l
Unity, Pennsylvania 53 R a
Unity Village, Missouri 61 Q b
Universal, Pennsylvania 53 R b
University, Mississippi 63 O d
University City, Missouri (51,249) 63 O d
University Park, Texas 65 N j
Unuk R., Alaska 77 W h
Upalco, Utah 68 F c
Upham, North Dakota 58 F b
Upland, California 75 H k
Upland, Indiana 57 H j
Upland, Nebraska 60 F d
Upnuk L., Alaska 76 H f
Upolu Pt., Hawaii 72 E e
Upper Alkali L., California 74 E c
Upper Arlington, Ohio (28,486), vicinity of Columbus
Upper Black Eddy, Pennsylvania 50 C d
Upper Darby, Pennsylvania (40,000), vicinity of Philadelphia
Upper Iowa R., Iowa 61 N a
Upper Klamath L., Oregon 73 J n
Upper Lake, California 74 C e
Upper Lehigh, Pennsylvania 50 B c
Upper Lehigh Junction, Pennsylvania 50 B c
Upper Marlboro, Maryland 53 K g
Upper New York B., New York 51 L f
Upper Red Hook, New York 50 F a
Upper Red L., Minnesota 59 M b
Upper Red Rock L., Montana 66 J e
Upper Sandusky, Ohio 52 C e
Upper Saranac L., New York 53 M a
Upper Tract, West Virginia 52 G g
Upperville, Virginia 52 J f
Upright, C., Alaska 76 A f
Upsala, Minnesota 59 M e
Upson, Wisconsin 56 C c
Upton, Kentucky 57 H m
Upton, Maine 49 E d
Upton, Massachusetts 51 K a
Upton, New Jersey 50 D f
Upton, Wyoming 67 Q e
Ural, Montana 66 E a
Urania, Louisiana 63 L g
Urbana, Illinois (27,294) 57 E j
Urbana, Indiana 57 H j
Urbana, Iowa 61 N b
Urbana, Missouri 61 L g
Urbana, Ohio 52 C e
Urbanna, Virginia 53 K h
Uriah, Alabama 54 D f
Urich, Missouri 61 K f
Urie, Wyoming 67 K h
Ursa, Illinois 57 B j
Ursine, Nevada 74 L g
Ushagat I., Alaska 76 L g
Usk, Washington 73 N g
Utah 68
Utah L., Utah 68 E c
Ute, Iowa 61 J b
Ute Cr., New Mexico 71 O d
Ute Park, New Mexico 71 M c
Utley, Texas 65 K e
Utleyville, Colorado 69 N f
Utica, Kansas 60 D f
Utica, Michigan 56 K g
Utica, Minnesota 59 P g
Utica, Mississippi 63 N f
Utica, Missouri 61 L e
Utica, Montana 67 K c
Utica, Nebraska 60 G d
Utica, New York (100,410) 53 L b
Utica, Ohio 52 D e
Utopia, Texas 65 H f
Utukok R., Alaska 76 G b
Uva, Wyoming 67 Q g
Uvada, Nevada 74 L e
Uvalda, Georgia 55 J e
Uvalde, Texas 65 H f
Uwekahuna, mt., Hawaii 72 E f
Uxbridge, Massachusetts 51 K a
Uyak B., Alaska 76 L h
Uzinki, Alaska 76 L h
Vacaville, California 74 C f
Vader, Washington 73 H j
Vadito, New Mexico 71 M c
Vadnais, L., Minnesota 59 R h
Vaiden, Mississippi 63 O e
Vail, Arizona 70 G g
Vails Gate, New York 50 E c
Valatie, New York 53 N c
Valders, Wisconsin 56 F e
Valdese, North Carolina 55 K b
Valdez, Alaska 77 O f
Valdez, Colorado 69 M f
Valdosta, Georgia (30,652) 54 H g
Vale, Oregon 73 N m
Vale, South Dakota 58 C f
Valentine, Arizona 70 D d
Valentine, Louisiana 63 N j
Valentine, Montana 67 M b
Valentine, Nebraska 60 D b
Valentine, Texas 64 C e
Valera, Texas 65 H d
Valhalla, New York 50 F c
Valiant, Oklahoma 62 H e
Valier, Montana 66 H a
Valle, Arizona 70 E d
Vallecito Mts., California 75 J l
Vallecito Res., Colorado 69 J f
Vallecitos, New Mexico 71 L c
Vallejo, California (60,877) 74 C f
Valley, Mississippi 63 N f
Valley, Wyoming 67 L e
Valley Center, Kansas 60 G g
Valley City, North Dakota 58 J d
Valley Falls, Kansas 61 J e
Valley Falls, Oregon 73 K n
Valley Forge, Pennsylvania 50 B e
Valley Head, Alabama 54 F c
Valley Head, West Virginia 52 F g
Valley Mills, Texas 65 K d
Valley of 10,000 Smokes, Alaska 76 K g
Valley Park, Missouri 61 O f
Valley Pass, Nevada 74 L c
Valley Station, Kentucky 57 H l
Valley Stream, New York (38,629) 50 F d
Valley View, Texas 65 K b
Vallonia, Indiana 57 G l
Valmont, New Mexico 71 M g
Valmy, Nevada 74 H d
Valparaiso, Florida 54 E g
Valparaiso, Indiana 57 F h
Valparaiso, Nebraska 60 H c
Valsetz, Oregon 73 G l
Val Verda, Utah 68 C g
Van, Texas 65 M c
Van Alstyne, Texas 65 L b
Vananda, Montana 67 N c
Van Buren, Arkansas 63 J c
Van Buren, Indiana 57 H j
Van Buren, Maine 49 G a
Van Buren, Missouri 61 N h
Vanceboro, Maine 49 H c
Vanceboro, North Carolina 55 O b
Vanceburg, Kentucky 57 K l
Vancouver, C., Alaska 76 E f
Vancouver, Washington (32,464) 73 H k
Vandalia, Illinois 57 E l
Vandalia, Missouri 61 N e
Vandemere, North Carolina 55 P b
Vanderbilt, Michigan 56 J d
Vanderbilt, Texas 65 L g
Vandergrift, Pennsylvania 52 G e
Vandervoort, Arkansas 63 J d
Vanduser, Missouri 61 P h
Van Duzen R., California 74 A d
Van Etten, New York 53 K c
Van Hiseville, New Jersey 50 E e
Van Hook, North Dakota 58 D c
Van Horn, Texas 64 C d
Van Houten, New Mexico 71 N c
Van Metre, South Dakota 58 F f
Vanoss, Oklahoma 62 G d
Vansant, Virginia 52 D h
Vantage, Washington 73 L j
Van Tassell, Nebraska 60 A b
Van Tassell, Wyoming 67 Q g
Van Wert, Iowa 61 L d
Van Wert, Ohio 52 B e
Vanzant, Missouri 61 M h
Vardaman, Mississippi 63 O e
Varina, North Carolina 55 N b
Varnado, Louisiana 63 O h
Varney, New Mexico 71 M e
Varnville, South Carolina 55 K e
Vashon, Washington 72 B j
Vashon Heights, Washington 72 B j
Vashon I., Washington 73 H h
Vashon I., Washington 72 B j
Vashti, North Dakota 58 G c
Vashti, Texas 65 J b
Vass, North Carolina 55 M b
Vassar, Michigan 56 K f
Vaucluse, South Carolina 55 K d
Vaughn, Montana 66 J b
Vaugn, New Mexico 71 M e
Veblen, South Dakota 58 J e
Veedersburg, Indiana 57 F j
Vega, New York 50 E a
Vega, Texas 64 B h
Vega Pt., Alaska 76 L j
Veguita, New Mexico 71 L e
Velarde, New Mexico 71 M c
Velasco, Texas 65 M g
Velva, North Dakota 58 F b
Venango, Nebraska 60 B d
Venator, Oregon 73 M m
Venetie, Alaska 77 O c
Venetie Landing, Alaska 77 O c
Veniaminof Vol., Alaska 76 H h
Venice, California 75 D m
Venice, Florida 55 M f
Venice, Illinois 61 Q d
Venice, Louisiana 63 O j
Venlo, North Dakota 58 J d
Ventnor, New Jersey 50 E g
Ventura, California (29,114) 75 F k
Venturia, North Dakota 58 G e
Venus, Florida 55 N f
Venus, Texas 65 K c
Vera, Texas 65 H b
Verbank, New York 50 F b
Verbena, Alabama 54 E e
Verde Hot Springs, Arizona 70 F e
Verdel, Nebraska 60 F b
Verden, Oklahoma 62 E c
Verde R., Arizona 70 F e
Verdi, California 74 E e
Verdigre, Nebraska 60 F b
Verdigris L., Oklahoma 62 H b
Verdigris R., Kansas 61 J g
Verdon, Nebraska 61 J d
Verendrye Nat. Mon., North Dakota 58 D c
Vergas, Minnesota 59 L d
Vergennes, Vermont 49 B d
Vermilion, Illinois 57 F k
Vermilion, Ohio 52 D d
Vermilion B., Louisiana 63 M j
Vermilion Cliffs, Utah 68 D f
Vermilion L., Minnesota 59 O c
Vermilion R., Louisiana 63 L h
Vermilion Ra., Minnesota 59 O c
Vermillion, Kansas 60 H e
Vermillion, South Dakota 59 K h
Vermillion R., Illinois 57 E h
Vermillion R., South Dakota 59 K h
Vermont 49
Vermont, Illinois 57 C j
Vernal, Utah 68 G c
Vernalis, California 74 D g
Verne, Wyoming 67 K h
Vernon, Alabama 54 C d
Vernon, Arizona 70 H e
Vernon, Colorado 69 O d
Vernon, Connecticut 51 J b
Vernon, Florida 54 F g
Vernon, Indiana 57 H l
Vernon, New Jersey 50 E c
Vernon, New York 53 L b
Vernon, Utah 68 D c
Vernon, Vermont 49 C f
Vernon, Texas 65 H a
Vernonia, Oregon 73 G k
Vero Beach, Florida 55 O f
Verona, Missouri 61 L h
Verona, New Jersey 51 J e
Verona, North Dakota 58 H d
Verona, Pennsylvania 53 R a
Verona, Wisconsin 56 D g
Verona, Wyoming 67 O e
Verplanck, New York 50 F c
Verret, L., Louisiana 63 M j
Versailles, Indiana 57 H k
Versailles, Kentucky 57 J l
Versailles, Missouri 61 M f
Versailles, Ohio 52 B e
Vesper, Kansas 60 F e
Vesper, Wisconsin 56 D e
Vesta, Minnesota 59 L f
Vestal Center, New York 53 L c
Vetal, South Dakota 58 E g
Veteran, New York 50 F a
Veteran, Wyoming 67 Q h
Vevay, Indiana 57 H l
Veyo, Utah 68 C f
Vian, Oklahoma 63 J c
Viborg, South Dakota 58 J g
Vici, Oklahoma 62 D b
Vicksburg, Arizona 70 D f
Vicksburg, Michigan 57 H g
Vicksburg, Mississippi (29,143) 63 N f
Vicksburg Nat. Mil. Park, Mississippi 63 N f
Victor, Colorado 69 L e
Victor, Idaho 66 J f
Victor, Iowa 61 M c
Victor, Montana 66 F c
Victor, New York 52 J c
Victoria, Kansas 60 E f
Victoria, Texas (33,047) 65 K g
Victoria, Virginia 52 H j
Victorville, California 75 H k
Vida, Montana 67 P b
Vida, Oregon 73 H l
Vidal, California 75 L k
Vidalia, Georgia 55 J e
Vidalia, Louisiana 63 M g
Vidauri, Texas 65 K g
Vienna, Georgia 54 H e
Vienna, Illinois 57 E m
Vienna, Maryland 53 L g
Vienna, Missouri 61 N f
Vienna, New Jersey 50 D d
Vienna, South Dakota 58 J f
Vienna, Virginia 53 J g
Vienna, West Virginia 52 E f
View, Texas 64 H c
Vilas, Colorado 69 O f
Vilas, Florida 54 G g
Village Cr., Texas 65 N e
Village Mills, Texas 65 N e
Villa Grove, Illinois 57 E k
Villanueva, New Mexico 71 M d
Villa Rica, Georgia 54 G d
Villas, New Jersey 50 D g
Villas, South Dakota 58 J g
Ville Platte, Louisiana 63 L h
Villisca, Iowa 61 K d
Vina, Alabama 54 C c
Vina, California 74 C e
Vinalhaven, Maine 49 G d
Vincennes, Indiana 57 F l
Vincent, Alabama 54 E d
Vincent, Ohio 52 E f
Vincent, Texas 64 F c
Vicente, Pt., California 75 G l
Vincentown, New Jersey 50 D f
Vineland, New Jersey (37,685) 50 C g
Vineyard Haven, Massachusetts 51 M c
Vineyard Sd., Massachusetts 51 M c
Vining, Minnesota 59 L d
Vinita, Oklahoma 62 H b
Vinland, Washington 72 A g
Vinson, Oklahoma 62 D d
Vinton, Iowa 61 M b
Vinton, Louisiana 63 K h
Vinton, Ohio 52 D g
Vinton, Virginia 52 G h
Viola, California 74 D d
Viola, Delaware 50 B g
Viola, Idaho 66 D c
Viola, Illinois 57 C h
Viola, Kansas 60 G g
Viola, Wisconsin 56 C f
Viola, Wyoming 67 K g
Virden, Illinois 57 D k
Virgelle, Montana 67 K a
Virgil, Kansas 61 H g
Virgil, South Dakota 58 H f
Virgilia, California 74 D d
Virgilina, Virginia 52 H j
Virginia 52-53
Virginia, Idaho 66 H g
Virginia, Illinois 57 C k
Virginia, Minnesota 59 O c
Virginia, Nebraska 60 H d
Virginia Beach, Virginia 53 K j
Virginia City, Montana 66 J d
Virginia City, Nevada 74 F e
Virginia Key, Florida 54 C d
Virgin Mts., Arizona 70 D c
Virgin Mts., Nevada 75 L h
Virgin R., Arizona 70 D c
Viroqua, Wisconsin 56 C f
Visalia, California 75 F h
Vista, California 75 H l
Vista Res., Nevada 74 K c
Vivian, Louisiana 63 K f
Vivian, South Dakota 58 F g
Voca, Texas 65 H d
Voda, Kansas 60 D e
Volborg, Montana 67 P d
Volcano, Colorado 69 K c
Volga, Iowa 61 N b
Volga, South Dakota 58 J f
Volga R., Iowa 61 N b
Volin, South Dakota 58 J h
Volney, Michigan 56 G f
Volta, California 75 D g
Voltaire, North Dakota 58 F b
Voluntown, Connecticut 51 K b
Vona, Colorado 69 O d
Von Frank Mt., Alaska 76 K e
Votaw, Texas 65 N e
Voth, Texas 65 N e
Vsevidof, Mt., Alaska 76 C k
Vulture Mts., Arizona 70 E f
Vya, Nevada 74 F c
Wabash, Arkansas 63 N d
Wabash, Indiana 57 H j
Wabasha, Minnesota 59 O f
Wabash R., Indiana 57 F l
Wabasso, Florida 55 O f
Wabasso, Minnesota 59 L f
Wabeno, Wisconsin 56 E d
Wabuska, Nevada 74 F e
Wacasassa B., Florida 55 J h
Waccamaw, L., North Carolina 55 N c
Waccamaw R., North Carolina 55 N c
Wachapreague, Virginia 53 L h
Wachusett Res., Massachusetts 49 D f
Wacker, Alaska 77 W j
Waco, Nebraska 60 G d
Waco, Texas (97,808) 65 K d
Waconia, Minnesota 59 N f
Waddington, New York 53 L a
Waddy, Kentucky 57 H l
Wade, North Carolina 55 N b
Wadena, Minnesota 59 L d
Wadesboro, North Carolina 55 L c
Wading R., New Jersey 50 D f
Wading River, New York 51 H d
Wadley, Alabama 54 F d
Wadley, Georgia 55 J e
Wadsworth, Nevada 74 F e
Wadsworth, Ohio 52 E d
Waelder, Texas 65 K f
Wagarville, Alabama 54 C f
Wagner, Montana 67 M a
Wagner, South Dakota 58 H g
Wagners, Pennsylvania 50 B c
Wagoner, Oklahoma 62 H c
Wagon Mound, New Mexico 71 N c
Wagon Wheel Gap, Colorado 69 K f
Wagontire, Oregon 73 L m
Wagram, North Carolina 55 M c
Waha, Idaho 66 D c
Wahiawa, Hawaii 72 C d
Wahoo, Nebraska 60 H c
Wahpeton, North Dakota 59 K d
Wah Wah Mts., Utah 68 C e
Waiahukini, Hawaii 72 E f
Waiakoa, Hawaii 72 D e
Waialua, Hawaii 72 C d
Waianae, Hawaii 72 C d
Waiateale, mt., Hawaii 72 B c
Waikane, Hawaii 72 C d
Waikii, Hawaii 72 E f
Wailuku, Hawaii 72 D e
Waimanalo, Hawaii 72 C d
Waimea, I. of Hawaii, Hawaii 72 E e
Waimea, I. of Kauai, Hawaii 72 B d
Waimea, I. of Oahu, Hawaii 72 C d

Wainiha, *Hawaii* 72 B c
Wainola, *Michigan* 56 E c
Wainwright, *Alaska* 76 G a
Waiohinu, *Hawaii* 72 E f
Waipahu, *Hawaii* 72 C d
Waipio, *Hawaii* 72 E e
Waitsburg, *Washington* 73 M j
Wakarusa, *Indiana* 57 G h
Wa Keeney, *Kansas* 60 E e
Wakefield, *Kansas* 60 G e
Wakefield, *Michigan* 56 D c
Wakefield, *Nebraska* 60 H b
Wakefield, *Rhode Island* 51 K b
Wakefield, *Virginia* 53 J j
Wake Forest, *North Carolina* 55 N b
Wakerton, *Indiana* 57 G h
Wakita, *Oklahoma* 62 F b
Wakpala, *South Dakota* 58 F e
Wakulla, *Florida* 54 G g
Walapai, *Arizona* 70 C d
Walbridge, *Ohio* 52 C d
Walcott, *Iowa* 61 O c
Walcott, *North Dakota* 59 K d
Walcott, *Wyoming* 67 O h
Walcott Res., *Idaho* 66 G g
Walden, *Colorado* 69 K c
Walden, *New York* 50 E b
Waldenburg, *Arkansas* 63 N c
Waldo, *Arkansas* 63 K e
Waldo, *Florida* 55 J h
Waldo, *Kansas* 60 F e
Waldo, *Missouri* 61 P b
Waldo, *Ohio* 52 C e
Waldo, *Wisconsin* 56 E f
Waldoboro, *Maine* 49 F d
Waldo L., *Oregon* 73 H m
Waldorf, *Maryland* 53 K g
Waldorf, *Minnesota* 59 N g
Waldport, *Oregon* 73 F l
Waldron, *Arkansas* 63 J d
Waldron, *Kansas* 61 O a
Wales, *Alaska* 76 C d
Wales, *Massachusetts* 51 J a
Wales, *Minnesota* 59 P c
Wales, *North Dakota* 58 H b
Wales, *Utah* 68 E d
Walhalla, *North Dakota* 58 J b
Walhalla, *South Carolina* 54 H c
Walk, L., *Texas* 64 G f
Walker, *California* 74 C c
Walker, *Iowa* 61 N b
Walker, *Kansas* 60 E f
Walker, *Louisiana* 63 N h
Walker, *Minnesota* 59 M c
Walker, *Missouri* 61 K g
Walker, *South Dakota* 58 E e
Walker L., *Alaska* 76 K c
Walker L., *Nevada* 74 G f
Walker Pass, *California* 75 G j
Walker R., *Nevada* 74 F e
Walkersville, *West Virginia* 52 F g
Walkertown, *North Carolina* 55 L a
Walker Valley, *New York* 50 E b
Walkerville, *Michigan* 56 G f
Walkerville, *Montana* 66 H c
Walkerville Junction, *Michigan* 57 L k
Wall, *South Dakota* 58 D f
Wallace, *Idaho* 66 D b
Wallace, *Kansas* 60 C f
Wallace, *Michigan* 56 F d
Wallace, *Nebraska* 60 C d
Wallace, *North Carolina* 55 O c
Wallace, *South Dakota* 58 J e
Wallace, *West Virginia* 52 F f
Wallace L., *Louisiana* 63 K f
Walla Walla, *Washington* 73 M j
Walla Walla R., *Oregon* 73 M k
Wallenpaupack, L., *Pennsylvania* 50 C c
Wallingford, *Connecticut* *(29,920)* 51 H c
Wallingford, *Vermont* 49 C e
Wallis, *Texas* 65 L f
Wallkill, *New York* 50 E b
Wallkill R., *New York* 50 E b
Wall Lake, *Iowa* 61 J b
Walloon L., *Michigan* 56 J d
Wallowa, *Oregon* 73 N k
Wallowa L., *Oregon* 73 N k
Wallowa Mts., *Oregon* 73 N k
Wallowa R., *Oregon* 73 N k
Wallula, L., *Washington* 73 M j
Wallula, *Washington* 73 M j
Walnut, *Illinois* 57 D h
Walnut, *Kansas* 61 J g
Walnut, *Mississippi* 63 P d
Walnut Canyon Nat. Mon., *Arizona* 70 F d
Walnut Cove, *North Carolina* 55 L a
Walnut Grove, *Mississippi* 63 O f
Walnut Grove, *Missouri* 61 L g
Walnut Hills, *Texas* 65 N j
Walnutport, *Pennsylvania* 50 B d
Walnut R., *Kansas* 60 E f
Walnut Ridge, *Arkansas* 63 N b
Walnut Springs, *Texas* 65 K c
Walpole, *Massachusetts* 51 L a
Walpole, *New Hampshire* 49 C e
Walrus I., *Alaska* 76 C h
Walrus Is., *Alaska* 76 G g
Walsenburg, *Colorado* 69 M f
Walsh, *Colorado* 69 O f
Walterboro, *South Carolina* 55 L e
Walters, *Oklahoma* 62 E d
Walthall, *Mississippi* 63 O e
Waltham, *Massachusetts* *(55,413)* 49 F h
Waltham, *Minnesota* 59 O g
Waltham, *Montana* 66 J b
Walthill, *Nebraska* 60 H b
Waltman, *Wyoming* 67 N f
Walton, *Indiana* 57 G j
Walton, *Kentucky* 57 J l
Walton, *New York* 53 L c
Walton, *West Virginia* 52 E g
Walton Junction, *Michigan* 56 H e
Waltonville, *Illinois* 57 D l
Walworth, *Wisconsin* 56 E g
Wamego, *Kansas* 60 H e
Wamic, *Oregon* 73 J k
Wampum, *Pennsylvania* 52 F e
Wamsutter, *Wyoming* 67 M h
Wanamakers, *Pennsylvania* 50 B d
Wanaque, *New Jersey* 50 E c
Wanaque Res., *New Jersey* 50 E c
Wanatah, *Indiana* 57 G h
Wanblee, *South Dakota* 58 E g
Wanchese, *North Carolina* 55 P d
Wanette, *Oklahoma* 62 F d
Wanilla, *Mississippi* 63 N g
Wannaska, *Minnesota* 59 L b
Wansa, *Nebraska* 60 G b
Wantagh, *New York* *(34,172)* 50 G d
Wapakoneta, *Ohio* 52 B e
Wapanucka, *Oklahoma* 62 G d
Wapato, *Washington* 73 K j
Wapello, *Idaho* 66 H f
Wapello, *Iowa* 61 N c
Wapiti Ra., *Wyoming* 67 L e
Wappapello L., *Missouri* 61 O h
Wapping, *Connecticut* 51 H b
Wappinger Cr., *New York* 50 F b
Wappinger Falls, *New York* 50 F b
Wapsipinicon R., *Iowa* 61 M b
Wapwallopen Cr., *Pennsylvania* 50 A c
Waquoit Village, *Massachusetts* 51 N b
War, *West Virginia* 52 E h
Waramaugh L., *Connecticut* 50 G b
Warba, *Minnesota* 59 N c
Ward, *Alabama* 54 C e
Warden, *Washington* 73 L j
Wardensville, *West Virginia* 52 H f
Wards I., *New York* 51 M e
Ware, *Massachusetts* 51 J a
Wareham, *Massachusetts* 51 M b
Warehouse Point, *Connecticut* 51 H b
Waresboro, *Georgia* 55 J f
Ware Shoals, *South Carolina* 55 J c
Waretown, *New Jersey* 50 E f
Waring, *Texas* 65 J f
Waring Mts., *Alaska* 76 H c
Warland, *Montana* 66 E a
Warm Spring, *Virginia* 52 G g
Warm Springs, *Georgia* 54 G e
Warm Springs, *Montana* 66 H c
Warm Springs, *Nevada* 74 J f
Warm Springs, *Nevada* 74 L e
Warm Springs, *Oregon* 73 J l
Warm Springs Res., *Oregon* 73 M m
Warner, *New Hampshire* 49 D e
Warner, *Oklahoma* 62 H c
Warner, *South Dakota* 58 H e
Warner Ls., *Oregon* 73 L n
Warner Ra., *California* 74 E c
Warner Robins, *Georgia* 54 H e
Warner Springs, *California* 75 J l
Warnertown, *Pennsylvania* 50 B c
Warren, *Arizona* 70 H h
Warren, *Arkansas* 63 L e
Warren, *Connecticut* 50 G b
Warren, *Idaho* 66 E d
Warren, *Illinois* 56 D g
Warren, *Indiana* 57 H j
Warren, *Massachusetts* 51 J a
Warren, *Michigan* *(89,246), vicinity of Detroit*
Warren, *Minnesota* 59 K b
Warren, *Montana* 67 M d
Warren, *New Hampshire* 49 D e
Warren, *Ohio* *(59,648)* 52 F d
Warren, *Pennsylvania* 52 G d
Warren, *Rhode Island* 51 L b
Warren, *Texas* 65 N e
Warren, *Virginia* 52 H h
Warren Grove, *New Jersey* 50 E f
Warren I., *Alaska* 77 V j
Warrens, *Wisconsin* 56 C e
Warrensburg, *Illinois* 57 D k
Warrensburg, *Missouri* 61 L f
Warrensburg, *New York* 53 N b
Warrenton, *Georgia* 55 J d
Warrenton, *Missouri* 61 N f
Warrenton, *North Carolina* 55 N a
Warrenton, *Oregon* 73 G j
Warrenton, *Virginia* 52 J g
Warrick, *Montana* 67 L a
Warrington, *Florida* 54 D g
Warrior, *Alabama* 54 E d
Warrior R., *Alabama* 54 D d
Warroad, *Minnesota* 59 L b
Warsaw, *Illinois* 57 B j
Warsaw, *Indiana* 57 H h
Warsaw, *Kentucky* 57 J l
Warsaw, *Missouri* 61 L f
Warsaw, *New York* 52 H c
Warsaw, *North Carolina* 55 N b
Warsaw, *Virginia* 53 K h
Wartrace, *Tennessee* 54 E b
Warwick, *Georgia* 54 H f
Warwick, *Maryland* 50 B g
Warwick, *New York* 50 E c
Warwick, *Rhode Island* *(68,504)* 51 L b
Warwick, *North Dakota* 58 H c
Warwick, *Pennsylvania* 50 B e
Wasatch Ra., *Utah* 68 E d
Wasco, *California* 75 F j
Wasco, *Oregon* 73 K k
Wascott, *Wisconsin* 56 B c
Waseca, *Minnesota* 59 N f
Washakie Needles, *Wyoming* 67 L f
Washburn, *Illinois* 57 D j
Washburn, *Maine* 49 G b
Washburn, Mt., *Wyoming* 67 K e
Washburn, *North Dakota* 58 E c
Washburn, *Texas* 64 C h
Washburn, *Wisconsin* 56 C c
Washington 73
Washington, *Arkansas* 63 K e
Washington, *Connecticut* 50 G b
Washington, *District of Columbia* *(763,956)* 53 K g
Washington, *Georgia* 55 J d
Washington, *Illinois* 57 D j
Washington, *Indiana* 57 F l
Washington, *Iowa* 61 N c
Washington, *Kansas* 60 G e
Washington, L., *Florida* 55 O e
Washington, *Louisiana* 63 L h
Washington, L., *Washington* 72 C h
Washington, *Missouri* 61 N f
Washington, Mt., *New Hampshire* 49 D d
Washington, *New Jersey* 50 D d
Washington, *New Hampshire* 49 C e
Washington, *North Carolina* 55 O b
Washington, *Pennsylvania* 53 O c
Washington, *Texas* 65 L e
Washington, *Utah* 68 C f
Washington, *Virginia* 52 H g
Washington, *West Virginia* 52 F e
Washington, *Wisconsin* 56 G d
Washington Court House, *Ohio* 52 C f
Washington Crossing, *Pennsylvania* 50 D e
Washington Highlands, *Maryland* 53 Q j
Washington I., *Wisconsin* 56 G d
Washington Nat. Airport 53 P h
Washingtonville, *New York* 50 E c
Washita R., *Oklahoma* 62 E c
Washoe, *Montana* 67 L d
Washougal, *Washington* 73 H k
Washtucna, *Washington* 73 M j
Wasilla, *Alaska* 76 N f
Waskish, *Minnesota* 59 M b
Waskom, *Texas* 65 N c
Wassaic, *New York* 50 F b
Wassaw Sd., *Georgia* 55 K f
Wassuk Ra., *Nevada* 74 G f
Wasta, *South Dakota* 58 D f
Wataga, *Illinois* 57 C h
Watauga, *South Dakota* 58 E e
Watauga, *Texas* 65 L j
Watauga L., *Tennessee* 55 K a
Watauga R., *Tennessee* 55 J a
Watch Hill, *Rhode Island* 51 K c
Waterboro, *Maine* 49 E e
Waterbury, *Connecticut* *(107,130)* 50 G b
Waterbury, *Vermont* 49 C d
Wateree Pond, *South Carolina* 55 L c
Wateree R., *South Carolina* 55 L c
Waterford, *California* 74 E g
Waterford, *Connecticut* 51 J c
Waterford, *Pennsylvania* 52 F d
Waterford Works, *New Jersey* 50 D f
Waterloo, *Alabama* 54 C c
Waterloo, *Arkansas* 63 K e
Waterloo, *Illinois* 57 C l
Waterloo, *Indiana* 57 H h
Waterloo, *Iowa* *(71,755)* 61 M b
Waterloo, *Montana* 66 H d
Waterloo, *New Jersey* 50 D d
Waterloo, *New York* 53 K c
Waterloo, *Wisconsin* 56 E f
Waterman, *Illinois* 57 E h
Water Mill, *New York* 51 J d
Waterproof, *Louisiana* 63 M g
Waters, *Michigan* 56 J e
Watersmeet, *Michigan* 56 D c
Waterton Glacier International Peace Park, *Montana* 66 G a
Watertown, *Connecticut* 50 G b
Watertown, *Massachusetts* *(39,092)* 49 F h
Watertown, *Minnesota* 59 N f
Watertown, *New York* *(33,306)* 53 L b
Watertown, *South Dakota* 58 J f
Watertown, *Tennessee* 54 E a
Watertown, *Wisconsin* 56 E f
Water Valley, *Mississippi* 63 O d
Water Valley, *Texas* 64 G d
Watervalley Res., *Arkansas-Louisiana* 63 M b
Watervalley Res., *Missouri-Arkansas* 61 N h
Waterville, *Connecticut* 51 G b
Waterville, *Maine* 49 F d
Waterville, *Minnesota* 59 N f
Waterville, *New York* 53 L c
Waterville, *Washington* 73 K h
Watford City, *North Dakota* 58 C c
Wathena, *Kansas* 61 K e
Watkins, *Colorado* 69 M d
Watkins, *Minnesota* 59 M e
Watkins Glen, *New York* 53 K c
Watkinsville, *Georgia* 54 H d
Watonga, *Oklahoma* 62 E c
Watrous, *New Mexico* 71 N d
Watseka, *Illinois* 57 F j
Watson, *Arkansas* 63 M e
Watson, *Minnesota* 59 L e
Watson, *Missouri* 61 J d
Watson, *Utah* 68 G d
Watsontown, *Pennsylvania* 53 K d
Watsonville, *California* 75 D h
Watts, *Oklahoma* 63 J b
Watts Bar Dam, *Tennessee* 54 G b
Watts Bar L., *Tennessee* 54 G b
Wattsburg, *Pennsylvania* 52 G c
Watuppa Pond, *Massachusetts* 51 L b
Waubay, *South Dakota* 58 J e
Waubay L., *South Dakota* 58 J e
Wauchula, *Florida* 55 N f
Waucoma, *Iowa* 61 M a
Wauconda, *Washington* 73 M g
Waukee, *Iowa* 61 L c
Waukegan, *Illinois* *(55,719)* 56 F g
Waukesha, *Wisconsin* *(30,004)* 56 E f
Waukomis, *Oklahoma* 62 F b
Waukon, *Iowa* 61 N a
Wauneta, *Nebraska* 60 C d
Waupaca, *Wisconsin* 56 D e
Waupun, *Wisconsin* 59 E f
Wauregan, *Connecticut* 51 K b
Waurika, *Oklahoma* 62 F d
Wausau, *Wisconsin* *(31,943)* 56 D e
Wausaukee, *Wisconsin* 56 F d
Wauseon, *Ohio* 52 B d
Wautoma, *Wisconsin* 56 D e
Wauwasota, *Wisconsin* 56 E f
Wauwatosa, *Wisconsin* *(56,923), vicinity of Milwaukee*
Wauwinet, *Massachusetts* 51 N c
Wauzeka, *Wisconsin* 56 C f
Waveland, *Indiana* 57 F k
Waveland, *Mississippi* 63 O h
Waverly, *Georgia* 55 K f
Waverly, *Illinois* 57 D k
Waverly, *Iowa* 61 M b
Waverly, *Kansas* 61 J f
Waverly, *Maryland* 53 Q e
Waverly, *Missouri* 61 L e
Waverly, *Nebraska* 60 H d
Waverly, *New York* 53 K c
Waverly, *Ohio* 52 C f
Waverly, *South Dakota* 59 K e
Waverly, *Tennessee* 54 D a
Waverly, *Virginia* 53 J h
Waverley, *Washington* 73 N h
Waverly Hall, *Georgia* 54 G e
Wawarsing, *New York* 50 E b
Wawasee, L., *Indiana* 57 H h
Wawona, *California* 74 F g
Waxahachie, *Texas* 65 L c
Waxhaw, *North Carolina* 55 L c
Way, *Mississippi* 63 N f
Wayan, *Idaho* 66 J g
Waycross, *Georgia* 55 J f
Wayland, *Iowa* 61 N c
Wayland, *Kentucky* 57 L m
Wayland, *Michigan* 56 H g
Wayland, *Missouri* 61 N d
Wayland, *New York* 52 J c
Wayne, *Maine* 49 F d
Wayne, *Michigan* 57 K g
Wayne, *Missouri* 61 L h
Wayne, *Nebraska* 60 H b
Wayne, *New York* 53 J c
Wayne, *Oklahoma* 62 F d
Wayne, *Pennsylvania* 50 C e
Wayne, *West Virginia* 52 D g
Wayne City, *Illinois* 57 E l
Waynesboro, *Georgia* 55 J d
Waynesboro, *Mississippi* 63 P g
Waynesboro, *Pennsylvania* 52 J f
Waynesboro, *Tennessee* 54 D b
Waynesboro, *Virginia* 52 H g
Waynesburg, *Ohio* 52 E e
Waynesburg, *Pennsylvania* 52 F f
Waynesville, *Illinois* 57 D j
Waynesville, *Missouri* 61 M g
Waynesville, *North Carolina* 54 H b
Waynesville, *Ohio* 52 B f
Waynoka, *Oklahoma* 62 E b
Wayside, *Nebraska* 60 A b
Wayside, *Texas* 64 C j
Weatherby, *Missouri* 61 K e
Weatherby L., *Kansas* 61 O a
Weatherford, *Oklahoma* 62 E c
Weatherford, *Texas* 65 K c
Weatherly, *Pennsylvania* 50 B d
Weaubleau, *Missouri* 61 L g
Weaver, *Alabama* 54 F d
Weaver, *Minnesota* 59 P f
Weaverville, *California* 74 C d
Webb, *Alabama* 54 F f
Webb, *Mississippi* 63 N e
Webb, *Texas* 65 H h
Webb City, *Missouri* 61 K g
Weber City, *New Mexico* 71 O e
Webster, *Colorado* 69 L d
Webster, *Florida* 55 J j
Webster, *Iowa* 61 M c
Webster, *Massachusetts* 51 K a
Webster, *New York* 53 J b
Webster, *North Dakota* 58 H b
Webster, *South Dakota* 58 J e
Webster, *Wisconsin* 56 A d
Webster City, *Iowa* 61 L b
Webster Groves, *Missouri* *(28,990)* 61 O f
Webster Res., *Kansas* 60 E e
Weches, *Texas* 65 M d
Wedderburn, *Oregon* 73 F n
Wedgefield, *South Carolina* 55 L d
Wedowee, *Alabama* 54 F d
Weed, *California* 74 C c
Weedsport, *New York* 53 K b
Weedville, *Pennsylvania* 52 H d
Weehawken, *New Jersey* 51 L e
Weeks, *Louisiana* 63 M j
Weeksbury, *Kentucky* 57 L m
Weekstown, *New Jersey* 50 D f
Weeksville, *North Carolina* 55 P a
Weeping Water, *Nebraska* 61 H d
Weesatche, *Texas* 65 K g
Weidman, *Michigan* 56 J f
Weimar, *Texas* 65 L f
Weiner, *Arkansas* 63 N c
Weinert, *Texas* 65 H b
Weippe, *Idaho* 66 E c
Weir, *Mississippi* 63 O e
Weir, *Texas* 65 K e
Weir City, *Kansas* 61 K g
Weirsdale, *Florida* 55 K j
Weirton, *West Virginia* *(28,201)* 52 F e
Weiser, *Idaho* 66 D e
Weiser R., *Idaho* 66 D e
Weiss Res., *Alabama* 54 F c
Weitschpec, *California* 74 B c
Welaka, *Florida* 55 K h
Welby, *Colorado* 69 O h
Welch, *Texas* 64 E c
Welch, *West Virginia* 52 E h
Welcome, *Minnesota* 59 M g
Weldon, *California* 75 G j
Weldon, *Illinois* 57 E j
Weldon, *Iowa* 61 L d
Weldon, *North Carolina* 55 O a
Weldon, *Texas* 65 M d
Weldona, *Colorado* 69 N c
Weldon R., *Missouri* 61 L d
Weleetka, *Oklahoma* 62 G c
Welfare I., *New York* 51 M f
Wellborn, *Florida* 55 J g
Wellborn, *Kansas* 61 O a
Wellesley, *Massachusetts* *(26,071)* 51 L a
Wellfleet, *Massachusetts* 51 N b
Wellfleet, *Nebraska* 60 D d
Wellfleet Harb., *Massachusetts* 51 N b
Wellington, *Alabama* 54 F d
Wellington, *Colorado* 69 L c
Wellington, *Illinois* 57 F j
Wellington, *Kansas* 60 G g
Wellington, *Nevada* 74 F f
Wellington, *Ohio* 52 D d
Wellington, *Texas* 64 D j
Wellington, *Utah* 68 F d
Wellman, *Texas* 64 E b
Wells, *Kansas* 60 G e
Wells, *Maine* 49 E e
Wells, *Minnesota* 59 N g
Wells, *Nevada* 74 L c
Wells, *New York* 53 M b
Wells, Pt., *Alaska* 77 N f
Wells, *Texas* 65 N d
Wellsboro, *Pennsylvania* 53 J d
Wellsburg, *Iowa* 61 M b
Wellsburg, *New York* 53 K c
Wellsburg, *West Virginia* 52 F e
Wells River, *Vermont* 49 C d
Wellston, *Ohio* 52 D f
Wellsville, *Missouri* 61 N e
Wellsville, *New York* 52 J c
Wellsville, *Utah* 68 E b
Wellton, *Arizona* 70 C g
Welsh, *Louisiana* 63 L h
Wenatchee L., *Washington* 73 K h
Wenatchee Mts., *Washington* 73 K h
Wenatchee R., *Washington* 73 K h
Wendel, *California* 74 E d
Wendell, *Idaho* 66 F g
Wendell, *Minnesota* 59 K d
Wendell, *North Carolina* 55 N b
Wenden, *Arizona* 70 D f
Wendling, *Oregon* 73 H l
Wendover, *Utah* 68 C c
Wendover, *Wyoming* 67 Q g
Wendte, *South Dakota* 58 F f
Wenona, *Illinois* 57 D h
Wenonah, *New Jersey* 50 C f
Wentworth, *New Hampshire* 49 D e
Wentworth, *South Dakota* 59 K g
Wentzville, *Missouri* 61 O f
Weohyakapka L., *Florida* 55 N f
Weott, *California* 74 B d
Werner, *North Dakota* 58 D c
Wernersville, *Pennsylvania* 50 A e
Weskan, *Kansas* 60 C f
Weslaco, *Texas* 65 K j
Wesley, *Iowa* 61 L a
Wesley, *Maine* 49 H d
Wesleyville, *Pennsylvania* 52 G c
Wessington, *South Dakota* 58 H f
Wessington Springs, *South Dakota* 58 H f
Wesson, *Arkansas* 63 L e
Wesson, *Mississippi* 63 N g
West, *Mississippi* 63 O e
West, *Pennsylvania* 53 Q c
West, *Texas* 65 K d
West Alexandria, *Ohio* 52 B f
West Allis, *Wisconsin* *(68,157)* 56 E g
West Athens, *New York* 50 F a
West B., *Florida* 54 F g
West B., *Louisiana* 63 O j
West B., *Texas* 65 N f
West Baldwin, *Maine* 49 E e
West Barnstable, *Massachusetts* 51 N b
Westbay, *Florida* 54 F g
West Bend, *Iowa* 61 K b
West Bend, *Wisconsin* 56 E f
West Blocton, *Alabama* 54 D d
Westboro, *Massachusetts* 51 K a
Westboro, *Missouri* 61 J d
Westboro, *Wisconsin* 56 C d
West Bountiful, *Utah* 68 C g
West Branch, *Iowa* 61 N c
West Branch, *Michigan* 56 J e
West Branch Res., *New York* 50 F c
West Bridgewater, *Massachusetts* 51 L a
Westbrook, *Connecticut* 51 J c
Westbrook, *Maine* 49 E e
Westbrook, *Minnesota* 59 L f
Westbrook, *Texas* 64 F c
West Brookfield, *Massachusetts* 51 J a
West Brookville, *New York* 50 D b
West Burke, *Vermont* 49 D d
Westbury, *New York* 50 F d
West Butte, mt., *Montana* 67 L a
Westby, *North Dakota* 58 C b
Westby, *Wisconsin* 56 C f
West C., *Alaska* 76 B e
West Camp, *New York* 50 F a
West Chazy, *New York* 53 N a
Westchester, *California* 75 D m
Westchester, *Connecticut* 51 J b
West Chester, *Pennsylvania* 50 B f
West Chicago, *Illinois* 57 E h
Westcliff, *Texas* 65 L j
Westcliffe, *Colorado* 69 L e
West Columbia, *Texas* 65 M f
West Concord, *Minnesota* 59 O f
West Conshohocken, *Pennsylvania* 50 C e
West Copake, *New York* 50 F a
West Cornwall, *Connecticut* 50 G b
Wescosville, *Pennsylvania* 50 B d
West Cote Blanche B., *Louisiana* 63 M j
West Covina, *California* *(50,645)* 75 G k
West Coxsackie, *New York* 50 F a
West Creek, *New Jersey* 50 E f
West Dallas, *Texas* 65 N j
West De Pere, *Wisconsin* 56 E e
West Des Moines, *Iowa* 61 L c
Westend, *California* 75 H j
West End, *Louisiana* 62 C e
West End, *North Carolina* 55 M b
West End, *Pennsylvania* 53 O b
Westerly, *Rhode Island* 51 K c
Western, *Nebraska* 60 G d
Westernport, *Maryland* 52 G f
Westfall, *Kansas* 60 F f
Westfall, *Oregon* 73 N m
West Falmouth, *Massachusetts* 51 M b
Westfield, *Illinois* 57 F k
Westfield, *Massachusetts* *(26,302)* 51 H a
Westfield, *New Jersey* *(31,447)* 50 E d
Westfield, *New York* 52 G c
Westfield, *Pennsylvania* 52 J d
Westfield, *Wisconsin* 56 D f
Westfield R., *Massachusetts* 51 H a
Westford, *Connecticut* 51 J b
West Fork, *Arkansas* 63 J c
West Fork, *Montana* 67 P a
West Frankfort, *Illinois* 57 E m
West Granville, *Massachusetts* 51 H a
West Green, *Georgia* 55 J f
West Greenwich Center, *Rhode Island* 51 K b
West Grove, *Pennsylvania* 50 B f
West Hamlin, *West Virginia* 52 D g
Westhampton, *New York* 51 H d
Westhampton Beach, *New York* 53 O e
West Hartford, *Connecticut* *(62,382)* 51 H b
West Hartland, *Connecticut* 51 H b
West Haven, *Connecticut* *(43,002)* 51 H c
West Haverstraw, *New York* 50 E c
West Helena, *Arkansas* 63 N d
Westhoff, *Texas* 65 K f
West Hollywood, *California* *(28,870), vicinity of Los Angeles*
Westhope, *North Dakota* 58 E b
West Hurley, *New York* 50 E b
West Jefferson, *North Carolina* 55 K a
West Jefferson, *Ohio* 52 C f
West Jordan, *Utah* 68 C j
West Kill, *New York* 50 E a
West Kingston, *Rhode Island* 51 K c
West L., *Nevada* 74 F c
West Lafayette, *Indiana* 57 E j
West La Fayette, *Ohio* 52 E e
Westlake, *Oregon* 73 F m
West Leyden, *New York* 53 L b
West Liberty, *Iowa* 61 N c
West Liberty, *Kentucky* 57 K m
West Liberty, *Ohio* 52 C e
West Liberty, *Pennsylvania* 53 P b

West UNITED STATES INDEX Wood

West Long Branch, *New Jersey* 50 E e
West Manchester, *Ohio* 52 B f
West Memphis, *Arkansas* 63 N c
West Miami, *Florida* 54 B d
West Middlesex, *Pennsylvania* 52 F d
West Mifflin, *Pennsylvania (27,289), vicinity of Pittsburgh*
West Milford, *New Jersey* 50 E c
West Milton, *Ohio* 52 B f
Westminster, *California (25,750), vicinity of Los Angeles*
Westminster, *Colorado* 69 O h
Westminster, *Maryland* 53 K f
Westminster, *South Carolina* 54 H c
Westminster, *Vermont* 49 C e
West Monroe, *Louisiana* 63 L f
Westmorland, *California* 75 K l
Westmoreland, *Kansas* 60 H e
Westmoreland, *New Hampshire* 49 C e
Westmoreland, *Tennessee* 54 E a
West Nanticoke, *Pennsylvania* 50 A c
West New York, *New Jersey (35,547)* 51 L e
West Nishnabotna R., *Iowa* 61 J c
West Nueces R., *Texas* 64 G f
West Okoboji L., *Iowa* 61 J a
West Olive, *Michigan* 56 G g
Weston, *Connecticut* 50 G c
Weston, *Idaho* 66 H g
Weston, *Michigan* 57 J h
Weston, *Missouri* 61 K e
Weston, *Nebraska* 60 H c
Weston, *Ohio* 52 C d
Weston, *Oregon* 73 M k
Weston, *West Virginia* 52 F f
Weston, *Wyoming* 67 P e
West Orange, *New Jersey (39,895)* 51 J e
Westover, *Texas* 65 H b
West Palm Beach, *Florida (56,208)* 55 O g
West Paris, *Maine* 49 E d
West Petersburg, *Alaska* 77 V h
Westphalia, *Indiana* 57 F l
Westphalia, *Kansas* 61 J f
West Pike, *Pennsylvania* 52 J d
West Pittston, *Pennsylvania* 50 B c
West Plains, *Missouri* 61 N h
West Point, *California* 74 E f
West Point, *Georgia* 54 F e
Westpoint, *Indiana* 57 F j
West Point, *Iowa* 61 N d
West Point, *Kentucky* 57 H m
West Point, *Mississippi* 63 P e
West Point, mt., *Alaska* 77 P d
West Point, *Nebraska* 60 H c
West Point, *New York* 50 E c
West Point, *Virginia* 53 K h
Westport, *California* 74 B e
Westport, *Connecticut* 50 G c
Westport, *Indiana* 57 H k
Westport, *New York* 53 N a
Westport, *Oregon* 73 G j
Westport, *South Dakota* 58 H e
Westport, *Tennessee* 54 C b
Westport, *Washington* 73 F j
West Portal, *New Jersey* 50 C d
West Reading, *Pennsylvania* 50 A e
West Roxbury, *Massachusetts* 49 F j
West Rutland, *Vermont* 49 C e
West St. Paul, *Minnesota* 59 R j
West Salem, *Illinois* 57 E l
West Salem, *Ohio* 52 D e
West Salem, *Wisconsin* 56 B f
West Saugerties, *New York* 50 E a
West Seattle, *Washington* 72 B h
West Shokan, *New York* 50 E b
Westside, *Iowa* 61 J b
West Side, *Oregon* 73 K n
West Springfield, *Massachusetts* 51 H a
West Stewartstown, *New Hampshire* 49 D d
West Stockbridge, *Massachusetts* 50 G a
West Suffield, *Connecticut* 51 H b
West Tisbury, *Massachusetts* 51 M c
Westtown, *New York* 50 D c
West Trenton, *New Jersey* 50 D e
West Union, *Illinois* 57 F k
West Union, *Iowa* 61 M b
West Union, *Ohio* 52 C g
West Union, *West Virginia* 52 F f
West Unity, *Ohio* 52 B d
West University Place, *Texas* 64 F j
West View, *Pennsylvania* 53 O a
Westville, *Florida* 54 F g
Westville, *Illinois* 57 F j
Westville, *Indiana* 57 G h
Westville, *New Jersey* 50 C f
Westville, *Oklahoma* 63 J c
West Virginia 52
West Walker R., *Nevada* 74 F f
West Warren, *Massachusetts* 51 J a
West Warwick, *Rhode Island* 51 K b
Westwater, *Utah* 68 G d
Westwego, *Louisiana* 62 B f
West Winfield, *New York* 53 L c
Westwood, *California* 74 E d
Westwood, *Massachusetts* 51 L a
Westwood, *New Jersey* 50 E d
Westworth, *Texas* 65 L j
West Yellowstone, *Montana* 66 J e
Wethersfield, *Connecticut* 51 H b
Wetmore, *Colorado* 69 L e
Wetmore, *Texas* 65 J f
Wet Mts., *Colorado* 69 L e
Wetonka, *South Dakota* 58 H e
Wetumpka, *Alabama* 54 E e
Wetumka, *Oklahoma* 62 G c
Wever, *Iowa* 61 N d
Wevertown, *New York* 53 M b
Wevok, *Alaska* 76 E b
Wewahitchka, *Florida* 54 F g
Wewoka, *Oklahoma* 62 G c
Weyauwega, *Wisconsin* 56 D e
Weyerhauser, *Wisconsin* 56 B d
Weymouth, *Massachusetts (48,177)* 51 M a
Whale B., *Alaska* 77 U h
Whalebone C., *Alaska* 76 D k
Whaleyville, *Virginia* 53 K j
Wharton, *New Jersey* 50 D d
Wharton, *Pennsylvania* 52 J d
Wharton, *Texas* 65 L f
What Cheer, *Iowa* 61 M c
Whatcom, L., *Washington* 73 H g
Whatley, *Alabama* 54 D f
Wheatfield, *Indiana* 57 F h
Wheatland, *California* 74 D e
Wheatland, *Iowa* 61 O c
Wheatland, *Wyoming* 67 Q g
Wheatland Res., *Wyoming* 67 P h
Wheatley, *Arkansas* 63 M d
Wheaton, *Illinois* 57 F h
Wheaton, *Kansas* 60 H e
Wheaton, *Maryland (54,635), vicinity of Washington, D.C.*
Wheaton, *Minnesota* 59 K e
Wheaton, *Missouri* 61 K h
Wheat Ridge, *Colorado* 69 O h
Wheeler, *Kansas* 60 C e
Wheeler, *Oregon* 73 G k
Wheeler, *Texas* 64 D h
Wheeler, *Wisconsin* 56 B d
Wheeler Dam, *Alabama* 54 D c
Wheeler L., *Alabama* 54 D c
Wheeler Pk., *Nevada* 74 L f
Wheeler Pk., *New Mexico* 71 M c
Wheeler Ridge, *California* 75 G j
Wheelersburg, *Ohio* 52 D g
Wheeler Springs, *California* 75 F k
Wheeling, *West Virginia (53,400)* 52 F e
Wheelock, *North Dakota* 58 C b
Wheelwright, *Kentucky* 57 L m
Whidbey I., *Washington* 73 H g
Whigham, *Georgia* 54 G g
Whipholt, *Minnesota* 59 M c
Whippany, *New Jersey* 50 E d
Whistler, *Alabama* 54 C g
Whitakers, *North Carolina* 55 O a
White, *South Dakota* 59 K f
White Bear L., *Minnesota* 59 R h
White Bear Lake, *Minnesota* 59 R h
White Bird, *Idaho* 66 D d
White Bluff, *Tennessee* 54 D a
White Bluffs, *Washington* 73 L j
White Butte, *South Dakota* 58 D e
White Castle, *Louisiana* 63 M h
White City, *Florida* 54 F h
White City, *Florida* 55 O f
White City, *Kansas* 60 H f
White Cloud, *Kansas* 61 J e
White Cloud, *Michigan* 56 H f
White Deer, *Texas* 64 C h
White Earth, *North Dakota* 58 D b
Whiteface, *Texas* 64 E b
Whiteface Mt., *New York* 53 M a
Whitefield, *New Hampshire* 49 D d
Whitefish, *Montana* 66 F a
Whitefish B., *Michigan* 56 J c
Whitefish Bay, *Wisconsin* 56 F f
Whitefish L., *Alaska* 76 K f
Whitefish L., *Alaska* 76 H f
Whitefish L., *Minnesota* 59 M d
Whitefish L., *Montana* 66 F a
Whitefish Pt., *Michigan* 56 J c
Whitefish R., *Michigan* 56 G c
Whitefish Ra., *Montana* 66 F a
Whiteflat, *Texas* 64 G a
White Hall, *Illinois* 57 C k
Whitehall, *Michigan* 56 G f
Whitehall, *Montana* 66 H d
Whitehall, *New York* 53 N b
Whitehall, *Pennsylvania* 53 P c
Whitehall, *Wisconsin* 56 B e
Whitehall Res., *Massachusetts* 51 K a
White Haven, *Pennsylvania* 50 B c
White Hills, *Alaska* 76 N b
White Hills, *Arizona* 70 C d
White Horse, *California* 74 D c
White Horse Beach, *Massachusetts* 51 M b
White Horse Pass, *Nevada* 74 L d
White House Station, *New Jersey* 50 D d
White L., *Louisiana* 63 L j
White L., *Michigan* 56 G f
White Lake, *New York* 50 D b
White Lake, *South Dakota* 58 H g
White Lake, *Wisconsin* 56 E d
Whiteland, *Indiana* 57 G k
Whitelocks Crossing, *South Dakota* 58 F e
White Mountain, *Alaska* 76 F d
White Mts., *Alaska* 77 O d
White Mts., *California* 74 G g
White Mts., *New Hampshire* 49 D d
White Oak, *Pennsylvania* 53 R c
White Oak Cr., *Texas* 65 M b
White Oak L., *Arkansas* 63 K e
White Oak Swamp, *North Carolina* 55 O c
White Owl, *South Dakota* 58 D f
White Pass, *Washington* 73 J j
White Pigeon, *Michigan* 57 H h
Whitepine, *Montana* 66 E b
White Pine, *Tennessee* 54 H a
White Pine Mine, *Michigan* 56 D c
White Pine Mts., *Nevada* 74 K e
White Plains, *New York (50,485)* 50 F d
White Plains, *North Carolina* 55 L a
Whiteport, *New York* 50 E b
White R., *Arizona* 70 G f
White R., *Arkansas* 63 M d
White R., *Indiana* 57 G k
White R., *Michigan* 56 G f
White R., *Nevada* 74 K f
White R., *South Dakota* 58 F g
White R., *Texas* 64 F b
White R., *Utah-Colorado* 68 G d
White R., *Vermont* 49 C e
White R., *Washington* 73 J h
White R., *Wisconsin* 56 C c
Whiteriver, *Arizona* 70 G f
White River, *South Dakota* 58 F g
White River Junction, *Vermont* 49 C e
White River Val., *Nevada* 74 K f
White Rock, *Nevada* 74 J c
White Rock, *Texas* 65 O j
White Rock Cr., *Kansas* 60 F e
White Rock L., *Texas* 65 O j
White Rock Pk., *Nevada* 74 L f
White Salmon, *Washington* 73 J k
White Sands Nat. Mon., *New Mexico* 71 L g
Whitesboro, *New York* 53 L b
Whitesboro, *Texas* 65 L b
Whitesburg, *Georgia* 54 G d
Whitesburg, *Kentucky* 57 L m
Whites City, *New Mexico* 71 N g
White Settlement, *Texas* 65 L j
Whiteson, *Oregon* 73 G k
White Springs, *Florida* 55 J g
White Springs, *Montana* 66 J c
Whitestone, *New York* 51 N e
White Sulphur Springs, *New York* 50 D b
White Sulphur Springs, *West Virginia* 52 F h
Whitesville, *Kentucky* 57 G m
Whitesville, *New Jersey* 50 E e
Whitesville, *New York* 52 J c
Whitesville, *West Virginia* 52 E h
White Swan, *Washington* 73 K j
Whitetail, *Montana* 67 P a
Whiteville, *North Carolina* 55 N c
Whiteville, *Tennessee* 54 B b
Whitewater, *Montana* 67 N a
Whitewater, *New Mexico* 71 J g
Whitewater, *Wisconsin* 56 E g
Whitewater B., *Florida* 55 N h
Whitewater R., *Indiana* 57 H k
Whitewood, L., *South Dakota* 58 J f
Whitewood, *South Dakota* 58 C f
Whitewright, *Texas* 65 L b
Whiting, *Iowa* 61 H b
Whiting, *Kansas* 61 J e
Whiting, *Maine* 49 H e
Whiting, *New Jersey* 50 E f
Whitingham Res., *Vermont* 49 B f
Whitinsville, *Massachusetts* 51 K a
Whitlash, *Montana* 66 J a
Whitley City, *Kentucky* 57 J n
Whitman, *Massachusetts* 51 M a
Whitman, *Nebraska* 60 C b
Whitman, *North Dakota* 58 H b
Whitman Nat. Mon., *Washington* 73 M j
Whitmire, *South Carolina* 55 K c
Whitney, L., *Texas* 65 K d
Whitney, Mt., *California* 75 G h
Whitney, *Nebraska* 60 A b
Whitney, *Nevada* 75 L h
Whitney, *Oregon* 73 M l
Whitney, *Texas* 65 K d
Whitsett, *Texas* 65 J g
Whitt, *Texas* 65 J c
Whittaker, *West Virginia* 52 F f
Whittemore, *Iowa* 61 K a
Whittemore, *Michigan* 56 K e
Whittier, *Alaska* 77 N f
Whittier, *California (33,663)* 75 H e
Whitwell, *Tennessee* 54 F b
Wibaux, *Montana* 67 Q c
Wichita, *Kansas (254,698)* 60 G g
Wichita Falls, *Texas (101,724)* 65 J b
Wichita Mts., *Oklahoma* 62 E d
Wichita R., *Texas* 65 J a
Wickatunk, *New Jersey* 50 E e
Wickenburg, *Arizona* 70 E f
Wickersham, *Washington* 73 H g
Wickett, *Texas* 64 D d
Wickford, *Rhode Island* 51 L b
Wickiup Res., *Oregon* 73 J m
Wickliffe, *Kentucky* 57 D n
Wide B., *Alaska* 76 J h
Widen, *West Virginia* 52 F g
Wien L., *Alaska* 76 M d
Wiergate, *Texas* 65 O d
Wiggins, *Colorado* 69 M c
Wiggins, *Mississippi* 63 O h
Wikieup, *Arizona* 70 D e
Wilber, *Nebraska* 60 H d
Wilborn, *Montana* 66 H c
Wilbraham, *Massachusetts* 51 J a
Wilbur, *Oregon* 73 G m
Wilbur, *Washington* 73 M h
Wilbur Dam, *Tennessee* 55 J a
Wilburton, *Oklahoma* 62 H d
Wilcox, *Missouri* 61 K d
Wilcox, *Nebraska* 60 E d
Wilcox, *Pennsylvania* 52 H d
Wildcat Pk., *Nevada* 74 J e
Wilder, *Tennessee* 54 F a
Wildersville, *Tennessee* 54 C b
Wild Horse Res., *Nevada* 74 K c
Wild L., *Alaska* 76 M c
Wildorado, *Texas* 64 B h
Wild Rice R., *Minnesota* 59 K c
Wild Rice R., *North Dakota* 59 K d
Wildrose, *North Dakota* 58 C b
Wild Rose, *Wisconsin* 56 D e
Wildwood, *Florida* 55 J j
Wildwood, *New Jersey* 50 D h
Wiley, *Colorado* 69 O e
Wilkes-Barre, *Pennsylvania (63,551)* 50 B c
Wilkesboro, *North Carolina* 55 K a
Wilkinsburg, *Pennsylvania (30,066)* 53 Q b
Willacoochee, *Georgia* 54 H f
Willaha, *Arizona* 70 E d
Willamette R., *Oregon* 73 G k
Willapa B., *Washington* 73 F j
Willapa R., *Washington* 73 G j
Willard, *Colorado* 69 N c
Willard, *Montana* 67 Q c
Willard, *New Mexico* 71 L e
Willard, *Ohio* 52 D d
Willard, *Utah* 68 D b
Willards, *Maryland* 53 L g
Willcox, *Arizona* 70 H g
Williams, *Arizona* 70 E d
Williams, *California* 74 C e
Williams, *Indiana* 57 G l
Williams, *Iowa* 61 L b
Williams, *Minnesota* 59 M b
Williams Bay, *Wisconsin* 56 E g
Williamsbridge, *New York* 51 N e
Williamsburg, *Iowa* 61 M c
Williamsburg, *Kentucky* 57 J n
Williamsburg, *Massachusetts* 49 C f
Williamsburg, *New York* 51 M f
Williamsburg, *Ohio* 52 B f
Williamsburg, *Pennsylvania* 52 H e
Williamsburg, *Virginia* 53 K h
Williamson, *Iowa* 61 L c
Williamson, *New York* 53 J b
Williamson, *West Virginia* 52 D h
Williamsport, *Indiana* 57 F j
Williamsport, *Maryland* 52 J f
Williamsport, *Pennsylvania (41,967)* 53 J d
Williamston, *Michigan* 56 J g
Williamston, *North Carolina* 55 O b
Williamston, *South Carolina* 55 J c
Williamstown, *Kentucky* 57 J l
Williamstown, *Massachusetts* 49 B f
Williamstown, *New Jersey* 50 D f
Williamstown, *Vermont* 49 C d
Williamstown, *West Virginia* 52 E f
Williamsville, *Missouri* 61 O h
Willimantic, *Connecticut* 51 J b
Willimantic R., *Connecticut* 51 J b
Willington, *Connecticut* 51 J b
Willis, *Texas* 65 M e
Willis, *Virginia* 52 F j
Williston, *Florida* 55 J h
Williston, *North Dakota* 58 C b
Williston, *South Carolina* 55 K d
Willisville, *Illinois* 57 D m
Willits, *California* 74 B e
Willmar, *Minnesota* 59 L e
Willoughby, L., *Vermont* 49 D d
Willoughby, *Ohio* 52 E d
Willow, *Alaska* 76 M f
Willow, *New York* 50 E a
Willow, *Oklahoma* 62 D c
Willow Bend, *Texas* 64 F j
Willow City, *North Dakota* 58 F b
Willow Cr., *California* 74 E d
Willow Cr., *Oregon* 73 N l
Willow Cr., *Oregon* 73 L k
Willow Cr., *Utah* 68 G d
Willow Cr., *Wyoming* 67 K h
Willow Creek, *Alaska* 77 P f
Willow Creek, *California* 74 B d
Willowemoc, *New York* 50 D b
Willowemoc Cr., *New York* 50 D b
Willow Grove, *Pennsylvania* 50 C e
Willow Lake, *South Dakota* 58 J f
Willowranch, *California* 74 E c
Willow Res., *Wisconsin* 56 D d
Willow River, *Minnesota* 59 O d
Willow Run, *Michigan* 57 K g
Willows, *California* 74 C e
Willow Springs, *Missouri* 61 N h
Willsboro, *New York* 53 N a
Wills Creek Res., *Ohio* 52 E e
Wills Point, *Texas* 65 L c
Wilmer, *Alabama* 54 C g
Wilmette, *Illinois (28,268)* 57 F g
Wilmington, *California* 75 E n
Wilmington, *Delaware (95,827)* 50 B f
Wilmington, *Illinois* 57 E h
Wilmington, *North Carolina (44,013)* 55 O c
Wilmington, *Ohio* 52 C f
Wilmington, *Vermont* 49 B f
Wilmont, *Minnesota* 59 L g
Wilmore, *Kansas* 60 E g
Wilmore, *Kentucky* 57 J m
Wilmot, *Arkansas* 63 M e
Wilmot, *Ohio* 52 E e
Wilsall, *Montana* 67 K c
Wilson, *Arkansas* 63 N c
Wilson, *Idaho* 66 D f
Wilson, *Kansas* 60 F f
Wilson, *Louisiana* 63 M h
Wilson, Mt., *Colorado* 68 H f
Wilson, Mt., *Nevada* 74 L f
Wilson, *New York* 52 H b
Wilson, *North Carolina (28,753)* 55 O b
Wilson, *Oklahoma* 62 F d
Wilson, *Pennsylvania* 50 C d
Wilson, *Texas* 64 F b
Wilson, *Wyoming* 67 K f
Wilson Cr., *Washington* 73 L h
Wilsoncreek, *Washington* 73 L h
Wilson Creek Ra., *Nevada* 74 L f
Wilson Dam, *Alabama* 54 D c
Wilson Junction, *Colorado* 69 O e
Wilson L., *Alabama* 54 D c
Wilson Res., *Kansas* 60 F f
Wilsonville, *Nebraska* 60 D d
Wilton, *Arkansas* 63 J e
Wilton, *Connecticut* 50 G c
Wilton, *Iowa* 61 N c
Wilton, *Maine* 49 E d
Wilton, *New Hampshire* 49 D f
Wilton, *North Dakota* 58 F c
Wilton, *Wisconsin* 56 C f
Wimauma, *Florida* 55 M f
Wimbledon, *North Dakota* 58 H c
Wimico, L., *Florida* 54 F h
Winamac, *Indiana* 57 G h
Winchell, *Texas* 65 H d
Winchendon, *Massachusetts* 49 D f
Winchester, *Idaho* 66 D c
Winchester, *Illinois* 57 C k
Winchester, *Indiana* 57 J j
Winchester, *Kentucky* 57 J m
Winchester, *Massachusetts* 49 F g
Winchester, *New Hampshire* 49 C f
Winchester, *Ohio* 52 C g
Winchester, *Tennessee* 54 E b
Winchester, *Texas* 65 K e
Winchester, *Virginia* 52 H f
Winchester Bay, *Oregon* 73 F m
Winchester Center, *Connecticut* 50 G b
Windam, *Montana* 67 K b
Windber, *Pennsylvania* 52 H e
Wind Cave Nat. Park, *South Dakota* 58 C g
Winder, *Georgia* 54 H d
Windfall, *Indiana* 57 H j
Wind Gap, *Pennsylvania* 50 C d
Windham, *Alaska* 77 V h
Windham, *Connecticut* 51 J b
Windham, *New York* 50 E a
Winding Stair Mts., *Oklahoma* 63 J d
Windmill Pt., *Virginia* 53 K h
Windom, *Kansas* 60 G f
Windom, *Minnesota* 59 L g
Windom Pk., *Colorado* 69 J f
Wind Pt., *Wisconsin* 56 F g
Wind R., *Wyoming* 67 M f
Wind River, *Wyoming* 67 M g
Wind River Ra., *Wyoming* 67 L f
Windsor, *Colorado* 69 M c
Windsor, *Connecticut* 51 H b
Windsor, *Illinois* 57 E k
Windsor, *Massachusetts* 49 C f
Windsor, *Michigan* 57 L k
Windsor, *Missouri* 61 L f
Windsor, *New York* 51 L c
Windsor, *North Carolina* 55 P a
Windsor, *South Carolina* 55 K d
Windsor, *Vermont* 49 C e
Windsor, *Virginia* 53 K j
Windsor Dam, *Massachusetts* 51 J a
Windsor Heights, *West Virginia* 52 F e
Windsor Locks, *Connecticut* 51 H b
Windthorst, *Texas* 65 J b
Windy, *Alaska* 77 N e
Winegars, *Michigan* 56 J f
Winehaven, *California* 75 B k
Winesap, *Washington* 73 K h
Winfield, *Alabama* 54 D d
Winfield, *Iowa* 61 N c
Winfield, *Kansas* 60 H g
Winfield, *Texas* 65 M b
Winifred, *Montana* 67 L b
Winifred, *South Dakota* 58 J g
Wing, *North Dakota* 58 F c
Wingate, *Indiana* 57 F j
Wingate, *New Mexico* 71 J d
Wingdale, *New York* 50 F b
Wingo, *Kentucky* 57 E n
Wink, *Texas* 64 D d
Winkelman, *Arizona* 70 G g
Winlock, *Washington* 73 H j
Winn, *Maine* 49 G c
Winn, *Michigan* 56 J f
Winnebago, L., *Wisconsin* 56 E e
Winnebago, *Minnesota* 59 M g
Winnebago, *Nebraska* 60 H b
Winneconne, *Wisconsin* 56 E e
Winnemucca, *Nevada* 74 H d
Winnemucca L., *Nevada* 74 F d
Winner, *South Dakota* 58 G g
Winnetka, *Illinois* 57 F g
Winnetoon, *Nebraska* 60 G b
Winnett, *Montana* 67 M b
Winnfield, *Louisiana* 63 L g
Winnibigoshish L., *Minnesota* 59 N c
Winnie, *Texas* 65 N f
Winnipesaukee, L., *New Hampshire* 49 D e
Winnsboro, *Louisiana* 63 M f
Winnsboro, *South Carolina* 55 K c
Winnsboro, *Texas* 65 M c
Winnwood, *Missouri* 61 Q a
Winokur, *Georgia* 55 J f
Winona, *Arizona* 70 F d
Winona, *Kansas* 60 C e
Winona, L., *Arkansas* 63 L d
Winona, *Michigan* 56 D c
Winona, *Minnesota* 59 P f
Winona, *Mississippi* 63 O e
Winona, *Missouri* 61 N g
Winona, *Texas* 65 M c
Winona, *Washington* 73 N j
Winooski, *Vermont* 49 B d
Winooski R., *Vermont* 49 C d
Winside, *Nebraska* 60 G b
Winslow, *Arizona* 70 G d
Winslow, *Arkansas* 63 J c
Winslow, *Indiana* 57 F l
Winslow, *Maine* 49 F d
Winslow, *Washington* 72 B h
Winsper, *Idaho* 66 H e
Winstead, *Connecticut* 51 G b
Winston, *Montana* 66 J c
Winston, *New Mexico* 71 K f
Winston-Salem, *North Carolina (111,135)* 55 L a
Winter Garden, *Florida* 55 K j
Winterhaven, *California* 75 L m
Winter Haven, *Florida* 55 N e
Winter Park, *Colorado* 69 L d
Winter Park, *Florida* 55 K j
Winters, *California* 74 C f
Winters, *Texas* 64 H d
Wintersburg, *Arizona* 70 E f
Winterset, *Iowa* 61 K c
Wintersport, *Maine* 49 G d
Winterton, *New York* 50 E b
Winthrop, *Maine* 49 F d
Winthrop, *Massachusetts* 49 H h
Winthrop, *Minnesota* 59 M f
Winthrop, *New York* 53 M a
Winthrop, *Washington* 73 K g
Winthrop Harbor, *Illinois* 56 F g
Winton, *Minnesota* 59 P c
Winton, *North Carolina* 55 P a
Winton, *Pennsylvania* 53 L d
Winton, *Washington* 73 K h
Winton, *Wyoming* 67 L h
Winyah B., *South Carolina* 55 M d
Wiota, *Iowa* 61 K c
Wirt, *Minnesota* 59 N c
Wiscasset, *Maine* 49 F d
Wisconsin 56
Wisconsin, L., *Wisconsin* 56 D f
Wisconsin Dells, *Wisconsin* 56 D f
Wisconsin R., *Wisconsin* 56 C f
Wisconsin Rapids, *Wisconsin* 56 D e
Wisdom, *Montana* 66 G d
Wise, *Virginia* 52 D h
Wiseman, *Alaska* 76 M c
Wise River, *Montana* 66 H d
Wishek, *North Dakota* 58 G d
Wishram, *Washington* 73 K k
Wisner, *Louisiana* 63 M g
Wisner, *Nebraska* 60 H c
Wisner, *New York* 50 E c
Wissota L., *Wisconsin* 56 B e
Wister, *Oklahoma* 63 J d
Wister Res., *Oklahoma* 63 J d
Witherbee, *New York* 53 N a
Witherspoon, Mt., *Alaska* 77 O f
Withington, Mt., *New Mexico* 71 K f
Withlacoochee R., *Florida* 54 H g
Withrow, *Washington* 73 L h
Witt, *Illinois* 57 D k
Witten, *South Dakota* 58 F g
Wittenberg, *Wisconsin* 56 D e
Wittmann, *Arizona* 70 E f
Woburn, *Massachusetts (31,214), vicinity of Boston*
Wofford, *Kentucky* 57 J n
Wolbach, *Nebraska* 60 F c
Wolcott, *Colorado* 69 K d
Wolcott, *Connecticut* 51 H b
Wolcott, *Kansas* 61 O a
Wolcott, *New York* 53 K b
Wolfeboro, *New Hampshire* 49 D e
Wolfe City, *Texas* 65 L b
Wolf Cr., *Texas* 64 D g
Wolf Creek, *Montana* 66 H b
Wolf Creek, *Oregon* 73 G n
Wolf Creek Dam, *Kentucky* 57 H n
Wolf Creek Pass, *Colorado* 69 K f
Wolfforth, *Texas* 64 F b
Wolf Hole, *Arizona* 70 D c
Wolf L., *Illinois* 57 D n
Wolf Mts., *Montana* 67 N d
Wolford, *North Dakota* 58 G b
Wolf Point, *Montana* 67 P a
Wolf R., *Mississippi* 63 O h
Wolf R., *Tennessee* 54 B b
Wolf R., *Wisconsin* 56 E d
Wolsey, *South Dakota* 58 H f
Wolverine, *Michigan* 56 J d
Wolverton, *Minnesota* 59 K d
Womelsdorf, *Pennsylvania* 50 A e
Wonder, *Oregon* 73 G n
Wonder L., *Alaska* 76 M e
Wood, Mt., *Montana* 67 L d
Wood, *South Dakota* 58 F g
Wood, *Pennsylvania* 52 H e
Woodbine, *Georgia* 55 K g

INDEX TO THE WORLD

(EXCEPT U.S.A.)

LIST OF ABBREVIATIONS

Afghan. Afghanistan
Afr. Africa
Alg. Algeria
Alta. Alberta (Canada)
Antarc. Antarctica
Arch., Archipel. Archipelago, Archipel
Argent. Argentina
Atl. Oc. Atlantic Ocean
Aust. Australia
Aut. Autonomous
Azerbai. Azerbaijan (Azerbaydzhanskaya)
B. Bay, Bahía, Baie, Bucht
Baluch. Baluchistan
B.C., etc. British Columbia (Canada)
Bech. Bechuanaland
Belg. Belgium, Belgian
Bol. Bolivia
Br. Bridge
Br., Brit., British
Bulg. Bulgaria
C. Cape, Cabo, Cap
Can. Canal
Cap. Capital
Car. Caroline
Cel. Celebes
Cent. Central
Ch. China
Chan. Channel
Co. County
Col. Colony
Colomb. Colombia
Cord. Cordillera (Mountains)
Cr. Creek
Czech. Czechoslovakia
Den. Denmark
Dep. Department
Des. Desert
Dist. District
Div. Division
Dom. Dominican
E. East, Eastern
Ecua. Ecuador
E.I. East Indies
Eng. England
Erit. Eritrea
Ethio. Ethiopia
Fd. Fiord, Fjord
Fed. Dist. Federal District
Fr. French, France
G. Gulf, Golfe, Golfo, Guba
Geb. Gebirge (Mountains)
Ger. Germany
G.F. Goldfield
Grp. Group
Gt. Great
Guat. Guatemala
Harb. Harbor, Harbour
Hd. Head
Hisp. Hispaniola
Hist. Historical
Hond. Honduras
Hung. Hungary
I. Island, Islet, Ile, Ilet, Isle
Ind. Res. Indian Reservation
Indon. Indonesia
Internat. International
Is. Islands, Isles, Iles
It. Italian, Italy
Iv. Cst. Ivory Coast
Jeb. Jebel (Mountain)
Junc. Junction
Kan. Kanal (Canal)
Kazakh. Kazakhstan (Kazakhskaya)
Kep. Kepulauan (Islands)
Kirgiz. Kirgizia (Kirgizskaya S.S.R.)
L. Lake, Loch, Lough, Lago, Lac, Lagoon, Lagôa
Ld. Land
Leb. Lebanon
Lit. Little
Lith. Lithuania
Lr. Lower
Lt. Ho. Light House
Madag. Madagascar (Malagasy Rep.)
Man. Manitoba (Canada)
Maur. Mauritania
Medit. Mediterranean
Me., Mex. Mexico
Mong. Mongolia
Mozamb. Mozambique
Mt. Mountain, Mount, Mont, Monte
N. North, Northern, New
Nat. National
N.B., etc. New Brunswick (Canada)
Neth., etc. Netherlands
Nfd., etc. Newfoundland (Canada)
Nic. Nicaragua
N. Ire. Northern Ireland
N.S. Nova Scotia (Canada)
N.-W. Terr., etc. North-West Territories (Canada)
N.Z., etc. New Zealand
O., Os. Ostrov (Island)
Ont. Ontario
Oc. Ocean
Ova. Ostrova (Islands)
Oz. Ozero (Lake)
Pac. Pacific
Pak. Pakistan
Pan. Panama
Para. Paraguay
Pass. Passage
P.E.I., etc. Prince Edward Island (Canada)
Pen. Peninsula
Phil. Philippines
Pk. Peak, Park
Plat. Plateau
Pol. Poluostrov (Peninsula)
Port. Portuguese, Portugal
Princip. Principality
Prom. Promontory
Prot. Protectorate
Prov. Province, Provincial
Pt., Pte. Point, Pointe
Pta. Punta (Point)
Pto. Puerto
Que. Quebec (Canada)
R. River, Río, Rivière
Ra. Range
Reg. Region
Rom. Romania
S. South, Southern, San, Santo
Sa. Serra, Sierra
Sard. Sardinia
Sask. Saskatchewan (Canada)
Scot. Scotland
Sd. Sound
Set. Settlement
Sol. Solomon
Som. Somaliland, Somali
Sp. Spanish, Spain
St., Ste., Sta. Saint, Sainte, Santa
Sta. Station
Str. Strait
Swed. Sweden
Switz. Switzerland
Tadzhik. Tadzhikistan (Tadzhikskaya)
Tang. Tanganyika
Terr. Territory, Territories
Trucial St. Trucial States
Turkmen. Turkmenistan (Turkmenskaya)
U.A.R. United Arab Republic
Ukr. Ukraine
Up. Upper
U.S.A. United States of America
Uzbek., Uzb. Uzbekistan (Uzbekskaya)
U.S.S.R. Union of Soviet Socialist Republics
Val. Valley
Vdkhr. Vodokhranilishche (Reservoir)
Venez. Venezuela
Viet. Vietnam
Vol. Volcano
W. West, Western
W.I. West Indies
Yugosl. Yugoslavia

Aachen, *Germany* 104 A c
Aalborg, *Denmark* 103 D h
Aalen, *Germany* 104 D d
Aalestrup, *Denmark* 103 C h
Aalsmeer, *Netherlands* 100 C b
Aalst. *See* Alost
Aalten, *Netherlands* 100 E c
Aarau, *Switzerland* 101 D a
Aarberg, *Switzerland* 101 C a
Aarburg, *Switzerland* 101 C a
Aardenburg, *Netherlands* 100 B c
Aare, R., *Switzerland* 101 C a
Aargau, canton, *Switzerland* 101 D a
Aarhus, *Denmark* 103 D h
Aars, *Denmark* 103 C h
Aarschot, *Belgium* 100 C d
Aba, *Congo* 121 G d
Abacaxis R., *Brazil* 92 F e
Abaco I., Gt., *Bahama Is.* 91 D a
Abaco I., Lit., *Bahama Is.* 91 D a
Abadan, *Iran* 124 E c
Abadeh, *Iran* 125 F c
Abaete, *Brazil* 93 H d
Abaiang, I., *Gilbert Is.* 78 H g
Abakan, *U.S.S.R.* 115 J c
Abal Dufaf, *Saudi Arabia* 124 D c
Abancay, *Peru* 92 C f
Abarqu, *Iran* 125 F c
Abashiri & B., *Japan* 133 J b
Abau, *New Guinea* 135 J b
Abaya L., *Ethiopia* 121 H c
Abbeville, *France* 108 D a
Abbey, *Saskatchewan* 86 J h
Abbotsford, *Br. Columbia* 88 H f
Abbottabad, *Pakistan* 126 D b
Abdul Aziz, Jebel, *Syria* 124 D b
Abdulino, *U.S.S.R.* 117 L d
Abéché, *Chad* 119 K f
Abee, *Alberta* 86 E d
Abeele, *Belgium* 100 A d
Abelessa, *Algeria* 118 F d
Abemama, I., *Gilbert Is.* 78 H g
Abengourou, *Ivory Coast* 118 E g
Abeokuta, *Nigeria* 118 F g
Aberayron, *Wales* 99 E h
Abercorn, *Quebec* 85 S g
Aberdare, *Wales* 99 E j
Aberdeen, *Saskatchewan* 86 L f
Aberdeen & co., *Scotland* 98 F c
Aberfeldy, *Scotland* 98 E d
Aberfoyle, *Scotland* 98 E d
Abergavenny, *Wales* 99 E j
Abernethy, *Manitoba* 87 O h
Aberystwyth, *Wales* 99 E h
Abha, *Saudi Arabia* 98 D f
Abidjan, *Ivory Coast* 118 E g
Abilene, *Alberta* 87 F d
Ab-i-Istada L., *Afghanistan* 125 J c
Abisko, *Sweden* 102 H b
Abitibi, *Ontario* 84 K c
Abitibi Canyon Dam, *Ont.* 84 J c
Abitibi L., *Ontario* 84 K d
Abitibi R., Little, *Ontario* 84 J b
Abitibi R., *Ontario* 84 J b
Abomey, *Dahomey* 118 F g
Abord à Plouffe, *Quebec* 85 Q j
Abound, *Saskatchewan* 87 M h
Abraham, Plains of, *Quebec* 85 S c
Abrantes, *Portugal* 106 A c
Abrud, *Romania* 112 D a
Abruzzi, dep., *Italy* 110 D d
Abruzzi, Mt., *Br. Columbia* 86 B h
Abtenau, *Austria* 104 E e
Abu, *India* 126 D d
Abu al Abyad, *Trucial States* 125 F e
Abu Arish, *Saudi Arabia* 124 D f
Abu Bahr, *Saudi Arabia* 124 E e
Abu Deleiq, *Sudan* 119 M e
Abu Dhabi, *Trucial States* 125 F e
Abu ed Duhur, *Syria* 123 F b
Abu el Jurdhan, *Jordan* 123 D g
Abu Jifan, *Saudi Arabia* 124 E e
Abu Kemal, *Syria* 124 D c
Abumombozi, *Congo* 120 E d
Abunã, *Brazil* 92 D e
Abu Qurqas, *Egypt* 119 M c
Abuta, *Japan* 133 G c
Abut Hd., *New Zealand* 135 Q l
Abuya Myeda, Mt., *Ethiopia* 121 H b
Abu Zabad, *Sudan* 119 L f
Abyei, *Sudan* 119 L g
Åbyn, *Sweden* 102 J d
Abyy, *U.S.S.R.* 115 P b
Acadia Valley, *Alberta* 86 G g
Acajutla, *Salvador* 91 B d
Acámbaro, *Mexico* 90 D c
Acaponeta, *Mexico* 90 C c
Acapulco, *Mexico* 90 D d
Acará & R., *Brazil* 93 H d
Acarigua, *Venezuela* 92 D b
Acatlán, *Mexico* 90 E d
Accra, *Ghana* 118 E g
Achaguas, *Venezuela* 92 D b
Achao, *Chile* 95 B f
Acheninni L., *Saskatchewan* 87 P d
Achigan, *Ontario* 84 F f
Achill I., *Eire* 99 A g
Achinsk, *U.S.S.R.* 115 J c
Achray, *Ontario* 85 N g
Acklins, I., *Bahamas Is.* 91 E b
Acme, *Alberta* 86 D g
Aconcagua, Mt., *Argentina* 94 C d
Açores, Is., *Atlantic Ocean* 118 B a
Acorizal, *Brazil* 93 F g
Acoyapa, *Nicaragua* 91 B d
Acre, *Israel* 123 D e
Actaeon Grp., *Tuamotu Archipelago* 79 N j
Acton, *Ontario* 84 K j
Acton Vale, *Quebec* 85 S g
Açú & R., *Brazil* 93 K e
Ada, *Okinawa* 78 C a
Adair, *Manitoba* 87 O h
Adak, I., *Aleutian Is.* 78 J b
Adalia. *See* Antalya
Adam, *Muscat & Oman* 125 G e
Adama, *Ethiopia* 121 H c
Adamant Mt., *Br. Columbia* 88 L e
Adamello, Mt., *Italy* 110 C b
Adam's Bridge, *India-Ceylon* 126 E g
Adams L., *Br. Columbia* 88 K e
Adam's Pk., *Ceylon* 126 F g
Adamsville, *Quebec* 85 S g
Adana, *Turkey* 124 C b
Adanac, *Saskatchewan* 86 H f
Adapazari, *Turkey* 124 B a
Adare, C., *Antarctica* 136 B d
Adare, *Eire* 99 B h
Adavale, *Australia* 135 H e
Addis Ababa, *Ethiopia* 121 H c
Addis Derra, *Ethiopia* 121 H b
Adelaer, C., *Greenland* 89 P c
Adelaide, *Australia* 135 G f
Adelaide, I., *Antarctica* 136 H e
Adelaide, Pt., *Australia* 134 G f
Adelaide, *South Africa* 122 D f
Adelaide River, *Australia* 134 G f
Adelboden, *Switzerland* 101 C b
Adélie Ld., *Antarctica* 136 T e
Ademuz, *Spain* 107 E b
Aden, *Aden* 124 E g
Aden, col. & prot., *South-West Asia* 124 D g
Aden, G. of, *Africa-Saudi Arabia* 121 K b
Adh Dhahiriya, *Jordan* 123 C f
Adhoi, *India* 126 D d
Adhra, *Syria* 123 E d
Adi, I., *New Guinea* 129 K l
Adi Kaie, *Eritrea* 121 H b
Adilabad, *India* 126 E e
Adi Ugri, *Eritrea* 121 H b
Adjuntas, *Puerto Rico* 54 C h
Adlavik Is., *Labrador* 81 O g
Admiral, *Saskatchewan* 86 J j
Admiralty G., *Australia* 134 E b
Admiralty Inlet, *N.-W. Terr.* 81 L c
Admiralty Is., *Pacific Ocean* 78 E g
Adolfo Alsina, *Argentina* 94 D e
Adoni, *India* 126 E e
Adoumré, *Cameroon* 119 H g
Adour R., *France* 109 C e
Adra, *Spain* 106 D d
Adraj, *Saudi Arabia* 125 F e
Adrano, *Sicily* 111 E g
Adrar, *Algeria* 118 E c
Adria, *Italy* 110 D c
Adriatic Sea, *Italy, etc.* 110 E d
Aduwa, *Ethiopia* 121 H b
Advocate Harbour, *Nova Scotia* 82 H h
Aegean Sea, *Greece* 113 E e
Aeltre, *Belgium* 100 B c
Ærösköbing, *Denmark* 103 D j
Aesch, *Switzerland* 101 C a
Aetna, *Alberta* 86 D j
Afetña, *Saipan-Tinian Is.* 78 A e
Afferden, *Netherlands* 100 E c
Affuá, *Brazil* 93 G d
Afghanistan, *Asia* 125 H c
Afif, *Saudi Arabia* 124 D e
Afogados de Ingazeira, *Brazil* 93 K e
Afono B., *Tutuila I.* 79 U o
Africa 118-122
Afrin, *Syria* 123 E a
Afula, *Israel* 123 D e
Afyon, *Turkey* 124 B b
Aga, *Truk Is.* 78 D n
Agab Workei, *Ethiopia* 121 H b
Agadès, *Niger* 118 G e
Agadir, *Morocco* 118 D b
Again, R., *Quebec* 85 L b
Agana, *Guam* 78 B l
Agartala, *India* 127 H d
Agassiz, *Br. Columbia* 88 J f
Agassiz, C., *Antarctica* 136 H e
Agat, *Guam* 78 A l
Agawa, *Ontario* 84 F e
Agawa, R., *Ontario* 84 F e
Agde, *France* 109 E e
Agen, *France* 109 D d
Agiabampo, *Mexico* 90 C b
Agidyen, *Jaluit I.* 79 U h
Agira, *Sicily* 111 E g
Agnébilékrou, *Ivory Coast* 118 E g
Agnes L., *Ontario* 87 L b
Agno, *Switzerland* 101 D c
Agordat, *Eritrea* 121 H a
Agram. *See* Zagreb
Agrigento, *Sicily* 111 D g
Agrínion, *Greece* 113 C e
Agropoli, *Italy* 111 E e
Agryz, *U.S.S.R.* 117 L b
Agua Clara, *Brazil* 93 G h
Aguadas, *Colombia* 92 B b
Aguadilla, *Puerto Rico* 91 F c
Aguadulce, *Panama* 91 C e
Aguanish, *Quebec* 83 K c
Aguanus R., *Quebec* 83 K c
Agua Prieta, *Mexico* 90 C a
Aguaray, *Argentina* 94 D b
Aguasabon Dam, *Ontario* 84 C d
Aguascalientes, *Mexico* 90 D c
Agudo, *Spain* 106 C c
Agudos, *Brazil* 93 H h
Aguijan, *Saipan-Tinian Is.* 78 A f
Águila, Pta., *Puerto Rico* 54 B j
Aguilar, *Spain* 106 C d
Aguilar de Campos, *Spain* 106 C a
Águilas, *Spain* 107 E d
Aguirre, B., *Argentina* 95 C j
Agujereada, Pta., *Puerto Rico* 54 B h
Agulhas C., *South Africa* 122 C f
Agusta, *Australia* 134 C f
Aha, *Okinawa* 78 C a
Ahar, *Iran* 124 E b
Ahmadnegar, *India* 126 D e
Ahmedabad, *India* 126 D d
Ahtopol, *Bulgaria* 112 F c
Ahuachapán, *Salvador* 91 A d
Ahualulco, *Mexico* 90 D c
Ahuntsic, *Quebec* 85 R j
Ahus, *Sweden* 103 F j
Ahvaz, *Iran* 124 E c
Ahvenanmaa, *Finland* 103 H f
Ahwar, *Aden* 124 E g
Ai, *Jaluit I.* 79 T j
Aibonito, *Puerto Rico* 54 C h
Aigle, L. à l', *Quebec* 82 G b
Aigle, *Switzerland* 101 B b
Aihunkiu, *China* 128 J a
Aijal, *India* 127 H d
Aikawa, *Japan* 133 F e
Aileron, *Australia* 134 F d
Ailinginae I., *Marshall Is.* 79 S a
Ailinglapalap I., *Marshall Is.* 79 T c
Ailsa Craig, *Ontario* 84 J j
Aim, *U.S.S.R.* 115 N c
Aimores, *Brazil* 93 J g
Ain, dep., *France* 108 F c
Aineman, *Jaluit I.* 79 U j
Aïn Galakka, *Chad* 118 J e
Aïn Safra, *Mauritania* 118 C e
Ainslie, L., C. Breton I., *Nova Scotia* 83 L g
Airai, *Palau Is.* 78 B m
Airdrie, *Alberta* 86 C g
Aire, *France* 109 C e
Aire, R., *England* 99 G g
Air Force I., *N.-W. Terr.* 81 M d
Airolo, *Switzerland* 101 D b
Aishihik & L., *Yukon* 77 T f
Aisne, dep., *France* 108 E b
Aiun, El, *Sp. Sahara* 118 C c
Aiwokako Passage, *Palau Is.* 78 B l
Aix, *France* 109 F e
Aix-la-Chapelle. *See* Aachen
Aiyansh, *Br. Columbia* 88 L c
Aiyina I., *Greece* 113 D f
Aiyion, *Greece* 113 C e
Aiyon, I., *Palau Is.* 78 C l
Aizpute, Latvia, *U.S.S.R.* 103 J h
Ajaccio & G. d', *Corsica* 111 B e
Ajaigarh, *India* 126 F d
Ajanta, *India* 126 E d
Ajanta Ra. *See* Sahiadriparvat

Campo Maior, *Portugal* 106 B c
Campos, *Brazil* 93 J h
Campos Novos, *Brazil* 94 F c
Campos Sales, *Brazil* 93 J e
Campulung, *Romania* 112 E b
Camrose, *Alberta* 86 E e
Camuy, *Puerto Rico* 54 C h
Canaan, *New Brunswick* 82 G g
Canaan R., *New Brunswick* 82 G h
Canada Bay, *Newfoundland* 83 Q c
Cañada de Gómez, *Argentina* 94 D d
Cañadón de las Vacas, *Argentina* 95 C h
Canakkale, *Turkey* 124 A a
Canal Flats, *Br. Columbia* 88 M e
Canama, *Brazil* 92 C e
Cananea, *Mexico* 90 B a
Cananeia, *Brazil* 94 G c
Cañar, *Ecuador* 92 B d
Canarias, Islas, *Atlantic Oc.* 118 B c
Canarreos, Arch. de los, *Cuba* 91 C b
Canary Is. See Canarias
Canas, *Portugal* 106 B b
Canatlán, *Mexico* 90 D c
Cañaveral, *Spain* 106 B c
Cañaveras, *Spain* 107 D b
Canavieiras, *Brazil* 93 K g
Canberra, *Australia* 135 J g
Candasnos, *Spain* 107 E b
Candia. See Iráklion
Candiac, *Manitoba* 87 O h
Candle L., *Saskatchewan* 87 M e
Candle Lake, *Saskatchewan* 87 M e
Cando, *Saskatchewan* 86 J f
Cane, *Ontario* 84 K e
Canea. See Khania
Canella, *Brazil* 94 F c
Canelones, *Uruguay* 94 E d
Cañete, *Chile* 95 B e
Cañete, *Peru* 92 B f
Cañete, *Spain* 107 E b
Cangamba, *Angola* 120 D g
Cangandala, *Angola* 120 D f
Cangas, *Spain* 106 B a
Canguaretama, *Brazil* 93 L e
Canha, *Portugal* 106 A c
Canica Island, *Quebec* 85 N c
Canicatti, *Sicily* 111 D g
Canim L., *Br. Columbia* 88 J j
Canindé, R., *Brazil* 93 J e
Çankiri, *Turkey* 124 B a
Canmore, *Alberta* 86 B g
Canna, I., *Scotland* 98 C c
Cannanore, *India* 126 E f
Cannes, *France* 109 G e
Canning, *Nova Scotia* 82 H h
Cannington, *Ontario* 85 L h
Canoe, L., *Saskatchewan* 86 J c
Canoe Passage, *Br. Columbia* 88 C d
Canoe R., *Br. Columbia* 88 K d
Canora, *Saskatchewan* 87 P g
Canosa, *Italy* 111 F e
Canso, C., *Nova Scotia* 83 M h
Canso, *Nova Scotia* 83 M h
Canso, Str. of, *Nova Scotia* 83 L h
Cantabrica, *Spain* 106 C a
Cantal, dep., *France* 109 E d
Cantanhede, *Portugal* 106 A b
Cantaur, *Saskatchewan* 86 J h
Canterbury, *England* 99 H j
Canterbury Bight, *New Zealand* 135 Q m
Canterbury Plains, *New Zealand* 135 Q m
Canterbury Sta., *N.B.* 82 E h
Can Tho, *S. Vietnam* 132 D e
Canton, *China* 131 F l
Canton I., *Phoenix Is.* 78 J g
Canuelas, *Argentina* 94 E e
Canutama, *Brazil* 92 E e
Canwood, *Saskatchewan* 86 L e
Canyon, *Ontario* 84 F e
Canyon Creek, *Alberta* 86 B c
Caopacho L., *Quebec* 82 F a
Caopacho R., *Quebec* 82 F b
Caopatina, L., *Quebec* 85 Q c
Capabarida, *Venezuela* 92 C a
Capakçur. See Bingol
Capana, *Brazil* 92 E e
Capão Bonito, *Brazil* 94 G b
Capassin, *Saskatchewan* 86 K e
Cap Chat, *Quebec* 82 F d
Cap de la Madeleine, *Quebec* 85 S f
Cap-d'Espoir, *New Brunswick* 82 H e
Cape Barren I., *Tasmania* 135 J h
Cape Breton Highlands Nat. Park, C. Breton I., *Nova Scotia* 83 M g
Cape Breton I., *Nova Scotia* 83 N g
Cape Broyle, *Newfoundland* 83 T f
Cape Charles, *Labrador* 83 R a
Cape Clear, *Eire* 99 A j
Cape Coast, *Ghana* 118 E g
Cape Dorset, *N.-W. Terr.* 81 M e
Cape Dyer, *N.-W. Terr.* 81 N d
Cape Hopes Advance, *Quebec* 81 N e
Cape La Hune, *Nfd.* 83 Q f
Capelinha, *Brazil* 93 J g
Capelle, La, *France* 108 E b
Cape Province, *South Africa* 122 C f
Cape Race, *Newfoundland* 83 T g
Cape Ray, *Newfoundland* 83 N f
Cape Sable I., *Nova Scotia* 82 G k
Cape St. Mary Lt. Ho., *Nova Scotia* 82 F j
Cape Tormentine, *N.B.* 82 J g
Cape Town, *South Africa* 122 B f
Cape Verde Is., *Atlantic Oc.* 118 B h
Cape York Pen., *Australia* 135 H b
Cap Haïtien, *Haiti* 91 E c
Capica, *Italy* 111 E e
Capilano R., *Br. Columbia* 88 D f
Capilla, *Argentina* 94 E d
Capilla del Monte, *Argentina* 94 D d
Capim, *Brazil* 93 H d
Capitachouane, R., *Quebec* 85 O e
Caplan, *Quebec* 82 G e
Capraia, I., *Italy* 110 B d
Capreol, *Ontario* 84 K f
Caprera, I., *Sardinia* 111 B e
Capri, I., *Italy* 111 E e
Capricorn Chan., *Australia* 135 K d
Caprivi Strip, *S.W. Africa* 122 C c
Capstick, *Cape Breton I.* 83 M g
Caquetá, R., *Colombia* 92 B c
Caquetá, R., *Venezuela* 92 C d
Carabaya, Cord. de, *Peru* 92 C f
Caracaraí, *Brazil* 92 E c
Caracas, *Venezuela* 92 D a
Caracol, *Brazil* 93 J e
Caraguatay, *Paraguay* 94 E b
Caramat, *Ontario* 84 D c
Caransebes, *Romania* 112 D b
Carapegua, *Paraguay* 94 E c
Caraquet & B., *N.B.* 82 H f
Caras, *Peru* 92 B e
Caratasca L., *Honduras* 91 C c
Caratinga, *Brazil* 93 J g
Carauari, *Brazil* 92 D d
Caravaca, *Spain* 107 D c
Caravelas, *Brazil* 93 K g
Caraveli, *Peru* 92 C g
Carballino, *Spain* 106 A a
Carballo, *Spain* 106 A a
Carberry, *Manitoba* 87 S j
Carbon, *Alberta* 86 D g
Carbonara, C., *Sardinia* 111 B f
Carbondale, *Alberta* 86 D e
Carbonear, *Newfoundland* 83 T f
Carcajou, *Alberta* 88 L b
Carcassonne, *France* 109 E e
Carcross, *Yukon* 77 U f
Cardamom Hills, *India* 126 E g
Cárdenas, *Cuba* 91 C b
Cárdenas, *Mexico* 90 E c
Cardiel, L., *Argentina* 95 B g
Cardiff, *Wales* 99 E j
Cardigan & B., *Wales* 99 D h
Cardigan B., *Prince Edward I.* 82 K g
Cardigan, co., *Wales* 99 E h
Cardigan, *Prince Edward I.* 82 K g
Cardona, *Spain* 107 F b
Cardross, *Saskatchewan* 87 M j
Cardston, *Alberta* 86 D j
Cardwell, *Australia* 135 J c
Carey, L., *Australia* 134 D e
Cargill, *Ontario* 84 J h
Carhaix, *France* 108 B b
Carhué. See Adolfo Alsina
Caribbean Sea, *West Indies, etc.* 91 D d
Cariboo Mts., *Br. Columbia* 88 J d
Caribou, L., *Ontario* 84 A b
Caribou, *Manitoba* 81 K f
Caribou Hide, *Br. Columbia* 88 F b
Caribou I., *Nova Scotia* 82 K h
Caribou I., *Ontario* 84 E e
Caribou Mts., *Alberta* 88 M a
Caribrod. See Dimitrovgrad
Carichic, *Mexico* 90 C b
Carievale, *Saskatchewan* 87 Q j
Carillon, *Quebec* 85 Q g
Cariñena, *Spain* 107 E b
Carinhanha, *Brazil* 93 J f
Caripito, *Venezuela* 92 E a
Cariús, *Brazil* 93 K e
Carlet, *Spain* 107 E c
Carleton, Mt., *New Brunswick* 82 F f
Carleton, *Quebec* 82 F e
Carleton Place, *Ontario* 85 O g
Carleton Pt., *Anticosti I., Quebec* 82 K d
Carlingford L., *Eire* 99 D g
Carlington, *Ontario* 84 C j
Carlisle, *England* 99 F f
Carlos Casares, *Argentina* 94 D e
Carlow & co., *Eire* 99 C h
Carlton, *Saskatchewan* 86 L f
Carlyle, *Saskatchewan* 87 P j
Carmacks, *Yukon* 77 T e
Carman, *Manitoba* 87 U j
Carmangay, *Alberta* 86 D h
Carmanville, *Newfoundland* 83 S d
Carmarthen & co., *Wales* 99 E j
Carmarthen B., *Wales* 99 D j
Carmaux, *France* 109 E d
Carmel, Mt., *Israel* 123 D e
Carmel, *Saskatchewan* 87 M f
Carmelo, *Uruguay* 94 E d
Carmen, *Bolivia* 92 D f
Carmen, *Colombia* 92 B b
Carmen, *Mexico* 90 F d
Carmen Alto, *Chile* 94 C b
Carmen de Patagones, *Argentina* 95 D f
Carmen I., *Mexico* 90 B b
Carmensa, *Argentina* 94 C e
Carmichael, *Saskatchewan* 86 J h
Carmona, *Angola* 120 D f
Carmona, *Spain* 106 C d
Carnamah, *Australia* 134 C e
Carnarvon, *Australia* 134 B d
Carnarvon, *South Africa* 122 C f
Carndonagh, *Eire* 98 C e
Carnduff, *Saskatchewan* 87 Q j
Carnegie, L., *Australia* 134 D e
Carnot, *Cent. Afr. Rep.* 119 J h
Carnsore Pt., *Eire* 99 C h
Carolina, *Brazil* 93 H e
Carolina, *Puerto Rico* 54 D h
Carolina, *South Africa* 122 E e
Caroline, *Alberta* 86 C f
Caroline I., *Pacific Ocean* 79 M h
Caroline Is., *Pacific Ocean* 78 E f
Caron, *Saskatchewan* 87 M h
Caroní, R., *Venezuela* 92 E b
Carora, *Venezuela* 92 C a
Carp, *Ontario* 85 O g
Carpathian Mts., *Cent. Eur.* 97 N f
Carpatii Sudici, *Romania* 112 D b
Carpentaria, G. of, *Australia* 134 G b
Carp L., *Br. Columbia* 88 H c
Carragana, *Saskatchewan* 87 O f
Carrara, *Italy* 110 C c
Carreño, *Spain* 106 C a
Carrickmacross, *Eire* 99 C g
Carrick-on-Shannon, *Eire* 99 B g
Carrick-on-Suir, *Eire* 99 C h
Carrière, L., *Quebec* 85 N e
Carrión de los Condes, *Spain* 106 C a
Carroll, *Manitoba* 87 R j
Carroll Inlet, *Antarctica* 136 G d
Carrot R., *Manitoba* 87 V d
Carrot R., *Saskatchewan* 87 N e
Carrot River, *Saskatchewan* 87 O e
Carrowmore L., *Eire* 99 A f
Carruthers, *Saskatchewan* 86 H f
Carsamba, *Turkey* 124 C a
Carseland, *Alberta* 86 D h
Carstairs, *Alberta* 86 C g
Carstairs, *Scotland* 98 E e
Carstensz, Mt., *New Guinea* 129 L l
Carswell L., *Saskatchewan* 88 P a
Cartagena, *Colombia* 92 B a
Cartagena, *Spain* 107 E d
Cartago, *Colombia* 92 B c
Cartago, *Costa Rica* 91 C e
Cartaxo, *Portugal* 106 A c
Cartaya, *Spain* 106 B d
Carteret, *France* 108 C b
Cartier, *Ontario* 84 J f
Cartierville, *Quebec* 85 R j
Cartierville Airport, *Quebec* 85 Q j
Cartwright, *Labrador* 81 O g
Cartwright, *Manitoba* 87 S j
Carúpano, *Venezuela* 92 E a
Carutaperá, *Brazil* 93 H d
Carvoeiro, *Brazil* 92 E d
Casablanca, *Chile* 94 B d
Casablanca, *Morocco* 118 D b
Casaccia, *Switzerland* 101 E b
Casapedia, *Quebec* 82 G e
Casapedia R., *Quebec* 82 F e
Casas Grandes, *Mexico* 90 C a
Casas Ibañez, *Spain* 107 E c
Cascade, *Br. Columbia* 88 K f
Cascade Mts., *Canada-U.S.A.* 88 J f
Cascade Pt., *New Zealand* 135 P l
Cascais, *Portugal* 106 A c
Caserta, *Italy* 111 E e
Casey B., *Antarctica* 136 P e
Casey, *Quebec* 85 Q e
Casey Ra., *Antarctica* 136 Q e
Cashel, *Eire* 99 B h
Casilda, *Argentina* 94 D d
Casilda, *Cuba* 91 D b
Casino, *Australia* 135 K e
Casma, *Peru* 92 B e
Caspe, *Spain* 107 E b
Caspian Sea, *Europe-Asia* 114 E e
Cassai, *Angola* 120 E g
Cassamba, *Angola* 120 E g
Cassel, *France* 108 E a
Casselman, *Ontario* 85 P g
Cassinga, *Angola* 122 B c
Cassino, *Brazil* 94 F d
Cassino, *Italy* 111 D e
Cassiparé, *Brazil* 93 G c
Cassis, *France* 109 F e
Cassou, *Upper Volta* 118 E f
Castanhal, *Brazil* 92 E e
Castanheiro, *Brazil* 92 D d
Castaño, *Argentina* 94 C d
Castasegna, *Switzerland* 101 E b
Casteljaloux, *France* 109 C d
Castellammare & G. di, *Sicily* 111 D f
Castellammare di Stabia, *Italy* 111 E e
Castellane, *France* 109 G e
Castellar de Santiago, *Spain* 106 D c
Castelli, *Argentina* 94 E e
Castellón de la Plana, *Spain* 107 E c
Castellote, *Spain* 107 E b
Castelnaudary, *France* 109 E e
Castelo Branco, *Portugal* 106 B c
Castelo de Vide, *Portugal* 106 B c
Castelsarrasin, *France* 109 D e
Castelvetrano, *Sicily* 111 D g
Casterle, *Belgium* 100 C c
Castets, *France* 109 C e
Castilletes, *Colombia* 92 C a
Castillo, Mt., *Chile* 95 B g
Castlebar, *Eire* 99 A g
Castle Douglas, *Scotland* 99 E f
Castlegar, *Br. Columbia* 88 L f
Castlerea, *Eire* 99 B g
Castlereagh, R., *Australia* 135 J f
Castor, *Alberta* 86 F f
Castres, *France* 109 E e
Castro, *Brazil* 94 F b
Castro, *Chile* 95 B f
Castro Marin, *Portugal* 106 B d
Castropol, *Spain* 106 B a
Castrovillari, *Italy* 111 F f
Castuera, *Spain* 106 C c
Catabola, *Angola* 120 D g
Catalina, *Newfoundland* 83 T e
Catalina Pt., *Guam* 78 B k
Catamaran, *Tasmania* 135 J h
Catamarca, *Argentina* 94 C c
Catanduanes, I., *Philippines* 129 H h
Catania & G. di, *Sicily* 111 E g
Catanzaro, *Italy* 111 F f
Catarman, *Philippines* 129 H h
Catastrophe, C., *Australia* 134 G g
Catbalogan, *Philippines* 129 H b
Cateau, Le, *France* 108 E a
Cater, *Saskatchewan* 86 J e
Cat I., *Bahama Is.* 91 D b
Cat Lake, *Ontario* 81 K g
Cato, I., *Coral Sea* 78 F k
Catorce, *Mexico* 90 D c
Catriló, *Argentina* 94 D e
Catuna, *Argentina* 94 C d
Cauchon L., *Manitoba* 87 V c
Caughnawaga, *Quebec* 85 R g
Caughnawaga Ind. Res., *Quebec* 85 R k
Caulfeild, *Br. Columbia* 88 C f
Caungula, *Angola* 120 D f
Cauquenes, *Chile* 94 B e
Causapscal, *Quebec* 82 E e
Cauto, R., *Cuba* 91 D b
Cauvery R., *India* 126 E f
Cavalcante, *Brazil* 93 H f
Cavan & co., *Eire* 99 C g
Cavell, *Ontario* 84 C b
Cavell, *Saskatchewan* 86 J f
Cavendish, *Alberta* 86 G h
Cavergno, *Switzerland* 101 D b
Cavers, *Ontario* 84 C d
Caviana, I., *Brazil* 93 G c
Cawnpore. See Kanpur
Cawood, *Quebec* 85 O g
Caxias, *Brazil* 92 C d
Caxias, *Brazil* 93 J d
Caxias do Sul, *Brazil* 94 F c
Cayambe, *Ecuador* 92 B c
Cayenne, *French Guiana* 93 G c
Cayes, Les, *Haiti* 91 E c
Cayey, *Puerto Rico* 54 C h
Cayley, *Alberta* 86 D h
Cayman Is., *W. Indies* 91 C c
Cayo, *British Honduras* 91 B c
Cayuga, *Ontario* 84 L k
Cazage, *Angola* 120 E g
Cazalla de la Sierra, *Spain* 106 C d
Cazin, *Yugoslavia* 110 E c
Cazorla, *Spain* 106 D d
Ceanannus Mór. See Kells
Ceará. See Fortaleza
Ceará Mirim, *Brazil* 93 K e
Ceba, *Saskatchewan* 87 P e
Cebaco, I., *Panama* 91 C e
Cebollar, *Argentina* 94 C c
Cebollera, Sa., *Spain* 107 D b
Cebu, *Philippines* 129 H h
Ceclavín, *Spain* 106 B c
Cedar L., *Manitoba* 87 R e
Cedar Springs, *Ontario* 84 H k
Cedoux, *Manitoba* 87 O j
Cedral, *Mexico* 90 D c
Cedros, I., *Mexico* 90 A b
Ceduna, *Australia* 134 F f
Cefalu, *Sicily* 111 E f
Cegled, *Hungary* 105 H e
Cehegin, *Spain* 107 E c
Ceiba, *Puerto Rico* 54 D h
Cejal, *Colombia* 92 D c
Celanova, *Spain* 106 B a
Celaya, *Mexico* 90 D c
Celebes, I., *Indonesia* 129 G l
Celebes Sea, *Indonesia* 129 H k
Celje, *Yugoslavia* 110 E b
Cella, *Spain* 107 E b
Celle, *Germany* 104 C b
Celles, *Belgium* 100 B d
Çemişgezek, *Turkey* 124 C b
Cenis, Mt., *France* 110 A c
Center L., *Palmyra I.* 79 U k
Central, Cord., *Peru* 92 B e
Central, Cord., *Dom. Rep.* 91 E c
Central African Republic, *Central Africa* 119 J g
Central America 91 B d
Central Butte, *Saskatchewan* 86 L h
Centralia, *Ontario* 84 J f
Centreville, *New Brunswick* 82 E g
Centreville, *Nova Scotia* 82 F j
Cephalonia. See Kefallinía
Ceram I., *Indonesia* 78 C h
Ceram Sea, *Indonesia* 129 J l
Cereal, *Alberta* 86 G g
Cerf, L. du, *Quebec* 85 P f
Cerignola, *Italy* 111 E e
Cerigo. See Kíthira I.
Cerigotto. See Andikíthira
Cerknica, *Yugoslavia* 110 E c
Çermik, *Turkey* 124 C b
Cernauti. See Chernovtsy
Cerralvo, I., *Mexico* 90 C c
Cerralvo, *Mexico* 90 E b
Cerreto Sannita, *Italy* 111 E e
Cerro de Pasco, *Peru* 92 B f
Cerro de Punta, Mt., *Puerto Rico* 54 C h
Cervera de Pisuerga, *Spain* 106 C a
Cesena, *Italy* 110 D c
Cēsis, *Latvia, U.S.S.R.* 103 L h
Česká Lipa, *Czechoslovakia* 104 F c
Česke Budějovice, *Czech.* 104 F d
Cessford, *Alberta* 86 F g
Cessnock, *Australia* 135 K f
Cetinje, *Yugoslavia* 112 B c
Cetraro, *Italy* 111 E f
Cette. See Sete
Cetti B., *Guam* 78 A l
Ceuta, B. de, *Mexico* 90 C c
Ceuta, *N. Africa* 118 D a
Cévennes, *France* 109 E e
Cevio, *Switzerland* 101 D b
Ceylon, I., *Indian Ocean* 126 F g
Ceylon, *Saskatchewan* 87 N j
Chablis, *France* 108 E c
Chacabuco, *Argentina* 94 D d
Chacance, *Chile* 94 C b
Chachapoyas, *Peru* 92 B e
Chachwengsao, *Thailand* 132 C d
Chad (Tchad), *Cent. Africa* 119 J f
Chad (Tchad) L., *Chad* 119 H f
Chagai, *Pakistan* 126 B c
Chagda, *U.S.S.R.* 115 N c
Chagny, *France* 108 F c
Chaguaramas, *Trinidad* 92 E a
Chāh Bahār, *Iran* 125 H d
Chaibassa, *India* 127 G d
Chaise Dieu, *France* 109 E d
Chakansur, *Afghanistan* 125 H c
Chakrata, *India* 126 E b
Chaksam, *Tibet* 127 H c
Chakwal, *Pakistan* 126 D b
Chala, *Peru* 92 C g
Chalan Kanoa, *Saipan-Tinian Is.* 78 A e
Chalchihuites, *Mexico* 90 D c
Chalcis. See Khalkís
Chaleur, B. de, *Quebec-New Brunswick* 82 H e
Chalham, I., *Chile* 95 C h
Chalhuanca, *Peru* 92 C f
Chaling, *China* 131 F j
Chalisgaon, *India* 126 D d
Chalk River, *Ontario* 85 N f
Chalky Inlet, *New Zealand* 135 P m
Challapata, *Bolivia* 92 D g
Challenger Mts., *N.-W. Terr.* 81 L a
Châlons-sur-Marne, *France* 108 F b
Châlons-sur-Saône, *France* 108 F c
Chalus, *France* 108 D d
Chalus, *Iran* 125 F b
Cham, *Germany* 104 E d
Chaman, *Pakistan* 126 C b
Chamba, *Tanganyika* 121 H g
Chambal R., *India* 126 E c
Chamberlain, *Saskatchewan* 87 M h
Chambéry, *France* 108 F d
Chambica, *Brazil* 93 H e
Chambord, *Quebec* 85 S d
Chamdo, *China* 128 C d
Chamical, *Argentina* 94 C d
Chamo, L., *Ethiopia* 121 H c
Chamonix, *France* 108 G d
Champa, *India* 126 E b
Champagne, prov., *France* 108 E b
Champcoeur, *Quebec* 85 N d
Champerico, *Guatemala* 90 F e
Champion, *Alberta* 86 D h
Champion, *Belgium* 100 D d
Champlain, *Quebec* 85 S f
Champlitte, *France* 108 F c
Champneuf, *Quebec* 85 N d
Chamusca, *Portugal* 106 A c
Chanchiang, *China* 131 E m
Chanchiang, *Hainan I., China* 131 D n
Chan-ching. See Tsamkong
Chanco, *Chile* 94 B e
Chancy, *Switzerland* 101 A b
Chanda, *India* 126 E d
Chandler, *Quebec* 82 H e
Chandod, *India* 126 D d
Chandpur, *East Pakistan* 127 H d
Chanf, *Iran* 125 H d
Chang-chia-k'on. See Changkiakow
Changchih, *China* 130 F d
Changchow, *China* 131 H k
Changchow, *China* 130 K g
Changchun, *China* 128 J b
Change Island, *Newfoundland* 83 S d
Changhsu Shan, *China* 131 K j
Changhsu Shan, I., *China* 131 K j
Changhua, *Taiwan* 131 K k
Changkiakow, *China* 130 G b
Changlang, *Kashmir* 126 E b
Changlo, *China* 130 J d
Changpeh, *China* 130 G b
Changping, *China* 130 H b
Changpu, *China* 131 H k
Changsha, *China* 131 F h
Changshan, *China* 131 J h
Changte. See Anyang
Changteh, *China* 131 E h
Changting, *China* 131 H k
Changyeh, *China* 128 D c
Channel, *Newfoundland* 83 N f
Channel Is., *English Channel* 99 A l
Channing, airfield, *Man.* 87 Q d
Chantada, *Spain* 106 B a
Chanthaburi, *Thailand* 132 C d
Chantilly, *France* 108 E b
Chany, Oz., *U.S.S.R.* 114 G c
Chao, R., *Thailand* 129 D g
Chaoan, *China* 131 H l
Chaochow, *China* 131 H l
Chao Hu, *China* 130 H g
Chaotung, *China* 131 A j
Chapais, *Quebec* 85 Q c
Chapala, L., *Mexico* 90 D c
Chapayevsk, *U.S.S.R.* 117 J d
Chapeau, *Quebec* 85 N g
Chapelle, L. de la, *Quebec* 83 L c
Chapleau, *Ontario* 84 G e
Chapleau, R., *Ontario* 84 G d
Chaplin, *Saskatchewan* 86 L h
Chapman, airfield, *Saskatchewan* 86 H e
Chapman, Mt., *Br. Columbia* 88 K e
Chaput Hughes, *Ontario* 84 K d
Char, *Mauritania* 118 C d
Chara, *U.S.S.R.* 115 L c
Charagua, *Bolivia* 92 E g
Charaña, *Bolivia* 92 D g
Charco Azul B., *Panama* 91 C e
Charcot, I., *Antarctica* 136 H e
Chard, *Alberta* 88 O c
Chardzhou, *Turkmen., U.S.S.R.* 114 F e
Charente, dep., *France* 108 D d
Charente, R., *France* 108 C d
Charente-Maritime, dep., *France* 108 C d
Charikar, *Afghanistan* 125 J c
Chari R., *Chad* 119 J f
Charité, La, *France* 108 E c
Charleroi, *Belgium* 100 C d
Charlesbourg, *Quebec* 85 R a
Charles I., *N.-W. Terr.* 81 M e
Charleville, *Australia* 135 J e
Charleville, *Eire* 99 B h
Charleville, *France* 108 F b
Charlie Lake, *Br. Columbia* 88 J b
Charlotte Amalie, *Virgin Is.* 54 E h
Charlotte L., *Br. Columbia* 88 G d
Charlottenburg, *Germany* 104 E b
Charlottetown, *Prince Edward I.* 82 J g
Charlton, *Australia* 135 H g
Charlton, *Ontario* 84 K e
Charlton I., *James Bay, North-West Territories* 81 M g
Charmey, *Switzerland* 101 C b
Charny, *Quebec* 82 A g
Charolles, *France* 108 F c
Charskiy, *Kazakh., U.S.S.R.* 117 H d
Charters Towers, *Australia* 135 J d
Charterville, *Quebec* 82 A h
Chartres, *France* 108 D b
Chartreuse, *France* 108 F d
Charvonnex, *France* 101 B c
Chascomús, *Argentina* 94 E e
Chase, *Br. Columbia* 88 O k
Chasm, *Br. Columbia* 88 J e
Chasseneuil, *France* 108 D d
Châteaubriant, *France* 108 C c
Château Chinon, *France* 108 E c
Château-du-Loir, *France* 108 D c
Châteaudun, *France* 108 D b
Château Gontier, *France* 108 C c
Château-la-Vallière, *France* 108 D c
Châteaulin, *France* 108 A b
Châteauneuf-en-Thymerais, *France* 108 D b
Châteaurenault, *France* 108 D c
Château Richer, *Quebec* 82 A f
Châteauroux, *France* 108 D c
Château Salins, *France* 108 G b
Château Thierry, *France* 108 E b
Châteauvert, L., *Quebec* 85 R e
Châteauvillain, *France* 108 F b
Châtelet, *Belgium* 100 C d
Châtellerault, *France* 108 D c
Châtel-St. Denis, *Switz.* 101 B b
Chatfield, *Manitoba* 87 U h
Chatham, *England* 99 H j
Chatham, *New Brunswick* 82 G f
Chatham, *Ontario* 84 H k
Chatham Is., *Pacific Ocean* 78 J m
Chatham Sd., *Br. Columbia* 88 D c
Cha Thing Phra, *Thailand* 132 C e
Châtillon-sur-Seine, *France* 108 F c
Chatra, *India* 127 F d
Chatrapur, *India* 127 G e
Châtre, La, *France* 108 E c
Chatsworth, *Ontario* 84 K h
Chaudière Falls, *Quebec* 84 C h
Chau-doc, *S. Vietnam* 132 C d
Chaumont-en-Bassigny, *France* 108 F b
Chaunskaya Guba, *U.S.S.R.* 115 R b
Chauvin, *Alberta* 86 G f
Chaux-de-Fonds, La, *Switz.* 101 B a
Chaves, *Brazil* 93 H d
Chaves, *Portugal* 106 B b
Chayu, *Tibet* 128 C e
Chazón, *Argentina* 94 D d
Cheadle, *Alberta* 86 D g
Cheb, *Czechoslovakia* 104 E c
Cheboksary, *U.S.S.R.* 117 H b
Chedabucto B., *Nova Scotia* 83 L h
Cheduba & I., *Burma* 127 H e
Cheecham, *Alberta* 88 O b
Cheepash, R., *Ontario* 84 J b
Cheeseman L., *Ontario* 87 O a
Che foo. See Yentai
Cheju Do, *Korea* 128 J d
Chekiang, prov., *China* 131 J h
Chekunda, *U.S.S.R.* 115 N c

Farmington, Br. Columbia 88 J c
Farne Is., England 98 F e
Farnes, Norway 103 B f
Farnham, Mt., Br. Columbia 88 L e
Farnham, Quebec 85 S g
Faro, Brazil 93 F d
Faro, Portugal 106 B d
Fårön, I., Sweden 103 H h
Farr B. Davis Sea, Antarctica 136 R e
Farrellton, Quebec 85 P g
Farrerdale, Saskatchewan 87 M g
Farrukhabad, India 126 E c
Fársala, Greece 113 D e
Farsi, Afghanistan 125 H c
Farsund, Norway 103 B g
Fasā, Iran 125 F d
Fatait ibn Kanat, Saudi Arabia 124 D d
Fatehgarh, India 126 E c
Fatehpur, India 126 D c
Father, Alberta 88 L c
Father L., Quebec 85 P c
Fatmomakke, Sweden 102 F d
Fatshan. See Namhoi
Fatu Hiva, I., Marquesas Is. 79 N h
Fauquier, Br. Columbia 88 L f
Faust, Alberta 86 B c
Fawcett, Alberta 86 C d
Fawcett L., Alberta 86 D c
Fawn, R., Ontario 81 L g
Faxaflói, Iceland 102 U m
Faya. See Largeau
Fazilka, India 126 D b
Feale R., Eire 99 A h
Fécamp, France 108 D b
Federación, Argentina 94 E d
Fefan, I., Truk Is. 78 E o
Fehmarn, I., Germany 104 D a
Feify. See Faifo
Feijó, Brazil 92 C e
Feira de Santana, Brazil 93 K f
Feldbach, Austria 105 F e
Feldkirch, Austria 104 C e
Felipe Carrillo Puerto, Mexico 90 G d
Félix U Gómez, Mexico 90 C a
Femund, L., Norway 102 D e
Fena Valley Res., Guam 78 A l
Fenelon Falls, Ontario 85 M h
Feng chên, China 130 F b
Fenghsien, China 130 H e
Fenghwang, China 131 D j
Fengkieh, China 130 D g
Fengsiang, China 130 C e
Fengyang, China 130 H f
Fenton, Saskatchewan 87 M e
Fenua Ura, I., Society Is. 79 L j
Fenwick, Ontario 85 L j
Fenwood, Saskatchewan 87 O g
Fenyang, China 130 E d
Feodosiya & B., U.S.S.R. 116 J j
Ferdow, Iran 125 G c
Fergus, Ontario 84 K j
Fergusson I., New Guinea 135 K a
Ferintosh, Alberta 86 E f
Ferland, Ontario 84 B b
Fermanagh, co., N. Ireland 99 B f
Ferme Neuve, Quebec 85 P f
Fermoy, Eire 99 B h
Fernando Poo, I., W. Africa 120 B d
Fernie, Br. Columbia 88 M f
Ferrara, Italy 110 C c
Ferrar Glacier, Antarctica 136 A c
Ferrato C., Sardinia 111 B f
Ferreira do Zezere, Portugal 106 A c
Ferreira Gomes, Brazil 93 G c
Ferrier, Alberta 86 C f
Ferolle Pt., Newfoundland 83 P b
Ferru, L., Quebec 83 N b
Ferryland, Newfoundland 83 T f
Fès, Morocco 118 D b
Fethard, Eire 99 B h
Fethiye, Turkey 124 A b
Fetlar I., Shetland 98 J a
Feu, L. du, Quebec 83 M c
Feudal, Saskatchewan 86 K g
Fez. See Fès
Fiambalá, Argentina 94 C c
Ficalho, Portugal 106 B d
Fichtel Geb., Germany 104 D c
Fideris, Switzerland 101 E b
Fidler L., Manitoba 87 V a
Field, Ontario 84 K f
Fielding, Saskatchewan 86 K f
Fier, Albania 113 B d
Fiesch, Switzerland 101 D b
Fife, co., Scotland 98 E d
Fife L., Saskatchewan 87 M j
Fife Lake, Saskatchewan 87 M j
Fife Ness, Scotland 98 F d
Figeac, France 109 E d
Figline Vald, Italy 110 C d
Figueira de Castelo Rodrigo, Portugal 106 B d
Figueras, Spain 107 G a
Figuig, Morocco 118 E b
Fiji Is., Pacific Ocean 78 H j
Filakovo, Czechoslovakia 105 H d
Filchner, C., Antarctica 136 R e
Filchner Ice Shelf, Antarctica 136 K c
File L., Manitoba 87 R d
Filiátes, Greece 113 C e
Filicudi, I., Italy 111 E f
Filipów, Poland 105 K a
Filippo Reef, Line Is. 79 L h
Filisur, Switzerland 101 E b
Fillmore, Manitoba 87 O j
Filonovsk, U.S.S.R. 117 F e
Finch, Ontario 85 P g
Findhorn R., Scotland 98 E c
Findlater, Saskatchewan 87 M h
Findlay, Mt., Br. Columbia 88 L e
Finhaut, Switzerland 101 B b
Finistère, dep., France 108 A b
Finisterre, C., Spain 106 A a
Finke, Australia 134 F e
Finke, R., Australia 134 F e
Finland, G. of, North-West Europe 103 L g
Finland, North Europe 102 L e
Finlay Forks, Br. Columbia 88 H c
Finlay R., Br. Columbia 88 G b
Finmark, Ontario 87 N b
Finnegan, Alberta 86 E g
Finschhafen, New Guinea 135 J a
Finspång, Sweden 103 F g
Finsteraarhorn, Switzerland 101 D b
Fintona, N. Ireland 99 C f
Fionnay, Switzerland 101 C b
Fiq, Syria 123 D e
Firat, R., Turkey 124 C b
Firebag R., Alberta 88 O b
Firenze (Florence), Italy 110 C d
Fire River, Ontario 84 G d
Firmat, Argentina 94 D d
Fir Mountain, Saskatchewan 86 L j
Firozabad, India 126 E c
Firūzābad, Iran 125 F d
Fisher, Quebec 85 N d
Fisher B., Antarctica 136 A e
Fisher B., Manitoba 87 U g
Fisher Branch, Manitoba 87 U g
Fisher Glacier, Antarctica 136 Q d
Fisher Str., N.-W. Terr. 81 L e
Fishguard, Wales 99 D j
Fishing Ls., The, Sask. 87 N h
Fiske, C., Antarctica 136 J d
Fiske, Saskatchewan 86 J g
Fitful Hd., Shetland 98 H b
Fitzcarrald, Peru 92 C f
Fitzhugh Sd., Br. Columbia 88 F e
Fitzpatrick, Quebec 85 S e
Fitzroy, Australia 134 E c
Fitzroy, R., Australia 135 J d
Fitzroy, R., Australia 134 D c
Fitzroy Harbour, Ontario 85 O g
Fitzwilliam I., Ontario 84 J g
Fiume. See Rijeka
Five Islands, Nova Scotia 82 H h
Fjällåsen, Sweden 102 J c
Flamborough Hd., England 99 G f
Flamingo B., New Guinea 129 L m
Flanders, Ontario 86 L b
Flanders. See Vlaanderen
Flat Bay, Newfoundland 83 O e
Flatbush, Alberta 86 C d
Flat I., Quebec 83 O c
Flat L., Alberta 86 E d
Flattery, C., Australia 135 J b
Flaxcombe, Saskatchewan 86 H g
Flèche, La, France 108 C c
Fleet, Alberta 86 F f
Fleetwood, England 99 E g
Flekkefjord, Norway 103 B g
Fleming, Saskatchewan 87 Q h
Flensburg, Germany 104 C a
Flers, France 108 C b
Flesherton, Ontario 84 K h
Fletcher Is., Antarctica 136 G d
Fleurance, France 109 D e
Fleur de Lys, Newfoundland 83 Q c
Fleur-de-Mai, L., Labrador 82 H b
Fleurier, Switzerland 101 B d
Fleuru, Belgium 100 C d
Flims, Switzerland 101 E b
Flinders I., Australia 134 F f
Flinders I., Tasmania 135 J g
Flinders R., Australia 135 H c
Flinders Ra., Australia 134 G f
Flin Flon, Manitoba 87 Q d
Flint & co., Wales 99 E g
Flint I., Pacific Ocean 79 L h
Flint L., Ontario 84 E c
Flintoft, Saskatchewan 86 L j
Flipper Pt., Wake I. 79 S d
Flisa, Norway 103 E f
Florac, France 109 E d
Floreffe, Belgium 100 C d
Florence. See Firenze
Florencia, Argentina 94 E c
Florencia, Argentina 94 D b
Florencia, Colombia 92 B c
Florennes, Belgium 100 C d
Florenville, Belgium 100 D e
Flores, Guatemala 90 F d
Flores, I., Atlantic Ocean 118 A a
Flores I., Vancouver I., British Columbia 88 F f
Flores I. & Sea, Indonesia 129 H m
Floriano, Brazil 93 J e
Floriano Peixoto, Brazil 92 D e
Florianópolis, Brazil 94 G c
Florida, Uruguay 94 E d
Floridia, Sicily 111 E g
Flórina, Greece 113 C d
Flörö, Norway 102 A f
Flotten L., Saskatchewan 86 J d
Flowerpot I. Nat. Park, Ontario 84 J g
Flower's Cove, Nfd. 83 Q b
Flüelen, Switzerland 101 D b
Flushing. See Vlissingen
Fly, R., New Guinea 135 H a
Flying Fish, C., Antarctica 136 F d
Foam Lake, Saskatchewan 87 O g
Foča, Yugoslavia 112 B c
Focşani, Romania 112 F b
Fofa Cahuel, Argentina 95 B f
Foggia, Italy 111 E e
Fogo & I., Newfoundland 83 S d
Föhr, I., Germany 104 C a
Foix & prov., France 109 D e
Fokis, Greece 113 D e
Folda, Fd., Norway 102 F c
Folégandros, I., Greece 113 E f
Foleyet, Ontario 84 H d
Foley I., N.-W. Territories 81 M d
Foligno, Italy 110 D d
Folkestone, England 99 H j
Follega, Netherlands 100 D b
Fonsagrada, Spain 106 B a
Fonseca, G. of, Honduras 91 B d
Fontaine, Belgium 100 C d
Fontainebleau, France 108 E b
Fontana, L., Argentina 95 B f
Fontas, Br. Columbia 88 J a
Fontas, R., Br. Columbia 88 J a
Fontenay-le-Comte, France 108 C c
Fonteneau, L., Quebec 83 L b
Fontenelle, Quebec 82 H e
Foochow, China 131 J j
Foothills, Alberta 88 L d
Forbes, Australia 135 J f
Forbes, Mt., Alberta 88 L e
Forcados, Nigeria 118 G g
Forcalquier, France 109 F e
Förde, Norway 103 A f
Fordlândia, Brazil 93 F d
Forel, Mt., Greenland 89 N c
Foremost, Alberta 86 F j
Forest, Ontario 84 H j
Forestburg, Alberta 86 E f
Forest Hill, Ontario 84 C j
Forest Lawn, Alberta 86 D g
Forestville, Quebec 82 C e
Forfar, Scotland 98 F d
Forgan, Saskatchewan 86 K g
Forget, Quebec 85 O d
Forget, Saskatchewan 87 P j
Fork River, Manitoba 87 S g
Forli, Italy 110 D c
Formentera I., Balearic Is. 107 F c
Formia, Italy 111 D e
Formiga, Brazil 93 H h
Formosa, Argentina 94 E c
Formosa, Brazil 93 H g
Formosa. See Taiwan, I.
Fornos d'Algôdres, Portugal 106 B b
Forres, Scotland 98 E c
Forrest, Australia 134 E f
Forrest, Manitoba 87 S j
Forrest L., Saskatchewan 88 P b
Forsa, Sweden 103 G f
Forsayth, Australia 135 H c
Forsnäs, Sweden 102 H c
Forssa, Finland 103 K f
Forster's Passage, Antarctica 136 K g
Forsythe, Quebec 85 O d
Fort Albany, Ontario 81 L g
Fortaleza, Acre, Brazil 92 D e
Fortaleza, Brazil 93 K d
Fort Ann Nat. Hist. Park, Nova Scotia 82 G j
Fort Archambault, Chad 118 J g
Fort Assiniboine, Alberta 88 M c
Fort Augustus, Scotland 98 D c
Fort Beaufort, South Africa 122 D f
Fort Beauséjour Nat. Hist. Park, Nova Scotia 82 H h
Fort Black, Saskatchewan 86 K c
Fort Chimo, Quebec 81 N f
Fort Chipewyan, Alberta 88 O a
Fort Coulonge, Quebec 85 O g
Fort Crampel, Central African Republic 119 J g
Fort Dauphin, Madagascar 121 N m
Forteau, Labrador 83 Q b
Fort Erie, Ontario 85 M k
Fortescue, R., Australia 134 C d
Fort Flatters, Algeria 118 G c
Fort Frances, Ontario 86 J b
Fort Fraser, Br. Columbia 88 G c
Fort Garry, Manitoba 87 U j
Fort George, Quebec 81 M g
Fort George, R., Quebec 81 M g
Fort Gouraud, Mauritania 118 C d
Fort Graham, Br. Columbia 88 G b
Forth, Firth of, Scotland 98 F d
Fort Hall, Kenya 121 H e
Fort Henrique, S.W. Africa 122 A c
Fort Hertz, Burma 127 J f
Fort Hill, Nyasaland 121 G f
Fort Hope, Ontario 81 L g
Forth R., Scotland 98 E d
Fortierville, Quebec 85 S f
Forties Settlement, N.S. 82 H j
Fortin, L., Quebec 82 E c
Fortín Avalos Sánchez, Paraguay 94 D b
Fortín Ayacucho, Paraguay 92 E g
Fortin Ballivian, Paraguay 92 E g
Fortín General Díaz, Paraguay 94 D b
Fortín López, Paraguay 94 D b
Fortín Teniente Montania, Paraguay 94 D b
Fort Jameson, N. Rhodesia 121 G g
Fort Johnston, Nyasaland 121 H g
Fort Kent, Alberta 86 G d
Fort Lallemand, Algeria 118 G b
Fort Lamy, Chad 119 J f
Fort Langley, Br. Columbia 88 F f
Fort Laperrine. See Tamanrasset
Fort Liard, N.-W. Territories 86 M e
Fort MacKay, Alberta 80 S g
Fort McKenzie, Quebec 81 N f
Fort Macleod, Alberta 86 D j
Fort Munro, W. Pakistan 126 C c
Fort Nelson, Br. Columbia 88 H a
Fort Nelson R., Br. Columbia 88 H a
Fort Polignac, Algeria 118 G c
Fort Portal, Uganda 121 G d
Fort Qu'Appelle, Sask. 87 O h
Fortress of Louisbourg Nat. Hist. Pk., C. Breton I., Nova Scotia 83 M h
Fortrose, Scotland 98 E c
Fort Roseberry, N. Rhodesia 121 F g
Fort Saint, Algeria 119 G b
Fort St. George. See Madras
Fort St. James, Br. Columbia 88 G c
Fort St. John, Br. Columbia 88 J b
Fort Sandeman, Pakistan 126 C b
Fort Saskatchewan, Alberta 86 D e
Fort Selkirk, Yukon 77 T e
Fort Severn, Ontario 81 L f
Fort Sibut, Cent. Afr. Rep. 119 J g
Fortuna, Spain 107 E c
Fortuna Ledge. See Marshall
Fortune & B., Newfoundland 83 R f
Fort Vermilion, Alberta 88 M a
Fort Victoria, S. Rhodesia 122 E d
Fort White, Burma 127 H d
Fort William, Ontario 87 O b
Fort William, Scotland 98 D d
Forty Mile, Yukon 77 R d
Forville, Belgium 100 C d
Forward, Saskatchewan 87 N j
Fosheim Pen., N.-W. Terr. 81 L b
Fosse, Belgium 100 C d
Fossmill, Ontario 85 L f
Fosston, Saskatchewan 87 O f
Foster, Quebec 85 S g
Foster Ls., Saskatchewan 88 R b
Foster R., Saskatchewan 88 R b
Fosterton, Saskatchewan 86 J h
Fougères, France 108 C b
Foul, I., Burma 127 H e
Foula, I., Scotland 98 H a
Foul B., Egypt 119 N d
Foulness, I., England 99 H j
Foulwind, C., New Zealand 135 Q l
Fourchu, C. Breton I., N.S. 83 M h
Fournel, L., Quebec 83 P b
Fournier, L., Quebec 82 G b
Foúrnoi, Is., Greece 113 F f
Fourup, I., Truk Is. 78 E o
Foveaux Strait, New Zealand 135 P m
Fowchow. See Fowling
Fowlers B., Australia 134 F f
Fowling, China 131 C h
Fowning, China 130 J f
Fowyang, China 130 G f
Fox, R., Manitoba 81 K f
Fox Bay, Anticosti I., Quebec 83 L d
Foxe Basin, N.-W. Territories 81 L d
Foxe Chan., N.-W. Territories 81 L d
Foxe Pen., N.-W. Territories 81 M e
Foxford, Saskatchewan 87 M e
Fox Harbour, Labrador 83 R a
Fox Pt., Anticosti I., Quebec 83 L d
Fox R., Br. Columbia 88 G b
Foxton, New Zealand 135 R l
Fox Valley, Saskatchewan 86 H h
Foxwarren, Manitoba 87 Q h
Foyle L., N. Ireland 98 C e
Foynes, Eire 99 A h
Foz do Aripuana, Brazil 92 E e
Foz do Cunene, Angola 122 A c
Foz do Jordão, Brazil 92 C e
Foz do Jutaí, Brazil 92 D d
Foz do Pauiní, Brazil 92 D e
Foz Embira, Brazil 92 C e
Fraire, Belgium 100 C d
Frameries, Belgium 100 B d
Franca, Brazil 93 H h
Francavilla Fontana, Italy 111 F e
France, W. Europe 108-109
Franceville, Gabon 120 C e
Franche-Comté, prov., France 108 G c
Francis, Manitoba 87 O h
Francis Harbour, Labrador 83 R a
Francis I., Antarctica 136 H e
Francistown, Bechuanaland 122 D d
François, Newfoundland 83 Q f
François L., Br. Columbia 88 G c
Frank, Alberta 86 C j
Frankford, Ontario 85 N h
Frankfurt-am-Main, Germany 104 C c
Frankfurt-an-der-Oder, Germany 104 F b
Fränkischer Jura, Germany 104 D d
Franklin, Dist. of, North-West Territories 80 H c
Franklin, I., Antarctica 136 B c
Franklin, Tasmania 135 J h
Franklin I., Ontario 84 K g
Franklin Str., N.-W. Terr. 81 K c
Franklyn, Mt., New Zealand 135 Q l
Frantsa Iosifa, Zemlya, Arctic Ocean 114 D a
Franz, Ontario 84 F d
Franz Josef Fd., Greenland 89 N b
Franz Josef Land. See Frantsa Iosifa, Zemlya
Fraser, R., Br. Columbia 88 K d
Fraserburg, South Africa 122 C f
Fraserburgh, Scotland 98 F c
Fraserdale, Ontario 84 J c
Fraser Mills, Br. Columbia 88 E f
Fraserwood, Manitoba 87 U h
Frasnes, Belgium 100 B d
Frater, Ontario 84 F e
Frauenfeld, Switzerland 101 D a
Fray Bentos, Uruguay 94 E d
Frazer L., Ontario 84 B c
Fredericia, Denmark 103 C j
Frederick House, R., Ontario 84 J c
Fredericton, New Brunswick 82 F h
Fredericton Junc., New Brunswick 82 F h
Frederik Hendrik I., New Guinea 129 L m
Frederikshaab, Greenland 89 P c
Frederikshavn, Denmark 103 D h
Fredonia, Colombia 92 B b
Fredrika, Sweden 102 H d
Fredrikstad, Norway 103 D g
Freeman R., Alberta 86 B d
Freeport, Bahama Is. 91 D a
Freeport, Nova Scotia 82 F j
Freetown, Prince Edward I. 82 J g
Freetown, Sierra Leone 118 C g
Fregenal de la Sierra, Spain 106 B c
Fréhel C., France 108 B b
Freiberg, Germany 104 E c
Freiburg, Germany 104 B d
Freirina, Chile 94 B c
Freistadt, Austria 104 F d
Freital, Germany 104 E c
Freixiel, Portugal 106 B b
Freixo, Portugal 106 B b
Fremantle, Australia 134 C f
French Guiana, S. America 93 G c
Frenchman Butte, Sask. 86 H e
Frenchman's Cove, Newfoundland 83 O d
French Somaliland, E. Africa 121 J b
Fresco, Ivory Coast 118 D g
Freshfield, C., Antarctica 136 A e
Freshwater, Newfoundland 83 T f
Fresnillo, Mexico 90 D c
Frewena, Australia 134 G c
Frias, Spain 106 D a
Fribourg & canton, Switzerland 101 C b
Fridtjof Nansen Mt., Antarctica 136 C a
Friedland, Germany 104 E b
Friesische Is., Nord, Germany 103 C j
Friesische Is., Ost, Germany 104 A b
Friesland, prov., Neth. 100 D a
Frio, C., S.W. Africa 122 A c
Friuli-Venezia Giulia, reg., Italy 110 D b
Frizzleton, Cape Breton I., Nova Scotia 83 L g
Frobisher, Saskatchewan 87 P j
Frobisher B., N.-W. Terr. 81 N e
Frobisher Bay, N.-W. Terr. 81 N e
Frobisher L., Saskatchewan 88 P b
Frog L., Alberta 86 G e
Fro Havet, Norway 102 C e
Frome, England 99 F j
Frome, L., Australia 134 H f
Fronteira, Portugal 106 B c
Frontera, Mexico 90 F d
Fronteras, Mexico 90 C a
Frontier, Saskatchewan 86 J j
Fronton de la Brea, Puerto Rico 54 C j
Frosinone, Italy 111 D e
Frost Glacier, Antarctica 136 T e
Frotet, L., Quebec 85 Q b
Froude, Saskatchewan 87 O j
Fröya, Norway 102 C e
Frunze, Kirgiz., U.S.S.R. 114 G d
Frutigen, Switzerland 101 C b
Frutuoso, Brazil 92 E f
Frývaldov, Czechoslovakia 105 G c
Fthiótis, Greece 113 D e
Fuchin, China 128 K a
Fu-chou. See Foochow
Fuchow. See Linchwan
Fu-chow, China 130 K c
Fuente-Alamo de Murcia, Spain 107 E d
Fuente del Arco, Spain 106 C c
Fuentes de Onoro, Spain 106 B b
Fuertaventura I., Canary Is. 118 C c
Fuerte, El, Mexico 90 C b
Fuerte, R., Mexico 90 C b
Fujiyama (Fuji san), Japan 133 F g
Fukien, prov., China 131 H j
Fuki Kaku, Taiwan 128 H e
Fukui, Japan 133 E f
Fukuoka, Japan 133 B h
Fukushima, Japan 133 G f
Fukuyama, Japan 133 G d
Fukuyama, Japan 133 C g
Fulda, R., Germany 104 C c
Funafuti, I., Ellice Is. 78 H h
Funchal, Madeira I. 118 B b
Fundão, Portugal 106 B b
Fundy, B. of, Nova Scotia-New Brunswick 82 G j
Fundy Nat. Park, New Brunswick 82 G h
Fünen. See Fyn
Fünfkurchen. See Péc
Funing. See Siapu
Fure, Japan 133 G b
Furg, Iran 125 G d
Furneaux Grp., Tasmania 135 J h
Furnes. See Veurne
Furness, Saskatchewan 86 H e
Furqlus, Syria 123 F c
Fürth, Germany 104 D d
Furue. See Kanoya
Furukawa, Japan 133 G e
Fury & Hecla Str., North-West Territories 81 L d
Fusagasugá, Colombia 92 C c
Fushih, China 130 D d
Fushimi, Japan 133 D g
Fu-shun, China 130 L b
Fusilier, Saskatchewan 86 H g
Fusin, China 130 K a
Fusio, Switzerland 101 D b
Futatsu ne, I., Iwo Jima 78 D a
Futemma, I., Okinawa 78 A c
Futiga, I., Tutuila I. 79 U o
Fuwa, Aden 124 E g
Fuyu, China 128 H a
Fyn, Denmark 103 D j
Fyne L., Scotland 98 D d
Fyzabad. See Faizabad
Gabarouse, Cape Breton I., Nova Scotia 83 M h
Gabarouse B., C. Breton I., Nova Scotia 83 M h
Gaberones, Bechuanaland 122 D d
Gabès & G. of, Tunisia 119 H b
Gąbin, Poland 105 H b
Gable Mt., Br. Columbia 88 F d
Gabon, Central Africa 120 C e
Gabrovo, Bulgaria 112 E c
Gach Saran, Iran 125 F c
Gadag, India 126 E e
Gadsby, Alberta 86 E f
Gael Hamkes B., Greenland 89 M b
Găeşti, Romania 112 E b
Gaeta & G. di, Italy 111 D e
Gafsa, Tunisia 119 G b
Gagan, I., Kwajalein Is. 79 U e
Gage, C., Prince Edward I. 82 H g
Gagetown, New Brunswick 82 F h
Gagil-Tomil, I., Yap I. 78 D l
Gagnon, L., Quebec 85 P f
Gagnon, Quebec 82 D b
Gaillac, France 109 D e
Gaillarbois, L., Quebec 82 E a
Gaima, New Guinea 135 H a
Gaimán, Argentina 95 C f
Gainsborough, England 99 G g
Gainsborough, Saskatchewan 87 Q j
Gairdner, L., Australia 134 G f
Gairloch, Scotland 98 D c
Galag. See Kalak
Galahad, Alberta 86 F f
Galangue, Angola 120 D g
Galap, I., Palau Is. 78 C l
Galápagos Is., Pacific Ocean 79 R h
Galashiels, Scotland 98 F e
Galathea B., Nicobar Is. 127 H g
Galati, Romania 112 G b
Galatz. See Galati
Galcaio, Somali Republic 121 K c
Galch Dar, Iran 125 F d
Galdhopiggen, Mt., Norway 103 C f
Galeana, Mexico 90 C a
Galeana, Mexico 90 E c
Galiano I., Br. Columbia 88 H f
Galich, U.S.S.R. 117 F a
Galilee, L., Australia 135 J d
Galilee, Sea of. See Tiberias L.
Galiote, Anticosti I., Quebec 82 J d
Galissonnière, L. la, Que. 82 K b
Galle, Ceylon 126 F g
Gallegos R., Argentina 95 B h
Gallet, L., Quebec 83 O b
Gallichan, Quebec 85 L d
Gallipoli, Italy 111 F e
Gallipoli. See Gelibolu
Gällivare, Sweden 102 J c
Galloway, Mull of, Scotland 99 D f
Galt, Ontario 84 K j
Galtee Mts., Eire 99 B h
Galvez, Argentina 94 D d
Galway B., Eire 99 A g
Galway (Gaillimh), Eire 99 A g
Gambaga, Ghana 118 E f
Gambia & R., N.W. Africa 118 B f
Gambier, Is., Pacific Ocean 79 N k
Gambier Mt., Australia 134 H g
Gambo, Newfoundland 83 S e
Gams, Switzerland 101 E a
Gananoque, Ontario 85 O h
Gand, Belgium 100 B c
Gandak R., India 127 F c
Gandava, Pakistan 126 C c
Gander, L., Newfoundland 83 S e
Gander & airport, Newfoundland 83 S e
Gander Bay South, Newfoundland 83 S d
Gander R., Newfoundland 83 R e
Gandesa, Spain 106 F b
Gandia, Spain 107 E c
Ganga. See Ganges
Gangaw, Burma 127 H d
Ganges (Ganga), R., India 127 G d
Gangtok, India 127 G c
Ganjam, India 127 G e
Gannat, France 108 E c
Gantheaume B., Australia 134 B e
Gao, Mali 118 E e
Gaoual, Guinea 118 C f
Garachiné, Panama 91 D e
Gara L., Eire 99 B g
Garanhuns, Brazil 93 K e
Garapan, I., Saipan-Tinian Is. 78 A e
Garba Tula, Kenya 121 H d
Gard, dep., France 109 F d

Herisau, Switzerland 101 E a
Herit, I., Truk Is. 78 F n
Heritage Ra., Antarctica 136 H b
Herlacher, C., Antarctica 136 F d
Herma Ness, Shetland 98 J a
Hermil, Lebanon 123 E c
Hermitage, Newfoundland 83 R f
Hermitage B., Newfoundland 83 Q f
Hermite, Is., Chile 95 C j
Hermon, Mt. See Jesh Sheikh
Hermosillo, Mexico 90 B b
Herning, Denmark 103 C h
Héron, Belgium 100 D d
Heron Bay, Ontario 84 D d
Heron I., Australia 135 K d
Hérons, I. aux, Quebec 85 S k
Herowabad, Iran 124 E b
Herräng, Sweden 103 H f
Herrera, Argentina 94 D c
Herrera di Pisuerga, Spain 106 C a
Herring Neck, Nfd. 83 S d
Herriot, Manitoba 87 Q b
Herschel, Saskatchewan 86 J g
Hersselt, Belgium 100 C c
Hertford & co., England 99 G j
's Hertogenbosch, Netherlands 100 D c
Herval. See Joacaba
Hervás, Spain 106 C b
Hervé, Belgium 100 D d
Hervey B., Australia 135 K d
Hervey Is., Cook Is. 79 L j
Hervey Junction, Quebec 85 S f
Herzberg, Germany 104 E c
Herzliya, Israel 123 C e
Herzogenbuchsee, Switzerland 101 C a
Hesdin, France 108 E a
Hespeler, Ontario 84 K j
Heught, Mt., Australia 134 F d
Heusden, Netherlands 100 D c
Hève, C. de la, France 108 D b
Heward, Manitoba 87 O j
Hexham, England 98 F f
Hiakiang, China 131 D k
Hickman's Harbour, Nfd. 83 T e
Hickson, Ontario 84 K j
Hidalgo, Mexico 90 E b
Hidalgo, state, Mexico 90 E c
Hieflau, Austria 104 F e
Hierro, I., Canary Is. 118 B c
Higashie Ue, I., Okinawa 78 A a
Higashi iwa, Iwo Jima 78 E a
Higashi Onna, Okinawa 78 B c
High Hill L., Manitoba 87 W c
Highland, Ontario 84 C j
High Point, Saskatchewan 86 K h
High Prairie, Alberta 88 L c
High River, Alberta 86 D h
Highrock & L., Manitoba 87 R c
Highrock L., Saskatchewan 88 R b
Higuro, Pta., Puerto Rico 54 B h
Hiimeji, Japan 133 D g
Hiiumaa, Estonia, U.S.S.R. 103 K g
Hijar, Spain 107 E b
Hijaz, Saudi Arabia 124 C e
Hikone, Japan 133 E g
Hikurangi, Mt., New Zealand 135 S k
Hikurangi, New Zealand 135 R j
Hilda, Alberta 86 G h
Hildesheim, Germany 104 C b
Hillah, al, Iraq 124 D c
Hillcrest, Alberta 86 C j
Hilliard, Alberta 86 E e
Hillmond, Saskatchewan 86 H e
Hillsborough, New Brunswick 82 H h
Hillsborough B., Prince Edward I. 82 J g
Hillsburgh, Ontario 84 K j
Hillsdale, Ontario 85 L h
Hillsport, Ontario 84 E c
Hillston, Australia 135 J f
Hilton Beach, Ontario 84 G f
Hilton Inlet, Antarctica 136 J d
Hilversum, Netherlands 100 D b
Hilyan, Saudi Arabia 124 D e
Himachal Pradesh, India 126 D b
Himalaya Mts., India, etc. 126 E b
Himanka, Finland 102 K d
Himare, Albania 113 B d
Hinchcliffe, Saskatchewan 87 P f
Hindeloopen, Netherlands 100 D b
Hinds Hill, pk., Nfd. 83 Q d
Hindubagh, Pakistan 126 C b
Hindu Kush, Mts., Afghanistan-Pakistan 126 C a
Hindupur, India 126 E f
Hindville, Alberta 86 G e
Hines Creek, Alberta 88 K b
Hingan, China 128 H a
Hingan. See Ankang
Hinganghat, India 126 E d
Hingho, China 130 F b
Hinghwa, China 130 J f
Hinghwa. See Putien
Hingi, China 131 B k
Hinglaj, Pakistan 126 C c
Hingoli, India 126 E e
Hingol R., Pakistan 126 C c
Hinis, Turkey 124 D b
Hinnöy, Norway 102 F b
Hinton, Alberta 88 L d
Hiro. See Birao
Hirosaki, Japan 133 G d
Hiroshima, Japan 133 C g
Hisarönü, Turkey 124 B a
Hisban, Jordan 123 D f
Hispaniola, I., West Indies 91 E c
Hissar, India 126 E c
Hissmofors, Sweden 102 F e
Hisya, Syria 123 E c
Hit, Iraq 124 D c
Hitchcock, Saskatchewan 87 O j
Hitra, Norway 102 C e
Hivaoa, I., Marquesas Is. 79 N h
Hiwasa, Japan 133 D h
Hjälmaren, L., Sweden 103 F g
Hjörring, Denmark 103 C h
Hkamti, Burma 127 J c
Hoadley, Alberta 86 C f
Hobart, Tasmania 135 J h
Hobbema, Alberta 86 D f
Hobbs Coast, Antarctica 136 E c
Hoboken, Belgium 100 C c
Hobro, Denmark 103 C h
Hobsogol, Mongolia 115 K c
Hochwan, China 131 C g
Hodeida, Yemen 124 D g
Hodges Hill, pk., Nfd. 83 R d
Hodgeville, Saskatchewan 86 L h
Hodgson, Manitoba 87 U g
Hódmezövásárhely, Hungary 105 J e
Hoek van Holland, Netherlands 100 C c
Hoey, Saskatchewan 87 M f
Hof, Germany 104 D c
Hofei, China 130 H g
Hofs Jökull, Iceland 102 Wm
Hofuf, Saudi Arabia 124 E d
Höganäs, Sweden 103 E h
Hogarth, Ontario 84 B c
Hogg L., Manitoba 87 V a
Hogs Back, Ontario 84 D j
Hohe Tauern, Austria 104 E e
Hohsien, China 131 E k
Hokianga Harb., New Zealand 135 Q j
Ho-kien-fu, China 130 H c
Hokitika, New Zealand 135 Q l
Hokkaido I., Japan 133 G c
Holap, I., Truk Is. 78 E m
Holbæk, Denmark 103 D j
Holden, Alberta 86 E e
Holdfast, Saskatchewan 87 M h
Holei, I., Palmyra I. 79 U k
Holguín, Cuba 91 D b
Holinkoerh, China 130 E b
Holland, Manitoba 87 T j
Holland, Noord, prov., Netherlands 100 C b
Holland, Zuid, prov., Netherlands 100 C b
Holland Centre, Ontario 84 K h
Hollandia, New Guinea. See Kotabaru
Hollange, Belgium 100 D e
Hollick-Kenyon Plateau, Antarctica 136 F c
Hollogne, Belgium 100 D d
Hollow Crique, Quebec 85 S c
Hollyburn, Br. Columbia 88 C f
Holmes L., Manitoba 87 V a
Holmestrand, Norway 103 D g
Holmfield, Manitoba 87 S j
Holmsund, Sweden 102 J e
Holstebro, Denmark 103 C h
Holstein, Germany 104 C b
Holstein, Ontario 84 K h
Holsteinsborg, Greenland 89 P c
Holten, Netherlands 100 E b
Holtyre, Ontario 84 K d
Holwerd, Netherlands 100 D a
Holyhead, Wales 99 D g
Holy I., England 98 F e
Holy I., Wales 99 D g
Holyoke, Alberta 86 G d
Holyrood, Newfoundland 83 T f
Home B., N.-W. Territories 81 N d
Homfray Str., Andaman Is. 127 H f
Hommelvik, Norway 102 D e
Homs, Libya 119 H b
Homs, Syria 123 E c
Honan, prov., China 130 F e
Honan. See Loyang
Honda, B., Cuba 91 C b
Honda, Colombia 92 C b
Hondo, Alberta 86 C c
Hondo, Mexico 90 D b
Honduras, C., Honduras 91 B c
Honduras, Cent. America 91 B d
Honduras, G. of, Brit. Hond. 91 B c
Hönefoss, Norway 103 D f
Honeywood, Ontario 84 K h
Honfleur, France 108 D b
Honghai B., China 131 G l
Hong Kong (Brit.), China 131 G l
Honshu I., Japan 133 C g
Hoofdplaat, Netherlands 100 B c
Hooger Smilde, Netherlands 100 E b
Hoogeveen, Netherlands 100 E b
Hoogezand, Netherlands 100 E a
Hooghalen, Netherlands 100 E b
Hooghly, India 127 G d
Hooghly R., India 127 G e
Hook Hd., Eire 99 C h
Hooping Harbour, Nfd. 83 Q c
Hoorn, Netherlands 100 D b
Hoorn Is., Pacific Ocean 78 J j
Hoosier, Saskatchewan 86 H g
Hope, Br. Columbia 88 J f
Hopedale, Labrador 81 N f
Hopeh, prov., China 130 G c
Hopen, I., Barents Sea 114 B a
Hopes Advance C., Quebec 82 N e
Hopetoun, Australia 134 D f
Hope Town, Andaman Is. 127 H f
Hopetown, South Africa 122 C e
Hopewell, Nova Scotia 82 K h
Hopewell Is., N.-W. Terr. 81 M f
Hoppo, China 131 D m
Horaždovice, Czechoslovakia 104 E d
Horburg, Alberta 86 B f
Horcasitas, Mexico 90 B b
Horgen, Switzerland 101 D a
Horizon, Saskatchewan 87 M j
Horka, Germany 104 F c
Horlick Mts., Antarctica 136 F a
Hormoz, Iran 125 F d
Hormoz I., Iran 125 G d
Hormuz, Str. of, Saudi Arabia-Iran 125 G d
Horn, Austria 105 F d
Horn, C. See Hornos, C. de
Horn, Iceland 102 U l
Hornavan, Sweden 102 G c
Hörnefors, Sweden 102 H e
Hornepayne, Ontario 84 F c
Hornopiren, Mt., Chile 95 B f
Hornos, C. de, Chile 95 C j
Hornsea, England 99 G g
Horo, Netherlands 100 D c
Horonobe, Japan 133 G b
Horqueta, Paraguay 94 E b
Horsefly, Br. Columbia 88 J d
Horse Is., Newfoundland 83 R c
Horse Islands, Newfoundland 83 R c
Horsens, Denmark 103 C j
Horse R., Alberta 86 F b
Horse Shoe, Australia 134 C e
Horseshoe B., Br. Columbia 88 C e
Horsham, Australia 134 H g
Horsham, England 99 G j
Horsham, Saskatchewan 86 H h
Horšovský Týn, Czechoslovakia 104 E d
Horst, Netherlands 100 E c
Horten, Norway 103 D g
Horwood L., Ontario 84 H d
Hoşap, Turkey 124 D b
Hose Ra., Sarawak 129 F k
Hoshangabad, India 126 E d
Hoshiarpur, India 126 E b
Hospel, India 126 E e
Hospenthal, Switzerland 101 D b
Hossegor, France 109 C e
Hoste, I., Chile 95 C j
Hosur, India 126 E f
Hotagen, Sweden 102 E e
Hotchkiss, Alberta 88 L b
Hotseh, China 130 G e
Hotton, Belgium 100 D d
Houdelaincourt, France 108 F b
Houffalize, Belgium 100 D d
Hourn L., Scotland 98 D c
House Harbour, Madeleine Is., Quebec 83 L f
House R., Alberta 86 E c
Houston, Br. Columbia 88 F c
Houten, Netherlands 100 D b
Houtman Abrolhos, Australia 134 B e
Howe Sd., Br. Columbia 88 H f
Howick, Quebec 85 R g
Howick, South Africa 122 E e
Howland I., Pacific Ocean 79 T l
Howley, Newfoundland 83 P d
Howser, Br. Columbia 88 L e
Hoyes, Spain 106 B b
Hoy I., Orkney 98 E b
Hoyle, Ontario 84 J d
Hoyt Station, New Brunswick 82 F h
Hoyun, China 128 F f
Hozat, Turkey 124 C b
Hrubieszów, Poland 105 K c
Hsawnghsup. See Thaungdut
Hsenwi, Burma 127 J d
Hsiachwan Shan, China 131 F m
Hsiamen. See Amoy
Hsi-an. See Sian
Hsi-ch'ang. See Sichang
Hsinchu, Taiwan 131 K k
Hsi-ning. See Sining
Hsinking. See Changchun
Hsipaw, Burma 127 J d
Hsüchang, China 130 F f
Hsuchow. See Hsüchang
Huachi, Bolivia 92 D g
Huacho, Peru 92 B f
Huacrachuco, Peru 92 B e
Hualgayoc, Peru 92 B e
Hualien, Taiwan 131 K l
Huanay, Bolivia 92 D g
Huancabamba, Peru 92 B e
Huancane, Peru 92 D g
Huancavelica, Peru 92 B f
Huancayo, Peru 92 B f
Huanchaca, Bolivia 92 D h
Huanchaco, Peru 92 B e
Huanta, Peru 92 C f
Huánuco, Peru 92 B e
Huaonta, Nicaragua 91 C d
Huara, Chile 94 C a
Huaras, Peru 92 B e
Huariaca, Peru 92 B f
Huario, Peru 92 B f
Huarmey, Peru 92 B f
Huascarán, Mt., Peru 92 B e
Huasco, Chile 94 B c
Huatusco. See Coatepec
Huaylas, Peru 92 B e
Hubbard, Nova Scotia 82 H j
Hubbard, Saskatchewan 87 O g
Huberdeau, Quebec 85 Q g
Hubli, India 126 E e
Hubner B., Tutuila I. 79 T o
Huddersfield, England 99 F g
Hudiksvall, Sweden 103 G f
Hudson, Ontario 86 K a
Hudson B., Canada 81 L f
Hudson Bay, Saskatchewan 87 P f
Hudson Hope, Br. Columbia 88 J b
Hudson Mts., Antarctica 136 G d
Hudson Str., Canada 81 M e
Hudwin L., Manitoba 87 W e
Hue, S. Vietnam 132 D c
Huedin, Romania 112 D a
Huehuetenango, Guatemala 90 F d
Huejutla, Mexico 90 E c
Huelva, Spain 106 B d
Huereal Overa, Spain 107 E d
Huete, Spain 107 D b
Hughenden, Alberta 86 F f
Hughenden, Australia 135 H d
Hughes R., Manitoba 86 R b
Hughton, Saskatchewan 86 K g
Huhehot, China 130 E b
Hŭichŏn, Korea 128 J b
Hukawng Valley, Burma 127 J c
Hukow, China 128 G e
Hukuntsi, Bechuanaland 122 C d
Hula L., Israel 123 D d
Hulin. See Linkiang
Hull, England 99 G g
Hull, Quebec 85 P g
Hull I., Phoenix Is. 78 J h
Hulst, Netherlands 100 C c
Hulun. See Hailar
Hulun Chih, China 128 G a
Hulutao, China 128 H b
Huma, China 115 M c
Humacao, Puerto Rico 54 D h
Humaitá, Brazil 92 E e
Humaitá, Paraguay 94 E c
Humansdorp, South Africa 122 C f
Humay, Peru 92 B f
Humbe. See Mutano
Humber B., Ontario 84 C k
Humbermouth, Newfoundland 83 P e
Humber R., England 99 H g
Humboldt, Saskatchewan 87 M f
Humboldt Glacier, Greenland 89 Q b
Humenné, Czechoslovakia 105 J d
Hume Res., Australia 135 J g
Hun, Libya 118 J c
Húna-floí, Iceland 102 V m
Hunan, prov., China 131 E j
Hundred Mile House, British Columbia 88 J e
Hungary, Central Europe 97 M g
Hungchiang, China 131 J j
Hungnam, Korea 128 J c
Hungtze Hu, China 130 J f
Hunsrück, Mts., Germany 104 B d
Hunta, Ontario 84 J c
Hunter I., Br. Columbia 88 E e
Hunter I., Pacific Ocean 78 H j
Hunter Is., Tasmania 135 H h
Hunters River, Prince Edward I. 82 J g
Hunting I., Quebec 82 J c
Huntingdon, Quebec 85 Q g
Huntingdon & co., England 99 G h
Huntly, New Zealand 135 R k
Huntly, Scotland 98 F c
Hunts Point, Nova Scotia 82 H k
Huntsville, Ontario 85 L g
Hunucma, Mexico 90 F c
Hun-yüan-chow, China 130 F c
Hunza, Kashmir 126 D a
Huon Pen., New Guinea 135 J a
Hupeh, prov., China 130 F g
Hurd C., Ontario 84 J g
Hurdman Bridge, Ontario 84 D h
Hurghada, Egypt 119 M c
Hurkeet, Ontario 84 B d
Huronia, reg., Ontario 84 L h
Huskvarna, Sweden 103 F h
Hussar, Alberta 86 E g
Husum, Germany 104 C a
Hüttenberg, Austria 104 F e
Hutton, Br. Columbia 88 J c
Huttwil, Switzerland 101 C a
Huxley, Alberta 86 D g
Huy, Belgium 100 D d
Hvar, I., Yugoslavia 110 F d
Hwahsien, China 131 F l
Hwaian, China 130 J f
Hwaijen, China 130 F c
Hwaiking. See Tsinyang
Hwaining, China 131 H g
Hwaiyang, China 130 G f
Hwaiyn. See Tsingkiang
Hwangchow. See Hwangkang
Hwang-Hai. See Yellow Sea
Hwang Ho, China 128 G c
Hwang Ho, Mouth of, China 130 J c
Hwanghsien, China 130 K d
Hwangkang, China 130 G g
Hweichow. See Sihsien
Hweimin, China 130 H d
Hweinan, China 128 J b
Hweitseh, China 131 A j
Hwohsien, China 130 E d
Hyakuna, I., Okinawa 78 B d
Hyas, Saskatchewan 87 P g
Hybla, Ontario 85 N g
Hyden, Australia 134 C f
Hyderabad, India 126 E e
Hyderabad, Pakistan 126 C c
Hyères, France 109 G e
Hyères, Is. d', France 109 G e
Hyland Post, Br. Columbia 88 E b
Hylo, Alberta 86 E d
Hyogo, Japan 133 D g
Hyrynsalmi, Finland 102 N d
Hythe, Alberta 88 K c
Hythe, England 99 H j
Iaşi, Romania 116 E h
Iauarete, Colombia 92 D c
Ibadan, Nigeria 118 F g
Ibagué, Colombia 92 B c
Ibarra, Ecuador 92 B c
Ibb, Yemen 124 D g
Ibembo, Congo 120 E d
Iberville, Quebec 85 R g
Ibiapaba, Sa. da, Brazil 93 J d
Ibicuí, Brazil 94 E c
Ibiza I., Balearic Is. 107 F c
Ibresi, U.S.S.R. 117 H c
Ibri, Muscat & Oman 125 G e
Ibu, I., Okinawa 78 C a
Ibwe Munyama, N. Rhodesia 122 D c
Ica, Peru 92 B f
Içá, R., Brazil 92 D d
Içana, Brazil 92 D c
Içel, Turkey 124 B b
Iceland, I., North Atlantic Ocean 102 Wm
Ichang, China 130 E g
Icheng, China 130 F g
Ichow. See Lini
Ichun, China 131 G j
Idah, Nigeria 118 G g
Iddesleigh, Alberta 86 F h
Ideles, Algeria 118 G d
Idfu, Egypt 119 M d
Idhra, I., Greece 113 D f
Idirtu, China 128 C c
Idlib, Syria 123 E b
Idutywa, South Africa 122 D f
Ieper, Belgium 100 A d
Ierissós, G. of, Greece 113 D d
Ie shima, Okinawa 78 B a
Ifakara, Tanganyika 121 H f
Iférouane, Niger 118 G e
Ifni, N.-W. Africa 118 C c
Igan, Sarawak 129 F k
Igarapé Miri, Brazil 93 H d
Igarka, U.S.S.R. 114 H b
Iglesias, Sardinia 111 B f
Igli, Algeria 118 E b
Igloolik, N.-W. Territories 81 L d
Ignace, Ontario 86 L a
Igoma, Tanganyika 121 G f
Igra, U.S.S.R. 117 L b
Iguacú & R., Brazil 94 F c
Iguala, Mexico 90 E d
Iguapé, Brazil 94 G b
Iguatú, Brazil 93 K e
Igumira, Tanganyika 121 G f
Igurin, I., Eniwetok 79 R d
Ihosy, Madagascar 121 N l
Ihtiman, Bulgaria 112 D c
Iida, Japan 133 E g
Iisalmi, Finland 102 M e
Ijebu-Ode, Nigeria 118 F g
IJselmonde, Netherlands 100 C c
IJselmuiden, Netherlands 100 D b
IJselstein, Netherlands 100 D b
IJssel Meer, Netherlands 100 D b
IJssel R., Netherlands 100 E b
Ijui, Brazil 94 F c
Ijzendijke, Netherlands 100 B c
Ikaría, I., Greece 113 F f
Ikei shima, Okinawa 78 B c
Ikisu, Tanganyika 121 G e
Ikla, Estonia, U.S.S.R. 103 L h
Ikushumbet, Japan 133 G c
Ilagan, Philippines 129 H g
Ilam, Iran 124 E c
Ilanz, Switzerland 101 E b
Iława, Poland 105 H b
Iławka, Poland 105 J a
Ilbunga, Australia 134 G e
Ilderton, Ontario 84 J j
Ile à la Crosse, L., Sask. 86 K c
Ile à la Crosse, Saskatchewan 86 K c
Ile-de-France, prov., France 108 E b
Ile Mayotte, I., Archipel des Comores 121 K g
Ilford, Manitoba 87 W b
Ilfracombe, England 99 E j
Ilhavo, Portugal 106 A b
Ilhéus, Brazil 93 K f
Ili, Kazakh., U.S.S.R. 114 G d
Ilia, Greece 113 C f
Ilic, Turkey 124 C b
Ilich, Kazakh., U.S.S.R. 114 F d
Iligan, Philippines 129 H j
Ilikotu. See Ankang
Ilimsk, U.S.S.R. 115 K c
Iliodhrómia, I., Greece 113 D e
Illapel, Chile 94 B d
Ille-et-Vilaine, dep., France 108 C b
Illescas, Spain 106 D b
Illimani, Mt., Bolivia 93 D g
Illora, Spain 106 D d
Il'men', Oz., U.S.S.R. 116 G b
Ilo, Peru 92 C g
Iloilo, Philippines 129 H h
Ilorin, Nigeria 118 F g
Ilots de Bass, Tubuai Is. 79 M k
Ilpi, U.S.S.R. 115 S b
Imabari, Japan 133 C g
Iman, U.S.S.R. 115 N d
Imandra, Oz., U.S.S.R. 114 C b
Imerimandroso, Madagascar 121 N k
Imi, Ethiopia 121 J c
Imieji Anchorage, Jaluit I. 79 U j
Immendingen, Germany 104 C e
Imperatriz, Brazil 92 D e
Imperatriz, Brazil 93 H e
Imperia, Italy 110 B d
Imperial, Saskatchewan 87 M g
Imperoyal, Nova Scotia 82 J j
Imphal, India 127 H d
Imrodj, I., Jaluit I. 79 T h
Imroz, I., Turkey 124 A a
Imtan, Syria 123 E e
Inaccessible Is., Antarctica 136 J f
Inagua, Gt., I., Bahama Is. 91 E b
Inagua, Lit., I., Bahama Is. 91 E b
Inarajan, Guam 78 A l
Inari & L., Finland 102 M b
Inchkeith, Scotland 98 E d
Inchŏn, Korea 128 J c
Incourt, Belgium 100 C d
Indaal, L., Scotland 98 C e
Indals Älv, Sweden 102 G e
Indaw, Burma 127 J d
Indawgyi L., Burma 127 J c
Independencia, Argentina 94 C d
India, S. Asia 126-127
Indian Arm, inlet, British Columbia 88 D f
Indian Brook, Cape Breton I., Nova Scotia 83 M g
Indian Des. See Thar
Indian Harbour, Labrador 83 O g
Indian Harbour, Nova Scotia 82 J j
Indian Head, Manitoba 87 O h
Indian Head, Saskatchewan 80 J g
Indian L., Northern, Man. 87 U a
Indian L., Southern, Man. 87 T a
Indicator L., Quebec 82 A b
Indiga, U.S.S.R. 114 D b
Indigirka, R., U.S.S.R 115 P b
Indispensable Reefs, Coral Sea 78 F j
Indonesia, S.-E. Asia 129 F l
Indore, India 126 E d
Indre, dep., France 108 D c
Indre-et-Loire, dep., France 108 N k
Indur (Nizamabad), India 126 E e
Indus, R., Pakistan, etc. 126 C d
Inebolu, Turkey 124 B a
Ingelmunster, Belgium 100 B d
Ingenika, R., Br. Columbia 88 G b
Ingersoll, Ontario 84 K j
Ingham, Australia 135 J c
Inglefield Inlet, Greenland 89 Q b
Inglefield Ld., Greenland 89 Q b
Ingleside, Ontario 85 R b
Inglis, Manitoba 87 Q h
Ing Luiggi, Argentina 94 D e
Ingolf, Ontario 86 G a
Ingolstadt, Germany 104 D d
Ingonish, C. Breton I., Nova Scotia 83 M g
Ingramport, Nova Scotia 82 H j
Ingrid Christensen Coast, Antarctica 136 R e
Inhambane, Mozambique 122 F d
Inírida, R., Colombia 92 D c
Inishark I., Eire 99 A g
Inishbofin, I., Eire 99 A g
Inishkea I., Eire 99 A f
Inishman, I., Eire 99 A g
Inishmore, I., Eire 99 A g
Inishmurray, I., Eire 99 B f
Inishtrahull, Eire 98 C e
Inishturk, I., Eire 99 A g
Injune, Australia 135 J e
Inkerman, New Brunswick 82 H f
Innertkirchen, Switzerland 101 D b
Innisfail, Alberta 86 D f
Innisfail, Australia 135 J c
Innisfree, Alberta 86 F e
Innsbruck, Austria 104 D e
Inowrocław, Poland 105 H b
Inquisivi, Bolivia 92 D g
Ins, Switzerland 101 C a
In Salah, Algeria 118 F c
Insar, U.S.S.R. 117 G d
Insein, Burma 127 J e
In Shan. See Yin Shan
Insinger, Saskatchewan 87 O g
Insterburg. See Chernyakhovsk
Instow, Saskatchewan 86 J j
Intelewa, Surinam 93 F c
Interlaken, Switzerland 101 C b
International Peace Garden, Canada-U.S.A. 87 R k
Interview I., Andaman Is. 127 H f
Intragna, Switzerland 101 D b
Inutil, B., Chile 95 C h
Inveraray, Scotland 98 D d
Invercargill, New Zealand 135 P m
Inverell, Australia 135 K e
Invermay, Saskatchewan 87 O g
Invermere, Br. Columbia 88 L e
Inverness, C. Breton I., Nova Scotia 83 L g
Inverness, Quebec 85 T f
Inverness & co., Scotland 98 E c
Inverurie, Scotland 98 F c
Investigator Str., Australia 134 G g
Inwood, Ontario 84 J k
Inyati, S. Rhodesia 122 D c
Inza, U.S.S.R. 117 H d
Inzer, U.S.S.R. 117 N c
Ioánnina, Greece 113 C e
Ioco, Br. Columbia 88 E f

Iona, C. Breton I., N.S. 83 M h
Iona I., Scotland 98 C d
Ionian Is., Greece 113 B e
Ionian Sea, Italy, etc. 97 M j
Ionishkis, Lithuania, U.S.S.R. 103 K h
Ios, I., Greece 113 E f
Ipala, Mexico 90 C c
Ipameri, Brazil 93 H g
Ipen. See Ypres
Ipiales, Colombia 90 B c
Ipin, China 131 B h
Ipiros, Greece 113 C e
Ipoh, Malaya 132 C f
Ipperwash Prov. Park, Ont. 84 J j
Ippy, Cent. Afr. Republic 119 K g
Ipswich, Australia 135 K e
Ipswich, England 99 H h
Ipú, Brazil 93 J d
Iquique, Chile 94 B b
Iquitos, Peru 90 C d
Iracoubo, French Guiana 93 G b
Iráklia, I., Greece 113 E f
Iráklion, Crete 113 E g
Iran (Persia), Asia 125 F c
Irapa, Venezuela 92 E a
Irapuato, Mexico 90 D c
Iraq, W. Asia 124 D c
Irazú, Vol., Costa Rica 91 C d
Irbid, Jordan 123 D e
Irbit, U.S.S.R. 117 R b
Ireland, Rep. of (Eire), British Isles 99 B g
Irendyk Khr., U.S.S.R. 117 N e
Irgiz, Kazakh., U.S.S.R. 114 F d
Iringa, Tanganyika 121 H f
Irish Sea, British Isles 99 D g
Irkutsk, U.S.S.R. 115 K c
Irkutskaya Oblast, U.S.S.R. 115 K c
Irma, Alberta 86 F f
Iron Bridge, Ontario 84 G f
Irondale, Ontario 85 M h
Iron Knob, Australia 134 G f
Iroquois Dam, Ontario 85 P b
Iroquois Falls, Ontario 84 K d
Irrawaddy, Burma 127 H e
Irrawaddy, R., Burma 127 H e
Irricana, Alberta 86 D g
Irtysh, R., U.S.S.R. 114 F c
Irumu, Congo 121 F d
Irvine, Alberta 86 G j
Isa, Mt., Australia 134 G d
Isaac L., Br. Columbia 88 J d
Isaacs Harbour, Nova Scotia 83 L h
Isabela I., Galápagos Is. 79 R g
Isabella, Manitoba 87 R h
Isabella, Puerto Rico 54 B h
Isabel Segundo, Puerto Rico 54 D h
Isaccea, Romania 112 G b
Isachsen, C., N.-W. Terr. 80 J b
Isachsen, N.-W. Terr. 80 J b
Isafjördhur, Iceland 102 U l
Isai Kalat, Pakistan 126 B c
Isangi, Congo 120 E d
Isari, Greece 113 D f
Ischia, I., Italy 111 D e
Ise, Japan 133 E g
Ise B., Japan 133 E g
Iseghem, Belgium 100 B d
Iseltwald, Switzerland 101 C b
Isère, dep. & R., France 109 F d
Isernia, Italy 111 E e
Isfandaqeh. See Gav Koshī
Isha Baidao, Somali Rep. 121 J d
Ishan, China 131 D k
Ishikari, Japan 133 H c
Ishikawa, I., Okinawa 78 B b
Ishim, U.S.S.R. 114 F c
Ishimbai, U.S.S.R. 117 N d
Ishinomaki B., Japan 133 G e
Ishkamish, Afghanistan 125 J b
Ishkanan, Iran 125 F d
Ishkasham, Afghanistan 125 K b
Isil Kul, U.S.S.R. 114 G c
Isiolo, Kenya 121 H d
Isisford, Australia 135 H d
Iskenderun, Turkey 124 C b
Iskilip, Turkey 124 B a
Iskitim, U.S.S.R. 114 H c
Iskut, R., Br. Columbia 88 D b
Iskwatam L., Saskatchewan 87 O c
Islamabad, Pakistan 126 E b
Island Falls, Ontario 84 J c
Island Falls, Saskatchewan 87 P c
Island L., Manitoba 81 K g
Island L., Newfoundland 83 Q e
Island L., Ontario 84 K g
Islands, B. of, Newfoundland 83 O d
Islands, B. of, New Zealand 135 R j
Islay, Alberta 86 G e
Islay I., Scotland 99 C e
Isle aux Morts, Nfd. 83 O f
Isle Maligne, Quebec 82 A e
Isle of Man, British Isles 99 E f
Isles, L. des, Saskatchewan 86 H d
Isle Verte, Quebec 82 C e
Ismailia, Egypt 119 M b
Ismail Khan, India 126 D b
Isna, Egypt 119 M c
Isoka, N. Rhodesia 121 G g
Isparta, Turkey 124 B b
Israel, W. Asia 123 C e
Isriya, Syria 123 F b
Issoudun, France 108 D c
Issyk Kul, Oz., Kirgiz., U.S.S.R. 114 G d
Istanbul, Turkey 124 A a
Isthmus B., Ontario 84 J g
Istmina, Colombia 92 B b
Istra, Yugoslavia 110 D c
Itabaiana, Brazil 93 K e
Itacare, Brazil 93 K f
Itacoatiara, Brazil 92 F d
Itaeté, Brazil 93 J f
Itaituba, Brazil 93 F d
Itajaí, Brazil 94 G c
Itajuí, Brazil 93 H f
Italy, Central Europe 110-111
Itapaci, Brazil 93 H f
Itapajé, Brazil 93 K d
Itapecurú-mirim, Brazil 93 J d
Itapemirim, Cachoeiro de, Brazil 93 J h
Itapetininga, Brazil 93 H h
Itapeva, Brazil 93 H h
Itaqüi, Brazil 94 E c
Itarsi, India 126 E d
Itatube, Brazil 92 E e
Itaúna, Brazil 93 J h
Itéa, Greece 113 D e
Itháci. See Ithaká
Ithaká, Greece 113 C e
Itiés, Greece 113 C d
Itoman, I., Okinawa 78 A d
Ituaçú, Brazil 93 J f
Itubera, Brazil 93 K f
Itula, Congo 121 F e
Ituna, Saskatchewan 87 O g
Iturbe, Argentina 94 C b
Ivailovgrad, Bulgaria 112 F d
Ivanhoe, Australia 135 H f
Ivanhoe, R., Ontario 84 H d
Ivanic Grad, Yugoslavia 110 F c
Ivanovka, U.S.S.R. 117 K d
Ivanovo, U.S.S.R. 116 M c
Ivdel, U.S.S.R. 114 F b
Iviza I. See Ibiza
Ivory Coast, West Africa 118 D g
Ivugivik, Quebec 81 M e
Iwakuni, Japan 133 C g
Iwaniska, Poland 105 J c
Iwo Jima, Pacific Ocean 78 E d
Ixiamas, Bolivia 92 D f
Ixtla, Mexico 90 E d
Ixtlán de Juárez, Mexico 90 E d
Iyang, China 131 H h
Iyella Ra., New Zealand 135 Q l
Iyo Nada, Japan 133 B h
Izabal & L., Guatemala 90 G d
Izegem (Iseghem), Belgium 100 B d
Izhevsk, U.S.S.R. 117 L b
Izhma & R., U.S.S.R. 114 E b
Izki, Muscat & Oman 125 G e
Izmail, Ukraine, U.S.S.R. 116 F j
Izmir, Turkey 124 A b
Izmit, Turkey 124 A a
Izra, Syria 123 E e
Iztapa, Guatemala 90 F e
Izu Pen., Japan 133 F g
Izu Shichito, Japan 133 F g
Izyum, Ukraine, U.S.S.R. 116 K g
Jääski. See Svetogorsk
Jabalpur, India 126 F d
Jabbeke, Belgium 100 B c
Jabbul, Syria 123 F a
Jablonec, Czechoslovakia 104 F c
Jabnoren, Jaluit I. 79 T g
Jabor, Jaluit I. 79 U j
Jaboti, Brazil 92 F d
Jabrin Oasis, Saudi Arabia 124 E e
Jaburú, Brazil 92 D d
Jabwot I., Marshall Is. 79 T c
Jaca, Spain 107 E a
Jacarezinho, Brazil 93 H h
Jachal, Argentina 94 C d
Jaci Paraná, Brazil 92 E e
Jack Fish, Ontario 84 D d
Jackfish L., Saskatchewan 86 J e
Jackhead Harbour, Manitoba 87 U g
Jack Lane B., Labrador 81 N f
Jackpine, Ontario 84 C c
Jackson B., New Zealand 135 P l
Jackson Bay, Br. Columbia 88 G e
Jackson's Arm, Newfoundland 83 Q d
Jacmel, Haiti 91 E c
Jacobabad, Pakistan 126 C c
Jacobina, Brazil 93 J f
Jacobs, Ontario 87 N a
Jacques Cartier, Mt., Quebec 82 G d
Jacques Cartier, Quebec 85 R g
Jacques Cartier, R., Quebec 85 T e
Jacques Cartier Pass, Quebec 82 H c
Jacquet River, New Brunswick 82 F f
Jade Mines, Burma 127 J c
Jadib, Aden 125 F f
Jadida, El. See Mazagan
Jadotville, Congo 120 F g
Jaén, Spain 106 D d
Jafarabad, India 126 D d
Jaffa (Yafo), Israel 123 C e
Jaffna, Ceylon 126 E g
Jaghbub, Libya 119 K c
Jaguarão, Brazil 94 F d
Jaguari, Brazil 94 F c
Jaguariaiva, Brazil 93 H h
Jaguaruna, Brazil 94 G c
Jahra, Kuwait 124 E d
Jahrom, Iran 125 F d
Jaicos, Brazil 93 J e
Jaipur, India 126 E c
Jaisalmer, India 126 D c
Jajarm, Iran 125 G b
Jajpur, India 127 G d
Jakarta. See Djakarta
Jäkkvik, Sweden 102 G c
Jakobi, Estonia, U.S.S.R. 103 M g
Jakobshavn, Greenland 81 O d
Jalalabad, Afghanistan 126 C b
Jalapa, Nicaragua 91 E d
Jalapa Enriquez, Mexico 90 E d
Jalasjärvi, Finland 102 K e
Jaldak, Afghanistan 125 J c
Jalgaon, India 126 E d
Jalisco, state, Mexico 90 D d
Jaloklab, Majuro Is. 79 T f
Jalor, India 126 D c
Jalpaiguri, India 127 G c
Jalq, Iran 125 H d
Jaluit, I., Marshall Is. 78 H g
Jaluit Lagoon, Jaluit I. 79 T h
Jam, Iran 125 F d
Jamaica, I., West Indies 91 D c
Jamaja, Estonia, U.S.S.R. 103 K g
Jamalabad, Iran 124 E b
Jamalpur, India 127 G c
Jambon, Pt., Quebec 82 F d
Jamdena, I., Indonesia 129 K m
James B., Ontario 81 L g
James Ras., Australia 134 F d
James Ross I., Antarctica 136 J f
Jamestown, Ontario 84 E d
Jamiltepec, Mexico 90 E d
Jammer Bugt, Denmark 103 C h
Jammu, Kashmir 126 E b
Jamnagar, India 126 D d
Jamrad, Afghanistan 125 J c
Jamrao, Pakistan 126 C c
Jämsä, Finland 103 L f
Jamshedpur, India 127 G d
Jamundi, Colombia 92 B c
Jandaq, Iran 125 F c
Janjira, India 126 D e
Jan L., Saskatchewan 87 P d
Jan Mayen I., Arctic Ocean 114 A a
Janos, Mexico 90 C a
Jansen, Saskatchewan 87 N g
Jansenville, South Africa 122 C f
Janaúria, Brazil 93 J g
Janze, France 108 C c
Jaora, India 126 E d
Japan & Sea of, E. Asia 133
Japen, I., New Guinea 129 L l
Japtan I., Eniwetok 79 S c
Japurá, Brazil 92 D d
Japvo Mt., India 127 H c
Jaragua, Brazil 93 H g
Jaragua, Brazil 94 G c
Jaramillo, Argentina 95 C g
Jarandilla, Spain 106 C b
Jaranwala, India 126 D b
Jardim, Brazil 93 K e
Jardine Brook, New Brunswick 82 E f
Jardines de la Reina, Cuba 91 D b
Jarí, R., Brazil 93 G c
Jarji, Nigeria 118 G f
Jarocin, Poland 105 G c
Jaromer, Czechoslovakia 105 F c
Jaroslaw, Poland 105 K c
Järpen, Sweden 102 E e
Jarrow, Alberta 86 F f
Jarvie, Alberta 86 D d
Jarvis, Ontario 84 K k
Jarvis I., Pacific Ocean 78 K g
Järvsö, Sweden 103 G f
Jashpurnagar, India 127 F d
Jask, Iran 125 G d
Jasmin, Saskatchewan 87 O g
Jason I., Falkland Is. 95 D h
Jason Pen., Antarctica 136 J e
Jasper, Alberta 88 K d
Jasper, Ontario 85 P h
Jasper Nat. Park, Alberta 88 K d
Jasper Place, Alberta 86 D e
Jassy. See Iasi
Jastrowie, Poland 105 G b
Jaszberény, Hungary 105 H e
Jataí, Brazil 93 G g
Jath, India 126 E e
Jativa, Spain 107 E c
Jatobá, Brazil 93 H d
Jaú, Brazil 93 H h
Jauche, Belgium 100 C d
Jauf. See Al Jawf
Jauja, Peru 92 B f
Jaumave, Mexico 90 E c
Jaunpur, India 127 F c
Jauuperí, Brazil 92 E c
Java, I., Indonesia 129 E m
Javarí, R., Peru-Brazil 92 C e
Javier, I., Chile 95 B g
Jawa, Nigeria 119 H f
Jayuya, Puerto Rico 54 C h
Jazir, Muscat & Oman 125 G f
Jebba, Nigeria 118 F g
Jebel Abiod, Tunisia 111 B g
Jeble, Syria 123 D b
Jech Doab, Pakistan 126 D b
Jedburgh, Saskatchewan 87 P g
Jedburgh, Scotland 98 F e
Jedede, Saudi Arabia 125 D e
Jēkabpils, Latvia, U.S.S.R. 103 L h
Jelgava (Yelgava), Latvia, U.S.S.R. 103 K h
Jellicoe, Ontario 84 C c
Jelsava, Czechoslovakia 105 J d
Jemeppe, Belgium 100 C d
Jemo I., Marshall Is. 79 T a
Jemseg, New Brunswick 82 F h
Jena, Germany 104 D c
Jenin, Jordan 123 D e
Jenipapo, Brazil 92 F e
Jenner, Alberta 86 F h
Jens Munk I., N.-W. Terr. 81 L d
Jeorg Plat., Antarctica 136 H c
Jeppo, Finland 102 K e
Jerablus, Syria 123 F a
Jerash, Jordan 123 D e
Jérémie, Haiti 91 E c
Jeremoabo, Brazil 93 K f
Jerez de la Frontera, Spain 106 B d
Jericho, Australia 135 J d
Jericho, Jordan 123 D f
Jerome, Ontario 84 H e
Jerruck, Pakistan 126 C c
Jersey, I., Channel Is. 108 B b
Jerusalem, Israel-Jordan 123 D f
Jervis I., New Guinea 135 H a
Jervis Inlet, Br. Columbia 88 H e
Jervois Ra., Australia 134 G d
Jesselton, N. Borneo 129 G j
Jessore, E. Pakistan 127 G d
Jésus, Ile, Quebec 85 Q h
Jetait, Manitoba 87 Q b
Jetalsar, India 126 D d
Jeypore, India 127 F e
Jezzin, Lebanon 123 D d
Jhal, Pakistan 126 C c
Jhalrapatan, India 126 E d
Jhang Maghiana, Pakistan 126 D b
Jhansi, India 126 E c
Jhau, Pakistan 126 C c
Jhelum, Pakistan 126 D b
Jhelum R., Pakistan 126 D b
Jhesh Sheikh, Syria 123 D d
Jhudo, Pakistan 126 C c
Jhunjhunu, India 126 E c
Jiachan, Tibet 126 F b
Jibhalanta, Mongolia 115 J d
Jicaro, Nicaragua 91 B d
Jičin, Czechoslovakia 104 F c
Jidd, Iraq 124 C c
Jiddah, Saudi Arabia 124 C e
Jiggitai L., Tibet 127 G a
Jihlava, Czechoslovakia 105 F d
Jildiah, Jebel, Saudi Arabia 124 D d
Jimena de la Frontera, Spain 106 C d
Jiménez, Mexico 90 D b
Jimma, Ethiopia 121 H c
Jinbal, Jaluit I. 79 T h
Jind, India 126 E c
Jinotega, Nicaragua 91 B d
Jipijapa, Ecuador 92 A d
Jirgalanta, Mongolia 115 J d
Jishah, Saudi Arabia 124 E d
Jisr esh Shughur, Syria 123 E b
Jiul R., Romania 112 D b
Jiza, Jordan 123 D f
Jizan, Saudi Arabia 124 D f
Joab L., Ontario 84 G a
Joacaba, Brazil 94 F c
João Pessoa, Brazil 93 L e
Jobrin, Ontario 84 D b
Jobson, Argentina 94 D c
Jodhpur, India 126 D c
Joe Batt's Arm, Nfd. 83 S d
Joensuu, Finland 102 N e
Jofane, Mozambique 122 E d
Joffre, Mt., Br. Columbia 88 M e
Joffre Oil Fields, Alberta 84 E b
Joggins, Nova Scotia 82 H h
Jogjakarta, Indonesia 129 F m
Jog L., Ontario 84 E b
Jogues, Ontario 84 G b
Johannesburg, South Africa 122 D e
Johan Pen., N.-W. Terr. 81 M b
John C., Nova Scotia 82 J h
John o' Groats, Scotland 98 E b
John Quincy Adams Glacier, Antarctica 136 S e
Johnstone Str., Br. Columbia 88 F e
Johnston I., Pacific Ocean 78 J e
Johore Bahru, Malaya 132 C f
Joinville, Brazil 94 G c
Joinville, France 108 F b
Joinville I., Antarctica 136 J f
Jokaj, I., Ponape I. 78 F n
Jokaj Passage, Ponape I. 78 F n
Jokkmökk, Sweden 102 H c
Joliette, Quebec 85 R f
Jolo & I., Philippines 129 H j
Jol Plat., Saudi Arabia 124 E f
Jonava, Lithuania, U.S.S.R. 103 L j
Jones, C., Quebec 81 M g
Jones Sd., N.-W. Territories 81 L b
Jönköping, Sweden 103 F h
Jonquière, Quebec 85 T d
Jonuta, Mexico 90 F d
Jordan, R., Israel-Jordan 123 D e
Jordan, W. Asia 124 C c
Jordan L., Nova Scotia 82 G j
Jorhat, India 127 H c
Jorje Montt, I., Chile 95 B h
Joseph, L., Labrador 81 N h
Joseph, L., Ontario 84 L h
Joseph Bonaparte Gulf, Australia 134 E b
Joseph Cook B., Antarctica 136 A e
Joseph Pt., Anticosti I., Quebec 83 K d
Jotunheimen, Norway 103 C f
Joussard, Alberta 86 B c
Joux, L. de, Switzerland 101 B b
Jowai, India 127 H c
Juan Fernández, Is., Pac. Oc. 79 R m
Juan Gallegos I., Canal Zone 91 F b
Juaniata, Saskatchewan 86 K f
Juan-les-Pins, France 109 G e
Juan Stuven, I., Chile 95 A g
Juárez, Argentina 95 E e
Juba, Sudan 119 M h
Juba R., Somali Republic 121 J d
Jubba, Saudi Arabia 124 D d
Jubbulpore. See Jabalpur
Jubeil, Lebanon 123 D c
Jubilee L., Newfoundland 83 R e
Jucaro, Cuba 91 D b
Juchitán, Mexico 90 E d
Jude I., Newfoundland 83 S f
Judeidat el Wadi, Syria 123 E d
Judenburg, Austria 104 F e
Judique, C. Breton I., Nova Scotia 83 L h
Jugoslavia. See Yugoslavia
Juian, China 131 K j
Juichow. See Kaoan
Juist, I., Germany 104 B b
Juiz de Fóra, Brazil 93 J h
Jujuy, Argentina 94 C b
Jukao, China 130 K f
Jukkasjarvi, Sweden 96 N b
Julaca, Bolivia 92 D h
Juli, Peru 92 D g
Juliaca, Peru 92 C g
Julia Creek, Australia 135 H d
Julianehaab, Greenland 89 P d
Julio de Castilhos, Brazil 94 F c
Jumaima, Iraq 124 D d
Jumet, Belgium 100 C d
Jumilla, Spain 107 E c
Jumin. See Juymand
Jumoo Mt., Br. Columbia 88 L e
Junagarh, India 126 D d
Junan, China 130 G f
Juncos, Puerto Rico 54 D h
Jundah, Australia 135 H d
Jundiaí, Brazil 93 H h
Junee, Australia 135 J f
Jungfrau, Mt., Switzerland 101 C b
Jungfraujoch, Switzerland 101 C b
Jungkiang, China 131 D k
Junín, Argentina 95 B e
Junín, Argentina 94 D d
Junín, Chile 94 B a
Junin, Peru 92 B f
Junina, R., India 126 E c
Juning. See Junan
Juniper, New Brunswick 82 E g
Juniye, Lebanon 123 D d
Junor, Saskatchewan 86 K e
Junsele, Sweden 102 G e
Juo Järvi, Finland 102 N e
Jupia, Brazil 93 G h
Jupiter R., Anticosti I., Quebec 82 J d
Juquila, Mexico 90 E d
Jura, dep., France 108 F c
Jura, Mts., France-Switzerland 108 G c
Juradó, Colombia 92 B b
Jura I. & Sd. of, Scotland 98 D d
Jurbarkas, Lithuania, U.S.S.R. 103 K j
Jurf ed Darawish, Jordan 123 D g
Jüri (Yüri), Estonia, U.S.S.R. 103 L g
Jurm, Afghanistan 125 K b
Juruá, R., Brazil 92 D d
Juruena & R., Brazil 92 F f
Jurutí, Brazil 93 F d
Jusiye, Syria 123 E c
Jussy, Switzerland 101 B b
Justice, Manitoba 87 S h
Justo Daract, Argentina 94 C d
Juticalpa, Honduras 91 B d
Jutland. See Jylland
Juuka, Finland 102 N e
Juwain, Afghanistan 125 H c
Juwarah, Muscat & Oman 125 G f
Juwer, Aden 124 E g
Juxtlahuaco, Mexico 90 E d
Juymand, Iran 125 G c
Jylland, Denmark 103 C h
Jylland, Syd, Denmark 103 C j
Jyväskylä, Finland 102 L e
Kabajana, I., Indonesia 129 H m
Kabala, Sierra Leone 118 C g
Kabale, Uganda 121 G e
Kabba, Nigeria 118 G g
Kåbbenbock, Jaluit I. 79 T j
Kabenung L., Ontario 84 E d
Kabinakagami, R., Ontario 84 F c
Kabinakagami L., Ontario 84 F d
Kabinda, Congo 120 E f
Kabongo, Congo 120 F f
Kabul & R., Afghanistan 125 J c
Kabunda, Congo 121 F g
Kačanik, Yugoslavia 112 C c
Kachiry, Kazakh., U.S.S.R. 114 G c
Kachkar, U.S.S.R. 117 Q c
Kachuga, U.S.S.R. 115 K c
Kadena, I., Okinawa 78 A c
Kadiger, China 130 A c
Kadiköy, Turkey 124 A a
Kadiri, India 124 E f
Kadiyevka, Ukraine, U.S.S.R. 116 L g
Kadom, U.S.S.R. 117 F c
Kadugli, Sudan 119 L f
Kaduna, Nigeria 118 G f
Kadur, India 126 E f
Kadyi, U.S.S.R. 117 F b
Kaegudeck L., Newfoundland 83 R e
Kaesong, Korea 128 J c
Kaf, Saudi Arabia 124 C c
Kafakumba, Congo 120 E f
Kafanchan, Nigeria 118 G g
Kafra, Chad 119 K e
Kafr Behum, Syria 123 E b
Kafrun, Syria 123 E c
Kagan, Uzbek., U.S.S.R. 114 F e
Kagawong, Ontario 84 H h
Kagi. See Chiai
Kagianagami L., Ontario 84 C b
Kagiano L., Ontario 84 D c
Kagoshima, Japan 133 B j
Kagoshima B., Japan 133 A j
Kagul, Moldavia, U.S.S.R. 116 F j
Kahafa, Saudi Arabia 124 D d
Kahama, Tanganyika 119 G e
Kahan, India 126 C c
Kahntah, Br. Columbia 88 J a
Kahnuj, Iran 125 G d
Kahta, Turkey 124 C b
Kahutara Pt., New Zealand 135 S k
Kaiama, Nigeria 118 F g
Kaiapoi, New Zealand 135 Q l
Kaiashk, R., Ontario 87 O a
Kai-chow, China 130 G e
Kaieteur Fall, Brit. Guiana 92 E b
Kai fêng, China 130 G e
Kaigo, Sudan 119 M g
Kaihwa. See Wenshan
Kai-Kep, Indonesia 129 K m
Kaikohe, New Zealand 135 Q j
Kaikoura, New Zealand 135 Q l
Kaikoura Ra., New Zealand 135 Q l
Kailas Ra., India-Tibet 126 E e
Kaimanawa Mts., New Zealand 135 R k
Kaimur Ra., India 126 F d
Kaipara Harb., New Zealand 135 Q k
Kaira, India 126 D d
Kairouan, Tunisia 119 H a
Kairovo, U.S.S.R. 117 N c
Kaisarie. See Kayseri
Kaiserlautern, Germany 104 B d
Kaitaia, New Zealand 135 Q j
Kaitangata, New Zealand 135 P m
Kai-yüan, China 130 M a
Kajaani, Finland 102 M d
Kajiado, Kenya 121 H e
Kajiki, Japan 133 B j
Kakabeka Falls, Ontario 87 N b
Kakagi L., Ontario 86 J a
Kakamari, Uganda 121 G d
Kakamega, Kenya 121 G d
Kakhk, Iran 125 G c
Kakhovskoye Vdkhr., Ukraine, U.S.S.R. 116 J h
Kakia, Bechuanaland 122 C d
Kaksha, U.S.S.R. 117 H a
Kakwa, R., Alberta 88 K c
Kalábáka, Greece 113 C e
Kalabera, I., Saipan-Tinian Is. 78 B e
Kala Bist. See Qala Bist
Kalabo, N. Rhodesia 122 C c
Kalabsha, Egypt 119 M d
Kalach, U.S.S.R. 117 E e
Kaladar, Ontario 85 N h
Kalahari Des., Bechuanaland 122 C d
Kalajoki, Finland 102 K d
Kalak, Iran 125 G d
Kalakan, U.S.S.R. 115 L c
Kalakepen, Sumatra 129 C k
Kalámai, Greece 113 D f
Kalamáta. See Kalámai
Kala Nao, Afghanistan 125 H c
Kalangali, Tanganyika 121 G f
Kalannie, Australia 134 C f
Kalarnian Ghat, India 126 F c
Kala Sarkari, Afghanistan 125 J b
Kalat, Pakistan 126 C c
Kalat-i-Ghilzai, Afghanistan 125 J c
Kalaw, Burma 127 J d
Kale, Burma 127 H d
Kalediran, Turkey 124 B b
Kalewa, Burma 127 H d
Kalgan. See Changkiakow
Kalgoorlie, Australia 134 D f
Kalhat, Muscat & Oman 125 G e
Kalikino, U.S.S.R. 117 M d
Kalimnos, I., Greece 113 F f
Kalingapatnam, India 127 F e
Kalinin, U.S.S.R. 116 J c
Kaliningrad, U.S.S.R. 103 J j
Kalisz, Poland 105 H c
Kaliua, Tanganyika 121 G f
Kalix Älv, Sweden 102 J c
Kalixfors, Sweden 102 J c
Kalkfeld, S.W. Africa 122 B d
Kalkfontein, Bechuanaland 122 C d
Kalkwerk, S.W. Africa 122 B e
Kallaste, Estonia, U.S.S.R. 103 M g
Kallavesi, Finland 102 M e
Kalloni, Greece 113 F e
Kall Sjön, Sweden 102 E e
Kalmar, Sweden 103 F h
Kalmar Sund, Sweden 103 G h
Kalmykovo, Kazakh., U.S.S.R. 114 E d
Kalocsa, Hungary 105 H e
Kalokhorio, Cyprus 123 A b
Kalone Pk., Br. Columbia 88 F d
Kaluga, U.S.S.R. 116 K d
Kalule, Congo 120 F f
Kalundborg, Denmark 103 D j
Kalundu, N. Rhodesia 121 F g
Kalutara, Ceylon 126 E g
Kalvarija, Lithuania, U.S.S.R. 103 K j
Kalyan, India 126 D e
Kalyazin, U.S.S.R. 116 K c
Kama, R., U.S.S.R. 114 E b
Kamaishi, Japan 133 G e
Kamalampaka, Tanganyika 121 G f

Kamaran, I., Red Sea 124 D f
Kamatsi, Saskatchewan 87 P b
Kamchatka, U.S.S.R. 115 R c
Kamchatskaya Oblast, U.S.S.R. 115 R c
Kamen, U.S.S.R. 114 H c
Kamenets Podolskiy, Ukraine, U.S.S.R. 116 E g
Kamenskoye, U.S.S.R. 115 R b
Kamensk Shakhtinski, U.S.S.R. 117 E f
Kamensk Ural'skiy, U.S.S.R. 117 Q b
Kamet, Mt., India 126 E b
Kami Iwani, Japan 133 C g
Kamina, Congo 120 E f
Kaminak L., N.-W. Terr. 81 K e
Kaministikwia, Ontario 87 N b
Kaminuriak L., N.-W. Terr. 81 K e
Kamiyama shima, Okinawa 78 A c
Kam Keut, Laos 132 C c
Kamloops, Br. Columbia 88 J e
Kamloops L., Br. Columbia 88 J e
Kamnik, Yugoslavia 110 E b
Kamouraska, Quebec 82 C f
Kampa Dzong, Tibet 127 G c
Kampala, Uganda 121 G d
Kampen, Netherlands 100 D b
Kampot, Cambodia 132 C d
Kamptee, India 126 E d
Kamsack, Saskatchewan 87 Q g
Kamuchawie L., Saskatchewan 87 P b
Kamyshin, U.S.S.R. 117 G e
Kamyshlov, U.S.S.R. 117 R b
Kanaaupscow & R., Quebec 81 M g
Kananaskis L., Alberta 86 B h
Kanayama. See Hachuman
Kanazawa, Japan 133 E f
Kanchanaburi, Thailand 132 B d
Kancheepuram, India 126 E f
Kanchow, China 131 G k
Kandahar, Afghanistan 125 J c
Kandahar, Saskatchewan 87 N g
Kandalaksha, U.S.S.R. 114 C b
Kandava, Latvia, U.S.S.R. 103 K h
Kandavu, I., Fiji Is. 78 H j
Kandole, Congo 120 E e
Kandy, Ceylon 126 F g
Kane Basin, Greenland 89 Q b
Kanev, Ukraine, U.S.S.R. 116 G g
Kang, Bechuanaland 122 C d
Kangan, Iran 125 F d
Kangar, Malaya 132 C e
Kangaroo I., Australia 134 G g
Kangāvar, Iran 124 E c
Kangchenjunga, Mt.,Nepal 127 G c
Kangeeak Pt., N.-W. Terr. 81 N d
Kangmar, Kashmir 126 E b
Kango, Gabon 120 C d
Kangoku iwa, Iwo Jima 78 D a
Kangpao, China 130 G b
Kangra, India 126 E b
Kangsa R., E. Pakistan 127 H c
Kani, Burma 127 H d
Kaniama, Congo 120 E f
Kaniapiskau, R., Quebec 81 N f
Kaniapiskau L., Quebec 81 N g
Kanibadam, Tadzhik., U.S.S.R. 125 K a
Kanif, Yap I. 78 C l
Kankan, Guinea 118 D f
Kanker, India 126 F d
Kankesanturai, Ceylon 126 E g
Kan Kiang, China 128 G e
Kannauj, India 126 E c
Kannus, Finland 102 K e
Kano, Nigeria 118 G f
Kanoya, Japan 133 B j
Kanpur, India 126 F c
Kansk, U.S.S.R. 115 J c
Kansu, prov., China 130 A e
Kantchari, Upper Volta 118 F f
Kanturk, Eire 99 B h
Kanuma, Japan 133 F f
Kanye, Bechuanaland 122 D e
Kaoan, China 131 G h
Kaocheng, China 130 G e
Kaohsiung, Taiwan 131 K l
Kaolack, Senegal 118 B f
Kaolan. See Lanchow
Kao Lu-ang, Mt., Thailand 132 B e
Kaomi, China 130 J d
Kaoyi, China 130 G d
Kaoyu, China 130 J f
Kaoyu Hu, China 130 J f
Kapal. See Taldy Kurgan
Kapaus, R., Borneo 129 F k
Kapfenberg, Austria 105 F e
Kapiri Mposhi, N. Rhodesia 121 F g
Kapiskau, Ontario 81 L g
Kapoeta, Sudan 119 M h
Kaposvár, Hungary 112 A a
Kapsabet, Kenya 121 H d
Kapsukas, Lithuania, U.S.S.R. 103 K j
Kapurthala, India 126 E b
Kapuskasing, Ontario 84 H c
Kapuskasing, R., Ontario 84 H d
Kar, Iran 124 E c
Kara, U.S.S.R. 114 F b
Kara Bogaz Gol, Turkmen., U.S.S.R. 114 E d
Karabuk, Turkey 124 B a
Karabuta, Iran 124 E b
Karacabey, Turkey 124 A a
Karaca Dagh, Turkey 124 B b
Karachev, U.S.S.R. 116 J e
Karachi, Pakistan 126 C d
Karaganda, Kazakh., U.S.S.R. 114 G d
Karaginskiy Os., U.S.S.R. 115 R c
Karaj, Iran 125 F b
Karak, Jordan 123 D f
Karak, Tibet 126 E b
Kara Kalpakskaya, Uzbek., U.S.S.R. 114 E d
Karakelong, I., Indonesia 129 J k
Karakoram Ra., Kashmir 126 D b
Karakose, Turkey 124 D b
Kara Kum, Turkmen., U.S.S.R. 114 E e
Kara Kum Can., Turkmen., U.S.S.R. 125 H b
Karaman, Turkey 124 B b
Karamea Bight, New Zealand 135 Q l
Karapiro, L., New Zealand 135 R k
Karasa, U.S.S.R. 117 K c
Karasburg, S.W. Africa 122 B e
Kara Sea, U.S.S.R. 114 G a
Karasjok, Norway 102 L b
Karatina, Kenya 121 H e
Karatsu, Japan 133 A h
Karaul, U.S.S.R. 114 H a
Karaurgan, Turkey 124 D a
Kardam, Tibet 126 F b
Kardhítsa, Greece 113 C e
Karelskaya A.S.S.R., U.S.S.R. 114 C b
Karenni, Burma 127 J e
Karesuando, Sweden 102 K b
Karganrud, Iran 124 E b
Kargil, Kashmir 126 E b
Kargopol, U.S.S.R. 116 L a
Kariba & L., S. Rhodesia 122 D c
Karibib, S.W. Africa 122 B d
Karikal, India 126 E f
Karimata, I., Indonesia 129 E l
Karin, Somali Republic 121 K b
Karind. See Kar
Karis, Finland 103 K f
Kariz, Iran 125 H c
Karkaralinsk, U.S.S.R. 114 G d
Karkkila, Finland 103 L f
Karlik Tagh, China 128 B b
Karl Marx Stadt, Germany 104 E c
Karlovac, Yugoslavia 110 E c
Karlovy Vary, Czechoslovakia 104 E c
Karlsbad. See Karlovy Vary
Karlsborg, Sweden 103 F g
Karlshamn, Sweden 103 F h
Karlskrona, Sweden 103 F h
Karlsruhe, Germany 104 C d
Karlstad, Sweden 103 E g
Karmöy, I., Norway 103 A g
Karnal, India 126 E c
Karnten, prov., Austria 104 E e
Karona Fall, Brit. Guiana 92 F c
Karora, Sudan 121 H a
Karpáthos, I. & Str., Greece 113 F g
Karperón, Greece 113 C e
Karroo, Great, S. Africa 122 C f
Kars, Turkey 124 D a
Karsakpay, Kazakh., U.S.S.R. 114 F d
Karsakuwigamak, L., Manitoba 87 S b
Kärsämäki, Finland 102 L e
Kārsava, Latvia, U.S.S.R. 103 M h
Karshi, Uzbek., U.S.S.R. 114 F e
Karstula, Finland 102 L e
Karsun, U.S.S.R. 117 H c
Kartaly, U.S.S.R. 117 Q d
Karungi, Sweden 102 K c
Karungu, Kenya 121 G e
Karunki, Finland 102 L c
Karur, India 126 E f
Karvina, Czechoslovakia 105 H d
Karwar, India 126 D f
Karymskoye, U.S.S.R. 115 L c
Kasai R., Congo 120 D e
Kasama, N. Rhodesia 121 G g
Kasanga, Tanganyika 121 G f
Kasempa, N. Rhodesia 120 F g
Kasenga, Congo 121 F g
Kasenga, N. Rhodesia 122 D c
Kashabowie, Ontario 87 M b
Kashan, Iran 125 F c
Kashgar, China 114 G e
Kashing, China 130 K g
Kashira, U.S.S.R. 116 L d
Kashishibog L., Ontario 87 N a
Kashiwazaki, Japan 133 F f
Kāshmar, Iran 125 G b
Kashmir, S. Asia 126 E b
Kashmor, Pakistan 126 C c
Kasimov, U.S.S.R. 117 E c
Kasinka, Bechuanaland 122 C c
Kaskinen, Finland 102 J e
Kas Kong, Cambodia 132 C d
Kaslo, Br. Columbia 88 L f
Kasongo, Congo 120 F e
Kásos, I., Greece 113 F g
Kásos Str., Crete 113 F g
Kaspichan, Bulgaria 112 F c
Kas Rong, Cambodia 132 C d
Kassala, Sudan 121 H a
Kassandra, Greece 113 D d
Kassel, Germany 104 C c
Kastamonu, Turkey 124 B a
Kastélli, Crete 113 D g
Kastéllion, Crete 113 E g
Kastoria, Greece 113 C d
Kastrosikiá, Greece 113 C e
Kasulu, Tanganyika 121 G e
Kasungu, Nyasaland 121 G g
Kasur, Pakistan 126 D b
Katabaru, I., Okinawa 78 B b
Katákolon, Greece 113 C f
Katanga, prov., Congo 120 E g
Katanning, Australia 134 C f
Katav Ivanovsk, U.S.S.R. 117 P c
Katepwe, Saskatchewan 87 O h
Katepwe Prov. Park, Sask. 87 O h
Katerini, Greece 113 D d
Kates Needle, Mt., B.C. 88 C b
Katha, Burma 127 J d
Katherine, Australia 134 F b
Kathgodam, India 126 E c
Kathiawar, India 126 D d
Kathryn, Alberta 86 D g
Katihar, India 127 G c
Katimik L., Manitoba 87 S f
Katmandu, Nepal 127 G c
Katni, India 126 F d
Kato Akhaia, Greece 113 C e
Katol, India 126 E d
Káto Nevrokópion, Greece 112 D d
Katoomba, Australia 135 K f
Katowice (Stalinogród), Poland 105 H c
Katrine, L., Scotland 98 D d
Katrineholm, Sweden 103 G g
Katsina, Nigeria 118 G f
Katsuren hantō, Okinawa 78 B c
Kattawagami L., Ontario 84 K c
Kattegat, Sweden-Denmark 103 D h
Kattowitz. See Katowice
Katwewe, Congo 121 F f
Katwijk-aan-Zee, Netherlands 100 C b
Kaufbeuren, Germany 104 D e
Kauhava, Finland 102 K e
Kaula I., Palmyra I. 79 U k
Kaunas, Lithuania, U.S.S.R. 103 K j
Kauriya, India 127 F d
Kautokeino, Norway 102 K b
Kavak, Turkey 124 C a
Kavali, India 126 E f
Kavála, Greece 113 E d
Kavála, prov., Greece 112 E d
Kavkaz Bolshoi & Maly, Mts., U.S.S.R. 114 D d
Kaw, French Guiana 93 G c
Kawactha Lakes, Ontario 85 M h
Kawagama L., Ontario 85 M g
Kawambwa, N. Rhodesia 121 F f
Kawanoe, Japan 133 C g
Kawardha, India 126 F d
Kawasaki, Japan 133 F g
Kawasak Passage, Palau Is. 78 C h
Kawene, Ontario 87 L a
Kawerau, New Zealand 135 R k
Kawhia, New Zealand 135 R k
Kawinaw L., Manitoba 87 S f
Kawkareik, Burma 127 J e
Kayes, Mali 118 C f
Kay Is., Antarctica 136 B d
Kayo, Okinawa 78 C b
Kayseri, Turkey 124 C b
Kayshyadoris, Lithuania, U.S.S.R. 103 L j
Kayville, Saskatchewan 87 M j
Kazabazua, Quebec 85 O g
Kazach'ye, U.S.S.R. 115 N a
Kazakhskaya, U.S.S.R. 114 F d
Kazakhstan. See Kazakhskaya
Kazalinsk, Kazakh., U.S.S.R. 114 F d
Kazan, U.S.S.R. 117 J c
Kazan L., Saskatchewan 86 J c
Kazanlŭk, Bulgaria 112 E c
Kazan R., N.-W. Territories 81 K e
Kazérun, Iran 125 F d
Kazvin. See Qazvin
Kdyne, Czechoslovakia 104 E d
Kéa, I., Greece 113 E f
Kearney, Ontario 85 L g
Keatley, Saskatchewan 86 K f
Keban Maden, Turkey 124 C b
Ke-bao I., N. Vietnam 132 D b
Kecskemét, Hungary 105 H e
Kedainiai, Lithuania, U.S.S.R. 103 K j
Kedgwick & R., N.B. 82 E f
Kediri, Indonesia 129 F m
Kedleston, Saskatchewan 87 M h
Keefers, Br. Columbia 88 J e
Keeler, Saskatchewan 87 M h
Keeley L., Saskatchewan 86 J d
Keels, Newfoundland 83 T e
Keely L., Saskatchewan 88 P c
Keetmanshoop, S.W. Africa 122 B e
Keewatin, Dist. of, North-West Territories 81 K e
Keewatin, Ontario 86 H a
Kefallinía, Greece 113 C e
Kegashka L., Quebec 83 L c
Kegaska, Quebec 83 L c
Keg River, Alberta 88 L b
Kegueur Tedi, Libya 119 J d
Keila, Estonia, U.S.S.R. 103 L g
Keita, Chad 119 K e
Keitele, Finland 102 M e
Keith, Scotland 98 F c
Keithley Creek, Br. Columbia 88 J d
Kekertuk, N.-W. Territories 81 N d
Keklau, Palau Is. 78 C m
Kelcyre, Albania 113 C d
Keller L., Saskatchewan 86 L b
Kellet, C., N.-W. Territories 80 G c
Kelliher, Saskatchewan 87 O g
Kelloselka, Finland 102 N c
Kells, Eire 99 C g
Kelme, Lithuania, U.S.S.R. 103 K j
Kelowna, Br. Columbia 88 K f
Kelsey, Manitoba 87 V b
Kelsey Bay, Vancouver I., British Columbia 88 G e
Kelsey L., Manitoba 87 Q e
Kelso, Saskatchewan 87 Q j
Kelso, Scotland 98 F e
Keltie, C., Antarctica 136 T e
Kelvington, Saskatchewan 87 O f
Kelvin I., Nipigon L., Ont. 84 B c
Kelwood, Manitoba 87 S h
Kem, U.S.S.R.-Finland 114 C b
Ké-Macina, Mali 118 D f
Kemano, Br. Columbia 88 F d
Kemel Paşa, Turkey 124 A b
Kemerovo, U.S.S.R. 114 H c
Kemi, Finland 102 L d
Kemijärvi, Finland 102 M c
Kemi Joki, Finland 102 L c
Kemnay, Manitoba 87 R j
Kempele, Finland 102 L d
Kemp Ld., Antarctica 136 P e
Kemp Pen., Antarctica 136 J d
Kempsey, Australia 135 K f
Kempt, L., Quebec 85 Q e
Kempten, Germany 104 D e
Kemptville, Ontario 85 P g
Kenabeek, Ontario 84 L e
Kenaston, Saskatchewan 86 L g
Kendal, England 99 F f
Kendal, Saskatchewan 87 O h
Kendall, C., N.-W. Terr. 81 L e
Kendari, Celebes 129 H l
Kendawangan, Borneo 129 F l
Kenema, Sierra Leone 118 C g
Kenge, Congo 120 D e
Keng-tung, Burma 127 J d
Kenhardt, South Africa 122 C e
Keniapiscau L., Quebec 85 O b
Kenitra. See Port Lyautey
Kenmare & R., Eire 99 A j
Kennedy, Saskatchewan 87 P h
Kennedy Chan., N.-W. Terr.-Greenland 81 N a
Kennedy L., Quebec 83 O b
Kennetcook, Nova Scotia 82 J h
Kenney Dam, Br. Columbia 88 G d
Kenogami, L., Quebec 85 T d
Kenogami, Quebec 85 T d
Kenogami, R., Ontario 84 E b
Kenogami Lake, Ontario 84 K d
Kenogamissi L., Ontario 84 J d
Kenonisca L., Quebec 85 O b
Kenora, Ontario 86 H a
Kensington, Prince Edward I. 82 J g
Kent, co., England 99 H j
Kent Bridge, Ontario 84 H k
Kent Junction, New Brunswick 82 G g
Kenton, Manitoba 87 R j
Kentville, Nova Scotia 82 H h
Kenville, Manitoba 87 Q g
Kenya, E. Africa 121 H d
Kenya, Mt., Kenya 121 H e
Keonjhar, India 127 G d
Kéos Tziá. See Kéa I.
Keppel, I., Falkland Is. 95 D h
Kerala, state, India 126 E f
Kerang, Australia 135 H g
Kerava, Finland 103 L f
Kerch, U.S.S.R. 116 K j
Kerchoual, Mali 118 F e
Kerema, New Guinea 135 J a
Keremeos, Br. Columbia 88 K f
Keren, Eritrea 121 H a
Kericho, Kenya 121 H e
Kerintji, Mt., Sumatra 129 D l
Kerkenbosch. See Zuidwolde
Kerkenna Is., Tunisia 119 H b
Kerki, Turkmen., U.S.S.R. 114 F e
Kérkira & I., Greece 113 B e
Kerkrade, Netherlands 100 D d
Kermadec Is., Pacific Ocean 78 J k
Kerman, Iran 125 G c
Kerman Des., Iran 125 G d
Kermanshah, Iran 124 E c
Kerrobert, Saskatchewan 86 H g
Kerry, co., Eire 99 A h
Kerulen R., Mongolia 128 F a
Kerzers, Switzerland 101 C b
Kesagami, R., Ontario 84 K b
Kesagami L., Ontario 84 K b
Kesteren, Netherlands 100 D c
Kestilä, Finland 102 M d
Keswick, England 99 E f
Keswick Ridge, New Brunswick 82 F h
Keszthely, Hungary 105 G e
Ketapang, Borneo 129 E l
Ketrzyn, Poland 105 J a
Kettering, England 99 G h
Kettle I., Quebec 84 D h
Kettlestone B., Quebec 81 M e
Kewagama, Quebec 85 M d
Keyes, Manitoba 87 S h
Key Harbour, Ontario 84 K g
Key Junction, Ontario 84 K g
Key L., Eire 99 B f
Keystown, Saskatchewan 87 M h
Kezhma, U.S.S.R. 115 K c
Khaapsalu, Estonia, U.S.S.R. 103 K g
Khabab, Syria 123 E d
Khabarovsk, U.S.S.R. 115 N d
Khabarovskiy Kroy, U.S.S.R. 115 N c
Khaburah, Muscat & Oman 125 G e
Khadhra, Saudi Arabia 124 D d
Khadro, Pakistan 126 C c
Khafs Maqran, Saudi Arabia 124 E e
Khaibar, Saudi Arabia 124 C d
Khairagarh, India 126 F d
Khairpur, Pakistan 126 C c
Khaitaksho, Kashmir 126 E b
Khaiwan, Yemen 124 D f
Khalis-ed-Daff, Saudi Arabia 124 C e
Khalki, I, Greece 113 F f
Khalkidhki, Greece 113 D d
Khalkís, Greece 113 D e
Khal-Mer-Sede. See Tazovskoye
Khalturin, U.S.S.R. 117 J a
Khaluf, Saudi Arabia 125 G e
Khamadhana, India 126 E c
Khamgaon, India 126 E d
Khamiab, Afghanistan 125 J b
Khamis, Mushait, Saudi Arabia 124 D f
Khamr, Yemen 124 D f
Khanabad, Afghanistan 125 J b
Khanaqin, Iraq 124 E c
Khān Baghdādī, Iraq 124 D c
Khandwa, India 126 E d
Khan-ez-Zebib, Jordan 123 E f
Khanfar, Aden 124 E g
Khanh-hoa, S. Vietnam 132 D d
Khaniá, Crete 113 D g
Khanka, Oz., U.S.S.R. 115 N d
Khan Sheikhun, Syria 123 E b
Khan Tengri. See Pobedy, Mt.
Khanty Mansiysk, U.S.S.R. 114 F b
Khanu. See Kahnuj
Khan Yunis, Egypt 123 C f
Kharaghoda, India 126 D d
Kharan, Pakistan 126 C c
Kharkov, Ukraine, U.S.S.R. 116 K g
Kharmanli, Bulgaria 112 E d
Kharovsk, U.S.S.R. 116 M b
Khartoum, Sudan 119 M e
Khasfah, Saudi Arabia 125 F f
Khash, Afghanistan 125 H c
Khasi Hills, India 127 H c
Khaskovo, Bulgaria 112 E d
Khasmel Girba, Sudan 119 N f
Khatanga, U.S.S.R. 115 K a
Khatangskiy Guba, Russia 115 L a
Khawak Pk., Afghanistan 126 D a
Kheralu, India 126 D d
Kheri, India 126 F c
Kherson, Ukraine, U.S.S.R. 116 H h
Khilok, U.S.S.R. 115 L c
Khinis. See Hinis
Khinjan, Afghanistan 126 C a
Khíos & I., Greece 113 F e
Khisfin, Syria 123 D e
Khiuma, Os. See Hiiumaa
Khiva, Uzbek., U.S.S.R. 114 F d
Khmel'nitskiy, Ukraine, U.S.S.R. 116 E g
Kholm, U.S.S.R. 116 G c
Kholmsk, U.S.S.R. 115 P d
Khomeyn, Iran 125 F c
Khong, Laos 132 D d
Khor, U.S.S.R. 115 N d
Khor-al-Amaya, Iraq 124 E d
Khóra Sfakion, Crete 112 E g
Khormali, China 128 A a
Khorramabad, Iran 124 E c
Khorramshahr, Iran 124 E c
Khotan, China 114 G e
Khrisoúpolis, Greece 112 E d
Khrojna, Bulgaria 112 E d
Khunsar, Iran 125 F c
Khur, Iran 125 G c
Khur. See Khvor
Khurmah, Saudi Arabia 124 D e
Khusf, Iran 125 G c
Khvaf, Iran 125 H c
Khvalynsk, U.S.S.R. 117 J d
Khvor, Iran 125 F c
Khvoy, Iran 124 D b
Khyber Pass, Pakistan 126 D b
Kiambi, Congo 121 F f
Kiamika, L., Quebec 85 P f
Kiamiki, Quebec 85 P f
Kiamusze, China 128 K a
Kian, China 131 G j
Kiangchow. See Kiangling
Kiangling, China 131 F g
Kiangpeh, China 131 C h
Kiangsi, prov., China 131 G j
Kiangsu, prov., China 130 J f
Kiangtu, China 130 J f
Kiangyin, China 130 K g
Kianto Järvi, Finland 102 N d
Kiao-chow B., China 130 K e
Kiaohsien, China 130 K d
Kiask L., Manitoba 87 U b
Kiating. See Loshan
Kibangula, Congo 120 F e
Kibombo, Congo 120 F e
Kibondo, Tanganyika 121 G e
Kičevo, Yugoslavia 112 C d
Kichiga, U.S.S.R. 115 R c
Kichiginsk, U.S.S.R. 117 Q c
Kicking Horse Pass, British Columbia 88 L e
Kidal, Mali 118 F e
Kidderminster, England 99 F h
Kidnappers, C., N. Zealand 135 R k
Kidodi, Tanganyika 121 H f
Kiel, Germany 104 D a
Kielce, Poland 105 J c
Kieldrecht, Belgium 100 C c
Kieler Bucht, Germany 104 D a
Kiel (Nord-Ostsee) Kan., Germany 104 C a
Kienchang. See Nancheng
Kiencheng, China 131 D h
Kienko, China 130 B f
Kienning, China 131 H j
Kienning. See Kienow
Kienow, China 131 J j
Kienping, China 130 J b
Kienshui, China 128 D f
Kienteh, China 131 J h
Kiev (Kiyev), Ukraine, U.S.S.R. 116 G f
Kiffa, Mauritania 118 C e
Kigali, Rwanda 121 G e
Kiganga, Tanganyika 121 G f
Kigoma, Tanganyika 121 F e
Kihsien, China 130 H b
Kii Chan, Japan 133 D h
Kijabe, Kenya 121 H e
Kijoka, I., Okinawa 78 C a
Kikhchik, U.S.S.R. 115 Q c
Kikinda, Yugoslavia 112 C b
Kikládhes, Is., Greece 113 E f
Kikori & R., New Guinea 135 H a
Kikuyu, Kenya 121 H e
Kikwissi, L., Quebec 85 M f
Kikwit, Congo 120 D f
Kilburn, New Brunswick 82 E g
Kilchu, Korea 128 J b
Kildala Arm, Br. Columbia 88 F d
Kildare, C., Prince Edward I. 82 J g
Kildare & co., Eire 99 C g
Kildonan, Br. Columbia 88 G f
Kilifi, Kenya 121 H e
Kili I., Marshall Is. 79 T c
Kilimanjaro, Mt., Tang. 121 H e
Kilindini, Kenya 121 H e
Kilkee, Eire 99 A h
Kilkenny & co., Eire 99 C h
Kilkieran B., Eire 99 A g
Kilkís, Greece 113 D d
Kilkís, prov., Greece 112 D d
Killala, Ontario 84 D c
Killala B., Eire 99 A f
Killaloe, Eire 99 B h
Killaloe Station, Ontario 85 N g
Killaly, Saskatchewan 87 P h
Killam, Alberta 86 F f
Killarney, Eire 99 A h
Killarney, Manitoba 87 S j
Killarney, Ontario 84 J g
Killary Harb., Eire 99 A g
Killdeer, Saskatchewan 86 L j
Killin, Scotland 98 E d
Killíni, Greece 113 C f
Killybegs, Eire 99 B f
Kilmarnock, Scotland 98 D e
Kil'mez, U.S.S.R. 117 K b
Kilosa, Tanganyika 121 H f
Kilrush, Eire 99 A h
Kilwa Kivinje, Tanganyika 121 H f
Kilwinning, Saskatchewan 86 L e
Kilworthy, Ontario 85 L h
Kima, Congo 120 F e
Kimberley, Br. Columbia 88 M f
Kimberley, Ontario 84 K h
Kimberley, South Africa 122 C e
Kimi, Greece 113 E e
Kimito, Finland 103 K f
Kimiwan L., Alberta 86 A c
Kimolos, I., Greece 113 E f
Kimvula, Congo 122 D f
Kin, I., Okinawa 78 B b
Kina, I., Okinawa 78 A c
Kinabulu, Mt., N. Borneo 129 G j
Kinadyeng, Jaluit I. 79 T h
Kinbrace, Scotland 98 E b
Kinbrook Island Prov. Park, Alberta 86 F h
Kincaid, Saskatchewan 86 K j
Kincardine, co., Scotland 98 F d
Kincardine, Ontario 84 J h
Kinchow Wan, China 130 K c
Kincolith, Br. Columbia 88 E c
Kindat, Burma 127 H d
Kindersley, Saskatchewan 86 H g
Kindia, Guinea 118 C f
Kindu-Port Empain, Congo 120 F e
Kinel', U.S.S.R. 117 K d
Kinel' Cherkkassy, U.S.S.R. 117 K d
Kineshma, U.S.S.R. 117 F b
Kingaroy, Australia 135 K e
King Christian I., N.-W. Terr. 80 J b
King Christian IX Ld., Greenland 89 N c
Kingcome Inlet, Br. Columbia 88 F e
King Edward VIII Fall, British Guiana 92 F b
King Frederick VI Land, Greenland 89 P c
King Frederick VIII Land, Greenland 89 N b
Kingfu, China 128 D e
King George, Mt., British Columbia 88 M e
King George I, I., South Shetlands 136 H f
King George Is., Hudson B., North-West Territories 81 M f
King George Sd., Australia 134 C g
King George VI Falls, British Guiana 92 E b
Kinghorn, Ontario 84 C c
King I., Antarctica 136 F d
King I., Br. Columbia 88 F d
King I., Burma 127 J f
King I., Tasmania 135 H g
Kingisepp, U.S.S.R. 103 N g
Kingku, China 128 D f
King Leopold Ra., Australia 134 E c
Kingman, Alberta 86 E e
Kingmen, China 130 F g
Kingoonya, Australia 134 G f

Kingsbridge, England 99 E k
Kingscourt, Eire 99 C g
King's Lynn, England 99 H h
King Sound, Australia 134 D c
Kingsport, Nova Scotia 82 H h
Kingston, Australia 134 H g
Kingston, Jamaica 91 D c
Kingston, New Zealand 135 P m
Kingston, Ontario 85 O h
Kingston-on-Thames, England 99 G j
Kingsussie, Scotland 98 E c
Kingsville, Ontario 84 H k
Kingtung, China 128 D f
Kingushi, Congo 120 D f
King William Ld., Greenland 89 N b
Kingyang, China 130 C d
Kingyüan. See Ishan
Kinhsien, China 130 K c
Kinhwa, China 131 J h
Kinistino, Saskatchewan 87 M f
Kinki, China 130 C d
Kinkora, Prince Edward I. 82 J g
Kinleith, New Zealand 135 R k
Kinley, Saskatchewan 86 K f
Kin misari, Okinawa 78 B b
Kinmount, Ontario 85 M h
Kinnaird, Br. Columbia 88 L f
Kino, Mexico 90 B b
Kinoosao, Saskatchewan 87 P a
Kinross & co., Scotland 98 E d
Kinsale, Eire 99 B j
Kinsale, Old Hd. of, Eire 99 B j
Kinsella, Alberta 86 F e
Kinsey, C., Antarctica 136 A e
Kintap, Borneo 129 G l
Kintyre, Mull of, Scotland 98 D e
Kintyre, Scotland 98 D e
Kinuso, Alberta 86 B c
Kin wan, Okinawa 78 B b
Kinyangiri, Tanganyika 121 G e
Kiosk, Ontario 85 M f
Kipanigan L., Manitoba-Saskatchewan 87 Q c
Kiparissía, G. of, Greece 113 C f
Kiparissía, Greece 113 C f
Kipawa, L., Quebec 85 M f
Kipawa, Quebec 85 M f
Kipini, Kenya 121 J e
Kipling, Saskatchewan 87 P h
Kipp, Alberta 86 E j
Kirby, Ontario 84 F f
Kirchberg, Switzerland 101 C a
Kirensk, U.S.S.R. 115 K c
Kirgizia. See Kirgizskaya
Kirgizskaya S.S.R., U.S.S.R. 114 G d
Kiri, Congo 120 D e
Kirin, China 128 J b
Kirit, Somali Republic 121 K c
Kiriwina, I., New Guinea 135 K a
Kiriwini Is. See Trobriand Is.
Kirkağaç, Turkey 124 A b
Kirkby Lonsdale, England 99 F f
Kirkcaldy, Alberta 86 D h
Kirkcaldy, Scotland 98 E d
Kirkcudbright & co., Scotland 98 E e
Kirkee, India 126 D e
Kirkella, Manitoba 87 Q h
Kirkenes, Norway 102 N a
Kirkland I., Br. Columbia 88 D g
Kirkland Lake, Ontario 84 K d
Kirkliston Ra., New Zealand 135 Q m
Kirkpatrick, Mt., Antarctica 136 A b
Kirk Pt., Ponape I. 78 F o
Kirkuk, Iraq 124 D b
Kirkwall, Orkney 98 F b
Kirov, U.S.S.R. 116 J d
Kirov, U.S.S.R. 117 J a
Kirovgrad, U.S.S.R. 117 P b
Kirovograd, Ukraine, U.S.S.R. 116 H g
Kirovsk, U.S.S.R. 114 C b
Kirriemuir, Alberta 86 G g
Kirriemuir, Scotland 98 E d
Kirsanov, U.S.S.R. 117 F d
Kirsehir, Turkey 124 B b
Kirthar Ra., Pakistan 126 C c
Kirun. See Chilung
Kiruna, Sweden 102 J c
Kiryū, Japan 133 F f
Kisamba, Congo 120 E f
Kisbér, Hungary 105 H e
Kisbey, Saskatchewan 87 P j
Kishan, China 130 C e
Kishanganj, India 126 G c
Kishangarh, India 126 D c
Kishi, Nigeria 118 F g
Kishinev, Moldavia, U.S.S.R. 116 F h
Kisii, Kenya 121 G e
Kisiju, Tanganyika 121 H f
Kiskittogisu L., Manitoba 87 T d
Kiskitto L., Manitoba 87 T d
Kiskunfélegyháza, Hungary 105 H e
Kismayu. See Chisimaio
Kispest, Hungary 105 H e
Kispiox, R., Br. Columbia 88 E c
Kissaraing I., Burma 127 J f
Kissidougou, Guinea 118 C g
Kississing. See Cold Lake
Kistawar, India 126 E b
Kistna R., India 126 E e
Kisujszállás, Hungary 105 J e
Kisumu, Kenya 121 G e
Kisvárda, Hungary 105 K d
Kiswe, Syria 123 E d
Kita, Mali 118 D f
Kitab, Uzbek., U.S.S.R. 114 F e
Kitale, Kenya 121 H d
Kitano hana, Iwo Jima 78 E a
Kitchener, Ontario 84 K j
Kitchioh, China 131 G l
Kitgum, Uganda 121 G d
Kíthira, I., Greece 113 D f
Kíthirai Chan., Greece 113 D g
Kíthnos, I., Greece 113 E f
Kitigan, Ontario 84 H c
Kitimat, Br. Columbia 88 E d
Kitimat Mill, Br. Columbia 88 E d
Kitscoty, Alberta 86 G e
Kittila, Finland 102 L c
Kitui, Kenya 121 H e
Kitwanga, Br. Columbia 88 F c
Kityang, China 131 H l
Kitzbühel, Austria 104 E e
Kitzingen, Germany 104 D d
Kiuchuan, China 128 C c
Kiukiang, China 131 H h
Kiungchow Str. See Hainan Str.
Kiuruvesi, Finland 102 M e
Kivi Järvi, Finland 102 L e
Kivu L., Congo 121 F e
Kivu Nat. Park, Congo 121 F e
Kiwai I., New Guinea 135 H a
Kiyan, Okinawa 78 A d
Kiyan misaki, Okinawa 78 A d
Kiyiu L., Saskatchewan 86 J g
Kiyma, Kazakh., U.S.S.R. 114 F c
Kizel, U.S.S.R. 114 E c
Kizil Irmak, Turkey 124 B a
Kizyl Arvat, Turkmen., U.S.S.R. 114 E e
Kizyl Jilga, Kashmir 126 E a
Kjerringöy, Norway 102 F c
Kjöge B., Greenland 89 N c
Kladanj, Yugoslavia 112 B b
Kladno, Czechoslovakia 104 F c
Klagenfurt, Austria 104 E e
Klaipeda. See Kaliningrad
Klang, Malaya 132 C f
Klappan R., Br. Columbia 88 E b
Klar Älv, Sweden 102 E f
Klausenburg. See Cluj
Kleczkowski L., Quebec 82 J c
Kleena Kleene, Br. Columbia 88 G e
Klemtu, Br. Columbia 88 E d
Klerksdorp, South Africa 122 D e
Kleszczele, Poland 105 K b
Klimpfjall, Sweden 102 F d
Klinaklini, R., Br. Columbia 88 G e
Klisura, Bulgaria 112 E c
Kliuchi, U.S.S.R. 117 G d
Ključ, Yugoslavia 110 F c
Klock, Ontario 85 M f
Klodawa, Poland 105 H b
Klofta, Norway 103 D f
Kłomnice, Poland 105 H c
Kloosterzande, Netherlands 100 C c
Klosters, Switzerland 101 E b
Kluirja, India 126 E c
Klundert, Netherlands 100 C c
Klyuchyevskaya Sopka, U.S.S.R. 115 R c
Knee L., Saskatchewan 86 K c
Knewstubb L., Br. Columbia 88 G d
Knight Inlet, Br. Columbia 88 F e
Knighton, Wales 99 E h
Knin, Yugoslavia 110 F c
Knob, C., Australia 134 C f
Knockmealdown Mts., Eire 99 B h
Knokke, Belgium 100 B c
Knowlton, Quebec 85 S g
Knox, C., Graham I., British Columbia 88 C c
Knox Coast, Antarctica 136 S e
Knysna, South Africa 122 C f
Knyszyn, Poland 105 K b
Koartak, Quebec 81 N e
Kobarid, Yugoslavia 110 D b
Kobe, Japan 133 D g
København (Copenhagen), Denmark 103 D j
Koblenz, Germany 104 B c
Kobrin, Belorussia, U.S.S.R. 116 D e
Kobroör, I., Indonesia 129 K m
Kocaeli. See Izmit
Kočani, Yugoslavia 112 D d
Kočevje, Yugoslavia 110 E c
Ko Chang, Thailand 132 C d
Kochi, Japan 133 C h
Koch I., N.-W. Territories 81 M d
Kochinda, I., Okinawa 78 A d
Kochiu, China 130 K d
Kochow. See Mowming
Kochumdek, U.S.S.R. 115 J b
Kodavere. See Kallaste
Koffiefontein, South Africa 122 D e
Koforidua, Ghana 118 E g
Kofu, Japan 133 F g
Kohat, India 126 D b
Kohima, India 127 H c
Kohler Ra., Antarctica 136 F c
Kojonup, Australia 134 C f
Kokand, Uzbek., U.S.S.R. 125 K a
Kokanee Glacier Prov. Park, British Columbia 88 L f
Kokchetav, Kazakh., U.S.S.R. 114 F c
Kokhtla Yarva, Estonia, U.S.S.R. 103 M g
Kokkola, Finland 102 K e
Kokoda, New Guinea 135 J a
Kokoshili Ra., Tibet 127 F a
Kokpekty, Kazakh., U.S.S.R. 114 H d
Koksoak, R., Quebec 81 N f
Kokstad, South Africa 122 D f
Kokura, Japan 133 B h
Ko Kut, Thailand 132 C d
Ko-lan-chow, China 130 E c
Kolar, India 126 E f
Kolari, Finland 102 K c
Kolarovgrad, Bulgaria 112 F c
Kolberg. See Kolobrzeg
Kolda, Senegal 118 B f
Kolding, Denmark 103 C j
Kole, Belgian Congo 120 F d
Kolguyev Ostrov, U.S.S.R. 114 D b
Kolhapur, India 126 D e
Kolin, Czechoslovakia 104 F c
Kolkas Rags, Latvia, U.S.S.R. 103 K h
Köln (Cologne), Germany 104 B c
Kolno, Poland 105 J b
Koło, Poland 105 H b
Kolo, Tanganyika 121 H e
Kołobrzeg, Poland 105 F a
Kologriv, U.S.S.R. 117 G a
Kolokani, Mali 118 D f
Kolomna, U.S.S.R. 116 L d
Kolomyya, Ukraine, U.S.S.R. 116 D g
Kolossia, Kenya 121 H d
Kolpakovskiy, U.S.S.R. 115 Q c
Kolpashevo, U.S.S.R. 114 H c
Kolpino, U.S.S.R. 116 G b
Kolwezi, Congo 120 F g
Kolyma, R., U.S.S.R. 115 Q b
Kolymskiy, Khrebet, U.S.S.R. 115 Q b
Komandorskiye Ova., U.S.S.R. 115 R c
Komariya, Ceylon 126 F g
Komarno, Czechoslovakia 105 H e
Komarno, Manitoba 87 U h
Komatsu, Japan 133 E f
Komebail Lagoon, Palau Is. 78 B m
Komi, U.S.S.R. 114 E b
Kommunisma Pk., Tadzhik., U.S.S.R. 117 G e
Komoran, I., New Guinea 129 L m
Komotini, Greece 112 E d
Kompong Cham, Cambodia 132 D d
Kompong Chhnang, Cambodia 132 C d
Kompong-thom, Cambodia 132 C d
Komsomolets, Kazakh., U.S.S.R. 117 R d
Komsomolets Ostrov, U.S.S.R. 115 J a
Komsomolsk, U.S.S.R. 115 N c
Kondiaronk, L., Quebec 85 O f
Kondinskoe, U.S.S.R. 114 F b
Kondoa, Tanganyika 121 H e
Kong, Ivory Coast 118 E g
Kongauru, Palau Is. 78 A o
Kong Karl's Land, Arctic Ocean 114 B a
Kongmoon, China 131 F l
Kongor, Sudan 119 M g
Kongsberg, Norway 103 C g
Kongsmoen, Norway 102 E d
Kongsvinger, Norway 103 E f
Kongwa, Tanganyika 121 H f
Königsberg. See Kaliningrad
Königshütte. See Chorzow
Konispol, Albania 113 C e
Konjic, Yugoslavia 112 A c
Konotop, Ukraine, U.S.S.R. 116 H f
Konrei, Palau Is. 78 C l
Konstantinovka, Ukraine, U.S.S.R. 116 K g
Konstantinovsk, U.S.S.R. 117 E g
Konstanz, Germany 104 C e
Kontiomäki, Finland 102 N d
Konya, Turkey 124 B b
Konza, Kenya 121 H e
Koostatak, Manitoba 87 U g
Kootenay L., Br. Columbia 88 L f
Kootenay Nat. Park, British Columbia 88 L e
Kootenay R., Br. Columbia 88 L f
Kootwijk, Netherlands 100 D b
Kopervik, Norway 103 A g
Kopeysk, U.S.S.R. 117 Q c
Köping, Sweden 103 F g
Kopparberg, Sweden 103 F g
Koppigen, Switzerland 101 C a
Koprivnica, Yugoslavia 110 F b
Korak, Palau Is. 78 C n
Korçë, Albania 113 C d
Korčula, I., Yugoslavia 110 F d
Korea, E. Asia 128 J c
Korea B., Korea 128 H c
Korea Kaikyo, Korea 128 J d
Korinthía & Argolís, Greece 113 D f
Kórinthos, G. of, Greece 113 D e
Kórinthos, Greece 113 D f
Koritza. See Korçë
Kormak, Ontario 84 H e
Kormakiti, C., Cyprus 123 A b
Kornat, I., Yugoslavia 110 E d
Korneuburg, Austria 105 G d
Korogwe, Tanganyika 121 H f
Koror, Palau Is. 78 B n
Koror Auluptagel, Palau Is. 78 B n
Körös, Hungary 112 C a
Korosten, Ukraine, U.S.S.R. 116 F f
Koro-Toro, Chad 119 J e
Korpo, Finland 103 J f
Korsakov, U.S.S.R. 115 P d
Korsnas, Finland 102 J e
Korsnes, Norway 102 G b
Kortgem, Netherlands 100 B c
Korthpulé, Albania 112 B d
Korti, Sudan 119 M e
Kortrijk. See Courtrai
Koryakskiy Khrebet, U.S.S.R. 115 R b
Kos, I., Greece 113 F f
Koscierzyna, Poland 105 G a
Kosha, Sudan 119 M d
Koshchagyl, Kazakh., U.S.S.R. 114 E d
Koshiki Retto, Japan 133 A j
Koshki, U.S.S.R. 117 K c
Košice, Czechoslovakia 105 J d
Kosima, Kuwait 124 E d
Koskaecodde L., Newfoundland 83 R f
Koslan, U.S.S.R. 114 D b
Köslin. See Koszalin
Kosovo Metohija, Yugoslavia 112 C c
Kossol Pass, Palau Is. 78 C k
Kostainica, Yugoslavia 110 F c
Kosti, Sudan 119 M f
Kostino, U.S.S.R. 114 H b
Kostroma, U.S.S.R. 116 M c
Koszalin, Poland 105 G b
Kotabaru, New Guinea 129 M l
Kota Bharu, Malaya 132 C e
Kotah, India 126 E c
Kota Kota, Nyasaland 121 G g
Kota Tinggi, Malaya 132 C f
Kotawara, India 126 E c
Kotcho, R., Br. Columbia 88 J a
Kotcho L., Br. Columbia 88 J a
Kotel, Bulgaria 112 F c
Kotelnich, U.S.S.R. 117 J a
Kotelnyy, Ostrov, U.S.S.R. 115 N a
Köthen, Germany 104 D c
Kotido, Uganda 121 G d
Kotka, Finland 103 M f
Kotlas, U.S.S.R. 114 D b
Kotonkoro, Nigeria 118 G f
Kotri, Pakistan 126 C c
Kottas Mts., Antarctica 136 L d
Kotturu, India 126 E f
Kouango, Cent. Afr. Rep. 119 K g
Koudougou, Upper Volta 118 E f
Koulikoro, Mali 118 D f
Koundé, Cent. Afr. Rep. 119 H g
Kouri shima, Okinawa 78 B a
Kourou, French Guiana 93 G b
Koutiala, Mali 118 D f
Kouvola, Finland 103 M f
Kovel', Ukraine, U.S.S.R. 116 D f
Kovno. See Kaunas
Kovrov, U.S.S.R. 117 E b
Kowkash, Ontario 84 C b
Kowloon, China 131 G l
Koyiu, China 131 F l
Koza, Okinawa 78 A c
Kozan, Turkey 124 C b
Kozáni, Greece 113 C d
Kra & Isthmus of, Thailand 132 B d
Kragerö, Norway 103 C g
Kragujevac, Yugoslavia 112 C b
Krakatau, I., Indonesia 129 E m
Kraków, Poland 105 H c
Kramatorsk, Ukraine, U.S.S.R. 116 K g
Kranj, Yugoslavia 110 E b
Kranystaw, Poland 105 K c
Krapina, Yugoslavia 110 E b
Krasino, Novaya Zemlya, U.S.S.R. 114 E a
Krasnobród, Poland 105 K c
Krasnodar, U.S.S.R. 114 C d
Krasnograd, Ukraine, U.S.S.R. 116 J g
Krasnoufimsk, U.S.S.R. 117 N b
Krasnovishersk, U.S.S.R. 114 E b
Krasnovodsk, Turkmen., U.S.S.R. 114 E d
Krasnoyarsk, U.S.S.R. 115 J c
Krasnoyarskiy Kroy, U.S.S.R. 115 J b
Krasnyi Kholm, U.S.S.R. 116 K b
Krasnyi Uzel, U.S.S.R. 117 G c
Krasny Kut, U.S.S.R. 117 H e
Krasnyy Yar, U.S.S.R. 117 G e
Kratie, Cambodia 132 D d
Kraul Mts, Antarctica 136 L d
Krefeld, Germany 104 B c
Kremenchug, Ukraine, U.S.S.R. 116 H g
Kremensk, U.S.S.R. 117 F f
Krems, Austria 105 F d
Kretinga, Lithuania, U.S.S.R. 103 J j
Kreuzlingen, Switzerland 101 E a
Kribi, Cameroon 119 G h
Krimml, Austria 104 E e
Krishnanagar, India 127 G d
Krishnaraja Res., India 126 E f
Kristiansand, Norway 103 C g
Kristianstad, Sweden 103 F h
Kristiansund, Norway 102 B e
Kristiinankaupunki, Finland 102 J e
Kristinehamn, Sweden 103 F g
Kríti, I. See Crete
Kriva Palanka, Yugoslavia 112 D c
Krivoy Rog, Ukraine, U.S.S.R. 116 H h
Krizevči, Yugoslavia 110 F b
Krk, I., Yugoslavia 110 E c
Krnov, Czechoslovakia 105 G c
Kroken, Norway 102 F d
Kroměříž, Czechoslovakia 105 G d
Kronau, Saskatchewan 87 N h
Kronoby, Finland 102 K e
Kronshtadt, U.S.S.R. 116 F a
Kroonstad, South Africa 122 D e
Kropotkin, U.S.S.R. 114 D d
Krotoszyn, Poland 105 G c
Krško, Yugoslavia 110 E c
Krüger, Mt., Antarctica 136 L d
Krugerdorf, Ontario 84 L e
Krugersdorp, South Africa 122 D e
Krujë, Albania 112 B d
Krumbach, Germany 104 D d
Krumlov, Czechoslovakia 104 F d
Krung Thep, Thailand 132 C d
Krupnik, Bulgaria 112 D d
Kruševac, Yugoslavia 112 C c
Kruševo, Yugoslavia 112 C d
Krustpils, Latvia, U.S.S.R. 103 L h
Krydor, Saskatchewan 86 K f
Krzyz, Poland 105 G b
Ksabi, Algeria 118 E c
Ksar el Kebir. See Alcazarquivir
Ktima, Cyprus 123 A c
Kuala, Sumatra 129 C k
Kuala Kangsar, Malaya 132 C f
Kuala Klawang, Malaya 132 C f
Kuala Krai, Malaya 129 D j
Kuala Lipis, Malaya 132 C f
Kuala Lumpur, Malaya 132 C f
Kuandang, Celebes 129 H k
Kuang-chow. See Canton
Kuang-hsi. See Kwangsi
Kuang-tung. See Kwangtung
Kuantan, Malaya 129 D k
Kub, S.W. Africa 122 B d
Kucha, China 114 H d
Kuching, Sarawak 129 F k
Kuchow. See Jungkiang
Kudat, N. Borneo 129 G j
Kudymkar, U.S.S.R. 114 E c
Kuei-chou. See Fengkieh
Kuei-lin. See Kweilin
Kueiteh, China 128 D c
Kuhak, Iran 125 H d
Kuh Banan, Iran 125 G c
Kuh-e-Bul, Iran 125 F c
Kuh Furgan, Iran 125 G d
Kuh-i-Dinar, Iran 125 F c
Kuhmo, Finland 102 N d
Kuhpayeh, Iran 125 F c
Kuhrud. See Qohoud
Kuhsan, Afghanistan 125 H c
Kuibis, S.W. Africa 122 B e
Kuikang, China 131 H h
Kuilenburg, Netherlands 100 D c
Kuinre, Netherlands 100 D b
Kui Nua, Thailand 132 B d
Kukatush, Ontario 84 H d
Kukawa, Nigeria 119 H f
Kukës, Albania 112 C c
Kukong, China 131 F k
Kukukus L., Ontario 86 L a
Kuku Pt., Wake I. 79 S d
Kuldīga, Latvia, U.S.S.R. 103 K h
Kuldja, China 114 H d
Kuldo, Br. Columbia 88 F c
Kulgera, Australia 134 F e
Kulhakangri Mt., Tibet 127 H c
Kuli, Truk Is. 78 D d
Kulin, China 131 B h
Kulmbach, Germany 104 D c
Kulunda, U.S.S.R. 114 G c
Kumai, Borneo 129 F l
Kumamoto, Japan 133 B h
Kumara, New Zealand 135 Q l
Kumara, U.S.S.R. 115 M c
Kumasi, Ghana 118 E g
Kumbakonam, India 126 E f
Kumora, U.S.S.R. 115 L c
Kumta, India 126 D f
Kunar, India 126 D b
Kunda, Estonia, U.S.S.R. 103 M g
Kundar, India 126 C b
Kunduz, Afghanistan 125 J b
Kungchang. See Lungsi
Kunghit I., Queen Charlotte Is., British Columbia 88 D d
Kungnang, India 127 H d
Kungrad, Uzbek., U.S.S.R. 114 E d
Kungur, U.S.S.R. 117 N b
Kunhsien, China 130 E f
Kunlun Mts., China-Tibet 127 F a
Kunming, China 128 D e
Kunsan, Korea 128 J c
Kuopio, Finland 102 M e
Kupang, Timor I. 129 H n
Kupa R., Yugoslavia 110 E c
Kupiškis, Lithuania, U.S.S.R. 103 L j
Kupyansk, Ukraine, U.S.S.R. 116 K g
Kure, Japan 133 C g
Kureika, U.S.S.R. 114 H b
Kurgan, U.S.S.R. 114 F c
Kuria Muria Is., Arabian Sea 125 G f
Kuril'skiye Ostrova, U.S.S.R. 115 P d
Kurnool, India 126 E e
Kuroki, Saskatchewan 87 O g
Kurow, New Zealand 135 Q m
Kurskiy Zaliv, U.S.S.R. 103 J j
Kursky, U.S.S.R. 116 K f
Kurtalan, Turkey 124 D b
Kuru, Finland 103 K f
Kuruman, South Africa 122 C e
Kurume, Japan 133 B h
Kurunegala, Ceylon 126 F g
Kusa, U.S.S.R. 117 P c
Kusaie, I., Caroline Is. 78 G g
Kushersk, U.S.S.R. 117 M a
Kushi, Okinawa 78 B b
Kushima, Japan 133 B j
Kushiro, Japan 133 J c
Kushk, Afghanistan 125 H c
Kushka, Turkmen., U.S.S.R. 114 F e
Kushva, U.S.S.R. 117 P a
Kustanay, Kazakh., U.S.S.R. 114 F c
Kütahya, Turkey 124 A b
Kutai R., Borneo 129 G k
Kutaka shima, Okinawa 78 B c
Kut-al-Hai. See Al Hayy
Kutaradja, Sumatra 129 C j
Kutch, Gt. Rann of, India 126 C d
Kutch & G. of, India 126 C d
Kutchian, Japan 133 G c
Kutina, Yugoslavia 110 F c
Kutno, Poland 105 H b
Kütsing, China 131 A k
Kutu, Ethiopia 121 G c
Kutum, Sudan 119 K f
Kuusamo, Finland 102 N d
Kuusjärvi, Finland 102 N e
Kuwait & state, Persian Gulf 124 E d
Kuyang, China 130 E b
Kuybyshev, U.S.S.R. 117 K d
Kuybyshev, U.S.S.R. 114 G c
Kuybyshevskoye Vdkhr., U.S.S.R. 117 J c
Kuytan, U.S.S.R. 115 K c
Kuzhbal, US.S.R. 117 G a
Kuzino, U.S.S.R. 117 P b
Kuzmin, Yugoslavia 112 B b
Kuznetsk, U.S.S.R. 117 H d
Kuzovatovo, U.S.S.R. 117 H d
Kvalöy, N., Norway 102 H a
Kvalöy, S., Norway 102 H b
Kvarken, Östra, chan., Swed. 102 J e
Kvarner, G. of, Yugoslavia 110 E c
Kvarnerolo, G. of, Yugoslavia 110 E c
Kvesmenes, Norway 102 J b
Kwajalein, Is., Marshall Is. 78 G f
Kwajalein Lagoon, Kwajalein Is. 79 T e
Kwakhanai, Bechuanaland 122 C d
Kwakoegron, Surinam 93 F b
Kwangchang, China 131 H j
Kwangchow Wan, China 131 E m
Kwangnan, China 131 B k
Kwangping. See Yungnien
Kwangshun, China 131 C j
Kwangsi, prov., China 131 C l
Kwangsin. See Shangjao
Kwangtung, prov., China 131 F l
Kwang-Tung Pen., China 130 K c
Kwania L., Uganda 121 G d
Kwataboahegan, R., Ontario 84 J a
Kweichih, China 131 H g
Kweichow, prov., China 131 B j
Kweichow. See Fengkieh
Kweihwa. See Huhehot
Kweihwa. See Tzeyun
Kweiki, China 131 H h
Kweilin, China 131 E k
Kweiping, China 131 E l
Kweisui. See Huhehot
Kweiteh. See Shangkiu
Kweiyang, China 131 C j
Kweiyang, China 131 F k
Kwi-chu. See Phu Qui
Kwidzyń, Poland 105 H b
Kwitao, Burma 127 J c
Kwoka, Mt., New Guinea 129 K l
Kyakhta, U.S.S.R. 115 K c
Kyancutta, Australia 135 G f
Kyangin, Burma 127 J e
Kyaukpadating, Burma 127 J e
Kyaukpyu, Burma 127 H e
Kyaukse, Burma 127 J d
Kyauktaw, Burma 127 H d
Kyi R., Tibet 127 H c
Kyle, Saskatchewan 86 J h
Kymi, Finland 103 M f
Kynšperk, Czechoslovakia 104 E c
Kynuna, Australia 135 H d
Kyoda, Okinawa 78 B b
Kyoga L., Uganda 121 G d
Kyoto, Japan 133 D g
Kyrenia, Cyprus 123 B b
Kyshtym, U.S.S.R. 117 Q c
Kythrea, Cyprus 123 B b
Kyuquot, Br. Columbia 88 F e
Kyushu, I., Japan 133 B h
Kyustendil, Bulgaria 112 D c
Kyusyur, U.S.S.R. 115 M a
Kyzyl, U.S.S.R. 115 J c
Kyzyl Kum, Uzbek., etc., U.S.S.R. 114 F d
Kyzylsk, U.S.S.R. 117 P d
Kzyl Orda, Kazakh., U.S.S.R. 114 F d
Laanila, Finland 102 M b
La Ascención, Mexico 90 C a
La Asunción, Margarita I., Venezuela 92 E a
Laban, Jordan 123 D g
La Banda, Argentina 94 D c
La Baneza, Spain 106 C a
Labang, Sarawak 129 F k
Labé, Guinea 118 C f
Labelle, Quebec 85 Q f
Labouheyre, France 109 C d
Laboulaye, Argentina 94 D d
Labrador, Coast of, dist., Newfoundland 81 N f
Labrador City, Nfd. 81 N g
Labrea, Brazil 92 E e
La Brea, Trinidad 92 E a
Labrieville. See Ste. Maurice de Labrieville
La Broquerie, Manitoba 86 E a
Labuan, I., N.-W. Borneo 129 G j
Labuk B., N. Borneo 129 G j
Lac à Beauce, Quebec 85 S e
Lacadena, Saskatchewan 86 J h

La Canoa, Venezuela 92 E b
La Carlota, Argentina 94 D d
La Carolina, Spain 106 D c
Lac au Saumon, Quebec 82 E e
Lac aux Brochets, Quebec 85 S e
Lac aux Sables, Quebec 85 S f
La Cave, Ontario 85 M f
Lac Baker, New Brunswick 82 D f
Lac Bouchette, Quebec 85 S d
Laccadive Is., Indian Ocean 126 D f
Lac Chat, Quebec 85 S e
Lac Édouard, Quebec 85 S e
La Ceiba, Honduras 90 G d
La Ceiba, Venezuela 92 C b
Lac Etchemin, Quebec 82 B g
Lac Frontière, Quebec 82 B g
Lac Gatineau, Quebec 85 P f
Lachen, Switzerland 101 D a
Lachine, Quebec 85 R k
Lachine, Rapides de, Quebec 85 R k
Lachine Canal, Montreal 85 R k
Lachlan R., Australia 135 J f
Lac Humqui, Quebec 82 E e
Lachute, Quebec 85 Q g
Lac la Biche, Alberta 86 F d
Lac La Hache, Br. Columbia 88 J e
Lac La Ronge Prov. Park, Saskatchewan 87 M c
La Cocha, Argentina 94 C c
Lacolle, Quebec 85 R g
Lacombe, Alberta 86 D f
La Conception, Quebec 85 Q f
La Copelina, Argentina 95 C e
Lacorne, Quebec 85 N d
La Coruña, Spain 106 A a
La Croche, Quebec 85 S e
La Croix, L., Minnesota-Ontario 86 L b
Lacroix, Mt., Antarctica 136 A e
La Cruz, Colombia 92 B c
La Cruz, Mexico 90 C b
Lac Saguay, Quebec 85 P f
Lac Ste. Anne, Alberta 86 C e
Lac Ste. Marie, Quebec 85 P g
Lac Ste. Thérèse, Ontario 84 G b
Lac Vert, Saskatchewan 87 N f
Ladakh Ra., Tibet-Kashmir 126 E b
Ladiz, Iran 125 H d
Ladner, Br. Columbia 88 D g
Ladoga L. See Ladozhskoye Oz.
La Dorado, Colombia 92 C b
Ladozhskoye Oz., U.S.S.R. 116 G a
Lady Ann Str., N.-W. Terr. 81 L b
Lady Beatrix L., Quebec 85 O b
Lady Evelyn L., Ontario 84 K e
Lady Neunes B., Antarctica 136 B d
Ladysmith, South Africa 122 D e
Ladysmith, Vancouver I., British Columbia 88 M f
Lae, I., Marshall Is. 79 S b
Lae, New Guinea 78 E h
Laeken, Belgium 100 C d
Læsö, I., Denmark 103 D h
La Esperanza, Honduras 91 B d
La Estrada, Spain 106 A a
Laferte, Quebec 85 M d
Laflamme, R., Quebec 85 N c
Lafleche, Saskatchewan 86 L j
Laforce, Quebec 85 M e
Laforest, Ontario 84 J e
La Fouly, Switzerland 101 C c
Lages, Brazil 93 K e
Laggan L., Scotland 98 E d
Laghouat, Algeria 118 F b
Lagonegro, Italy 111 E e
Lagos, Mexico 90 D c
Lagos, Nigeria 118 F g
Lagos, Portugal 106 A d
La Grange, Australia 134 D c
La Granja, Spain 106 C b
La Guaira, Venezuela 92 D a
La Guardia, Argentina 94 C c
La Guardia, Spain 106 A b
Laguna, Brazil 94 G c
Lagunas, Peru 92 B e
Lagunillas, Bolivia 92 E g
Lahave, Nova Scotia 82 H j
Lahave Is., Nova Scotia 82 H j
Lahej, Aden 124 D g
Lahijan, Iran 125 F b
Laholm, Sweden 103 E h
Lahore, Pakistan 126 D b
Lahti, Finland 103 L f
Lai, C., N. Vietnam 132 D c
Laibach. See Ljubljana
Lai-chau, N. Vietnam 132 C b
Laichow. See Yehsien
Laigle, France 108 D b
Laila, Saudi Arabia 124 E e
Laingsburg, South Africa 122 C f
Laird, Saskatchewan 86 L f
Lairet, R., Quebec 83 Q h
Lairg, Scotland 98 E b
Laisamis, Kenya 121 H d
Laishev, U.S.S.R. 117 J c
Laives, Italy 101 G b
Laja, L., Chile 95 B e
La Japonesa, Argentina 95 C e
Lajes, Brazil 94 F c
Lajord, Saskatchewan 87 N h
La Junquera, Spain 107 G a
Lakaträsk, Sweden 102 J c
Lake Alma, Saskatchewan 87 N j
Lake Eliza, Alberta 86 F e
Lakefield, Ontario 85 M h
Lake Grace, Australia 134 C f
Lake Harbour, N.-W. Terr. 81 N e
Lake King, Australia 134 C f
Lake Lenore, Saskatchewan 87 N f
Lake Louise, Alberta 88 L e
Lake Nash, Australia 134 G d
Lake River, Ontario 81 L g
Lake Superior Prov. Park, Ontario 84 F e
Lake Traverse, Ontario 85 M g
Lake Valley, Saskatchewan 86 L h
Lakhimpur, India 127 H c
Lakki, Pakistan 126 D b
Lakkor Tso, Tibet 127 F b
Lakonía, G. of, Greece 113 D f
Lakonía, Greece 113 D f
Lakota, Ivory Coast 118 D g
Lakse Fd., Norway 102 M a
Lakselv, Norway 102 L a
Laktsang, Tibet 127 F b
La Libertad, Ecuador 92 A d
La Libertad, Guatemala 90 F d
La Libertad, Nicaragua 91 B d
La Ligua, Chile 94 B d
Lalin, Spain 106 A a
La Loche, Lac, Saskatchewan 86 H b
La Loche, Saskatchewan 86 H b
La Loche West, Saskatchewan 86 H b
La Maddalena, I., Sardinia 111 B e
La Malbaie, Quebec 82 B f
Lamaline, Newfoundland 83 R g
Lamartine, Quebec 82 B f
Lamastre, France 109 F d
Lambach, Austria 104 E d
Lamballe, France 108 B b
Lambaréné, Gabon 120 C e
Lambayeque, Peru 92 B e
Lambert Glacier, Antarctica 136 Q d
Lambert's Ld., Greenland 89 M b
Lambeth, Ontario 84 J k
Lámbia, Greece 113 C f
Lambton, Quebec 85 T g
Lambton Mills, Ontario 84 C k
Lamé, Chad 119 H g
Lamégo, Portugal 106 B b
Lamía, Greece 113 D e
Lamlam, Mt., Guam 78 A l
Lammermuir Hills, Scotland 98 F e
Lamoil, Truk Is. 78 D m
Lamont, Alberta 86 E e
La Montaña, Peru 92 C f
La Motte, Quebec 85 M d
Lampazos, Mexico 90 D b
Lampedusa, I., Medit. Sea 119 H a
Lampeter, Wales 99 E h
Lamphun, Thailand 132 B c
Lampi, I., Burma 127 J f
Lampman, Saskatchewan 87 P j
Lamu, Kenya 121 J e
Lamud, Peru 92 B e
Lanark, Ontario 85 O g
Lanark & co., Scotland 98 E e
Lancashire, co., England 99 F g
Lancaster, England 99 F f
Lancaster, New Brunswick 82 F h
Lancaster, Ontario 85 Q g
Lancaster Sd., N.-W. Terr. 81 L c
Lancer, Saskatchewan 86 J h
Lanchow, China 130 D c
Landeck, Austria 104 D e
Landen, Belgium 100 D d
Landerneau, France 108 A b
Landes, dep., France 109 C d
Landfall, I. See Recalada
Landing L., Manitoba 87 U c
Landis, Saskatchewan 86 J f
Landon, Sweden 102 F e
Landrienne, Quebec 85 N d
Landsberg, Germany 104 D d
Landsberg. See Gorzów
Lands End, C., N.-W. Terr. 80 G b
Land's End, England 99 D k
Landshut, Germany 104 E d
Landskrona, Sweden 103 E j
Lanfine, Alberta 86 G g
Lang, Saskatchewan 87 N j
Langaa, Denmark 103 C h
Langadhas, Greece 113 D d
Langana L., Ethiopia 121 H c
Langara I., Queen Charlotte Is., British Columbia 88 C c
Langbank, Saskatchewan 87 P h
Langchung, China 130 C g
Langdon, Alberta 86 D h
Langeac, France 109 E d
Langeland, I., Denmark 103 D j
Längelmavesi, Finland 103 L f
Langenburg, Saskatchewan 87 Q h
Langenthal, Switzerland 101 C a
Langham, Saskatchewan 86 L f
Langholm, Scotland 98 F e
Lang Jökull, Iceland 102 V m
Langkawi, I., Malaya 132 B e
Langlade, Quebec 85 P d
Langley, Br. Columbia 88 F g
Langley, co., Br. Columbia 88 F g
Langlois Village, Quebec 85 N d
Langogne, France 109 E d
Langon, France 109 C d
Langöy, Norway 102 F b
Langres, France 108 F c
Langruth, Manitoba 87 T h
Langsa, Sumatra 129 C k
Långsele, Sweden 102 G e
Lang-Son, N. Vietnam 132 D b
Långträsk, Sweden 102 J d
Languedoc, prov., France 109 E e
Laniel, Quebec 85 L e
Lanigan, Saskatchewan 87 M g
Lanklaer, Belgium 100 D c
Lankor Tso, Tibet 127 F b
Lannion, France 108 B b
L'Annonciation, Quebec 85 Q f
Lanoraie, Quebec 85 R g
Lansdowne, Ontario 85 O h
Lansdowne House, Ontario 81 L g
L'Anse-Amour, Labrador 83 Q b
L'Anse au Loup, Labrador 83 Q b
Lanusei, Sardinia 111 B f
Lanzarote, I., Canary Is. 118 C c
Laoag, Philippines 129 H g
Lao Bao, Laos 132 D c
Lao-chang-Ho R., China 130 H d
Lao Kay, N. Vietnam 132 C b
Laon, France 108 E b
La Oroya, Peru 92 B f
Laos, S.-E. Asia 132 C c
Lao shan, China 130 K d
Lapalisse, France 108 E c
La Paragua, Venezuela 92 E b
La Passe Dangereuse, Quebec 82 A d
La Patrie, Quebec 85 T g
La Paz, Argentina 94 E d
La Paz, Argentina 94 C d
La Paz, Bolivia 92 D g
La Paz, Honduras 91 B d
La Paz, Mexico 90 B c
Lapchung L., Tibet 127 G b
La Pelada, Argentina 94 D d
La Perouse, Manitoba 87 U c
La Perouse Str., U.S.S.R.-Japan 133 G b
La Piedad, Mexico 90 D c
Lapinlahti, Finland 102 M e
Lapithos, Cyprus 123 B b
La Plata, Argentina 94 E d
Laporte, Saskatchewan 86 H g
Lapovo, Yugoslavia 112 C b
Lappa Järvi, Finland 102 K e
Lappeenranta, Finland 103 N f
Lappland, N. Europe 89 K c
Lappträsk, Sweden 102 K c
Laprairie, Quebec 85 R g
Laprairie Basin, Quebec 85 S k
Laprida, Argentina 95 D e
Laptevykh Sea, U.S.S.R. 115 L a
La Purísima, Mexico 90 B b
Lăpuşul Românesc. See Targul Lapusul
Łapy, Poland 105 K b
La Quiaca, Argentina 94 C b
Lar, Iran 125 F d
Larache, Morocco 118 D a
Laragne, France 109 F d
Laramate, Peru 92 C f
Laranjeiras, Brazil 93 K f
La Rasse, Switzerland 101 B a
Larder Lake, Ontario 85 L d
L'Ardoise, C. Breton I., Nova Scotia 83 M h
La Reine, Quebec 85 L d
La Réole, France 109 C d
Largeau (Faya), Chad 120 D a
Large I., Quebec 82 J c
Largs, Scotland 98 D e
Larino, Italy 111 E e
La Rioja, Argentina 94 C c
Larisa, Greece 113 D e
La Rivière, Manitoba 87 T j
Larkana, Pakistan 126 C c
Larnaca & B., Cyprus 123 B c
Larne, N. Ireland 99 D f
La Robla, Spain 106 C a
La Roca, Spain 106 B c
Laroche, Belgium 100 D d
La Rochelle, France 108 C c
La Roche-sur-Yon, France 108 C c
La Roda, Spain 107 D c
La Ronge & L., Saskatchewan 87 M c
La Rosa, Switzerland 101 F b
Larrimah, Australia 134 F c
Larry's River, Nova Scotia 83 L h
Lars Christensen Coast, Antarctica 136 Q d
Larsen Ice Shelf, Antarctica 136 H e
Larson, Ontario 87 N a
Laruns, France 109 C e
Larvik, Norway 103 D g
Laryak, U.S.S.R. 114 G b
La Salle, Manitoba 87 U j
La Salle, Ontario 84 G k
La Salle, Quebec 85 R k
Las Anod, Somali Republic 121 K c
La Sarre, Quebec 85 L d
Las-Cejas, Argentina 94 D c
La Scie, Newfoundland 83 R d
Las Colorados, Argentina 95 B e
Las Cruces, Mexico 90 C b
La Serena, Chile 94 B c
Las Flores, Argentina 94 E e
Lash. See Khash
Lashburn, Saskatchewan 86 H e
Las Heras, Argentina 95 C g
Lashio, Burma 127 J d
Lashkar, India 126 E c
La Sila, Italy 111 F f
Lasíthi, Crete 113 E g
Lasjerd, Iran 125 F b
Las Khoreh, Somali Republic 121 K b
Las Lajas, Argentina 95 B e
Las Lomitas, Argentina 94 D b
La Souterraine, France 108 D c
Las Palmas, Canary Is. 118 B c
La Spezia, Italy 110 B c
Las Plumas, Argentina 95 C f
Lasqueti I., Br. Columbia 88 G f
L'Assomption, Quebec 85 R g
Las Tablas, Panama 91 C e
Last Mountain, ra., Sask. 87 N g
Last Mountain L., Sask. 87 M g
Lastovo, I., Yugoslavia 110 F d
Las Varas, Mexico 90 C c
Laswari, India 126 E c
Lata, Manua Is. 79 S o
Latacunga, Ecuador 92 B d
Latady I., Antarctica 136 H d
Latady Mts., Antarctica 136 H c
Latakia, Syria 123 D b
Latchford, Ontario 84 L e
Latina, Italy 111 D e
La Tour du Pin, France 108 F d
La Trève, L., Quebec 85 P c
Latrun, Jordan 123 C f
La Tuque, Quebec 85 S e
Latvia, U.S.S.R. 103 K h
Lauder, Manitoba 87 R j
Laufen, Switzerland 101 C a
Lau Group, Fiji Is. 78 J j
Lauhkaung. See Launggyang
Lauli'i, Tutuila I. 79 U o
Launay Station, Quebec 85 M d
Launceston, England 99 E k
Launceston, Tasmania 135 J h
Launggyang, Burma 127 J c
La Unión, Chile 95 B f
La Unión, Mexico 90 D d
La Unión, Salvador 91 B d
La Unión, Spain 107 E d
Laura, Australia 135 H c
Laura, Saskatchewan 86 K g
La Urbana, Venezuela 92 D b
Laurel, Ontario 85 K j
Laurentian Basin, Arctic Oc. 89 T a
Laurentides, Parc des, Quebec 85 T e
Lauria, Italy 111 E e
Laurie, I., South Orkneys 136 J f
Laurie L. & R., Manitoba 87 Q b
Laurier, Manitoba 87 S h
Laurie River, Manitoba 87 R b
Laurierville, Quebec 85 T f
Lausanne, Switzerland 101 B b
Lautaro, Chile 95 B e
Lautem. See Vila Nova de Malaca
Lauzon, Quebec 82 A g
Lavacherie, Belgium 100 D d
Laval, France 108 C b
Laval des Rapides, Quebec 85 R j
Lavalle, Argentina 94 C d
Lavalleja. See Minas
Lavamünd, Austria 104 F e
Lavant, Ontario 85 O g
Lavardac, France 109 D d
La Vega, Dominican Republic 91 E c
Laveille, L., Ontario 85 M g
La Vela, Venezuela 92 D a
Laverton, Australia 134 D e
Lavongai, Bismarck Arch. 78 E g
Lavos, Portugal 106 A b
Lavoy, Alberta 86 F e
Lavras, Brazil 93 H h
Lavras, Brazil 94 F d
Lavras, Brazil 93 K e
Lavrentiya, U.S.S.R. 115 T b
Lávrion, Greece 113 E f
Lawford L., Manitoba 87 V d
Lawk Sawk, Burma 127 J d
Lawlers, Australia 134 D e
Lawn, Newfoundland 83 R g
Lawra, Ghana 118 E f
Lawrence Station, N.B. 82 E h
Lawrencetown, Nova Scotia 82 J j
Lawson, Saskatchewan 86 L h
Lazarevac, Yugoslavia 112 C b
Lazio, reg., Italy 111 D d
Leach I., Ontario 84 F e
Leader, Saskatchewan 86 H h
Leaf L., Saskatchewan 87 P e
Leaf R., Quebec 81 M f
Leahy, C., Antarctica 136 F d
Leamington, England 99 F h
Leamington, Ontario 84 H k
Leamy I. & Cr., Quebec 84 C h
Learmonth, Australia 134 B d
Leaside, Ontario 84 D j
Leask, Saskatchewan 86 L e
Łeba, Poland 105 G a
Lebanon, W. Asia 123 D d
Lebesby, Norway 102 M a
Le Blanc, France 108 D c
Lebombo Mts., South Africa 122 E e
Lebork, Poland 105 G a
Lebret, Manitoba 87 O h
Lebu, Chile 95 B e
Lebwa, Lebanon 123 E c
Le Carroz, Switzerland 101 B b
Lecce, Italy 111 G e
Lecco, Italy 110 B c
L'Echourie, Quebec 82 H d
Leckie Ra., Antarctica 136 P e
Le Creusot, France 108 F c
Lectoure, France 109 D e
Ledbury, England 99 F h
Ledesma, Argentina 94 D b
Ledesma, Spain 106 C b
Ledo, India 127 J c
Le Dorat, France 108 D c
Leduc, Alberta 86 D e
Leech L., Saskatchewan 87 P g
Leeds, England 99 F g
Leende, Netherlands 100 D c
Lee R., Eire 99 B j
Leerbeek, Belgium 100 C d
Leerdam, Netherlands 100 D c
Leeuwarden, Netherlands 100 D a
Leeuwin, C., Australia 134 B f
Leeward Is., West Indies 91 G c
Lefebvre, Quebec 82 C f
Lefka, Cyprus 123 A b
Lefkara, Cyprus 123 B c
Lefkoniko, Cyprus 123 B b
Lefroy, L., Australia 134 D f
Leftrook L., Manitoba 87 T b
Legal, Alberta 86 D e
Legan, Kwajalein Is. 79 U e
Legaré, L., Quebec 85 R f
Legaspi, Philippines 129 H h
Legge Pk., Tasmania 135 J h
Leghorn. See Livorno
Le Gîte, Quebec 85 T d
Legnica, Poland 105 G c
Le Havre, France 108 D b
Lehututu, Bechuanaland 122 C d
Leiah, Pakistan 126 D b
Leicester & co., England 99 G h
Leichhardt, R., Australia 134 G c
Leichou. See Haikang
Leiden, Netherlands 100 C b
Leigh Creek, Australia 134 G f
Leighton Buzzard, England 99 G j
Leignon, Belgium 100 D d
Leimuiden, Netherlands 100 C b
Leinan, Saskatchewan 86 K h
Leinster, prov., Eire 99 C g
Leipzig, Germany 104 E c
Leipzig, Saskatchewan 86 J f
Leith, Scotland 98 E e
Leitrim, co., Eire 99 B f
Leix (Laoighis), co., Eire 99 C h
Leiyang, China 131 F j
Leka, Norway 102 D d
Le Kef, Tunisia 119 G a
Leksands Noret, Sweden 103 F f
Leksvik, Norway 102 D e
Leleque, Argentina 95 B f
Le Locle, Switzerland 101 B a
Lelom Pass, Truk Is. 78 C n
Le Maire, Estrecho de, Argentina 95 D h
Léman, Lac, Switzerland 101 B b
Le Mans, France 108 D b
Lemberg, Manitoba 87 O h
Lemberg. See Lvov
Lemieux, Quebec 85 S f
Lemieux Is., N.-W. Terr. 81 N e
Lemnos. See Limnos, I.
Lempriere, Br. Columbia 88 K d
Lemsford, Saskatchewan 86 H h
Lemyethna, Burma 127 J e
Lena, R., U.S.S.R. 115 M b
Leney, Saskatchewan 86 K f
Lenina, Pk., Kirgiz., U.S.S.R. 114 G e
Leninabad, Uzbek., U.S.S.R. 114 F d
Leninakan, Armyanskaya, U.S.S.R. 114 D d
Leningrad, U.S.S.R. 116 G b
Leninka, U.S.S.R. 115 S b
Leninogorsk, Kazakh., U.S.S.R. 114 H c
Leninogorsk, U.S.S.R. 117 L d
Leninsk Kuznetskiy, U.S.S.R. 114 H c
Lenk, Switzerland 101 C b
Lennox, I, Chile & Argentina 95 C j
Lennoxville, Quebec 85 T g
Lenore, Manitoba 87 R j
Lenore L., Saskatchewan 87 M f
Lens, France 108 E a
Lent, Netherlands 100 D c
Lentiira, Finland 102 N d
Lenvik, Norway 102 H b
Lenya, Burma 127 J f
Lenz, Switzerland 101 E b
Lenzerheide, Switzerland 101 E b
Leoben, Austria 104 F e
Leominster, England 99 F h
Léon, France 109 C e
León, Mexico 90 D c
León, Montañas de, Spain 106 B a
León, Nicaragua 91 B d
León, Spain 106 C a
Leone, B., Tutuila I. 79 T o
Leone, I., Tutuila I. 79 T o
Leonforte, Sicily 111 E g
Leonidhion, Greece 113 D f
Leonora, Australia 134 D e
Leontevo, U.S.S.R. 116 K b
Leopold & Astrid Coast, Antarctica 136 R e
Léopold II L., Congo 120 D e
Léopoldville, Congo 120 D e
Leoville, Saskatchewan 86 K e
Lephepe, Bechuanaland 122 D d
L'Épiphanie, Quebec 85 R g
Lepontine, Alps, Switzerland-Italy 101 D b
Lepreau, New Brunswick 82 F h
Lepreau, Pt., New Brunswick 82 F h
Le Puy, France 109 E d
Lercara Friddi, Sicily 111 D g
Lerdo, Mexico 90 D b
Le Relais, Quebec 85 T e
Lerida, Spain 107 F b
Lerma, Argentina 94 C b
Lerma, Spain 107 D a
Lermoos, Austria 104 D e
Léros, I., Greece 113 F f
Leross, Manitoba 87 O g
Leroy, Saskatchewan 87 N g
Lerwick, Scotland 98 J a
Les Abrets, France 108 F d
Lesbos. See Lesvos, I.
Les Éboulements, Quebec 82 B f
Les Escoumains, Quebec 82 C e
Les Étroits, Quebec 82 D f
Les Haudères, Switzerland 101 C b
Leskovac, Yugoslavia 112 C c
Leslieville, Alberta 86 C f
Les Mechins, Quebec 82 F e
Lesnoy, U.S.S.R. 114 C b
Lesozavodsk, U.S.S.R. 115 N d
Lesparre, France 109 C d
Les Ponts, Switzerland 101 B b
Les Sables d'Olonne, France 108 C c
Lessines, Belgium 100 B d
Lestijärvi, Finland 102 L e
Lestock, Saskatchewan 87 N g
Lesvos (Lesbos), I., Greece 113 E e
Leszno, Poland 105 G c
Letea I., Romania 112 G b
Letellier, Manitoba 87 U j
Lethbridge, Alberta 86 E j
Lethbridge, Newfoundland 83 T e
Leticia, Colombia 92 D d
Leti Kep., Indonesia 129 J m
Le Touquet, France 108 D a
Letpadan, Burma 127 J e
Le Tréport, France 108 D a
Letterkenny, Eire 98 B f
Letur, Spain 107 D c
Leucate, France 109 E e
Leuk, Switzerland 101 C b
Leuser, Mt., Sumatra 129 C k
Leusoali'i, I., Manua Is. 79 S o
Leuven. See Louvain
Leuze, Belgium 100 B d
Levack, Ontario 84 J f
Levádhia, Greece 113 D e
Levanger, Norway 102 D e
Leven L., Scotland 98 E d
Levêque, C., Australia 134 D c
Leverett Glacier, Antarctica 136 D a
Leviče, Czechoslovakia 105 H d
Levick, Mt., Antarctica 136 B d
Le Vigan, France 109 E e
Levin, New Zealand 135 R l
Lévis, Pte., Quebec 85 T b
Lévis, Quebec 82 A g
Levítha, I., Greece 113 F f
Levkás, I., Greece 113 C e
Levoča, Czechoslovakia 105 J d
Lewes, England 99 H k
Lewis, Butt of, Scotland 98 C b
Lewis, I., Scotland 98 C b
Lewis Hills, Newfoundland 83 O e
Lewis Pass, New Zealand 135 Q l
Lewisporte, Newfoundland 83 R d
Lewvan, Saskatchewan 87 N h
Leydsdorp, South Africa 122 E d
Leysele, Belgium 100 A d
Leyte, I., Philippines 129 H h
Lezajsk, Poland 105 K c
Lha-kang Dzong, Tibet 127 H c
Lhasa, Tibet 127 H c
Lha-tse Dzong, Tibet 127 G c
Lhontse Dzong, Tibet 127 H c
Liangchow. See Wuwei
Liangsian, China 130 H c
Liant, C., Thailand 132 C d
Liaocheng, China 130 H d
Liaohsien, China 130 F d
Liao R., China 128 H b
Liao-tung, G. of, China 130 K c
Liaoyang, China 130 L b
Liari, Pakistan 126 C c
Liberec, Czechoslovakia 104 F c
Liberia, Costa Rica 91 B d
Liberia, W. Africa 118 C g
Liberty, Saskatchewan 87 M g
Lib I., Marshall Is. 79 S b
Libiron, I., Eniwetok 79 R d
Libnan, Jebel, Lebanon 123 D c
Libourne, France 109 C d
Libreville, Gabon 120 B d
Libya, N. Africa 119 H c
Licata, Sicily 111 D g
Lichan, I., Saipan-Tinian Is. 78 B d
Licheng. See Tsinan
Lichfield, England 99 F h
Lida, Belorussia, U.S.S.R. 116 D e
Lida-di-Roma, Italy 111 D e
Liddes, Switzerland 101 C c
Lidilbut, I., Eniwetok 79 R b
Lidköping, Sweden 103 E g
Lidzbark, Poland 105 J a
Liebenthal, Saskatchewan 86 H h
Liechtenstein, Europe 101 E a
Liège & prov., Belgium 100 D d
Liegnitz. See Legnica
Lieksa, Finland 102 P e
Lienkong, China 131 J j
Lienyunkang, China 130 J e
Lienz, Austria 104 E e
Liepāja, Latvia, U.S.S.R. 103 J h
Lier, Belgium 100 C c
Lierneux, Belgium 100 D d
Liestal, Switzerland 101 C a
Lièvre, R. du, Quebec 85 P g
Lièvres, I. aux, Quebec 82 C f
Ligure, Appennino, Mts., Italy 110 B c
Liguria, reg., Italy 110 B c
Ligurian Sea, Italy 110 B d
Lihou Reef, Coral Sea 78 F j
Lihsien, China 131 E h
Lijeron, I., Jaluit I. 79 T h
Likely, Br. Columbia 88 J d
Likiang, China 128 D e
Likiep, I., Marshall Is. 79 T b
Likimi, Congo 120 E d

Mackenzie King I., *North-West Territories* 80 H b
McKenzie L., *Ontario* 87 L b
McKenzie L., *Saskatchewan* 87 P d
Mackenzie Plains, *New Zealand* 135 Q m
MacKerracher L., *Manitoba* 87 S a
McKirdy, *Ontario* 84 B c
Macklin, *Saskatchewan* 86 H f
McKnight L., *Manitoba* 87 Q b
McLaughlin, *Alberta* 86 G f
McLaughlin R., *Manitoba* 87 U e
McLean, *Manitoba* 87 N h
McLean L., *Saskatchewan* 86 H b
McLennan, *Alberta* 88 L c
McLeod Lake, *British Columbia* 88 H c
McLeod R., *Alberta* 86 B e
Macloutsie, *Bechuanaland* 122 D d
MacMahon, *Algeria* 118 F c
McMahon, *Saskatchewan* 86 K h
Macmillan Ra., *Yukon* 80 F e
McMorran, *Saskatchewan* 86 J g
McMunn, *Manitoba* 87 F a
McMurdo Sd., *Antarctica* 136 B c
McMurphy, *Br. Columbia* 88 K e
McMurray, *Alberta* 88 O b
McNamara I., *Antarctica* 136 G d
MacNutt, *Saskatchewan* 87 Q g
McNutt I., *Nova Scotia* 82 G k
Macomer, *Sardinia* 111 B e
Macon, *Belgium* 100 C d
Mâcon, *France* 108 F c
Macoun, *Saskatchewan* 87 O j
Macoun L., *Saskatchewan* 88 S b
Macouria, *Fr. Guiana* 93 G c
Macpherson Ra., *Australia* 135 K e
Macquarie, R., *Australia* 135 J f
Macquarie Harb., *Tasmania* 135 J h
MacRobertson Coast, *Antarctica* 136 Q e
Macroom, *Eire* 99 B j
Macrorie, *Saskatchewan* 86 K g
McTaggart, *Saskatchewan* 87 N j
McTavish, *Manitoba* 87 U j
MacTier, *Ontario* 85 L g
Macuje, *Colombia* 92 C c
Macusani, *Peru* 92 C f
McVeigh, *Manitoba* 87 Q b
McWatters, *Quebec* 85 M d
Madaba, *Jordan* 123 D f
Madadi, *Chad* 119 K e
Madagascar (Malagasy Rep.), I., *Indian Ocean* 121 N l
Madain Salih, *Saudi Arabia* 124 C d
Madalai, I., *Palau Is.* 78 B n
Madame I., *C. Breton I., Nova Scotia* 83 M h
Madan, *Iran* 125 G b
Madang, *New Guinea* 78 E h
Madaripur, *E. Pakistan* 127 H d
Madawaska, *Ontario* 85 N g
Madawaska R., *Ontario* 85 N g
Madawaska R., *Quebec-New Brunswick* 82 D f
Madeira, Is., *Atlantic Oc.* 118 B b
Madeira, R., *Brazil* 92 E e
Madeleine, C. de la, *Quebec* 82 G d
Madeleine, Is. de la, *Quebec* 82 K f
Madge, L., *Saskatchewan* 86 K c
Madhopur, *India* 126 E c
Madhya Pradesh, *India* 126 E d
Madigan Nunatak, *Antarc.* 136 A e
Madison, *Saskatchewan* 86 J g
Madoc, *Ontario* 85 N h
Madona, *Latvia, U.S.S.R.* 103 M h
Madras, *India* 126 F f
Madre, Sa., *Mexico* 90 C b
Madre Austral, L. de la, *Mexico* 90 E c
Madre de Dios, I., *Chile* 95 A h
Madre de Dios, R., *Peru-Bolivia* 92 D f
Madre del Sur, Sa., *Mexico* 90 D d
Madrid, *Spain* 106 D b
Madridejos, *Spain* 106 D c
Madura, I., *Indonesia* 129 F m
Madurai, *India* 126 E g
Maebashi, *Japan* 133 F f
Maestra, Sa., *Cuba* 91 D b
Maevatanana, *Madagascar* 121 N k
Mafeking, *Manitoba* 87 Q k
Mafeking, *South Africa* 122 D e
Mafia I., *Tanganyika* 121 H f
Mafra, *Portugal* 106 A c
Mafraq, *Jordan* 123 E e
Magadan, *U.S.S.R.* 115 Q c
Magadi & L., *Kenya* 121 H e
Magadino, *Switzerland* 101 D b
Magad Plat. See Jol Plat.
Magaguadavic L., *New Brunswick* 82 E h
Magallanes, & Estrecho de, *Chile* 95 B h
Magangué, *Colombia* 92 C b
Magari saki, *Okinawa* 78 C b
Magas. See Panāh
Magaz, *Spain* 106 C b
Magburaka, *Sierra Leone* 118 C g
Magdala, *Ethiopia* 121 H b
Magdalena, B., *Mexico* 90 B c
Magdalena, *Bolivia* 92 E f
Magdalena, I., *Chile* 95 B f
Magdalena, *Mexico* 90 B a
Magdalena, R., *Colombia* 92 C b
Magdalena, R., *Mexico* 90 B a
Magdalen Is. See Madeleine, Is. de la
Magdanskaya Oblast, *U.S.S.R.* 115 R b
Magdeburg, *Germany* 104 D b
Magellan, Str. of, *Chile* 95 C h
Mageröya, *Norway* 102 M a
Maggia, *Switzerland* 101 D b
Maggiore, L., *Italy* 110 B b
Maghang Tsangpo R., *Tibet* 127 G c
Maghara, Mt., *Egypt* 123 B g
Magherafelt, *N. Ireland* 99 C f
Maglaj, *Yugoslavia* 112 B b
Maglie, *Italy* 111 G e
Magnet, *Manitoba* 87 S g
Magnetawan, *Ontario* 85 L g
Magnet B., *Antarctica* 136 P e
Magnetic I., *Australia* 135 J c
Magnetic Pole, N., *North-West Territories* 80 J c
Magnitogorsk, *U.S.S.R.* 117 P d
Magog, *Quebec* 85 S g
Magosol, *Mexico* 90 E c
Magpie, *Quebec* 82 H c
Magpie L., *Quebec* 82 H c
Magpie R., *Ontario* 84 F d
Magpie R., *Quebec* 82 H c
Magpie R., West, *Quebec* 82 G b
Magrath, *Alberta* 86 E j
Magua, I., *Guam* 78 B k
Maguse River, *N.-W. Terr.* 81 K e
Magwe, *Burma* 127 J d
Mahabad, *Iran* 124 E b
Mahabaleshwar, *India* 126 D e
Mahaddei Uen, *Somali Rep.* 121 K d
Mahadeo Hills, *India* 126 E d
Mahail, *Saudi Arabia* 124 D f
Mahajamba, B. de, *Madag.* 121 N k
Mahalapye, *Bechuanaland* 122 D d
Mahallat, *Iran* 125 F c
Mahanadi R., *India* 127 F d
Mahanoro, *Madagascar* 121 N k
Mahbubnagar, *India* 126 E e
Mahdia, *Tunisia* 119 H a
Mahe, *India* 126 E f
Mahendragiri, Mt., *India* 127 F e
Maher, *Ontario* 84 J c
Mahia Pen., *New Zealand* 135 S k
Mahmed-Hussein-magala. See Shahsavar
Mahmudabad, *Iran* 125 F b
Mahone Bay, *Nova Scotia* 82 H j
Mahua, *Mozambique* 121 H g
Mahuva, *India* 126 D d
Maiā, I., *Manua Is.* 79 S o
Maicasagi R., *Quebec* 85 O c
Maida, *Yemen* 124 D f
Maidan, *Afghanistan* 125 J c
Maidstone, *England* 99 H j
Maidstone, *Saskatchewan* 86 H e
Maiduguri, *Nigeria* 119 H f
Maienfeld, *Switzerland* 101 E a
Maihar, *India* 126 F d
Maikal Ra., *India* 126 F d
Maikop, *U.S.S.R.* 114 D d
Maillardville, *Br. Columbia* 88 E f
Maimana, *Afghanistan* 125 H b
Main-à-Dieu, *C. Breton I., Nova Scotia* 83 N h
Main Barrier Ra., *Australia* 135 H f
Main Brook, *Newfoundland* 83 Q b
Main Centre, *Saskatchewan* 86 K h
Main Chan., *Ontario* 84 J g
Main Duck I., *Ontario* 85 O j
Maine, prov., *France* 108 C b
Maine-et-Loire, dep., *France* 108 C c
Maing Kaing, *Burma* 127 J d
Maingkwan, *Burma* 127 J c
Mainpuri, *India* 126 E c
Main R., *Germany* 104 C d
Main Topsail, pk., *Nfd.* 83 Q d
Mainz, *Germany* 104 C d
Maipo, Mt., *Argentina* 94 C d
Maipú, *Argentina* 94 E e
Maiquetía, *Venezuela* 92 D a
Maison Carrée, *Algeria* 118 F a
Maisonneuve, *Quebec* 85 S j
Maissin, *Belgium* 100 D e
Mait & I., *Somali Republic* 121 K b
Maitland, *Australia* 135 K f
Maitland, L., *Australia* 134 D e
Maitland, *Nova Scotia* 82 J h
Maitland Bridge, *Nova Scotia* 82 G j
Maiz, *Mexico* 90 E c
Maizuru, *Japan* 133 D g
Maja, I., *Indonesia* 129 E l
Majagual, *Colombia* 92 C b
Majmaa, *Saudi Arabia* 124 E d
Major, *Saskatchewan* 86 H g
Majorca (Mallorca), *Balearic Is.* 107 G c
Majunga, *Madagascar* 121 N k
Majuro, Is., *Marshall Is.* 79 U g
Majuro Lagoon, *Majuro Is.* 79 U g
Makabe, I., *Okinawa* 78 A d
Makale, *Ethiopia* 121 H b
Makania, *Tanganyika* 121 H e
Makariev, *U.S.S.R.* 117 F b
Makarvey, *U.S.S.R.* 117 G b
Makassar, *Celebes* 129 G m
Makassar Str., *Indonesia* 129 G l
Makedhonia, *Greece* 113 C d
Makemo, I., *Tuamotu Arch.* 79 M j
Makeruru, I., *Palau Is.* 78 B n
Makeyevka, Ukraine, *U.S.S.R.* 116 K g
Makhach Kala, *U.S.S.R.* 114 D d
Makhai, *China* 128 B c
Makin, I., *Gilbert Is.* 78 H g
Makinak, *Manitoba* 86 S h
Makindu, *Kenya* 121 H e
Makinson Inlet, *N.-W. Terr.* 81 M b
Makkinga, *Netherlands* 100 E b
Makkovik, *Labrador* 81 O f
Makla, Jeb. el, *Saudi Arabia* 124 C d
Makó, *Hungary* 112 C a
Makokibatan L., *Ontario* 84 C a
Makongolosi, *Tanganyika* 121 G f
Makorako, Mt., *New Zealand* 135 R k
Makram, *Saudi Arabia* 124 C e
Makri, *India* 126 F e
Makri. See Fethiye
Maksamaa, *Finland* 102 K e
Maksmo. See Maksamaa
Maku, *Iran* 124 D b
Makum, *India* 127 J c
Makurdi, *Nigeria* 118 G g
Makwa L., *Saskatchewan* 86 H d
Makwiro, *S. Rhodesia* 122 E c
Malá, *Peru* 92 B f
Malabang, *Philippines* 129 H j
Malabar Coast, *India* 126 D f
Malabu, *Nigeria* 119 H g
Malacca, *Malaya* 129 D k
Malacca, Str. of, *Sumatra-Malaya* 129 D k
Malachi, *Ontario* 86 G a
Maladeta, Mt., *Spain* 107 F a
Málaga, *Spain* 106 C d
Malagasy Rep. (Madagascar), *Indian Ocean* 121 N l
Malaita, *Solomon Is.* 78 F h
Malakal, I., *Palau Is.* 78 B n
Malakal, *Sudan* 119 M g
Malakal Harb., *Palau Is.* 78 B n
Malakal Pass, *Palau Is.* 78 B n
Malakand & Pass, *Pakistan* 126 D b
Malån, *Sweden* 102 H d
Malang, *Java* 129 F m
Malanje, *Angola* 120 D f
Mälaren, L., *Sweden* 103 G g
Malargüe, *Argentina* 94 C e
Malartic, L., *Quebec* 85 M d
Malartic, *Quebec* 85 M d
Malaspina Str., *Br. Columbia* 88 G f
Malathia, *Kenya* 121 H e
Malatya, *Turkey* 120 C b
Malaya, *S.-E. Asia* 132 C f
Malayer, *Iran* 124 E c
Malaysia, Federation of, *South-East Asia* 129 F j
Malazgirt, *Turkey* 124 D b
Mal B., *Quebec* 82 H e
Malbaie R., *Quebec* 82 B f
Malbork, *Poland* 105 H a
Malchow, *Germany* 104 E b
Malda, *India* 127 G c
Maldegem, *Belgium* 100 B c
Malden I., *Pacific Ocean* 79 L h
Maldon, *England* 99 H j
Maldonado, *Uruguay* 94 F d
Maléa, C., *Greece* 113 D f
Malé Karpaty, *Czech.* 105 G d
Malekula, I., *New Hebrides* 78 G j
Máleme, *Crete* 113 D g
Malesherbes, *France* 108 E b
Mali, *W. Africa* 118 E e
Malignant Cove, *Nova Scotia* 83 K h
Maliksha, *India* 126 E a
Malinau, *Borneo* 129 G k
Malindi, *Kenya* 121 J e
Malines, *Belgium* 100 C c
Malin Hd., *Eire* 98 C e
Malkangiri, *India* 127 F e
Malko Tŭrnovo, *Bulgaria* 112 F d
Mallaig, *Alberta* 86 F d
Mallaig, *Scotland* 98 D c
Mállia G., *Crete* 113 E g
Mallorca. See Majorca
Mallorytown, *Ontario* 85 P h
Mallow, *Eire* 99 B h
Malmberget, *Sweden* 102 J c
Malmédy, *Belgium* 100 E d
Malmesbury, *England* 99 F j
Malmö, *Sweden* 103 E j
Malmyzh, *U.S.S.R.* 117 K b
Maloelap, I., *Marshall Is.* 79 U b
Maloggia, *Switzerland* 101 E b
Malolos, I., *Guam* 78 A l
Malombe L., *Nyasaland* 121 H g
Malone, *Ontario* 85 N h
Malonga, *Congo* 120 E g
Malpelo I., *Pacific Ocean* 79 S g
Malpeque B., *Prince Edward I.* 82 J g
Malta, I., *Mediterranean Sea* 111 E h
Malta Chan., *Medit. Sea* 111 E g
Malters, *Switzerland* 101 D a
Malton, airport, *Ontario* 85 L j
Malton, *England* 99 G f
Malung, *Sweden* 103 E f
Malvaglia, *Switzerland* 101 D b
Malvan, *India* 126 D e
Malvern Hills, *England* 99 F h
Malvinas, Islas. See Falkland Is.
Malwa, *India* 126 F c
Mama, *U.S.S.R.* 115 L c
Mamainse Point, *Ontario* 84 F e
Mamantel, *Mexico* 90 F d
Mambasa, *Congo* 121 F d
Mameigweiss L., *Ontario* 86 L a
Ma-me-o Beach, *Alberta* 86 D f
Mammamattawa, *Ontario* 84 F b
Mamonal, *Colombia* 92 B a
Mamou, *Guinea* 118 C f
Mampoko, *Congo* 120 D d
Mamu, *Afghanistan* 125 H d
Mamudju, *Celebes* 129 G l
Man, I. of, *Irish Sea* 99 E f
Man, *Ivory Coast* 118 D g
Manacapurú, *Brazil* 92 E d
Manacor, *Balearic Is.* 107 G c
Manado, *Celebes* 129 H k
Mañagaha, I., *Saipan-Tinian Is.* 78 A d
Managua, *Nicaragua* 91 B d
Managua L., *Nicaragua* 91 B d
Manakha, *Yemen* 124 D f
Manamah, *Bahrein I.* 124 F d
Mananjary, *Madagascar* 121 N l
Manantenina, *Madagascar* 121 N l
Manapouri L., *New Zealand* 135 P m
Manasarowar, L., *Tibet* 126 F b
Manati, *Puerto Rico* 54 C h
Manaus, *Brazil* 92 F d
Manawan L., *Saskatchewan* 87 O c
Manche, dep., *France* 108 C b
Manchester, *England* 99 F g
Manchouli, *China* 128 G a
Manchuria, *China* 128 H a
Mancora, *Peru* 92 A d
Manda, *Tanganyika* 121 G g
Mandal, *Norway* 103 B g
Mandalay, *Burma* 127 J d
Mandal Gobi, *Mongolia* 128 E a
Mandarin B., *China* 131 E m
Mander, *Netherlands* 100 E b
Mandera, *Kenya* 121 J d
Mandi, *India* 126 E b
Mandih, *Philippines* 129 H j
Mandla, *India* 126 F d
Mandritsara, *Madagascar* 121 N k
Mandvi, *India* 126 C d
Manfredonia, G. di, *Italy* 111 F e
Manfuha, *Saudi Arabia* 124 E e
Mangaia, I., *Cook Is.* 78 K j
Mangaldai, *India* 127 H c
Mangalme, *Chad* 119 J f
Mangalore, *India* 126 D f
Mangaréva, I., *Tuamotu Arch.* 79 N k
Mangfall Geb., *Germany* 104 D e
Manglaralto, *Ecuador* 92 A d
Mangrol, *India* 126 D d
Mangualde, *Portugal* 106 B b
Mangueira, L. da, *Brazil* 94 F d
Manhay, *Belgium* 100 D d
Manhuaçu, *Brazil* 93 J h
Manicoré, *Brazil* 92 E e
Manicouagan L., *Quebec* 82 D b
Manicouagan Pen. & R., *Quebec* 82 D d
Manifold, C., *Australia* 135 K d
Manigotan, *Manitoba* 87 V g
Manihiki, I., *Pacific Ocean* 78 K h
Manikpur, *E. Pakistan* 126 F c
Manila, *Philippines* 129 H h
Manipur (Imphal), *India* 127 H c
Manisa, *Turkey* 124 A b
Manitoba, L., *Manitoba* 87 T h
Manitoba, prov., *Canada* 80 J f
Manito L., *Saskatchewan* 86 H f
Manitou, *Manitoba* 87 T j
Manitou Beach, *Sask.* 87 M g
Manitou L., Lower, *Ontario* 86 K a
Manitou L., *Ontario* 84 J g
Manitou L., *Quebec* 82 J c
Manitou L., Upper, *Ontario* 86 J a
Manitoulin I., *Ontario* 84 H g
Manitou R., *Quebec* 82 G b
Manitouwadge, *Ontario* 84 E c
Manitouwadge L., *Ontario* 84 E c
Manitowaning, *Ontario* 84 J g
Manitowik L., *Ontario* 84 F d
Maniwaki, *Quebec* 85 P f
Maniyah, *Iraq* 124 D c
Manizales, *Colombia* 92 B b
Manja, *Madagascar* 121 M l
Manjimup, *Australia* 134 C f
Manka, *Taiwan* 131 K k
Mankota, *Saskatchewan* 86 K j
Manlleu, *Spain* 107 G a
Manmad, *India* 126 D d
Mann, I., *Kwajalein Is.* 79 U e
Mannar, *Ceylon* 126 E g
Mannar, G. of, *India* 126 E g
Mannargudi, *India* 126 E f
Mannheim, *Germany* 104 C d
Manning, *Alberta* 88 L b
Manning Prov. Park, *British Columbia* 88 J f
Mannville, *Alberta* 86 F e
Manoa, *Bolivia* 92 D e
Manokwari, *New Guinea* 129 K l
Manono, *Congo* 120 F f
Manor, *Saskatchewan* 87 P j
Manosque, *France* 109 F e
Manouane, R., *Quebec* 85 Q e
Manouane L. & R., *Quebec* 82 B c
Manresa, *Spain* 107 F b
Manseau, *Quebec* 85 T f
Mansel I., *N.-W. Territories* 81 L e
Mansfield, *England* 99 G g
Mansi, *Burma* 127 J d
Mansilla de Las Mulas, *Spain* 106 C a
Manson Creek, *Br. Columbia* 88 G c
Manta, *Ecuador* 92 A d
Mantario, *Saskatchewan* 86 H g
Mant I., *Ponape I.* 78 G n
Mantova. See Mantua
Mantua, *Italy* 110 C c
Manú, *Peru* 92 C f
Manua Is., *Samoa* 78 K j
Manuan, *Quebec* 85 Q e
Manuanis L., *Quebec* 82 B c
Manuel Rodriguez, I., *Chile* 95 B h
Manujan, *Iran* 125 G d
Manukau Harb., *N. Zealand* 135 R k
Manus I., *Admiralty Is.* 78 E g
Manyberries, *Alberta* 86 G j
Many Island L., *Alberta* 86 G h
Manyoni, *Tanganyika* 121 G f
Manzala L., *Egypt* 119 M b
Manzanares, *Spain* 106 D c
Manzanillo, *Cuba* 91 D b
Manzanillo, *Mexico* 90 D d
Manzanillo, Pta., *Panama* 91 D e
Manzini, *Swaziland* 122 E e
Mao, *Chad* 119 J f
Map, I., *Yap I.* 78 D l
Mapia Is., *Pacific Ocean* 78 D g
Mapimí, *Mexico* 90 D b
Mapire, *Venezuela* 92 E b
Maple Creek, *Saskatchewan* 86 H j
Maqainama, *Saudi Arabia* 124 E e
Maqatin, *Aden* 124 E g
Maqna, *Saudi Arabia* 124 B d
Maquela do Zombo, *Angola* 120 D f
Maquereau, Pte. au, cape, *Quebec* 82 H e
Maquinchao, *Argentina* 95 C f
Mara, *South Africa* 122 D d
Maraã, *Brazil* 92 D d
Marabá, *Brazil* 93 H e
Maracá, I. de, *Brazil* 93 G c
Maracaçumé, *Brazil* 93 H d
Maracaibo, L. de, *Venezuela* 92 C b
Maracaibo, *Venezuela* 92 C a
Maracanã, *Brazil* 93 H d
Maracay, *Venezuela* 92 D a
Marada, *Libya* 119 J c
Maradi, *Niger* 118 G f
Maragheh, *Iran* 124 E b
Maragogi, *Brazil* 93 K e
Marajó, *Brazil* 93 H d
Marakei, I., *Gilbert Is.* 78 H g
Marakwet, *Kenya* 121 H d
Maralinga, *Australia* 134 F f
Maramures, *Romania* 105 K e
Marand, *Iran* 124 E b
Maranguape, *Brazil* 93 K d
Marañon, R., *Peru* 92 B d
Maras, *Turkey* 124 C b
Marathon, *Ontario* 84 D d
Maraú, *Brazil* 93 K f
Maravilha, *Brazil* 92 D e
Marbella, *Spain* 106 C d
Marble Bar, *Australia* 134 C d
Marbleton, *Quebec* 85 T g
Marc, L., *Labrador* 82 J a
Marceau L., *Quebec* 82 F b
Marcelin, *Saskatchewan* 86 L f
Marcelino, *Brazil* 92 D c
Marchand, *Manitoba* 86 F a
Marche, *Belgium* 100 D d
Marche, reg., *Italy* 110 D d
Marchena, *Spain* 106 C d
Marchin, *Belgium* 100 D d
Mar Chiquita, *Argentina* 94 D d
Marcus I., *Pacific Ocean* 78 F d
Mardan, *Pakistan* 126 D b
Mar del Plata, *Argentina* 95 E e
Mardin, *Turkey* 124 D b
Marechal Deodoro. See Alagoas
Maree, L., *Scotland* 98 D c
Mareeba, *Australia* 135 J c
Marengo, *Saskatchewan* 86 H g
Marganets, Ukraine, *U.S.S.R.* 116 J h
Margaree Harbour, *Cape Breton I., Nova Scotia* 83 L g
Margaret Bay, *Br. Columbia* 88 F e
Margarita, I., *Venezuela* 92 E a
Margarites, *Crete* 113 E g
Margate, *England* 99 H j
Margie, *Alberta* 88 O c
Margo, *Saskatchewan* 87 O g
Marguerite, *Br. Columbia* 88 H d
Marguerite B., *Antarctica* 136 H e
Marguerite B., *Quebec* 82 F d
Maria, *Quebec* 82 F e
Maria I., *Tabuai Is.* 79 L j
Marianao, *Cuba* 91 C b
Marianas, Is., *Pacific Ocean* 78 E e
Marianske Lázně. See Marienbad
Mariapolis, *Manitoba* 87 T j
Maria van Diemen, C., *New Zealand* 135 Q j
Marib, *Yemen* 124 D f
Maribor, *Yugoslavia* 110 E b
Maridi, *Sudan* 119 L h
Marie Byrd Ld., *Antarctica* 136 D b
Mariefred, *Sweden* 103 G g
Marie Galante, I., *Leeward Is.* 91 G c
Mariehamn, *Finland* 103 H f
Marie L., *Alberta* 86 G d
Marienbad (Marianske Lázně), *Czechoslovakia* 104 E d
Marienberg, *Netherlands* 100 E b
Marienbourg, *Belgium* 100 C d
Marienburg. See Malbork
Mariental, *S.W. Africa* 122 B d
Mariestad, *Sweden* 103 E g
Marieville, *Quebec* 85 R g
Mariiru Pt., *Rota I.* 78 A j
Marina Fall, *British Guiana* 92 F b
Marinha Grande, *Portugal* 106 A c
Maritsa R., *Bulgaria, etc.* 112 E d
Mariyampole. See Kapsukas
Mariyskaya A.S.S.R., *U.S.S.R.* 114 D c
Marj, el, *Libya* 119 K b
Marjamaa, *Estonia, U.S.S.R.* 103 L g
Markala, *Mali* 118 D f
Markapur, *India* 126 E e
Markdale, *Ontario* 84 K h
Markelo, *Netherlands* 100 E b
Marken, I., *Netherlands* 100 D b
Market Drayton, *England* 99 F h
Market Harborough, *England* 99 G h
Markham, L., *Tibet* 127 F a
Markham, Mt., *Antarctica* 136 A b
Markham, *Ontario* 85 L j
Markham Inlet, *N.-W. Terr.* 81 N a
Markinch, *Saskatchewan* 87 N h
Markovo, *U.S.S.R.* 115 S b
Marks, *U.S.S.R.* 117 H e
Markstay, *Ontario* 84 K f
Marlbank, *Ontario* 85 N h
Marlborough, *Br. Guiana* 92 F b
Marmagão, *India* 126 D e
Marmande, *France* 109 D d
Marmara, Sea of, *Turkey* 124 A a
Marmaris, *Turkey* 124 A b
Marmion L., *Ontario* 86 L a
Marmora, *Ontario* 85 N h
Marne, dep., *France* 108 F b
Maroua, *Cameroon* 119 H f
Marouf Junction, *Quebec* 85 L d
Marouini, R., *Fr. Guiana* 93 G c
Marquesas Is., *Pacific Ocean* 79 N h
Marquette, *Manitoba* 87 U h
Marquina, *Spain* 107 D a
Marquis, *Saskatchewan* 87 M h
Marrakech. See Marrakesh
Marrakesh, *Morocco* 118 D b
Marree, *Australia* 134 G e
Marris, *India* 126 C c
Marsabit, *Kenya* 121 H d
Marsa Hali, *Saudi Arabia* 124 D f
Marsala, *Sicily* 111 D g
Marsden, *Saskatchewan* 86 H f
Marseille, *France* 109 F e
Marshall, *Saskatchewan* 85 H e
Marshall Is., *Pacific Ocean* 78 G f
Marshall L., *Ontario* 84 C b
Marsh Harbour, *Bahama Is.* 91 D a
Marstrand, *Sweden* 103 D h
Marsum, *Netherlands* 100 D a
Martaban, *Burma* 127 J e
Martaban, G. of, *Burma* 127 J e
Martelange, *Belgium* 100 D e
Marten R., *Quebec* 85 P a
Martigny Ville, *Switzerland* 101 C b
Martina, *Switzerland* 101 F b
Martinho, *Brazil* 93 F e
Martinique I., *Windward Is.* 91 G d
Martin Pen., *Antarctica* 136 F d
Marton, *New Zealand* 135 R l
Martos, *Spain* 106 D d
Maruf, *Afghanistan* 125 J c
Marugame, *Japan* 133 C g
Marum, *Netherlands* 100 E a
Marvejols, *France* 109 E d
Marwayne, *Alberta* 86 G e
Mary, Turkmen., *U.S.S.R.* 114 F e
Maryborough, *Australia* 135 H g
Maryborough, *Australia* 135 K e
Maryborough. See Portlaoise
Marydale, *South Africa* 122 C e
Maryfield, *Saskatchewan* 87 Q j
Mary Henry, Mt., *British Columbia* 88 G a
Mary Kathleen, *Australia* 135 H d
Maryport, *England* 99 E f
Mary's Harbour, *Labrador* 83 R a
Marystown, *Newfoundland* 83 R f
Marysville, *New Brunswick* 82 F h
Más Afuera, I., *Pacific Oc.* 79 R m
Masaka, *Uganda* 121 G e
Masalog, I., *Guam* 78 B l
Masangena, *Mozambique* 122 E d
Masara, *Mozambique* 122 E c
Masasi, *Tanganyika* 121 H g
Más-á-Tierra, *Juan Fernández Is.* 79 R m
Masaya, *Nicaragua* 91 B d
Masbate, I., *Philippines* 129 H h
Mascara, *Algeria* 119 F a
Masefau B., *Tutuila I.* 79 U o
Masefield, *Saskatchewan* 86 K j
Masères, L., *Quebec* 85 P d
Maseru, *Basutoland* 122 D e
Mashaki, *Afghanistan* 125 J c
Mashhad, *Iran* 125 G b
Mashkode, *Ontario* 84 F e
Mashkol, Hamun-i-, *Pakistan* 126 B c
Masi-Manimba, *Congo* 120 D e
Masindi, *Uganda* 121 G d
Masira, G. of, *Saudi Arabia* 125 G f
Masira Chan., *Saudi Arabia* 125 G e
Masira I., *Muscat & Oman* 125 G e
Masjed Soleyman, *Iran* 124 E c
Maskinongé, *Quebec* 85 R f
Mask L., *Eire* 99 A g
Masoala C., *Madagascar* 119 P k
Mason Creek, *Br. Columbia* 88 H b
Masöy, *Norway* 102 L a
Massa, *Italy* 110 C c
Massafra, *Italy* 111 F e
Massakori, *Chad* 119 J f
Massapê, *Brazil* 93 J d
Massawa, *Eritrea* 121 H a
Massénya, *Chad* 119 J f
Masset, Graham I., *British Columbia* 88 C d
Masset Inlet, Queen Charlotte Is., *British Columbia* 88 C d
Masseube, *France* 109 D e
Massey, *Ontario* 84 H f
Massinga, *Mozambique* 122 F d

Mobert, Ontario 84 E d
Mocajuba, Brazil 93 H d
Moçambique, Mozambique 121 J h
Mocâmedes, Angola 120 C h
Mocha, Yemen 124 D g
Mochudi, Bechuanaland 122 D d
Mocimboa-de-Praia, Mozambique 121 J g
Mocoa, Colombia 92 B c
Mocorito, Mexico 90 C b
Moctezuma, Mexico 90 D c
Moctezuma, Mexico 90 C b
Mocuba, Mozambique 122 F c
Mocuburi, Mozambique 121 H g
Modane, France 109 G d
Modave, Belgium 100 D d
Modena, Italy 110 C c
Modica, Sicily 111 E g
Modjamboli, Congo 120 E d
Mo-duc, S. Vietnam 132 D d
Modung, China 128 C e
Moen, Truk Is. 78 E n
Moengo, Surinam 93 G b
Mofa, Ethiopia 121 J b
Moffat, Scotland 98 E e
Mogadiscio (Mogadishu), Somali Republic 121 K d
Mogadishu. See Mogadiscio
Mogador, Morocco 118 D b
Mogadouro, Portugal 106 B b
Mogar, Ethiopia 121 H c
Mogaung, Burma 127 J c
Mogilev, Belorussia, U.S.S.R. 116 G e
Mogilev Podol'skiy, Ukraine, U.S.S.R. 116 F g
Mogocha, U.S.S.R. 115 L c
Mogochin, U.S.S.R. 114 H c
Mogok, Burma 127 J d
Mogu, Ethiopia 121 J d
Moguer, Spain 106 B d
Mohács, Hungary 112 B b
Moheli I, Comores Arch 121 J g
Moho, China 115 M c
Mohoro, Tanganyika 121 H f
Moirang, India 127 H d
Moisie & R., Quebec 82 F c
Moissac, France 109 D d
Moji, Brazil 93 H h
Mojikit L., Ontario 84 B b
Moju & R., Brazil 93 H d
Mokai, New Zealand 135 R k
Mokau R., New Zealand 135 R k
Mokolo, Cameroon 119 H f
Mokpo, Korea 128 J d
Mokshany, U.S.S.R. 117 G d
Molanosa, Saskatchewan 87 M d
Moldava, Czechoslovakia 105 J d
Moldavia, Romania 112 F a
Moldavia, U.S.S.R. 116 F h
Molde & Fd., Norway 102 B e
Moldova Veche, Romania 112 C b
Molepolole, Bechuanaland 122 D d
Môle St. Nicolas, Haiti 91 E c
Molfetta, Italy 111 F e
Molina, Chile 94 B e
Molina, Spain 107 E c
Molina, Spain 107 E b
Moliro, Congo 121 G f
Moll, Belgium 100 D c
Mollendo, Peru 92 C g
Mollis, Switzerland 101 E a
Mollosund, Sweden 103 D g
Molndal, Sweden 103 E h
Molotov. See Perm
Molotovsk, U.S.S.R. 114 C b
Molotovsk, U.S.S.R. 117 J b
Molson, Manitoba 86 E a
Molson L., Manitoba 87 V d
Moltke Nunatak, Antarctica 136 K c
Molucca Pass, Indonesia 129 J k
Moluccas, Is., Indonesia 129 J l
Moma, Mozambique 121 H h
Mombasa, Kenya 121 H e
Mombetsu, Japan 133 H b
Momchilgrad, Bulgaria 112 E d
Momeik. See Mong-mit
Momignies, Belgium 100 C d
Momotombo, Nicaragua 91 B d
Mompós, Colombia 92 C b
Mön, I., Denmark 103 E j
Mona, I., Puerto Rico 54 B h
Monå Fd., Finland 102 K e
Monach I., Scotland 98 B c
Monaco, S. Europe 109 G e
Monadhliath Mts., Scotland 98 E c
Monaghan & co., Eire 99 C f
Mona Pass, West Indies 91 F c
Monarch, Alberta 86 D j
Monarch Mt., Br. Columbia 88 G e
Monashee Mts., British Columbia 80 H g
Monasterace Marina, Italy 111 F f
Monastir, Sardinia 111 B f
Monastir, Tunisia 119 H a
Monbuey, Spain 106 B a
Monchique, Portugal 106 A d
Monclova, Mexico 90 D b
Moncton, New Brunswick 82 H g
Mondoñedo, Spain 106 B a
Mondul, Tanganyika 121 H e
Monemvasia, Greece 113 D f
Monet, Quebec 85 P d
Monetny, U.S.S.R. 117 Q b
Moneva, Spain 107 E b
Monforte, Portugal 106 B c
Monga, Congo 120 E d
Mongalla, Sudan 119 M g
Monger, L., Australia 134 C e
Möng-Hsu, Burma 127 J d
Monghyr, India 127 G c
Möng Kiang. See Mong Yai
Möng Kung, Burma 127 J d
Mong-mit, Burma 127 J d
Mongo, Chad 119 J f
Mongolia, East Asia 115 J d
Mongolia, Inner, China 115 K d
Mongonu, Nigeria 119 H f
Mongoumba, Cent. Afr. Rep. 119 J h
Möng-pai, Burma 127 J e
Möng Pan, Burma 127 J d
Möng Pawn, Burma 127 J d
Möng-Sit, Burma 127 J d
Mongu, N. Rhodesia 122 C c
Mong Yai, Burma 127 J d
Moniquira, Colombia 92 C b
Monitor, Alberta 86 G g
Monkira, Australia 134 H d
Monkton, Ontario 84 J j
Monmouth, Mt., British Columbia 88 H e
Monmouth & co., Wales 99 F j
Monnikendam, Netherlands 100 D b
Monopoli, Italy 111 F e
Monovar, Spain 107 E c
Monreal del Campo, Spain 107 E b
Monrovia, Liberia 118 C g
Mons, Belgium 100 B d
Monsanto, Portugal 106 B b
Monserrato, Sardinia 111 B f
Monster, Netherlands 100 C b
Mönsterås, Sweden 103 G h
Mont, Belgium 100 D d
Montagne Tremblante, Parc de la, Quebec 85 Q f
Montagny, Quebec 82 B g
Montague, Prince Edward I. 82 K g
Montague I., Antarctica 136 K g
Montaigu, Belgium 100 C d
Montalbán, Spain 107 E b
Montánchez, Spain 106 B c
Montargis, France 108 E c
Montauban, France 109 D d
Montbard, France 108 F c
Montblanch, Spain 107 F b
Montbrison, France 108 F d
Montcevelles, L., Quebec 83 M b
Montcornet, France 108 F b
Mont de Marsan, France 109 C e
Montdidier, France 108 E b
Mont Dore, Le, France 108 E d
Monte Alegre, Brazil 93 G d
Monte Alegre, Brazil 93 H g
Montebello, Quebec 85 Q g
Monte Carlo, Monaco 109 G e
Monte Carmelo, Brazil 93 H g
Monte Caseros, Argentina 94 E d
Monte Comán, Argentina 94 C d
Monte Cristi, Dom. Rep. 91 E c
Montecristo, I., Italy 110 C d
Montefrío, Spain 106 C d
Montego Bay, Jamaica 91 D c
Montélimar, France 109 F d
Montemorelos, Mexico 90 E b
Montenegro, Yugoslavia 112 B c
Montereau, France 108 E b
Montería, Colombia 92 B b
Montero, Bolivia 92 E g
Monteros, Argentina 94 C c
Monterrey, Mexico 90 D b
Monte Sant' Angelo, Italy 111 E e
Montes Claros, Brazil 93 J g
Montevideo, Uruguay 94 E d
Montfort-sur-Meu, France 108 B b
Montgomery, Pakistan 126 D b
Montgomery & co., Wales 99 E h
Monthey, Switzerland 101 B b
Montijo, B. de, Panama 91 C e
Montilla, Spain 106 C d
Mont Joli, Quebec 82 D e
Mont Laurier, Quebec 85 P f
Mont Louis, Quebec 82 G d
Montluçon, France 108 E c
Montmagny, Quebec 82 B g
Montmartre, Saskatchewan 87 O h
Montmédy, France 108 F b
Montmirail, France 108 E b
Montmorency, Quebec 82 A g
Montmorency R., Quebec 82 A f
Montoro, Spain 106 C c
Montpellier, France 109 E e
Montpellier, Quebec 85 P g
Montreal, L., Ontario 84 F e
Montreal, Quebec 85 R g
Montreal, R., Ontario 84 K e
Montreal I., Ontario 84 F e
Montreal L. & R., Sask. 87 M d
Montreal Lake, Saskatchewan 87 M d
Montréal Nord, Montreal, Quebec 85 R h
Montréal Ouest, Montreal, Quebec 85 R k
Montreal River, Ontario 84 F e
Montréal Sud, Montreal, Quebec 85 T j
Montrejeau, France 109 D e
Montreuil, France 108 D a
Montreuil, Quebec 85 L e
Montreuil Bellay, France 108 C c
Montreux, Switzerland 101 B b
Montrock, Ontario 84 K d
Montrose, Scotland 98 F d
Mont Royal, dist., Montreal 85 R j
Monts, Pte. des, Quebec 81 N h
Mont-St.-Jean, Belgium 100 C d
Mont-St.-Michel & B., France 108 C b
Montserrat, I., Leeward Is. 91 G c
Mont Tremblant, Quebec 85 Q f
Monywa, Burma 127 J d
Monza, Italy 110 B c
Monze, N. Rhodesia 122 D c
Monzón, Spain 107 F b
Moonbeam, Ontario 84 H c
Moora, Australia 134 C f
Moore, L., Australia 134 C e
Moore's Mills, New Brunswick 82 E h
Moorfoot Hills, Scotland 98 E e
Moor Lake Sta., Ontario 85 N f
Moorsel, Belgium 100 C d
Moorslede, Belgium 100 B d
Moose Factory, Ontario 84 K a
Moose Hill, Ontario 87 N b
Moosehorn, Manitoba 87 T g
Moose I., Manitoba 87 U g
Moose Jaw, Saskatchewan 87 M h
Moosejaw Cr., Saskatchewan 87 N h
Moose L., Manitoba 87 R d
Moose Lake, Manitoba 87 R e
Moose Mt. Prov. Park, Saskatchewan 87 P j
Moose Nose L., Manitoba 87 W b
Moose R., Ontario 84 J b
Moose River, Ontario 84 J b
Moosomin, Saskatchewan 87 Q h
Moosonee, Ontario 84 K a
Mopti, Mali 118 E f
Moquegua, Peru 92 C g
Mor, Truk Is. 78 E n
Mora, Cameroon 119 H f
Mora, Ethiopia 121 H b
Mora, Portugal 106 A c
Mora, Spain 106 D c
Mora, Sweden 102 F f
Moradabad, India 126 E c
Mora de Rubielos, Spain 107 E b
Moramanga, Madagascar 121 N k
Morano Calabro, Italy 111 F f
Morar L., Scotland 98 D d
Morat. See Murten
Moratalla, Spain 107 E c
Morava, Czechoslovakia 105 G d
Morava R., Yugoslavia 112 C b
Moravska Trebova, Czechoslovakia 105 G d
Morawhanna, British Guiana 92 F b
Moray, co., Scotland 98 E c
Moray Firth, Scotland 98 E c
Morbihan, dep., France 108 B c
Morbihan, L. De, Quebec 82 K b
Morden, Manitoba 87 T j
Morden, Nova Scotia 82 H h
Mordova, U.S.S.R. 117 E d
Mordovskaya, U.S.S.R. 114 D c
Morecambe & B., England 99 F f
Moreda, Spain 106 D d
Moree, Australia 135 J e
Moreira, Brazil 92 E d
Mörel, Switzerland 101 D b
Morelia, Mexico 90 D d
Morella, Spain 107 E b
Morelos, Mexico 90 D b
Morelos, Mexico 90 C b
Morelos, state, Mexico 90 E d
Morena, Sa., Spain 106 C c
Moreni, Romania 112 E b
Moresby I., Br. Columbia 88 C d
Moreton B., Australia 135 K e
Morez, France 108 G c
Morgan, Australia 134 G f
Morgat, France 108 A b
Morges, Switzerland 101 B b
Morgins, Switzerland 101 B b
Moriani, India 127 H c
Morice L., Br. Columbia 88 F c
Morin Creek, Saskatchewan 86 J d
Morinville, Alberta 86 D e
Morioka, Japan 133 G e
Morisset Station, Quebec 82 B g
Morlaix, France 108 B b
Morley, Alberta 86 C g
Mornington, I., Chile 95 A g
Mornington I., Australia 134 G c
Morobe, New Guinea 135 J a
Morocco, N.-W. Africa 118 D b
Moro G., Philippines 129 H j
Morogoro, Tanganyika 121 H f
Morokwen, South Africa 122 C e
Morón, Cuba 91 D b
Morona, Ecuador 92 B d
Morondava, Madagascar 121 M l
Morón de la Frontera, Spain 106 C d
Morotai, I., Indonesia 129 J k
Moroto, Uganda 121 G d
Morpeth, England 98 F e
Morpeth, Ontario 84 J k
Morphou & B., Cyprus 123 A b
Morrin, Alberta 86 E g
Morrinhos, Brazil 93 H g
Morrinsville, New Zealand 135 R k
Morris, Manitoba 87 U j
Morrisburg, Ontario 85 P h
Morris Jesup, C., Arctic Oc. 89 N a
Morrosquillo, G. de, Colombia 92 B b
Mors, Denmark 103 C h
Morse, Saskatchewan 86 K h
Morshansk, U.S.S.R. 117 E d
Morson, Ontario 86 H a
Mortagne, France 108 D b
Mortagua, Portugal 106 A b
Mortain, France 108 C b
Mortlach, Saskatchewan 87 L h
Mortlock Is., Pacific Ocean 78 F f
Morven, Australia 135 J e
Morvi, India 126 D d
Moscow (Moskva), U.S.S.R. 116 K d
Mose, C., Antarctica 136 T e
Moselle, dep., France 108 G b
Moselle, R., France 108 G b
Mosera, I. See Masira I.
Mosers River, Nova Scotia 83 K j
Mosgiel, New Zealand 135 Q m
Mosher, Ontario 84 F d
Moshupa, Bechuanaland 122 D d
Mosjöen, Norway 102 E d
Moskenesöy, Norway 102 E c
Moskva. See Moscow
Mosonmagyarovar, Hungary 108 G e
Mosqueiro, Brazil 93 H d
Mosquera, Colombia 92 B c
Moss, Norway 103 D g
Mossâmedes, Angola 122 A c
Mossbank, Saskatchewan 87 M j
Mosselbaai, South Africa 122 C f
Mossendjo, Congo 120 C e
Moss L., Manitoba 87 T a
Mossoró, Brazil 93 K e
Mossy Pt., Manitoba 87 U f
Mossy R., Saskatchewan 87 O d
Mossuma, Angola 120 E g
Mossurize, Mozambique 122 E d
Most, Czechoslovakia 104 E c
Mostaganem, Algeria 118 F a
Mostar, Yugoslavia 112 A c
Mostardas, Brazil 94 F d
Mostoos Hills, Saskatchewan 88 P c
Mosul, Iraq 124 D b
Mota del Marqués, Spain 106 C b
Motala, Sweden 103 F g
Motatán, Venezuela 92 C b
Motherwell, Scotland 98 E e
Môtier, Switzerland 101 C b
Môtiers, Switzerland 101 B b
Motihari, India 127 G c
Motôt, Switzerland 101 C b
Moto Yama, Iwo Jima 78 D a
Motril, Spain 106 D d
Motte, C. de la, Antarctica 136 A e
Motueka, New Zealand 135 Q l
Motul, Mexico 90 G c
Moubray B., Antarctica 136 B d
Moudhros, Greece 113 E e
Moudon, Switzerland 101 B b
Mouila, Gabon 120 C e
Moukden. See Shenyang
Mould Bay, North-West Territories 80 H b
Moulins, France 108 E c
Moulmein, Burma 127 J e
Moulouya R., Morocco 118 E b
Mountain Park, Alberta 88 L d
Mountain View, Alberta 86 D j
Mount Assiniboine Prov. Park, Alberta 86 B h
Mount Bellew, Eire 99 B g
Mount Brydges, Ontario 84 J k
Mount Carmel, Nfd. 83 T f
Mount Dennis, Ontario 84 C k
Mount Dutton, Australia 135 G e
Mount Forest, Ontario 84 K j
Mount Gambier, Australia 135 H g
Mount Lofty Ra., Australia 135 G f
Mount Magnet, Australia 134 C e
Mount Morgan, Australia 135 K d
Mount Revelstoke Nat. Park, British Columbia 88 K e
Mounts B., England 99 D k
Mount Stewart, Prince Edward I. 82 K g
Mount Uniacke, Nova Scotia 82 J j
Mount Vernon, Australia 134 C d
Moura, Brazil 92 E d
Moura, Portugal 106 B c
Mourão, Portugal 106 B c
Mourne Mts., N. Ireland 99 C f
Moussoro, Chad 119 J f
Moutier, Switzerland 101 C a
Mouton I., Nova Scotia 82 H k
Mowming, China 131 E m
Mowping, China 130 K d
Moyale, Kenya 121 H d
Moyie, British Columbia 88 M f
Moyobamba, Peru 92 B e
Mozambique, Southern Africa 122 E d
Mozhabong L., Ontario 84 H f
Mozhga, U.S.S.R. 117 L b
Mozyr, Belorussia, U.S.S.R. 116 F e
Mpanda, Tanganyika 121 G f
Mporokoso, N. Rhodesia 121 G f
Mstislavl, Belorussia, U.S.S.R. 116 G d
Mtakuja, Tanganyika 121 G f
Mtito Andei, Kenya 121 H e
Mtoko, S. Rhodesia 122 E c
Mtsensk, U.S.S.R. 116 K e
Mu, R., Burma 127 J d
Muádhdham, el, Saudi Arabia 124 C d
Muang Chaiya, Thailand 132 B e
Muang Nan, Thailand 132 C c
Muang Palien, Thailand 132 B e
Mubarraz, Saudi Arabia 124 E d
Mubende, Uganda 121 G d
Muchinga Mts., N. Rhodesia 121 G g
Mucuri, Brazil 93 K g
Mudanya, Turkey 124 A a
Mudawwara, Jordan 123 D h
Mud B., British Columbia 88 E g
Muddus Järvi, Finland 102 M b
Muddy L., Saskatchewan 86 H f
Mudgee, Australia 135 J f
Mudhnib, Saudi Arabia 124 D d
Mudjatik, R., Saskatchewan 88 Q b
Mueda, Mozambique 121 H g
Muenster, Saskatchewan 87 N f
Muggendorf, Germany 104 D d
Mugía, Spain 106 A a
Muğla, Turkey 124 A b
Muglad, Sudan 119 L f
Muhammadabad. See Darreh Gaz
Muharraq, Persian Gulf 125 F d
Mühldorf, Germany 104 E d
Mühlehorn, Switzerland 101 E a
Mühlig-Hofmann Mts., Antarctica 136 M d
Muhu, Estonia, U.S.S.R. 103 K g
Muinak, Uzbek., U.S.S.R. 114 E d
Muine Bheag, Eire 99 C h
Mujinkarikku, Eniwetok 79 S b
Mukalla, Aden Prot. 124 E g
Mukdahan, Thailand 132 C c
Mukden. See Shenyang
Mukeru, Palau Is. 78 B m
Mukhtuya, U.S.S.R. 115 L b
Mukhu Väin, Estonia, U.S.S.R. 102 K g
Muktinath, Nepal 127 F c
Mukutawa R., Manitoba 87 U e
Mula, Spain 107 E c
Mulchen, Chile 95 B e
Mulege, Mexico 90 B b
Mulgrave, Nova Scotia 83 L h
Mülhausen, Germany 104 D c
Mülheim, Germany 104 B c
Mulhouse, France 108 G c
Mulki, India 126 D f
Mullaittivu, Ceylon 126 F g
Muller Geb., Mts., Borneo 129 F k
Mullewa, Australia 134 C e
Müllheim, Switzerland 101 E a
Mull I., Scotland 98 D d
Mullingar, Eire 99 C g
Multan, Pakistan 126 D b
Multia, Finland 102 L e
Mulvihill, Manitoba 87 T h
Mumbondo, Angola 120 C g
Mumbwa, N. Rhodesia 120 F g
Muna, I., Indonesia 129 H m
München. See Munich
München Gladbach, Germany 104 B c
Muncho Lake, British Columbia 88 G a
Muncho Lake Prov. Park, British Columbia 88 G a
Mundare, Alberta 86 E e
Mundiwindi, Australia 134 D d
Mundo Novo, Brazil 93 J f
Mundrabilla, Australia 134 E f
Mungari, Mozambique 122 E c
Munich (München), Germany 104 D d
Muniesa, Spain 107 E b
Munk, Manitoba 87 W c
Munkfors, Sweden 103 E g
Munnerstadt, Germany 104 D c
Muñoz Gamero, Pen., Chile 95 B h
Munson, Alberta 86 E g
Münster, Germany 104 B c
Munster, prov., Eire 99 A h
Münster, Switzerland 101 F b
Münster, Switzerland 101 D b
Münster, Switzerland 101 D a
Muntok, Bangka I., Indonesia 129 E l
Muong Attopeu, Laos 132 D d
Muong Borikone, Laos 132 C c
Muong Saravane, Laos 132 D c
Muonio, R., Sweden-Finland 102 K c
Muonionalusta, Sweden 102 K c
Muotathal, Switzerland 101 D b
Mur, Yemen 124 D f
Murakami, Japan 133 F e
Murat, R., Turkey 124 D b
Murat Dagh, Turkey 124 A b
Murayama, Japan 133 G e
Murça, Portugal 106 B b
Murcheh Khur, Iran 125 F c
Murchison, Mt., Antarctica 136 B d
Murchison, R., Australia 134 C e
Murchison Falls, Uganda 121 G d
Murcia, Spain 107 E d
Murdochville, Quebec 82 G e
Muresul (Maros), R., Romania 112 C a
Murgon, Australia 135 K e
Muri, Switzerland 101 D a
Muriae, Brazil 93 J h
Murias de Paredes, Spain 106 B a
Muriel L., Alberta 86 G d
Murillo, Ontario 87 O b
Müritz See, Germany 104 E b
Murjo, Mt., Java 129 F m
Murmansk, U.S.S.R. 129 C b
Murom, U.S.S.R. 117 F c
Muroran, Japan 133 G c
Muros, Spain 106 A a
Murphy, Mt., Antarctica 136 F d
Murray, R., Australia 135 J g
Murray Bridge, Australia 134 G g
Murray Harbour, Prince Edward I. 82 K g
Murray Head, Prince Edward I. 82 K h
Murray R., Br. Columbia 88 J c
Murray River, Prince Edward I. 82 K h
Murrayville, Br. Columbia 88 F g
Mürren, Switzerland 101 C b
Murrumbidgee, R., Australia 135 J f
Mursir. See Ash
Murten & See, Switzerland 101 C b
Murtle L., Br. Columbia 88 K d
Mururoa I., Tuamotu Arch. 79 M k
Murwara, India 126 F d
Murzuq, Libya 119 H c
Muş, Turkey 124 D b
Musa Kala, Afghanistan 125 H c
Musalamiya, Saudi Arabia 124 E d
Muscat, Muscat & Oman 125 G e
Muscat & Oman, Arabian Peninsula 125 G e
Musemir, Aden 124 D g
Musgrave, Australia 135 H b
Musgrave Ra., Australia 134 F e
Musgravetown, Nfd. 83 T e
Mushalagan L., Quebec 82 C b
Mushalagan R., Quebec 82 C a
Mushie, Congo 120 D e
Muskeg L., Ontario 87 N a
Muskoka L., Ontario 85 L g
Muskwa, Br. Columbia 88 H a
Muskwa, L., Alberta 86 C b
Muskwa R., Alberta 86 C b
Musmar, Sudan 119 N e
Musoma, Tanganyika 121 G e
Musquanus L., Quebec 83 L c
Musquaro, L., Quebec 83 L c
Musquaro, Quebec 83 L c
Musquash, New Brunswick 83 F h
Musquodoboit, Nova Scotia 82 J h
Musquodoboit Harb., Nova Scotia 83 J j
Mussau, I., Pacific Ocean 78 E g
Mussidan, France 109 D d
Mustahil, Ethiopia 121 J c
Mustajidda, Saudi Arabia 124 D d
Mustang, Nepal 127 F c
Musters, L., Argentina 95 C g
Muswellbrook, Australia 135 K f
Mut, Egypt 119 L c
Mut, Turkey 124 B b
Mutanda, N. Rhodesia 120 F g
Mutano, Angola 122 A c
Muti, Eniwetok 79 S c
Mutok, Ponape I. 78 G o
Mutok Harb., Ponape I. 78 G o
Mutoray, U.S.S.R. 115 K b
Mutsu B., Japan 133 G d
Mutton Bay, Quebec 83 N c
Mutton I., Eire 99 A h
Mutumbo, Angola 120 D g
Mutupet, India 126 E f
Muwale, Tanganyika 121 G f
Muy, Le, France 109 G e
Muya, Japan 133 D g
Muya, U.S.S.R. 115 L c
Muy Muy, Nicaragua 91 B d
Muzaffarabad, Kashmir 126 D b
Muzaffargarh, Pakistan 126 D b
Muzaffarnagar, India 127 F c
Muzaffarpur, India 127 F c
Muzhi, U.S.S.R. 114 F b
Múzquiz, Mexico 90 D b
Mwanza, Tanganyika 121 G e
Mweelrea, Eire 99 A g
Mweru L., Congo 121 F f
Mwinilunga, N. Rhodesia 120 E g
Myadaung, Burma 127 J d
Myanaung, Burma 127 J e
Myaungmya, Burma 127 J e
Myebon, Burma 127 H d
Myingyan, Burma 127 J d
Myinmolettka, Mt., Burma 127 J f
Myitkyina, Burma 127 J c
Myjava, Czechoslovakia 105 G d
Mymensingh, East Pakistan 127 H d
Myohaung, Burma 127 H d
Myrdal, Norway 103 B f
Myrnam, Alberta 86 F e
Myrtle, Manitoba 87 U j
Myrtle, Ontario 85 M h
Myslowice, Poland 105 H c
Mysore, India 126 E f
Mystery L., Manitoba 87 U c
My Tho, S. Vietnam 129 E h
Myzakyula, Estonia, U.S.S.R. 103 L g
Mziha, Tanganyika 121 H f
Mzimba, Nyasaland 121 G g
Na, Ponape I. 78 G o
Naantali, Finland 103 K f
Naarden, Netherlands 100 D b
Naas, Eire 99 C g
Nabatiya, Lebanon 123 D d
Nabberu, L., Australia 134 D e
Nabisipi R., Quebec 83 K c
Nablus, Jordan 123 D e
Nacaome, Honduras 91 B d
Nacimiento, Mexico 90 D b
Nacmine, Alberta 86 E g
Nacozari de Garcia, Mexico 90 C a
Nadiad, India 126 D d
Nærøy, Norway 102 D d
Næstved, Denmark 103 D j
Nafels, Switzerland 101 E a
Naft, Iran 124 E c
Nafud Des., Saudi Arabia 124 C d
Naga, Aden 124 E g
Naga, Philippines 129 H h
Nagagami, Ontario 84 F c
Nagagami, R., Ontario 84 F c
Nagagami L., Ontario 84 E c
Nagagamisis L., Ontario 84 F c

Naga Hills, India 127 H c
Nagalama, Uganda 121 G d
Nagano, Japan 133 F f
Nagaoka, Japan 133 F f
Nagapattinam, India 126 E f
Nagar, Kashmir 126 D a
Nagar Karnul, India 126 E e
Nagar Parkar, India 126 D d
Nagasaki, Japan 133 A h
Nagato, Japan 133 B g
Nagaur, India 126 D c
Nagda, India 126 E d
Nagercoil, India 126 E g
Nagha Kalat, Pakistan 126 C c
Nagina, India 126 E c
Nago, Okinawa 78 B b
Nagoya, Japan 133 E g
Nago wan, Okinawa 78 B b
Nagpur, India 126 E d
Nagu, Finland 103 J f
Naguabo, Puerto Rico 54 D h
Nagykanizsa, Hungary 105 G e
Naha, Japan 133 M p
Naha, Okinawa 78 A c
Nahael Niyeu, Argentina 95 C f
Nahan, India 126 E b
Nahariya, Israel 123 D d
Nahavendi, Iran 124 E e
Naicam, Saskatchewan 87 N f
Naifar, Iraq 124 E c
Nain, Iran 125 F c
Nain, Labrador 81 N f
Naini Tal, India 126 E c
Nain Sing Ra., Tibet 126 F b
Nairn, Ontario 84 J f
Nairn & co., Scotland 98 E c
Nairobi, Kenya 121 H e
Naisecho, Kenya 121 H d
Naivasha & L., Kenya 121 H e
Najd, Saudi Arabia 124 D d
Najera, Spain 107 D a
Najin, Korea 128 K b
Najira, Saudi Arabia 124 E d
Nakagusuku, Okinawa 78 B c
Nakajo, Japan 133 F e
Nakama, Okinawa 78 A c
Nakaoshi, Okinawa 78 B b
Nakatsu, Japan 133 B h
Nakfa, Eritrea 121 H a
Nakhichevan, U.S.S.R. 114 D e
Nakhla, Saudi Arabia 125 F e
Nakhon Pathom, Thailand 132 C d
Nakhon Phanom, Thailand 132 C c
Nakhon Ratchasima, Thailand 132 C d
Nakhon Sawan, Thailand 132 C c
Nakhon Si Thammarat, Thailand 132 C e
Nakijin, Okinawa 78 B a
Nakina, Ontario 84 D b
Nakl Mubarak, Saudi Arabia 124 C e
Nakuru, Kenya 121 H e
Nakusp, Br. Columbia 88 L e
Nalgonda, India 126 E e
Nallamalai Hills, India 126 E e
Nalusa, N. Rhodesia 120 E g
Nalut, Libya 119 H b
Namai, B., Palau Is. 78 C m
Namaka, Alberta 86 D h
Namangan, Uzbek., U.S.S.R. 114 G d
Namarik I., Marshall Is. 79 T c
Namasagali, Uganda 121 G d
Namatail, Mozambique 121 H h
Nambala, N. Rhodesia 120 F h
Namcha Barwa, China 128 C e
Nam-dinh, N. Vietnam 132 D b
Namelakl Passage, Palau Is. 78 C m
Namew L., Saskatchewan 87 P d
Namhoi, China 131 F l
Namib Des., S.W. Africa 122 A d
Namlea, I., Indonesia 129 J l
Namling Dzong, Tibet 127 G c
Nam Mao R. See Shweli R.
Namonuito, Is., Carolina Is. 78 E f
Namorona, Madagascar 121 N l
Nampa, Alberta 88 L b
Nampula, Mozambique 121 H h
Namsen R., Norway 102 E d
Namsos, Norway 102 D d
Nams Vatn, Norway 102 E d
Namtsy, U.S.S.R. 115 M b
Namu, Br. Columbia 88 F e
Namu I., Marshall Is. 79 T b
Namur, Quebec 85 Q g
Namur & prov., Belgium 100 C d
Namur L., Alberta 88 N b
Namutoni, S.W. Africa 122 B c
Namwala, N. Rhodesia 122 D c
Namyang, China 131 G k
Nanaimo, Vancouver I., British Columbia 88 H f
Nana Kru, Liberia 118 D h
Nanan. See Tayü
Nanao, Japan 133 E f
Nanchang, China 131 G h
Nancheng, China 131 H j
Nancheng. See Hanchung
Nan-ching. See Nanking
Nanchung, China 130 C g
Nancy, France 108 G b
Nanda Devi, Mt., India 126 E b
Nanded, India 126 E e
Nanga Parbat, Kashmir 126 D a
Nanjangud, India 126 E f
Nanking, China 130 J g
Nanmatol Is., Ponape I. 78 G o
Nannine, Australia 134 C e
Nanning, China 131 D l
Nanortalik, Greenland 89 P d
Nanping, China 131 J j
Nanripo, Mozambique 121 H g
Nansei Shoto. See Ryukyu Shoto
Nansen Sd., N.-W. Terr. 81 K a
Nan Shan, China 124 C c
Nantais, L., Quebec 81 M e
Nantan, China 131 C k
Nantes, France 108 C c
Nanticoke, Ontario 84 K k
Nanton, Alberta 86 D h
Nantucket Inlet, Antarctica 136 J d
Nantung, China 130 K f
Nanue, Ponape I. 78 G o
Nanumanga, I., Ellice Is. 78 H h
Nanumea, I., Ellice Is. 78 H h
Nanuque, Brazil 93 J g
Nanyang, China 130 F f
Nanyuki, Kenya 121 H d
Naococane L., Quebec 81 M g
Naoetsu, Japan 133 F f
Naoshera, Kashmir 126 D b
Napadogan, New Brunswick 82 F g
Napanee, Ontario 85 O h
Napas, U.S.S.R. 114 H c
Napetipi R., Quebec 83 O b
Napier, New Zealand 135 R k
Napier Mts., Antarctica 136 P e
Napierville, Quebec 85 R g
Napinka, Manitoba 87 R j
Naples (Napoli), Italy 111 D e
Napoli, G. di, Italy 111 D e
Napoli. See Naples
Naqb Ashtar, Jordan 123 D g
Nara, Japan 133 D g
Nara, Mali 118 D e
Naracoorte, Australia 134 H g
Naramata, Br. Columbia 88 K f
Narathiwat, Thailand 132 C e
Narayanganj, E. Pakistan 127 H d
Narbonne, France 109 E e
Nares Ld., Greenland 89 P a
Narino, Colombia 92 B c
Nari R., Pakistan 126 C c
Narken, Sweden 102 K c
Narmada R., India 126 D d
Narmidj, Jaluit I. 79 T h
Narnaul, India 126 E c
Narok, Kenya 121 H e
Narovchat, U.S.S.R. 117 F d
Narrabri, Australia 135 J f
Narranderra, Australia 135 J f
Narrogin, Australia 134 C f
Narsimhapur, India 126 E d
Narsinghgarh, India 126 E d
Narva, Estonia, U.S.S.R 103 N g
Narva Laht, Estonia, U.S.S.R. 103 M g
Narvik, Norway 102 G b
Naryan Mar, U.S.S.R. 114 E b
Narykary, U.S.S.R. 114 F b
Narym, U.S.S.R. 114 H c
Naryn, Kirgiz., U.S.S.R. 114 H c
Narynkol, Kazakh., U.S.S.R. 117 H d
Naseby, New Zealand 135 Q m
Nash Creek, New Brunswick 82 F f
Nasi Järvi, Finland 103 K f
Nasian, Ghana 118 E g
Nasik, India 126 D d
Nasirabad, India 126 D c
Nassau, Bahama Is. 91 D a
Nassau, B. de, Chile 95 C j
Nassau, I., Pacific Ocean 78 K h
Nässjö, Sweden 103 F h
Nass R., Br. Columbia 88 E c
Nastapoka Is., N.-W. Terr. 81 M f
Nata, Panama 91 C e
Natal, Br. Columbia 86 C j
Natal, Brazil 92 E e
Natal, Brazil 93 K e
Natal, prov., South Africa 122 E e
Natal, Sumatra 129 C k
Natashquan, Quebec 83 L c
Natashquan R., Labrador-Quebec 82 K a
Nation R., Br. Columbia 88 G c
Natiskotek B., Anticosti I., Quebec 83 K d
Natividade, Brazil 93 H f
Natron L., Tanganyika 121 H e
Nattavaara, Sweden 102 J c
Natuna Besar. See Bunguran I.
Natuna Selatan, I., Indonesia 129 E k
Naturaliste, C., Australia 134 B f
Naudville, Quebec 85 T d
Naujoji Vilnia, Lithuania, U.S.S.R. 103 L j
Naukhas, S. W. Africa 122 B d
Naumburg, Germany 104 D c
Nauplia. See Navplion
Naur, Jordan 123 D f
Nauru, I., Pacific Ocean 78 G g
Naushahro, Pakistan 126 C c
Naushki, U.S.S.R. 115 K c
Nauta, Peru 92 C d
Nautla, Mexico 90 E c
Nava del Rey, Spain 106 C b
Navalcarnero, Spain 106 C b
Navalmoral, Spain 106 C c
Navan, Eire 99 C g
Navarino, I., Chile 95 C j
Navarre, prov., France 109 C e
Navarro, Argentina 94 E e
Navojoa, Mexico 90 C b
Navplion, Greece 113 D f
Navrongo, Ghana 118 E f
Navsari, India 126 D d
Nawa, Syria 123 E e
Nawai, India 126 E c
Náxos, I., Greece 113 E f
Nayakhan, U.S.S.R. 115 Q b
Nayarit, Sa. de, Mexico 90 D c
Nayarit, state, Mexico 90 C c
Nay Band, Iran 125 F d
Nayfah, Saudi Arabia 125 F f
Nayoro, Japan 133 H b
Nazaré da Mata, Brazil 93 K e
Nazareth, Israel 123 D e
Nazas, Mexico 90 D b
Nazca, Peru 92 C f
Naze, The. See Lindesnes
Nazilli, Turkey 124 A b
Nazimovo, U.S.S.R. 115 J c
Nazko, British Columbia 88 H d
Nazko, R., Br. Columbia 88 H d
Ncheu, Nyasaland 121 G g
Ndala, Tanganyika 121 G e
Ndeni, I., Santa Cruz Is. 78 G h
Ndjolé, Gabon 120 C e
Ndola, N. Rhodesia 121 F g
Neagh L., N. Ireland 99 C f
Neápolis, Crete 113 E g
Neath, Wales 99 E j
Nebikon, Switzerland 101 C a
Nebit-Dag, Turkmen., U.S.S.R. 114 E e
Nechako, R., Br. Columbia 88 G d
Neckar, R., Germany 104 C d
Necochea, Argentina 95 E e
Nedelec, Quebec 85 L e
Nederweert, Netherlands 100 D c
Neede, Netherlands 100 E b
Needles, The, England 99 F k
Neelin, Manitoba 87 S j
Neemuch, India 126 D d
Neepawa, Manitoba 87 S h
Neergaard L., N.-W. Terr. 81 L c
Neerpelt, Belgium 100 D c
Negev, Israel 123 C g
Negombo, Ceylon 126 E g
Negrais, C., Burma 127 H e
Negra Pt., Philippines 129 H g
Negritos, Peru 92 A d
Negro, R., Argentina 95 D e
Negro, R., Brazil 92 E d
Negro, R., Uruguay 94 E d
Negros, I., Philippines 129 H j
Negru Vodă, Romania 112 G c
Nehbandān, Iran 125 H c
Neidpath, Saskatchewan 86 K h
Neilburg, Saskatchewan 86 H f
Neils Harbour, Cape Breton I., Nova Scotia 83 M g
Neisse. See Nysa
Neiva, Colombia 92 B c
Neksö, Bornholm I., Denmark 103 F j
Nelkan, U.S.S.R. 115 N c
Nell, Kwajalein Is. 79 T e
Nellore, India 124 F f
Nelma, U.S.S.R. 115 N d
Nelson, Br. Columbia 88 L f
Nelson, New Zealand 135 Q l
Nelson, R., Manitoba 81 K f
Nelson House, Manitoba 87 T c
Nelson I., Antarctica 136 J f
Néma, Mauritania 118 D e
Neman, U.S.S.R. 103 K j
Nemegos, Ontario 84 G e
Nemegosenda L., Ontario 84 G d
Nemeiben L., Saskatchewan 87 M c
Nemiscau, Quebec 81 M g
Nemiscau L., Quebec 85 O a
Nemours, Algeria 118 E a
Nemours, France 108 E b
Nemunas, R., Lithuania, U.S.S.R. 103 K j
Nemuro, Japan 133 J c
Nemuro B., Japan 133 J c
Nenagh, Eire 99 B h
Nendeln, Liechtenstein 101 E a
Nen R., England 99 G h
Neópolis, Brazil 93 K f
Nepa, U.S.S.R. 115 K c
Nepal, Asia 127 F c
Nephton, Ontario 85 N h
Neptune, Saskatchewan 87 N j
Nérac, France 109 D d
Nerchinsk, U.S.S.R. 115 L c
Neringa, Lithuania, U.S.S.R. 103 J j
Nerpio, Spain 107 D c
Nes, U.S.S.R. 114 D b
Nesle, L., Quebec 83 N c
Nesna, Norway 102 E c
Nesset, Norway 102 C e
Ness L., Scotland 98 E c
Nesslau, Switzerland 101 E a
Nesterville, Ontario 84 G f
Nesthorn, Mt., Switzerland 101 C b
Nestor Falls, Ontario 86 H a
Nesttun, Norway 103 A f
Netanya, Israel 123 C e
Netherhill, Saskatchewan 86 H g
Netherlands, W. Europe 100 C b
Nettilling L., N.-W. Terr. 81 M d
Nettuno, Italy 111 D e
Neubrandenburg, Germany 104 E b
Neuburg, Germany 104 D d
Neuchâtel, L. de, Switzerland 101 B b
Neuchâtel & canton, Switzerland 101 B a
Neudorf, Saskatchewan 87 P h
Neufchâteau, Belgium 100 D e
Neufchâteau, France 108 F b
Neufchâtel, France 108 D b
Neufelden, Austria 104 E d
Neuhausen, Switzerland 101 D a
Neumünster, Germany 104 C a
Neunkirch, Switzerland 101 D a
Neuquén, Argentina 95 C e
Neusiedler See, Austria 105 G e
Neuss, Germany 104 B c
Neustadt, Germany 104 D a
Neustettin. See Szczecinek
Neustrelitz, Germany 104 E b
Neu Ulm, Germany 104 D d
Neuve Église. See Nieuwkerke
Neuveville, Switzerland 101 C a
Neuvitas, Cuba 91 D b
Neuwerk, I., Germany 104 C b
Nevada, Sa., Mts., Spain 106 D d
Nevel, U.S.S.R. 116 F c
Nevel'sk, U.S.S.R. 115 P d
Nevers, France 108 E c
Nevesinje, Yugoslavia 112 B c
Neveyezhkino, U.S.S.R. 117 G e
Neville, Saskatchewan 86 K j
Nevis, Alberta 86 D f
Nevis, I., Leeward Is. 91 G c
Nevşehir, Turkey 124 B b
Nevyansk, U.S.S.R. 117 Q b
New Amsterdam, British Guiana 93 F b
Newark, England 99 G g
New Bedford Inlet, Antarctica 136 J d
Newboro, Ontario 85 O h
New Brigden, Alberta 86 G g
New Britain, Bismarck Arch. 78 E h
Newbrook, Alberta 86 E d
New Brunswick, prov., Canada 81 N h
Newburgh, Ontario 85 O h
New Burnt Cove, Newfoundland 83 T e
Newbury, England 99 G j
New Caledonia, Pacific Oc. 78 G j
New Carlisle, Quebec 82 G e
Newcastle, Australia 135 K f
Newcastle, New Brunswick 82 G f
Newcastle, N. Ireland 99 C f
Newcastle, Ontario 85 M j
Newcastle, South Africa 122 D e
Newcastle Bridge, New Brunswick 82 F g
Newcastle Emlyn, Wales 99 D h
Newcastle Mine, Alberta 86 E g
Newcastle-under-Lyme, England 99 F g
Newcastle-upon-Tyne, England 99 F e
Newcastle Waters, Australia 134 F c
Newchwang. See Yingkow
Newdale, Manitoba 87 R h
New Dayton, Alberta 86 E j
New Delhi. See Delhi
New Denmark, New Brunswick 82 E g
New Edinburgh, dist., Ottawa 84 D h
Newell L., Alberta 86 E h
New England Ra., Australia 135 K f
New Fish Creek, Alberta 88 L c
New Forest, England 99 F k
Newfoundland, I. & prov., Canada 81 O g
New Galloway, Scotland 98 E e
Newgate, Br. Columbia 86 B j
New Georgia, I., Solomon Is. 78 F h
New Germany, Nova Scotia 82 H j
New Glasgow, Nova Scotia 82 K h
New Guinea, Pacific Ocean 78 D h
New Hamburg, Ontario 84 K j
Newhaven, England 99 H k
New Hazelton, Br. Columbia 88 F c
New Hebrides, Is., Pacific Ocean 78 G j
New Ireland, Bismarck Arch. 78 F h
New Liskeard, Ontario 85 L e
Newman's Cove, Newfoundland 83 T e
Newmarket, Eire 99 B h
Newmarket, England 99 H h
Newmarket, Ontario 85 L h
New Norfolk, Tasmania 135 J h
New Norway, Alberta 86 E f
New Osgoode, Saskatchewan 87 O f
New Plymouth, New Zealand 135 Q k
Newport, Isle of Wight, England 99 G k
Newport, Quebec 82 H e
Newport, Wales 99 F j
New Providence, I., Bahama Is. 91 D b
Newquay, England 99 D k
New Quebec Crater, Quebec 81 M e
New Richmond, Quebec 82 G e
New Ross, Eire 99 C h
Newry, N. Ireland 99 C f
New Schwabenland, Antarctica 136 M d
New Siberian Islands. See Novosibirskiye Ostrova
New South Wales, state, Australia 135 J f
Newton Abbott, England 99 E k
Newton Stewart, Scotland 99 E f
New Toronto, Ontario 85 L j
Newtown, Newfoundland 83 T d
Newtown, Wales 99 E h
Newtownards, N. Ireland 99 D f
New Waterford, C. Breton I., Nova Scotia 83 M g
New Westminster, British Columbia 88 H f
New World I., Newfoundland 83 S d
New Zealand 135
New Zealand Claim, Antarctica 136 C c
Nexö. See Neksö
Neya, U.S.S.R. 117 H a
Neyriz, Iran 125 F d
Neyshābūr, Iran 125 G b
Nezhin, Ukraine, U.S.S.R. 116 G f
Ngain, Jaluit I. 79 T h
Nganglaring Tso, Tibet 127 F b
N'Gaoundéré, Cameroon 119 H g
Ngardmau, Palau Is. 78 B m
Ngardmau B., Palau Is. 78 C l
Ngardololok, Palau Is. 78 A o
Ngaregur, Palau Is. 78 C l
Ngaremediu, Palau Is. 78 B n
Ngatapa, New Zealand 135 R k
Ngatik, I., Caroline Is. 78 F g
Ngauruhoe, Mt., New Zealand 135 R k
Ngemelis Is., Palau Is 78 A o
Ngeregong, Palau Is. 78 B o
Ngergoi, Palau Is. 78 A o
Ngesebus, Palau Is. 78 A o
Ngeuni, Sudan 119 L g
Ngobasangel, Palau Is. 78 B n
Ngong, Kenya 121 H e
Ngoring Nor, China 128 C d
Nguigmi, Niger 119 H f
Ngwasi, Tanganyika 121 H f
Nha-Trang, S. Vietnam 132 D d
Nhill, Australia 134 H g
Niafounké, Mali 118 E e
Niagara Falls, Ontario 85 L j
Niagara on the Lake, Ont. 85 L j
Niah, Sarawak 129 F k
Niamey, Niger 118 F f
Nia Nia, Congo 121 F d
Niapa, Mt., Borneo 129 G k
Nias, I., Indonesia 129 C k
Nicaragua, Cent. Amer. 91 B d
Nicaragua L., Nicaragua 91 B d
Nicastro, Italy 111 F f
Nice, France 109 G e
Nichicun L., Quebec 81 M g
Nichinan, Japan 133 B j
Nicholson, Ontario 84 G e
Nickel Lake, Ontario 86 J b
Nicman, Quebec 82 G c
Nicobar Is., Indian Ocean 127 H g
Nicola, Br. Columbia 88 J e
Nicolet, Quebec 85 S f
Nicosia, Cyprus 123 B b
Nicoya & Pen., Costa Rica 91 B d
Nictau, New Brunswick 82 E f
Nictaux Falls, Nova Scotia 82 G j
Nidau, Switzerland 101 C a
Nidzica, Poland 105 J b
Niedere Tauern, Austria 104 E e
Niedersachsen, Germany 104 C b
Niellé, Ivory Coast 118 D f
Nielson B., Antarctica 136 Q e
Niére, Chad 119 K f
Nieuw Amsterdam, Surinam 93 F b
Nieuwendijk, Netherlands 100 C c
Nieuwersluis, Netherlands 100 C b
Nieuwkerke, Belgium 100 A d
Nieuwkoop, Netherlands 100 C b
Nieuw Nickerie, Surinam 93 F b
Nieuwpoort, Belgium 100 C c
Nieuwpoort, Netherlands 100 C c
Nieves, Mexico 90 D c
Nièvre, dep., France 108 E c
Nif, Yap I. 78 C m
Nigadoo, New Brunswick 82 G f
Nigde, Turkey 124 B b
Nigeria, W. Africa 118 G e
Nigeria, W. Africa 118 G g
Niger R., W. Africa 118 F f
Nighthawk L., Ontario 84 K d
Nigula, Estonia, U.S.S.R. 103 M g
Niigata, Japan 133 F f
Niitaka Chain, Taiwan 131 K l
Nijil, Jordan 123 D g
Nijkerk, Netherlands 100 D b
Nijmegen, Netherlands 100 D j
Nikaria. See Ikaría, I.
Nikel, U.S.S.R. 117 B b
Nikiforos, Greece 112 E d
Nikki, Dahomey 118 F g
Nikko Nat. Park, Japan 133 F f
Nikolayev, Ukraine, U.S.S.R. 116 G h
Nikolayevskiy, U.S.S.R. 117 G e
Nikolayevsk-na-Amure, U.S.S.R. 115 P c
Nikolo-Berezovka, U.S.S.R. 117 M b
Nikolo-Kozel'sk, Ukraine, U.S.S.R. 116 H h
Nikol'skaya Pestrovka, U.S.S.R. 117 G d
Nikopol, Ukraine, U.S.S.R. 116 J h
Niksar, Turkey 124 C a
Nikšić, Yugoslavia 112 B c
Nila, I., Indonesia 129 J m
Nile, R., N. Africa 119 M e
Nilgault, L., Quebec 85 N f
Nilgiri, India 127 G d
Nilgiri Hills, India 126 E f
Nimach (Neemuch), India 126 D d
Nîmes, France 109 F e
Nimgiri, Mt., India 127 F e
Nimrod Glacier, Antarctica 136 A b
Ninette, Manitoba 87 S j
Nineveh, Iraq 124 D b
Ningan, China 128 J b
Ninganpao, China 130 B d
Ningerh. See Puerh
Ninghai, China 131 K h
Ninghsien, China 131 F j
Ninghsien (Ningpo), China 131 K h
Ningi, Kwajalein Is. 79 U e
Ningkwo. See Suancheng
Ninglingting. See Kinki
Ningpo, China 131 K h
Ning-sia, China 130 C c
Ningsia Hui Aut. Reg., China 130 B d
Ningsiang, China 131 F h
Ningteh. See Yingchwan
Ning-wu-fu, China 130 F c
Ning-yüan chow, China 130 K b
Ning-yüan-ting, China 130 F b
Ninh-binh, N. Vietnam 132 D b
Ninh Hoa. See Nha Trang
Ninigo I., Admiralty Is. 78 E g
Ninnis Glacier, Antarctica 136 A e
Ninove, Belgium 100 C d
Nioro, Mali 118 D e
Niort, France 108 C c
Níos. See Íos, I.
Nipawin, Saskatchewan 87 N e
Nipawin Prov. Park, Saskatchewan 87 N d
Nipe, B. de, Cuba 91 D b
Nipigon, L. & R., Ontario 84 B c
Nipigon, Ontario 84 B c
Nipigon B., Ontario 84 B d
Nipin R., Saskatchewan 86 H c
Nipisiguit B., New Brunswick 82 G f
Nipisiguit R., New Brunswick 82 F f
Nipisi R., Alberta 86 C c
Nipissing, L., Ontario 85 L f
Nipissing Junc., Ontario 85 L f
Nipissis L. & R., Quebec 82 F c
Nipisso L., Quebec 82 G c
Niquelandia, Brazil 93 H f
Nirmal, India 126 E e
Nis, Yugoslavia 112 C c
Nischu, Kashmir 126 E b
Nish. See Nis
Nishapur. See Neyshābūr
Nishio, Japan 133 E g
Nishiwaki, Japan 133 D g
Nisiros, I., Greece 113 F f
Nissan, Solomon Is. 78 G h
Nissi, Estonia, U.S.S.R. 103 L g
Nitchequon, Quebec 81 M g
Niterói, Brazil 93 J h
Nith R., Scotland 98 E e
Nitra, Czechoslovakia 105 H d
Nitrianske Pravno, Czechoslovakia 105 H d
Niue, I., Pacific Ocean 78 K j
Niut, Mt., Borneo 129 E k
Nivala, Finland 102 L e
Nivelles, Belgium 100 C d
Nivernais, prov., France 108 E c
Niverville, Manitoba 87 U j
Nizamabad, India 126 E e
Nizampatam, India 126 F e
Nizana, Israel 123 C g
Nizhne Udinsk, U.S.S.R. 115 J c
Nizhniye Kresty, U.S.S.R. 115 R b
Nizhniy Lomov, U.S.S.R. 117 F d
Nizhniy Tagil, U.S.S.R. 117 P b
Nizhnyaya Pesha, U.S.S.R. 114 D b
Nizke Tatry, Czechoslovakia 105 H d
Njombe, Tanganyika 121 G f
Nkonde, Tanganyika 121 G f
N'Kongsamba, Cameroon 119 G h
Nmai R., Burma 127 J c
Noagarh, India 127 F d
Noakhali. See Sudharam
Noanama, Colombia 92 B c
Nobel, Ontario 84 K g
Nobleford, Alberta 86 D j
Nocera, Italy 111 E e
Nochistlán, Mexico 90 E d
Noel Paul's Brook, Newfoundland 83 Q e
Noelville, Ontario 84 K f
Noemfoor, I., New Guinea 129 K l
Nœrbö, Norway 103 A g
Nogaro, France 109 C e
Nogent-le-Rotrou, France 108 D b
Nogent-sur-Seine, France 108 E b
Noginsk, U.S.S.R. 116 L d
Noire, R., Quebec 85 N f
Noirmoutier, I. de, France 108 B c
Nokhtuysk, U.S.S.R. 115 L c
Nokomis, Saskatchewan 87 N g
Nokomis L., Saskatchewan 88 S b
Nola, Cent. Afr. Rep. 120 D d
Nola, Italy 111 E e
Nolalu, Ontario 87 N b
Nominingue, Quebec 85 P f
Nonancourt, France 108 D b
Nong-han, Thailand 132 C c
Nong Khai, Thailand 132 C c
Nongoma, South Africa 122 E e
Nonni (Nun), R., China 128 H a
Nonno, Ethiopia 121 H c
Nonoava, Mexico 90 C b
Nõo, Estonia, U.S.S.R. 103 M g
Noonkanbah, Australia 134 D c
Noordeloos, Netherlands 100 C c

Noordwolde, Netherlands 100 E b
Nootka & Sd., Br. Columbia 88 F f
Nootka I., Vancouver I., British Columbia 88 F f
Nora, Saskatchewan 87 O f
Nora, Sweden 103 F g
Noranda, Quebec 85 L d
Nord, dep., France 108 E a
Nord Cap. See Horn, Iceland
Norddal, Norway 102 B e
Nordegg R., Alberta 86 B f
Nordenshelda, Arch., U.S.S.R. 115 J a
Nordhausen, Germany 104 D c
Nordkapp, Norway 102 L a
Nordkinn Halvöya, Norway 102 M a
Nördlingen, Germany 104 D d
Nordreisa, Norway 102 J b
Nordrhein-Westfalen, Germany 104 B c
Nord Slesvig. See Jylland, S.
Nordstrand I., Germany 104 C a
Nordvik, U.S.S.R. 115 L a
Nore, Norway 103 C f
Norembego, Ontario 84 K d
Nore R., Eire 99 C h
Norfolk, co., England 99 H h
Norfolk I., Pacific Ocean 78 H k
Norgama, Pakistan 126 C c
Norheimsund, Norway 103 B f
Norily, U.S.S.R. 114 H b
Normanby I., New Guinea 135 K a
Normandie, prov., France 108 C b
Normandin, Quebec 85 S d
Normanton, Australia 135 H c
Normetal, Quebec 85 L d
Norquay, Saskatchewan 87 P g
Norquiñ, Argentina 95 B e
Norquiñco, Argentina 95 B f
Norris Arm, Newfoundland 83 R d
Norrköping, Sweden 103 G g
Norrsundet, Sweden 103 G f
Norrtalje, Sweden 103 H g
Norseman, Australia 134 D f
Norsholm, Sweden 103 F g
Northallerton, England 99 G f
Northam, Australia 134 C f
Northampton, Australia 134 B e
Northampton & co., England 99 G h
North Aulatsivik I., Labrador 81 N f
North Battleford, Saskatchewan 86 J f
North Bay, Newfoundland 83 O f
North Bay, Ontario 85 L f
North Berwick, Scotland 98 F d
North Borneo, Borneo 129 G j
North Branch, Ontario 86 H a
North Brook, Ontario 85 N h
North C., Antarctica 136 B d
North C., C. Breton I., Nova Scotia 83 M f
North C., New Zealand 135 Q j
North Caribou L., Ontario 81 K g
North Chan., Ontario 84 G f
North Chan., Scotland-Northern Ireland 98 D e
North Devon, New Brunswick 82 F h
North Downs, England 99 H j
North-East Foreland, Greenland 89 M a
Northeast I., Truk Is. 78 E m
Northeast Pt., Belle Isle, Newfoundland 83 R a
Northern Bight, Newfoundland 83 S e
Northern Circars, India 126 F e
Northern Head, New Brunswick 82 F j
Northern Ireland, Brit. Isles 99 C f
Northern Light L., Ontario 87 M b
Northern Rhodesia, Central Africa 122 D b
Northern Territory, Australia 134 F c
North French R., Ontario 84 J b
Northgate, Saskatchewan 87 P j
North Head, New Brunswick 82 F j
North Head, Newfoundland 83 O d
North I., New Zealand 135 R k
North Kent I., N.-W. Terr. 81 L b
North Knife L., Manitoba 87 V a
North Land. See Severnaya Zemlya
North McIntyre, Ontario 87 O b
North Magnetic Pole 89 M b
North Pole, Arctic Ocean 89 A a
Northport, Nova Scotia 82 J h
North Pt., Prince Edward I. 82 H f
North Riding, Yorkshire, England 99 F f
North River Bridge, C. Breton I., Nova Scotia 83 M g
North Ronaldsay, I., Orkney 98 F a
North Rustico, Prince Edward I. 82 J g
North Sea, W. Europe 96 G d
Northside, Canton I. 79 S m
North Star, Alberta 88 L b
North Sydney, C. Breton I., Nova Scotia 83 M g
North Taranaki Bight, New Zealand 135 R k
Northumberland, co., England 98 F e
Northumberland Str., Nova Scotia 82 J g
North Vancouver, British Columbia 88 H f
North Vermilion, Alberta 88 L a
North West C., Australia 134 B d
North West River, Labrador 81 N g
North West St. Augustin R., Quebec 83 N b
Northwest Territories, political region, Canada 80 H d
North York, Ontario 84 C j
Norton, New Brunswick 82 G h
Norvegia, C., Antarctica 136 L d
Norway, North-West Europe 102-103
Norway House, Manitoba 80 K g
Norway I., N.-W. Terr. 80 G c
Norwegian B., N.-W. Terr. 81 K b
Norwich, England 99 H h
Norwich, Ontario 84 K k
Norwood, Ontario 85 M h
Noshiro, Japan 133 F d
Nosseghem, Belgium 100 C d
Nossi Bé, I., Madagascar 121 N j
Notikewin, R., Alberta 88 K b
Noto, Sicily 111 E g
Notodden, Norway 103 C g
Noto Pen., Japan 133 E f
Notre Dame, New Brunswick 82 H g
Notre Dame, Quebec 82 A h
Notre Dame B., Newfoundland 83 R d
Notre Dame de la Dorée, Quebec 85 S d
Notre Dame-de-Lévis, Quebec 85 T c
Notre Dame de Lourdes, Manitoba 87 T j
Notre Dame de Rimouski, Quebec 82 D e
Notre Dame du Lac, Quebec 82 D f
Notre Dame du Laus, Quebec 85 P f
Notre Dame Mts., Quebec 82 B g
Nottawasaga B., Ontario 84 K h
Nottaway R., Quebec 85 M b
Nottingham & co., England 99 G h
Nottingham I., North-West Territories 81 M e
Nouakchott, Mauritania 118 B e
Nouméa, Pacific Ocean 78 G k
Nouvelle, L., Quebec 82 D c
Nouvelle, Quebec 82 F e
Nova Bečej, Yugoslavia 112 C b
Nova Chaves, Angola 120 E g
Nova Cruz, Brazil 93 K e
Nova Freixo, Mozambique 121 H g
Nova Gaia, Angola 120 D g
Nova Goa, India 126 D e
Nova Iorque, Brazil 93 J e
Nova Lisboa, Angola 120 D g
Novara, Italy 110 B c
Nova Scotia, prov., Canada 81 N j
Nova Sofala, Mozambique 122 E d
Nova Venecia, Brazil 93 J g
Novaya Sibir, I., U.S.S.R. 115 Q a
Novaya Zemlya, I., U.S.S.R. 114 E a
Nové Zámky, Czechoslovakia 105 H e
Novgorod, U.S.S.R. 116 G b
Novi, Yugoslavia 110 E c
Novi Pazar, Bulgaria 112 F c
Novi Pazar, Yugoslavia 112 C c
Novi Sad, Yugoslavia 112 B b
Novocherkassk, U.S.S.R. 117 E g
Novokuznetsk, U.S.S.R. 114 H c
Novo Mesto, Yugoslavia 110 E c
Novomoskovsk, Ukraine, U.S.S.R. 116 J g
Novomoskovsk, U.S.S.R. 116 L d
Novo Redondo, Angola 120 C g
Novorossiysk, U.S.S.R. 114 C d
Novoshakhtinsk, U.S.S.R. 117 D g
Novosibirsk, U.S.S.R. 114 H c
Novosibirskaya Oblast, U.S.S.R. 114 G c
Novosibirskiye Ostrova, Is., U.S.S.R. 115 N a
Novo Troitsk, U.S.S.R. 117 P e
Novourgench. See Urgench
Novska, Yugoslavia 110 F c
Novy Jičin, Czechoslovakia 105 H d
Novyy Port, U.S.S.R. 114 G b
Nowa Wilejka. See Naujoji Vilnia
Nowgong, India 127 H c
Nowra, Australia 135 K f
Nowy Sacz, Poland 105 J d
Nowy Targ, Poland 105 J d
Nowy Tomysl, Poland 105 G b
Noya, Spain 106 A a
Noyrot, L., Quebec 83 O b
Nozay, France 108 C c
Ntungamo, Uganda 121 G e
Nuanetsi, S. Rhodesia 122 E d
Nuassuak Pen., Greenland 89 P b
Nueltin L., North-West Territories 81 K e
Nueva, I., Chile & Argentina 95 C j
Nueva Imperial, Chile 95 B e
Nueva Lubeca, Argentina 95 B f
Nueve de Julio, Argentina 94 D e
Nuevo, G., Argentina 95 D f
Nuevo Laredo, Mexico 90 E b
Nuevo León, state, Mexico 90 D b
Nui, I., Ellice Is. 78 H h
Nuits-St. Georges, France 108 F c
Nuku'alofa, Tonga Is. 78 J j
Nuku Hiva, I., Marquesas Is. 79 M h
Nukulaelae, I., Ellice Is. 78 J h
Nukunono, I., Tokelau Is. 78 J h
Nukuoro, I., Caroline Is. 78 F g
Nukus, Uzbek., U.S.S.R. 114 E d
Nules, Spain 107 E c
Nullabor, Australia 134 F f
Nullagine, Australia 134 D d
Nullarbor Plain, Australia 134 E f
Numata, Japan 133 F f
Numazu, Japan 133 F g
Nunchía, Colombia 92 C b
Nunkiang, China 128 J a
Nuoro, Sardinia 111 B e
Nuquí, Colombia 92 B b
Nuremberg. See Nürnberg
Nurmes, Finland 102 N e
Nürnberg (Nuremberg), Germany 104 D d
Nurri, Sardinia 111 B f
Nusaybin, Turkey 124 D b
Nushki, Pakistan 126 C c
Nutak, Labrador 81 N f
Nut L., Saskatchewan 87 O f
Nut Mountain, ra., Saskatchewan 87 P f
Nut Mountain, Saskatchewan 87 O f
Nutrias, Venezuela 92 D b
Nuu, Manua Is. 79 R o
Nu'uuli, Tutuila I. 79 U o
Nuvukjuak, North-West Territories 81 M d
Nuwara Eliya, Ceylon 126 F g
Nyada, Sweden 102 G e
Nyåker, Sweden 102 H e
Nyala, Sudan 119 K f
Nyalikungu, Tanganyika 121 G e
Nyamlell, Sudan 119 L g
Nyandoma, U.S.S.R. 114 D b
Nyantakara, Tanganyika 121 G e
Nyanza, Rwanda 121 F e
Nyasa, L., Nyasaland 121 G g
Nyasaland, E. Africa 121 G g
Nyazepetrovsk, U.S.S.R. 117 P b
Nyda, U.S.S.R. 114 G b
Nyeri, Kenya 121 H e
Nyhammar, Sweden 103 F f
Nyiregyháza, Hungary 105 J e
Nyköbing, Denmark 103 D j
Nyköbing, Denmark 103 C h
Nyköping, Sweden 103 G g
Nylstroom, South Africa 122 D d
Nymagee, Australia 135 J f
Nyngan, Australia 135 J f
Nyon, Switzerland 101 B b
Nyonga, Tanganyika 121 G f
Nyons, France 109 F d
Nysa, Poland 105 G c
Nysted, Denmark 103 D j
Nyurba, U.S.S.R. 115 L b
Nyuya, U.S.S.R. 115 L b
Nzega, Tanganyika 121 G e
Oakan, Japan 133 J c
Oak Bay, New Brunswick 82 E h
Oakburn, Manitoba 87 R h
Oakham, England 99 G h
Oak L., Manitoba 87 R j
Oak Lake, Manitoba 87 R j
Oakland, Ontario 84 K j
Oakner, Manitoba 87 R h
Oak Point, Manitoba 87 T h
Oak River, Manitoba 87 R h
Oakville, Manitoba 87 T j
Oakville, Ontario 85 L j
Oamaru, New Zealand 135 Q m
Oates Coast, Antarctica 136 A d
Oates Ld., Antarctica 136 A d
Oaxaca & state, Mexico 90 E d
Ob, R., U.S.S.R. 114 F b
Oba, L., Ontario 84 F d
Oba, Ontario 84 F c
Obakamiga L., Ontario 84 E c
Obama, Japan 133 D g
Oban, New Zealand 135 P m
Oban, Saskatchewan 86 J f
Oban, Scotland 98 D d
Obatogamau L., Quebec 85 Q c
Obbia, Somali Republic 121 K c
Obed, Alberta 88 L d
Obeh, Afghanistan 125 H c
Oberammergau, Germany 104 D e
Oberhausen, Germany 104 B c
Oberriet, Switzerland 101 E a
Oberwald, Switzerland 101 D b
Obi, I., Indonesia 129 J l
Obidos, Brazil 93 F d
Obidos, Portugal 106 A c
Obihiro, Japan 133 H c
Obo, Cent. Afr. Rep. 119 L g
Obo, Mongolia 128 D b
Obock, Fr. Somaliland 121 J b
Obonga L., Ontario 87 O a
Oborona, U.S.S.R. 117 E d
Obrayera, Nicaragua 91 C d
O'Brien, Ontario 84 K e
Observatory Inlet, British Columbia 88 E c
Obskaya Guba, U.S.S.R. 114 G b
Ocampo, Mexico 90 E c
Ocana, Colombia 92 C b
Ocaña, Spain 106 D c
Occidental, Cord., Colombia 92 B c
Ocean Falls, Br. Columbia 88 F d
Oceania, Pacific Ocean 78-79
Ocean Park, Br. Columbia 88 E g
Ochil Hills, Scotland 98 E d
Ochre River, Manitoba 87 S g
Ocland, Romania 112 E a
Ocoa, B. de, Dom. Rep. 91 E c
Ocoña, Peru 92 C g
Ocos, Guatemala 90 F e
Ocotal, Nicaragua 91 B d
Octopus, Ontario 84 D c
Ocumare, Venezuela 92 D a
Ocussi Ambeno, Timor 134 D a
Oda, Ghana 118 E g
Odaka, Japan 133 G f
Odate, Japan 133 G d
Odawara, Japan 133 F g
Odemira, Portugal 106 A d
Odemiş, Turkey 124 A b
Odense, Denmark 103 D j
Oder R., Germany 104 F b
Odessa, Manitoba 87 O h
Odessa, Ontario 85 O h
Odessa, Ukraine, U.S.S.R. 116 G h
Odhill, Manitoba 87 T c
Odienné, Ivory Coast 118 D g
Odom Inlet, Antarctica 136 J d
Odoorn, Netherlands 100 E b
Odorhei, Romania 112 E a
Odra R., Poland 104 F b
Odzala, Congo 120 C d
Oedelem, Belgium 100 B c
Oeiras, Brazil 93 J e
Oeno, I., Pacific Ocean 79 N k
Of, Turkey 124 D a
Offaly (Ui Failghe), co., Eire 99 B g
Offenbach, Germany 104 C c
Ofu, Manua Is. 79 R o
Ogahalla, Ontario 84 E b
Ogaki, Japan 133 E g
Ogascanan, L., Quebec 85 M e
Ogden, Mt., Alaska-British Columbia 88 C a
Ogden, Nova Scotia 83 L h
Ogema, Saskatchewan 87 N j
Ogidaki, Ontario 84 F f
Ogimi, Okinawa 78 C a
Ogoja, Nigeria 118 G g
Ogoki, Ontario 81 L g
Ogoki, R., Ontario 84 D b
Ogoki L., Ontario 84 C b
Ogoki Res., Ontario 84 B b
Ogr, Sudan 119 L f
Ogulin, Yugoslavia 110 E c
Ohakune, New Zealand 135 R k
Ohaton, Alberta 86 E f
Ohau, L., New Zealand 135 P m
Ohey, Belgium 100 D d
O'Higgins, Mt., Chile 95 B g
Ohrid, Yugoslavia 112 C d
Ohridsko Jezero, Yugoslavia 112 C d
Oiapoque, R., Brazil, etc. 93 G c
Oignies, Belgium 100 C d
Oil Springs, Ontario 84 H k
Oirschot, Netherlands 100 D c
Oise, dep., France 108 E b
Oita, Japan 133 B h
Oiticica, Brazil 93 J e
Ojinaga, Mexico 90 D b
Ojiya, Japan 133 F f
Ojocaliente, Mexico 90 D c
Ojo de Agua, Argentina 94 D c
Ojo del Toro, Pico, Cuba 91 D c
Oka, Quebec 85 Q g
Okahandja, S.W. Africa 122 B d
Okaihau, New Zealand 135 Q j
Okak Is., Labrador 81 N f
Okanagan Centre, British Columbia 88 K e
Okanagan Falls, British Columbia 88 K f
Okanagan L., Br. Columbia 88 K e
Okanagan Landing, British Columbia 88 K e
Oka R., U.S.S.R. 117 F c
Okau, Yap I. 78 D l
Okaukuejo, S.W. Africa 122 B c
Okavango, R., Angola 122 B c
Okayama, Japan 133 C g
Okehampton, England 99 E k
Okha, U.S.S.R. 115 P c
Okhansk, U.S.S.R. 117 M b
Okhotsk, Sea of, U.S.S.R. 115 P c
Okhotsk, U.S.S.R. 115 P c
Oki gunto, Japan 133 C f
Okinawa, Ryukyu Is. 78 D d
Okotoks, Alberta 86 D h
Oktyabr'skiy, U.S.S.R. 117 L c
Oktyabrskoy Revolyutsiy, Os., U.S.S.R. 115 J a
Oku, Okinawa 78 C a
Okučani, Yugoslavia 110 F c
Okuma B., Antarctica 136 C c
Okuru, New Zealand 135 P e
Okushiri I., Japan 133 F c
Olaine, Latvia, U.S.S.R. 103 K h
Olamane R., Quebec 83 M c
Olanchito, Honduras 91 B c
Öland, I., Sweden 103 G h
Olasan, Ethiopia 121 K c
Olavarría, Argentina 94 D e
Oława, Poland 105 G c
Olbia, Sardinia 111 B e
Oldcastle, Eire 99 C g
Oldenburg, Germany 104 D a
Oldenburg, Germany 104 C b
Oldenzaal, Netherlands 100 E b
Old Fort Bay, Quebec 83 P b
Oldham, England 99 F g
Old Hogem, Br. Columbia 88 G c
Oldman R., Alberta 88 M f
Old Perlican, Newfoundland 83 T e
Old Post Pt., Quebec 83 L c
Olds, Alberta 86 C g
Old Wives & L., Saskatchewan 87 M h
O'Leary, Prince Edward I. 82 H g
Olecko, Poland 105 K a
Olekminsk, U.S.S.R. 115 M b
Olenek, R., U.S.S.R. 115 M a
Olenek, U.S.S.R. 115 L b
Olenekskiy Zaliv, U.S.S.R. 115 M a
Oléron, I. d', France 108 C d
Olga, U.S.S.R. 115 N d
Olga L., Quebec 85 N c
Olifants Kloof, Bechuanaland 122 C d
Olimbos, Mts., Greece 113 D d
Oliva de Jerez, Spain 106 B c
Olivares, Cerro de, Argentina 94 C d
Olivares, Spain 107 D c
Oliveira, Brazil 93 J f
Olivenza, Spain 106 B c
Oliver, Br. Columbia 88 K f
Olivone, Switzerland 101 D b
Ollagüe, Chile 94 C b
Ollagüe, Mt., Bolivia 94 C b
Ollan, Truk Is. 78 D o
Olmedo, Spain 106 C b
Olomatimu, Manua Is. 79 S o
Olomouc, Czechoslovakia 105 G d
Olosega, Manua Is. 79 R o
Olot, Spain 107 G a
Olovyannaya, U.S.S.R. 115 L c
Olpe, Germany 104 B c
Olst, Netherlands 100 E b
Olsztyn, Poland 105 J b
Olten, Switzerland 101 C a
Oltu, Turkey 124 D a
Oltul R., Romania 112 E b
Olvera, Spain 106 C d
Olympia, Greece 113 C f
Olympus. See Olimbos
Olyutorskiy Zaliv, U.S.S.R. 115 R b
Omagh, N. Ireland 99 C f
Omaguas, Peru 92 C d
Oman, G. of, Saudi Arabia-Iran 125 G e
Oman, Muscat & Oman 125 G e
Omaok, Palau Is. 78 A o
Omaruru, S.W. Africa 122 B d
Ombabika B., Ontario 84 B b
Ombombo, S.W. Africa 122 A c
Omdurman, Sudan 119 M e
Omemee, Ontario 85 M h
Ometepec, Mexico 90 E d
Omin, Yap I. 78 D l
Omineca, R., Br. Columbia 88 G c
Omineca Mts., Br. Columbia 88 F b
Ommanney B., North-West Territories 80 J c
Ommen, Netherlands 100 E b
Omoa, Honduras 91 B c
Omsk, U.S.S.R. 114 G c
Omskaya Oblast, U.S.S.R. 114 G c
Omuta, Japan 133 B h
Omutninsk, U.S.S.R. 117 L a
Onakawana, Ontario 84 J b
Onakwahegan, R., Ontario 84 J a
Onaman L., Ontario 84 C b
Onamue, Truk Is. 78 D o
Onaping L., Ontario 84 J e
Onatchiway L., Quebec 82 A d
Öndör Hän, Mongolia 128 F a
Onega & R., U.S.S.R. 114 C b
Onehunga, New Zealand 135 R k
Onemak, Kwajalein Is. 79 U e
One Sided Lake, Ontario 86 J a
Onezhskoye Oz., U.S.S.R. 114 C b
Ongole, India 84 F e
Ongudai, U.S.S.R. 114 H c
Oniiba, S.W. Africa 122 B c
Onion Lake, Saskatchewan 86 H e
Onistagan L., Quebec 82 A c
Onitsha, Nigeria 118 G g
Onjül, Mongolia 128 E a
Onna, Okinawa 78 B b
Onnaram, Truk Is. 78 F o
Onoto, Venezuela 92 D b
Onoway, Alberta 86 C e
Onslow, Australia 134 B d
Ontario, prov., Canada 81 K g
Onteniente, Spain 107 E c
Ontiñena, Spain 107 F b
Ooa, Jaluit I. 79 T j
Oodnadatta, Australia 134 G e
Ooldea, Australia 134 F f
Oostburg, Netherlands 100 B c
Oostcamp, Belgium 100 B c
Oostende. See Ostende
Ooster Schelde, Netherlands 100 B c
Oosterwolde, Netherlands 100 E b
Oosthuizen, Netherlands 100 D b
Oostmalle, Belgium 100 C c
Oostvoorne, Netherlands 100 C c
Ootacamund, India 126 E f
Ootsa L., Br. Columbia 88 G d
Opochuanau L., Manitoba 87 S b
Opal, Alberta 86 D e
Opala, U.S.S.R. 115 Q c
Opari, Sudan 119 M h
Opasatika, Ontario 84 H c
Opasatika L., Ontario 84 H c
Opataka L., Quebec 85 Q b
Opatija, Yugoslavia 110 E c
Opava, Czechoslovakia 105 G d
Opawica L. & R., Quebec 85 P c
Opemisca L., Quebec 85 Q c
Opemisha, Ontario 84 D b
Opeongo L., Ontario 85 M g
Ophir, Mt., Malaya 132 C f
Ophoven, Belgium 100 D c
Opochka, U.S.S.R. 116 F c
Opocopa L., Quebec 82 F a
Opodepe, Mexico 90 B a
Opole, Poland 105 G c
Oporto. See Porto
Opotiki, New Zealand 135 R k
Oppa B., Japan 133 G e
Oppein. See Opole
Optic Lake, Manitoba 87 Q d
Oputo, Mexico 90 C a
Oqair. See Uqair
Oradea, Romania 112 C a
Oran, Algeria 118 E a
Orán, Argentina 92 E h
Orange, France 109 F d
Orangedale, C. Breton I., Nova Scotia 83 L h
Orange Free State, prov., South Africa 122 D e
Orange R., S. Africa 122 B e
Orangeville, Ontario 84 K j
Oranje Geb., Mts., Surinam 93 F c
Oranjestad, Aruba, Dutch West Indies 91 E d
Oras, Philippines 129 J h
Orăştie, Romania 112 D b
Orasul Stalin. See Braşov
Oravita, Romania 112 C b
Oravská Magura, Czechoslovakia 105 H d
Orawia, New Zealand 135 P m
Orbe, Switzerland 101 B b
Orcera, Spain 107 D c
Ord, Mt., Australia 134 E c
Ordale, Saskatchewan 84 L e
Ordenes, Spain 106 A a
Ord River, Australia 134 E c
Ordu, Turkey 124 C a
Ordzhonikidze, U.S.S.R. 114 D d
Ordzhonikidzegrad. See Bezhitsa
Oreba, Kwajalein Is. 79 T d
Orebro, Sweden 103 F g
Öregrund, Sweden 103 H f
Orekhovo Zuyevo, U.S.S.R. 116 L d
Orel, U.S.S.R. 116 K e
Orellana, Peru 92 B e
Orellana, Spain 106 C c
Orenburg, U.S.S.R. 117 M e
Orense, Spain 106 B a
Oresund, Denmark-Sweden 103 E j
Orgaña, Spain 107 F a
Orgaz, Spain 106 D c
Orhon R., Mongolia 128 D a
Oriental, Cord., Colombia 92 C b
Oriental, Cord., Peru 92 B e
Orient Bay, Ontario 84 B c
Orihuela, Spain 107 E c
Orillia, Ontario 85 L h
Orinoco, R., Venezuela 92 E b
Orion, Alberta 86 G j
Orissa, state, India 127 F d
Oristano & G. di, Sardinia 111 B f
Orivesi, Finland 102 N e
Oriximiná, Brazil 93 F d
Orizaba, Mexico 90 E d
Orizare, Bulgaria 112 F c
Orizona, Brazil 93 H g
Orkanger, Norway 102 C e
Orkney, Saskatchewan 86 K j
Orkney, Scotland 98 F b
Örland, Norway 102 C e
Orléanais, prov., France 108 D c
Orléans, France 108 D c
Orleans, I. d', Quebec 82 A g
Orléansville, Algeria 118 F a
Orman, Syria 123 E e
Ormara, Pakistan 126 B c
Ormiston, Saskatchewan 87 M j
Ormsby, Ontario 85 N h
Ormstown, Quebec 85 R g
Ornach, Pakistan 126 C c
Orne, dep., France 108 C b
Örnsköldsvik, Sweden 102 H e
Orochen, U.S.S.R. 115 M c
Orocué, Colombia 92 C c
Oroku, Okinawa 78 A c
Oroluk, I., Caroline Is. 78 F f
Oromocto & L., New Brunswick 82 F h
Oron. See Kochumdek
Orono, Ontario 85 M j
Orontes, R., Syria 124 C b
Orosei, G. di, Sardinia 111 B e
Orosi, Vol., Costa Rica 91 B d
Orote Pen., Guam 78 A l
Orr L., Manitoba 87 U b
Orsa, Sweden 103 F f
Orsha, Belorussia, U.S.S.R. 116 G d
Orsières, Switzerland 101 C b
Orsk, U.S.S.R. 117 P e
Orsova, Romania 112 D b
Ortegal, C., Spain 106 B a
Orthez, France 109 C e
Ortiz, Mexico 90 C b
Ortiz, Venezuela 92 D b
Orugueira, Spain 106 B a
Orukuizu, Palau Is. 78 A n
Oruro, Bolivia 92 D g
Orust, Sweden 103 D g
Orvieto, Italy 110 D d
Oryekhovo, U.S.S.R. 117 G e
Osa, U.S.S.R. 117 G e
Osa, U.S.S.R. 117 M b
Osage, Manitoba 87 O j
Osaka, Japan 133 D g
Oschiri, Sardinia 111 B e
Osen, Norway 102 D d
Osgoode Station, Ontario 85 P g

Osh, Kirgiz., U.S.S.R. 114 G d
Oshawa, Ontario 85 M j
O Shima, Japan 133 F g
Oshnoviyeh, Iran 124 E b
Osijek, Yugoslavia 112 B b
Osilo, Sardinia 111 B e
Osipenko, U.S.S.R. 115 N c
Osipovichi, Belorussia, U.S.S.R. 116 F e
Osire Sud, S.W. Africa 122 B d
Oskarshamn, Sweden 103 G h
Oskelaneo, Quebec 85 P d
Osler, Saskatchewan 86 L f
Oslo, Norway 103 D g
Oslo Fd., Norway 103 D g
Osmanabad, India 126 E e
Osmancik, Turkey 124 B a
Osnabrück, Germany 104 C b
Osorio, Brazil 94 F c
Osorno, Chile 95 B f
Osorno, Spain 106 C a
Osoyoos, Br. Columbia 88 K f
Osowiec, Poland 105 K b
Ospika, R., Br. Columbia 88 H b
Oss, Netherlands 100 D c
Ostaboningue, L., Quebec 85 M e
Ostavall, Sweden 102 F e
Ostende (Oostende), Belgium 100 A c
Österreich, Nieder, prov., Austria 105 F d
Österreich, Ober, prov., Austria 104 F d
Östersund, Sweden 102 F e
Östhammar, Sweden 103 H f
Ostrava, Czechoslovakia 105 H d
Ostroda, Poland 105 H b
Ostrołeka, Poland 105 J b
Ostrom, Ontario 84 J e
Ostrov, Romania 112 G b
Ostrov, U.S.S.R. 116 F c
Ostrovno, U.S.S.R. 115 R b
Ostrowiec, Poland 105 J c
Ostrów Mazowiecki, Poland 105 K b
Ostuni, Italy 111 F e
Ostvågöy, Norway 102 F b
O'Sullivan L., Ontario 84 C b
O'Sullivan L., Quebec 85 P e
Osumi Kaikyo, Japan 133 B j
Osuna, Spain 106 C d
Oswestry, England 99 E h
Ota, Japan 133 C g
Otago Peninsula, New Zealand 135 P m
Otahunu, New Zealand 135 R k
Otaki, New Zealand 135 R l
Otaru & B., Japan 133 G c
Otasuts, Japan 133 G c
Otavalo, Ecuador 92 B c
Otepää, Estonia, U.S.S.R. 103 M g
Othris, Mts., Greece 103 D e
Otira, New Zealand 135 Q l
Otish Mts., Quebec 82 B a
Otjiwarongo, S.W. Africa 122 B d
Otoçac, Yugoslavia 110 E c
Otoineppu, Japan 133 H b
Otosquen, Saskatchewan 87 P e
Otpor, U.S.S.R. 115 L d
Otranto, Str. of, Italy-Albania 113 B d
Otsu, Japan 133 D g
Otta, Truk Is. 78 E o
Ottawa, Ontario 85 P g
Ottawa Is., North-West Territories 81 L f
Ottawa R., Quebec-Ontario 85 M f
Ottawa West, Ontario 84 C j
Otter, Anticosti I., Quebec 82 J d
Otter I., Ontario 84 D d
Otter L., Saskatchewan 87 N c
Otter Lake, Ontario 84 L g
Otterlo, Netherlands 100 D b
Otteröy, Norway 102 B e
Otthon, Saskatchewan 87 P g
Ottignies, Belgium 100 C d
Ötting, Germany 104 E d
Otto Fd., North-West Territories 81 L a
Otukamanoan L., Ontario 86 K a
Otus, U.S.S.R. 116 J j
Otway, B., Chile 95 B h
Otway, C., Australia 135 H g
Otwock, Poland 105 J b
Ötz, Austria 104 D e
Ötztaler Alpen, Mts., Italy-Austria 110 C b
Ouagadougou, Upper Volta 118 E f
Ouahigouya, Upper Volta 118 E f
Ouangolodougou, Ivory Coast 118 D g
Ouargla, Algeria 118 G b
Oubangui R., Congo 120 D d
Oud, India 126 F c
Ouddorp, Netherlands 100 B c
Oudecappelle, Belgium 100 A c
Oudenaarde. See Audenard
Oudenbosch, Netherlands 100 C c
Oudtshoorn, South Africa 122 C f
Ouessant, I. d', France 108 A b
Ouezzane, Morocco 118 D b
Ouidah, Dahomey 118 F g
Ouimet, Ontario 87 P a
Oulu, Finland 102 L d
Oulu Järvi, Finland 102 M d
Oulu Joki, Finland 102 M d
Oum Chalouba, Chad 119 K e
Ounas Joki, Finland 102 L c
Oura wan, Okinawa 78 B b
Ouricuri, Brazil 93 J e
Ourinhos, Brazil 93 H h
Ouro Preto, Brazil 93 J h
Ouse, R., England 99 G f
Ouse, R., England 99 H h
Outarde B., Quebec 82 D d
Outardes, R. aux, Quebec 82 D d
Outer I., Quebec 83 O b
Outjo, S.W. Africa 122 B d
Outlook, Saskatchewan 86 K g
Outremont, Quebec 85 S j
Ouyen, Australia 135 H g
Ovalle, Chile 94 B d
Ovar, Portugal 106 A b
Overbrook, Ontario 84 D h
Over Flakkee I., Netherlands 100 C c
Overflowing R., Manitoba-Saskatchewan 87 Q e
Overijssel, prov., Netherlands 100 E b
Överkalix, Sweden 102 K c
Övermark, Finland 102 J e
Overpelt, Belgium 100 D c
Övertornea, Sweden 102 K c
Oviedo, Spain 106 C a
Ovruch, Ukraine, U.S.S.R. 116 F f
Owen I., Burma 127 J f
Owen Sd., Ontario 84 K h
Owen Sound, Ontario 84 K h
Owen Stanley Ra., New Guinea 135 J a
Owerri, Nigeria 118 G g
Owikeno L., Br. Columbia 88 F e
Owo, Nigeria 118 G g
Oxbow, Saskatchewan 87 P j
Oxdrift, Ontario 86 J a
Oxford, Nova Scotia 82 J h
Oxford & co., England 99 G j
Oxford House, Manitoba 87 W d
Oxford L., Manitoba 87 W d
Oxley's Pk., Australia 135 J f
Oyem, Gabon 120 C d
Oyen, Alberta 86 G g
Oymyakon, U.S.S.R. 115 P b
Oyo, Nigeria 118 F g
Oyster B., Tasmania 135 J h
Ozd, Hungary 105 J d
Ozerki, U.S.S.R. 117 G d
Ozhogino, U.S.S.R. 115 P b
Ozieri, Sardinia 111 B e
Ozun, Romania 112 E b
Paan, Burma 127 J e
Paan, China 128 C e
Paarl, South Africa 122 B f
Pabaži, Latvia, U.S.S.R. 103 L h
Pabianice, Poland 105 H c
Pabna, E. Pakistan 127 G d
Pacajá, R., Brazil 93 G d
Pacaraima, Sa., Brazil, etc. 92 E c
Pacasmayo, Peru 92 B e
Pachbhadra, India 126 D c
Pachen, Tibet 128 B d
Pachmarhi, India 126 E d
Pachow. See Pachung
Pachuca, Mexico 90 E c
Pachung, China 130 C g
Paços, Portugal 106 A b
Pacquet, Newfoundland 83 R d
Padam, Kashmir 126 E b
Padang, Sumatra 129 D l
Paddle Prairie, Alberta 88 L b
Paddle R., Alberta 86 C d
Paddockwood, Saskatchewan 87 M e
Paderborn, Germany 104 C c
Padilla, Bolivia 92 E g
Padlei, North-West Territories 81 K e
Padloping Island, North-West Territories 81 N d
Padoue, Quebec 82 E e
Padova, Italy 110 C c
Padstow, England 99 D k
Padua. See Padova
Padul, Spain 106 D d
Paeroa, New Zealand 135 R k
Pafuri, Mozambique 122 E d
Pagai Is., Indonesia 129 D l
Pagan, Burma 127 H d
Pagasai, G. of, Greece 113 D e
Pagato R., Saskatchewan 87 P b
Pago, I., Yugoslavia 110 E c
Pago B., Guam 78 B l
Pagong L., Kashmir-Tibet 126 E b
Pago Pago, Tutuila I. 79 T o
Pago Pago Harb., Tutuila I. 79 U o
Pagwachuan, Ontario 84 D c
Pagwachuan, R., Ontario 84 E c
Pagwa River, Ontario 84 E b
Pahiatua, New Zealand 135 R l
Pahlavi, Bandar-e, Iran 124 E b
Pahlavi Dezh, Iran 125 F b
Pahsien, China 130 H c
Pahsien. See Chungking
Paignton, England 99 E k
Paiho, China 130 E f
Paijanne, L., Finland 103 L f
Pai-Khoi Krebet, U.S.S.R. 114 F b
Pailingmiao, China 128 F b
Paimpol, France 108 B b
Paincourt, Ontario 84 H k
Paint L., Manitoba 87 T c
Paisley, Ontario 84 J h
Paisley, Scotland 98 E e
Paita, Peru 92 A e
Pai Tu Hu, China 130 H g
Pajakumbuh, Sumatra 129 D l
Pajala, Sweden 102 K c
Pajares, Spain 106 C a
Pajde, Estonia, U.S.S.R. 103 L g
Pakanbaru, Sumatra 129 D k
Pakashkan L., Ontario 87 N a
Pakchan, Burma 127 J f
Pakenham, Ontario 85 O g
Pak-hoi, China 131 D m
Pakistan, E., S. Asia 127 G d
Pakistan, W., S. Asia 126 C c
Pak-lay, Laos 132 C c
Pakokku, Burma 127 J d
Pakowki L., Alberta 86 F j
Pakrac, Yugoslavia 110 F c
Paks, Hungary 105 H e
Pakse, Laos 132 D c
Pakwa L., Manitoba 87 S d
Palafrugell, Spain 107 G b
Palaiokhóra, Crete 113 D g
Palamau, India 127 F d
Palamcottah, India 126 E g
Palamós, Spain 107 G b
Palamuse, Estonia, U.S.S.R. 103 M g
Palana, India 126 D c
Palana, U.S.S.R. 115 R c
Palanpur, India 126 D d
Palapye Road, Bechuanaland 122 D d
Palau Is., Pacific Ocean 78 D f
Palaw, Burma 132 B d
Palawan, I., Philippines 129 G j
Paldiski, Estonia, U.S.S.R. 103 L g
Palembang, Sumatra 129 D l
Palena, Chile 95 B f
Palencia, Spain 106 C a
Palenque, Mexico 90 F d
Paleokhorio, Cyprus 123 B b
Palermo, Argentina 94 D b
Palermo, Ontario 84 L j
Palermo, Sicily 111 D f
Palestina, Chile 94 C b
Palestine, W. Asia 124 C c
Paletwa, Burma 127 H d
Palghat, India 126 E f
Palgrave Pt., S.W. Africa 122 A d
Palgu Tso, Tibet 127 G c
Palhoça, Brazil 94 G c
Pali, India 126 D c
Palimé, Togo 118 F g
Paliseul, Belgium 100 D e
Palizada, Mexico 90 F d
Palk Str., India 126 E g
Palliser B., New Zealand 135 R l
Palma, Balearic Is. 107 G c
Palma, I., Canary Is. 118 B c
Palma, Mozambique 121 J g
Palmares, Brazil 94 F d
Palmas, B., Mexico 90 C c
Palmas, Brazil 94 F c
Palmas, C., Liberia 118 D h
Palmas, G. of, Sardinia 111 B f
Palma Sola, Venezuela 92 D a
Palmeira, Brazil 94 F c
Palmer, C., Antarctica 136 G d
Palmer, Saskatchewan 86 L j
Palmer Arch., Antarctica 136 H f
Palmerston, Ontario 84 K j
Palmerston I., Cook Is. 78 K j
Palmerston North, New Zealand 135 R l
Palmerston South, New Zealand 135 Q m
Palm I., Australia 135 J c
Palmira, Colombia 92 B c
Palmyra, Syria 124 C c
Palmyra I., Pacific Ocean 78 K f
Palni Hills, India 126 E f
Paloh, Borneo 129 E k
Paloich, Sudan 119 M f
Palo Santo, Argentina 94 E c
Palpa, Nepal 127 F c
Palu, Turkey 124 D b
Palz do Vinho, Portugal 106 B b
Pamban Chan., India 126 E g
Pambrun, Saskatchewan 86 K j
Pamekasan, Indonesia 129 F m
Pamiers, France 109 D e
Pamir, Mts., U.S.S.R. 114 G e
Pampas, Peru 92 C f
Pamplona, Colombia 92 C b
Pamplona, Spain 107 E a
Panache, L., Ontario 84 J f
Panagyurishte, Bulgaria 112 E c
Panāh, Iran 125 H d
Panama, G. of, Panama 91 D e
Panama & rep., Central America 91 D e
Panama Canal, Central America 91 G b
Panarea, I., Italy 111 E f
Panay, I., Philippines 129 H h
Pančevo, Yugoslavia 112 C b
Panciu, Romania 112 F b
Pandan, Philippines 129 H h
Pan de Azucar, Chile 94 B c
Pandharpur, India 126 E e
Pando, Uruguay 94 E d
Pandora, Costa Rica 91 C e
Panevėžys, Lithuania, U.S.S.R. 103 J k
Panfilov, Kazakh., U.S.S.R. 114 H d
Panfilovo, U.S.S.R. 117 F e
Pangala, Congo 120 C e
Pangkiang, China 128 F b
Pangman, Saskatchewan 87 N j
Pangnirtung, North-West Territories 81 N d
Panhook L., Nova Scotia 82 H j
Pania Mutombo, Congo 120 E f
Panipat, India 126 E c
Panja, China 128 B c
Panjim. See Nova Goa
Panjkora R., India 126 D a
Panjshir, India 126 C a
Panna, India 126 F d
Pannerden, Netherlands 100 E c
Panruti, India 126 E f
Pantanaw, Burma 127 J e
Pantar, I., Indonesia 129 H m
Pantelleria, I., Mediterranean Sea 111 D g
Pao-an-chow, China 130 G b
Paochang, China 130 G a
Paochi. See Paoki
Pão de Açúcar, Brazil 93 K e
Paoki, China 130 C e
Paoking. See Shaoyang
Paola, Italy 111 F f
Paoning. See Langchung
Paosham, China 128 C e
Paoting, China 130 G c
Pao-tow, China 130 D b
Papakura, New Zealand 135 R k
Papantla, Mexico 90 E c
Papa Stour I., Scotland 98 H a
Papa Westray, I., Orkney Is. 98 F a
Papeete, Tahiti 79 M j
Papenburg, Germany 104 B b
Papendrecht, Netherlands 100 C c
Paphos, Cyprus 123 A c
Papineauville, Quebec 85 P g
Paposo, Chile 94 B c
Papua, G. of, New Guinea 135 H a
Papua. See New Guinea
Papun, Burma 127 J e
Pará, R., Brazil 93 H d
Pará. See Belém
Paracatú, Brazil 93 H g
Paracel Is. & Reefs, South China Sea 132 E c
Parachinar, India 126 C b
Paracin, Yugoslavia 112 C c
Paracurú, Brazil 93 K d
Paradis, Quebec 85 O d
Paradise Hill, Saskatchewan 86 H e
Paradise I., Palmyra I. 79 T k
Paradise Valley, Alberta 86 G e
Parag. See Park
Paraguaná, Venezuela 92 D a
Paraguarí, Paraguay 94 E c
Paraguassú, R., Brazil 93 K f
Paraguay, R., Argentina, etc. 94 E c
Paraguay, S. America 94 E b
Parah, Afghanistan 125 H c
Parakes, Bechuanaland 122 C c
Parakou, Dahomey 118 F g
Param, Ponape I. 78 G n
Param, Truk Is. 78 E o
Paramaribo, Surinam 93 F b
Paramonga, Peru 92 B f
Paramoshir, U.S.S.R. 115 Q c
Paraná, Argentina 94 D d
Paraná, Brazil 93 H f
Paraná, R., Argentina 94 E c
Paranaguá, Brazil 94 G c
Paranaíba & R., Brazil 93 G g
Parang, Philippines 129 H j
Paranga, Uganda 121 G d
Parang La, Kashmir 126 E b
Parapóla, I., Greece 113 D f
Paratinga, Brazil 93 J f
Parbati R., India 126 E d
Parbhani, India 126 E e
Parc de Mont Orford, Quebec 85 S g
Parchim, Germany 104 D b
Pardubice, Czechoslovakia 105 F c
Parece Vela Reef, Pacific Ocean 78 E e
Parecis, Sa. dos, Brazil 92 E f
Parent, L., Quebec 85 O d
Parent, Quebec 85 Q e
Pariaguán, Venezuela 92 E b
Parika, British Guiana 92 F b
Parinari, Peru 92 C d
Parintins, Brazil 93 F d
Paris, France 108 E b
Paris, Ontario 84 K j
Parisienne, I., Ontario 84 F f
Parita, B. de, Panama 91 C e
Pariz, Iran 125 G d
Park, Iran 125 H d
Parkbeg, Saskatchewan 86 L h
Parkerview, Saskatchewan 87 O g
Parkes, Australia 135 J f
Park Hill, Ontario 84 J j
Park Lake Prov. Park, Alberta 86 E j
Parkland, Alberta 86 D h
Parkman, Saskatchewan 87 Q j
Parkside, Saskatchewan 86 L e
Parma, Italy 110 C c
Parnaguá, Brazil 93 J f
Parnaíba, Brazil 93 J d
Parnaíba, R., Brazil 93 J d
Parnassós, Mt., Greece 113 D e
Pärnu & G., Estonia, U.S.S.R. 103 L g
Paron, India 126 E d
Parral, Chile 94 B e
Parral, Mexico 90 C b
Parramatta, Australia 135 K f
Parras, Mexico 90 D b
Parrsboro, Nova Scotia 82 H h
Parry, Saskatchewan 87 N j
Parry B., North-West Territories 81 L d
Parry I., Eniwetok 79 S d
Parry I., Ontario 84 K g
Parry Is., North-West Territories 80 H b
Parry Sd., Ontario 84 K g
Parry Sound, Ontario 84 K g
Parsnip, R., Br. Columbia 88 H c
Parson's Pond, Newfoundland 83 P c
Partabgarh, India 126 D d
Partabpur, India 127 G c
Parthenay, France 108 C c
Partinico, Sicily 111 D f
Partridge, R., Ontario 84 K b
Partridgeberry Hills, Newfoundland 83 R e
Partridge Breast L., Manitoba 87 U a
Pas, The, Manitoba 87 Q e
Pasargadae, Iran 125 F c
Pasawng, Burma 129 J e
Pascalis, Quebec 85 N d
Pascopee, Ontario 84 A b
Pas-de-Calais, dep., France 108 E a
Pasfield L., Saskatchewan 88 R a
Paska, Ontario 84 C b
Paskuh, Iran 125 H d
Pasley, C., Australia 134 D f
Pasni, Pakistan 126 B c
Paso de Indios, Argentina 95 C f
Paso de los Libres, Argentina 94 E c
Paso de los Toros, Uruguay 94 E d
Paso Limay, Argentina 95 B f
Paspebiac, Quebec 82 G e
Pasqua, Saskatchewan 87 M h
Pasquia Hills, Saskatchewan 87 O e
Pasquia R., Manitoba-Saskatchewan 87 Q e
Passau, Germany 104 E d
Passchendaele, Belgium 100 B d
Passero, C., Sicily 111 E g
Pass Lake, Ontario 84 B d
Passo Fundo, Brazil 94 F c
Passos, Brazil 93 H h
Pasteur, L., Quebec 82 F c
Pasto, Colombia 92 B c
Pastrana, Spain 106 D b
Pasvik Elv, Norway 102 N b
Paswegin, Saskatchewan 87 O f
Pásztó, Hungary 105 H e
Patan, India 126 D d
Patan, Nepal 127 G c
Pataz, Peru 92 B e
Patea, New Zealand 135 R k
Paterno, Sicily 111 E g
Paterson Inlet, New Zealand 135 P m
Pathankot, India 126 E b
Pathlow, Saskatchewan 87 N f
Patiala, India 126 E b
Pati Pt., Guam 78 B k
Patkai Hills, Burma 127 J c
Pátmos, I., Greece 113 F f
Patna, India 127 G c
Patos, Brazil 93 K e
Patos, L. dos, Brazil 94 F d
Patos de Minas, Brazil 93 H g
Patquia, Argentina 94 C d
Pátrai, G. of, Greece 113 C e
Pátrai, Greece 113 C e
Patras. See Pátrai
Patricia, Alberta 86 F h
Patricio Lynch, I., Chile 95 A g
Patrocinio, Brazil 93 H g
Pattani, Thailand 132 C e
Patti, Sicily 111 E f
Pattullo, Mt., British Columbia 88 E b
Patuanak, Saskatchewan 88 Q c
Pátzcuaro, Mexico 90 D d
Pau, France 109 C e
Pau d'Arco, Brazil 93 H e
Pau dos Ferros, Brazil 93 K e
Paugan Falls, Quebec 85 P g
Paul Block B., Antarctica 136 D c
Paulding B., Antarctica 136 T e
Paul I., Labrador 81 N f
Paulistana, Brazil 93 J e
Paungde, Burma 127 J e
Pauni, India 126 E d
Pauri, India 126 E b
Pautrask, Sweden 102 G d
Pavia, Italy 110 B c
Pavilion, British Columbia 88 J e
Pāvilosta, Latvia, U.S.S.R. 103 J h
Pavlodar, Kazakh., U.S.S.R. 114 G c
Pavlograd, Ukraine, U.S.S.R. 116 J g
Pavlovka, U.S.S.R. 117 F e
Pavlovo, U.S.S.R. 117 F c
Pavlovsk, U.S.S.R. 117 E e
Pavlovski, U.S.S.R. 116 L d
Paxoi, I., Greece 113 C e
Payerne, Switzerland 101 B b
Payne, R., Quebec 81 M f
Payne Bay, Quebec 81 M e
Payne L., Quebec 81 M e
Paynes Find, Australia 134 C e
Paynton, Saskatchewan 86 J e
Paysandú, Uruguay 94 E d
Paz, R., Salvador 91 A d
Pazar, India 126 E b
Pazardzhik, Bulgaria 112 E c
Peace R., Alberta 88 M a
Peace R., Br. Columbia 88 H b
Peace River, Alberta 88 L b
Peachland, Br. Columbia 88 K f
Peacock B., Antarctica 136 F d
Peacock Pt., Wake I. 79 S e
Peak, The, England 99 F g
Peak Hill, Australia 134 C e
Peale I., Wake I. 79 S d
Peale Inlet, Antarctica 136 G d
Pearce, Alberta 86 D j
Pearl, Ontario 84 B d
Pearson L., Manitoba 87 U b
Peary Chan., North-West Territories 80 J b
Peary Ld., Greenland 89 N a
Pebane, Mozambique 121 H h
Pebas, Peru 92 C d
Pebble I., Falkland Is. 95 E h
Pébo, Central African Republic 119 J g
Peć, Yugoslavia 112 C c
Pechenga, U.S.S.R. 114 C b
Pechora, R., U.S.S.R. 114 E b
Pechora, U.S.S.R. 117 E b
Pécs, Hungary 112 B a
Pedernales, Venezuela 92 E b
Pedhoulas, Cyprus 123 A c
Pedregal, Panama 91 C e
Pedreiras, Brazil 93 J d
Pedro Afonso, Brazil 93 H e
Pedro Azul, Brazil 93 J g
Pedro Juan Caballero, Paraguay 94 E b
Pedroll, Brazil 93 J d
Pedro Luro, Argentina 95 D e
Pedro Pt., Ceylon 126 F g
Peebles, Saskatchewan 87 P h
Peebles & co., Scotland 98 E e
Peel, New Brunswick 82 E g
Peel Pt., North-West Territories 80 H c
Peel Sd., North-West Territories 81 K c
Peenemünde, Germany 104 E a
Peera Peera Poolanna L., Australia 134 G e
Peerless L., Alberta 88 M b
Peers, Alberta 88 M d
Peetri, Estonia, U.S.S.R. 103 L g
Pegasus B., New Zealand 135 Q l
Pegu, Burma 127 J e
Pegu Yoma, Burma 127 J e
Pehan, China 128 J a
Pehchen, China 130 K b
Pehuajó, Argentina 94 D e
Peineta, Mt., Chile 95 B h
Peiping. See Peking
Peipus, L. See Chudskoye Oz.
Peixe, Brazil 93 H f
Pekan, Malaya 132 C f
Peking, China 130 H b
Pekisko, Alberta 88 N e
Pelagie Is., Mediterranean Sea 119 H a
Pélagos, I., Greece 113 D e
Peleduy, U.S.S.R. 115 L c
Pelee I. & Pt., Ontario 84 H k
Peleliu, Palau Is. 78 A o
Peleng, I., Indonesia 129 H l
Pelican B., Manitoba 87 R f
Pelican L., Alberta 86 D c
Pelican L., Manitoba 87 S j
Pelican L., Manitoba 87 R f
Pelican L., Saskatchewan 87 O c
Pelican Mts., Alberta 86 D c
Pelican Narrows, Saskatchewan 87 P c
Pelican Portage, Alberta 86 E c
Pelican Rapids, Manitoba 87 R f
Peljesac Pen., Yugoslavia 110 F d
Pelkosenniemi, Finland 102 M c
Pella, Greece 113 C d
Pellegrini, Argentina 94 D e
Pelletier L., Manitoba 87 U b
Pellworm I., Germany 104 C a
Pelly, Saskatchewan 87 Q g
Pelly Pt., British Columbia 88 C f
Peloponnisos, Greece 113 C f
Pelotas, Brazil 94 F d
Pemba Is., East Africa 121 H f
Pemberton, British Columbia 88 H e
Pembina Mt., ra., Manitoba 87 T j
Pembina Oil Fields & R., Alberta 86 B e
Pembroke, C., Falkland Is. 95 E h
Pembroke, Ontario 85 N g
Pembroke & co., Wales 99 D j
Penafiel, Portugal 106 A b
Peñafiel, Spain 106 C b
Penalva, Brazil 93 J d
Penambo Ra., Sarawak 129 F k
Peña Negra, Sa. de, Spain 106 B a
Penang, I., Malaya 132 C e
Penápolis, Brazil 93 G h
Peñaranda de Bracamonte, Spain 106 C b
Peñarroya, Spain 106 C c
Penas, G. de, Chile 95 A g
Penck, C., Antarctica 136 R e
Penck Trough, Antarctica 136 L d
Pendembu, Sierra Leone 118 C g
Penedo, Brazil 93 K f
Penedono, Portugal 106 B b
Penetanguishene, Ontario 84 L h
Penggaram, Malaya 132 C f
Penghu, Is., China 131 J l
Penglai, China 130 K d
Pengpu, China 128 G d
Penguin Spit, Palmyra I. 79 T k
Penhall, Ontario 84 G c
Penhalonga, Southern Rhodesia 122 E c
Penhold, Alberta 86 D f
Penhurst, Ontario 84 F c
Peniche, Portugal 106 A c
Peñiscola, Spain 107 F b

Penn, *Saskatchewan* 86 K e
Pennant, *Saskatchewan* 86 J h
Pennant Pt., *Nova Scotia* 82 J j
Pennfield, *New Brunswick* 82 F h
Pennine, Alpi, Mts., *Switzerland* 101 C b
Pennine Chain, *England* 99 F f
Penny Highland, Mt., *North-West Territories* 81 N d
Penobsquis, *New Brunswick* 82 G h
Penong, *Australia* 134 F f
Penonome, *Panama* 91 C e
Penrith, *England* 99 F f
Pensacola Mts., *Antarctica* 136 J b
Pense, *Saskatchewan* 87 N h
Pentecôte, L., *Quebec* 82 E d
Penticton, *British Columbia* 88 K f
Pentland Firth, *Scotland* 98 E b
Pentland Hills, *Scotland* 98 E e
Penza, *U.S.S.R.* 117 G d
Penzance, *England* 99 D k
Penzance, *Saskatchewan* 87 M g
Penzhino, *U.S.S.R.* 115 R b
Penzhinskaya Guba, *U.S.S.R.* 115 R b
Peperga, *Netherlands* 100 E b
Pepinster, *Belgium* 100 D d
Peqin, *Albania* 112 B d
Peralta, *Spain* 107 E a
Percé, *Quebec* 82 H e
Perdido, Mt., *Spain* 107 F a
Perdu, L., *Quebec* 82 B c
Perdue, *Saskatchewan* 86 K f
Pereira, *Colombia* 92 B c
Perello, *Spain* 107 F b
Pérez, *Chile* 94 C c
Pergamino, *Argentina* 94 D d
Perho, *Finland* 102 L e
Péribonca, *Quebec* 85 S d
Peribonca L., *Quebec* 82 A c
Peribonca R., *Quebec* 82 A d
Perico, *Argentina* 94 C b
Perigueux, *France* 109 D d
Perijá, Sa. de, *Venezuela* 92 C a
Peril Rock, *Quebec* 83 P b
Perim I., *Red Sea* 124 D g
Peristéra I., *Greece* 113 E e
Perlas, Arch. de las, *Panama* 91 D e
Perlas & L. de las, *Nicaragua* 91 C d
Perm, *U.S.S.R.* 117 N b
Pernambuco. *See* Recife
Péronne, *France* 108 E b
Péronnes, *Belgium* 100 C d
Perpignan, *France* 109 E e
Perron, *Quebec* 85 N d
Perry, *Ontario* 84 F e
Perry L., *Ontario* 84 D b
Perryvale, *Alberta* 86 D d
Persepolis, *Iran* 125 F d
Pershing, *Quebec* 85 O d
Persia. *See* Iran
Persian Gulf, *Saudi Arabia, etc.* 124 E d
Perth, *Australia* 134 C f
Perth, *New Brunswick* 82 E g
Perth, *Ontario* 85 O h
Perth & co., *Scotland* 98 E d
Peru, *South America* 92 C f
Perufune, *Japan* 133 H c
Perugia, *Italy* 110 D d
Peruibe, *Brazil* 93 H h
Peruwelz, *Belgium* 100 B d
Pervijze, *Belgium* 100 A c
Pervomaysk, Ukraine, *U.S.S.R.* 116 G g
Perwez, *Belgium* 100 C d
Pesaro, *Italy* 110 D d
Pescadores, Is. *See* Penghu, Is.
Pescara, *Italy* 110 E d
Peschici, *Italy* 111 F e
Peshawar, *Pakistan* 84 D b
Pêso da Régua, *Portugal* 106 B b
Pesqueira, *Brazil* 93 K e
Pestravka, *U.S.S.R.* 117 J d
Petah Tiqva, *Israel* 123 C e
Petalioí, G. of, *Greece* 113 E f
Petalioí, I., *Greece* 113 E f
Petawaga, L., *Quebec* 85 P f
Petawawa, *Ontario* 85 N g
Peterbell, *Ontario* 84 G d
Peterborough, *Australia* 134 G f
Peterborough, *England* 99 G h
Peterborough, *Ontario* 85 M h
Peterhead, *Scotland* 98 F c
Peter I Island, *Antarctica* 136 G e
Petermann Fd., *Greenland* 89 P a
Petermann Pk., *Greenland* 89 N b
Petermann Ra., *Australia* 134 E e
Peter Pond L., *Saskatchewan* 86 H b
Peters Arm South, *Newfoundland* 83 R d
Petersfield, *Manitoba* 87 V h
Petitcodiac, *New Brunswick* 82 G h
Petite Rivière, *Quebec* 82 B f
Petite Rivière Bridge, *Nova Scotia* 82 H j
Petit Étang, C. Breton I., *Nova Scotia* 83 L g
Petit Jardin, *Newfoundland* 83 N e
Petit Matane, *Quebec* 82 E e
Petit Rocher, *New Brunswick* 82 G f
Petit Vallée, *Quebec* 82 H d
Peto, *Mexico* 90 G c
Petone, *New Zealand* 135 R l
Petorca, *Chile* 94 B d
Petra, *Jordan* 123 D g
Petras, Mt., *Antarctica* 136 E c
Petra Velikogo Zaliv, *U.S.S.R.* 115 N d
Petre, Pt., *Ontario* 85 N j
Petrich, *Bulgaria* 112 D d
Petrila, *Romania* 112 D b
Petrinja, *Yugoslavia* 110 F c
Petrodvorets, *U.S.S.R.* 116 F b
Petrolândia, *Brazil* 93 K e
Petrolia, *Ontario* 84 H k
Petrolina, *Brazil* 93 J e
Petropavlovsk, Kazakh., *U.S.S.R.* 114 F c
Petropavlovsk, *U.S.S.R.* 115 Q c
Petrópolis, *Brazil* 93 J h
Petrovac, *Yugoslavia* 112 C b
Petrovsk, *U.S.S.R.* 117 N d
Petrovsk, *U.S.S.R.* 115 K c
Petrovsk, *U.S.S.R.* 117 G d
Petrozavodsk, *U.S.S.R.* 114 C b
Petsamo. *See* Pechenga
Petty Harbour, *Newfoundland* 83 T f
Pevek, *U.S.S.R.* 115 S b
Pézenas, *France* 109 E e
Pforzheim, *Germany* 104 C d
Phalodi, *India* 126 D c
Phanon Dang Raek, *Thailand* 132 C d
Phan Rang, *S. Vietnam* 132 D d
Phan-Thiet & B. of, *South Vietnam* 132 D d
Phatthalung, *Thailand* 132 B e
Phet Buri, *Thailand* 132 B d
Philippeville, *Belgium* 100 C d
Philippeville & G. of, *Algeria* 118 G a
Philippi, L., *Australia* 134 G d
Philippines, Is., *East Indies* 129 H h
Philippine Sea, *Philippines* 78 D e
Philippopolis. *See* Plovdiv
Philipsburg, *Quebec* 85 R g
Phillips B., *N.-W. Territories* 81 L a
Philomena, *Alberta* 88 O c
Philpots Pen., *N.-W. Terr.* 81 M c
Phippen, *Saskatchewan* 86 J f
Phitsanulok Muang, *Thailand* 132 C c
Phnom-Penh, *Cambodia* 132 C d
Phoenix I., *Phoenix Is.* 78 J h
Phoenix Is., *Pacific Ocean* 78 J g
Pho-mo-chang-thang Tso, *Tibet* 127 H c
Phou San, Mt., *Laos* 132 C c
Phu-dien, *N. Vietnam* 132 D c
Phuket, *Thailand* 129 C j
Phulji, *Pakistan* 126 C c
Phu Qui, *N. Vietnam* 132 D c
Phu-Quoc, I., *S. Vietnam* 132 C d
Piacenza, *Italy* 110 B c
Piakoudie L., *Quebec* 82 B b
Pianosa, I., *Italy* 110 C d
Piapot, *Saskatchewan* 86 H j
Pias, *Portugal* 106 B c
Piashti L., *Quebec* 82 K c
Piatra Neamt, *Romania* 112 F a
Piazza Armerina, *Sicily* 111 E g
Piazzi, I., *Chile* 95 B h
Pibor Post, *Sudan* 119 M g
Pibroch, *Alberta* 86 D d
Piccadilly, *Newfoundland* 83 O e
Pichanal, *Argentina* 94 D b
Pichilemu, *Chile* 94 B d
Pickardville, *Alberta* 86 D d
Pickerel, *Ontario* 84 K g
Pickerel L., *Ontario* 86 L b
Pickerel River, *Ontario* 84 K f
Pickering, *England* 99 G f
Pickle Lake, *Ontario* 81 K g
Pic R., *Ontario* 84 D d
Picton, *Australia* 135 K f
Picton, *New Zealand* 135 Q l
Picton, *Ontario* 85 N h
Pictou & I., *Nova Scotia* 82 K h
Picture Butte, *Alberta* 86 E j
Picun Leufú, *Argentina* 95 C e
Pidark, *Pakistan* 126 B c
Piedmont. *See* Piemonte
Piedrahita, *Spain* 106 C b
Piedras Negras, *Mexico* 90 D b
Piedra Sola, *Uruguay* 94 E d
Pie I., *Ontario* 87 O b
Pieksämäki, *Finland* 102 M e
Pielinen, *Finland* 102 N e
Piemonte, region, *Italy* 110 A c
Pierre L., *Ontario* 84 K c
Pierreville, *Quebec* 85 S f
Pierson, *Manitoba* 87 Q j
Pietarsaari, *Finland* 102 K e
Pietermaritzburg, *South Africa* 122 E e
Pietersburg, *South Africa* 122 D d
Pigeon B., *Ontario* 84 H k
Pigeon L., *Alberta* 86 D e
Pigeon L., *Ontario* 85 M h
Pigeon R., *Manitoba* 87 V f
Pigeon River, *Ontario* 87 N b
Pigüe, *Argentina* 95 D e
Pihtipudas, *Finland* 102 L e
Piirai, *Eniwetok* 79 S c
Pikangikum L., *Ontario* 81 K g
Pikwitonei, *Manitoba* 87 U c
Pila, *Argentina* 94 E e
Piła, *Poland* 105 G b
Pilão Arcado, *Brazil* 93 J f
Pilar, *Argentina* 94 D d
Pilar, C., *Chile* 95 B h
Pilar, *Paraguay* 94 E c
Pilcaniyeu, *Argentina* 95 B f
Pilger, *Saskatchewan* 87 M f
Pilibhit, *India* 126 E c
Pilley's I., *Newfoundland* 83 R d
Pílos, *Greece* 113 C f
Pilot Butte, *Saskatchewan* 87 N h
Pilot Mound, *Manitoba* 87 T j
Pilsen, *Czechoslovakia* 104 E d
Piltene, *Latvia, U.S.S.R.* 103 J h
Pi Mai, *Thailand* 132 C c
Pimentel, *Peru* 92 B e
Piña, *Canal Zone* 91 F b
Pina, *Spain* 107 E b
Pinarbasi, *Turkey* 124 C b
Pinar del Río, *Cuba* 91 C b
Pincher Creek, *Alberta* 86 D j
Pincher Station, *Alberta* 86 D j
Pinchi, *British Columbia* 88 G c
Pindhos, Mts., *Greece* 113 C e
Pine, C., *Newfoundland* 83 T g
Pinebluff L., *Saskatchewan* 87 P d
Pine Creek, *Australia* 134 F b
Pinedale, *Alberta* 88 L d
Pinehouse L., *Saskatchewan* 86 L c
Pinehouse Lake, *Sask.* 86 L c
Pinehurst L., *Alberta* 86 F d
Pine Island B., *Antarctica* 136 F d
Pine Portage, *Ontario* 84 B c
Pine R., *Alberta* 86 D d
Pine R., *British Columbia* 88 J c
Pine River, *Manitoba* 87 R g
Pine River, *Saskatchewan* 86 K c
Pineros, I., *Puerto Rico* 54 D h
Pinery Prov. Pk., *Ontario* 84 H k
Pinetown, *South Africa* 122 E e
Pinewood, *Ontario* 86 H b
Piney, *Manitoba* 86 F a
Ping-chüan-chow, *China* 130 J b
Pingelap, I., *Caroline Is.* 78 F f
Pingelly, *Australia* 134 C f
Pingkiang, *China* 131 F h
Pinglap, I., *Jaluit I.* 79 T j
Pingliang, *China* 130 C e
Pinglo, *China* 131 E k
Pingrup, *Australia* 134 C f
Ping-ting-chow, *China* 130 F d
Pingwu, *China* 130 B f
Pingyang. *See* Linfen
Pingyüan, *China* 130 H d
Pinhel, *Portugal* 106 B b
Pini, I., *Indonesia* 129 C k
Pinjarra, *Australia* 134 B f
Pinkham, *Saskatchewan* 86 H g
Pinkiang, *China* 128 J a
Pink Mountain, *British Columbia* 88 H b
Pinnaroo, *Australia* 135 H g
Pinos, I. de, *Cuba* 91 C b
Pinos, *Mexico* 90 D c
Pinrang, *Celebes* 129 G l
Pins, Pte. aux, *Ontario* 84 J k
Pinsk, *Belorussia, U.S.S.R.* 116 E e
Pintados, *Chile* 94 C b
Pinto, *Argentina* 94 D c
Pinto Butte, Mt., *Saskatchewan* 86 K j
Pinware R. & B., *Labrador* 83 Q b
Pioneer, Os., *U.S.S.R.* 115 J a
Piotrkow, *Poland* 105 H c
Pipar, *India* 126 D c
Pipestone, *Manitoba* 87 R j
Pipestone Creek, *Manitoba-Saskatchewan* 87 Q j
Pipinas, *Argentina* 94 E e
Pipmuacan Lake Res., *Quebec* 82 B d
Pippli, *India* 127 G d
Piracuruca, *Brazil* 93 J d
Piraeus. *See* Piraievs
Piraievs, *Greece* 113 D f
Pirámide, Mt., *Chile* 94 B g
Piranhaquara, *Brazil* 93 G d
Piranhas, *Brazil* 93 K e
Pirapora, *Brazil* 93 J g
Piratini, *Brazil* 94 F d
Piraube L., *Quebec* 82 A c
Piray, *Argentina* 94 F c
Pírgos, *Crete* 113 E g
Pírgos, *Greece* 113 D f
Pírgos, *Greece* 113 C f
Pirin Planina, *Bulgaria* 112 D d
Piripiri, *Brazil* 93 J d
Piritu, *Venezuela* 92 E a
Pirmasens, *Germany* 104 B d
Pirna, *Germany* 104 E c
Pirot, *Yugoslavia* 112 D c
Pir Panjal Ra., *Kashmir* 126 D b
Pis, I., *Truk Is.* 78 E m
Pisa, *Italy* 110 C d
Pisagua, *Chile* 94 B a
Pisco, *Peru* 92 B f
Pisek, *Czechoslovakia* 104 F d
Pishin, *Iran* 125 H d
Pishin, *Pakistan* 126 C b
Pisticci, *Italy* 111 F e
Pistolet B., *Newfoundland* 83 R b
Pitaga, *Labrador* 82 G a
Pitangüi, *Brazil* 93 J g
Pitcairn I., *Pacific Ocean* 79 N k
Piteå, *Sweden* 102 J d
Pite Älv, *Sweden* 102 H d
Piterka, *U.S.S.R.* 117 H e
Piteşti, *Romania* 112 E b
Pithiviers, *France* 108 E b
Piti, I., *Guam* 78 A l
Pitlochry, *Scotland* 98 E d
Pitt I., *British Columbia* 88 D d
Pitt Meadows, *British Columbia* 88 E f
Pitt R., *Br. Columbia* 88 F f
Piuà-Petri, *Romania* 112 F b
Piumafua, I., *Manua Is.* 79 S o
Piura, *Peru* 92 A e
Pivabiska, R., *Ontario* 84 G b
Piza, *Latvia, U.S.S.R.* 103 J h
Pizeau, Pte., *Quebec* 83 Q j
Piz Sardona, *Switzerland* 101 E b
Pkulagalid, I., *Palau Is.* 78 B l
Pkulagasemieg, *Palau Is.* 78 B n
Pkulngril, I., *Palau Is.* 78 B m
Pkurengel, I., *Palau Is.* 78 B m
Placentia, *Newfoundland* 83 T f
Placentia B., *Newfoundland* 83 S f
Placer Guadalupe, *Mexico* 90 C b
Placetas, *Cuba* 91 D b
Plagua, I., *Saipan-Tinian Is.* 78 B d
Plain of Sharon, *Israel* 123 C e
Pláka B., *Crete* 113 E g
Plakoti, C., *Cyprus* 123 C b
Plamondon, *Alberta* 86 E d
Plana, *Czechoslovakia* 104 E d
Planaltina, *Brazil* 93 H g
Planina, *Yugoslavia* 110 E c
Plasencia, *Spain* 106 B b
Plaški, *Yugoslavia* 110 E c
Plassen, *Norway* 103 E f
Plaster Rock, *New Brunswick* 82 E g
Plastun, *U.S.S.R.* 115 N d
Plata, R. de la, *Argentina* 94 E d
Platamón, *Greece* 113 D d
Plate Cove, *Newfoundland* 83 T e
Platí, *Greece* 113 D d
Plato, *Saskatchewan* 86 J g
Platres, *Cyprus* 123 A c
Plauen, *Germany* 104 E c
Plav, *Yugoslavia* 112 B c
Plavnica, *Yugoslavia* 112 B c
Playas, *Ecuador* 92 A d
Playgreen L., *Manitoba* 87 T e
Plaza Huincul, *Argentina* 95 C e
Pleasantdale, *Saskatchewan* 87 N f
Pleasant Mt., *New Brunswick* 82 F g
Pleasant Point, *Manitoba* 87 S j
Pledger L., *Ontario* 84 G b
Pleiku, *S. Vietnam* 129 E h
Plenty, B. of, *New Zealand* 135 R k
Plenty, *Saskatchewan* 86 J g
Plessisville, *Quebec* 85 T f
Pletipi L., *Quebec* 82 B b
Plettenberg B., *South Africa* 122 C f
Pleven, *Bulgaria* 112 E c
Pljevlja, *Yugoslavia* 112 B c
Płock, *Poland* 105 H b
Ploeşti, *Romania* 112 F b
Plomarion, *Greece* 113 F e
Plön, *Germany* 104 D a
Plonge, L. la, *Saskatchewan* 86 K c
Płońsk, *Poland* 105 J b
Plovdiv, *Bulgaria* 112 E c
Plum Coulee, *Manitoba* 87 U j
Plumtree, *S. Rhodesia* 122 D d
Plunkett, *Saskatchewan* 87 M g
Plymouth & Sd., *England* 99 E k
Plympton, *Nova Scotia* 82 G j
Plynlimmon, *Wales* 99 E h
Plzeň. *See* Pilsen
Po, R., *Italy* 110 D c
Poai, *China* 130 F e
Pobedy, Mt., Kirgiz., *U.S.S.R.* 114 H d
Pobla de Segur, *Spain* 107 F a
Pochinki, *U.S.S.R.* 117 G c
Pochutla, *Mexico* 90 E d
Podkamennaya Tunguska, *U.S.S.R.* 114 H b
Podlubovo, *U.S.S.R.* 117 M c
Podolsk, *U.S.S.R.* 116 K d
Podporozh'ye, *U.S.S.R.* 116 J a
Pogamasing, *Ontario* 84 J f
Pohai, G. of, *China* 130 J c
Pohai, Str. of, *China* 130 K c
Poincaré, L., *Quebec* 83 O b
Poinsett, C., *Antarctica* 136 S e
Point-à-Maurier, *Quebec* 83 N c
Point à Pitre, *Leeward Is.* 91 G c
Point du Chêne, *New Brunswick* 82 H g
Pointe à Gatineau, *Quebec* 84 D h
Pointe au Baril Station, *Ontario* 84 K g
Pointe au Pic, *Quebec* 82 B f
Pointe aux Anglais, *Quebec* 82 E d
Pointe aux Trembles, *Quebec* 85 R g
Pointe Bleue, *Quebec* 85 S d
Pointe Claire, *Quebec* 85 R g
Point Edward, *Ontario* 84 H j
Pointe Verte, *New Brunswick* 82 G f
Point Leamington, *Newfoundland* 83 R d
Point Pelee Nat. Park, *Ontario* 84 H k
Poisson Blanc, L., *Quebec* 85 P f
Poitiers, *France* 108 D c
Poitoumarche, prov., *France* 108 C c
Poix, *Belgium* 100 D d
Poix, *France* 108 D b
Pok, I., *Ponape I.* 78 G o
Pokaran, *India* 126 D c
Pokhra, *Nepal* 127 F c
Pokka, *Finland* 102 L b
Pokrovsk (Engels), *U.S.S.R.* 117 H e
Pokrovsk, *U.S.S.R.* 117 F d
Pokrovsk, *U.S.S.R.* 117 D g
Pokrovskoe, *U.S.S.R.* 115 M b
Pola, I., *Tutuila Is.* 79 U o
Pola. *See* Pula
Pola de Laviana, *Spain* 106 C a
Poland, *Central Europe* 105 G c
Polesk, *U.S.S.R.* 103 J j
Polevskoi, *U.S.S.R.* 117 Q b
Polgahawela, *Ceylon* 126 F g
Polgar, *Hungary* 105 J e
Poli, *Cameroon* 119 H g
Políaigos, I., *Greece* 113 E f
Policastro, G. di, *Italy* 111 E f
Poligny, *France* 108 F c
Polillo Is., *Philippines* 129 H h
Pólinos. *See* Políaigos, I.
Polis, *Cyprus* 123 A b
Pollensa, *Balearic Is.* 107 G b
Pollet, L., *Quebec* 82 A a
Pollockville, *Alberta* 86 F g
Pollux, *New Zealand* 135 P m
Polotsk, *Belorussia, U.S.S.R.* 116 F d
Poltava, *Ukraine, U.S.S.R.* 116 J g
Poltimore, *Quebec* 85 P g
Põltsamaa, *Estonia, U.S.S.R.* 103 M g
Poluostrov Buzachi, Kazakh., *U.S.S.R.* 114 E d
Põlva, *Estonia, U.S.S.R.* 103 M g
Polwarth, *Saskatchewan* 86 L e
Polynesia, *Pacific Ocean* 78 K l
Pomán, *Argentina* 94 C c
Pombal, *Brazil* 93 K e
Pombal, *Portugal* 106 A c
Pombetsu, *Japan* 133 H c
Pomene, *Mozambique* 122 F d
Pommersche B., *Germany* 104 F a
Pomorie, *Bulgaria* 112 F c
Pomos, Pt., *Cyprus* 123 A b
Pomquet, *Nova Scotia* 83 L h
Ponape, I., *Caroline Is.* 78 F f
Ponape, *Ponape I.* 78 G n
Ponape Harb., *Ponape I.* 78 F n
Ponass L., *Saskatchewan* 87 O f
Ponce, *Puerto Rico* 54 C h
Pondicherry, *India* 126 E f
Pond Inlet, *North-West Territories* 81 M c
Ponente, Riviera di, *Italy* 110 A d
Pones, I., *Truk Is.* 78 F o
Ponferrada, *Spain* 106 B a
Ponhook L., *Nova Scotia* 82 H j
Ponoka, *Alberta* 86 D f
Ponoy, *U.S.S.R.* 114 D b
Pons, *France* 108 C d
Pons, *Spain* 107 F b
Ponta Grossa, *Brazil* 94 F c
Pont-Audemer, *France* 108 D b
Pontbriand B., *Quebec* 82 K c
Pont Château, *France* 108 B c
Pont d'Ain, *France* 108 F c
Ponte, *Switzerland* 101 E b
Ponte da Barca, *Portugal* 106 A b
Ponte de Sôr, *Portugal* 106 A c
Ponteix, *Saskatchewan* 86 K j
Ponte Nova, *Brazil* 93 J h
Pontevedra, *Spain* 106 A a
Pontianak, *Borneo* 129 E l
Pontivy, *France* 108 B b
Pont Lafrance, *New Brunswick* 82 H f
Ponto Berrío, *Colombia* 92 C b
Ponto Carreño, *Venezuela* 92 D b
Pontoise, *France* 108 E b
Ponton, *Manitoba* 87 S d
Ponto Piñasco, *Paraguay* 92 F h
Pontresina, *Switzerland* 101 E b
Pontrilas, *Saskatchewan* 87 N e
Pont Rouge, *Quebec* 85 T f
Pont Viau, *Quebec* 85 R j
Pontypool, *Ontario* 85 M h
Pontypool, *Wales* 99 E j
Pontypridd, *Wales* 99 E j
Ponza, I., *Italy* 111 D e
Poole, *England* 99 F k
Poona, *India* 126 D e
Pooncarie, *Australia* 135 H f
Poopo, *Bolivia* 92 D g
Poopo, L., *Bolivia* 92 D g
Popa Mt., *Burma* 127 J d
Popayán, *Colombia* 92 B c
Poperinge, *Belgium* 100 A d
Poplarfield, *Manitoba* 87 U h
Poplar Point, *Manitoba* 87 U h
Poplar Pt., *Manitoba* 87 U f
Poplar R., *Manitoba* 87 U f
Popocatapetl, Mt., *Mexico* 90 E d
Popokabaka, *Congo* 120 D f
Popovača, *Yugoslavia* 110 F c
Poppel, *Belgium* 100 D c
Porbandar, *India* 126 C d
Porcher I., *Br. Columbia* 88 D d
Porcupine Hills, *Alberta* 86 C h
Porcupine Mt., ra., *Manitoba-Saskatchewan* 87 Q f
Porcupine Plain, *Saskatchewan* 87 O f
Poreč, *Yugoslavia* 110 D c
Pori, *Finland* 103 J f
Porjus, *Sweden* 102 H c
Porkhov, *U.S.S.R.* 116 F c
Porkkala, *Finland* 103 L g
Porlamar, Margarita I., *Venezuela* 92 E a
Pornic, *France* 108 B c
Poronaysk, *U.S.S.R.* 115 P d
Póros I., *Greece* 113 D f
Porpoise B., *Antarctica* 136 T e
Porquis Junction, *Ontario* 84 K d
Porsanger Fd., *Norway* 102 L a
Porsanger Halvöy, *Norway* 102 L a
Porsgrund, *Norway* 103 C g
Portachuelo, *Bolivia* 92 E g
Port Adelaide, *Australia* 135 G f
Portadown, *N. Ireland* 99 C f
Portage, *Prince Edward I.* 82 H g
Portage I., *New Brunswick* 82 G f
Portage la Prairie, *Manitoba* 87 T j
Port Alberni, Vancouver I., *British Columbia* 88 G f
Port Albert, *Ontario* 84 J j
Portalegre, *Portugal* 106 B c
Port Alfred, *Quebec* 82 B e
Port Alice, Vancouver I., *British Columbia* 88 F e
Port Antonio, *Jamaica* 91 D c
Portarlington, *Eire* 99 C g
Port Arthur, *Ontario* 87 O b
Port Arthur (Lushun), *China* 128 H c
Port Augusta, *Australia* 134 G f
Port-au-Port & B., *Newfoundland* 83 O e
Port-au-Port Pen., *Newfoundland* 83 N e
Port-au-Prince, *Haiti* 91 E c
Port aux Basques, *Newfoundland* 83 N f
Port Blair, *Andaman Is.* 127 H f
Port Blandford, *Nfd.* 83 S e
Port Borden, *Prince Edward I.* 82 J g
Port Bruce, *Ontario* 84 K k
Port Burwell, *Ontario* 84 K k
Port Carling, *Ontario* 85 L g
Port Cartier, *Quebec* 81 N g
Port Cartier, *Quebec* 82 F c
Port Chalmers, *New Zealand* 135 Q m
Port Clements, Queen Charlotte Is., *Br. Columbia* 88 C d
Port Colborne, *Ontario* 85 L k
Port Coquitlam, *British Columbia* 88 H f
Port Cornwallis, *Andaman Is.* 127 H f
Port Credit, *Ontario* 85 L j
Port Dalhousie, *Ontario* 85 L j
Port Daniel, *Quebec* 82 H e
Port Darwin, *Falkland Is.* 95 E h
Port de Paix, *Haiti* 91 E b
Port Dickson, *Malaya* 132 C f
Port Douglas, *Australia* 135 J c
Port Dover, *Ontario* 84 K k
Port Dufferin, *Nova Scotia* 83 K j
Port Edward, *Br. Columbia* 88 D c
Portel, *Brazil* 93 G d
Port Elgin, *New Brunswick* 82 H g
Port Elgin, *Ontario* 84 J h
Port Elizabeth, *South Africa* 122 D f
Port Ellen, *Scotland* 98 C e
Porter L., *Saskatchewan* 88 Q b
Porter Landing, *Br. Columbia* 88 D a
Port Étienne, *Mauritania* 118 B d
Port Felix, *Nova Scotia* 83 L h
Port George, *Nova Scotia* 82 G j
Port Greville, *Nova Scotia* 82 H h
Port Guichon, *Br. Columbia* 88 D g
Port Harcourt, *Nigeria* 118 G h
Port Hardy, Vancouver I., *British Columbia* 88 F e
Port Harrison, *Quebec* 81 M f
Port Hastings, C. Breton I., *Nova Scotia* 83 L h
Port Hawkesbury, C. Breton I., *Nova Scotia* 83 L h
Port Hedland, *Australia* 134 C d
Port Hood, C. Breton I., *Nova Scotia* 83 L h
Port Hope, *Ontario* 85 M j
Port Hope Simpson, *Labrador* 83 Q a
Portimão, *Portugal* 106 A d
Port Jackson, *Australia* 135 K f
Port Kells, *British Columbia* 88 E g
Port Kembla, *Australia* 135 K f
Portland, *Australia* 134 H g
Portland, *Ontario* 85 O h
Portland Bill, *England* 99 F k
Portland Can., *Alaska-British Columbia* 88 D c
Portland Creek Pond, *Nfd.* 83 P c
Portland Inlet, *Br. Columbia* 88 D c
Portland Point, *Jamaica* 91 D c
Portlaoise, *Eire* 99 C g
Port Lincoln, *Australia* 135 G f
Port Loko, *Sierra Leone* 118 C g
Port Loring, *Ontario* 84 L g
Port Lyautey, *Morocco* 118 D b
Port McNicoll, *Ontario* 84 L h
Port Macquarie, *Australia* 135 K f
Portmadoc, *Wales* 99 E h
Port Maitland, *Nova Scotia* 82 F k
Port Maitland, *Ontario* 85 L k
Port Manvers, *Labrador* 81 N f
Port Martin, *Antarctica* 136 A e
Port Medway, *Nova Scotia* 82 H j
Port Menier, Anticosti I., *Quebec* 82 H d
Port Moody, *British Columbia* 88 H f
Port Moody, inlet, *B.C.* 88 E f
Port Moody Conservation Reserve, *British Columbia* 88 E e
Port Moresby, *New Guinea* 135 J a
Port Morien, C. Breton I., *Nova Scotia* 83 N g
Port Mouton, *Nova Scotia* 82 H k
Portneuf, L., *Quebec* 82 B d
Portneuf, *Quebec* 85 T f
Portneuf, R., *Quebec* 82 C e
Portneuf sur Mer, *Quebec* 82 C e
Port Nicholson, *New Zealand* 135 R l
Port Nolloth, *South Africa* 122 B e
Porto, *Portugal* 106 A b
Pôrto Acre, *Brazil* 92 D e

Ross & Cromarty, co., Scotland 98 D c
Rossano, Italy 111 F f
Rosseau, Ontario 85 L g
Rossel I., New Guinea 135 K b
Rossendale, Manitoba 87 T j
Ross I., Burma 127 J f
Ross I., Manitoba 87 U d
Ross Ice Shelf, Antarctica 136 C b
Rossignol, Belgium 100 D e
Rossignol, L., Nova Scotia 82 G j
Rossland, British Columbia 88 L f
Rosslare Harb., Eire 99 C h
Rossport, Ontario 84 C d
Ross Sea, Antarctica 136 C d
Rossway, Nova Scotia 82 G j
Rosswood, British Columbia 88 E c
Rosta, Norway 102 H b
Rosthern, Saskatchewan 86 L f
Rostock, Germany 104 E a
Rostov, U.S.S.R. 117 D g
Rostov, U.S.S.R. 116 L c
Rös Vatn, Norway 102 F d
Rota, I., Mariana Is. 78 E e
Rothenburg, Germany 104 D d
Rotherham, England 99 G g
Rothesay, New Brunswick 82 G h
Rothesay, Scotland 98 D e
Rothschild I., Antarctica 136 H e
Roti, I., Indonesia 129 H n
Rotorua, New Zealand 135 R k
Rotterdam, Netherlands 100 C c
Rotuma, I., Fiji Is. 78 H h
Roubaix, France 108 E a
Rouen, France 108 D b
Rõuge, Estonia, U.S.S.R. 103 M h
Rouleau, Saskatchewan 87 N h
Roulers, Belgium 100 B d
Roumania. See Romania
Round Harbour, Newfoundland 83 R d
Round Hill, Alberta 86 E e
Round Pond, Newfoundland 83 R e
Rounthwaite, Manitoba 87 S j
Roura, Fr. Guiana 93 G c
Rous, Pen., Chile 95 C j
Rousay I., Orkney, Scotland 98 E a
Rousbrugge, Belgium 100 A d
Rouse, C., Antarctica 136 Q e
Roussillon Oriental, prov., France 109 E e
Routhierville, Quebec 82 E e
Rouveen, Netherlands 100 E b
Rouvray, L., Quebec 82 B d
Rouyn, Quebec 85 M d
Rovaniemi, Finland 102 L c
Roveredo, Switzerland 101 E b
Rovigo, Italy 110 C c
Rovinari, Romania 112 D b
Rovno, Ukraine, U.S.S.R. 116 E f
Rowan L., Ontario 86 J a
Rowley, Alberta 86 E g
Rowley I., North-West Territories 81 M d
Roxas, Philippines 129 H h
Roxburgh, co., Scotland 98 F e
Roxburgh, New Zealand 135 P m
Roxton, Quebec 85 S g
Roy, L., Quebec 82 C d
Royal, Mt., Ontario 84 B c
Royal Canal, Eire 99 C g
Royalties, Alberta 86 C h
Royan, France 108 C d
Rožňava, Czechoslovakia 105 J d
R. Scott Glacier, Antarctica 136 D a
Rtishchevo, U.S.S.R. 117 F d
Rua, I., Jaluit I. 79 T h
Ruac, I., Truk Is. 78 E m
Ruahine Ra., New Zealand 135 R k
Ruanda. See Rwanda
Ruanda-Urundi. See Rwanda, Burundi
Ruapehu, Mt., New Zealand 135 R k
Ruapuke I., New Zealand 135 P m
Rubtsovsk, U.S.S.R. 114 H c
Rudbar, Afghanistan 125 H c
Ruddell, Saskatchewan 86 K f
Ruddervoorde, Belgium 100 B c
Rudköbing, Denmark 103 D j
Rudok, Tibet 126 E b
Rudolf L., Kenya 121 H d
Ruel, Ontario 84 J e
Ruffec, France 108 D c
Rufino, Argentina 94 D d
Rugby, England 99 G h
Rügen, I., Germany 104 E a
Rui Barbosa, Brazil 93 J f
Rujiena, Latvia, U.S.S.R. 103 L h
Rujiyaru, I., Eniwetok 79 R c
Ruk, Pakistan 126 C c
Rukwa L., Tanganyika 121 G f
Rum, I., Scotland 98 C d
Rumania. See Romania
Rumbek, Sudan 119 L g
Rumburk, Czechoslovakia 104 F c
Rum Cay, Bahama Is. 91 E b
Rumegies, France 100 B d
Rumigny, France 100 C e
Rumillies, Belgium 100 B d
Rum Jungle, Australia 134 F b
Rumoi, Japan 133 G c
Rumsey, Alberta 86 E g
Rumung, I., Yap I. 78 D l
Rumuruti, Kenya 121 H d
Runanga, New Zealand 135 Q l
Rungwa, Tanganyika 121 G f
Rungwe Mt., Tanganyika 121 G f
Runit, I., Eniwetok 79 S c
Runnymede, Saskatchewan 87 Q g
Runu, I., Yap I. 78 D l
Rupert, R., Quebec 81 M g
Rupert B., Quebec 85 L a
Rupert House, Quebec 81 M a
Rupert R., Quebec 81 N a
Ruppert Coast, Antarctica 136 D c
Rupshu, India 126 E b
Rurrenabaque, Bolivia 92 D f
Rurutu, I., Austral Is. 79 L k
Rusape, S. Rhodesia 122 E c
Ruseifa, Jordan 123 E e
Rusele, Sweden 102 H d
Ruse (Ruschuk), Bulgaria 112 E c
Rush Lake, Saskatchewan 86 K h
Rusne, R., Lithuania, U.S.S.R. 103 J j
Russas, Brazil 93 K d
Russelkonda, India 127 F e
Russell, Manitoba 87 Q h
Russell, New Zealand 135 R j
Russell, Ontario 81 P g
Russell I., North-West Territories 81 K c
Russell L., Manitoba 87 Q b
Russell L., Saskatchewan 88 R b
Russia. See Union of Soviet Socialist Republics
Russkoye Ust'ye, U.S.S.R. 115 P a
Russo, Switzerland 101 D b
Rustak, Afghanistan 125 J b
Rutbah, Iraq 124 D c
Rutherglen, Ontario 85 L f
Rüthi, Switzerland 101 E a
Ruthilda, Saskatchewan 86 J g
Ruthin, Wales 99 E g
Rutland, co., England 99 G h
Rutland I., Andaman Is. 127 H f
Rutland Station, Saskatchewan 86 H f
Rutter, Ontario 84 K f
Ruurlo, Netherlands 100 E b
Ruvuma R., Mozambique 121 H g
Ruweiba, Sudan 119 L e
Ruwenzori, Mt., Uganda 121 G d
Ružomberok, Czechoslovakia 105 H d
Rvazhsk, U.S.S.R. 116 M e
Rwanda, Cent. Africa 121 F e
Ryan, L., Scotland 98 D f
Ryazan, U.S.S.R. 116 L d
Rybachiy, Pol., U.S.S.R. 114 C b
Rybinsk, U.S.S.R. 116 L b
Rybinskoye Vdkhr., U.S.S.R. 116 L b
Rybnoye, U.S.S.R. 115 K a
Rycroft, Alberta 88 K c
Rydal Bank, Ontario 84 G f
Ryde, Isle of Wight, England 99 G k
Rye, England 99 H k
Ryerson, Saskatchewan 87 Q j
Ryland, Ontario 84 G c
Ryley, Alberta 86 E e
Rymarov, Czechoslovakia 105 G d
Rypin, Poland 105 H b
Ryukyu Retto, Is., Japan 128 H j
Rzeszów, Poland 105 J c
Rzhev, U.S.S.R. 116 J c
Saalfeld, Germany 104 D c
Saanen, Switzerland 101 C b
Saanich, Br. Columbia 88 H f
Saarbrucken, West Germany 104 B d
Saaremaa, Os., Lithuania, U.S.S.R. 103 K g
Saari Selkä, Finland 102 N b
Saarland, Europe 104 B d
Saarlouis, West Germany 104 B d
Saas Grund, Switzerland 101 C b
Saavedra, Argentina 95 D e
Saavedra, Chile 95 B e
Šabac, Yugoslavia 112 B b
Sabadell, Spain 107 G b
Sabalan, Mt., Iran 124 E b
Sabalgarh, India 126 E c
Sabana, Arch. de, Cuba 91 C b
Sabanalarga, Colombia 92 C a
Sabancuy, Mexico 90 F d
Sab Biyar, Syria 123 F d
Sabha, Jordan 123 E e
Sabile, Latvia, U.S.S.R. 103 K h
Sabiñanigo, Spain 107 E a
Sabinas, Mexico 90 D b
Sabine, C., North-West Territories 81 M b
Sabine Mt., Antarctica 136 B d
Sabi R., India 126 E c
Sable, C., Nova Scotia 82 G k
Sable, France 108 C c
Sable I., Nova Scotia 83 N k
Sable Island Bank, Nova Scotia 83 M k
Sable River, Nova Scotia 82 G k
Sables, R. aux, Ontario 84 H f
Sabrina Coast, Antarctica 136 S e
Sabzawar, Iran 125 G b
Sabzevar (Shindand), Afghanistan 125 H c
Sacaca, Bolivia 92 D g
Sacedón, Spain 107 D b
Săcele, Romania 112 E b
Sachigo, R., Ontario 81 K g
Sachs Harbour, North-West Territories 80 G c
Sackville, New Brunswick 82 H h
Sacramento, Brazil 93 H g
Sacré-Coeur Saguenay, Quebec 82 C e
Sada, Yemen 124 D f
Sádaba, Spain 107 E a
Sá da Bandeira, Angola 120 C g
Sadad, Syria 123 E c
Sadaich. See Sadīj
Sadīj, Iran 125 G d
Sadiya, India 127 J c
Sa 'diya, Jeb., Saudi Arabia 125 D e
Sadmarda, Afghanistan 125 J b
Sado, I., Japan 133 F e
Sadra, India 126 D d
Sadulpur, India 126 E c
Saeki, Japan 133 B h
Safad, Israel 123 E d
Safed Koh Ra., Afghanistan-Pakistan 126 C b
Safi, Morocco 118 D b
Safi, Syria 123 D f
Safidabeh, Iran 125 H c
Safita, Syria 123 E c
Safonovo, U.S.S.R. 116 H d
Safranbolu, Turkey 124 B a
Saga, Japan 133 B h
Sagaing, Burma 127 J d
Sagami, B., Japan 133 F g
Saganaga L., Ontario 87 M b
Saganash L., Ontario 84 H c
Sagar, India 126 E d
Saglek B., Labrador 81 N f
Sagone, G. de, Corsica 110 B d
Sagres, Portugal 106 A d
Sagua la Grande, Cuba 91 C b
Saguenay, R., Quebec 82 B e
Sagunto, Spain 107 E c
Saham, Muscat & Oman 125 G e
Sahand, Mt., Iran 124 E b
Sahara, reg., Algeria 118 E c
Sahara Des., Africa 118 D d
Saharanpur, India 126 E c
Saharien Atlas, Mts., Algeria 118 F b
Sahiadriparvat Ra., India 126 E d
Sahuaripa, Mexico 90 C b
Sahuayo, Mexico 90 D c
Sahugun, Spain 106 C a
Sahun, Aden 124 E g
Sahy, Czechoslovakia 105 H d
Sahyadri Mts., India 124 D e
Saibai, I., New Guinea 135 H a
Saida. See Sidon
Saidabad, Iran 125 G d
Saidapet, India 124 F f
Said Bundas, Sudan 119 K g
Saidu Sharif, Pakistan 126 D b
Saignelégier, Switzerland 101 B a
Saigon, S. Vietnam 132 D d
Sailana, India 126 D d
Saimaa, L., Finland 103 M f
Saimaa Kanal, Finland-U.S.S.R. 103 N f
Saimbeyli, Turkey 124 B c
St. Abbs Hd., Scotland 98 F e
Ste. Adelaide, Quebec 82 H e
Ste. Adèle, Quebec 85 Q g
St. Affrique, France 109 E e
St. Agapit, Manitoba 85 T f
Ste. Agathe, Manitoba 87 U j
Ste. Agathe des Monts, Quebec 85 Q f
Ste. Agnes, Quebec 85 L d
St. Agrève, France 109 F d
St. Albans, England 99 G j
St. Alban's, Newfoundland 83 R f
St. Albert, Alberta 86 D e
St. Alexandre, Quebec 82 C f
St. Alexis des Monts, Quebec 85 R f
St. Ambroise, Quebec 85 T d
St. Amour, France 108 F c
St. Anaclet, Quebec 82 D e
St. André, C., Madagascar 121 M k
St. Andrew's, New Brunswick 82 E h
St. Andrew's, Newfoundland 83 N f
St. Andrews, Scotland 98 F d
St. Andrew's Chan., Cape Breton I., Nova Scotia 83 M g
Ste. Ann, Manitoba 87 E a
St. Ann B., Cape Breton I., Nova Scotia 83 M g
Ste. Anne, L., Quebec 82 E c
Ste. Anne, Quebec 85 T d
Ste. Anne, R., Quebec 82 B f
Ste. Anne de Beaupré, Quebec 82 B f
Ste. Anne de Chicoutimi, Quebec 82 A e
Ste. Anne de la Pérade, Que. 85 S f
Ste. Anne de la Pocatière, Quebec 82 B f
Ste. Anne-des-Monts, Que. 82 F d
Ste. Anne du Lac, Quebec 85 P f
St. Anns, Cape Breton I., Nova Scotia 83 M g
St. Anns Bay, Jamaica 91 D c
St. Anthonis, Netherlands 100 D c
St. Anthony, Newfoundland 83 R b
St. Antönien, Switzerland 101 E b
St. Antonin, Quebec 82 C f
St. Arsène, Quebec 82 C f
St. Athanase, Quebec 82 C f
St. Aubert, Quebec 82 B f
St. Augustin, C. de, Madagascar 121 M l
St. Augustin B., Quebec 83 O b
St. Augustin R., Quebec 83 N b
St. Augustin-Saguenay, Quebec 83 O b
St. Austell, England 99 D k
St. Barnabé Nord, Quebec 85 S f
St. Barthélemi, Quebec 85 R f
St. Barthélemy, I., Leeward Is. 91 G c
St. Béat, France 109 D e
St. Benedict, Saskatchewan 87 M f
St. Benoit Labre, Quebec 82 B g
St. Bernard, I., Quebec 85 Q k
St. Bernard Pass, Grand, Switzerland-Italy 110 A c
Ste. Blandine, Quebec 82 D e
St. Boniface, Manitoba 87 U j
St. Boswells, Saskatchewan 86 L h
St. Brendan's, Newfoundland 83 T e
St. Bride, Mt., Alberta 86 B g
St. Bride's, Newfoundland 83 S g
St. Bride's B., Wales 99 D j
St. Brieuc, France 108 B b
St. Brieux, Saskatchewan 87 N f
St. Bruno de Guigues, Quebec 85 L e
St. Calais, France 108 D c
St. Camille, Quebec 82 B g
St. Casimir, Quebec 85 S f
St. Catharines, Ontario 85 L j
St. Catherine Lock, Quebec 85 S k
St. Cécile, Quebec 82 B h
St. Césaire, Quebec 85 R g
St. Chamond, France 108 F d
St. Charles, Quebec 82 B g
St. Charles R., Quebec 83 P h
St. Chély d'Apcher, France 109 E d
St. Christopher (St. Kitts), I., Leeward Is. 91 G c
St. Clair, L., Ontario-Michigan 84 H k
St. Clair R., Ontario-Michigan 84 H j
St. Claude, Manitoba 87 T j
St. Clement, Quebec 82 C f
Ste. Clothilde, Quebec 85 S g
St. Coeur de Marie, Quebec 85 T d
St. Côme, Quebec 85 R f
St. Côme. See Linière
St. Croix, I., West Indies 54 E j
Ste. Croix, New Brunswick 82 E h
Ste. Croix, Switzerland 101 B b
Ste. Croix R., Maine-New Brunswick 82 E h
St. Cyprien, Quebec 82 C f
St. Cyrille, Quebec 85 S g
St. Cyr Lake, Saskatchewan 86 J d
St. Damien, Quebec 82 B g
St. David-de-Lévis, Quebec 85 S c
St. David's, Newfoundland 83 O e
St. David's Hd., Wales 99 D j
St. Denis, France 108 E b
St. Denis, Quebec 82 C f
St. di Nova Siri, Italy 111 F e
St. Dizier, France 108 F b
St. Donat, Quebec 85 Q f
Ste. Élisabeth, Quebec 85 S d
St. Eloi, Quebec 82 C e
St. Elzéar de Laval, Quebec 85 R h
Ste. Émélie de l'Énergie, Quebec 85 R f
St. Éphrem, Quebec 82 B g
St. Étienne, France 108 F d
St. Eugène, Quebec 85 M d
St. Eusèbe, Quebec 82 D f
St. Eustache, Quebec 85 R g
St. Eustatius, I., Leeward Is. 91 G c
St. Fabien, Quebec 82 D e
Ste. Famille, Quebec 82 B g
Ste. Famille d'Aumond, Quebec 85 P f
St. Fargeau, France 108 E c
St. Félicien, Quebec 85 S d
Ste. Félicité, Quebec 82 E e
St. Félix de Valois, Quebec 85 R f
St. Filipsland, Netherlands 100 C c
St. Fintan's, Newfoundland 83 O e
St. Flavien, Quebec 85 T f
Ste. Florence, Quebec 82 E e
St. Florent & G. de, Corsica 110 B d
St. Florentin, France 108 E b
St. Flour, France 109 E d
St. Fortunat, Quebec 85 T g
St. Francis, C., Newfoundland 83 T f
St. Francis, L., Quebec 85 Q g
St. Francis B., S.W. Africa 122 A e
St. François, L., Quebec 85 T g
St. François, R., Quebec 85 S f
St. François Xavier, Quebec 85 S g
St. Fulgent, France 108 C c
St. Gabriel de Brandon, Quebec 85 R f
St. Gallen & canton, Switzerland 101 E a
St. Gaudens, France 109 D e
St. Gédéon, Quebec 82 B h
St. Gédéon, Quebec 85 T d
Ste. Geneviève B., Newfoundland 83 Q b
St. George, C., Newfoundland 83 N e
St. George, New Brunswick 82 F h
St. Georges, Fr. Guiana 93 G c
St. George's, Nfd. 83 O e
St. Georges, Quebec 82 B g
St. Georges, Quebec 82 H e
St. George's B., Newfoundland 83 N e
St. George's Chan., Ireland-Wales 99 C j
St. Gérard, Belgium 100 C d
St. Gérard, Quebec 85 M d
St. Gérard, Quebec 85 T g
St. Germain, France 108 E b
Ste. Germaine, Quebec 82 B g
St. Gervais, Quebec 82 B g
St. Gheorghe, I., Romania 112 G b
St. Ghislain, Belgium 100 B d
St. Giles, Quebec 85 T f
St. Gilgen, Austria 104 E e
St. Gilles, Belgium 100 C c
St. Gilles, France 109 F e
St. Gillis-Waas, Belgium 100 C c
St. Gingolph, Switzerland 101 B b
St. Girons, France 109 D e
St. Godefroy, Quebec 82 G e
St. Gotthard, pass, Switzerland 101 D b
St. Gregor, Saskatchewan 87 N f
St. Gregory, Mt., Newfoundland 83 O d
St. Guénolé, France 108 A c
St. Guillaume, Quebec 85 S g
St. Helena, I., Atlantic Ocean 120 A h
St. Helena B., South Africa 122 B f
Ste. Hélène, I., Quebec 85 S j
Ste. Hélène, Quebec 82 C f
St. Helens, England 99 E g
St. Helier, Quebec 82 H d
St. Hénédine, Quebec 82 B g
St. Henri, Quebec 82 A g
St. Herménégilde, Quebec 85 T g
St. Honoré, Quebec 82 C f
St. Honoré, Quebec 82 A e
St. Hubert, Belgium 100 D d
St. Hyacinthe, Quebec 85 S g
St. Ignace, Ontario 84 B d
St. Ignace du Lac, Quebec 85 R f
St. Imier, Switzerland 101 B a
St. Irénée, Quebec 82 B f
St. Isidore, Quebec 85 L e
St. Isidore, Quebec 85 T g
St. Ives, England 99 D k
St. Jacques, New Brunswick 82 D f
St. Jacques, Quebec 85 R g
St. James, C., British Columbia 88 D d
St. Janvier, Quebec 85 L d
St. Jean, Belgium 100 A d
St. Jean, France 108 G d
St. Jean, L., Quebec 85 S d
St. Jean, Quebec 85 R g
St. Jean, R., Quebec 82 H c
St. Jean Baptiste, Manitoba 87 U j
St. Jean Bosco, Quebec 85 S e
St. Jean d'Angély, France 108 C d
St. Jean de Dieu, Quebec 82 C e
St. Jean de Luz, France 109 C e
St. Jean de Matha, Quebec 85 R f
St. Jean Port Joli, Quebec 82 B f
St. Jérôme, Quebec 85 Q g
St. Jérôme, Quebec 85 T d
St. Joachim, Quebec 85 S g
St. Joachim, Quebec 82 B f
St. John, New Brunswick 82 F h
St. John B. & I., Newfoundland 83 P c
St. John I., Virgin Is. 54 E h
St. John R., Maine-New Brunswick 82 E g
St. John R., Quebec 82 G e
St. John's, Newfoundland 83 T f
St. Joseph, L., Ontario 81 K g
St. Joseph, Quebec 82 B g
St. Joseph d'Alma. See Alma
St. Joseph de Lévis, Quebec 85 U b
St. Joseph I., Ontario 84 G f
St. Joseph's, Newfoundland 83 T f
St. Jovite, Quebec 85 Q f
St. Kilda, I., Scotland 98 B c
St. Lambert, Quebec 85 T f
St. Lambert, Quebec 85 R g
St. Laurent, Fr. Guiana 93 G b
St. Laurent, Manitoba 87 U h
St. Laurent, Quebec 85 R j
St. Laurent R., Quebec 83 Q j
St. Lawrence, Australia 135 J d
St. Lawrence, C., Cape Breton I., Nova Scotia 83 M f
St. Lawrence, G. of, Canada 82 K f
St. Lawrence, Newfoundland 83 R g
St. Lawrence I., Bering Sea 80 B e
St. Lawrence Islands Nat. Park, Ontario 85 O h
St. Lawrence R., Canada-U.S.A. 81 N h
St. Lawrence Seaway, Quebec-New York 85 P h
St. Lazare, Manitoba 87 Q h
St. Leger, Belgium 100 D e
St. Léon, Quebec 85 T d
St. Léon, Quebec 82 E e
St. Léonard, Belgium 100 C c
St. Léonard, France 108 D d
St. Leonard, New Brunswick 82 E f
St. Leonard, Quebec 85 S f
St. Léonard de Port Maurice, Quebec 85 R h
St. Léon-de-Standon, Quebec 82 B g
St. Lewis R., Labrador 83 P a
St. Liboire, Quebec 85 S g
St. Lin, Quebec 85 R g
St. Lô, France 108 C b
St. Louis, L., Quebec 85 R g
St. Louis, Mauritania 118 B e
St. Louis, Prince Edward I. 82 H g
St. Louis, Saskatchewan 87 M f
St. Louis de Kent, New Brunswick 82 H g
St. Louis du Ha Ha, Quebec 82 D f
Ste. Louise, Quebec 82 B f
St. Lucia, C., South Africa 122 E e
St. Lucia, I., Windward Is. 91 G d
St. Lucia L., South Africa 122 E e
Ste. Lucie, Quebec 85 Q f
St. Ludger, Quebec 82 B h
St. Luke's I., Burma 127 J f
St. Lunaire B., Newfoundland 83 R b
St. Maartensdijk, Netherlands 100 C c
St. Magnus B., Shetland 98 H a
St. Maixent, France 108 C c
St. Malachie, Quebec 82 B g
St. Malo & G. de, France 108 B b
St. Marc, Haiti 91 E c
St. Marc des Carrières, Quebec 85 S f
St. Marcel, Quebec 82 B g
St. Mard, Belgium 100 D e
St. Margaret B., Newfoundland 83 P b
St. Margaret B., Nova Scotia 82 J j
Ste. Marguerite, R., Quebec 82 B e
Ste. Marguerite, R., Quebec 82 F c
Ste. Marie, C., Madagascar 121 N m
Ste. Marie, Quebec 82 A g
Ste. Marie I., Madagascar 121 N k
Ste. Marthe de Gaspé, Quebec 82 F d
St. Martin, I., Leeward Is. 91 G c
St. Martin L., Manitoba 87 T g
St. Martins, New Brunswick 82 G h
St. Mary, C., Nova Scotia 82 F j
St. Mary B., Nova Scotia 82 F j
St. Mary Is., India 126 D f
St. Mary Is., Quebec 83 N c
St. Mary Reefs, Quebec 83 N c
St. Mary Res., Alberta 86 D j
St. Mary's, Newfoundland 83 T g
St. Mary's, Ontario 84 J j
St. Mary's, Tasmania 134 J h
St. Mary's B., Newfoundland 83 T g
St. Mary's C., Newfoundland 83 S g
St. Mary's L., Scotland 98 E e
St. Mary's Pk., Australia 135 G f
St. Mary's R., Nova Scotia 83 K h
St. Mathieu, Quebec 82 D e
St. Mathieu, Quebec 85 M d
St. Matthew I., Bering Sea 80 B e
St. Matthew's I., Burma 127 J g
St. Maurice, R., Quebec 85 R e
St. Maurice, Switzerland 101 B b
Ste. Maurice de Labrieville, Quebec 82 C d
St. Maximin, France 109 F e
St. Maxine, Quebec 82 A g
St. Meen, France 108 B b
St. Michel de Laval, Quebec 85 R j
St. Michel des Saints, Quebec 85 R f
St. Moritz, Switzerland 101 E b
St. Nazaire, France 108 B c
St. Nicolaasga, Netherlands 100 D b
St. Nicolas. See St. Niklaas
St. Niklaas, Belgium 100 C c
St. Niklau, Switzerland 101 C b
St. Norbert, Manitoba 87 U j
St. Odilienberg, Netherlands 100 E c
St. Omer, France 108 E a
St. Omer, Quebec 82 F e
St. Ours, Quebec 85 R g
St. Pacôme, Quebec 83 C f
St. Pamphile, Quebec 82 C g
St. Pascal, Quebec 82 C f
St. Patrice, L., Quebec 85 N f
St. Paul, Alberta 86 F d
St. Paul, Quebec 82 C f
St. Paul de Fenouillet, France 109 E e
St. Paul-de-Montminy, Quebec 82 B g
St. Paul du Nord, Quebec 82 C e
St. Paul I., Cape Breton I., Nova Scotia 83 M f
St. Paulin, Quebec 85 R f
St. Paul R., Quebec 83 P b
St. Pauls Inlet, Nfd. 83 P d
Ste. Perpétue, Quebec 82 C f
St. Peter, Pt., Quebec 82 H e
St. Peter B., Labrador 83 R a
St. Peter's, Cape Breton I., Nova Scotia 83 M h
St. Peter's, Prince Edward I. 82 K g
Ste. Pétronille, Quebec 85 U b
St. Philémon, Quebec 82 B g
St. Pie, Quebec 85 S g
St. Pierre, L., Quebec 85 S f
St. Pierre, Manitoba 86 E a
St. Pierre, Martinique, West Indies 91 G d
St. Pierre, Quebec 85 R k
St. Pierre & I., Atlantic Ocean 83 Q g
St. Pol, France 108 E a
St. Pölten, Austria 105 F d
St. Pons, France 109 E e
St. Pourçain, France 108 E c
St. Prime, Quebec 85 S d
St. Quentin, France 108 E b
St. Quentin, New Brunswick 82 E f
St. Raphaël, Quebec 82 B g
St. Raymond, Quebec 85 T f
St. Rémi, Quebec 85 R g
St. Rémi d'Amherst, Quebec 85 Q f
St. Robert, Quebec 85 R g

St. Romaine, *Quebec* 82 A h
St. Rose, *Quebec* 85 R g
Ste. Rose du Dégelé, *Quebec* 82 D f
Ste. Rose du Lac, *Manitoba* 87 S g
St. Samuel, *Quebec* 82 B h
St. Sauveur, *Quebec* 85 R b
St. Sébastien, C., *Madagascar* 121 N j
St. Sernin-sur-Rance, *France* 109 E e
St. Servan, *France* 108 B b
St. Sever, *France* 109 C e
St. Shott's, *Newfoundland* 83 T g
St. Siméon, *Quebec* 82 C f
St. Simon, *Quebec* 82 C e
St. Stephen, *New Brunswick* 82 E h
St. Sylvestre, *Quebec* 85 T f
Ste. Thècle, *Quebec* 85 S f
St. Théophile, *Quebec* 82 B h
Ste. Thérèse, *Quebec* 85 R g
St. Thomas, I., *Virgin Is.* 54 E h
St. Thomas, *Ontario* 84 J k
St. Thomas Dydime, *Quebec* 85 S d
St. Tite, *Quebec* 85 S f
St. Tite des Caps, *Quebec* 82 B f
St. Trond. See St. Truiden
St. Tropez, *France* 109 G e
St. Truiden, *Belgium* 100 D d
St. Urbain, *Quebec* 82 B f
St. Valéry, *France* 108 D a
St. Valéry-en-Caux, *France* 108 D b
St. Vallier, *Quebec* 82 B g
St. Veit, *Austria* 104 F e
Ste. Véronique, *Quebec* 85 Q f
St. Victor, *Quebec* 82 B g
St. Vincent, C., *Madagascar* 121 M l
St. Vincent, G., *Australia* 135 G g
St. Vincent, *Windward Is.* 91 G d
St. Vincent de Paul, *Quebec* 85 R h
St. Vincent's, *Newfoundland* 83 T g
St. Vith, *Belgium* 100 E d
St. Walburg, *Saskatchewan* 86 H e
St. Williams, *Ontario* 84 K k
St. Yvon, *Quebec* 82 H d
Saintes, *France* 108 C d
Saintonge, prov., *France* 108 C d
Saipan, I., *Mariana Is.* 78 E e
Saipan Chan., *Saipan-Tinian Is.* 78 A e
Saiping. See Sinyang
Saiun (Saywūn), *Aden* 124 E f
Saivomuotka, *Sweden* 102 K b
Saka Dzong, *Tibet* 127 G c
Sakai, *Japan* 133 D g
Sakakah, *Saudi Arabia* 124 D d
Saka Kalat, *Pakistan* 126 C c
Sakami L., *Quebec* 81 M g
Sakania, *Congo* 121 F g
Sakarya, R., *Turkey* 124 B b
Sakata, *Japan* 133 F e
Sakha, *Saudi Arabia* 124 D e
Sakhalin, *U.S.S.R.* 115 P c
Sakhalinskaya Oblast, *U.S.S.R.* 115 P c
Sakahlinskiy Zaliv, *U.S.S.R.* 115 P c
Saki, *U.S.S.R.* 116 H j
Šakiai, Lithuania, *U.S.S.R.* 103 K j
Sakishima Gunto, Is., *Japan* 133 K k
Sakti, *India* 127 F d
Sakylä, *Finland* 103 K f
Sala, *Czechoslovakia* 105 G d
Sala, *Sweden* 103 G g
Salacgrîva, Latvia, *U.S.S.R.* 103 L h
Sala Consilina, *Italy* 111 E e
Salada, L., *Mexico* 90 A a
Salado, R., *Argentina* 94 D c
Salaga, *Ghana* 118 E g
Salahiya, *Syria* 123 D c
Salajar, I., *Indonesia* 129 H m
Salala, *Muscat & Oman* 125 F f
Salama, *Guatemala* 90 F d
Salamanca, *Mexico* 90 D c
Salamanca, *Spain* 106 C b
Salamaua, *New Guinea* 135 J a
Salamina, *Colombia* 92 B b
Salamis & I., *Greece* 113 D f
Salangen, *Norway* 102 G b
Salas, *Spain* 106 B a
Salas de los Infantes, *Spain* 106 D a
Salat, I., *Truk Is.* 78 F o
Salat Pass, *Truk Is.* 78 F o
Salatsgriva. See Salacgrîva
Salaverry, *Peru* 92 B e
Sala-y-Gomez, I., *Pacific Ocean* 79 Q k
Salbris, *France* 108 E c
Saldaña, *Spain* 106 C a
Saldus, Latvia, *U.S.S.R.* 103 K h
Sale, *Australia* 135 J g
Salekhard, *U.S.S.R.* 114 F b
Salem, *India* 126 E f
Salemi, *Sicily* 111 D g
Sälen, *Sweden* 103 E f
Salerno, G. di, *Italy* 111 E e
Salerno, *Italy* 111 E e
Salford, *England* 99 F g
Salgueiro, *Brazil* 93 K e
Salima, *Nyasaland* 121 G g
Salina, I., *Italy* 111 E f
Salina Cruz, *Mexico* 90 E d
Salinas, *Ecuador* 92 A d
Salinas, *Mexico* 90 D c
Salinas, *Mexico* 90 D b
Salinas, Pta., *Puerto Rico* 54 C h
Salinas, *Puerto Rico* 54 C j
Salinas. See Salinópolis
Salinitas, *Chile* 94 B b
Salinópolis, *Brazil* 93 H d
Salins, *France* 108 F c
Salisbury, *England* 99 F j
Salisbury, L., *Uganda* 121 G d
Salisbury, *New Brunswick* 82 G g
Salisbury, *Southern Rhodesia* 122 E c
Salisbury I., *North-West Territories* 81 M e
Salisbury Plain, *England* 99 F j
Salkhad, *Syria* 123 E e
Sallyana, *Nepal* 127 F c
Salmo, *British Columbia* 88 L f
Salmon, R., *British Columbia* 88 H c
Salmon Arm, *British Columbia* 88 K e
Salmon Bay, *Quebec* 83 P b
Salmon Gums, *Australia* 134 D f
Salmon R., Anticosti I., *Quebec* 82 K d
Salmon R., *New Brunswick* 82 F g
Salo, *Finland* 103 K f
Salon, *France* 109 F e
Salonica. See Thessaloníki
Salonta, *Romania* 112 C a
Salqin, *Syria* 123 E a
Salsette I., *India* 126 D e
Salta, *Argentina* 94 C b
Saltcoats, *Saskatchewan* 87 P g
Saltdal, *Norway* 102 F c
Saltee, Is., *Eire* 99 C h
Salt Fd., *Norway* 102 F c
Saltillo, *Mexico* 90 D b
Salt L., *Australia* 134 B d
Salt Ls., *Australia* 134 E e
Salto, *Argentina* 94 D d
Salto, *Uruguay* 94 E d
Salto da Divisa, *Brazil* 93 K g
Salt Ra., *Pakistan* 126 D b
Saltrou, *Haiti* 91 E c
Salûm & G. of, *Egypt* 119 L b
Salumaua, *New Guinea* 135 J a
Salur, *India* 127 F e
Salut, Is. du, *French Guiana* 93 G b
Saluzzo, *Italy* 110 A c
Salvador, El, *Central America* 91 B d
Salvador, *Saskatchewan* 86 H f
Salvador (Bahia), *Brazil* 93 K f
Salvage, *Newfoundland* 83 T e
Salvaterra, *Portugal* 106 A c
Salvatierra, *Mexico* 90 D c
Salvus, *Br. Columbia* 88 E c
Salzburg, *Austria* 104 E e
Salzwedel, *Germany* 104 D b
Samahala, *Bechuanaland* 122 C c
Samalut, *Egypt* 119 M c
Samaná & B. de, *Dominican Republic* 91 F c
Samar, I., *Philippines* 129 J h
Samarai, *New Guinea* 135 K b
Samarinda, *Borneo* 129 G l
Samarkand, Uzbek., *U.S.S.R.* 114 F e
Samarra Balad, *Iraq* 124 D c
Samasala, *India* 126 D c
Samāwa, *Iraq* 124 E c
Sambalpur, *India* 127 F d
Sambava, *Madagascar* 121 P j
Sambeek, *Netherlands* 100 D c
Sambhal, *India* 126 E c
Sambhar, *India* 126 D c
Sambor, Ukraine, *U.S.S.R.* 116 C g
Samborombón B., *Argentina* 94 E e
Sambre, R., *Belgium* 100 C d
Samedan, *Switzerland* 101 E b
Sameminato, *Japan* 133 G d
Sami, *Pakistan* 126 B c
Samira, *Saudi Arabia* 124 D d
Sam Ka, *Burma* 127 J d
Sam-nua, *Laos* 132 C b
Samoa, Is., *Pacific Ocean* 78 J h
Samokov, *Bulgaria* 112 D c
Samorogouan, *Upper Volta* 118 E f
Sámos, I., *Greece* 113 F f
Samothrace. See Samothráki, I.
Samothráki, I., *Greece* 113 E d
Sampacho, *Argentina* 94 D d
Sampit, *Borneo* 129 F l
Samrée, *Belgium* 100 D d
Samsat, *Turkey* 124 C b
Samshui, *China* 131 F l
Samsö, I., *Denmark* 103 D j
Samsu, *Korea* 128 J b
Samsun, *Turkey* 124 C a
San, *Mali* 118 E f
San'a, *Yemen* 124 D f
Sanam, Jebel, *Iraq* 124 E c
San Ambrosio I., *Pacific Oc.* 78 R l
Sanandaj, *Iran* 124 E b
San Antioco, I., *Sardinia* 111 B f
San Antonio, C., *Argentina* 94 E e
San Antonio, C., *Cuba* 91 C b
San Antonio, *Chile* 94 C b
San Antonio, *Chile* 94 B d
San Antonio, *Mexico* 90 C c
San Antonio Oeste, *Argentina* 95 D f
San Bartolomeu de Messines, *Portugal* 106 A d
San Benedetto del Tronto, *Italy* 110 D d
San Benito Is., *Mexico* 90 A b
San Bernardo, *Chile* 94 B d
San Blas, *Argentina* 95 D f
San Blas, G. de, *Panama* 91 D e
San Blas, *Mexico* 90 C c
San Blas, *Mexico* 90 C b
San Borja, *Mexico* 90 B b
San Carlos, Amazonas, *Venezuela* 92 D c
San Carlos, *Argentina* 94 C c
San Carlos, *Argentina* 94 C d
San Carlos, *Argentina* 94 C d
San Carlos, *Chile* 94 B e
San Carlos, Cojedes, *Venezuela* 92 D b
San Carlos, *Mexico* 90 E c
San Carlos, *Nicaragua* 91 C d
San Carlos de Bariloche, *Argentina* 95 B f
San Carlos del Zulia, *Venezuela* 92 C b
Sanchez, *Dominican Republic* 91 F c
San Clemente, *Spain* 107 D c
San Cosme, *Paraguay* 94 E c
San Cristóbal, *Argentina* 94 D d
San Cristóbal, I., *Galápagos Is.* 92 A h
San Cristóbal, I., *Solomon Is.* 78 G h
San Cristóbal, *Mexico* 90 F d
San Cristóbal, *Venezuela* 92 C b
Sancti Spíritus, *Cuba* 91 D b
Sanctuary, *Saskatchewan* 86 J g
Sand, *Norway* 103 B g
Sandakan, *N. Borneo* 129 G j
Sanday I., *Orkney Is.* 98 F a
Sandbank L., *Ontario* 84 H a
Sandefjord, *Norway* 103 D g
Sandfly L., *Saskatchewan* 86 L c
Sandgate, *Australia* 135 K e
Sand Hills, Great, *Saskatchewan* 86 H h
Sand Hills, Middle, *Alberta* 86 G h
Sandhornöy, *Norway* 102 E c
Sand I., *Palmyra I.* 79 T k
Sand I., *Truk Is.* 78 E n
Sandia, *Peru* 92 D f
San Diego, C., *Argentina* 95 C h
San Diego de Cabrutica, *Venezuela* 92 E b
Sandikli, *Turkey* 124 B b
Sandilands, *Manitoba* 86 F a
San Dimas, *Mexico* 90 C c
Sand L., Big, *Manitoba* 87 S a
Sand L., Little, *Manitoba* 87 T a
Sand L., *Ontario* 86 H a
Sand Lake, *Ontario* 84 F e
Sandnes, *Norway* 103 A g
Sandoa, *Congo* 120 E f
San Domingos, *Portugal* 106 B d
Sandoway, *Burma* 127 H e
Sand R., *Alberta* 86 F d
Sandspit, Moresby I., *British Columbia* 88 D d
Sandstone, *Australia* 134 C e
Sandtop, C., Anticosti I., *Quebec* 83 L d
Sandträsk, *Sweden* 102 J c
Sandvig, Bornholm I., *Denmark* 103 F j
Sandwich B., *Labrador* 81 O g
Sandwith, *Saskatchewan* 86 J e
Sandybeach L., *Ontario* 86 K a
Sandy C., *Australia* 135 K d
Sandy Creek, *Quebec* 85 O g
Sandy Falls, *Ontario* 84 J d
Sandy L., *Newfoundland* 83 Q d
Sandy L., *Ontario* 81 K g
Sandy Lake, *Manitoba* 87 R h
Sandy Lake, *Saskatchewan* 88 Q b
Sandy Narrows, *Saskatchewan* 87 O c
San Esteban de Gormaz, *Spain* 106 D b
San Felipe, *Chile* 94 B d
San Felipe, *Guatemala* 90 F e
San Felipe, *Mexico* 90 F d
San Felipe, *Mexico* 90 D c
San Felipe, *Venezuela* 92 D a
San Feliu de Guixols, *Spain* 107 G b
San Feliu de Llobregat, *Spain* 107 F b
San Félix, I., *Pacific Ocean* 79 R l
San Félix, *Venezuela* 92 E b
San Fernando, *Chile* 94 B d
San Fernando, *Mexico* 90 E c
San Fernando, *Mexico* 90 A b
San Fernando, *Philippines* 129 H g
San Fernando, *Trinidad* 92 E a
San Fernando de Apure, *Venezuela* 92 D b
San Fernando de Atabapo, *Venezuela* 92 D c
Sanford, *Manitoba* 87 U j
San Francisco del Chañar, *Argentina* 94 D d
San Francisco do Maranhão, *Brazil* 93 J e
Sanga, *Angola* 120 D g
Sangareddipet, *India* 126 E e
San Germán, *Puerto Rico* 54 B h
Sanggau, *Borneo* 129 F k
Sangihe Kep. (Sangi Is.), *Indonesia* 129 J k
Sangi Is. See Sangihe Kep.
San Giovanni in Fiore, *Italy* 111 F f
Sangkulirang, *Borneo* 129 G k
Sangre Grande, *Trinidad* 92 E a
Sangudo, *Alberta* 86 C e
Sanguin, *Liberia* 118 D g
San Ignacio, *Bolivia* 92 D f
San Ignacio, *Bolivia* 92 E g
San Ignacio, *Mexico* 90 C c
San Ignacio, *Mexico* 90 B b
San Ignacio, *Paraguay* 94 E c
San Javier, *Argentina* 94 E d
San Javier, *Bolivia* 92 E g
San Javier, *Chile* 94 B e
San João, *Portugal* 106 B b
San Joaquim, *Bolivia* 92 E f
San Jorge, G., *Argentina* 95 C g
San José, *Bolivia* 92 E g
San José, *Colombia* 92 C c
San José, *Costa Rica* 91 C e
San José, G., *Argentina* 95 D f
San José, *Guatemala* 90 F e
San José, I., *Mexico* 90 B b
San José, *Uruguay* 94 E d
San José Carpizo, *Mexico* 90 F d
San José de Amacuro, *Venezuela* 92 E b
San José de Feliciano, *Argentina* 94 E d
San José del Cabo, *Mexico* 90 C c
San José de Ocuné, *Colombia* 92 C c
San Josef Bay, *British Columbia* 88 E e
San Juan, *Bolivia* 90 F g
San Juan, Cabezas de, *Puerto Rico* 54 D h
San Juan, *Peru* 92 B g
San Juan, *Puerto Rico* 54 C h
San Juan, *Venezuela* 92 D a
San Juan & R., *Argentina* 94 C d
San Juan, C., *Argentina* 95 D h
San Juan, R., *Mexico* 90 E d
San Juan, R., *Nicaragua* 91 B d
San Juan de Camarones, *Mexico* 90 C b
San Juan de Guadalupe, *Mexico* 90 D c
San Juan del Norte, *Nicaragua* 91 C d
San Juan de los Lagos, *Mexico* 90 D c
San Juan del Río, *Mexico* 90 E c
San Juan del Sur, *Nicaragua* 91 B d
San Julián, *Argentina* 95 C g
San Justo, *Argentina* 94 D d
Sankeimo, I., *Okinawa* 78 B b
Sankuri Post, *Kenya* 121 H e
San Lázaro, C., *Mexico* 90 B c
San Lorenzo, *Argentina* 94 D d
San Lorenzo, *Ecuador* 92 B c
San Lorenzo, *Honduras* 91 B d
San Lorenzo, *Mexico* 90 B b
San Lorenzo, *Peru* 92 D f
San Lorenzo, *Puerto Rico* 54 D h
San Lorenzo del Escorial, *Spain* 106 C b
San Lorenzo Is., *Mexico* 90 B b
Sanlucar la Mayor, *Spain* 106 B d
San Lucas, *Bolivia* 92 D h
San Lucas, C., *Mexico* 90 C c
San Luis, *Argentina* 94 E c
San Luis, *Argentina* 94 C d
San Luis, *Cuba* 91 D b
San Luis de la Paz, *Mexico* 90 D c
San Luis Potosí & state, *Mexico* 90 D c
Sanluri, *Sardinia* 111 B f
San Marcos, *Colombia* 92 B b
San Marino, rep., *Italy* 110 D d
San Martín, *Argentina* 94 C d
San Martín, *Colombia* 92 C c
San Martín, L., *Chile-Argentina* 95 B g
San Martín, R., *Bolivia* 92 E g
San Martín de los Andes, *Argentina* 95 B f
San Martín de Valdeiglesais, *Spain* 106 C b
San Martinho, *Portugal* 106 A c
San Mateo, *Spain* 107 F b
San Matías, *Bolivia* 92 F g
San Matías, G., *Argentina* 95 D f
San Maura. See Levkás, I.
Sanmenhsia, *China* 130 E e
San Miguel, B. de, *Panama* 91 D e
San Miguel, *Bolivia* 92 E g
San Miguel, *Mexico* 90 D c
San Miguel, *Peru* 92 C f
San Miguel, R., *Bolivia* 92 E g
San Miguel, *Salvador* 91 B d
San Miguel. See Rey, I. del
San Miguel de Tucumán, *Argentina* 94 C c
San Nicolás, *Argentina* 94 D d
San Pablo, *Bolivia* 92 D h
San Pablo, C., *Argentina* 95 C h
San Pedro, *Argentina* 94 E d
San Pedro, *British Honduras* 91 B c
San Pedro, *Ivory Coast* 118 D h
San Pedro, *Mexico* 90 D b
San Pedro, *Paraguay* 94 E b
San Pedro de Arimena, *Colombia* 92 C c
San Pedro del Gallo, *Mexico* 90 D b
San Pedro de Lloc, *Peru* 92 B e
San Pedro de Macoris, *Dominican Republic* 91 F c
San Pedro do Sul, *Portugal* 106 A b
San Pedro Sula, *Honduras* 91 B c
San Pietro I., *Sardinia* 111 B f
San Quintín & B., *Mexico* 90 A a
San Rafael, *Argentina* 94 C d
San Ramón, *Peru* 92 B f
San Remo, *Italy* 110 A d
San Roque, *Argentina* 94 E c
San Salvador, *Angola* 120 C f
San Salvador, *Salvador* 91 B d
San Salvador (Guanahani), *Bahama Is.* 91 E b
Sansanne Mango, *Togo* 118 F f
San Sebastián, *Puerto Rico* 54 C h
San Sebastián, *Spain* 107 D a
San Sebastián & B. de, *Argentina* 95 C h
San Severo, *Italy* 111 E e
Santa, *Peru* 92 B e
Santa Ana, *Bolivia* 92 D f
Santa Ana, *Bolivia* 92 F g
Santa Ana, *Ecuador* 92 A d
Santa Ana, *Mexico* 90 B a
Santa Ana, *Salvador* 91 B d
Santa Anna (do Bananal), I. de, *Brazil* 93 G f
Santa Bárbara, *Honduras* 91 B d
Santa Bárbara, *Venezuela* 92 E b
Santa Baturité, *Brazil* 93 K d
Santa Catalina, *Chile* 94 C c
Santa Catalina, I., *Mexico* 90 B b
Santa Catalina, Mt. See Encantada, Cerro de
Santa Catarina, I., *Brazil* 94 G c
Santa Catarina, *Mexico* 90 C c
Santa Clara, *Brazil* 92 D d
Santa Clara, *Cuba* 91 C b
Santa Clara, Sa., *Mexico* 90 B b
Santa Coloma de Farnes, *Spain* 107 G b
Santa Cruz, *Argentina* 95 C h
Santa Cruz, *Bolivia* 92 E g
Santa Cruz, *Chile* 94 B d
Santa Cruz, *Mexico* 90 B a
Santa Cruz, *Peru* 92 B e
Santa Cruz, *Philippines* 129 H h
Santa Cruz, R., *Argentina* 95 B h
Santa Cruz de la Zarza, *Spain* 106 D c
Santa Cruz del Sur, *Cuba* 91 D b
Santa Cruz de Tenerife, *Canary Is.* 118 B c
Santa Cruz Is., *Pacific Ocean* 78 G h
Santa de Unturán, *Venezuela* 92 D c
Santa dos Dois Irmãos, *Brazil* 93 J e
Santa Elena, *Ecuador* 92 A d
Santa Eufemia, G. di, *Italy* 111 F f
Santa Fé, *Argentina* 94 D d
Santa Fé, *Cuba* 91 C b
Santa Filomena, *Brazil* 93 H e
Santa Helena, *Brazil* 94 F b
Santa Helena, *Brazil* 93 H d
Santa Helena, *Brazil* 93 F e
Santai, *China* 130 B g
Santa Inés, B., *Mexico* 90 B b
Santa Inés, I., *Chile* 95 B h
Santa Isabel, *Argentina* 94 C e
Santa Isabel, *Fernando Poo* 118 G h
Santa Isabel, *Puerto Rico* 54 C j
Santa Isabel, *Solomon Is.* 78 F h
Santa Lucía, *Cuba* 91 D b
Santa Margarita, I., *Mexico* 90 B c
Santa María, *Argentina* 94 C c
Santa María, *Brazil* 94 F c
Santa Maria, I., *Atlantic Ocean* 118 B b
Santa María, I., *Chile* 95 B e
Santa María, *Mexico* 90 C b
Santa María, Mt., *Argentina* 94 C e
Santa María del Río, *Mexico* 90 D c
Santa Maria di Leuca, C., *Italy* 111 G f
Santa María la Real de Nieva, *Spain* 106 C b
Santa Marta, *Colombia* 92 C a
Santander, *Colombia* 92 B c
Santander, *Spain* 106 D a
Santa Quiteria, *Brazil* 93 J d
Santarém, *Brazil* 93 G d
Santarém, *Portugal* 106 A c
Santa Rita, *Brazil* 93 F e
Santa Rita, I., *Guam* 78 A l
Santa Rita, *Venezuela* 92 C a
Santa Rosa, *Argentina* 94 C d
Santa Rosa, *Argentina* 94 C d
Santa Rosa, *Bolivia* 92 E g
Santa Rosa, *Brazil* 94 F c
Santa Rosa, *Honduras* 91 B d
Santa Rosa de Toay, *Argentina* 94 D e
Santa Rosalía, *Mexico* 90 B b
Santa Rosa Mt., *Guam* 78 B k
Santa Sylvina, *Argentina* 94 D c
Santa Vitoria do Palmar, *Brazil* 94 F d
Santiago, Baja California, *Mexico* 90 C c
Santiago, *Brazil* 94 F c
Santiago, Cerro, *Panama* 91 C e
Santiago, *Chile* 94 B d
Santiago, *Dominican Republic* 91 E c
Santiago, *Mexico* 90 C c
Santiago, *Panama* 91 C e
Santiago, Sa. de, *Bolivia* 92 F g
Santiago de Compostela, *Spain* 106 A a
Santiago de Cuba, *Cuba* 91 D c
Santiago del Estero, *Argentina* 94 D c
Santillana, *Spain* 106 C a
Santis, Mt., *Switzerland* 101 E a
Santo Angelo, *Brazil* 94 F c
Santo António, *Brazil* 92 E f
Santo António da C., *Brazil* 93 G d
Santo António do Zaire, *Angola* 120 C f
Santo Corazón, *Bolivia* 92 F g
Santo Domingo, *Cuba* 91 C b
Santo Domingo, *Dominican Republic* 91 F c
Santo Domingo, *Mexico* 90 A a
San Tomé, *Venezuela* 92 E b
Santoríni. See Thíra, I.
Santos, *Brazil* 93 H h
Santo Tomás, *Mexico* 90 A a
Santo Tomás, *Peru* 92 C f
Santvliet, *Belgium* 100 C c
San Urbano, *Argentina* 94 D d
San Vicente, *Salvador* 91 B d
San Vicente del Caguán, *Colombia* 92 C c
San Vito, C., *Italy* 111 F e
São Antonio do Içá, *Brazil* 92 D d
São Bento do Norte, *Brazil* 93 K e
São Borja, *Brazil* 94 E c
São Carlos, *Brazil* 93 H h
São Cristovão, *Brazil* 93 K f
São Domingos, *Brazil* 93 H f
São Felix, *Brazil* 93 G e
São Francisco, *Brazil* 93 J e
São Francisco, *Brazil* 93 J g
São Francisco, R., *Brazil* 93 K e
São Francisco do Sul & I. de, *Brazil* 94 G c
Sao Hill, *Tanganyika* 121 H f
São Jerónimo, *Brazil* 94 F c
São João da Barra, *Brazil* 93 J h
São João da Boa Vista, *Brazil* 94 G b
São João del Rei, *Brazil* 93 J h
São João do Araguaya, *Brazil* 93 H e
São João do Piauí, *Brazil* 93 J e
São Joaquim, *Brazil* 92 D c
São José, *Brazil* 94 G c
São José, *Brazil* 92 D d
São José do Mipibú, *Brazil* 93 K e
São José do Norte, *Brazil* 94 F d
São José do Rio Prêto, *Brazil* 93 H h
São Lourenço & R., *Brazil* 93 F g
São Luis, *Brazil* 93 J d
São Luis, I. de, *Brazil* 93 J d
São Luiz Gonzaga, *Brazil* 94 F c
São Mateus, *Brazil* 93 K g
São Mateus do Sul, *Brazil* 94 F c
São Miguel, I., *Atlantic Ocean* 118 B a
Saona, I., *Dominican Republic* 91 F c
Saône, R., *France* 108 F c
Saône-et-Loire, dep., *France* 108 F c
São Paulo, *Brazil* 93 H h
São Paulo de Luanda, *Angola* 120 C f
São Paulo de Olivença, *Brazil* 92 D d
São Raimundo Nonato, *Brazil* 93 J e
São Romão, *Brazil* 92 D e
São Sebastião, *Brazil* 92 E e
São Sebastião & I. da, *Brazil* 93 H h
São Simão, *Brazil* 93 H h
São Tomé, I., *G. of Guinea* 120 B d
Saoura, *Algeria* 118 E c
São Vicente, *Brazil* 93 H h
Sapiéntza, I., *Greece* 113 C f
Saposoa, *Peru* 92 B e
Sapporo, *Japan* 133 G c
Sapri, *Italy* 111 E e
Saqqez, *Iran* 124 E b
Saragossa (Zaragoza), *Spain* 107 E b
Saraguro, *Ecuador* 92 B d
Saraikela, *India* 127 G d
Sarajevo, *Yugoslavia* 112 B c
Saraktash, *U.S.S.R.* 117 N e
Sarala, *U.S.S.R.* 114 H c
Sarandí del Yi, *Uruguay* 94 E d
Sarangarh, *India* 127 F d
Saransk, *U.S.S.R.* 117 G c
Sarapul, *U.S.S.R.* 117 L b
Saratov, *U.S.S.R.* 117 G e
Saratsi-ting, *China* 130 E b
Sarawak, *Borneo* 129 F k
Sarbaz, *Iran* 125 H d
Sárbogárd, *Hungary* 105 H e
Sarco, *Chile* 94 B c
Sardarshahr, *India* 126 D c
Sardasht, *Iran* 124 E b
Sardegna. See Sardinia
Sardinia (Sardegna), *Italy* 111 B e
Sardoal, *Portugal* 106 A c
Sareks Nat. Park, *Sweden* 102 G c
Sargans, *Switzerland* 101 E a
Sari, *Iran* 125 F b
Sarikamis, *Turkey* 124 D a
Sarina, *Australia* 135 J d
Sariñena, *Spain* 107 E b
Sar-i-Pul, *Afghanistan* 125 J b
Sar-i-pul, *Iran* 124 E c
Sark, I., *Channel Is.* 108 B b
Sarkad, *Hungary* 105 J e
Sarlat, *France* 109 D d
Sarmi, *New Guinea* 129 L l
Sarmiento, Mt., *Chile* 95 B h
Sarna, *Sweden* 103 E f
Sarnen, *Switzerland* 101 D b
Sarnia, *Ontario* 84 H k
Sarno, *Italy* 111 E e
Saronic G., *Greece* 113 D f
Saronno, *Italy* 110 B c
Sar Passage, *Palau Is.* 78 B n
Sarpsborg, *Norway* 103 D g
Sarpul. See Shahsavar
Sarrebourg, *France* 108 G b
Sarreguemines, *France* 108 G b
Sarre Union, *France* 108 G b
Sarria, *Spain* 106 B a
Sart, *Belgium* 100 D d

Sartène, Corsica 111 B e
Sarthe, R. & dep., France 108 D c
Sarufutsu, Japan 133 H b
Saruru, Japan 133 H c
Sarvar, Hungary 105 G e
Sasa Baneh, Ethiopia 121 J c
Sasamat, L., Br. Columbia 88 E f
Sascumica L., Quebec 85 N b
Sasebo, Japan 133 A h
Saskatchewan, prov., Canada 80 J g
Saskatchewan R., N., Alberta-Saskatchewan 86 K f
Saskatchewan R., S., Saskatchewan 86 J h
Saskatoon, Saskatchewan 86 L f
Saskeram L., Manitoba 87 Q e
Saskylakh, U.S.S.R. 115 L a
Sasovo, U.S.S.R. 117 E c
Sassandra & R., Ivory Coast 118 D h
Sassari, Sardinia 111 B e
Sassnitz, Germany 104 E a
Sastre, Argentina 94 D d
Sas-van-Gent, Netherlands 100 B c
Satadougou, Mali 118 C f
Satara, India 126 D e
Satellite B., North-West Territories 80 H b
Säter, Sweden 103 F f
Satevo, Mexico 90 C b
Satka, U.S.S.R. 117 P c
Sátoraljaújhely, Hungary 105 J d
Satpura Ra., India 126 D d
Satu Mare, Romania 105 K e
Satun, Thailand 132 C e
Sauda, Norway 103 B g
Saudhárkrókur, Iceland 102 W m
Saudi Arabia, South-West Asia 124 D e
Saugeen, R., Ontario 84 J h
Saugstad, Mt., Br. Columbia 88 F d
Saulieu, France 108 F c
Saulnierville, Nova Scotia 82 F j
Sault au Mouton, Quebec 82 C e
Sault-aux-Cochons, R., Quebec 82 C e
Sault Ste. Marie, Ontario 84 F f
Saumur, France 108 C c
Saumur, L., Quebec 82 K b
Saunders, Alberta 86 B f
Saunders, C., New Zealand 135 Q m
Saurashtra. See Kathiawar
Sauterelles, L. aux, Quebec 82 J b
Sava, R., Yugoslavia 112 B b
Savai'i, I., Samoa 78 J j
Savane R., Quebec 82 A b
Savannakhet, Laos 132 C c
Savanna la Mar, Jamaica 91 D c
Savant Lake, Ontario 87 M a
Savantvadi, India 126 D e
Savanur, India 126 E f
Save, Dahomey 118 F g
Saveh, Iran 125 F b
Savenay, France 108 C c
Save R., Mozambique 122 E d
Savoff, Ontario 84 F c
Savoie, dep., France 108 G d
Savoie, prov., France 108 G d
Savona, British Columbia 88 J e
Savona, Italy 110 B c
Savonlinna, Finland 102 N f
Savukoski, Finland 102 N c
Savu Sea, Indonesia 129 H m
Sawa, Aden 124 E f
Sawahlunto, Sumatra 129 D l
Sawayan Pt., Quebec 85 L a
Sawbill, Manitoba 87 Q a
Sawdy, Alberta 86 D d
Sawle Pt., Palmyra I. 79 T k
Sawqirah B., Muscat & Oman 125 G f
Sawyerville, Quebec 85 T g
Saxnäs, Sweden 102 F d
Saya, Syria 123 D b
Sayabac, Quebec 82 E e
Saya Buri. See Pak-lay
Sayán, Peru 92 B f
Sayan, Vostochnyy, U.S.S.R. 115 J c
Sayan, Zapadnyy, U.S.S.R. 115 J c
Sayhut, Aden 125 F f
Sayula, Mexico 90 D d
Sayward, British Columbia 88 G e
Scafell Pike, England 99 E f
Scalea, Italy 111 E f
Scandia, Alberta 86 E h
Scânteia, Romania 112 F a
Scanterbury, Manitoba 87 V h
Scanzano, Italy 111 F e
Scapa, Alberta 86 F g
Scapa Flow, Orkney Is. 98 E b
Scarborough, England 99 G f
Scarborough, Ontario 84 E k
Scarborough Bluffs, Ontario 84 E k
Scărisoara, Romania 112 D a
Scarth, Manitoba 87 R j
Scatari I., Cape Breton I., Nova Scotia 83 N g
Sceptre, Saskatchewan 86 H h
Schaffhausen & canton, Switzerland 101 D a
Scharhörn, I., Germany 104 C b
Schefferville, Labrador 81 N g
Scheiben I., Truk Is. 78 E n
Schelde, Ooster & Wester, Netherlands 100 B c
Scheveningen, Netherlands 100 C b
Schiedam, Netherlands 100 C c
Schiermonnikoog I., Netherlands 100 E a
Schiphol, Netherlands 100 C b
Schleins, Switzerland 101 F b
Schleswig, Germany 104 C a
Schleswig-Holstein, Germany 100 C a
Schneidemühl. See Pila
Schönberg, Germany 104 D b
Schönbuhl, Switzerland 101 C a
Schönebeck, Germany 104 D c
Schongau, Germany 104 D e
Schoonhoven, Netherlands 100 C c
Schötz, Switzerland 101 D a
Schouwen I., Netherlands 100 B c
Schreiber, Ontario 84 C d
Schuchinsk, Kazakh., U.S.S.R. 114 G c
Schuler, Alberta 86 G h
Schull, Eire 99 A j
Schuls, Switzerland 101 F b
Schultz L., North-West Territories 80 K e
Schumacher, Ontario 84 J d
Schüpfheim, Switzerland 101 D b
Schwabach, Germany 104 D d
Schwäbisch Hall. See Hall
Schwägalp, Switzerland 101 E a
Schwandorf, Germany 104 E d
Schwaner Geb., Mts., Borneo 129 F l
Schwarzhorn, Mt., Switzerland 101 C b
Schwarzwald, Germany 104 C d
Schwedt, Germany 104 F b
Schweidnitz. See Swidnica
Schweinfurt, Germany 104 D c
Schwerin, Germany 104 D b
Schwyz & canton, Switzerland 101 D a
Sciacca, Sicily 111 D g
Scie, R. à la, Quebec 83 R k
Scilly, Is. of, England 99 C l
Sclater, Manitoba 87 R g
Scollard, Alberta 86 E g
Scoresby Ld., Greenland 89 N b
Scoresby Sd., Greenland 89 N b
Scotch Bay, Manitoba 87 T h
Scotia, Ontario 85 L g
Scotia Sea, Antarctica 136 K g
Scotland, Great Britain 98 D c
Scotsburn, Nova Scotia 82 K h
Scotsguard, Saskatchewan 86 J j
Scotstown, Quebec 85 T g
Scott, C., Vancouver I., British Columbia 88 E e
Scott, Saskatchewan 86 J f
Scott Glacier, Antarctica 136 S e
Scott I., Antarctica 78 K o
Scott Inlet, North-West Territories 81 M c
Scott Is., Br. Columbia 88 E e
Scottsdale, Tasmania 135 J h
Scottsville, Cape Breton I., Nova Scotia 83 L g
Scout Lake, Saskatchewan 87 M j
Scudder, Ontario 84 H k
Scugog, L., Ontario 85 M h
Scutari. See Shkodër
Scutari. See Uskudar
Seaforth, Ontario 84 J j
Seager Wheeler L., Saskatchewan 87 O d
Seahorse Pt., North-West Territories 81 L e
Sea I., British Columbia 88 C f
Seal Bight, Labrador 83 R a
Seal Cove, New Brunswick 82 F j
Seal Cove, Newfoundland 83 Q d
Sea Lion Is., Falkland Is. 95 E h
Seal R., Manitoba 81 K f
Searchmont, Ontario 84 F f
Searston, Newfoundland 83 N f
Seba Beach, Alberta 86 C e
Sebastián Vizcaino, B. de, Mexico 90 B b
Sebenico. See Sibenik
Sebha, Libya 119 H c
Sebin Karahisar, Turkey 124 C a
Séchelles, L., Quebec 82 C a
Sechelt, British Columbia 88 H f
Sečovce, Czechoslovakia 105 J d
Secretan, Saskatchewan 86 L h
Secretary I., New Zealand 135 P m
Secunderabad, India 126 E e
Seda, Lithuania, U.S.S.R. 103 K h
Sedalia, Alberta 86 G g
Sedan, France 108 F b
Sedano, Spain 106 D a
Seddonville, New Zealand 135 Q l
Sedgewick, Alberta 86 F f
Sedhiou, Senegal 118 B f
Sedley, Manitoba 87 O h
Sedom, Israel 123 D f
Sedrun, Switzerland 101 D b
Seebe, Alberta 86 C g
Seeheim, S.W. Africa 122 B e
Seeleys Bay, Ontario 85 O h
Seelisberg, Switzerland 101 D b
Sées, France 108 D b
Seewis, Switzerland 101 E b
Sefrou, Morocco 118 E b
Segorbe, Spain 107 E c
Ségou, Mali 118 D f
Segovia, R., Nicaragua 91 C d
Segovia, Spain 106 C b
Séguéla, Ivory Coast 118 D g
Sehkuheh, Iran 125 H c
Sehwan, Pakistan 126 C c
Seibo, Dominican Republic 91 F c
Seignelay, R., Quebec 82 C a
Seiland, Norway 102 K a
Seine, R., France 108 D b
Seine-et-Marne, dep., France 108 E b
Seine-et-Oise, dep., France 108 D b
Seine Maritime, dep., France 108 D b
Seitler, U.S.S.R. 116 J j
Seiyala, Egypt 119 M d
Sekenke, Tanganyika 121 G e
Seki, Japan 133 E g
Sekieshan I., China 131 L g
Sekondi, Ghana 118 E g
Sektyakh, U.S.S.R. 115 M a
Selborne, C., Antarctica 136 B b
Selby, England 99 G g
Seldom, Newfoundland 83 S d
Selemiya, Syria 123 F b
Selenge, R., Mongolia-U.S.S.R. 115 K d
Selima Oasis, Sudan 119 L d
Selkirk, Manitoba 87 V h
Selkirk, Ontario 84 L k
Selkirk & co., Scotland 98 F e
Selkirk I., Manitoba 87 S e
Selkirk Mts., British Columbia-Montana 80 H g
Selle, Sa. de la, Haiti 91 E c
Selles, France 108 D c
Selva, Argentina 94 D c
Selwyn, Australia 135 H d
Selwyn Ra., Australia 134 G d
Sem, Norway 103 D g
Semans, Saskatchewan 87 N g
Semarang, Indonesia 129 F m
Semawe, Jeb. See Har Sagī
Semipalatinsk, Kazakh., U.S.S.R. 114 H c
Semnan, Iran 125 F b
Semuida, I., Okinawa 78 B a
Senador Pompeu, Brazil 93 K e
Sena Madureira, Brazil 92 D e
Senate, Saskatchewan 86 H j
Sendai, Japan 133 G e
Senegal (Sénégal), W. Africa 118 B f
Sénégal R., W. Africa 118 C e
Senga Hill, N. Rhodesia 121 G f
Sengilei, U.S.S.R. 117 J d
Senhor do Bonfim, Brazil 93 J f
Senise, Italy 111 F e
Senj, Yugoslavia 110 E c
Senja, Norway 102 G b
Senlac, Saskatchewan 86 H f
Senneterre, Quebec 85 N d
Sens, France 108 E b
Senta, Yugoslavia 112 C b
Sentinel Pk., British Columbia 88 J c
Sentinel Ra., Antarctica 136 G c
Seoni, India 126 E d
Seoul, Korea 128 J c
Sepólno, Poland 105 G b
Sept Iles, Quebec 82 F c
Sept-Milles, L., Quebec 82 B b
Sepúlveda, Spain 106 D b
Sequeros, Spain 106 B b
Ser, Mt., India 126 E b
Serai, Syria 123 D b
Serakhs, Turkmen., U.S.S.R. 114 F e
Seram I., Indonesia 129 J l
Serbia (Srbija), Yugoslavia 112 C c
Serdeles, Libya 119 H c
Serdobsk, U.S.S.R. 117 G d
Serengeti Nat. Park, Tanganyika 121 G e
Sergach, U.S.S.R. 117 G c
Sergiyevsk, U.S.S.R. 117 K c
Sérifos, I., Greece 113 E f
Sermata, I., Indonesia 129 J m
Serov, U.S.S.R. 114 F c
Serowe, Bechuanaland 122 D d
Serpa, Portugal 106 B d
Serpent, R. au, Quebec 82 A d
Serpentine R., British Columbia 88 E g
Serpins, Portugal 106 A b
Serpukhov, U.S.S.R. 116 K d
Serra do Gurupí, Brazil 93 H d
Sérrai, Greece 112 D d
Serre San Bruno, Italy 111 F f
Serrezuela, Argentina 94 C d
Sertã, Portugal 106 A c
Sertañia, Brazil 93 K e
Sertão, Brazil 93 J e
Sertig, Switzerland 101 E b
Sérvia, Greece 113 D d
Seseganaga L., Ontario 87 N a
Sesekinika Lake, Ontario 84 K d
Seseko shima, Okinawa 78 A b
Sesheke, Northern Rhodesia 122 C c
Sète, France 109 E e
Sete Lagoas, Brazil 93 J g
Sétif, Algeria 118 G a
Settee L., Manitoba 87 U a
Setting L., Manitoba 87 T c
Settlement, Wake I. 79 S e
Setubal, Portugal 106 A c
Seul, L., Manitoba 81 K g
Seul, Lac, Ontario 81 K g
Sevan, Oz., Armyanskaya 114 D d
Sevastopol, U.S.S.R. 116 H j
Sevelen, Switzerland 101 E a
Seven Islands. See Sept Iles
Seven Persons, Alberta 86 G j
Seventy Mile House, British Columbia 88 J e
Séverac-le-Château, France 109 E d
Severn, Ontario 81 L f
Severn, R., England 99 F j
Severn, R., Ontario 81 L f
Severn, South Africa 122 C e
Severnaya Dvina, U.S.S.R. 114 D b
Severnaya Zemlya, U.S.S.R. 115 K a
Sevilla. See Seville
Seville (Sevilla), Spain 106 C d
Seward Mts., Antarctica 136 H d
Sexsmith, Alberta 88 K c
Seybaplaya, Mexico 90 F d
Seychelles, Is., Indian Ocean 121 K a
Seydhisfjördhur, Iceland 102 Z a
Seyhan, Turkey 124 C b
Seymchan, U.S.S.R. 115 Q b
Seymour, Mt., British Columbia 88 D e
Seymour R., British Columbia 88 D e
Seyne, France 109 G d
Sézanne, France 108 E b
Sfakiá. See Khóra Sfakion
Sfântu Gheorghe, Romania 112 E b
Sfax, Tunisia 119 H b
Sfira, Syria 123 F a
Shaam, Trucial States 125 G d
Shabaqua, Ontario 87 N b
Shackleton, Saskatchewan 86 J h
Shackleton Glacier, Antarctica 136 C b
Shackleton Ice Shelf, Antarctica 136 R e
Shackleton Inlet, Antarctica 136 B b
Shackleton Ra., Antarctica 136 K b
Shadegan, Iran 124 E c
Shadrinsk, U.S.S.R. 117 R b
Shadwan, I., Egypt 119 M c
Shaftesbury, England 99 F j
Shag Rocks, Atlantic Ocean 136 J g
Shahba, Syria 123 E e
Shahbandar, Pakistan 126 C d
Shahdād, Iran 125 G c
Shahdadkot, Pakistan 126 C c
Shahdadpur, Pakistan 126 C c
Shahgarh, India 126 C c
Shahhat, Libya 119 K b
Shahidula, India 126 E a
Shahin, Iran 124 E b
Shahjahanpur, India 126 E c
Shahjui, Afghanistan 125 J c
Shāhpūr, Iran 124 D b
Shahpura, India 126 D c
Shahrakht, Iran 125 H c
Shahr-e-Babak, Iran 125 G c
Shahreza, Iran 125 F c
Shahr-i-Zabul. See Zabol
Shahrud, Iran 125 G b
Shahsavar, Iran 125 F b
Shahsien, China 131 H j
Shaiba, Saudi Arabia 124 D d
Shajara, Saudi Arabia 124 E e
Shakespeare I., Ontario 84 B c
Shakhty, U.S.S.R. 117 E g
Shakpets. See Shakubetsueki
Shakubetsueki, Japan 133 H c
Shala L., Ethiopia 121 H c
Shalasha, Sudan 119 L f
Shalath, Br. Columbia 88 H e
Shallop, Anticosti I., Quebec 82 K d
Shallow Lake, Ontario 84 J g
Shamil, Iran 125 G d
Shammar, Jabal, Saudi Arabia 124 D d
Shamrock, Saskatchewan 86 L h
Shanghai, China 130 K g
Shangjao, China 131 H h
Shangkiu, China 130 G e
Shangtung, prov., China 130 H d
Shangyiu, China 131 G k
Shan-hai-kwan. See Linyu
Shanhsien. See Sanmenhsia
Shannah, Saudi Arabia 125 F f
Shannon, Eire 99 B h
Shannon, I., Greenland 89 M b
Shannon R., Eire 99 B g
Shansi, prov., China 130 E c
Shantarskiye Os., U.S.S.R. 115 N c
Shantou. See Swatow
Shantung Pen., China 118 H c
Shaohing, China 131 K g
Shaowu, China 131 H j
Shaoyang, China 131 E j
Shapinsay, I., Orkney Is. 98 F a
Shaqa, Saudi Arabia 124 D f
Shaqra, Saudi Arabia 124 E d
Sharbot Lake, Ontario 85 O h
Sharjah, Trucial States 125 G d
Shark B., Australia 134 B e
Sharqi, Jeb. esh, Lebanon-Syria 123 E d
Sharr, Jebel el, Saudi Arabia 124 C d
Sharya, U.S.S.R. 117 G a
Shasi, China 131 F g
Shatra, Iraq 124 E c
Shatt-al-Arab, Iraq 124 E c
Shaubek, Jordan 123 D g
Shaunavon, Saskatchewan 86 J j
Shawanaga, Ontario 84 K g
Shawbridge, Quebec 85 Q g
Shawinigan, Quebec 85 S f
Shawville, Quebec 85 O g
Shchors, Ukraine, U.S.S.R. 116 G f
Shebandowan L., Ontario 87 M b
Shedden, Ontario 84 J k
Shediac, New Brunswick 82 H g
Sheelin L., Eire 99 C g
Sheenborough, Quebec 85 N g
Sheenjik R., Alaska 80 E f
Sheep Cr., Alberta 88 K d
Sheep Haven, Eire 98 B e
Sheerness, Alberta 86 F g
Sheerness, England 99 H j
Sheet Harbour, Nova Scotia 82 K j
Sheffield, England 99 G g
Sheguindah, Ontario 84 J g
Sheho, Saskatchewan 87 O g
Shehuen. See Chalia, R.
Sheikh, Jeb. esh (Mt. Hermon), Syria 123 D d
Sheikh 'Abd er Rahman. See Arka, Aden
Sheikh Miskin, Syria 123 E e
Sheikh 'Othman, Aden 124 E g
Sheik Seraq, Syria 123 F d
Shekak, R., Ontario 84 F c
Shekha, Aden 124 E f
Sheklung, China 131 F l
Shelburne, Nova Scotia 82 G k
Shelburne, Ontario 84 K h
Sheldrake, Quebec 82 H c
Shelekhova, Zaliv, U.S.S.R. 115 Q c
Shellbrook, Saskatchewan 86 L e
Shell Lake, Saskatchewan 86 K e
Shellmouth, Manitoba 87 Q h
Shelter Bay, Quebec 82 F c
Shenchow. See Yüanling
Shendam, Nigeria 119 G g
Shendi, Sudan 119 M e
Shëngjin, Albania 112 B d
Shenkursk, U.S.S.R. 114 D b
Shensi, prov., China 130 D e
Shenyang, China 130 L b
Sheopur, India 126 E c
Shepard, Alberta 86 D g
Shepard I., Antarctica 136 E d
Shepetovka, Ukraine, U.S.S.R. 116 E f
Sheppard, Mt., British Columbia 88 C b
Shepparton, Australia 135 J g
Sherada, Ethiopia 121 H c
Sherard, C., North-West Territories 81 L c
Sherard Osborn Fd., Greenland 89 P a
Sherbro I., Sierra Leone 118 C g
Sherbrooke, Nova Scotia 83 L c
Sherbrooke, Quebec 85 T g
Sherbrooke L., Nova Scotia 82 H j
Sher Dahan, Mt., India 126 C b
Sheridan, C., North-West Territories 81 N a
Sherridon, Manitoba 87 Q c
Sheslay, British Columbia 88 D a
Sheslay, R., British Columbia 88 D a
Shetland (Zetland), Is., Scotland 98 J a
Shevaroy Hills, India 126 E f
Shiant Is., Scotland 98 C c
Shibam, Aden 124 E f
Shibarghan, Afghanistan 125 J b
Shibata, Japan 133 F f
Shibetsi, Japan 133 J c
Shibin el Kom, Egypt 119 M b
Shichiyo Is., Truk Is. 78 D n
Shickshock Mts., Quebec 82 F e
Shiel, L., Scotland 98 D d
Shigatse, Tibet 127 G c
Shigawake, Quebec 82 G e
Shihnan. See Enshih
Shih Pao Shan, China 128 E e
Shihshow, China 131 F h
Shihtao, China 130 L d
Shihtsien, China 131 D j
Shikag L., Ontario 87 M a
Shikarpur, Pakistan 126 C c
Shiki Is., Truk Is. 78 E n
Shikoku, I., Japan 133 C h
Shilka & R., U.S.S.R. 115 L c
Shillelagh, Eire 99 C h
Shillington, Ontario 84 K d
Shillong, India 127 H c
Shilongol. See Silinhot
Shimoga, India 126 E f
Shimo Jima, Japan 133 A h
Shimoni, Kenya 121 H e
Shimonoseki, Japan 133 B g
Shin, L., Scotland 98 E b
Shinapaaru, I., Rota I. 78 A h
Shinas, Muscat & Oman 125 G e
Shingshal & Pass, Kashmir 126 E a
Shingu, Japan 133 D h
Shining Tree, Ontario 84 J e
Shinjo, Japan 133 G e
Shinshar, Syria 123 E c
Shinyanga, Tanganyika 121 G e
Ship Cove, Newfoundland 83 S f
Shipets. See Shibetsi
Shipman, Saskatchewan 87 N e
Shippegan & I., New Brunswick 82 H f
Shipshaw, R., Quebec 85 T d
Shipshaw Dam, Quebec 85 T d
Shiraishi, Japan 133 G f
Shiraz, Iran 125 F d
Shireza, Pakistan 126 C c
Shisur, Saudi Arabia 125 F f
Shiuchow. See Kukong
Shiuhing. See Koyiu
Shivpuri, India 126 E c
Shizugawa, Japan 133 G e
Shizuoka, Japan 133 F g
Shklov, Belorussia, U.S.S.R. 116 G d
Shkodër, Albania 112 B c
Shoal Harbour, Newfoundland 83 T e
Shoal L., Ontario 86 G a
Shoal Lake, Manitoba 87 R h
Shoal Ls., Manitoba 87 U h
Shoe Cove, Newfoundland 83 R d
Shoka. See Changhua
Sholapur, India 126 E e
Shonai. See Tsuruoka
Shonian Harb., Palau Is. 78 A o
Shortdale, Manitoba 87 R g
Shouldice, Alberta 86 E h
Shovo Tso, Tibet 127 F b
Shrewsbury, England 99 F h
Shropshire, co., England 99 F h
Shtora, Lebanon 123 D d
Shubenacadie, Nova Scotia 82 J h
Shubenacadie L., Nova Scotia 82 J j
Shuikow, China 131 J j
Shumaisa, Saudi Arabia 124 E e
Shumen. See Kolarovgrad
Shumerlya, U.S.S.R. 117 H c
Shunking. See Nanchung
Shunteh. See Singtai
Shuqra, Aden 124 E g
Shurab, Iran 125 G c
Shuri, I., Okinawa 78 A c
Shurma, Saudi Arabia 124 D e
Shuru Tso, Tibet 127 G b
Shusf, Iran 125 H c
Shushal, Kashmir 126 E b
Shushtar, Iran 124 E c
Shuswap L., British Columbia 88 K e
Shuya, U.S.S.R. 117 E b
Shuyang, China 130 J e
Shwebo, Burma 127 J d
Shwedaung, Burma 127 J e
Shwegyin, Burma 127 J e
Shweli R., Burma 127 J d
Shyok, India 126 E b
Sialkot, Pakistan 126 D b
Siam, G. of, See Thailand, G. of
Siam. See Thailand
Sian, China 130 D e
Siangtan, China 131 F j
Siangyang, China 130 F f
Siangyin, China 131 F h
Siapu, China 131 J j
Siargao, I., Philippines 129 J j
Siaton, Philippines 129 H j
Šiauliai, Lithuania, U.S.S.R. 103 K j
Sib, Muscat & Oman 125 G e
Sibbald, Alberta 86 G g
Sibenik, Yugoslavia 110 E d
Siberut, I., Indonesia 129 C l
Sibi, Pakistan 126 C c
Sibiu, Romania 112 E b
Sibley Prov. Park, Ontario 84 B d
Sibolga, Sumatra 129 C k
Sibsagar, India 127 H c
Sibu, Sarawak 129 F k
Sicasica, Bolivia 92 D g
Sichang, China 128 D e
Sicié, C., France 109 F e
Sicilia, I. See Sicily
Sicilian Chan., Mediterranean Sea 111 C g
Sicily (Sicilia), I., Italy 111 D g
Sickle L., Manitoba 87 R b
Sicuani, Peru 92 C f
Šid, Yugoslavia 112 B b
Sideby, Finland 103 J e
Siderno Marina, Italy 111 F f
Sidewood, Saskatchewan 86 H h
Sidhout, India 126 E f
Sidi Barrani, Egypt 119 L b
Sidi-bel-Abbès, Algeria 118 E a
Sidi Ifni, Ifni, North-West Africa 118 C c
Sidlaw Hills, Scotland 98 E d
Sidley, Mt., Antarctica 136 E c
Sidney, Manitoba 87 S j
Sidney, Vancouver I., British Columbia 88 H f
Sidon, Lebanon 123 D d
Sidri, G. of, Libya 119 J b
Siedlce, Poland 105 K b
Siegen, Germany 104 C c
Siem Reap, Cambodia 132 C d
Siena, Italy 110 C d
Sieradz, Poland 105 H c
Siero, Spain 106 C a
Sierra Colorada, Argentina 95 C f
Sierra Grande, Argentina 95 C f
Sierra Leone, W. Africa 118 C g
Sierra Madre, Mexico 90 C b
Sierra Mojada, Mexico 90 D b
Sierra Rosada, Argentina 95 C f
Sífnos, I., Greece 113 E f
Sifton, Manitoba 87 R g
Sifton Pass, Br. Columbia 88 F b
Sigean, France 109 E e
Sighet, Romania 105 K e
Sighisoara, Romania 112 E a
Siglufjördhur, Iceland 102 W l
Sigmaringen, Germany 104 C d
Sigsig, Ecuador 92 B d
Sigüenza, Spain 106 D b
Siguiri, Guinea 118 D f
Sigulda, Latvia, U.S.S.R. 103 L h
Sihl See, Switzerland 101 D a
Sihsien, China 131 J h
Siilinjärvi, Finland 102 M e
Sikanni Chief R., B.C. 88 H b
Sikar, India 126 E c

Sikasso, *Mali* 118 D f
Si Kiang, R., *China* 128 F f
Siking. *See* Sian
Sikinos, I., *Greece* 113 E f
Sikkim, *India* 127 G c
Silairsk, *U.S.S.R.* 117 N d
Silao, *Mexico* 90 D c
Silchar, *India* 127 H d
Silenen, *Switzerland* 101 D b
Silenrieux, *Belgium* 100 C d
Sil Garhi, *Nepal* 126 F c
Sili, I., *Manua Is.* 79 S o
Silifke, *Turkey* 124 B b
Silinhot, *China* 128 G b
Silistra, *Bulgaria* 112 F b
Siljan, L., *Sweden* 103 F f
Silkeborg, *Denmark* 103 C h
Sillery, dist., *Quebec* 85 S e
Silloth, *England* 98 E f
Sils, *Switzerland* 101 E b
Silsby L., *Manitoba* 87 W c
Silton, *Saskatchewan* 87 N h
Silvânia, *Brazil* 93 H g
Silvaplana, *Switzerland* 101 E b
Silva Porto, *Angola* 120 D g
Silver Centre, *Ontario* 85 L e
Silver Heights, *Alberta* 86 F f
Silver Islet, *Ontario* 84 B d
Silver Mt., *Newfoundland* 83 P d
Silver R., *Nova Scotia* 82 G j
Silver Star Prov. Park, *British Columbia* 88 K e
Silverthrone Mt., *British Columbia* 88 F e
Silves, *Brazil* 92 F d
Silves, *Portugal* 106 A d
Silvretta, Mts., *Austria-Switzerland* 104 C e
Simanggang, *Sarawak* 129 F k
Simard, L., *Quebec* 85 M e
Simcoe, *Ontario* 84 K k
Simcoe L., *Ontario* 85 L h
Simeulue, I., *Indonesia* 129 C k
Simferopol, *U.S.S.R.* 116 J j
Simi, I., *Greece* 113 F f
Simleul Silvaniei, *Romania* 105 K e
Simmie, *Saskatchewan* 86 J j
Simo, *Finland* 102 L d
Simö Järvi, L., *Finland* 102 M c
Simola, *Finland* 103 N f
Simonette, R., *Alberta* 88 K c
Simonhouse, *Manitoba* 87 Q d
Simon L., *Quebec* 85 P g
Simoom Sound, *British Columbia* 88 F e
Simpelveld, *Netherlands* 100 D d
Simplon & Pass, *Switzerland* 101 D b
Simpson, I., *Chile* 95 B g
Simpson, *Saskatchewan* 87 M g
Simpson Des., *Australia* 134 G e
Simpson I., *Ontario* 84 C d
Simpson Pen., *North-West Territories* 81 L d
Simuna, *Estonia, U.S.S.R.* 103 M g
Sinai, Pen., *Egypt* 119 M c
Sinaloa, state, *Mexico* 90 C b
Sinaloa & R., *Mexico* 90 C b
Sinamaica, *Venezuela* 92 C a
Sinbo, *Burma* 127 J d
Sinchang, *China* 131 K h
Sin-chow, *China* 130 G c
Sindel, *Bulgaria* 112 F c
Sindhi R., *India* 126 E c
Sind Sagar Doab, *Pakistan* 126 D b
Sines, *Portugal* 106 A d
Singa, *Sudan* 119 M f
Singapore, & Str., *South Asia* 132 C f
Singaradja, *Bali I., Indonesia* 129 G m
Singen, *Germany* 104 C e
Singida, *Tanganyika* 121 G e
Singitic G., *Greece* 113 D d
Singkawang, *Borneo* 129 E k
Singkep, I., *Riouw Arch., Indonesia* 129 D l
Singora. *See* Songkhla
Singsingsia, *China* 128 B b
Singtai, *China* 130 G d
Singtze, *China* 131 H h
Sinho, *China* 130 G d
Sinhsien, *China* 128 F c
Sinhwa, *China* 131 E j
Sining, *China* 128 D c
Siniscola, *Sardinia* 111 B e
Sinj, *Yugoslavia* 110 F d
Sinjar & Jebel, *Iraq* 124 D b
Sinjil, *Palestine* 123 D e
Sinkiang, *China* 114 H d
Sin-min-fu, *China* 130 L b
Sinnamary, *Fr. Guiana* 93 G b
Sinning, *China* 131 E j
Sinoe L., *Romania* 112 G b
Sinoia, *Southern Rhodesia* 122 E c
Sinop, *Turkey* 124 C a
Sintaluta, *Manitoba* 87 O h
Sintang, *Borneo* 129 F k
Sintra, *Portugal* 106 A c
Sinuiju, *Korea* 128 H b
Sinyang, *China* 128 F d
Sion, *Switzerland* 101 C b
Sioux Lookout, *Ontario* 86 L a
Siparia, *Trinidad* 92 E a
Sipiwesk, *Manitoba* 87 U c
Sipiwesk L., *Manitoba* 87 U c
Siple, Mt., *Antarctica* 136 E d
Sipolilo, *Southern Rhodesia* 122 E c
Sipora, I., *Indonesia* 129 C l
Siquisique, *Venezuela* 92 D a
Sira, *India* 126 E f
Sira. *See* Síros, I.
Siracusa. *See* Syracuse
Sirajganj, *E. Pakistan* 127 H d
Sir Alexander, Mt., *British Columbia* 88 J d
Sir Charles Hamilton Sd., *Newfoundland* 83 S d
Sir Douglas, Mt., *Alberta-British Columbia* 86 B h
Sir Edward Pellew Group, Is., *Australia* 134 G c
Siretul, R., *Romania* 112 F a
Siri, *Ethiopia* 121 H c
Sirjan, *Iran* 125 G d
Sirna, I., *Greece* 113 F f
Sironcha, *India* 126 F e
Sironj, *India* 126 E d
Síros, I., *Greece* 113 E f
Sirsa, *India* 126 D c
Sir Sanford, Mt., *British Columbia* 88 L e
Sirsi, *India* 126 D f
Sirte & G. of, *Libya* 119 J b
Sir Wilfred Laurier, Mt., *British Columbia* 88 K d
Sisak, *Yugoslavia* 110 F c
Sisaket, *Thailand* 132 C c
Sisal, *Mexico* 90 F c
Sisi, *Bechuanaland* 122 D d
Sisib L., *Manitoba* 87 S f
Sisipuk L., *Manitoba-Saskatchewan* 87 Q c
Sisopon, *Cambodia* 132 C d
Sisteron, *France* 109 F d
Sitamau, *India* 126 E d
Sitapur, *India* 126 F c
Sitara, *Saudi Arabia* 124 E e
Sithonia, *Greece* 113 D d
Sitía, *Crete* 113 F g
Sittang, *Burma* 127 J e
Sittang, R., *Burma* 127 J e
Sittard, *Netherlands* 100 D d
Sitten. *See* Sion
Si'ufaga, I., *Manua Is.* 79 S o
Siulagi Pt., *Manua Is.* 79 S o
Sivand, *Iran* 125 F d
Sivas, *Turkey* 124 C b
Siverek, *Turkey* 124 C b
Sivrihisar, *Turkey* 124 B b
Sivry, *Belgium* 100 C d
Siwa, *Egypt* 119 L c
Siwalik Hills, *India* 126 E b
Sjælland, *Denmark* 103 D j
Sjötorp, *Sweden* 103 E g
Skadarsko Jezero, *Yugoslavia-Albania* 112 B c
Skagafjörd, *Iceland* 102 W l
Skagens, *Denmark* 103 D h
Skagerrak, Chan., *Norway-Denmark* 103 B h
Skara, *Sweden* 103 E g
Skardu, *Kashmir* 126 E a
Skarnes, *Norway* 103 D f
Skead, *Ontario* 84 K d
Skead, *Ontario* 84 K f
Skeena, R., *Br. Columbia* 88 E c
Skeena Crossing, *British Columbia* 88 F c
Skeena Mts., *Br. Columbia* 88 E b
Skegness, *England* 99 H g
Skellefte Älv, *Sweden* 102 H d
Skellefteå, *Sweden* 102 J d
Skelton Glacier, *Antarctica* 136 A e
Skiathos, I., *Greece* 113 D e
Skibbereen, *Eire* 99 A j
Skidegate, *Graham I., British Columbia* 88 C d
Skien, *Norway* 103 C g
Skierniewice, *Poland* 105 J c
Skiff, *Alberta* 86 F j
Skiftet Kihti, *Finland* 103 J f
Skipton, *England* 99 F g
Skiros, I., *Greece* 113 E e
Skive, *Denmark* 103 C h
Skofja Loka, *Yugoslavia* 110 E b
Skookumchuk, *Br. Columbia* 88 M f
Skópelos, I., *Greece* 113 D e
Skopin, *U.S.S.R.* 116 L e
Skopje, *Yugoslavia* 112 C c
Skövde, *Sweden* 103 E g
Skovorodino, *U.S.S.R.* 115 M c
Skownan, *Manitoba* 87 S g
Skradin, *Yugoslavia* 110 E d
Skrunda, *Latvia, U.S.S.R.* 103 K h
Skudeneshavn, *Norway* 103 A g
Skuodas, *Lithuania, U.S.S.R.* 103 J h
Skye, I., *Scotland* 98 C c
Slagelse, *Denmark* 103 D j
Slamet, Mt., *Indonesia* 129 E m
Slaney R., *Eire* 99 C h
Slate Is., *Ontario* 84 D d
Slatina, *Romania* 112 E b
Slatina, *Yugoslavia* 112 A b
Slave L., Lesser, *Alberta* 86 B c
Slave Lake, *Alberta* 86 C c
Slåveni, *Romania* 112 E b
Slave R., Lesser, *Alberta* 86 C c
Slavgorod, *U.S.S.R.* 114 G c
Slavonia, *Yugoslavia* 112 A b
Slavonski Brod, *Yugoslavia* 112 A l
Slavyansk, *Ukraine, U.S.S.R.* 116 K g
Slea Hd., *Eire* 99 A h
Sleat, Sd. of, *Scotland* 98 D c
Sled L., *Saskatchewan* 86 K d
Sleeper Is., *North-West Territories* 81 L f
Slessor Glacier, *Antarctica* 136 K c
Sleydinge, *Belgium* 100 B c
Sliedrecht, *Netherlands* 100 C c
Slieve Aughty, Mts., *Eire* 99 B g
Slieve Bloom Mts., *Eire* 99 B g
Slieve Mish, Mts., *Eire* 99 A h
Sligo & co., *Eire* 99 B f
Sligo B., *Eire* 99 B f
Slite, *Sweden* 103 H h
Sliven, *Bulgaria* 112 F c
Slobodskoy, *U.S.S.R.* 117 K a
Slocan, *Br. Columbia* 88 L f
Slocan L., *Br. Columbia* 88 L f
Sloka, *Latvia, U.S.S.R.* 116 C d
Slonim, *Belorussia, U.S.S.R.* 116 D e
Sloten, *Netherlands* 100 D b
Slough, *England* 99 G j
Slovakia (Slovensko), reg., *Czechoslovakia* 105 H d
Slovenija, *Yugoslavia* 110 E c
Slovensko. *See* Slovakia
Sluis, *Netherlands* 100 B c
Sluiskil, *Netherlands* 100 B c
Slunj, *Yugoslavia* 110 E c
Słupsk, *Poland* 105 G a
Slussfors, *Sweden* 102 G d
Slutsk, *Belorussia, U.S.S.R.* 116 E e
Slyne Hd., *Eire* 99 A g
Slyudyanka, *U.S.S.R.* 115 K c
Small I., *Truk Is.* 78 F n
Small L., *Manitoba* 87 U a
Smeaton, *Saskatchewan* 86 N e
Smilde, *Netherlands* 100 E b
Smiley, *Saskatchewan* 86 H g
Smiltene, *Latvia, U.S.S.R.* 103 L h
Smith, *Alberta* 86 C c
Smith, I., *N.-W. Territories* 81 M e
Smith, I., *Quebec* 81 M e
Smith, I., *South Shetlands* 136 H f
Smith B., *N.-W. Territories* 81 M b
Smithers, *Br. Columbia* 88 E c
Smith Pt., *Nova Scotia* 82 J h
Smith Sd., *N.-W. Territories* 81 M b
Smiths Falls, *Ontario* 85 O h
Smithton, *Tasmania* 135 H h
Smoky C., *C. Breton I., Nova Scotia* 83 M g
Smoky Falls, *Ontario* 84 H b
Smoky Lake, *Alberta* 86 E d
Smoky R., *Alberta* 88 L c
Smoky R., Lit., *Alberta* 88 L c
Smöla, *Norway* 102 B e
Smolensk, *U.S.S.R.* 116 H d
Smooth Rock Falls, *Ontario* 84 J d
Smoothrock L., *Ontario* 84 A b
Smoothstone L., *Saskatchewan* 86 L d
Smoothstone R., *Saskatchewan* 86 L c
Smyley, C., *Antarctica* 136 H d
Smyrna (Izmir), *Turkey* 124 A b
Snaefell, *Isle of Man* 99 D f
Snare, L., *Saskatchewan* 88 Q a
Snåsa, *Norway* 102 E d
Snåsa Vatn, *Norway* 102 D d
Sneek, *Netherlands* 100 D a
Sneen, *Eire* 99 A j
Sneeuw Gebergte, Mts., *New Guinea* 129 L l
Snipe L., *Alberta* 86 A c
Snizort L., *Scotland* 98 C c
Snöhetta, Mt., *Norway* 102 C e
Snowden, *Saskatchewan* 87 N e
Snowdon, *Wales* 99 E g
Snowflake, *Manitoba* 87 T j
Snow Hill I., *Antarctica* 136 J f
Snow I., *Antarctica* 136 H f
Snow Lake, *Manitoba* 87 S d
Snow Road, *Ontario* 85 O h
Snowy Mts., *Australia* 135 J g
Soazza, *Switzerland* 101 E b
Sobakin, *U.S.S.R.* 117 J d
Sobinka, *U.S.S.R.* 116 M d
Sobrado, *Brazil* 93 G e
Sobral, *Brazil* 93 J d
Sobrance, *Czechoslovakia* 105 K d
Sochi, *U.S.S.R.* 117 C d
Society Is., *Pacific Ocean* 79 L j
Socorro, *Colombia* 92 C b
Socorro I., *Mexico* 90 B d
Socotra I., *Indian Ocean* 121 L b
Soc-trang, *S. Vietnam* 132 D e
Soda Creek, *Br. Columbia* 88 H d
Sodankylä, *Finland* 102 M c
Söderfors, *Sweden* 103 G f
Söderhamn, *Sweden* 103 G f
Söderköping, *Sweden* 103 G g
Södertälje, *Sweden* 103 G g
Sodiri, *Sudan* 119 L f
Soepiori, I., *New Guinea* 129 L l
Soest, *Germany* 104 C c
Soest, *Netherlands* 100 D b
Soeurs, I. des, *Quebec* 85 S k
Sofia (Sofiya), *Bulgaria* 112 D c
Sofiya. *See* Sofia
Sogamoso, *Colombia* 92 C b
Sogndal, *Norway* 103 B g
Sogne Fd., *Norway* 103 A f
Söğut, *Turkey* 124 B a
Sohag, *Egypt* 119 M c
Sohan R., *Pakistan* 126 D b
Sohar, *Muscat & Oman* 125 G e
Soheb, *Aden* 124 E g
Soignies, *Belgium* 100 C d
Soissons, *France* 108 E b
Soke, *England* 99 G h
Soke, *Turkey* 124 A b
Sok Gomba. *See* Pachen
Sok Karmalinsk, *U.S.S.R.* 117 L c
Sokode, *Togo* 118 F g
Sokol, *U.S.S.R.* 116 L b
Sokolo, *Mali* 118 D f
Sokoniya, I., *Okinawa* 78 C b
Sokota, *Ethiopia* 121 H b
Sokoto, *Nigeria* 118 F f
Solai, *Kenya* 121 H d
Solbad Hall, *Austria* 104 D e
Soledad, *Venezuela* 92 E b
Soledade, *Brazil* 92 D e
Solent, The, Chan., *England* 99 G k
Solenzara, *Corsica* 111 B e
Sol Iletsk, *U.S.S.R.* 114 E c
Solimões, R. *See* Amazonas
Solingen, *Germany* 104 B c
Sollefteå, *Sweden* 102 G e
Sollum. *See* Salûm
Solok, *Sumatra* 129 D l
Solomon Is., *Pacific Ocean* 78 G h
Solomon Sea, *Pacific Ocean* 135 K a
Solothurn & canton, *Switzerland* 101 C a
Solsona, *Spain* 107 F a
Solstad, *Norway* 102 D d
Soltau, *Germany* 104 C b
Solund, I., *Norway* 103 A f
Solway Firth, *England-Scotland* 98 E f
Solwezi, *N. Rhodesia* 120 F g
Soma, *Turkey* 124 A b
Somalia. *See* Somali Republic
Somali Republic (Somalia), *East Africa* 121 J d
Sombor, *Yugoslavia* 112 B b
Sombra, *Ontario* 84 H k
Sombreiro Chan., *Nicobar Is.* 127 H g
Sombrerete, *Mexico* 90 D c
Sombrero I., *Leeward Is.* 91 G c
Somcuța Mare, *Romania* 105 K e
Someren, *Netherlands* 100 D c
Somerset, *Australia* 135 H b
Somerset, co., *England* 99 E j
Somerset, *Manitoba* 87 T j
Somerset I., *North-West Territories* 81 K c
Somme, *Belgium* 100 D d
Somme, dep., *France* 108 E b
Somme, R., *France* 108 D a
Sommières, *France* 109 F e
Somoto, *Nicaragua* 91 B d
Somovit, *Bulgaria* 112 E c
Somzee, *Belgium* 100 C d
Sonaripur, *India* 127 G c
Sönderborg, *Denmark* 103 C j
Song-Cau, *S. Vietnam* 132 D d
Songea, *Tanganyika* 121 H g
Songkhla, *Thailand* 132 C e
Song-koi, R., *China, etc.* 132 C b
Sonkajärvi, *Finland* 102 M e
Sonkovo, *U.S.S.R.* 116 K c
Sonmiani, *Pakistan* 126 C c
Sonneberg, *Germany* 104 D c
Sonningdale, *Saskatchewan* 86 K f
Sonogno, *Switzerland* 101 D b
Sonora, *Nova Scotia* 83 L h
Sonora, state & R., *Mexico* 90 B b
Sonoyta, *Mexico* 90 B a
Sonpur, *India* 127 F d
Sonsón, *Colombia* 92 B b
Sonsorol Is., *Pacific Ocean* 78 D g
Soochow, *China* 130 K g
Sooke, *Br. Columbia* 88 H f
Soping. *See* Yuyu
Soppero, *Sweden* 102 J b
Sopron, *Hungary* 110 F b
Sop's Arm, *Newfoundland* 83 Q d
Sora, *Italy* 111 D e
Sorata, *Bolivia* 92 D g
Sorbas, *Spain* 107 D d
Sorel, *Quebec* 85 R f
Sorell, *Tasmania* 135 J h
Sörenberg, *Switzerland* 101 D b
Sörfold, *Norway* 102 F c
Sorgono, *Sardinia* 111 B e
Soria, *Spain* 107 D b
Soriano, *Uruguay* 94 E d
Sornico, *Switzerland* 101 D b
Sorocaba, *Brazil* 93 H h
Soroka, *U.S.S.R.* 117 L d
Soroki, *Moldavia, U.S.S.R.* 116 F g
Sorol, I., *Caroline Is.* 78 E f
Soromesis, *Bechuanaland* 122 C c
Soron, *India* 126 E c
Sororoca, *Brazil* 92 E c
Soroti, *Uganda* 121 G d
Söröya, I., *Norway* 102 K a
Sorrento, *Br. Columbia* 88 K e
Sorrento, *Italy* 111 E e
Sör-Rondane Mts., *Antarctica* 136 N d
Sorsele, *Sweden* 102 G d
Sortavala, *U.S.S.R.* 102 P f
Sosanjaya B., *Rota I.* 78 A j
Sosanlag B., *Rota I.* 78 A j
Sosnovka, *U.S.S.R.* 117 E d
Sosnovo, Ozerskoye, *U.S.S.R.* 115 L c
Sosnowiec, *Poland* 105 H c
Sosu, I., *Okinawa* 78 C a
Sosva, *U.S.S.R.* 114 F c
Soto la Marina, *Mexico* 90 E c
Sotra, I., *Norway* 103 A f
Sotuta, *Mexico* 90 G c
Souanke, *Congo* 120 C d
Soudan, *Australia* 134 G d
Souflíon, *Greece* 112 F d
Souillac, *France* 109 D d
Soulanges Can., *Quebec* 85 Q g
Sŏul. *See* Seoul
Sounding L., *Alberta* 86 G f
Soure, *Brazil* 93 H d
Soure, *Portugal* 106 A b
Souris, *Manitoba* 87 R j
Souris, *Prince Edward I.* 83 K g
Souris R., *Manitoba-North Dakota* 80 J h
Sousel, *Brazil* 93 G d
Sousse, *Tunisia* 119 H a
South Africa, Rep. of, *Africa* 122 C e
South America 92-95
Southampton, C., *N.-W. Terr.* 81 L e
Southampton, *England* 99 F k
Southampton, I., *N.-W. Terr.* 81 L e
Southampton, *Nova Scotia* 82 H h
Southampton, *Ontario* 84 J h
Southard, C., *Antarctica* 136 T e
South Aulatsivik I., *Labrador* 81 N f
South Australia, state, *Australia* 134 F e
South B., *Ontario* 84 J g
South Baymouth, *Ontario* 84 H g
South Brook, *Newfoundland* 83 Q d
South Brookfield, *Nova Scotia* 82 H j
South Chan., *Eniwetok* 79 S d
South China Sea, *Asia* 78 B f
South Downs, *England* 99 G k
South-East C., *Tasmania* 135 J h
Southeast Pass, *Jaluit I.* 79 U j
Southend, *England* 99 H j
Southend, *Saskatchewan* 88 S b
Southern Alps, *New Zealand* 135 Q l
Southern Cross, *Australia* 134 C f
Southern Harbour, *Newfoundland* 83 S f
Southern Rhodesia, *Central Africa* 122 D c
Southey, *Saskatchewan* 87 N h
South Fork, *Saskatchewan* 86 J j
South Georgia, I., *Atlantic Ocean* 136 K g
South Harbour, *Cape Breton I., Nova Scotia* 83 M g
South Henik L., *N.-W. Terr.* 81 K e
South I., *New Zealand* 135 Q m
South Indian Lake, *Manitoba* 87 T b
South Inlet, *Antarctica* 136 B d
South Junction, *Manitoba* 86 F a
South Lochaber, *Nova Scotia* 83 K h
South Nelson, *New Brunswick* 82 G g
South Orkneys, Is., *Atlantic Ocean* 136 J f
South Pass, *Truk Is.* 78 E o
South Polar Plateau, *Antarctica* 136 C a
South Pole, *Antarctica* 136 A a
South Porcupine, *Ontario* 84 J d
Southport, *Australia* 135 K e
Southport, *England* 99 E g
South Pt., *Anticosti I., Quebec* 83 K d
South Pt., *Jaluit I.* 79 U j
South River, *Ontario* 85 L g
South Ronaldsay I., *Orkney Is.* 98 F b
South Sask. Dam, *Sask.* 86 L g
South Seal R., *Manitoba* 87 S a
South Shetland Is., *Antarc.* 136 H f
South Shields, *England* 98 G f
Southside, *Canton I.* 79 S n
South Slocan, *Br. Columbia* 88 L f
South Taranari Bight, *New Zealand* 135 R k
South West Africa, *Southern Africa* 122 B d
Southwest C., *Madeleine Is., Quebec* 83 L f
South West C., *Tasmania* 135 J h
South Westminster, *British Columbia* 88 E g
Southwest Pass, *Jaluit I.* 79 T j
Southwest Passage, *Eniwetok* 79 R c
Southwest Pt., *Anticosti I., Quebec* 82 J a
Southwold, *England* 99 J h
Souza, *Brazil* 93 K e
Souzel, *Portugal* 106 B c
Sovereign, *Saskatchewan* 86 K g
Sovetsk, *U.S.S.R.* 103 J j
Sovetskaya Gavan, *U.S.S.R.* 115 P d
Sovietsk, *U.S.S.R.* 117 J b
Soviet Union (U.S.S.R.), *Europe-Asia* 114-115
Sowden L., *Ontario* 87 M a
Soy, *Kenya* 121 H d
Soya & B., *Japan* 133 G b
Soya Misaki, *Japan* 133 H b
Soya Str., *Japan* 133 G b
Soyopa, *Mexico* 90 C b
Spa, *Belgium* 100 D d
Spain, *W. Europe* 106-107
Spalato. *See* Split
Spalding, *England* 99 G h
Spalding, *Saskatchewan* 87 N f
Spandau, *Germany* 104 E b
Spaniard's Bay, *Nfd.* 83 T f
Spanish, *Ontario* 84 H f
Spanish R., *Ontario* 84 J f
Spanish Sahara, *W. Africa* 118 C c
Spanish Town, *Jamaica* 91 D c
Sparta, *Greece* 113 D f
Sparti. *See* Sparta
Spartivento, C., *Italy* 111 F g
Spassk, *U.S.S.R.* 117 F d
Spassk Dalniy, *U.S.S.R.* 118 K b
Spassk-Ryszanskiy, *U.S.S.R.* 117 E c
Spearhill, *Manitoba* 87 T g
Spedden, *Alberta* 86 F d
Speers, *Saskatchewan* 86 K f
Spence Bay, *N.-W. Terr.* 81 K d
Spencer G., *Australia* 134 G f
Spences Bridge, *British Columbia* 88 J e
Sperling, *Manitoba* 87 U j
Sperrin Mts., *N. Ireland* 99 C f
Spétsai I., *Greece* 113 D f
Speyer, *Germany* 104 C d
Spey R., *Scotland* 98 E c
Spezand, *Pakistan* 126 C b
Spinazzola, *Italy* 111 F e
Spiringen, *Switzerland* 101 D b
Spirit River, *Alberta* 88 K c
Spiritwood, *Saskatchewan* 86 K e
Spitsbergen, *Arctic Ocean* 114 A a
Spitsbergen, Vest, *Arctic Oc.* 114 A a
Spittal, *Austria* 104 E e
Split, C., *Nova Scotia* 82 H h
Split, *Yugoslavia* 110 F d
Split L., *Manitoba* 87 V b
Split Lake, *Manitoba* 87 V b
Splügen, Pass, *Switz.-Italy* 101 E b
Splügen, *Switzerland* 101 E b
Spoleto, *Italy* 110 D d
Spondin, *Alberta* 86 F g
Spontin, *Belgium* 100 C d
Sporadhes, Is., *Aegean Sea* 113 F f
Sporadhes, Voriai, Is., *Aegean Sea* 113 E e
Spragge, *Ontario* 84 H f
Sprague, *Manitoba* 86 F a
Spree, R., *Germany* 104 E b
Spremberg, *Germany* 104 F c
Sprimont, *Belgium* 100 D d
Springbok, *South Africa* 122 B e
Springburn, *Alberta* 88 L c
Spring Coulee, *Alberta* 86 D j
Springdale, *Newfoundland* 83 Q d
Springer, Mt., *Quebec* 85 Q c
Springfield, *New Brunswick* 82 G h
Springfield, *Nova Scotia* 82 H j
Springfield, *Ontario* 84 K k
Springfontein, *South Africa* 122 D f
Springhill, *Nova Scotia* 82 H h
Springhill, *Quebec* 82 A h
Springside, *Saskatchewan* 87 P g
Springsure, *Australia* 135 J d
Spring Valley, *Saskatchewan* 87 M j
Springwater, *Saskatchewan* 86 J g
Spruce Brook, *Nfd.* 83 O e
Sprucedale, *Ontario* 85 L g
Spruce Lake, *Saskatchewan* 86 H e
Spruga, *Switzerland* 101 D b
Spurfield, *Alberta* 86 C c
Spy Hill, *Saskatchewan* 87 Q h
Squamish, *Br. Columbia* 88 H f
Squattack, *Quebec* 82 D f
Squaw L., *Quebec* 83 L c
Squillace, G. di, *Italy* 111 F f
Srbija (Serbia), *Yugoslavia* 112 C c
Srebrenica, *Yugoslavia* 112 B b
Sredinnyy, Khrebet, Mts., *U.S.S.R.* 115 R c
Sredne Kamchatsk, *U.S.S.R.* 115 R c
Sredne Kolymak, *U.S.S.R.* 115 Q b
Sredne Vilyuysk, *U.S.S.R.* 115 M b
Śrem, *Poland* 105 G b
Srepok, *Cambodia* 132 D d
Sretensk, *U.S.S.R.* 115 L c
Srikakulam, *India* 127 F e
Sri Kolayatji, *India* 126 D c
Srinagar, *Kashmir* 126 D b
Srirangapatnar, *India* 126 E f
Srivilliputtur, *India* 126 E g
Srnetica, *Yugoslavia* 110 F c
Środa, *Poland* 105 G b
Stackpool, *Ontario* 84 J e
Staden, *Belgium* 100 A d
Staffa I., *Scotland* 98 C d
Stafford & co., *England* 99 F h
Stalingrad. *See* Volgograd
Stalin Mt., *Br. Columbia* 88 G a
Stallworthy, C., *N.-W. Terr.* 81 K a
Stalwart, *Saskatchewan* 87 M g
Stamprooi, *Netherlands* 100 D c
Stanchik, *U.S.S.R.* 115 Q a
Standard, *Alberta* 86 E g
Standerton, *South Africa* 122 D e
Stange, *Norway* 103 D f
Stanislav, *Ukraine, U.S.S.R.* 116 D g
Stanley, *Falkland Is.* 95 E h
Stanley, *New Brunswick* 82 F g
Stanley Falls, *Congo* 120 F d
Stanley Mission, *Saskatchewan* 87 N c
Stanleyville, *Congo* 120 F d
Stanmore, *Alberta* 86 F g
Stann Creek, *Brit. Honduras* 91 B c
Stanovoy Khrebet, Mts., *U.S.S.R.* 115 M c
Stans, *Switzerland* 101 D b
Stansmore Ra., *Australia* 134 E d
Stanthorpe, *Australia* 135 K e
Staphorst, *Netherlands* 100 E b
Starachowice, *Poland* 105 J c
Stara Planina, *Bulgaria* 112 E c
Staraya Russa, *U.S.S.R.* 116 G c
Stara Zagora, *Bulgaria* 112 E c
Starbuck, I., *Pacific Ocean* 79 L h
Starbuck, *Manitoba* 87 U j
Star City, *Saskatchewan* 87 N f
Stargard, *Poland* 104 F b

Taoan, *China* 128 H a
Taochow. See Kadiger
Taofu, *China* 128 D d
Taongi, I., *Marshall Is.* 78 G f
Taormina, *Sicily* 111 E g
Tapa, *Estonia, U.S.S.R.* 103 L g
Tapachula, *Mexico* 90 F e
Tapah, *Malaya* 132 C f
Tapajós, R., *Brazil* 93 F d
Tapak, I., *Ponape I.* 78 G n
Tapalque, *Argentina* 94 D e
Tapan, *Sumatra* 129 D l
Tapanui, *New Zealand* 135 P m
Tapa Shan, *China* 130 D f
Tapauá, *Brazil* 92 E e
Taplang Dzong, *Nepal* 127 G c
Tapti R., *India* 126 E d
Tapuaenuku, Mt., *New Zealand* 135 Q l
Taputimu, I., *Tutuila I.* 79 T o
Taqa, *Muscat & Oman* 125 F f
Taquara, *Brazil* 94 F c
Taquaritinga, *Brazil* 93 K e
Tara, *Ontario* 84 J h
Tara, *U.S.S.R.* 114 G c
Taradale, *New Zealand* 135 R k
Tarahumare, Sa., *Mexico* 90 C b
Tarakan, *Borneo* 129 G k
Tarakli, *Turkey* 124 B a
Taranaki Bight, N., *New Zealand* 135 R k
Taranaki Bight, S., *New Zealand* 135 R k
Tarancón, *Spain* 106 D b
Taranto, G. di, *Italy* 111 F f
Taranto, *Italy* 111 F e
Tarapoto, *Peru* 92 B e
Taraqua, *Brazil* 92 D d
Tararua Ra., *New Zealand* 135 R l
Tarascon, *France* 109 D e
Tarasp, *Switzerland* 101 F b
Tarata, *Peru* 92 C g
Tarauaca, *Brazil* 92 C e
Tarawa, I., *Gilbert Is.* 78 H g
Tarawera, *New Zealand* 135 R k
Tarazona, *Spain* 107 E b
Tarazona de la Mancha, *Spain* 107 E c
Tarbagatai Khrebet, *Kazakh., U.S.S.R.* 114 H d
Tarbat Ness, *Scotland* 98 E c
Tarbert, *Scotland* 98 D e
Tarbert, *Scotland* 98 C c
Tarbes, *France* 109 D e
Tarchan, *Tibet* 126 F b
Tarcoola, *Australia* 134 F f
Taree, *Australia* 135 K f
Tärendö, *Sweden* 102 K c
Târgu Jiu, *Romania* 112 D b
Târgul Lapusul, *Romania* 105 K e
Târgul Ocna, *Romania* 112 F a
Târgu Mureş, *Romania* 112 E a
Tarija, *Bolivia* 92 E h
Tarik, I., *Truk Is.* 78 E o
Tarim, *Saudi Arabia* 124 E f
Tarlac, *Philippines* 129 H h
Tarma, *Peru* 92 B f
Tarn, dep. & R., *France* 109 E e
Tärna, *Sweden* 102 F d
Tarn-et-Garonne, dep., *Fr.* 109 D d
Tarnobrzeg, *Poland* 105 J c
Tarnopol, *Saskatchewan* 87 M f
Tarnów, *Poland* 105 J c
Tarnowskie Gory, *Poland* 105 H c
Tarnu Măgurele, *Romania* 112 E c
Taroom, *Australia* 135 J e
Taroudant, *Morocco* 118 D b
Tarragona, *Spain* 107 F b
Tarrega, *Spain* 107 F b
Tarsale, *U.S.S.R.* 114 G b
Tarso Muri, Mt. See Kegueur Tedi
Tarsus, *Turkey* 124 B b
Tartagal, *Argentina* 92 E h
Tartas, *France* 109 C e
Tartu, *Estonia, U.S.S.R.* 103 M g
Tartus, *Syria* 123 D c
Tarum, *Iran* 125 G d
Tarzwell, *Ontario* 84 K d
Taschereau, *Quebec* 85 M d
Taseevo, *U.S.S.R.* 115 J c
Taseko, Mt., *Br. Columbia* 88 H e
Taseko, R., *Br. Columbia* 88 H e
Tashi Bhup Tso, *Tibet* 127 F b
Tashihto, *China* 128 B b
Tashkent, *Uzbek., U.S.S.R.* 114 F d
Tashkurghan, *Afghanistan* 125 J b
Tashota, *Ontario* 84 C b
Tasil, *Syria* 123 D e
Taskan, *U.S.S.R.* 115 Q b
Tasman, Mt., *New Zealand* 135 Q l
Tasman B., *New Zealand* 135 Q l
Tasmania, I. & state, *Australia* 135 J h
Tasman Mts., *New Zealand* 135 Q l
Tasman Sea, *New Zealand, etc.* 78 G l
Tassgong, *Bhutan* 127 H c
Tast, L. du, *Quebec* 85 N a
Tata, *Hungary* 105 H e
Tataacho Pt., *Rota I.* 78 A h
Tatamagouche, *Nova Scotia* 82 J h
Tatarsk, *Iran* 114 G c
Tatarskaya, *U.S.S.R.* 114 E c
Tatarskiy Proliv, *U.S.S.R.* 115 P d
Tate, *Saskatchewan* 87 N g
Tating, *China* 131 B j
Tatla L., *Br. Columbia* 88 G e
Tatlayoko Lake, *British Columbia* 88 G e
Tatlow, Mt., *Br. Columbia* 88 H e
Tatnam, C., *Manitoba* 81 K f
Tatranská Lomnica, *Czechoslovakia* 105 J d
Tatry, Mts., *Poland-Czech.* 105 H d
Tatta, *Pakistan* 126 C d
Tatu, R., *China* 128 D d
Tatuhí, *Brazil* 93 H h
Tatung, *China* 130 F b
Tatung Ho, R., *China* 128 D c
Ta'u, I., *Manua Is.* 79 S o
Tauá, *Brazil* 93 J e
Tauak Pass, *Ponape I.* 78 F o
Taualap Pass, *Truk Is.* 78 D n
Tauapeçaçú, *Brazil* 92 E d
Taubaté, *Brazil* 93 H h
Taulaga, I., *Swains I.* 79 Q o
Taumarunui, *New Zealand* 135 R k
Taungdwingyi, *Burma* 127 J d
Taung-gyi, *Burma* 127 J d
Taungup, *Burma* 127 H e
Taunton, *England* 99 E k
Taunus, Mts., *Germany* 104 C c
Taupo & L., *New Zealand* 135 R k
Tauragé, *Lithuania, U.S.S.R.* 103 K j
Tauranga & Harb., *New Zealand* 135 R k
Taureau L., *Quebec* 85 R f
Tauroa Pt., *New Zealand* 135 Q j
Tauste, *Spain* 107 E b
Tauysk, *U.S.S.R.* 115 P c
Tavani, *N.-W. Territories* 81 K e
Tavda, *U.S.S.R.* 114 F c
Taverne, *Switzerland* 101 D b
Taverner B., *N.-W. Terr.* 81 M d
Tavistock, *England* 99 E k
Tavistock, *Ontario* 84 K j
Tavolara, I., *Sardinia* 111 B e
Tävoy & R., *Burma* 127 J f
Tävoy I., *Burma* 127 J f
Tavrichanka, *U.S.S.R.* 117 B c
Tavsanli, *Turkey* 124 A b
Tawang, *India* 127 H c
Tawatinaw & R., *Alberta* 86 D d
Tawau, *N. Borneo* 129 G k
Tawitawi, I., *Philippines* 129 H j
Taxco, *Mexico* 90 E d
Tay, Firth of & R., *Scotland* 98 E d
Tayga, *U.S.S.R.* 114 H c
Tay L., *Scotland* 98 E d
Taylor, *Br. Columbia* 88 J b
Taymouth, *New Brunswick* 82 F g
Taymyr, Ozero, *U.S.S.R.* 115 K a
Taytay, *Philippines* 129 G h
Tayü, *China* 131 G k
Tayung, *China* 131 E h
Taza, *Morocco* 118 E b
Tazovskaya G., *U.S.S.R.* 114 G b
Tazovskoye, *U.S.S.R.* 114 G b
Tbilisi, *U.S.S.R.* 114 D d
Tchad. See Chad
Tchad, L. See Chad, L.
Tchaourou, *Dahomey* 118 F g
Tczew, *Poland* 105 H a
Te Anau, L., *New Zealand* 135 P m
Teano Ra., *Australia* 134 C d
Teapa, *Mexico* 90 F d
Te Aroha, *New Zealand* 135 R k
Tea Tree, *Australia* 134 F d
Te Awamutu, *New Zealand* 135 R k
Teboursouk, *Tunisia* 119 G a
Tebyulyakh, *U.S.S.R.* 115 P b
Tecamachalco, *Mexico* 90 E d
Tecka & R., *Argentina* 95 B f
Tecolutla, *Mexico* 90 E c
Tecpan, *Mexico* 90 D d
Tecumseh, *Ontario* 84 H k
Tedzhen, *Turkmen., U.S.S.R.* 114 F e
Teema, I., *Okinawa* 78 B b
Tees, *Alberta* 86 D f
Tees, R., *England* 99 G f
Teeswater, *Ontario* 84 J j
Tefé, *Brazil* 92 E d
Tegerhi, *Libya* 119 H d
Tegucigalpa, *Honduras* 91 B d
Tehchow, *China* 130 H d
Tehek L., *N.-W. Territories* 81 K d
Teheran. See Tehran
Tehran, *Iran* 125 F b
Tehri, *India* 126 E b
Tehsien. See Tehchow
Tehuacán, *Mexico* 90 E d
Tehuantepec, G. of, *Mexico* 90 E d
Tehuantepec, Isthmus of, *Mexico* 90 E d
Tehuantepec, *Mexico* 90 E d
Teian, See Anlu
Teifi R., *Wales* 99 E h
Teign R., *England* 99 E k
Tekapo, L., *New Zealand* 135 Q l
Tekirdağ, *Turkey* 124 A a
Te Kuiti, *New Zealand* 135 R k
Tela, *Honduras* 91 B c
Tel Aviv, *Israel* 123 C e
Telegraph Creek, *British Columbia* 88 H g
Telen, *Argentina* 94 C e
Telkalakh, *Syria* 123 E c
Telkwa, *Br. Columbia* 88 F c
Tell Bise, *Syria* 123 E c
Tellicherry, *India* 126 E f
Tellier, *Quebec* 82 F c
Telok Anson, *Malaya* 132 C f
Teloloapan, *Mexico* 90 E d
Telpos-iz, *U.S.S.R.* 114 E b
Telsen, *Argentina* 95 C f
Telshyay, *Lithuania, U.S.S.R.* 103 K j
Teltaka, *Ontario* 84 E c
Telukbetung, *Sumatra* 129 E m
Tembeling, *Malaya* 132 C f
Temblador, *Venezuela* 92 E b
Temesvar. See Timisoara
Temir, *Kazakh., U.S.S.R.* 114 E d
Temir Tau, *U.S.S.R.* 114 H c
Temiscamie L., *Quebec* 82 A b
Temiscamie R., *Quebec* 82 A b
Temiscouata, L., *Quebec* 82 D f
Témiskaming, *Quebec* 85 L f
Temnikov, *U.S.S.R.* 117 F c
Temosachic, *Mexico* 90 C b
Tempio, *Sardinia* 111 B e
Temta, *U.S.S.R.* 111 G b
Temuco, *Chile* 95 B e
Tenanzingo, *Mexico* 90 E d
Tenasique, *Mexico* 90 F d
Tenasserim, *Burma* 127 J f
Tenasserim R., *Burma* 127 J f
Tenby, *Wales* 99 D j
Tenby Bay, *Ontario* 84 G f
Ten Degrees Chan., *Andaman Is.* 127 H g
Tenerife, I., *Canary Is.* 118 B c
Ténès, *Algeria* 118 F a
Tengchow. See Penglai
Tengiz, Oz., *Kazakh., U.S.S.R.* 114 F c
Tenke, *Congo* 120 F g
Ten Mile L., *Newfoundland* 83 Q b
Tennant's Creek, *Australia* 134 F c
Tenterfield, *Australia* 135 K e
Teocaltiche, *Mexico* 90 D c
Teophilo Otoni, *Brazil* 93 J g
Tepatitlán, *Mexico* 90 D c
Tepehuanes, *Mexico* 90 C b
Tepelene, *Albania* 113 C d
Tepic, *Mexico* 90 D c
Teramo, *Italy* 110 D d
Ter Apel, *Netherlands* 100 E b
Terban, Jebel, *Saudi Arabia* 124 D f
Terborg, *Netherlands* 100 E c
Terence, *Manitoba* 87 R f
Teresina, *Brazil* 93 J e
Teressa, I., *Nicobar Is.* 127 H g
Terezin, *Czechoslovakia* 104 F c
Teri Nam Tso, *Tibet* 127 G b
Termez, *Uzbek., U.S.S.R.* 114 F e
Termini Imerese, *Sicily* 111 D f
Termoli, *Italy* 111 E e
Termonde, *Belgium* 100 C c
Ternate, *Halmahera I.* 129 J k
Terneuzen, *Netherlands* 100 B c
Terni, *Italy* 110 D d
Ternopol, *Ukraine, U.S.S.R.* 116 D g
Terpeniya, C., *U.S.S.R.* 115 P d
Terrace, *Br. Columbia* 88 E c
Terrace Bay, *Ontario* 84 C d
Terracina, *Italy* 111 D e
Terralba, *Sardinia* 111 B f
Terra Nova & R., *Nfd.* 83 S e
Terra Nova B., *Antarctica* 136 B c
Terra Santa, *Brazil* 93 F d
Terrebonne, *Quebec* 85 R g
Terrence Bay, *Nova Scotia* 82 J j
Terrenceville, *Newfoundland* 83 S f
Terror Mt., *Antarctica* 136 B c
Terschelling I., *Netherlands* 100 D a
Teruel, *Spain* 107 E b
Tervola, *Finland* 102 L c
Tervueren, *Belgium* 100 C d
Tesecau L., *Quebec* 85 P a
Teshio, *Japan* 133 H b
Teslin, *Yukon* 77 V f
Tessaoua, *Niger* 118 G f
Tessenderloo, *Belgium* 100 D c
Tessier, *Saskatchewan* 86 K g
Tetachuck L., *Br. Columbia* 89 G d
Tetagouche R., *New Brunswick* 82 F f
Tetas, Pta., *Chile* 94 B b
Tete, *Mozambique* 122 E c
Tête à la Baleine, *Quebec* 83 N c
Tetreauville, *Quebec* 85 S h
Tetuan, *Morocco* 118 D a
Tetyukhe, *U.S.S.R.* 115 N d
Tetyushi, *U.S.S.R.* 117 J c
Teulada, *Sardinia* 111 B f
Teulada C., *Sardinia* 111 B f
Teulon, *Manitoba* 87 U h
Teutoburger Wald, *Germany* 104 B b
Tevere. See Tiber
Teviot R., *Scotland* 98 F e
Tevriz, *U.S.S.R.* 114 G c
Te Waewae B., *New Zealand* 135 P m
Texada I., *Br. Columbia* 88 G f
Texcoco, *Mexico* 90 E d
Texel I., *Netherlands* 100 C a
Tezpur, *India* 127 H c
Thachap Kangri, *Tibet* 127 F b
Thadiq, *Saudi Arabia* 124 E d
Thailand, G. of, *S.-E. Asia* 132 C c
Thailand (Siam), *S.-E. Asia* 132 C c
Thakhek, *Laos* 132 C c
Thal, *Pakistan* 126 D b
Thale Sap, L., *Thailand* 132 C d
Thalkirch, *Switzerland* 101 E b
Thames, Firth of, *New Zealand* 135 R k
Thames, *New Zealand* 135 R k
Thames, R., *England* 99 H j
Thames, R., *Ontario* 84 H k
Thamesville, *Ontario* 84 J k
Thana, *India* 126 D e
Thanh-hoa, *N. Vietnam* 132 D c
Thanjavur, *India* 126 E f
Thann, *France* 108 G c
Thar Des., *India* 126 D c
Thargomindah, *Australia* 135 H e
Tharrawaddy, *Burma* 127 J e
Tharsis, *Spain* 106 B d
Thásos, I., *Greece* 113 E d
Thásos Str., *Greece* 113 E d
Thaton, *Burma* 127 J e
Thaungdut, *Burma* 127 H d
Thayetmyo, *Burma* 127 H e
Thazi, *Burma* 127 J d
Thedford, *Ontario* 84 J j
Theodore, *Australia* 135 K e
Theodore, *Saskatchewan* 87 P g
Therien, *Alberta* 86 F d
Thérmai, G. of, *Greece* 113 D d
Thermiá. See Kithnos, I.
Thermopylae, *Greece* 113 D e
Theron Mts., *Antarctica* 136 K c
Thesiger B., *N.-W. Terr.* 80 G c
Thesprotía, *Greece* 113 C e
Thessalía, *Greece* 113 D e
Thessalon, *Ontario* 84 G f
Thessaloníki, *Greece* 113 D d
Thetford, *England* 99 H h
Thetford Mines, *Quebec* 85 T f
Theux, *Belgium* 100 D d
Thicket Portage, *Manitoba* 87 U c
Thickwood Hills, *Alberta* 86 E b
Thiel Mts., *Antarctica* 136 G a
Thielt, *Belgium* 100 B c
Thiers, *France* 108 E d
Thiès, *Senegal* 118 B f
Thingvalla vatn, *Iceland* 102 V m
Thio, *Eritrea* 121 J b
Thionville, *France* 108 G b
Thíra, I., *Greece* 113 E f
Thirsk, *England* 99 G f
Thirty Thousand Is., *Ont.* 84 K g
Thisted, *Denmark* 103 C h
Thistilfjord, *Iceland* 102 Y l
Thityabin, *Burma* 127 J d
Thiviers, *France* 108 D d
Thjórsá, R., *Iceland* 102 W m
Thok Jalung, *Tibet* 126 F b
Thomastown, *Eire* 99 C h
Thom Bay, *N.-W. Territories* 80 K c
Thompson, *Manitoba* 87 U c
Thompson R., *Br. Columbia* 88 J e
Thomson R., *Australia* 135 H d
Thongwa, *Burma* 127 J e
Thorburn, *Nova Scotia* 83 K h
Thorhild, *Alberta* 86 D d
Thorn. See Torun
Thornbury, *Ontario* 84 K h
Thorndale, *Ontario* 84 J j
Thorne Glacier, *Antarctica* 136 D a
Thornhill, *Ontario* 85 L j
Thornhill, *Scotland* 98 E e
Thorold, *Ontario* 85 L j
Thorsby, *Alberta* 86 C e
Thorshavn, *Faeroe Is.* 96 F c
Thórshöfn, *Iceland* 102 Y l
Thorsteinson, L., *Manitoba* 87 U a
Thorvard Nilsen Mts., *Antarctica* 136 C a
Thouars, *France* 108 C c
Thourout, *Belgium* 100 B c
Thraki, Dhitiki, *Greece* 112 E d
Three Hills, *Alberta* 86 D g
Three Kings Is., *New Zealand* 135 Q j
Threepoint L., *Manitoba* 87 T c
Three Points C., *Ghana* 118 E h
Three Rivers. See Trois Rivières
Three Rock Cove, *Nfd.* 83 N e
Throssel Ra., *Australia* 134 D d
Thueyts, *France* 109 F d
Thuin, *Belgium* 100 C d
Thule, *Greenland* 81 N b
Thule, I., *Antarctica* 136 K g
Thun, *Switzerland* 101 C b
Thunder B., *Ontario* 87 O b
Thunderhouse Falls, *Ont.* 84 G b
Thuner See, *Switzerland* 101 C b
Thur, R., *Switzerland* 101 D a
Thurgau, canton, *Switz.* 101 D a
Thüringer Wald, *Germany* 104 D c
Thurles, *Eire* 99 B h
Thursday I., *Australia* 135 H b
Thurso, *Quebec* 85 P g
Thurso, *Scotland* 98 E b
Thurston I., *Antarctica* 136 F d
Thusis, *Switzerland* 101 E b
Thutade L., *Br. Columbia* 88 F b
Tiaret, *Algeria* 118 F a
Tiassale, *Ivory Coast* 118 D g
Tibati, *Cameroon* 119 H g
Tiber, R., *Italy* 110 D d
Tiberias & L., *Israel* 123 D e
Tibet, *S. Asia* 127 G b
Tiblemont, *Quebec* 84 N d
Tiburon, *Haiti* 91 E c
Tiburón, I., *Mexico* 90 B b
Tichborne, *Ontario* 85 O h
Tichfield, *Saskatchewan* 86 K g
Ticino, canton, *Switzerland* 101 D b
Ticul, *Mexico* 90 G c
Tide Head, *New Brunswick* 82 F f
Tide L., *Alberta* 86 F h
Tidjikja, *Mauritania* 118 C e
Tidnish, *Nova Scotia* 82 J h
Tiébissou, *Ivory Coast* 118 D g
Tiefencastel, *Switzerland* 101 E b
Tieh-ling, *China* 130 L a
Tiel, *Netherlands* 100 D c
Tielt, *Belgium* 100 B c
Tien Chih, *China* 128 D f
Tien-ching. See Tientsin
Tien-chwang-tai, *China* 130 K b
Tienen. See Tirlemont
Tienpao, *China* 131 C l
Tienpaoshan, *China* 130 H b
Tienshai, *China* 130 B e
Tien Shan, *Central Asia* 114 G d
Tiensha Pass, *China* 130 C e
Tienshui, *China* 128 E d
Tientsin, *China* 130 H c
Tiermas, *Spain* 107 E a
Tierra del Fuego, *Chile-Argentina* 95 C h
Tigăneşti, *Romania* 112 F b
Tighina. See Bendery
Tigil, *U.S.S.R.* 115 Q c
Tignish, *Prince Edward I.* 82 H g
Tigris, R., *Iraq* 124 E c
Tijoca, *Brazil* 93 H d
Tika, *Quebec* 82 G c
Tikhvin, *U.S.S.R.* 116 H b
Tikrit, *Iraq* 124 D c
Tiksi, *U.S.S.R.* 115 M a
Tilburg, *Netherlands* 100 D c
Tilbury, *England* 99 H j
Tilbury, *Ontario* 84 H k
Tilbury I., *Br. Columbia* 88 D g
Tilcara, *Argentina* 94 C b
Tilichiki, *U.S.S.R.* 115 R b
Tillangchong I., *Nicobar Is.* 127 H g
Tilley, *Alberta* 86 F h
Tillsonburg, *Ontario* 84 K k
Tílos, I., *Greece* 113 F f
Tilsit. See Sovetsk
Tilston, *Manitoba* 87 Q j
Tilting, *Newfoundland* 83 S d
Timagami, *Ontario* 85 L e
Timagami L., *Ontario* 84 K f
Timanski Kryazh, *U.S.S.R.* 114 E b
Timaru, *New Zealand* 135 Q m
Timashevo, *U.S.S.R.* 117 K d
Timbuktu (Tombouctou), *Mali* 118 E e
Timiskaming, L., *Que.-Ont.* 85 L e
Timisoara, *Romania* 112 C b
Timmins, *Ontario* 84 J d
Timoneng, I., *Guam* 78 B k
Timor, I. & Sea, *Indonesia* 129 H n
Timote, *Argentina* 94 D e
Tinaea Pt., *Philippines* 129 J j
Tindouf, *Algeria* 118 D c
Tineo, *Spain* 106 B a
Tingchow. See Changting
Tinghsien, *China* 130 G c
Tingnan, *China* 131 G k
Tingo Maria, *Peru* 92 B e
Tingri Dzong, *Tibet* 127 G c
Tingwick, *Quebec* 85 T g
Tinian & I., *Saipan-Tinian Is.* 78 A e
Tinian Chan., *Saipan-Tinian Is.* 78 A f
Tinian Harb., *Saipan-Tinian Is.* 78 A e
Tinnevelly. See Tirunelveli
Tinogasta, *Argentina* 94 C c
Tínos, I., *Greece* 113 E f
Tinsukia, *India* 127 J c
Tintigny, *Belgium* 100 D e
Tintina, *Argentina* 94 D c
Tioman, Palau, I., *Malaya* 132 C f
Tionaga, *Ontario* 84 H d
Tipperary & co., *Eire* 99 B h
Tip Top Hill, *Ontario* 84 D d
Tiracumbá, Sa. de, *Brazil* 93 H d
Tiran, I., *Saudi Arabia* 124 B d
Tirana. See Tiranë
Tiranë, *Albania* 112 B d
Tiraspol, *Moldavia, U.S.S.R.* 116 F h
Tire, *Turkey* 124 A b
Tireboli, *Turkey* 124 C a
Tiree I., *Scotland* 98 C d
Tîrgovista, *Romania* 112 E b
Tirich Mir, *Pakistan* 126 D a
Tirlemont, *Belgium* 100 C d
Tirlyanski, *U.S.S.R.* 117 P c
Tirnavos, *Greece* 113 D e
Tirol (Tyrol), reg., *Austria* 104 D e
Tirua Pt., *New Zealand* 135 R k
Tiruchchirappalli, *India* 126 E f
Tiruchendur, *India* 126 E g
Tiru Kona Malai. See Trincomalee
Tirunelveli, *India* 126 E g
Tirupati, *India* 126 E f
Tiruvannamalai, *India* 126 E f
Tisa, R., *Yugoslavia* 112 C b
Tisdale, *Saskatchewan* 87 N f
Tisiye, *Syria* 123 E e
Tissa, *Nigeria* 119 H g
Tisza, R., *Hungary* 105 J e
Titicaca, L., *Bolivia-Peru* 92 D g
Titisee, *Germany* 104 C e
Titograd, *Yugoslavia* 112 B c
Titovo Užice, *Yugoslavia* 112 B c
Titov-Veles, *Yugoslavia* 112 C d
Titu, *Romania* 112 E b
Tiverton, *England* 99 E k
Tiverton, *Nova Scotia* 82 F j
Tiverton, *Ontario* 84 J h
Tivoli, *Italy* 111 D e
Tiwi, *Muscat & Oman* 125 G e
Tixkokob, *Mexico* 90 G c
Tixtla, *Mexico* 90 E d
Tizimín, *Mexico* 90 G c
Tizi Ouzou, *Algeria* 118 F a
Tjalang, *Sumatra* 129 C k
Tjilatjap, *Indonesia* 129 E m
Tjirebon, *Indonesia* 129 E m
Tjörn, I., *Sweden* 103 D g
Tlacotalpan, *Mexico* 90 E d
Tlaltenango, *Mexico* 90 D c
Tlapa, *Mexico* 90 E d
Tlaxcala, *Mexico* 90 E d
Tlaxiaco, *Mexico* 90 E d
Tlell, *Br. Columbia* 88 D d
Tlemcen, *Algeria* 118 E b
Tméssa, *Libya* 119 J c
Tmiet, I., *Jaluit I.* 79 U h
Toad R., *Br. Columbia* 88 G a
Toay, *Argentina* 94 D e
Toba, Donau, *Sumatra* 129 C k
Toba, *Japan* 133 E g
Tobago, I., *Windward Is.* 91 G d
Toba Inlet, *Br. Columbia* 88 G e
Tobarro, *Spain* 107 E c
Tobel, *Switzerland* 101 E a
Tobelo, *Halmahera I.* 129 J k
Tobermory, *Ontario* 84 J g
Tobermory, *Scotland* 98 C d
Tobi, I., *Pacific Ocean* 78 D g
Tobiishi hana, *Iwo Jima* 78 D b
Tobique R., *New Brunswick* 82 E f
Toboali, *Bangka I., Indon.* 129 E l
Toboli, *Celebes* 129 H l
Tobolsk, *U.S.S.R.* 114 F c
Tobruk, *Libya* 119 K b
Tocantinópolis, *Brazil* 93 H e
Tocina, *Spain* 106 C d
Toco, *Chile* 94 C b
Tocopilla, *Chile* 94 B b
Tocoripa, *Mexico* 90 C b
Tocuyo, *Venezuela* 92 C b
Todd Mt., *New Brunswick* 82 F g
Todenyang, *Kenya* 121 H d
Todmorden, *Ontario* 84 D j
Todos Santos, B., *Mexico* 90 A a
Todos Santos, *Mexico* 90 B c
Tofield, *Alberta* 86 E e
Tofino, *Vancouver I., British Columbia* 88 G f
Togarakaikyo, *Japan* 133 A j
Toghraqbulaq, *China* 128 B b
Togo, *Saskatchewan* 87 Q g
Togo, *West Africa* 118 F g
Toguchi, I., *Okinawa* 78 B b
To Huping Tso, *Tibet* 127 F b
Tojo, *Japan* 133 C g
Tokachi Dake, *Japan* 133 H c
Tokanga, *U.S.S.R.* 114 D b
Tokanui, *New Zealand* 135 P m
Tokar, *Sudan* 121 H a
Tokara Retto, *Japan* 133 N n
Tokat, *Turkey* 124 C a
Tokelau Is., *Pacific Ocean* 78 K h
Toki Pt., *Wake I.* 79 S d
Tokmak, *Kirgiz., U.S.S.R.* 114 G d
Tokoto, *China* 130 E b
Tokushima, *Japan* 133 D h
Tokuyama, *Japan* 133 B g
Tokyo & B., *Japan* 133 F g
Tol, I., *Truk Is.* 78 D o
Tolaga Bay, *New Zealand* 135 S k
Tolbukhin, *Bulgaria* 112 F c
Toledo, *Chile* 94 B c
Toledo, Mts., *Spain* 106 C c
Toledo, *Spain* 106 C c
Tolen & I., *Netherlands* 100 C c
Tolmin, *Yugoslavia* 110 D b
Tolo, G. of, *Celebes* 129 H d
Toluca, *Mexico* 90 E d
Tolun, *China* 130 H a
Tölz, Bad, *Germany* 104 D e
Tomar, *Portugal* 106 A c
Tomari, *U.S.S.R.* 115 P d
Tomaszów Mazowiecki, *Poland* 105 J c
Tomatumari, *British Guiana* 92 F b
Tombouctou. See Timbuktu
Tome, *Chile* 94 B e
Tomiko, *Ontario* 85 L f
Tomil, I., *Yap I.* 78 D l
Tomini, G. of, *Celebes* 129 H l
Tomkinson Ra., *Australia* 134 E e
Tommot, *U.S.S.R.* 115 M c
Tompkins, *Saskatchewan* 86 J h
Tomsk, *U.S.S.R.* 115 H c
Tomskaya Oblast, *U.S.S.R.* 114 G c
Tonala, *Mexico* 90 F d
Tönder, *Denmark* 103 C j
Tondern, *Ontario* 84 E c
Tondi, *India* 126 E g
Tonelik, I., *Truk Is.* 78 E m
Tonga, Is., *Pacific Ocean* 78 J j
Tonga, *Sudan* 119 M g
Tongareva, I., *Pacific Ocean* 78 K h
Tongatapu, I., *Tonga Is.* 78 K j
Tongeren, *Belgium* 100 D d
Tongking, *N. Vietnam* 131 B m
Tongobory, *Madagascar* 121 M l
Tongoy, *Chile* 94 B d
Tongres. See Tongeren
Tongue, *Scotland* 98 E b
Tonichi, *Mexico* 90 C b
Tonk, *India* 126 E c
Tonkhil, *Mongolia* 128 B a
Tonking, G. of, *China, etc.* 132 D b
Tonkova, *U.S.S.R.* 114 H b
Tonle Sap, *Cambodia* 132 C d
Tonneins, *France* 109 D d
Tonnerre, *France* 108 F c
Tönsberg, *Norway* 103 D g
Toowoomba, *Australia* 135 K e
Topland, *Alberta* 86 B d
Topley Lodge, *Br. Columbia* 88 F c
Topolčany, *Czechoslovakia* 105 H d